KṚṢṆA

THE SUPREME PERSONALITY OF GODHEAD

BOOKS by
His Divine Grace
A. C. Bhaktivedanta Swami Prabhupāda

Bhagavad-gītā As It Is
Śrīmad-Bhāgavatam, Cantos 1-10 (12 vols.)
Śrī Caitanya-caritāmṛta (17 vols.)
Teachings of Lord Caitanya
The Nectar of Devotion
The Nectar of Instruction
Śrī Īśopaniṣad
Easy Journey to Other Planets
Kṛṣṇa, The Supreme Personality of Godhead (2 vols.)
Kṛṣṇa Consciousness: The Topmost Yoga System
Perfect Questions, Perfect Answers
Teachings of Lord Kapila, the Son of Devahūti
Transcendental Teachings of Prahlāda Mahārāja
Teachings of Queen Kuntī
Kṛṣṇa, the Reservoir of Pleasure
The Science of Self-Realization
The Path of Perfection
Search for Liberation
The Journey of Self-Discovery
A Second Chance
Laws of Nature
Message of Godhead
Civilization and Transcendence
Life Comes From Life
The Perfection of Yoga
Beyond Birth and Death
On the Way to Kṛṣṇa
Rāja-vidyā: The King of Knowledge
Elevation to Kṛṣṇa Consciousness
Kṛṣṇa Consciousness: The Matchless Gift
Wisdom Through Renunciation
Back to Godhead magazine (founder)

available from:

The Bhaktivedanta Book Trust
P. O. Box 324, Borehamwood
Herts. WD6 1NB, England
Telephone: 0181-905 1244

The Bhaktivedanta Book Trust
3764 Watseka Avenue
Los Angeles, California 90034
USA

The Bhaktivedanta Book Trust
P.O. Box 262
Botany, N.S.W. 2019
Australia

KṚṢṆA

The Supreme Personality of Godhead

A Summary Study of
Śrīla Vyāsadeva's
Śrīmad-Bhāgavatam,
Tenth Canto

Volume Two

His Divine Grace
A.C. Bhaktivedanta Swami Prabhupāda
Founder-Ācārya of the International Society
for Krishna Consciousness

THE BHAKTIVEDANTA BOOK TRUST

Readers interested in the subject matter of this book are invited by the International Society for Krishna Consciousness to correspond with its Secretary at either of the following addresses:

International Society for Krishna Consciousness
P.O. Box 324, Borehamwood
Herts. WD6 1NB, England
Telephone: 0181-905 1244
e-mail: bbl@com.bbt.se

International Society for Krishna Consciousness
3764 Watseka Avenue
Los Angeles, California 90034, USA
e-mail: letters@iskcon.com

International Society for Krishna Consciousness
P.O. Box 262, Botany
N.S.W. 2019, Australia

World Wide Web:
http://www.algonet.se/~krishna
http://www.harekrishna.com/~ara

First Edition: 1970
1996 Edition: 70,000 copies

ISBN (volume 2): 91-7149-349-2
Set (two volumes): 91-7149-350-6

Words from George Harrison

Everybody is looking for KṚṢṆA.

Some don't realize that they are, but they are.

KṚṢṆA is GOD, the Source of all that exists, the Cause of all that is, was, or ever will be.

As GOD is unlimited, HE has many Names.

Allah-Buddha-Jehovah-Rāma: All are KṚṢṆA, all are ONE.

God is not abstract; He has both the impersonal and the personal aspects to His personality, which is SUPREME, ETERNAL, BLISSFUL, and full of KNOWLEDGE. As a single drop of water has the same qualities as an ocean of water, so has our consciousness the qualities of GOD'S consciousness . . . but through our identification and attachment with material energy (physical body, sense pleasures, material possessions, ego, etc.) our true TRANSCENDENTAL CONSCIOUSNESS has been polluted, and like a dirty mirror it is unable to reflect a pure image.

With many lives our association with the TEMPORARY has grown. This impermanent body, a bag of bones and flesh, is mistaken for our true self, and we have accepted this temporary condition to be final.

Through all ages, great SAINTS have remained as living proof that this nontemporary, permanent state of GOD CONSCIOUSNESS can be revived in all living Souls. Each Soul is potentially divine.

Kṛṣṇa says in *Bhagavad-gītā:* "Steady in the Self, being freed from all material contamination, the yogi achieves the highest perfectional stage of happiness in touch with the Supreme Consciousness." (VI, 28)

YOGA (a scientific method for GOD (SELF) realization)

is the process by which we purify our consciousness, stop further pollution, and arrive at the state of Perfection, full KNOWLEDGE, full BLISS.

If there's a God, I want to see Him. It's pointless to believe in something without proof, and Kṛṣṇa Consciousness and meditation are methods where you can actually obtain GOD perception. You can actually see God, and hear Him, play with Him. It might sound crazy, but He is actually there, actually with you.

There are many yogic Paths—Rāja, Jñāna, Haṭha, Kriyā, Karma, Bhakti—which are *all* acclaimed by the MASTERS of each method.

SWAMI BHAKTIVEDANTA is, as his title says, a BHAKTI Yogi following the path of DEVOTION. By serving GOD through each thought, word, and DEED, and by chanting of HIS Holy Names, the devotee quickly develops God-consciousness. By chanting

Hare Kṛṣṇa, Hare Kṛṣṇa
Kṛṣṇa Kṛṣṇa, Hare Hare
Hare Rāma, Hare Rāma
Rāma Rāma, Hare Hare

one inevitably arrives at KṚṢṆA Consciousness. (The proof of the pudding is in the eating!)

I request that you take advantage of this book, *KṚṢṆA*, and enter into its understanding. I also request that you make an appointment to meet your God now, through the self-liberating process of YOGA (UNION) and GIVE PEACE A CHANCE.

ALL YOU NEED IS LOVE (KRISHNA) HARI BOL.

George Harrison

Contents

Preface

nivṛtta-tarṣair upagīyamānād
bhavauṣadhāc chrotra-mano-'bhirāmāt
ka uttamaśloka-guṇānuvādāt
pumān virajyeta vinā paśu-ghnāt
(*Śrīmad-Bhāgavatam* 10.1.4)

In the Western countries, when someone sees the cover of a book like *Kṛṣṇa,* he immediately asks, "Who is Kṛṣṇa? Who is the girl with Kṛṣṇa?" etc.

The immediate answer is that Kṛṣṇa is the Supreme Personality of Godhead. How is that? Because He conforms in exact detail to descriptions of the Supreme Being, the Godhead. In other words, Kṛṣṇa is the Godhead because He is all-attractive. Outside the principle of all-attraction, there is no meaning to the word "Godhead." How is it one can be all-attractive? First of all, if one is very wealthy, if he has great riches, he becomes attractive to the people in general. Similarly, if someone is very powerful, he also becomes attractive, and if someone is very famous, he also becomes attractive, and if someone is very beautiful or wise or unattached to all kinds of possessions, he also becomes attractive. So from practical experience we can observe that one is attractive due to (1) wealth, (2) power, (3) fame, (4) beauty, (5) wisdom and (6) renunciation. One who is in possession of all six of these opulences at the same time, who possesses them to an unlimited degree, is understood to be the Supreme Personality of Godhead. These opulences of the Godhead are delineated by Parāśara Muni, a great Vedic authority.

We have seen many rich persons, many powerful persons, many famous persons, many beautiful persons, many learned and scholarly persons, and persons in the renounced order of life unattached to material possessions. But we have never seen any one person who is unlimitedly and simultaneously wealthy, powerful, famous, beautiful, wise and unattached, like Kṛṣṇa, in the history of humanity. Kṛṣṇa, the Supreme Personality of Godhead, is a historical person who appeared on this earth 5,000 years ago. He stayed on this earth for 125 years and played exactly like a human being, but His activities were unparalleled. From the very moment of His appearance to the moment of His disappearance, every one of His activities is unparalleled in the history of the world, and therefore anyone who knows what we mean by Godhead will accept Kṛṣṇa as the Supreme Personality of Godhead. No one is equal to the Godhead, and no one is greater than Him. That is the import of the familiar saying "God is great."

There are various classes of men in the world who speak of God in different ways, but according to the Vedic literature and according to the great *ācāryas,* the authorized persons versed in the knowledge of God in all ages, like *ācāryas* Śaṅkara, Rāmānuja, Madhva, Viṣṇu Svāmī, Lord Caitanya and all their followers by disciplic succession, all unanimously agree that Kṛṣṇa is the Supreme Personality of Godhead. As far as we, the followers of Vedic civilization, are concerned, we accept the Vedic history of the whole universe, which consists of different planetary systems called Svargalokas, or the higher planetary system, Martyalokas, or the intermediary planetary system, and Pātālalokas, or the lower planetary system. The modern historians of this earth cannot supply historical evidences of events that occurred before 5,000 years ago, and the anthropologists say that 40,000 years ago *Homo sapiens* had not appeared on this planet because evolution had not reached that point. But the Vedic histories, the *Purā-*

ṇas and *Mahābhārata,* relate human histories which extend millions and billions of years into the past.

For example, from these literatures we are given the histories of Kṛṣṇa's appearances and disappearances millions and billions of years ago. In the Fourth Chapter of the *Bhagavad-gītā* Kṛṣṇa tells Arjuna that both He and Arjuna had had many births before and that He (Kṛṣṇa) could remember all of them and that Arjuna could not. This illustrates the difference between the knowledge of Kṛṣṇa and that of Arjuna. Arjuna might have been a very great warrior, a well-cultured member of the Kuru dynasty, but after all, he was an ordinary human being, whereas Kṛṣṇa, the Supreme Personality of Godhead, is the possessor of unlimited knowledge. Because He possesses unlimited knowledge, Kṛṣṇa has a memory that is boundless.

Kṛṣṇa's knowledge is so perfect that He remembers all the incidents of His appearances some millions and billions of years in the past, but Arjuna's memory and knowledge are limited by time and space, for he is an ordinary human being. In the Fourth Chapter Kṛṣṇa states that He can remember instructing the lessons of the *Bhagavad-gītā* some millions of years ago to the sun-god, Vivasvān.

Nowadays it is the fashion of the atheistic class of men to try to become God by following some mystic process. Generally the atheists claim to be God by dint of their imagination or their meditational prowess. Kṛṣṇa is not that kind of God. He does not become God by manufacturing some mystic process of meditation, nor does He become God by undergoing the severe austerities of the mystic yogic exercises. Properly speaking, He never *becomes* God because He is the Godhead in all circumstances.

Within the prison of His maternal uncle Kaṁsa, where His father and mother were confined, Kṛṣṇa appeared outside His mother's body as the four-handed Viṣṇu-Nārāyaṇa. Then He turned Himself into a baby and told His father to carry

Him to the house of Nanda Mahārāja and his wife Yaśodā. When Kṛṣṇa was just a small baby the gigantic demoness Pūtanā attempted to kill Him, but when He sucked her breast He pulled out her life. That is the difference between the real Godhead and a God manufactured in the mystic factory. Kṛṣṇa had no chance to practice the mystic *yoga* process, yet He manifested Himself as the Supreme Personality of Godhead at every step, from infancy to childhood, from childhood to boyhood, and from boyhood to young manhood. In this book, *Kṛṣṇa,* all of His activities as a human being are described. Although Kṛṣṇa plays like a human being, He always maintains His identity as the Supreme Personality of Godhead.

Since Kṛṣṇa is all-attractive, one should know that all his desires should be focused on Kṛṣṇa. In the *Bhagavad-gītā* it is said that the individual person is the proprietor or master of his own body but that Kṛṣṇa, who is the Supersoul present in everyone's heart, is the supreme proprietor and supreme master of each and every individual body. As such, if we concentrate our loving propensities upon Kṛṣṇa only, then immediately universal love, unity and tranquillity will be automatically realized. When one waters the root of a tree, he automatically waters the branches, twigs, leaves and flowers; when one supplies food to the stomach through the mouth, he satisfies all the various parts of the body.

The art of focusing one's attention on the Supreme and giving one's love to Him is called Kṛṣṇa consciousness. We have inaugurated the Kṛṣṇa consciousness movement so that everyone can satisfy his propensity for loving others simply by directing his love toward Kṛṣṇa. The whole world is very eager to satisfy the dormant propensity of love for others, but the various invented methods like socialism, communism, altruism, humanitarianism and nationalism, along with whatever else may be manufactured for the peace and prosperity of the world, are all useless and frustrating because of our gross ignorance of the art of loving Kṛṣṇa. Generally people think that by advancing the cause of moral principles and religious rites they will be happy. Others may think that happiness can be achieved by economic development, and yet others think that simply by sense gratification they will be happy. But the real fact is that people can be happy only by loving Kṛṣṇa.

Kṛṣṇa can perfectly reciprocate one's loving propensities in different relationships called mellows, or *rasas.* Basically there are twelve loving relationships. One can love Kṛṣṇa as the supreme unknown, as the supreme master, the supreme friend, the supreme child, the supreme lover. These are the five basic love *rasas.* One can also love Kṛṣṇa indirectly in seven different relationships, which are apparently different from the five primary relationships. All in all, however, if one simply reposes his dormant loving propensity in Kṛṣṇa, then his life becomes successful. This is not a fiction but is a fact that can be realized by practical application. One can directly perceive the effects that love for Kṛṣṇa has on his life.

In the Ninth Chapter of the *Bhagavad-gītā* this science of Kṛṣṇa consciousness is called the king of all knowledge, the king of all confidential things, and the supreme science of transcendental realization. Yet we can directly experience the results of this science of Kṛṣṇa consciousness because it is very easy to practice and is very pleasurable. Whatever percentage of Kṛṣṇa consciousness we can perform will become an eternal asset to our life, for it is imperishable in all circumstances. It has now been actually proved that today's confused and frustrated younger generation in the Western countries can directly perceive the results of channeling the loving propensity toward Kṛṣṇa alone.

It is said that although one executes severe austerities, penances and sacrifices in his life, if he fails to awaken his dormant love for Kṛṣṇa, then all his penances are to be considered useless. On the other hand, if one has awakened his dormant love for Kṛṣṇa, then what is the use in executing austerities and penances unnecessarily?

The Kṛṣṇa consciousness movement is the unique gift of Lord Caitanya to the fallen souls of this age. It is a very simple method which has actually been carried out during the last four years in the Western countries, and there is no doubt that this movement can satisfy the dormant loving propensities of humanity. This book, *Kṛṣṇa,* is another presentation to help the Kṛṣṇa consciousness movement in the Western world. This transcendental literature is published with profuse illustrations. People love to read various kinds of fiction to spend their time and energy. Now this tendency can be directed to Kṛṣṇa. The result will be the imperishable satisfaction of the soul, both individually and collectively.

It is said in the *Bhagavad-gītā* that even a little effort expended on the path of Kṛṣṇa consciousness can save one from the greatest danger. Hundreds of thousands of examples can be cited of people who have escaped the greatest dangers of life due to a slight advancement in Kṛṣṇa consciousness. We therefore request everyone to take advantage of this great transcendental literary work. One will find that by reading one page after another, an immense treasure of knowledge in art, science, literature, philosophy and religion will be revealed, and ultimately, by reading this one book, *Kṛṣṇa,* love of Godhead will fructify.

My grateful acknowledgment is due to Śrīmān George Harrison, now chanting Hare Kṛṣṇa, for his liberal contribution of $19,000 to meet the entire cost of printing this volume. May Kṛṣṇa bestow upon this nice boy further advancement in Kṛṣṇa consciousness.

And at last my ever-willing blessings are bestowed upon Śrīmān Śyāmasundara dāsa Adhikārī, Śrīmān Brahmānanda dāsa Brahmacārī, Śrīmān Hayagrīva dāsa Adhikārī, Śrīmān Satsvarūpa dāsa Adhikārī, Śrīmatī Devahūti-devī dāsī, Śrīmatī

Jadurāṇī-devī dāsī, Śrīmān Muralīdhara dāsa Brahmacārī, Śrīmān Bhāradvāja dāsa Adhikārī and Śrīmān Pradyumna dāsa Adhikārī, etc., for their hard labor in different ways to make this publication a great success.

Hare Kṛṣṇa.

A. C. Bhaktivedanta Swami

Advent Day of
Śrīla Bhaktisiddhānta Sarasvatī
February 26th, 1970
ISKCON Headquarters
3764 Watseka Avenue
Los Angeles, California

CHAPTER FIFTY-SIX

The Story of the Syamantaka Jewel

There was a king of the name Satrājit within the jurisdiction of Dvārakā-dhāma. He was a great devotee of the sun-god, who awarded him the benediction of a jewel known as Syamantaka. Because of this Syamantaka jewel, there was a misunderstanding between King Satrājit and the Yadu dynasty. Later the matter was settled when Satrājit voluntarily offered Kṛṣṇa his daughter, Satyabhāmā, along with the Syamantaka jewel. Not only Satyabhāmā but also Jāmbavatī, the daughter of Jāmbavān, was married to Kṛṣṇa on account of the Syamantaka jewel. These two marriages took place before the appearance of Pradyumna, which was described in the last chapter. How King Satrājit offended the Yadu dynasty and how he later came to his senses and offered his daughter and the Syamantaka jewel to Kṛṣṇa are described as follows.

Since he was a great devotee of the sun-god, King Satrājit gradually entered into a very friendly relationship with him. The sun-god was pleased with him and delivered to him an exceptional jewel known as Syamantaka. When Satrājit wore this jewel in a locket around his neck, he appeared exactly like an imitation sun-god. Putting on this jewel, he entered the city of Dvārakā, and people thought that the sun-god had come into the city to see Kṛṣṇa. They knew that Kṛṣṇa, being the Supreme Personality of Godhead, was sometimes visited by the demigods, so while Satrājit was visiting the city of Dvārakā all the inhabitants except Kṛṣṇa took him to be the sun-god himself. Although King Satrājit was known to everyone, he could not be recognized because of the dazzling effulgence of the Syamantaka jewel.

Mistaking Satrājit to be the sun-god, some of the important citizens of Dvārakā immediately went to Kṛṣṇa to inform Him that the sun-god had arrived to see Him. At that time, Kṛṣṇa was playing chess. One of the important residents of Dvārakā spoke thus: "My dear Lord Nārāyaṇa, You are the Supreme Personality of Godhead. In Your plenary portion as Nārāyaṇa, or Viṣṇu, You have four hands with different symbols—the conchshell, disc, club and lotus flower. You are actually the owner of everything, but in spite of Your being the Supreme Personality of Godhead, Nārāyaṇa, You descended in Vṛndāvana to act as the child of Yaśodāmātā, who sometimes used to tie You up with her ropes, and You are celebrated, therefore, by the name Dāmodara."

That Lord Kṛṣṇa is the Supreme Personality of Godhead, Nārāyaṇa, as accepted by the citizens of Dvārakā, was later confirmed by the great Māyāvādī philosophical leader Śaṅkarācārya. By accepting the Lord as impersonal, he did not reject the Lord's personal form. Everything which has form in this material world is subject to creation, maintenance and annihilation, but because the Supreme Personality of Godhead, Nārāyaṇa, does not have a material form subject to these limitations, Śaṅkarācārya, to convince the less intelligent men who take Kṛṣṇa to be an ordinary human being, said that God is impersonal. This impersonality means that He is not a person of this material condition. He is a transcendental personality without a material body.

The citizens of Dvārakā addressed Lord Kṛṣṇa not only as Dāmodara but also as Govinda, which indicates that Kṛṣṇa is very affectionate to the cows and calves; and just to refer to their intimate connection with Kṛṣṇa, they addressed Him as Yadunandana because He was born the son of Vasudeva in the Yadu dynasty. The citizens of Dvārakā concluded by addressing Kṛṣṇa as the supreme master of the whole universe. They addressed Kṛṣṇa in many different ways, proud of being citizens of Dvārakā who could see Kṛṣṇa daily.

When Satrājit was visiting the city of Dvārakā, the citizens felt great pride to think that although Kṛṣṇa was living in Dvārakā like an ordinary human being, the demigods were coming to see Him. Thus they informed Lord Kṛṣṇa that the sun-god, with his glaring bodily effulgence, was coming to see Him. The citizens of Dvārakā confirmed that the sun-god's coming into Dvārakā was not very wonderful, because people all over the universe who were searching after the Supreme Personality of Godhead knew that He had appeared in the Yadu dynasty and was living in Dvārakā as one of the members of that family. Thus the citizens expressed their joy on this occasion. On hearing the statements of His citizens, the all-pervasive Personality of Godhead, Kṛṣṇa, simply smiled. Being pleased with the citizens of Dvārakā, Kṛṣṇa informed them that the person they described as the sun-god was actually King Satrājit, who had come to visit Dvārakā City to show his opulence in the form of the valuable jewel obtained from the sun-god.

Satrājit, however, did not come to see Kṛṣṇa; he was instead overwhelmed by the Syamantaka jewel. He installed the jewel in a temple to be worshiped by *brāhmaṇas* he engaged for this purpose. This is an example of a less intelligent person worshiping a material thing. In the *Bhagavad-gītā* it is stated that less intelligent persons, in order to get immediate results from their fruitive activities, worship the demigods created within this universe. The word "materialist" means one concerned with gratification of the senses within this material world. Although Kṛṣṇa later asked for this Syamantaka jewel, King Satrājit did not deliver it; on the contrary, he installed the jewel for his own purposes of worship. And who would not worship that jewel? The Syamantaka jewel was so powerful that daily it produced a large quantity of gold. A quantity of gold is counted by a measurement called a *bhāra.* According to Vedic formulas, one *bhāra* is equal to about twenty-one pounds, and one *mound* equals about eighty-two pounds. The jewel was producing about 170 pounds of gold every day. Besides that, it is learned from the Vedic literature that in whatever part of the world this jewel was worshiped there was no possibility of famine, and wherever the jewel was present, there was no possibility of anything inauspicious, such as pestilence.

Lord Kṛṣṇa wanted to teach the world that the best of everything should be offered to the ruling chief of the country. King Ugrasena was the overlord of many dynasties and happened to be the grandfather of Kṛṣṇa, so Kṛṣṇa asked Satrājit to present the Syamantaka jewel to King Ugrasena. Kṛṣṇa pleaded that the best should be offered to the King. But Satrājit, being a worshiper of the demigods, had become too materialistic and, instead of accepting the request of Kṛṣṇa, thought it wiser to worship the jewel to get the 170 pounds of gold every day. Materialistic persons who can achieve such huge quantities of gold are not interested in Kṛṣṇa consciousness. Sometimes, therefore, to show special favor, Kṛṣṇa takes away one's great accumulations of materialistic wealth and thus makes one a great devotee. But Satrājit refused to abide by the order of Kṛṣṇa and did not deliver the jewel.

After this incident, Satrājit's younger brother, in order to display the opulence of the family, took the jewel, put it on his neck and rode on horseback into the forest, making a show of his material opulence. While Satrājit's brother, who was known as Prasena, was moving here and there in the forest, a big lion attacked him, killed both him and the horse on which he was riding, and took away the jewel to his cave. News of this was received by the gorilla king, Jāmbavān, who then killed that lion in the cave and took away the jewel. Jāmbavān had been a great devotee of the Lord since the time of Lord Rāmacandra, so he did not take the valuable jewel as something he very much needed. He gave it to his young son to play with as a toy.

In the city, when Satrājit's younger brother Prasena did not return from the forest with the jewel, Satrājit became very upset. He did not know that his brother had been killed by a lion and that the lion had been killed by Jāmbavān. He thought instead that because Kṛṣṇa wanted that jewel, which had not been delivered to Him, Kṛṣṇa might have therefore taken the jewel from Prasena by force and killed him. This idea grew into a rumor, which Satrājit spread in every part of Dvārakā.

The false rumor that Kṛṣṇa had killed Prasena and taken away the jewel spread everywhere like wildfire. Kṛṣṇa did not like to be defamed in that way, and therefore He decided that He would go to the forest and find the Syamantaka jewel. Taking with Him some of the important inhabitants of Dvārakā, Kṛṣṇa went to search out Prasena, the brother of Satrājit, and found him dead, killed by the lion. At the same time, Kṛṣṇa also found the lion killed by Jāmbavān, who is generally called Ṛkṣa. It was found that the lion had been killed by the hand of Ṛkṣa without the assistance of any weapon. Kṛṣṇa and the citizens of Dvārakā then found in the forest a great tunnel, said to be the path to Ṛkṣa's house. Kṛṣṇa knew that the inhabitants of Dvārakā would be afraid to enter the tunnel; therefore He asked them to remain outside, and He Himself entered the dark tunnel alone to find Ṛkṣa, Jāmbavān. After entering the tunnel, Kṛṣṇa saw that the valuable jewel known as Syamantaka had been given to the son of Ṛkṣa as a toy. To take the jewel from the child, Kṛṣṇa approached and stood before him. When the nurse taking care of Ṛkṣa's child saw Kṛṣṇa standing before her, she was afraid, thinking He might take away the valuable Syamantaka jewel, and she cried out loudly in fear.

Hearing the nurse's cries, Jāmbavān appeared on the scene in a very angry mood. Jāmbavān was actually a great devotee of Lord Kṛṣṇa, but because he was angry he could not recognize his master and thought Him to be an ordinary man. This brings to mind the statement of the *Bhagavad-gītā* in which the Lord advises Arjuna to get free from anger, greed and lust in order to rise to the spiritual platform. Lust, anger and greed run parallel in the heart and check one's progress on the spiritual path.

Not recognizing his master, Jāmbavān challenged Him to fight. There was then a great fight between Kṛṣṇa and Jāmbavān, in which they fought like two opposing vultures. Whenever there is an eatable corpse the vultures fight heartily over the prey. Kṛṣṇa and Jāmbavān first of all fought with weapons, then with stones, then with big trees, then hand to hand, until at last they were hitting each other with their fists, their blows like the striking of thunderbolts. Each expected victory over the other, but the fighting continued for twenty-eight days, both in daytime and at night, without stopping.

Although Jāmbavān was the strongest living entity of that time, practically all the joints of his bodily limbs became slackened and his strength was reduced practically to nil, for he was struck constantly by the fists of Śrī Kṛṣṇa. Feeling very tired, with perspiration all over his body, Jāmbavān was astonished. Who was this opponent who was fighting so hard with him? Jāmbavān was quite aware of his own superhuman bodily strength, but when he felt tired from being struck by Kṛṣṇa, he could understand that Kṛṣṇa was no one else but his worshipable Lord, the Supreme Personality of Godhead. This incident has special significance for devotees. In the beginning, Jāmbavān could not understand Kṛṣṇa because his vision was obscured by material attachment. He was attached to his boy and to the greatly valuable Syamantaka jewel, which he did not want to spare for Kṛṣṇa. In fact, when Kṛṣṇa came there he was angry, thinking that Kṛṣṇa had come to take away the jewel. This is the material position: although one is very strong in body, that cannot help him understand Kṛṣṇa.

In a sporting attitude, Kṛṣṇa wanted to engage in a mock fight with His devotee. As we have experienced from the pages of *Śrīmad-Bhāgavatam,* the Supreme Personality of Godhead has all the propensities and instincts of a human being. Sometimes, in a sportive spirit, He wishes to fight to make a show of bodily strength, and when He so desires, He selects one of His suitable devotees to give Him that pleasure. Kṛṣṇa desired this pleasure of mock fighting with Jāmbavān. Although Jāmbavān was a devotee by nature, he did not know that his opponent was Kṛṣṇa while he gave service to the Lord by his bodily strength. But as soon as Kṛṣṇa was pleased by the fighting, Jāmbavān immediately understood that his opponent was none other than the Supreme Lord Himself. The conclusion is that he could understand Kṛṣṇa by his service, for Kṛṣṇa is sometimes satisfied by fighting also.

Jāmbavān therefore said to the Lord, "My dear Lord, I can now understand who You are. You are the Supreme Personality of Godhead, Lord Viṣṇu, the source of everyone's strength, wealth, reputation, beauty, wisdom and renunciation." This statement is confirmed by the *Vedānta-sūtra,* wherein the Supreme Lord is declared to be the source of everything. Jāmbavān identified Lord Kṛṣṇa as the Supreme Personality, Lord Viṣṇu: "My dear Lord, You are the creator of the creators of .the universal affairs." This statement is very instructive to the ordinary man, who is amazed by the activities of a person with an exceptional brain. The ordinary man is surprised to see the inventions of a great scientist, but the statement of Jāmbavān confirms that although a scientist may be a creator of many wonderful things, Kṛṣṇa is the creator of the scientist. He is the creator of not only one scientist but of millions and trillions, all over the universe. Jāmbavān said further, "Not only are You the creator of the creators, but You are also the creator of the material elements which the so-called creators manipulate." Scientists utilize the physical elements or laws of material nature to do something wonderful, but actually such laws and elements are also the creation of Kṛṣṇa. This is actual scientific understanding. Less intelligent men do not try to understand who created the brain of the scientist; they are satisfied simply to see the wonderful creation or invention of the scientist.

Jāmbavān continued, "My dear Lord, the time factor, which combines all the physical elements, is also Your representative. You are the supreme time factor, in which all creation takes place, is maintained and is finally annihilated. And beyond the physical elements and the time factor, the persons who manipulate the ingredients and advantages of creation are part and parcel of You. The living entity is not, therefore, an independent creator. By studying all factors in the right perspective, one can see that You are the supreme controller and Lord of everything. My dear Lord, I can therefore understand that You are the same Supreme Personality of Godhead whom I worship as Lord Rāmacandra. My Lord Rāmacandra wanted to construct a bridge over the ocean, and I saw personally how the ocean became agitated simply by my Lord's glancing over it. And when the whole ocean became agitated, the living entities like the whales, alligators and *timiṅgila* fish all became perturbed. [The *timiṅgila* fish in the ocean can swallow big aquatics like whales in one gulp.] In this way the ocean was forced to give way and allow Rāmacandra to cross to the island known as Laṅkā. [This island is now said to be Ceylon. Lord Rāmacandra's construction of a bridge over the ocean from Cape Comorin to Ceylon is still well known to everyone.] After the construction of the bridge, a fire was set all over the kingdom of Rāvaṇa. During the fighting with Rāvaṇa, every part of his limbs was slashed to pieces by Your sharp arrows, and his heads fell to the face of the earth. Now I can understand that You are none other than my Lord Rāmacandra. No one else has such immeasurable strength; no one else could defeat me in this way."

Lord Kṛṣṇa was satisfied by the prayers and statements of Jāmbavān, and to mitigate Jāmbavān's pain, He began to stroke the lotus palm of His hand all over Jāmbavān's body. Thus Jāmbavān at once felt relieved from the fatigue of the great fight. Lord Kṛṣṇa then addressed him as King Jāmbavān because he, and not the lion, was actually the king of the forest, having killed a lion with his bare hands, without a weapon. Kṛṣṇa informed Jāmbavān that He had come to ask for the Syamantaka jewel because ever since the Syamantaka jewel had been stolen His name had been defamed by the less intelligent. Kṛṣṇa plainly informed him that He had come there to ask for the jewel in order to be free from this defamation. Jāmbavān understood the whole situation, and to satisfy the Lord he immediately delivered not only the Syamantaka jewel but also his daughter Jāmbavatī, who was of marriageable age, and presented her to Lord Kṛṣṇa.

The episode of Jāmbavatī's marriage with Lord Kṛṣṇa and the delivery of the jewel known as Syamantaka was finished within the mountain cave. Although the fighting between Kṛṣṇa and Jāmbavān went on for twenty-eight days, the inhabitants of Dvārakā waited outside the tunnel for twelve days, and after that they decided that something undesirable must have happened. They could not understand for certain what had actually happened, and being very sorry and tired they returned to the city of Dvārakā.

All the members of the family, namely Kṛṣṇa's mother, Devakī, His father, Vasudeva, and His chief wife, Rukmiṇī, along with all other friends, relatives and residents of the palace, were very sorry when the citizens returned home without Kṛṣṇa. Because of their natural affection for Kṛṣṇa, they began to call Satrājit ill names, for he was the cause of Kṛṣṇa's disappearance. They went to worship the goddess Candrabhāgā, praying for the return of Kṛṣṇa. The goddess was satisfied by the prayers of the citizens of Dvārakā, and she immediately offered them her benediction. Simultaneously, Kṛṣṇa appeared on the scene, accompanied by His new wife, Jāmbavatī, and all the inhabitants of Dvārakā and relatives of Kṛṣṇa became joyful. The inhabitants of Dvārakā were as joyful as someone receiving a dear relative back from the dead. They had concluded that Kṛṣṇa had been put into great difficulties due to the fighting; therefore, they had become almost hopeless of His return. But when they saw that Kṛṣṇa had actually returned, not alone but with a new wife, Jāmbavatī, they immediately performed a ceremony of celebration.

King Ugrasena then called for a meeting of all important kings and chiefs. He also invited Satrājit, and before the whole assembly Kṛṣṇa explained the incident of the recovery of the jewel from Jāmbavān. Kṛṣṇa wanted to return the valuable jewel to King Satrājit. Satrājit, however, was ashamed because he had unnecessarily defamed Kṛṣṇa. He accepted the jewel in his hand, but he remained silent, bending his head downwards, and without saying anything in the assembly of the kings and chiefs, he returned home with the jewel. Then he thought about how he could clear himself of the abominable act he had performed by defaming Kṛṣṇa. He was conscious that he had offended Kṛṣṇa very grievously and that he had to find a remedial measure so that Kṛṣṇa would again be pleased with him.

King Satrājit was eager to get relief from the anxiety he had foolishly created due to being attracted by a material thing, specifically the Syamantaka jewel. Truly afflicted by the offense he had committed against Kṛṣṇa, he sincerely wanted to rectify it. From within, Kṛṣṇa gave him good intelligence, and Satrājit decided to hand over to Kṛṣṇa both the jewel and his beautiful daughter, Satyabhāmā. There was no alternative for mitigating the situation, and therefore he arranged the marriage ceremony of Kṛṣṇa and his daughter. He gave in charity both the jewel and his daughter to the Supreme Personality of Godhead. Satyabhāmā was so beautiful and qualified that Satrājit, in spite of being asked for her hand by many princes, was waiting to find a suitable son-in-law. By the grace of Kṛṣṇa he decided to hand his daughter over to Him.

Lord Kṛṣṇa, being pleased with Satrājit, informed him that He did not have any need of the Syamantaka jewel. "It is better to let it remain in the temple as you have kept it," He said, "and every one of us will derive benefit from the jewel. Because of the jewel's presence in the city of Dvārakā, there will be no more famines or disturbances created by pestilence or excessive heat and cold."

Thus ends the Bhaktivedanta purport of the Fifty-sixth Chapter of Kṛṣṇa, *"The Story of the Syamantaka Jewel."*

CHAPTER FIFTY-SEVEN

The Killing of Satrājit and Śatadhanvā

After Akrūra visited Hastināpura and reported the condition of the Pāṇḍavas to Kṛṣṇa, there were further developments. The Pāṇḍavas were transferred to a house which was made of lac and was later set ablaze, and everyone believed that the Pāṇḍavas, along with their mother, Kuntī, had been killed. This information was also sent to Lord Kṛṣṇa and Balarāma. After consulting together, They decided to go to Hastināpura to show sympathy to Their relatives. Kṛṣṇa and Balarāma certainly knew that the Pāṇḍavas could not have been killed in the devastating fire, but in spite of this knowledge They wanted to go to Hastināpura to take part in the bereavement. On arriving in Hastināpura, Kṛṣṇa and Balarāma first went to see Bhīṣmadeva because he was the chief of the Kuru dynasty. They then saw Kṛpācārya, Vidura, Gāndhārī and Droṇa. Other members of the Kuru dynasty were not sorry, because they wanted the Pāṇḍavas and their mother to be killed. But some family members, headed by

Bhīṣma, were actually very sorry for the incident, and Kṛṣṇa and Balarāma expressed equal sorrow, without disclosing the actual situation.

When Kṛṣṇa and Balarāma were away from the city of Dvārakā, there was a conspiracy to take the Syamantaka jewel away from Satrājit. The chief conspirator was Śatadhanvā, who was among those who had wanted to marry Satyabhāmā, Satrājit's beautiful daughter. Satrājit had promised that he would give his beautiful daughter in charity to various candidates, but later the decision was changed, and Satyabhāmā was given to Kṛṣṇa along with the Syamantaka jewel. Satrājit had no desire to give the jewel away with his daughter, and Kṛṣṇa, knowing his mentality, accepted his daughter but returned the jewel. After getting back the jewel from Kṛṣṇa, he was satisfied and kept it with him always. But in the absence of Kṛṣṇa and Balarāma there was a conspiracy by many men, including even Akrūra and Kṛtavarmā, who were devotees of Lord Kṛṣṇa, to take the jewel from Satrājit. Akrūra and Kṛtavarmā joined the conspiracy because they wanted the jewel for Kṛṣṇa. They knew that Kṛṣṇa wanted the jewel and that Satrājit had not delivered it properly. Others joined the conspiracy because they were disappointed in not having the hand of Satyabhāmā. Some of them incited Śatadhanvā to kill Satrājit and take away the jewel.

The question is generally raised, Why did a great devotee like Akrūra join this conspiracy? And why did Kṛtavarmā, although a devotee of the Lord, join the conspiracy also? The answer given by great authorities like Jīva Gosvāmī is that although Akrūra was a great devotee, he was cursed by the inhabitants of Vṛndāvana because of his taking Kṛṣṇa away from their midst. Because of wounding their feelings, Akrūra was forced to join the conspiracy declared by sinful men. Similarly, Kṛtavarmā was a devotee, but because of his intimate association with Kaṁsa, he was contaminated by sinful reactions, and he also joined the conspiracy.

Being inspired by all the members of the conspiracy, Śatadhanvā one night entered the house of Satrājit and killed him while he was sleeping. Śatadhanvā was a sinful man of abominable character, and although due to his sinful activities he was not to live for many days, he decided to kill Satrājit while Satrājit was sleeping at home. When he entered the house to kill Satrājit, all the women there cried very loudly, but in spite of their great protests, Śatadhanvā mercilessly butchered Satrājit without hesitation, exactly as a butcher kills an animal in the slaughterhouse. Since Kṛṣṇa was absent from home, His wife Satyabhāmā was present on the night Satrājit was murdered, and she began to cry, "My dear father! My dear father! How mercilessly you have been killed!" The dead body of Satrājit was not immediately removed for cremation because Satyabhāmā wanted to go to Kṛṣṇa in Hastināpura. Therefore the body was preserved in a tank of oil so that Kṛṣṇa could come back and see the dead body of Satrājit and take real action against Śatadhanvā. Satyabhāmā immediately started for Hastināpura to inform Kṛṣṇa about the ghastly death of her father.

When Kṛṣṇa was informed by Satyabhāmā of the murder of His father-in-law, He began to lament like an ordinary man. His great sorrow is, again, a strange thing. Lord Kṛṣṇa has nothing to do with action and reaction, but because He was playing the part of a human being, He expressed His full sympathy for the bereavement of Satyabhāmā, and His eyes filled with tears when He heard about the death of His father-in-law. He thus began to lament, "Oh, what unhappy incidents have taken place!" Then Kṛṣṇa and Balarāma, along with Satyabhāmā, immediately returned to Dvārakā and began to make plans to kill Śatadhanvā and take away the jewel. Although he was a great outlaw in the city, Śatadhanvā was still very much afraid of Kṛṣṇa's power, and thus when Kṛṣṇa arrived he became most afraid.

Understanding Kṛṣṇa's plan to kill him, he immediately

went to take shelter of Kṛtavarmā. But Kṛtavarmā said, "I shall never be able to offend Lord Kṛṣṇa and Balarāma, for They are not ordinary persons. They are the Supreme Personality of Godhead. Who can be saved from death if he has offended Balarāma and Kṛṣṇa? No one can be saved from Their wrath." Kṛtavarmā further said that Kaṁsa, although powerful and assisted by many demons, could not be saved from Kṛṣṇa's wrath, and what to speak of Jarāsandha, who had been defeated by Kṛṣṇa seventeen times and each time had to return from the fighting in disappointment.

When Śatadhanvā was refused help by Kṛtavarmā, he went to Akrūra and implored him to help. But Akrūra also replied, "Balarāma and Kṛṣṇa are Themselves the Supreme Personality of Godhead, and anyone who knows Their unlimited strength would never dare offend Them or fight with Them." He further informed Śatadhanvā, "Kṛṣṇa and Balarāma are so powerful that simply by willing They create, maintain and dissolve the whole cosmic manifestation. Unfortunately, persons bewildered by the illusory energy cannot understand the strength of Kṛṣṇa, although the whole cosmic manifestation is fully under His control." He cited, as an example, that Kṛṣṇa, even at the age of seven years, had lifted Govardhana Hill and had continued to hold up the mountain for seven days, exactly as a child carries a small umbrella. Akrūra plainly informed Śatadhanvā that he would always offer his most respectful obeisances to Kṛṣṇa, the Supersoul of everything created and the original cause of all causes. When Akrūra also refused to give him shelter, Śatadhanvā decided to deliver the Syamantaka jewel into the hands of Akrūra. Then, riding on a horse which could run at great speed and up to four hundred miles at a stretch, he fled the city.

When Kṛṣṇa and Balarāma were informed of the flight of Śatadhanvā, They mounted Their chariot, its flag marked by a picture of Garuḍa, and followed immediately. Kṛṣṇa was particularly angry with Śatadhanvā and wanted to kill him because he had killed Satrājit, a superior personality. Satrājit happened to be the father-in-law of Kṛṣṇa, and it is the injunction of the *śāstras* that one who is *guru-druhaḥ,* who has rebelled against a superior person, must be punished in proportion to the severity of the offense. Because Śatadhanvā had killed His father-in-law, Kṛṣṇa was determined to kill him by any means.

Śatadhanvā's horse became exhausted and died near a garden house in Mithilā. Unable to take help of the horse, Śatadhanvā began to run with great speed. In order to be fair to Śatadhanvā, Kṛṣṇa and Balarāma also left Their chariot and began to follow Śatadhanvā on foot. While Śatadhanvā and Kṛṣṇa were running, Kṛṣṇa took His disc and cut off Śatadhanvā's head. After Śatadhanvā was killed, Kṛṣṇa searched through his clothing for the Syamantaka jewel, but He could not find it. He then returned to Balarāma and said, "We have killed this person uselessly, for the jewel is not to be found on his body." Śrī Balarāma suggested, "The jewel might have been kept in the custody of another man in Dvārakā, so You'd better return and search it out." Śrī Balarāma expressed His desire to remain in Mithilā City for some days because He enjoyed an intimate friendship with the King. Therefore, Kṛṣṇa returned to Dvārakā, and Balarāma entered the city of Mithilā.

When the King of Mithilā saw the arrival of Śrī Balarāma in his city, he was most pleased and received the Lord with great honor and hospitality. He gave many valuable presents to Balarāmajī in order to seek His pleasure. At this time Śrī Balarāma lived in the city for several years as the honored guest of the King of Mithilā, Janaka Mahārāja. During this time, Duryodhana, the eldest son of Dhṛtarāṣṭra, took the opportunity to come to Balarāma and learn from Him the art of fighting with a club.

After killing Śatadhanvā, Kṛṣṇa returned to Dvārakā, and in order to please His wife Satyabhāmā, He informed her of the death of Śatadhanvā, the killer of her father. But He also informed her that the jewel had not been found in his possession. Then, according to religious principles, Kṛṣṇa, along with Satyabhāmā, performed ceremonies in honor of His departed father-in-law. In those ceremonies all the friends and relatives of the family joined together.

Akrūra and Kṛtavarmā were prominent members in the conspiracy to kill Satrājit, having incited Śatadhanvā to kill him. So when they heard of the death of Śatadhanvā at Kṛṣṇa's hand, and when they also heard that Kṛṣṇa had returned to Dvārakā, they both immediately left the city. The citizens of Dvārakā felt themselves threatened with pestilence and natural disturbances due to the absence of Akrūra from the city. This was a kind of superstition, because while Lord Kṛṣṇa was present there could not be any pestilence, famine or natural disturbances. But in the absence of Akrūra there were apparently some disturbances in Dvārakā. The superstition arose for the following reason: Once in the province of Kāśī (Vārāṇasī) there was severe drought—practically no rain fell. At that time the King of Kāśī arranged the marriage of his daughter, known as Gāndinī, with Śvaphalka, the father of Akrūra. This was done by the King of Kāśī on the advice of an astrologer, and actually it so happened that after the marriage of the King's daughter with Śvaphalka there was sufficient rainfall in the province. Due to this supernatural power of Śvaphalka, his son Akrūra was considered equally powerful, and people were under the impression that wherever Akrūra or his father stayed there would be no natural disturbances, such as famine or drought. That kingdom is considered happy where there is no famine, pestilence or excessive heat and cold and where people are happy mentally, spiritually and physically. As soon as there was some disturbance in Dvārakā, people considered the cause to be the absence of an auspicious personality in the city. Thus there was a rumor that because of the absence of Akrūra inauspicious things were happening.

After the departure of Akrūra, some of the elderly residents of the city also began to perceive inauspicious signs due to the absence of the Syamantaka jewel. When Lord Śrī Kṛṣṇa heard these rumors spread by the people, He decided to summon Akrūra from the kingdom of Kāśī.

Akrūra was Kṛṣṇa's uncle; therefore, when he came back to Dvārakā, Lord Kṛṣṇa first of all gave him a welcome befitting a superior person. Kṛṣṇa is the Supersoul in everyone and knows everything going on in everyone's heart. He knew everything that had happened in connection with Akrūra's conspiracy with Śatadhanvā. Therefore, He smilingly began to speak to Akrūra. Addressing him as the chief among munificent men, Kṛṣṇa said, "My dear uncle, it is already known to Me that the Syamantaka jewel was left by Śatadhanvā with you. Presently there is no direct claimant of the Syamantaka jewel, for King Satrājit has no male issue. His daughter Satyabhāmā is not very eager for this jewel, yet her expected son, as a grandson of Satrājit's, would, after performing the regulative principles of inheritance, be the legal claimant of the jewel." Lord Kṛṣṇa indicated by this statement that Satyabhāmā was already pregnant and that her son would be the real claimant of the jewel and would certainly take the jewel from Akrūra.

Kṛṣṇa continued, "This jewel is so powerful that no ordinary man is able to keep it. I know that you are very pious in activities, so there is no objection to the jewel's being kept with you. There is one difficulty, and that is that My elder brother, Śrī Balarāma, does not believe My version that the jewel is with you. I therefore request you, O large-hearted one, to show Me the jewel just once before My other relatives so that they may be pacified and reject various kinds of rumors. You cannot deny that the jewel is with you because we can understand that you have enhanced your opulence and are performing sacrifices on an altar made of solid gold." The properties of the jewel were known: wherever the jewel remained, it would produce for the keeper more than two *mounds* of pure gold daily. Akrūra was getting gold in that proportion and distributing it profusely at sacrificial performances. Lord Kṛṣṇa cited Akrūra's lavishly spending gold as positive evidence of his possessing the Syamantaka jewel.

When Lord Kṛṣṇa, in friendly terms and sweet language, impressed Akrūra about the real fact and Akrūra understood that nothing could be concealed from the knowledge of Śrī Kṛṣṇa, he brought out the valuable jewel, covered by cloth but shining like the sun, and presented it before Kṛṣṇa. Lord Kṛṣṇa took the Syamantaka jewel in His hand and showed it to all His relatives and friends present and then returned the jewel to Akrūra in their presence, so that they would know that the jewel was actually being kept by Akrūra in Dvārakā City.

This story of the Syamantaka jewel is very significant. In *Śrīmad-Bhāgavatam* it is said that anyone who hears the story of the Syamantaka jewel or describes it or simply remembers it will be free from all kinds of defamation and the reactions of all impious activities and thus will attain the highest perfectional condition of peace.

Thus ends the Bhaktivedanta purport of the Fifty-seventh Chapter of Kṛṣṇa, *"The Killing of Satrājit and Śatadhanvā."*

CHAPTER FIFTY-EIGHT

Five Queens Married by Kṛṣṇa

As mentioned in the last chapter, there was a great rumor that the five Pāṇḍava brothers, along with their mother, Kuntī, had died, according to the plan of the sons of Dhṛtarāṣṭra, in a fire accident in the house of lac in which they were living. But then the five brothers were detected at the marriage ceremony of Draupadī, so another rumor spread that the Pāṇḍavas and their mother were not dead. It was a rumor, but actually it was so; they returned to their capital city, Hastināpura, and people saw them face to face. When this news was carried to Kṛṣṇa and Balarāma, Kṛṣṇa wanted to see them personally, and therefore He decided to go to Hastināpura.

This time Kṛṣṇa visited Hastināpura in state, as a royal prince, accompanied by His commander in chief, Yuyudhāna, and by many other soldiers. He had not actually been invited to visit the city, yet He went to see the Pāṇḍavas out of His affection for His great devotees. He visited the Pāṇḍavas without warning, and all of them got up from their respective seats as soon as they saw Him. Kṛṣṇa is called Mukunda because as soon as one comes in constant touch with Kṛṣṇa or sees

Him in full Kṛṣṇa consciousness, one immediately becomes freed from all material anxieties. Not only that, but one is immediately blessed with all spiritual bliss.

Receiving Kṛṣṇa, the Pāṇḍavas were enlivened, just as if awakened from unconsciousness or loss of life. When a man is lying unconscious, his senses and the different parts of his body are inactive, but when he regains his consciousness the senses immediately become active. Similarly, the Pāṇḍavas received Kṛṣṇa as if they had just regained their consciousness, and so they were very much enlivened. Lord Kṛṣṇa embraced every one of them, and by the touch of the Supreme Personality of Godhead the Pāṇḍavas immediately became freed from all reactions of material contamination and were therefore smiling in spiritual bliss. By seeing the face of Lord Kṛṣṇa, everyone was transcendentally satisfied. Lord Kṛṣṇa, although the Supreme Personality of Godhead, was playing the part of an ordinary human being, and thus He immediately touched the feet of Yudhiṣṭhira and Bhīma because they were His two older cousins. Arjuna embraced Kṛṣṇa as a friend of the same age, whereas the two younger brothers, namely Nakula and Sahadeva, touched the lotus feet of Kṛṣṇa to show Him respect. After an exchange of greetings according to the social etiquette befitting the position of the Pāṇḍavas and Lord Kṛṣṇa, Kṛṣṇa was offered an exalted seat. When He was comfortably seated, the newly married Draupadī, young and very beautiful in her natural feminine gracefulness, came before Lord Kṛṣṇa to offer her respectful greetings. The Yādavas who accompanied Kṛṣṇa to Hastināpura were also very respectfully received; specifically, Sātyaki, or Yuyudhāna, was also offered a nice seat. In this way, when everyone else was properly seated, the five brothers took their seats near Lord Kṛṣṇa.

After meeting with the five brothers, Lord Kṛṣṇa personally went to visit Śrīmatī Kuntīdevī, the mother of the Pāṇḍavas, who was also Kṛṣṇa's paternal aunt. In offering His respects to His aunt, Kṛṣṇa also touched her feet. Kuntīdevī's eyes became wet, and, in great love, she feelingly embraced Lord Kṛṣṇa. She then inquired from Him about the well-being of her paternal family members—her brother Vasudeva, his wives and other members of the family. Similarly, Kṛṣṇa also inquired from His aunt about the welfare of the Pāṇḍava family. Although Kuntīdevī was related to Kṛṣṇa by family ties, she knew immediately after meeting Him that He is the Supreme Personality of Godhead. She remembered the past calamities of her life and how by the grace of Kṛṣṇa she and her sons, the Pāṇḍavas, had been saved. She knew perfectly well that without Kṛṣṇa's grace no one could have saved them from the fire "accident" designed by the sons of Dhṛtarāṣṭra. In a choked-up voice, she began to narrate before Kṛṣṇa the history of their life.

Śrīmatī Kuntī said, "My dear Kṛṣṇa, I remember the day when You sent my brother Akrūra to gather information about us. This means that You always remember us automatically. When You sent Akrūra, I could understand that there was no possibility of our being put in danger. All good fortune in our life began when You sent Akrūra to us. Since then, I have been convinced that we are not without protection. We may be put into various types of dangerous conditions by our family members, the Kurus, but I am confident that You remember us and always keep us safe and sound. Even ordinary devotees who simply think of You are always immune to all kinds of material danger, and what to speak of ourselves, who are personally remembered by You. So, my dear Kṛṣṇa, there is no question of bad luck; we are always in an auspicious position because of Your grace. But although You have bestowed a special favor on us, people should not mistakenly think that You are partial to some and inattentive to others. You make no such distinction. No one is Your favorite and no one is Your enemy. As the Supreme Personality of Godhead, You are equal to everyone, and everyone can take advantage of Your special protection. The fact is that although You are equal to everyone, You are especially inclined to the devotees who always think of You. The devotees are related to You by ties of love. As such, they cannot forget You even for a moment. You are present in everyone's heart, but because the devotees always remember You, You respond accordingly. Although the mother has affection for all the children, she takes special care of the one who is fully dependent. I know certainly, my dear Kṛṣṇa, that being seated in everyone's heart, You always create auspicious situations for Your unalloyed devotees."

Then King Yudhiṣṭhira also praised Kṛṣṇa as the Supreme Personality and universal friend of everyone, but because Kṛṣṇa was taking special care of the Pāṇḍavas, King Yudhiṣṭhira said, "My dear Kṛṣṇa, we do not know what sort of pious activities we have executed in our past lives that have made You so kind and gracious to us. We know very well that the great mystics who always engage in meditation to capture You do not find it easy to obtain such grace, nor can they draw any personal attention from You. I cannot understand why You are so kind to us. We are not *yogīs;* on the contrary, we are attached to material contaminations. We are householders dealing in politics, worldly affairs. I do not know why You are so kind to us."

Being requested by King Yudhiṣṭhira, Kṛṣṇa agreed to stay in Hastināpura for four months during the rainy season. The four months of the rainy season are called Cāturmāsya. During this period, the generally itinerant preachers and *brāhmaṇas* stop at a certain place and live under rigid regulative principles. Although Lord Kṛṣṇa is above all regulative principles, He agreed to stay at Hastināpura out of affection for the Pāṇḍavas. Taking this opportunity of Kṛṣṇa's residence in Hastināpura, all the citizens of the city got the privilege of seeing Him now and then, and thus they merged into transcendental bliss simply by seeing Lord Kṛṣṇa face to face.

One day, while Kṛṣṇa was staying with the Pāṇḍavas, He

and Arjuna prepared themselves to go to the forest to hunt. Both of them sat down on Arjuna's chariot, which flew a flag with a picture of Hanumān. Arjuna's special chariot is always marked with the picture of Hanumān, and therefore he is also named Kapidhvaja. (*Kapi* means Hanumān, and *dhvaja* means "flag.") Thus Arjuna prepared to go to the forest with his bow and infallible arrows. He dressed himself with suitable protective garments, for he was to practice for the time when he would be killing many enemies on the battlefield. He specifically entered that part of the forest where there were many tigers, deer and various other animals. The reason Kṛṣṇa went with Arjuna was not to practice animal-killing, for He doesn't have to practice anything; He is self-sufficient. He accompanied Arjuna to see how he was practicing because in the future he would have to kill many enemies. After entering the forest, Arjuna killed many tigers, boars, bison, *gavayas* (a kind of wild animal), rhinoceroses, deer, hares, porcupines and similar other animals, which he pierced with his arrows. Some of the dead animals that were fit to be offered in sacrifices were carried by servants and sent to King Yudhiṣṭhira. The ferocious animals, such as tigers and rhinoceroses, were killed only to stop disturbances in the forest. Since there are many sages and saintly persons who are residents of the forest, it is the duty of the *kṣatriya* kings to keep even the forest in a peaceful condition for living.

Arjuna felt tired and thirsty from hunting, and therefore he went to the bank of the Yamunā along with Kṛṣṇa. When both the Kṛṣṇas, namely Kṛṣṇa and Arjuna, reached the bank of the Yamunā (Arjuna is sometimes called Kṛṣṇa, as is Draupadī), they washed their hands, feet and mouths and drank the clear water of the Yamunā. While resting and drinking water, they saw a beautiful girl of marriageable age walking alone on the bank of the Yamunā. Kṛṣṇa asked His friend Arjuna to go forward and ask the girl who she was. By the order of Kṛṣṇa, Arjuna immediately approached the girl, who was very beautiful. She had an attractive body, nice, glittering teeth and a smiling face. Arjuna inquired, "My dear girl, you are so beautiful with your raised breasts. May I ask you who you are? We are surprised to see you loitering here alone. What is your purpose in coming here? We can guess only that you are searching after a suitable husband. If you don't mind, you can disclose your purpose. I shall try to satisfy you."

The beautiful girl was the river Yamunā personified. She replied, "Sir, I am the daughter of the sun-god, and I am now performing penance and austerity to have Lord Viṣṇu as my husband. I think He is the Supreme Person and just suitable to become my husband. I disclose my desire thus because you wanted to know it."

The girl continued, "My dear sir, I know that you are the hero Arjuna; so I may further say that I shall not accept anyone as my husband besides Lord Viṣṇu, because He is the only protector of all living entities and the bestower of liberation for all conditioned souls. I shall be thankful unto you if you pray to Lord Viṣṇu to be pleased with me." The girl Yamunā knew it well that Arjuna was a great devotee of Lord Kṛṣṇa and that if he would pray, Kṛṣṇa would never deny his request. To approach Kṛṣṇa directly may sometimes be futile, but to approach Kṛṣṇa through His devotee is sure to be successful. She further told Arjuna, "My name is Kālindī, and I live within the waters of the Yamunā. My father was kind enough to construct a special house for me within the waters of the Yamunā, and I have vowed to remain in the water as long as I cannot find Lord Kṛṣṇa." Arjuna duly carried the message of the girl Kālindī to Kṛṣṇa, although Kṛṣṇa, as the Supersoul in everyone's heart, knew everything. Without further discussion, Kṛṣṇa immediately accepted Kālindī and asked her to sit down on the chariot. Then all of them approached King Yudhiṣṭhira.

After this, Kṛṣṇa was asked by King Yudhiṣṭhira to help in constructing a suitable house to be planned by the great architect Viśvakarmā, the celestial engineer in the heavenly kingdom. Kṛṣṇa immediately called for Viśvakarmā and made him construct a wonderful city according to the desire of King Yudhiṣṭhira. When this city was constructed, Mahārāja Yudhiṣṭhira requested Kṛṣṇa to live with them a few days more to give them the pleasure of His association. Lord Kṛṣṇa accepted the request of Mahārāja Yudhiṣṭhira and remained there for many days more.

In the meantime, Kṛṣṇa engaged in the pastime of offering the Khāṇḍava forest, which belonged to King Indra. Kṛṣṇa wanted to give it to Agni, the fire-god. The Khāṇḍava forest contained many varieties of drugs, and Agni required to eat them for rejuvenation. Agni, however, did not touch the Khāṇḍava forest directly but requested Kṛṣṇa to help him. Agni knew that Kṛṣṇa was very pleased with him because he had formerly given Him the Sudarśana disc. So in order to satisfy Agni, Kṛṣṇa became the chariot driver of Arjuna, and both went to the Khāṇḍava forest. After Agni had eaten up the Khāṇḍava forest, he was very pleased. At this time he offered Arjuna a specific bow known as Gāṇḍīva, four white horses, one chariot and an invincible quiver with two specific arrows considered to be talismans, which had so much power that no warrior could counteract them. When the Khāṇḍava forest was being devoured by the fire-god, Agni, there was a demon of the name Maya who was saved by Arjuna from the devastating fire. For this reason, that former demon became a great friend of Arjuna, and in order to please Arjuna he constructed a nice assembly house within the city constructed by Viśvakarmā. This assembly house had some corners so puzzling that when Duryodhana came to visit this house he was misdirected, accepting water as land and land as water. Duryodhana was thus insulted by the opulence of the Pāṇḍavas, and he became their determined enemy.

After a few days, Lord Kṛṣṇa took permission from King Yudhiṣṭhira to return to Dvārakā. When He got permission,

He returned to His country accompanied by Sātyaki, the leader of the Yadus who were living in Hastināpura with Him. Kālindī also returned with Kṛṣṇa to Dvārakā. After returning, Kṛṣṇa consulted many learned astrologers to find the suitable moment at which to marry Kālindī, and then He married her with great pomp. This marriage ceremony gave much pleasure to the relatives of both parties, and all of them enjoyed the great occasion.

The kings of Avantipura (now known as Ujjain) were named Vindya and Anuvindya. Both kings were under the control of Duryodhana. They had one sister, named Mitravindā, who was a very qualified, learned and elegant girl, the daughter of one of Kṛṣṇa's aunts. She was to select her husband in an assembly of princes, but she strongly desired to have Kṛṣṇa as her husband. During the assembly for selecting her husband, Kṛṣṇa was present, and He forcibly carried away Mitravindā in the presence of all the other royal princes. Being unable to resist Kṛṣṇa, the princes were left simply looking at each other.

After this incident, Kṛṣṇa married the daughter of the King of Kośala. The King of Kośala Province was called Nagnajit. He was very pious and was a follower of the Vedic ritualistic ceremonies. His most beautiful daughter was named Satyā. Sometimes Satyā was called Nāgnajitī, for she was the daughter of King Nagnajit. King Nagnajit wanted to give the hand of his daughter to any prince who could defeat seven very strong, stalwart bulls maintained by him. No one in the princely order could defeat the seven bulls, and therefore no one could claim the hand of Satyā. The seven bulls were very strong, and they could hardly bear even the smell of any prince. Many princes visited this kingdom and tried to subdue the bulls, but instead of controlling them, they themselves were defeated. This news spread all over the country, and when Kṛṣṇa heard that one could achieve the girl Satyā only by defeating the seven bulls, He prepared Himself to go to the kingdom of Kośala. With many soldiers, He approached that part of the country, known as Ayodhyā, making a regular state visit.

When it was known to the King of Kośala that Kṛṣṇa had come to ask the hand of his daughter, he was very pleased. With great respect and pomp, he welcomed Kṛṣṇa to the kingdom. When Kṛṣṇa approached him, he offered the Lord a suitable sitting place and articles for reception. Everything appeared very elegant. Kṛṣṇa also offered him respectful obeisances, thinking him to be His future father-in-law.

When Satyā understood that Kṛṣṇa Himself had come to marry her, she was very pleased that the husband of the goddess of fortune had so kindly come there to accept her. For a long time she had cherished the idea of marrying Kṛṣṇa and was following the principles of austerities to obtain her desired husband. She then began to think, "If I have performed any pious activities to the best of my ability, and if I have sincerely thought all along to have Kṛṣṇa as my husband, then Kṛṣṇa may be pleased to fulfill my long-cherished desire." She began to offer prayers to Kṛṣṇa mentally, thinking, "I do not know how the Supreme Personality of Godhead can be pleased with me. He is the master and Lord of everyone. Even the goddess of fortune, whose place is next to the Supreme Personality of Godhead, and Lord Śiva, Lord Brahmā and many other demigods of different planets always offer their respectful obeisances unto the Lord. The Lord also sometimes descends to this earth in different incarnations to fulfill the desire of His devotees. He is so exalted and great that I do not know how to satisfy Him." She thought that the Supreme Personality of Godhead could be pleased only out of His own causeless mercy upon the devotee; otherwise, there was no means to please Him. Lord Caitanya, in the same way, prayed in His *Śikṣāṣṭaka* verses, "My Lord, I am Your eternal servant. Somehow or other I have fallen into this material existence. If You kindly pick Me up and fix Me as an atom of dust at Your lotus feet, it will be a great favor to Your eternal servant." The Lord can be pleased only by a humble attitude in the service spirit. The more we render service unto the Lord under the direction of the spiritual master, the more we make advancement on the path approaching the Lord. We cannot demand any grace or mercy from the Lord because of our service rendered to Him. He may accept or not accept our service, but the only means to satisfy the Lord is through the service attitude, and nothing else.

King Nagnajit was a pious king, and having Lord Kṛṣṇa in his palace, he began to worship Him to the best of his knowledge and ability. He presented himself before the Lord thus: "My dear Lord, You are the proprietor of the whole cosmic manifestation, and You are Nārāyaṇa, the resting place of all living creatures. You are self-sufficient and pleased with Your personal opulences, so how can I offer You anything? And how could I please You by such an offering? It is not possible, because I am an insignificant living being. Actually I have no ability to render any service unto You."

Kṛṣṇa is the Supersoul of all living creatures, so He could understand the mind of Satyā. He was also very pleased with the respectful worship of the King in offering Him a sitting place, eatables, a residence and so on. He was appreciative, therefore, that both the girl and her father were eager to have Him as their intimate relative. He smiled and in a grave voice said, "My dear King Nagnajit, you know very well that anyone in the princely order who is regular in his position will never ask anything from anyone, however exalted he may be. Such requests by a *kṣatriya* king have been deliberately forbidden by the learned Vedic followers. If a *kṣatriya* breaks this regulation, his action is condemned by learned scholars. But in spite of this rigid regulative principle, I am asking you for the hand of your beautiful daughter just to establish our relationship in return for your great reception of Me. You may also be pleased to be informed that in Our family tradition there is no scope for Our offering anything in exchange for accepting your daughter. We cannot pay any price you may impose for delivering her." In other words, Kṛṣṇa wanted the hand of Satyā from the King without fulfilling the condition of defeating the seven bulls.

After hearing the statement of Lord Kṛṣṇa, King Nagnajit said, "My dear Lord, You are the reservoir of all pleasure, all opulences and all qualities. The goddess of fortune, Lakṣmījī, always lives on Your chest. Under these circumstances, who can be a better husband for my daughter? Both my daughter and I have always prayed for this opportunity. You are the chief of the Yadu dynasty. You may kindly know that from the very beginning I have made a vow to marry my daughter to a suitable candidate, one who can come out victorious in the test I have devised. I have imposed this test just to understand the prowess and position of my intended son-in-law. You, Lord Kṛṣṇa, are the chief of all heroes. I am sure You will be able to bring these seven bulls under control without any difficulty. Until now they have never been subdued by any prince; anyone who has attempted to bring them under control has simply had his limbs broken."

King Nagnajit continued his request: "Kṛṣṇa, if You'll kindly bridle the seven bulls and bring them under control, then undoubtedly You will be selected as the desired husband of my daughter, Satyā." After hearing this statement, Kṛṣṇa could understand that the King did not want to break his vow. Thus, in order to fulfill his desire, He tightened His belt and prepared to fight with the bulls. He immediately divided Himself into seven Kṛṣṇas, and each one of Them immediately caught hold of a bull and bridled its nose, thus bringing it under control as if it were a plaything.

Kṛṣṇa's dividing Himself into seven is very significant. It was known to Satyā that Kṛṣṇa had already married many other wives, but still she was attached to Kṛṣṇa. In order to encourage her, Kṛṣṇa immediately expanded Himself into seven. The purport is that Kṛṣṇa is one, but He has unlimited forms of expansions. He married many thousands of wives, but this does not mean that while He was with one wife the others were bereft of His association. Kṛṣṇa could associate with each and every wife by His expansions.

When Kṛṣṇa brought the bulls under His control by bridling their noses, their strength and pride were immediately smashed. The name and fame which the bulls had attained was thus vanquished. When Kṛṣṇa had the bulls bridled, He pulled them strongly, just as a child pulls a toy wooden bull. Upon seeing this advantage of Kṛṣṇa, King Nagnajit became very much astonished and immediately, with great pleasure, brought his daughter Satyā before Kṛṣṇa and handed her over to Him. Kṛṣṇa also immediately accepted Satyā as His wife. Then there was a marriage ceremony with great pomp. The queens of King Nagnajit were also very pleased because their daughter Satyā got Kṛṣṇa as her husband. Since the King and queens were very pleased on this auspicious occasion, there was a celebration all over the city in honor of the marriage. Everywhere were heard the sounds of the conchshell and kettledrum and various other vibrations of music and song. The learned *brāhmaṇas* showered their blessings upon the newly married couple. In jubilation, all the inhabitants of the city dressed themselves with colorful garments and ornaments. King Nagnajit was so pleased that he gave a dowry to his daughter and son-in-law, as follows.

First of all he gave them 10,000 cows and 3,000 well-dressed young maidservants, ornamented up to their necks. This system of dowry is still current in India, especially for *kṣatriya* princes. When a *kṣatriya* prince is married, at least a dozen maidservants of similar age are given along with the bride. After giving the cows and maidservants, the King enriched the dowry by giving 9,000 elephants and a hundred times more chariots than elephants. This means that he gave 900,000 chariots. And he gave a hundred times more horses than chariots, or 90,000,000 horses, and a hundred times more menservants than horses. Royal princes maintained such menservants and maidservants with all provisions, as if they were their own children or family members. After giving this dowry, the King of Kośala Province bade his daughter and great son-in-law be seated on a chariot and allowed them to go to their home, guarded by a division of well-equipped soldiers. As they traveled fast to their new home, the King's heart was enlivened with affection for them.

Before this marriage of Satyā with Kṛṣṇa, there had been many competitive engagements with the bulls of King Nagnajit, and many other princes of the Yadu dynasty and of other dynasties as well had tried to win the hand of Satyā. When the frustrated princes of the other dynasties heard that Kṛṣṇa was successful in getting the hand of Satyā by subduing the bulls, naturally they became envious. While Kṛṣṇa was traveling to Dvārakā, all the frustrated and defeated princes encircled Him and began to shower their arrows on the bridal party. When they attacked Kṛṣṇa's party and shot arrows like incessant torrents of rain, Arjuna, the best friend of Kṛṣṇa, took charge of the challenge, and he alone very easily drove them off to please his great friend Kṛṣṇa on the occasion of His marriage. He immediately took up his bow, Gāṇḍīva, and chased away all the princes; exactly as a lion drives away all small animals simply by chasing them, Arjuna drove away all the princes, without killing even one of them. After this, the chief of the Yadu dynasty, Lord Kṛṣṇa, along with His newly married wife and the huge dowry, entered the city of Dvārakā with great pomp. Kṛṣṇa then lived there with His wife very peacefully.

Besides Kuntīdevī, Kṛṣṇa had another paternal aunt; her name was Śrutakīrti, and she was married and lived in Kekaya Province. She had a daughter whose name was Bhadrā. Bhadrā wanted to marry Kṛṣṇa, and her brother handed her over to Him unconditionally. Kṛṣṇa accepted her as His bona fide wife. Thereafter, Kṛṣṇa married a daughter of the King of

Madras Province. Her name was Lakṣmaṇā. Lakṣmaṇā had all good qualities. She was also forcibly married by Kṛṣṇa, who took her in the same way that Garuḍa snatched the jar of nectar from the hands of the demigods. Kṛṣṇa kidnapped this girl in the presence of many other princes in the assembly of her *svayaṁvara.* The *svayaṁvara* is a ceremony in which the bride can select her own husband from an assembly of many princes.

The description of Kṛṣṇa's marriage with the five girls mentioned in this chapter is not sufficient. He had many other thousands of wives besides them. Kṛṣṇa accepted the other thousands of wives after killing a demon named Bhaumāsura. All these thousands of girls were held captive in the palace of Bhaumāsura, and Kṛṣṇa released them and married them.

Thus ends the Bhaktivedanta purport of the Fifty-eighth Chapter of Kṛṣṇa, *"Five Queens Married by Kṛṣṇa."*

CHAPTER FIFTY-NINE

The Deliverance of the Demon Bhaumāsura

The story of Bhaumāsura—how he kidnapped and made captive sixteen thousand princesses by collecting them from the palaces of various kings and how he was killed by Kṛṣṇa, the Supreme Lord of wonderful character—is all described by Śukadeva Gosvāmī to King Parīkṣit in *Śrīmad-Bhāgavatam.* Generally, the demons are always against the demigods. This demon, Bhaumāsura, having become very powerful, took by force the umbrella from the throne of the demigod Varuṇa. He also took the earrings of Aditi, the mother of the demigods. He conquered a portion of heavenly Mount Meru and occupied the portion known as Maṇi-parvata. The King of the heavenly planets, Indra, therefore came to Dvārakā to complain about Bhaumāsura before Lord Kṛṣṇa.

Hearing this complaint by Indra, the King of heaven, Lord Kṛṣṇa, accompanied by His wife Satyabhāmā, immediately started for the abode of Bhaumāsura. The two of them rode on the back of Garuḍa, who flew them to Prāgjyotiṣa-pura,

Bhaumāsura's capital city. To enter the city of Prāgjyotiṣapura was not a very easy task, because it was very well fortified. First of all, there were four strongholds guarding the four directions of the city, which was well protected on all sides by formidable military strength. The next boundary was a water canal all around the city, and in addition the whole city was surrounded by electric wires. The next fortification was of *anila,* a gaseous substance. After this, there was a network of barbed wiring constructed by a demon of the name Mura. The city appeared well protected even in terms of today's scientific advancements.

When Kṛṣṇa arrived, He broke all the strongholds to pieces by the strokes of His club and scattered the military strength here and there by the constant onslaught of His arrows. With His celebrated Sudarśana *cakra* He counteracted the electrified boundary, annihilated the canal of water and the gaseous boundary, and cut to pieces the electrified network fabricated by the demon Mura. By the vibration of His conchshell, He broke the hearts of the great fighters and also broke the fighting machines that were there. Similarly, He broke the walls around the city with His invincible club.

The vibration of Lord Kṛṣṇa's conchshell sounded like a thunderbolt at the time of the dissolution of the whole cosmic manifestation. The demon Mura heard the vibration of the conchshell, awakened from his sleep and came out to see what had happened. He had five heads and had long been living within the water. The Mura demon was as brilliant as the sun at the time of the dissolution of the cosmos, and his temper was like blazing fire. The effulgence of his body was so dazzling that he was difficult to see with open eyes. When he came out, he first took out his trident and rushed the Supreme Personality of Godhead. The demon Mura in his onslaught was like a big snake attacking Garuḍa. His angry mood was very severe, and he appeared ready to devour the three worlds. First of all he attacked the carrier of Kṛṣṇa, Garuḍa, by whirling and then throwing his trident, and through his five mouths he vibrated sounds like the roaring of a lion. These roaring vibrations spread all over the atmosphere until they extended all over the world and into outer space, up and down and out to the ten directions, rumbling throughout the entire universe.

Lord Kṛṣṇa saw that the trident of the Mura demon was rushing toward His carrier, Garuḍa. Immediately, by a trick of His hand, He took two arrows and threw them toward the trident, cutting it to pieces. Simultaneously, using many arrows, He pierced the mouths of the demon Mura. When the Mura demon saw himself outmaneuvered by the Supreme Personality of Godhead, he immediately began to strike the Lord in great anger with his club. But Lord Kṛṣṇa, with His own club, broke the club of Mura to pieces before it could reach Him. The demon, bereft of his weapon, decided to attack Kṛṣṇa with his strong arms, but Kṛṣṇa, with the aid of His Sudarśana *cakra,* immediately separated the demon's five heads from his body. The demon then fell into the water, just as the peak of a mountain falls into the ocean after being struck by the thunderbolt of Indra.

This demon Mura had seven sons, named Tāmra, Antarikṣa, Śravaṇa, Vibhāvasu, Vasu, Nabhasvān and Aruṇa. All of them became puffed up and vengeful because of the death of their father, and to retaliate they prepared in great anger to fight with Kṛṣṇa. They equipped themselves with necessary weapons and situated Pīṭha, another demon, to act as commander in the battle. By the order of Bhaumāsura, all of them combinedly attacked Kṛṣṇa.

When they came before Lord Kṛṣṇa, they began to shower Him with many kinds of weapons, like swords, clubs, lances, arrows and tridents. But they did not know that the strength of the Supreme Personality of Godhead is unlimited and invincible. Kṛṣṇa, with His arrows, cut all the weapons of the men of Bhaumāsura into pieces, like grains. Kṛṣṇa then threw His weapons, and Bhaumāsura's commander in chief, Pīṭha, along with his assistants, fell down, their military dress cut off and their heads, legs, arms and thighs severed. All of them were sent to the superintendent of death, Yamarāja.

Bhaumāsura, who was also known as Narakāsura, happened to be the son of the earth personified. When he saw that all his soldiers, commanders and fighters had been killed on the battlefield by the strokes of the weapons of the Personality of Godhead, he became exceedingly angry at the Lord. He then came out of the city with a great number of elephants who had all been born and brought up on the seashore. All of them were highly intoxicated. When they came out, they saw that Lord Kṛṣṇa and His wife were beautifully situated high in outer space just like a blackish cloud about the sun, glittering with the light of electricity. The demon Bhaumāsura immediately released a weapon called Śataghnī, by which he could kill hundreds of warriors with one stroke, and all his assistants simultaneously threw their respective weapons at the Supreme Personality of Godhead. Lord Kṛṣṇa counteracted all these weapons by releasing His feathered arrows. The result of this fight was that all the soldiers and commanders of Bhaumāsura fell to the ground, their arms, legs and heads separated from their trunks, and all their horses and elephants also fell with them. In this way, all the weapons released by Bhaumāsura were cut to pieces by the Lord's arrows.

The Lord was fighting on the back of Garuḍa, who was helping the Lord by striking the horses and elephants with his wings and scratching their heads with his nails and sharp beak. The elephants, feeling much pain from Garuḍa's attack on them, all dispersed from the battlefield. Bhaumāsura alone remained on the battlefield, and he engaged himself in fighting with Kṛṣṇa. He saw that Kṛṣṇa's carrier, Garuḍa, had caused great disturbance to his soldiers and elephants, and in great anger he struck Garuḍa with all his strength, which defied the strength of a thunderbolt. Fortunately, Garuḍa was not an ordinary bird, and he felt the strokes given by Bhaumāsura just as a great elephant feels the impact of a garland of flowers.

Bhaumāsura thus came to see that none of his tricks would act upon Kṛṣṇa, and he became aware that all his attempts to kill Kṛṣṇa would be frustrated. Yet he tried for the last time, taking a trident in his hand to strike Him. Kṛṣṇa was so dexterous that before Bhaumāsura could throw his trident, his head was cut off by the sharp Sudarśana *cakra.* His head, illuminated by earrings and a helmet, fell down on the battlefield. On the occasion of Bhaumāsura's being killed by Lord Kṛṣṇa, all the demon's relatives screamed in disappointment, and the saintly persons glorified the chivalrous activities of the Lord. Taking this opportunity, the denizens of the heavenly planets showered flowers on the Lord.

At this time, the earth personified appeared before Lord Kṛṣṇa and greeted Him with a Vaijayantī flower garland. She then returned the dazzling earrings of Aditi, bedecked with jewels and gold. She also returned the umbrella of Varuṇa, along with a valuable jewel, which she presented to Kṛṣṇa. After this, the earth personified offered her prayers to Kṛṣṇa, the Supreme Personality and master of the world, who is always worshiped by exalted demigods. She fell down in obeisances and, in great devotional ecstasy, began to speak.

"Let me offer my respectful obeisances unto the Lord, who is always present with four symbols, namely His conchshell, disc, lotus and club, and who is the Lord of all demigods. Please accept my respectful obeisances unto You. My dear Lord, You are the Supersoul, and in order to satisfy the aspirations of Your devotees, You descend on the earth in Your various transcendental incarnations, which are just appropriate to the devotees' worshipful desire. Kindly accept my respectful obeisances.

"My dear Lord, the lotus flower grows out of Your navel, and You are always decorated with a garland of lotus flowers.

Your eyes are always spread like the petals of the lotus flower, and therefore they are all-pleasing to the eyes of others. Your soft and delicate lotus feet are always worshiped by Your unalloyed devotees, and those lotus feet pacify their lotuslike hearts. I therefore repeatedly offer my respectful obeisances unto You.

"You possess all beauty, strength, fame, property, knowledge and renunciation; You are the shelter of all six opulences. Although You are all-pervading, You have appeared as the son of Vasudeva. Please, therefore, accept my respectful obeisances. You are the original Supreme Personality of Godhead and the supreme cause of all causes. Only Your Lordship is the reservoir of all knowledge. Let me offer my respectful obeisances unto You. Personally You are unborn; still, You are the father of the whole cosmic manifestation. You are the reservoir and shelter of all kinds of energies. The manifested appearance of this world is caused by You, and You are both the cause and effect of this cosmic manifestation. Please therefore accept my respectful obeisances.

"My dear Lord, as for the three gods Brahmā, Viṣṇu and Śiva, they are not independent of You. When there is a necessity of creating this cosmic manifestation, You create Your passionate appearance of Brahmā, and when You want to maintain this cosmic manifestation You expand Yourself as Lord Viṣṇu, the reservoir of all goodness. Similarly, You appear as Lord Śiva, master of the mode of ignorance, and thus dissolve the whole creation. You always maintain Your transcendental position, in spite of creating these three modes of material nature. You are never entangled in these modes of nature, as the ordinary living entities are.

"Actually, my Lord, You are the material nature, You are the father of the universe, and You are eternal time, which has caused the combination of the elements of nature and the manifestation of the material creation. Still, You are always transcendental to all these material activities. My dear

Lord, O Supreme Personality of Godhead, I know that earth, water, fire, air, sky, the five sense objects, mind, the senses and their deities, egotism, and the total material energy—everything animate and inanimate in this phenomenal world—rests upon You. Since everything is produced of You, nothing can be separate from You. Yet since You are transcendentally situated, nothing material can be identified with Your personality. Everything is therefore simultaneously one with You and different from You, and the philosophers who try to separate everything from You are certainly mistaken in their viewpoint.

"My dear Lord, may I inform You that this boy, whose name is Bhagadatta, is the son of my son, Bhaumāsura. He has been very much affected by the ghastly situation created by the death of his father and has become very much confused and afraid. I have therefore brought him to surrender unto Your lotus feet. I request Your Lordship to give shelter to this boy and bless him with Your lotus feet. I bring him to You so that he may be relieved of the reactions of all the sinful activities of his father."

When Lord Kṛṣṇa heard the prayers of mother Earth, He immediately assured her of immunity from all fearful situations. He said to Bhagadatta, "Don't be afraid." Then He entered the palace of Bhaumāsura, which was equipped with all kinds of opulences. In the palace of Bhaumāsura, Lord Kṛṣṇa saw 16,100 young princesses, who had been kidnapped and held captive there. When the princesses saw the Supreme Personality of Godhead, Kṛṣṇa, enter the palace, they immediately became captivated by the beauty of the Lord and prayed for His causeless mercy. Within their minds, they decided to accept Lord Kṛṣṇa as their husband without hesitation. Each one of them prayed to Providence that Kṛṣṇa might become her husband. Sincerely and seriously, they offered their hearts to the lotus feet of Kṛṣṇa with an unalloyed devotional attitude. As the Supersoul in everyone's heart, Kṛṣṇa could understand their uncontaminated desire, and He agreed to accept them as His wives. Thus He arranged for suitable garments and ornaments for them, and each of them, seated on a palanquin, was dispatched to Dvārakā City. Kṛṣṇa also collected unlimited wealth from the palace, a treasure of chariots, horses, jewels and so on. He took from the palace fifty white elephants, each with four tusks, and all of them were dispatched to Dvārakā.

After this incident, Lord Kṛṣṇa and Satyabhāmā entered Amarāvatī, the capital city of the heavenly planets, and they immediately entered the palace of King Indra and his wife, Śacīdevī, who welcomed them. Kṛṣṇa then presented Indra with the earrings of Aditi.

When Kṛṣṇa and Satyabhāmā were returning from the capital city of Indra, Satyabhāmā remembered Kṛṣṇa's promise to give her a *pārijāta* tree. Taking the opportunity of having come to the heavenly kingdom, she uprooted a *pārijāta* tree and placed it on the back of Garuḍa. Once Nārada had taken a *pārijāta* flower and presented it to Kṛṣṇa's senior wife, Śrī Rukmiṇīdevī. On account of this, Satyabhāmā had developed an inferiority complex; she also wanted such a flower from Kṛṣṇa. Kṛṣṇa had understood the competitive womanly nature of His co-wives, and He smiled. He had immediately asked Satyabhāmā, "Why are you asking for only one flower? I would like to give you a whole tree of *pārijāta* flowers."

Actually, Kṛṣṇa had purposely taken His wife Satyabhāmā with Him so that she could collect the *pārijāta* with her own hand. But the denizens of the heavenly planets, including Indra, were very irritated. Without their permission, Satyabhāmā had uprooted a *pārijāta* tree, which is not to be found on the earth planet. Indra, along with other demigods, offered opposition to Kṛṣṇa and Satyabhāmā for taking away the tree, but in order to please His favorite wife Satyabhāmā, Kṛṣṇa became determined and adamant, so there was a fight between the demigods and Kṛṣṇa. As usual, Kṛṣṇa came out victorious, and He triumphantly brought the *pārijāta* tree chosen by His wife to this earth planet, to Dvārakā. After this, the tree was installed in the palace garden of Satyabhāmā. On account of this extraordinary tree, the garden house of Satyabhāmā became extraordinarily beautiful. As the *pārijāta* tree came down to the earthly planet, the fragrance of the flowers also came down, and the celestial drones migrated to this earth in search of their fragrance and honey.

King Indra's behavior toward Kṛṣṇa was not very much appreciated by great sages like Śukadeva Gosvāmī. Out of His causeless mercy, Kṛṣṇa had gone to the heavenly kingdom, Amarāvatī, to present King Indra with his mother's earrings, which had been lost to Bhaumāsura, and Indra had been very glad to receive them. But when a *pārijāta* tree from the heavenly kingdom was taken by Kṛṣṇa, Indra offered to fight with Him. This was self-interest on the part of Indra. He offered his prayer, tipping down his head to the lotus feet of Kṛṣṇa, but as soon as his purpose was served, he became a different creature. That is the way of the dealings of materialistic men. Materialistic men are always interested in their own profit. For this purpose they can offer any kind of respect to anyone, but when their personal interest is over, they are no longer friends. This selfish nature is found not only among the richer class of men on this planet but even in personalities like Indra and other demigods. Too much wealth makes a man selfish. A selfish man is not prepared to take to Kṛṣṇa consciousness and is condemned by great devotees like Śukadeva Gosvāmī. In other words, possession of too many worldly riches is a disqualification for advancement in Kṛṣṇa consciousness.

After defeating Indra, Kṛṣṇa arranged to marry the 16,100 girls brought from the custody of Bhaumāsura. By expanding Himself into 16,100 forms, He simultaneously married them all in different palaces at the same auspicious moment. He thus established the truth that Kṛṣṇa and no one else is the

Supreme Personality of Godhead. There is nothing impossible for Kṛṣṇa, the Supreme Personality of Godhead; He is all-powerful, omnipresent and imperishable, and as such there is nothing wonderful in this pastime. All the palaces of the more than 16,000 queens of Kṛṣṇa were full with suitable gardens, furniture and other paraphernalia, of which there is no parallel in this world. There is no exaggeration in this story from *Śrīmad-Bhāgavatam.* The queens of Kṛṣṇa were all expansions of the goddess of fortune, Lakṣmījī. Kṛṣṇa lived with them in different palaces, and He treated them exactly the same way an ordinary man treats his wife.

We should always remember that the Supreme Personality of Godhead, Kṛṣṇa, was playing exactly like a human being; although He showed His extraordinary opulences by simultaneously marrying more than sixteen thousand wives in more than sixteen thousand palaces, He behaved with them just like an ordinary man, and He strictly followed the relationship between husband and wife required in ordinary homes. Therefore, it is very difficult to understand the characteristics of the Supreme Brahman, the Personality of Godhead. Even demigods like Brahmā are unable to probe into the transcendental pastimes of the Lord. The wives of Kṛṣṇa were so fortunate that they got the Supreme Personality of Godhead as their husband, although their husband's personality was unknown even to Brahmā and the other demigods.

In their dealings as husband and wife, Kṛṣṇa and His queens would smile, talk, joke, embrace and so on, and their conjugal relationship ever-increasingly developed. In this way, Kṛṣṇa and the queens enjoyed transcendental happiness in their household life. Although each and every queen had thousands of maidservants engaged for her service, the queens were all personally attentive in serving Kṛṣṇa. Each one of them used to receive Kṛṣṇa personally when He entered the palace. They engaged in seating Him on a nice couch, worshiping Him with all kinds of paraphernalia, washing His lotus feet with Ganges water, offering Him betel nuts and massaging His legs. In this way, they gave Him relief from the fatigue He felt after being away from home. They fanned Him nicely, offered Him fragrant essential floral oil, decorated Him with flower garlands, dressed His hair, asked Him to lie down to take rest, bathed Him personally and fed Him palatable dishes. Each queen did all these things herself and did not wait for the maidservants. In other words, Kṛṣṇa and His different queens displayed on this earth an ideal household life.

Thus ends the Bhaktivedanta purport of the Fifty-ninth Chapter of Kṛṣṇa, *"The Deliverance of the Demon Bhaumāsura."*

CHAPTER SIXTY

Talks Between Kṛṣṇa and Rukmiṇī

Once upon a time, Lord Kṛṣṇa, the Supreme Personality of Godhead, the bestower of all knowledge upon all living entities, from Brahmā to the insignificant ant, was sitting in the bedroom of Rukmiṇī, who was engaged in the service of the Lord along with her assistant maidservants. Kṛṣṇa was sitting on the bedstead of Rukmiṇī, and the maidservants were fanning Him with *cāmaras* (yak-tail fly-whisks).

Lord Kṛṣṇa's dealings with Rukmiṇī as a perfect husband are a perfect manifestation of the supreme perfection of the Personality of Godhead. There are many philosophers who propound a concept of the Absolute Truth in which God cannot do this or that. They deny the incarnation of God, or the Supreme Absolute Truth in human form. But actually the fact is different: God cannot be subject to our imperfect sensual activities. He is the all-powerful, omnipresent Personality of Godhead, and by His supreme will He can not only create, maintain and annihilate the whole cosmic manifestation but can also descend as an ordinary human being to execute the highest mission. As stated in the *Bhagavad-gītā,* whenever there are discrepancies in the discharge of human occupational duties, He descends. He is not forced to appear by any external agency, but He descends by His own internal potency in order to reestablish the standard functions of human activities and simultaneously annihilate the disturbing elements in the progressive march of human civilization. In accordance with this principle of the transcendental pastimes of the Supreme Personality of Godhead, He descended in His eternal form as Śrī Kṛṣṇa in the dynasty of the Yadus.

The palace of Rukmiṇī was wonderfully furnished. There were many canopies hanging on the ceiling with laces bedecked with pearl garlands, and the whole palace was illuminated by the effulgence of valuable jewels. There were many flower groves of *mallikā* and *cāmeli,* which are considered the most fragrant flowers in India. There were many clusters of these plants, with blooming flowers enhancing the beauty of the palace. And because of the exquisite fragrance of the flowers, little groups of humming bees gathered around the trees, and at night the pleasing moonshine glittered through the network of holes in the windows. There were many heavily flowered trees of *pārijāta,* and the mild wind stirred the fragrance of the flowers all around. Incense burned within the walls of the palace, and the fragrant smoke leaked out of the window shutters. Within the room were mattresses covered with white bedsheets; the bedding was as soft and white as milk foam. In this situation, Lord Śrī Kṛṣṇa sat very comfortably and enjoyed the service of Rukmiṇījī, who was assisted by her maidservants.

Rukmiṇī was also very eager to get the opportunity to serve her husband, the Supreme Personality of Godhead. She therefore wanted to serve the Lord personally and took the handle of the *cāmara* from the hand of a maidservant and began to move the fan. The handle of the *cāmara* was made of gold and bedecked with valuable jewels, and it became more beautiful when taken by Rukmiṇī because all of her fingers were beautifully set with jeweled rings. Her legs were decorated with jeweled ankle bells, which rang very softly between the pleats of her sari. Rukmiṇī's raised breasts were smeared with *kuṅkuma* and saffron; thus her beauty was enhanced by the reflection of the reddish color emanating from her covered breasts. Her high hips were decorated with a jeweled lace girdle, and a locket of great effulgence hung on her neck. Above all, because she was engaged in the service of Lord Kṛṣṇa—although at that time she was old enough to have grown-up sons—her beautiful body was beyond compare in the three worlds. When we take account of her beautiful face, it appears that the curling hair on her head, the beautiful earrings on her ears, her smiling mouth and her necklace of gold all combined to shower rains of nectar, and thus it was definitely proved that Rukmiṇī was none other than the original goddess of fortune, who is always engaged in the service of the lotus feet of Nārāyaṇa.

The pastimes of Kṛṣṇa and Rukmiṇī in Dvārakā are accepted by great authorities as manifestations of those of Nārāyaṇa and Lakṣmī, which are of an exalted opulence. The pastimes of Rādhā and Kṛṣṇa in Vṛndāvana are simple and rural, distinguished from the polished urban characteristics of those of Dvārakā. The characteristics of Rukmiṇī were unusually bright, and Kṛṣṇa was very much satisfied with her behavior.

Kṛṣṇa had experienced that when Rukmiṇī was offered a *pārijāta* flower by Nārada Muni, Satyabhāmā had become envious of her co-wife and had immediately demanded a similar flower from Kṛṣṇa. In fact, she could not be pacified until she was promised the whole tree. And Kṛṣṇa actually fulfilled His promise: He brought the tree down to the earth planet from the heavenly kingdom. After this episode, Kṛṣṇa expected that because Satyabhāmā had been rewarded by a full tree of *pārijāta,* Rukmiṇī would also demand something.

Rukmiṇī did not mention anything of the incident, however, for she was grave and simply satisfied in her service. Kṛṣṇa wanted to see her a bit irritated, and therefore He schemed to see the beautiful face of Rukmiṇī in an irritated condition. Although Kṛṣṇa had more than 16,100 wives, He used to behave with each of them with familial affection; He would create a particular situation between Himself and His wife in which the wife would criticize Him in the irritation of love, and Kṛṣṇa would enjoy this. In this case, because Kṛṣṇa could not find any fault with Rukmiṇī, for she was very grave and always engaged in His service, He smilingly, in great love, began to speak to her just to provoke her loving anger. Rukmiṇī was the daughter of King Bhīṣmaka, a powerful king. Thus Kṛṣṇa did not address her as Rukmiṇī; He addressed her this time as the princess. "My dear princess, it is very surprising. Many great personalities in the royal order wanted to marry you. Although not all of them were kings, all possessed the opulence and riches of the kingly order; they were well behaved, learned, famous among kings, beautiful in their bodily features and personal qualifications, liberal, very powerful in strength and advanced in every respect. They were not unfit in any way, and over and above that, your father and your brother had no objection to such a marriage. On the contrary, they gave their word of honor that you would be married with Śiśupāla. Indeed, the marriage was sanctioned by both your parents. Śiśupāla was a great king and was so lusty and mad after your beauty that if he had married you I think he would always have remained with you just like your faithful servant.

"In comparison to Śiśupāla, with his personal qualities, I am nothing. And you may personally realize it. I am surprised that you rejected the marriage with Śiśupāla and accepted Me, who am inferior in comparison to Śiśupāla. I think Myself completely unfit to be your husband because you are so beautiful, sober, grave and exalted. May I inquire from you the reason that induced you to accept Me? Now, of course, I may address you as My beautiful wife, but still I may inform you of My actual position—that I am inferior to all those princes who wanted to marry you.

"First of all, you may know that I was so much afraid of Jarāsandha that I could not dare live on the land, and thus I have constructed this house within the water of the sea. It is not My business to disclose this secret to others, but you must know that I am not very heroic; I am a coward and am afraid of My enemies. Still I am not safe, because all the great kings of the land are inimical to Me. I have personally created this inimical feeling by fighting with them in many ways. Another fault is that although I am on the throne of Dvārakā, I have no immediate claim. Although I got a kingdom by killing My maternal uncle, Kaṁsa, the kingdom was to go to My grandfather; so actually I have no possession of a kingdom. Besides that, I have no fixed aim in life. People cannot understand Me very well. What is the ultimate goal of My life? They know very well that I was a cowherd boy in Vṛndāvana. People expected that I would follow in the footsteps of My foster father, Nanda Mahārāja, and be faithful to Śrīmatī Rādhārāṇī and all Her friends in the village of Vṛndāvana. But all of a sudden I left them. I wanted to become a famous prince. Still I could not have any kingdom, nor could I rule as a prince. People are bewildered about My ultimate goal of life; they do not know whether I am a cowherd boy or a prince, whether I am the son of Nanda Mahārāja or the son of Vasudeva. Because I have no fixed aim in life, people may call Me a vagabond. Therefore, I am surprised that you could select such a vagabond husband.

"Besides this, I am not very much polished, even in social etiquette. A person should be satisfied with one wife, but you see that I have married many times, and I have more than sixteen thousand wives. I cannot please all of them as a polished husband. My behavior with them is not very nice, and I know that you are very conscious of it. I sometimes create a situation with My wives which is not very happy. Because I was trained in a village in My childhood, I am not well acquainted with the etiquette of urban life. I do not know the way to please a wife with nice words and behavior. And from practical experience it is found that any woman who follows My way or becomes attracted by Me is ultimately left to cry for the rest of her life. In Vṛndāvana, many *gopīs* were attracted to Me, and now I have left them, and they are living but are simply crying for Me in separation. I have heard from Akrūra and Uddhava that since I left Vṛndāvana, all My cowherd boyfriends, the *gopīs* and Rādhārāṇī, and My foster father, Nanda Mahārāja, are simply crying constantly for Me. I have left Vṛndāvana for good and am now engaged with the queens in Dvārakā, but I am not well behaved with any of you. So you can very easily understand that I have no steadiness of character; I am not a very reliable husband. The net result of being attracted to Me is to acquire a life of bereavement only.

"My dear beautiful princess, you may also know that I am always penniless. Just after My birth, I was carried penniless to the house of Nanda Mahārāja, and I was raised just like a cowherd boy. Although My foster father possessed many hundreds of thousands of cows, I was not the proprietor of even one of them. I was simply entrusted with taking care of them and tending them, but I was not the proprietor. Here also I am not the proprietor of anything but am always penniless. There is no cause to lament for such a penniless condition; I possessed nothing in the past, so why should I lament that I do not possess anything at present? You may note also that My devotees are not very opulent; they also are very poor in worldly goods. Persons who are very rich, possessing worldly wealth, are not interested in devotion to Me, or Kṛṣṇa consciousness. On the contrary, when a person becomes penniless, whether by force or by circumstances, he may become interested in Me if he gets the proper opportunity. Persons who are proud of their riches, even if they are offered association with My devotees, do not take advantage of consciousness of Me. In other words, the poorer class of men may have some interest in Me, but rich men have no interest. I think, therefore, that your selection of Me was not very intelligent. You appear very intelligent, trained by your father and brother, but ultimately you have made a great mistake in selecting your life's companion.

"But there is no harm; the mistake can still be rectified, and it is better late than never. You are at liberty to select a suitable husband who is actually an equal to you in opulence, family tradition, wealth, beauty, education—in all respects. Whatever mistakes you may have made may be forgotten. Now you may chalk out your own lucrative path of life. Usually a person does not establish a marital relationship with a person who is either higher or lower than his position. My dear daughter of the King of Vidarbha, I think you did not consider very sagaciously before your marriage. Thus you made a wrong selection by choosing Me as your husband. You mistakenly heard about My having very exalted character, although factually I was nothing more than a beggar. Without seeing Me and My actual position, simply by hearing about Me, you selected Me as your husband. That was not very rightly done. Therefore, since it is better late than never, I advise you that you may now select one of the great *kṣatriya* princes and accept him as your life's companion, and you may reject Me."

Kṛṣṇa was proposing that Rukmiṇī divorce Him at a time when Rukmiṇī already had many grown-up children. Therefore Kṛṣṇa's whole proposition appeared to be something unexpected because according to the Vedic culture there was no such thing as separation of husband and wife by divorce. Nor was it possible for Rukmiṇī to choose a new husband at her advanced age, when she had many married sons. To Rukmiṇī every one of Kṛṣṇa's proposals appeared crazy, and she was surprised that Kṛṣṇa could say such things. Simple as she was, her anxiety was increasing more and more at the thought of separation from Kṛṣṇa.

Kṛṣṇa continued, "After all, you have to prepare yourself for your next life. I therefore advise that you select someone who can help you in both this life and the next, for I am completely unable to help. My dear beautiful princess, you know that all the members of the princely order, including Śiśupāla, Śālva, Jarāsandha, Dantavakra and even your elder brother Rukmī, are My enemies; they do not like Me at all. They hate Me from the cores of their hearts. All these princes were very much puffed up with their worldly possessions and did not care a fig for anyone who came before them. In order to teach them some lessons, I agreed to kidnap you according to your desire; otherwise I actually have no love for you, although you loved Me even before the marriage.

"As I have already explained, I am not very interested in family life or love between husband and wife. By nature, I am not very fond of family life, wife, children, home and opulences. As My devotees are always neglectful of all these worldly possessions, I am also like that. Actually, I am interested in self-realization; that gives Me pleasure, and not this family life." After submitting His statement, Lord Kṛṣṇa suddenly stopped.

The great authority Śukadeva Gosvāmī remarks that Kṛṣṇa almost always passed His time with Rukmiṇī, and Rukmiṇī was a bit proud to be so fortunate that Kṛṣṇa never left her even for a moment. Kṛṣṇa, however, does not like any of His devotees to be proud. As soon as a devotee becomes so, by some tactic He cuts down that pride. In this case also, Kṛṣṇa said many things which were hard for Rukmiṇī to hear. She could only conclude that although she was proud of her position, Kṛṣṇa could be separated from her at any moment.

Rukmiṇī was conscious that her husband was not an ordinary human being. He was the Supreme Personality of Godhead, the master of the three worlds. By the way He was speaking, she was afraid of being separated from the

Lord, for she had never heard such harsh words from Kṛṣṇa before. Thus she became perplexed with fear of separation, and her heart began to palpitate. Without replying to a word of Kṛṣṇa's statement, she simply cried in great anxiety, as if drowning in an ocean of grief. She silently scratched the floor with the nails of her toes, which reflected reddish light on the floor. The tears from her eyes mixed with the black cosmetic ointment from her eyelids and dropped down, washing the *kuṅkuma* and saffron from her breasts. Choked up on account of great anxiety, unable to speak even a word, she kept her head downward and remained standing just like a stick. Due to extremely painful fear and lamentation, she lost all her powers of reason and became weak, her body losing so much weight that the bangles on her wrists became slack. The *cāmara* with which she was serving Kṛṣṇa immediately fell from her hand. Her brain and memory became puzzled, and she lost consciousness. The nicely combed hair on her head scattered here and there, and she fell down straight, like a banana tree cut down by a whirlwind.

Lord Kṛṣṇa immediately realized that Rukmiṇī had not taken His words in a joking spirit. She had taken them very seriously, and in her extreme anxiety over immediate separation from Him, she had fallen into this condition. Lord Śrī Kṛṣṇa is naturally very affectionate toward His devotees, and when He saw Rukmiṇī's condition, His heart immediately softened. At once He became merciful to her. The relationship between Rukmiṇī and Kṛṣṇa was like that between Lakṣmī and Nārāyaṇa; therefore, Kṛṣṇa appeared before Rukmiṇī in His four-handed manifestation of Nārāyaṇa. He got down from the bedstead, lifted her up by her hands and, placing His cooling hands on her face, smoothed the scattered hair on her head. Lord Kṛṣṇa dried the wet breasts of Rukmiṇījī with His hand. Understanding the seriousness of Rukmiṇī's love for Him, He embraced her to His chest.

The Supreme Personality is expert in putting a thing reasonably for one's understanding, and thus He tried to retract all that He had said before. He is the only resort for all devotees, and so He knows very well how to satisfy His pure devotees. Kṛṣṇa understood that Rukmiṇī could not follow the statements He had made in a joking way. To counteract her confusion, He spoke as follows.

"My dear daughter of King Vidarbha, My dear Rukmiṇī, please do not misunderstand Me. Don't be unkind to Me like this. I know that you are sincerely and seriously attached to Me; you are My eternal companion. The words which have affected you so much are not factual. I wanted to irritate you a bit, and I was expecting you to make counteranswers to those joking words. Unfortunately, you have taken them seriously; I am very sorry for it. I expected that your red lips would tremble in anger when you heard My statement and that you would chastise Me in many words. O perfection of love, I never expected that your condition would be like this. I expected that you would cast your blinking glance upon Me in retaliation and that I would thus be able to see your beautiful face in that angry mood.

"My dear beautiful wife, you know that because we are householders we are always busy in many household affairs and long for a time when we can enjoy some joking words between us. That is our ultimate gain in household life." Actually, householders work very hard day and night, but all fatigue of the day's labor is minimized as soon as they meet, husband and wife together, and enjoy life in many ways. Lord Kṛṣṇa wanted to exhibit Himself as being like an ordinary householder who delights himself by exchanging joking words with his wife. He therefore repeatedly requested Rukmiṇī not to take those words very seriously.

In this way, when Lord Kṛṣṇa pacified Rukmiṇī by His sweet words, she could understand that what He had formerly said was not actually meant seriously but was spoken to evoke some joking pleasure between themselves. She was therefore pacified by hearing the words of Kṛṣṇa. Gradually she was freed from all fear of separation from Him, and she began to look at His face very cheerfully with her naturally smiling face. She said, "My dear lotus-eyed Lord, Your statement that we are not a fit combination is completely right. It is not possible for me to come to an equal level with You, for You are the reservoir of all qualities, the unlimited Supreme Personality of Godhead. How can I be a fit match for You? There is no possibility of comparison with You, who are the master of all greatness, the controller of the three qualities and the object of worship for great demigods like Brahmā and Lord Śiva. As far as I am concerned, I am a product of the three modes of material nature, which impede the progressive advancement of devotional service. When and where can I be a fit match for You? My dear husband, You have rightly said that You have taken shelter in the water of the sea as if You were afraid of the kings. But who are the kings of this material world? I do not think that the so-called royal families are kings of the material world. The kings of the material world are the three modes of material nature, who are actually its controllers. You are situated in the core of everyone's heart, where You remain completely aloof from the touch of the three modes of material nature, and there is no doubt about it.

"You say You always maintain enmity with the worldly kings. But who are the worldly kings? I think the worldly kings are the senses. They are most formidable, and they control everyone. Certainly You maintain enmity with these material senses. You are never under the control of the senses; rather, You are the controller of the senses, Hṛṣīkeśa. My dear Lord, You have said that You are bereft of all royal power, and that is also correct. Not only are You bereft of supremacy over the material world, but even Your servants, those who have some attachment to Your lotus feet, also give up supremacy over the material world because they consider the material position to be the darkest region, which checks the progress of spiritual enlightenment. Your servants do not like material supremacy, so what to speak of You? My dear Lord, Your statement that You do not act as an ordinary person with a particular aim in life is also perfectly correct. Even Your great devotees and servants, known as great sages and saintly persons, remain in such a state that no one can get any clue as to the aim of their lives. Human society considers them crazy and cynical. Their aim of life remains a mystery to the common human being; the lowest of mankind can know neither You nor Your servants. A contaminated human being cannot even imagine the pastimes of You and Your devotees. O unlimited one, when the activities and endeavors of Your devotees remain a mystery to the common human beings, how can Your motives and endeavors be understood by them? All kinds of energies and opulences are engaged in Your service, but still they rest at Your shelter.

"You have described Yourself as penniless, but this condition is not poverty. Since there is nothing in existence but You, You do not need to possess anything—You Yourself are everything. Unlike others, You do not require to purchase anything extraneously. With You all contrary things can be adjusted because You are absolute. You do not possess anything, but no one is richer than You. In the material world, no one can be rich without possessing. Since Your Lordship is absolute, You can adjust the contradiction of possessing nothing but at the same time being the richest. In the *Vedas* it is stated that although You have no material hands and legs, You accept everything offered in devotion by the devotees. You have no material eyes and ears, but still You can see and hear everything everywhere. Although You do not possess anything, the great demigods who accept prayers and worship from others come and worship You to solicit Your mercy. How can You be categorized among the poor?

"My dear Lord, You have also stated that the richest section of human society does not worship You. This is also correct, because persons who are puffed up with material possessions think of utilizing their property for sense gratification. When a poverty-stricken man becomes rich, he makes a program for sense gratification due to his ignorance of how to utilize his hard-earned money. Under the spell of the external energy, he thinks that his money is properly employed in sense gratification, and thus he neglects to render You transcendental service. My dear Lord, You have stated that persons who possess nothing are very dear to You; renouncing everything, Your devotee wants to possess You only. I see, therefore, that a great sage like Nārada Muni, who does not possess any material property, is still very dear to You. And such persons do not care for anything but Your Lordship.

"My dear Lord, You have stated that a marriage between persons equal in social standing, beauty, riches, strength, influence and renunciation can be a suitable match. But this status of life can be possible only by Your grace. You are the supreme perfectional source of all opulences. Whatever opulent status one may have is all derived from You. As described in the *Vedānta-sūtra, janmādy asya yataḥ*—You are the supreme source from which everything emanates, the reservoir of all pleasures. Therefore, persons endowed with knowledge desire only to achieve You, and nothing else. To achieve Your favor, they give up everything—even the transcendental realization of Brahman. You are the supreme, ultimate goal of life. You are the reservoir of all interests of the living entities. Those who are actually well motivated desire only You, and for this reason they give up everything to attain success. They therefore deserve to associate with You. In the society of the servitors and served in Kṛṣṇa consciousness, one is not subjected to the pains and pleasures of material society, which functions according to sex attraction. Therefore, everyone, whether man or woman, should seek to be an associate in Your society of servitors and served. You are the Supreme Personality of Godhead; no one can excel You, nor can anyone come up to an equal level with You. The perfect social system is that in which You remain in the center, being served as the Supreme, and all others engage as Your servitors. In such a perfectly constructed society, everyone can remain eternally happy and blissful.

"My Lord, You have stated that only the beggars praise Your glories, and that is also perfectly correct. But who are those beggars? Those beggars are all exalted devotees, liberated personalities and those in the renounced order of life. They are all great souls and devotees who have no other business than to glorify You. Such great souls forgive even the worst offenders. These so-called beggars execute their spiritual advancement in life, tolerating all tribulations in the material world. My dear husband, do not think that I accepted You as my husband out of my inexperience; actually, I followed all these great souls. I followed the path of these great beggars and decided to surrender my life unto Your lotus feet.

"You have said that You are penniless, and that is correct, for You distribute Yourself completely to these great souls and devotees. Knowing this fact perfectly well, I rejected even such great personalities as Lord Brahmā and King Indra. My Lord, the great time factor acts under Your direction only. The time factor is so great and powerful that within moments it can effect devastation anywhere within the creation. Considering all these factors, I thought Jarāsandha, Śiśupāla and similar princes who wanted to marry me to be no more important than ordinary insects.

"My dear all-powerful son of Vasudeva, Your statement that You have taken shelter within the water of the ocean, being afraid of all the great princes, is quite unsuitable, for my experience with You contradicts this. I have actually seen that You kidnapped me forcibly in the presence of all these princes. At the time of my marriage ceremony, simply by giving a jerk to the string of Your bow, You very easily drove the others away and kindly gave me shelter at Your lotus feet. I still remember vividly how You kidnapped me in the same way that a lion forcibly takes its share of hunted booty, driving away all small animals within the twinkling of an eye.

"My dear lotus-eyed Lord, I cannot understand Your statement that women and other persons who have taken shelter under Your lotus feet pass their days only in bereavement.

From the history of the world we can see that princes like Aṅga, Pṛthu, Bharata, Yayāti and Gaya were all great emperors of the world, and there were no competitors to their exalted positions. But in order to achieve the favor of Your lotus feet, they renounced their exalted positions and entered the forest to practice penances and austerities. When they voluntarily accepted such a position, accepting Your lotus feet as all in all, does it mean that they were in lamentation and bereavement?

"My dear Lord, You have advised me that I can still select another from the princely order and divorce myself from Your companionship. But, my dear Lord, it is perfectly well known to me that You are the reservoir of all good qualities. Great saintly persons like Nārada Muni are always engaged simply in glorifying Your transcendental characteristics. Someone who simply takes shelter of such a saintly person immediately becomes freed from all material contamination. And when he comes in direct contact with Your service, the goddess of fortune agrees to bestow all her blessings. Under the circumstances, what woman who has once heard of Your glories from authoritative sources and has somehow or other relished the nectarean fragrance of Your lotus feet would be foolish enough to agree to marry someone of this material world, who is always afraid of death, disease, old age and rebirth? I have therefore accepted Your lotus feet not without consideration but after mature and deliberate decision. My dear Lord, You are the master of the three worlds. You can fulfill all the desires of all Your devotees in this world and the next because You are the Supreme Soul of everyone. I have therefore selected You as my husband, considering You to be the only fit personality. You may throw me in any species of life according to the reactions of my fruitive activities, and I haven't the least concern for this. My only ambition is that I may always remain fast to Your lotus feet, for You can deliver Your devotees from illusory material existence and are always prepared to distribute Yourself to Your devotees.

"My dear Lord, You have advised me to select one of the princes such as Śiśupāla, Jarāsandha or Dantavakra, but what is their position in this world? They are always engaged in hard labor to maintain their household life, just like the bulls working hard day and night with an oil-pressing machine. They are compared to asses, beasts of burden. They are always dishonored like dogs, and they are miserly like cats. They have sold themselves like slaves to their wives. Any unfortunate woman who has never heard of Your glories may accept such a man as her husband, but a woman who has learned about You—that You are praised not only in this world but in the halls of the great demigods like Lord Brahmā and Lord Śiva—will not accept anyone besides You as her husband. A man within this material world is just a dead body. In fact, superficially, the living entity is covered by this body, which is nothing but a bag of skin decorated with a beard and mustache, hairs on the body, nails on the fingers, and hairs on the head. Within this decorated bag are bunches of muscles, bundles of bones, and pools of blood, always mixed with stool, urine, mucus, bile and polluted air and enjoyed by different kinds of insects and germs. A foolish woman accepts such a dead body as her husband and, in sheer misunderstanding, loves him as her dear companion. This is possible only because such a woman has never relished the ever-blissful fragrance of Your lotus feet.

"My dear lotus-eyed husband, You are self-satisfied. You do not care whether or not I am beautiful or qualified; You are not at all concerned about it. Therefore Your nonattachment for me is not at all astonishing; it is quite natural. You cannot be attached to any woman, however exalted her position and beauty. Whether You are attached to me or not, may my devotion and attention be always engaged at Your lotus feet. The material mode of passion is also Your creation, so when You passionately glance upon me, I accept it as the greatest boon of my life. I am ambitious only for such auspicious moments."

After hearing Rukmiṇī's statement and her clarification of each and every word He had used to arouse her anger of love toward Him, Kṛṣṇa addressed Rukmiṇī as follows: "My dear chaste wife, My dear princess, I expected such an explanation from you, and only for this purpose did I speak all those joking words, so that you might be cheated of the real point of view. Now My purpose has been served. The wonderful explanation you have given of My every word is completely factual and approved by Me. O most beautiful Rukmiṇī, you are My dearmost wife. I am greatly pleased to understand how much love you have for Me. Please take it for granted that no matter what ambition and desire you might have and no matter what you might expect from Me, I am always at your service. And it is a fact also that My devotees, My dearmost friends and servitors, are always free from material contamination, even though they are not inclined to ask such liberation from Me. My devotees never desire anything from Me except to be engaged in My service. And yet because they are completely dependent upon Me, even if they are found to ask something from Me, that is not material. Such ambitions and desires, instead of becoming the cause of material bondage, become the source of liberation from this material world.

"My dear chaste and pious wife, I have tested, on the basis of strict chastity, your love for your husband, and you have passed the examination most successfully. I have purposely agitated you by speaking many words not applicable to your character, but I am surprised to see that not a pinch of your devotion to Me has been deviated from its fixed position. My dear wife, I am the bestower of all benedictions, even up to the standard of liberation from this material world, and it is I only who can stop the continuation of material existence and call one back home, back to Godhead. One whose devotion for Me is adulterated worships Me for some material benefit, just to keep himself in the world of material happiness, culminating in the pleasure of sex life. One who engages himself in severe penances and austerities just to attain this material happiness is certainly under the illusion of My external energy. Persons who are engaged in My devotional service simply for the purpose of material gain and sense gratification are certainly very foolish, for material happiness based on sex life is available in the most abominable species of life, such as the hogs and dogs. No one should try to approach Me for such happiness, which is available even if one is put into a hellish condition of life. It is better, therefore, for persons who are simply after material happiness and not after Me to remain in that hellish condition."

Material contamination is so strong that everyone is working very hard day and night for material happiness. The show of religion, austerity, penance, humanitarianism, philanthropy, politics, science—everything is aimed at realizing some material benefit. For the immediate success of material benefit, materialistic persons generally worship different demigods, and under the spell of material propensities they sometimes take to the devotional service of the Lord. But sometimes it so happens that if a person sincerely serves the Lord and at the same time maintains material ambitions, the Lord very kindly removes the sources of material happiness. Not finding any recourse in material happiness, the devotee then engages himself absolutely in pure devotional service.

Lord Kṛṣṇa continued, "My dear best of queens, I clearly understand that you have no material ambition; your only purpose is to serve Me, and you have long been engaged in unalloyed service. Exemplary unalloyed devotional service not only can bestow upon the devotee liberation from this material world, but it also promotes him to the spiritual world to be eternally engaged in My service. Persons too much addicted to material happiness cannot render such service. Women whose hearts are polluted and full of material desires devise various means of sense gratification while outwardly showing themselves to be great devotees.

"My dear honored wife, although I have thousands of

wives, I do not think that any one of them can love Me more than you. The practical proof of your extraordinary position is that you had never seen Me before our marriage; you had simply heard about Me from a third person, and still your faith in Me was so much fixed that even in the presence of many qualified, rich and beautiful men of the royal order, you did not select any one of them as your husband but insisted on having Me. You neglected all the princes present, and very politely you sent Me a confidential letter inviting Me to kidnap you. While I was kidnapping you, your elder brother Rukmī violently protested and fought with Me. As a result of the fight, I defeated him mercilessly and disfigured his body. At the time of Aniruddha's marriage, when we were all playing chess, there was another fight with your brother Rukmī on a controversial verbal point, and My elder brother, Balarāma, finally killed him. I was surprised to see that you did not utter even a word of protest over this incident. Because of your great anxiety that you might be separated from Me, you suffered all the consequences without speaking even a word. As the result of this great silence, My dear wife, you have purchased Me for all time; I have come eternally under your control. You sent your messenger inviting Me to kidnap you, and when you found that there was a little delay in My arriving on the spot, you saw the whole world as vacant. At that time you concluded that your beautiful body was not fit to be touched by anyone else; therefore, thinking that I was not coming, you decided to commit suicide and immediately end that body. My dear Rukmiṇī, such great and exalted love for Me will always remain within My soul. As far as I am concerned, it is not within My power to repay you for your unalloyed devotion to Me."

The Supreme Personality of Godhead, Kṛṣṇa, certainly has no business being anyone's husband or son or father, because everything belongs to Him and everyone is under His control. He does not require anyone's help for His satisfaction. He is *ātmārāma,* self-satisfied; He can derive all pleasure by

Himself, without anyone's help. But when the Lord descends to play the part of a human being, He plays a role either as a husband, son, friend or enemy in full perfection. As such, when He was playing as the perfect husband of the queens, especially of Rukmiṇījī, He enjoyed conjugal love in complete perfection.

According to Vedic culture, although polygamy is allowed, none of one's wives should be ill-treated. In other words, one may take many wives only if he is able to satisfy all of them equally as an ideal householder; otherwise it is not allowed. Lord Kṛṣṇa is the world teacher; therefore, even though He had no need for a wife, He expanded Himself into as many forms as He had wives, and He lived with them as an ideal householder, observing the regulative principles, rules and commitments in accordance with the Vedic injunctions and the social laws and customs of society. For each of His 16,108 wives, He simultaneously maintained different palaces, different establishments and different atmospheres. Thus the Lord, although one, exhibited Himself as 16,108 ideal householders.

Thus ends the Bhaktivedanta purport of the Sixtieth Chapter of Kṛṣṇa, *"Talks Between Kṛṣṇa and Rukmiṇī."*

CHAPTER SIXTY-ONE

The Genealogy of the Family of Kṛṣṇa

Kṛṣṇa had 16,108 wives, and in each of them He begot ten sons, all of them equal to their father in the opulences of strength, beauty, wisdom, fame, wealth and renunciation. "Like father, like son." All the 16,108 wives of Kṛṣṇa were princesses, and when each saw that Kṛṣṇa was always present in her respective palace and did not leave home, she considered Kṛṣṇa a henpecked husband who was very much attached to her. Every one of them thought that Kṛṣṇa was her very obedient husband, but actually Kṛṣṇa had no attraction for any of them. Although each thought that she was the only wife of Kṛṣṇa and was very, very dear to Him, Lord Kṛṣṇa, being *ātmārāma,* self-sufficient, felt neither attraction nor enmity toward any one of them; He was equal to all the wives and treated them as a perfect husband just to please them. For Him, there was no need of even a single wife. In fact, since they were women, the wives could not understand the exalted position of Kṛṣṇa, nor the truths about Him.

All the princesses who were wives of Kṛṣṇa were exquisitely beautiful, and each one of them was attracted by Kṛṣṇa's eyes, which were just like lotus petals, and by His beautiful face, long arms, beautiful ears, pleasing smile, humorous talk and sweet words. Influenced by these features of Kṛṣṇa, they all used to dress themselves very attractively, desiring to attract Him by their feminine bodily appeal. They exhibited their feminine characteristics by smiling and moving their eyebrows, thus shooting sharp arrows of conjugal love just to awaken Kṛṣṇa's lusty desires for them. Still, they could not arouse Kṛṣṇa's mind or His sexual appetite. This means that Kṛṣṇa never had any sexual relations with any of His many wives, save and except to beget children.

The queens of Dvārakā were so fortunate that they got Lord Śrī Kṛṣṇa as their husband and personal companion, although He is not approachable by exalted demigods like Brahmā. Lord Kṛṣṇa and His queens remained together as husband and wife, and Kṛṣṇa, as an ideal husband, treated them in such a way that at every moment there was an increase of transcendental bliss in their smiling exchanges, talking and mixing together. Each and every wife had hundreds and thousands of maidservants, yet when Kṛṣṇa entered the palaces of His thousands of wives, each one of them used to receive Kṛṣṇa personally by seating Him in a nice chair, worshiping Him with all requisite paraphernalia, personally washing His lotus feet, offering Him betel nuts, massaging His legs to relieve them of fatigue, fanning Him to make Him comfortable, offering all kinds of scented sandalwood pulp, oils and aromatics, putting flower garlands on His neck, dressing His hair, getting Him to lie down on the bed and assisting Him in taking His bath. Thus they served always in every respect, especially when Kṛṣṇa was eating. They always engaged in the service of the Lord.

Of the 16,108 queens of Kṛṣṇa, each of whom had ten sons, there is the following list of the sons of the first eight queens. By Rukmiṇī, Kṛṣṇa had the following ten sons: Pradyumna, Cārudeṣṇa, Sudeṣṇa, Cārudeha, Sucāru, Cārugupta, Bhadracāru, Cārucandra, Vicāru and Cāru. None of them were inferior in their qualities to their divine father, Lord Kṛṣṇa. The names of Satyabhāmā's ten sons are as follows: Bhānu, Subhānu, Svarbhānu, Prabhānu, Bhānumān, Candrabhānu, Bṛhadbhānu, Atibhānu, Śrībhānu and Pratibhānu. The ten sons of the next queen, Jāmbavatī, were headed by Sāmba. Their names are as follows: Sāmba, Sumitra, Purujit, Śatajit, Sahasrajit, Vijaya, Citraketu, Vasumān, Draviḍa and Kratu. Lord Kṛṣṇa was specifically very affectionate to the sons of Jāmbavatī. The ten sons Lord Kṛṣṇa had by His wife Satyā, the daughter of King Nagnajit, were as follows: Vīra, Candra, Aśvasena, Citragu, Vegavān, Vṛṣa, Āma, Śaṅku, Vasu and Kunti. Amongst all of them, Kunti was very powerful. Kṛṣṇa's ten sons by Kālindī were as follows: Śruta, Kavi, Vṛṣa, Vīra, Subāhu, Bhadra, Śānti, Darśa, Pūrṇamāsa and Somaka, the youngest son. The ten sons Lord Kṛṣṇa begot in His next wife, Lakṣmaṇā, the daughter of the King of Madras Province, were named Praghoṣa, Gātravān, Siṁha, Bala, Prabala, Ūrdhaga, Mahāśakti, Saha, Oja and Aparājita. The ten sons of His next wife, Mitravindā, were as follows: Vṛka, Harṣa, Anila, Gṛdhra, Vardhana, Unnāda, Mahāṁsa, Pāvana, Vahni and Kṣudhi. The ten sons of His next wife, Bhadrā, were named Saṅgrāmajit, Bṛhatsena, Śūra, Praharaṇa, Arijit, Jaya, Subhadra, Vāma, Āyur and Satyaka. Besides these eight chief queens, Kṛṣṇa had 16,100 other wives, and all of them also had ten sons each.

The eldest son of Rukmiṇī, Pradyumna, was married with Māyāvatī from his very birth, and afterwards he married Rukmavatī, the daughter of his maternal uncle, Rukmī. From Rukmavatī, Pradyumna had a son named Aniruddha. In this way, Kṛṣṇa's family—Kṛṣṇa and His wives, along with their sons and grandsons and even great-grandsons—all combined together to include very nearly one billion family members.

Rukmī, the elder brother of Kṛṣṇa's first wife, Rukmiṇī, was greatly harassed and insulted in his fight with Kṛṣṇa, but on the request of Rukmiṇī his life was spared. Since then Rukmī held a great grudge against Kṛṣṇa and was always inimical toward Him. Nevertheless, his daughter married Kṛṣṇa's son, and his granddaughter married Kṛṣṇa's grandson Aniruddha. This fact appeared a little astonishing to Mahārāja Parīkṣit when he heard it from Śukadeva Gosvāmī, and the King addressed him as follows: "I am surprised that Rukmī and Kṛṣṇa, who were so greatly inimical to one another, could again be united by marital relationships between their descendants." Parīkṣit Mahārāja was curious about the mystery of this incident, and therefore he inquired from Śukadeva Gosvāmī. Because Śukadeva Gosvāmī was a perfect *yogī,* nothing was hidden from his power of insight. A perfect *yogī* like Śukadeva Gosvāmī can see past, present and future in all details. Therefore, from such *yogīs* or mystics nothing can be concealed. When Parīkṣit Mahārāja inquired from Śukadeva Gosvāmī, Śukadeva Gosvāmī answered as follows.

Pradyumna, the eldest son of Kṛṣṇa, born of Rukmiṇī, was Cupid himself. He was so beautiful and attractive that the daughter of Rukmī, namely Rukmavatī, could not select any husband other than Pradyumna during her *svayaṁvara.* Therefore, in that selection meeting she garlanded Pradyumna in the presence of all the other princes. When there was a fight among the princes, Pradyumna came out victorious, and therefore Rukmī was obliged to offer his beautiful daughter to Pradyumna. Although enmity always blazed in Rukmī's heart because of his having been insulted by Kṛṣṇa's kidnapping of his sister, Rukmiṇī, Rukmī could not resist consenting to the marriage ceremony just to please Rukmiṇī when his daughter selected Pradyumna as her husband. And so Pradyumna became the son-in-law as well as the nephew of Rukmī. Besides the ten sons described above, Rukmiṇī had one beautiful daughter with big eyes, and she was married to Kṛtavarmā's son, whose name was Balī.

Although Rukmī was a veritable enemy of Kṛṣṇa, he had great affection for his sister, Rukmiṇī, and wanted to please her in all respects. On this account, when Rukmiṇī's grandson Aniruddha was to be married, Rukmī offered his granddaughter Rocanā to Aniruddha. Such marriage between immediate cousins is not very much sanctioned by the Vedic culture, but in order to please Rukmiṇī, Rukmī offered his daughter and granddaughter to the son and grandson of Kṛṣṇa, respectively. In this way, when the negotiation of the marriage of Aniruddha with Rocanā was complete, a big marriage party accompanied Aniruddha and started from Dvārakā. They traveled until they reached Bhojakaṭa, which Rukmī had colonized after his sister had been kidnapped by Kṛṣṇa. This marriage party was led by the grandfather, namely Lord Kṛṣṇa, accompanied by Lord Balarāma, and it included Kṛṣṇa's first wife, Rukmiṇī, His son Pradyumna, Jāmbavatī's son Sāṃba and many other relatives and family members. They reached the town of Bhojakaṭa, and the marriage ceremony was peacefully performed.

The King of Kaliṅga was a friend of Rukmī and gave him the ill advice to play chess with Balarāma and thus defeat Him in a bet. Among *kṣatriya* kings, betting and gambling in chess was not uncommon. If someone challenged a *kṣatriya* to play on the chessboard, the *kṣatriya* could not refuse the challenge. Śrī Balarāmajī was not a very expert chess player, and this was known to the King of Kaliṅga. So Rukmī was advised to retaliate against the family members of Kṛṣṇa by challenging Balarāma to play chess. Although not an expert chess player, Śrī Balarāmajī was very enthusiastic in sporting activities. He accepted Rukmī's challenge and sat down to play. Betting was with gold coins, and Balarāma first of all challenged with one hundred coins, then one thousand coins, then ten thousand coins. Each time, Balarāma lost, and Rukmī was victorious.

Śrī Balarāma's losing the game was an opportunity for the King of Kaliṅga to criticize Kṛṣṇa and Balarāma. Thus the King of Kaliṅga was talking jokingly while purposefully showing his teeth to Balarāma. Because Balarāma was the loser in the game, He was a little intolerant of the sarcastic joking words and became somewhat agitated. Rukmī again challenged Balarāma and made a bet of a hundred thousand gold coins, but fortunately this time Balarāma won. Nonetheless, out of cunningness Rukmī claimed that Balarāma was the loser and that he himself had won. Because of this lie, Balarāmajī became most angry with Rukmī. His agitation was so sudden and great that it appeared like a tidal wave in the ocean on a full-moon day. Balarāma's eyes are naturally reddish, and when He became agitated and angry His eyes became more reddish. This time He challenged and made a bet of a hundred million coins.

Again Balarāma was the winner according to the rules of chess, but Rukmī again cunningly claimed that he had won. Rukmī appealed to the princes present, and he especially mentioned the name of the King of Kaliṅga. During the dispute there was a voice from the sky, and it announced that for all honest purposes Balarāma was the actual winner of this game, that He was being abused, and that the statement of Rukmī that he had won was absolutely false.

In spite of this divine voice, Rukmī insisted that Balarāma had lost, and by his persistence it appeared that he had death upon his head. Falsely puffed up by the ill advice of his friend, he did not give much importance to the oracle, and he began to criticize Balarāmajī. He said, "My dear Balarāmajī, You two brothers, cowherd boys only, may be very expert in tending cows, but how can You be expert in playing chess or shooting arrows on the battlefield? These arts are well known only to the princely order." Hearing this kind of pinching talk by Rukmī and hearing the loud laughter of all the other princes present there, Lord Balarāma became as agitated as burning cinders. He immediately took His club in His hand and, without further talk, struck Rukmī on the head. From that one blow, Rukmī fell down immediately and was dead and gone. Thus Rukmī was killed by Balarāma on that auspicious occasion of Aniruddha's marriage. These things are not very uncommon in *kṣatriya* society.

The King of Kaliṅga, afraid that he would be the next one attacked, fled from the scene. Before he could escape even a few steps, however, Balarāmajī immediately captured him, and because the King had always shown his teeth while criticizing Balarāma and Kṛṣṇa, Balarāma broke all the King's teeth with His club. The other princes supporting the King of Kaliṅga and Rukmī were also captured, and Balarāma beat them with His club, breaking their legs and hands. They did not try to retaliate but thought it wise to run away from the bloody scene.

During this strife between Balarāma and Rukmī, Lord Kṛṣṇa did not utter a word, for He knew that if He supported Balarāma, Rukmiṇī would be unhappy, and if He said that the killing of Rukmī was unjust, then Balarāma would be unhappy. Therefore, Lord Kṛṣṇa was silent on the death of His brother-in-law Rukmī on the occasion of His grandson's marriage. He did not disturb His affectionate relationship with either Balarāma or Rukmiṇī. After this, the bride and bridegroom were ceremoniously seated on the chariot, and they started for Dvārakā, accompanied by the bridegroom's party. The bridegroom's party was always protected by Lord Kṛṣṇa, the killer of the Madhu demon. Thus they left Rukmī's kingdom, Bhojakaṭa, and happily started for Dvārakā.

Thus ends the Bhaktivedanta purport of the Sixty-first Chapter of Kṛṣṇa, *"The Genealogy of the Family of Kṛṣṇa."*

CHAPTER SIXTY-TWO

The Meeting of Ūṣā and Aniruddha

The meeting of Aniruddha and Ūṣā, which caused a great fight between Lord Kṛṣṇa and Lord Śiva, is very mysterious and interesting. Mahārāja Parīkṣit was eager to hear the whole story from Śukadeva Gosvāmī, and thus Śukadeva narrated it. "My dear King, you must have heard the name of King Bali. He was a great devotee who gave away in charity all that he had—namely, the whole world—to Lord Vāmana, the incarnation of Viṣṇu as a dwarf *brāhmaṇa.* King Bali had one hundred sons, and the eldest of all of them was Bāṇāsura."

This great hero Bāṇāsura, born of Mahārāja Bali, was a great devotee of Lord Śiva and was always ready to render service unto him. Because of his devotion, Bāṇāsura achieved a great position in society, and he was honored in every respect. Actually, he was very intelligent and liberal also, and his activities are all praiseworthy because he never deviated from his promise and word of honor; he was very truthful and fixed in his vow. In those days, he was ruling over the city of Śoṇitapura. By the grace of Lord Śiva, Bāṇāsura had one thousand arms, and he became so powerful that even demigods like King Indra were serving him most obediently.

Long ago, when Lord Śiva was dancing in his celebrated fashion called *tāṇḍava-nṛtya,* for which he is known as Naṭarāja, Bāṇāsura helped Lord Śiva in his dancing by rhythmically beating drums with his one thousand hands. Lord Śiva is well known as Āśutoṣa ("very easily pleased"), and he is also very affectionate to his devotees. He is a great protector for persons who take shelter of him and is the master of all living entities in this material world. Being pleased with Bāṇāsura, he said, "Whatever you desire you can have from me, for I am very pleased with you." Bāṇāsura replied, "My dear lord, if you please, you can remain in my city just to protect me from the hands of my enemies."

Once upon a time, Bāṇāsura came to offer his respects to Lord Śiva. By touching the lotus feet of Lord Śiva with his helmet, which was shining like the sun globe, he offered his obeisances unto him. While offering his respectful obeisances, Bāṇāsura said, "My dear lord, anyone who has not fulfilled his ambition will be able to do so by taking shelter of your lotus feet, which are just like a desire tree from which one can take anything he desires. My dear lord, you have given me one thousand arms, but I do not know what to do with them. They are simply a burden; I cannot use them properly in fighting, since I cannot find anyone competent to fight with me except Your Lordship, the original father of the material world. Sometimes I feel a great tendency to fight with my arms, and I go out to find a suitable warrior. Unfortunately, everyone flees, knowing my extraordinary power. Being baffled at not finding a match, I satisfy the itching of my arms by beating them against the mountains. In this way, I tear many great mountains to pieces."

Lord Śiva realized that his benediction had become troublesome for Bāṇāsura and addressed him, "You rascal! You are very eager to fight, but since you have no one to fight with, you are distressed. Although you think that there is no one in the world to oppose you except me, I say that you will eventually find such a competent person. At that time your days will come to an end, and your flag of victory will no longer fly. Then you will see your false prestige smashed to pieces!"

After hearing Lord Śiva's statement, Bāṇāsura, who was very much puffed up with his power, became elated that he would meet someone able to smash him to pieces. Bāṇāsura then returned home with great pleasure, and he always waited for the day when the suitable fighter would come to cut down his strength. He was such a foolish demon. It appears that foolish, demoniac human beings, when unnecessarily overpowered with material opulences, want to exhibit these opulences, and such foolish people feel satisfaction when these opulences are exhausted. The idea is that they do not know how to expend their energy for right causes, being unaware of the benefit of Kṛṣṇa consciousness. Actually, there are two classes of men—one is Kṛṣṇa conscious, the other is non–Kṛṣṇa conscious. The non–Kṛṣṇa conscious men are generally devoted to the demigods, whereas the Kṛṣṇa conscious men are devoted to the Supreme Personality of Godhead. Kṛṣṇa conscious persons utilize everything for the service of the Lord. The non–Kṛṣṇa conscious persons utilize everything for sense gratification, and Bāṇāsura is a perfect example of such a person. For his own satisfaction, he was very eager to utilize his extraordinary power to fight. Not finding any combatant, he struck his powerful hands against the mountains, breaking them to pieces. In contrast to this, Arjuna also possessed extraordinary powers for fighting, but he utilized them only for Kṛṣṇa.

Bāṇāsura had a very beautiful daughter, whose name was Ūṣā. When she had attained the age of marriage and was sleeping amongst her many girlfriends, she dreamt one night that Aniruddha was by her side and that she was enjoying a conjugal relationship with him, although she had never actually seen him or heard of him before. She awoke from her dream exclaiming very loudly, "My dear beloved, where are you?" Being exposed to her other friends in this way, she became a little bit ashamed. One of Ūṣā's girlfriends was Citralekhā, who was the daughter of Bāṇāsura's prime minister. Citralekhā and Ūṣā were intimate friends, and out of great curiosity Citralekhā asked, "My dear beautiful princess, as of yet you are not married to any young boy, nor have you seen any boys until now; so I am surprised that you are exclaiming like this. Who are you searching after? Who is your suitable match?"

On hearing Citralekhā's inquiries, Ūṣā replied, "My dear friend, in my dream I saw a nice young man who is very, very beautiful. His complexion is swarthy, his eyes are just like lotus petals, and he is dressed in yellow garments. His arms are very long, and his general bodily features are so pleasing that any young girl would be attracted. I feel much pride in saying that this beautiful young man was kissing me, and I was very much enjoying the nectar of his kissing. But I am sorry to inform you that just after this he disappeared, and I have been thrown into the whirlpool of disappointment. My dear friend, I am very anxious to find this wonderful young man, the desired lord of my heart."

After hearing Ūṣā's words, Citralekhā immediately replied, "I can understand your bereavement, and I assure you that if this boy is within these three worlds—the upper, middle and lower planetary systems—I must find him for your satisfaction. If you can identify him from your dream, I shall bring you peace of mind. Now, let me draw some pictures for you to inspect, and as soon as you find the picture of your desired husband, let me know. It doesn't matter where he is; I know the art of bringing him here. So, as soon as you identify him, I shall immediately arrange for it."

Citralekhā, while talking, began to draw many pictures of the demigods inhabiting the higher planetary systems, then pictures of the Gandharvas, Siddhas, Cāraṇas, Pannagas, Daityas, Vidyādharas and Yakṣas, as well as many pictures of human beings. (The statements of *Śrīmad-Bhāgavatam* and other Vedic literatures prove definitely that on each and every planet there are living entities of different varieties. Therefore, it is foolish to assert that there are no living entities but those on this earth.) Citralekhā painted many pictures. Among those of the human beings were the members of the Vṛṣṇi dynasty, including Vasudeva, the father of Kṛṣṇa; Śūrasena, the grandfather of Kṛṣṇa; Śrī Balarāmajī; Lord Kṛṣṇa; and many others. When Ūṣā saw the picture of Pradyumna, she became a little bashful, but when she saw the picture of Aniruddha, she became so bashful that she immediately lowered her head and smiled, having found the man she was seeking. She identified the picture to Citralekhā as that of the man who had stolen her heart.

Citralekhā was a great mystic *yoginī,* and as soon as Ūṣā identified the picture, Citralekhā could immediately understand that it was of Aniruddha, a grandson of Kṛṣṇa, although neither she nor Ūṣā had previously known his name or ever seen him. That very night, she traveled in outer space and within a very short time reached the city of Dvārakā, which was well protected by Lord Kṛṣṇa. She entered the palace and found Aniruddha sleeping in his bedroom on a very opulent bed. Citralekhā, by her mystic power, immediately brought Aniruddha, in that sleeping condition, to the city of Śoṇitapura so that Ūṣā might see her desired husband. Ūṣā immediately bloomed in happiness and began to enjoy the company of Aniruddha with great satisfaction.

The palace in which Ūṣā and Citralekhā lived was so well fortified that it was impossible for any male to either enter or see inside. Ūṣā and Aniruddha lived together in the palace, and day after day Ūṣā's love for Aniruddha grew four times upon four. Ūṣā pleased Aniruddha with valuable garments, flowers, garlands, scents and incense. By his bedside sitting place were other paraphernalia for residential purposes—nice drinks such as milk and sherbet and nice eatables which could be chewed or swallowed. Above all, she pleased him with sweet words and very obliging service. Ūṣā worshiped Aniruddha as if he were the Supreme Personality of Godhead. By her excellent service, Ūṣā made Aniruddha forget all other things and was able to draw his attention and love to her without deviation. In such an atmosphere of love and service, Aniruddha practically forgot himself and could not recall how many days he had been away from his real home.

In due course of time, Ūṣā exhibited some bodily symptoms by which it could be understood that she was having intercourse with a male friend. The symptoms were so prominent that her actions could no longer be concealed from anyone. Ūṣā was always cheerful in the association of Aniruddha, and she did not know the bounds of her satisfaction. The housekeeper and the guards of the palace could guess very easily that she was having relations with a male friend, and without waiting for further developments, all of them informed their master, Bāṇāsura. In Vedic culture, an unmarried girl having association with a male is the greatest disgrace to the family, and so the caretakers cautiously informed their master that Ūṣā was showing symptoms indicating a disgraceful association. The servants informed their master that they were not at all neglectful in guarding the house, being alert day and night against any young man who might enter. They were so careful that a male could not even see what was going on there, and so they were surprised that she had become contaminated. Since they could not trace out the reason for it, they submitted the whole situation before their master.

Bāṇāsura was shocked to understand that his daughter Ūṣā was no longer a virgin maiden. This weighed heavily on his heart, and without delay he rushed toward the palace where Ūṣā was living. There he saw that Ūṣā and Aniruddha were sitting together and talking. They looked very beautiful together, Aniruddha being the son of Pradyumna, who was Cupid himself. Bāṇāsura saw his daughter and Aniruddha as a suitable match, yet for family prestige he did not like the combination at all. Bāṇāsura could not understand who the boy actually was. He appreciated the fact that Ūṣā could not have selected anyone in the three worlds more beautiful. Aniruddha's complexion was brilliant and swarthy. He was dressed in yellow garments and had eyes just like lotus petals. His arms were very long, and he had nice, curling, bluish hair. The glaring rays of his glittering earrings and the beautiful smile on his lips were certainly captivating. Still, Bāṇāsura was very angry.

When Bāṇāsura saw him, Aniruddha was engaged in playing with Ūṣā. Aniruddha was nicely dressed, and Ūṣā had garlanded him with various beautiful flowers. The reddish *kuṅkuma* powder put on the breasts of women was spotted here and there on the garland, indicating that Ūṣā had embraced him. Bāṇāsura was struck with wonder that, even in his presence, Aniruddha was peacefully sitting in front of Ūṣā. Aniruddha knew, however, that his would-be father-in-law was not at all pleased and that he was gathering many soldiers in the palace to attack him.

Thus, not finding any other weapon, Aniruddha took hold of a big iron rod and stood up before Bāṇāsura and his soldiers. He firmly took a posture indicating that if attacked he would strike all of the soldiers down to the ground with the iron rod. Bāṇāsura and his company of soldiers saw that the boy was standing before them just like the superintendent of death with his invincible rod. Now, under the order of Bāṇāsura, the soldiers from all sides attempted to capture and arrest him. When they dared to come before him, Aniruddha struck them with the rod, breaking their heads, legs, arms and thighs, and one after another they fell to the ground. He killed them just as the leader of a pack of boars kills barking dogs one after another. In this way, Aniruddha was able to escape the palace.

Bāṇāsura knew various arts of fighting, and by the grace of Lord Śiva he knew how to arrest his enemy by the use of a *nāga-pāśa,* snake-noose, and thus he seized Aniruddha as he came out of the palace. When Ūṣā received the news that her father had arrested Aniruddha, she was overwhelmed with grief and confusion. Tears glided down from her eyes, and being unable to check herself, she began to cry very loudly.

Thus ends the Bhaktivedanta purport of the Sixty-second Chapter of Kṛṣṇa, *"The Meeting of Ūṣā and Aniruddha."*

CHAPTER SIXTY-THREE

Lord Kṛṣṇa Fights with Bāṇāsura

When the four months of the rainy season passed and Aniruddha had still not returned home, all the members of the Yadu family became much perturbed. They could not understand how the boy was missing. Fortunately, one day the great sage Nārada came and informed the family about Aniruddha's disappearance from the palace. He explained how Aniruddha had been carried to the city of Śoṇitapura, the capital of Bāṇāsura's empire, and how Bāṇāsura had arrested him with the *nāga-pāśa,* even though Aniruddha had defeated his soldiers. This news was given in detail by Nārada, and the whole story was disclosed. Then the members of the Yadu dynasty, all of whom had great affection for Kṛṣṇa, prepared to attack the city of Śoṇitapura. Practically all the leaders of the family, including Pradyumna, Sātyaki, Gada, Sāmba, Sāraṇa, Nanda, Upananda and Bhadra, combined together and gathered eighteen *akṣauhiṇī* military divisions into phalanxes. Then they all went to Śoṇitapura and surrounded it with soldiers, elephants, horses and chariots.

Bāṇāsura heard that the soldiers of the Yadu dynasty were attacking the whole city, tearing down various walls, gates and nearby gardens. Becoming very angry, he immediately ordered his soldiers, who were of equal caliber, to go and face them. Lord Śiva was so kind to Bāṇāsura that he personally came as the commander in chief of the military force, assisted by his heroic sons Kārttikeya and Gaṇapati. Nandīśvara, Lord Śiva, seated on his favorite bull, led the fighting against Lord Kṛṣṇa and Balarāma. We can simply imagine how fierce the fighting was—Lord Śiva with his valiant sons on one side, and Lord Kṛṣṇa, the Supreme Personality of Godhead, and His elder brother, Śrī Balarāmajī, on the other. The fighting was so fierce that those who saw the battle were struck with wonder, and the hairs on their bodies stood up. Lord Śiva was engaged in fighting directly with Lord Kṛṣṇa, Pradyumna was engaged with Kārttikeya, and Lord Balarāma was engaged with Bāṇāsura's commander in chief, Kumbhāṇḍa, who was assisted by Kūpakarṇa. Sāmba, the son of Kṛṣṇa, fought the son of Bāṇāsura, and Bāṇāsura fought Sātyaki, commander in chief of the Yadu dynasty. In this way the fighting was waged.

News of the fighting spread all over the universe. Demigods such as Lord Brahmā, from higher planetary systems, along with great sages and saintly persons, Siddhas, Cāraṇas and Gandharvas, all being very curious to see the fight between Lord Śiva and Lord Kṛṣṇa and their assistants, hovered over the battlefield in their airplanes. Lord Śiva is called the Bhūta-nātha because he is assisted by various types of powerful ghosts and denizens of the inferno—Bhūtas, Pretas, Pramathas, Guhyakas, Ḍākinīs, Piśācas, Kuṣmāṇḍas, Vetālas, Vināyakas and Brahma-rākṣasas. (Of all kinds of ghosts, the Brahma-rākṣasas are the most powerful. They are *brāhmaṇas* who after death have entered the ghostly species of life.)

The Supreme Personality of Godhead, Śrī Kṛṣṇa, simply drove all these ghosts away from the battlefield with the arrows from His celebrated bow, Śārṅga-dhanur. Lord Śiva then began to release all his selected weapons against the Personality of Godhead. Lord Śrī Kṛṣṇa, without any difficulty, counteracted all these weapons with counterweapons. He counteracted the *brahmāstra,* similar to the atomic bomb, with another *brahmāstra,* and an air weapon with a mountain weapon. When Lord Śiva released a particular weapon bringing about a violent hurricane on the battlefield, Lord Kṛṣṇa presented just the opposing element, a mountain weapon, which checked the hurricane on the spot. Similarly, when Lord Śiva released his weapon of devastating fire, Kṛṣṇa counteracted it with torrents of rain.

At last, when Lord Śiva released his personal weapon, called Pāśupata-astra, Kṛṣṇa immediately counteracted it with the Nārāyaṇa-astra. Lord Śiva then became exasperated in fighting with Lord Kṛṣṇa. Kṛṣṇa then took the opportunity to release His yawning weapon. When this weapon is released, the opposing party becomes tired, stops fighting and begins to yawn. Consequently, Lord Śiva became so fatigued that he refused to fight anymore and began yawning. Kṛṣṇa was now able to turn His attention from the attack of Lord Śiva to the efforts of Bāṇāsura, and He began to kill Bāṇāsura's personal soldiers with swords and clubs. Meanwhile, Lord Kṛṣṇa's son Pradyumna was fighting fiercely with Kārttikeya, the commander in chief of the demigods. Kārttikeya was wounded, and his body was bleeding profusely. In this condition, he left the battlefield and, without fighting anymore, rode away on the back of his peacock carrier. Similarly, Lord Balarāma smashed Bāṇāsura's commander in chief, Kumbhāṇḍa, with the strokes of His club. Kūpakarṇa was also wounded in this way, and both he and Kumbhāṇḍa fell on the battlefield, Kumbhāṇḍa being fatally wounded. Without guidance, all of Bāṇāsura's soldiers scattered here and there.

When Bāṇāsura saw that his soldiers and commanders had been defeated, his anger only increased. He thought it wise to stop fighting with Sātyaki, Kṛṣṇa's commander in chief, and

and Lord Śiva act only in one capacity: Lord Brahmā can create, and Lord Śiva can annihilate. But neither of them can maintain. Lord Viṣṇu, however, not only maintains but creates and annihilates also. Factually, the creation is not effected by Brahmā, because Brahmā himself is created by Lord Viṣṇu. And Lord Śiva is created, or born, of Brahmā. The Śiva-jvara thus understood that without Kṛṣṇa, or Nārāyaṇa, no one could help him. He therefore rightly took shelter of Lord Kṛṣṇa and, with folded hands, began to pray as follows.

"My dear Lord, I offer my respectful obeisances unto You because You have unlimited potencies. No one can surpass Your potencies, and thus You are the Lord of everyone. Generally people consider Lord Śiva the most powerful personality in the material world, but Lord Śiva is not all-powerful; You are all-powerful. This is factual. You are the original consciousness, or knowledge. Without knowledge, or consciousness, nothing can be powerful. A material thing may be very powerful, but without the touch of consciousness it cannot act. A material machine may be gigantic and wonderful, but without the touch of someone conscious and in knowledge, the material machine is useless for all purposes. My Lord, You are complete knowledge, and there is not a pinch of material contamination in Your personality. Lord Śiva may be a powerful demigod because of his specific power to annihilate the whole creation, and, similarly, Lord Brahmā may be very powerful because he can create the entire universe, but actually neither Brahmā nor Lord Śiva is the original cause of this cosmic manifestation. You are the Absolute Truth, the Supreme Brahman, and You are the original cause. The original cause of the cosmic manifestation is not the impersonal Brahman effulgence. That impersonal Brahman effulgence rests on Your personality." As confirmed in the *Bhagavad-gītā,* the cause of the impersonal Brahman is Lord Kṛṣṇa. This Brahman effulgence is likened to the sunshine, which emanates from the sun globe. Therefore, impersonal Brahman is not the ultimate cause. The ultimate cause of everything is the supreme eternal form of Kṛṣṇa. All material actions and reactions take place in the impersonal Brahman, but in the personal Brahman, the eternal form of Kṛṣṇa, there is no action and reaction.

The Śiva-jvara continued, "Therefore, my Lord, Your body is completely peaceful, completely blissful and devoid of material contamination. In the material body there are actions and reactions of the three modes of material nature. The time factor is the most important element, above all others, because the material manifestation is effected by the agitation of time. Thus natural phenomena come into existence, and as soon as phenomena appear, fruitive activities are visible. As the result of these fruitive activities, a living entity takes his form. He acquires a particular nature packed up in a subtle body and gross body formed by the life air, the ego, the ten sense organs, the mind and the five gross elements. These then create the type of body which later becomes the root cause of various other bodies, which are acquired one after another by means of the transmigration of the soul. All these phenomenal manifestations are the combined actions of Your material energy. You, however, are the cause of this external energy, and thus You remain unaffected by the action and reaction of the different elements. And because You are transcendental to such compulsions of material energy, You are the supreme tranquillity. You are the last word in freedom from material contamination. I therefore take shelter at Your lotus feet, giving up all other shelter.

"My dear Lord, Your appearance as the son of Vasudeva in Your role as a human being is one of the pastimes of Your complete freedom. To benefit Your devotees and vanquish the nondevotees, You appear in multi-incarnations. All such incarnations descend in fulfillment of Your promise in the *Bhagavad-gītā* that You appear as soon as there are discrepancies in the system of progressive life. When there are disturbances by irregular principles, my dear Lord, You appear by Your internal potency. Your main business is to protect and maintain the demigods and spiritually inclined persons and to maintain the standard of material law and order. Considering Your mission to maintain such law and order, Your violence toward the miscreants and demons is quite befitting. This is not the first time You have incarnated; it is to be understood that You have done so many, many times before.

"My dear Lord, I beg to submit that I have been very greatly chastised by the release of Your Nārāyaṇa-jvara, which is certainly very cooling yet at the same time severely dangerous and unbearable for all of us. My dear Lord, as long as one is forgetful of Kṛṣṇa consciousness, driven by the spell of material desires and ignorant of the ultimate shelter at Your lotus feet, one who has accepted this material body becomes disturbed by the three miserable conditions of material nature. Because one does not surrender unto You, he continues to suffer perpetually."

After hearing the Śiva-jvara, Lord Kṛṣṇa replied, "O three-headed one, I am pleased with your statement. Be assured that there will be no more suffering for you from the Nārāyaṇa-jvara. Not only are you now free from fear of the Nārāyaṇa-jvara, but anyone in the future who simply recollects this fight between you and the Nārāyaṇa-jvara will also be freed from all kinds of fear." After hearing the Supreme Personality of Godhead, the Śiva-jvara offered respectful obeisances unto His lotus feet and left.

In the meantime, Bāṇāsura somehow or other recovered from his setbacks and, with rejuvenated energy, returned to fight. This time Bāṇāsura appeared before Lord Kṛṣṇa, who was seated on His chariot, with different kinds of weapons in his one thousand hands. Very much agitated, Bāṇāsura splashed his different weapons upon the body of Lord Kṛṣṇa like torrents of rain. When Lord Kṛṣṇa saw the weapons of Bāṇāsura coming at Him, like water coming out of a strainer, He took His sharp-edged Sudarśana disc and began to cut off the demon's one thousand arms, one after another, just as a gardener trims the twigs of a tree with sharp cutters. When Lord Śiva saw that his devotee Bāṇāsura could not be saved even in his presence, he came to his senses and personally came before Lord Kṛṣṇa and began to pacify Him by offering the following prayers.

Lord Śiva said, "My dear Lord, You are the worshipable object of the Vedic hymns. One who does not know You considers the impersonal *brahmajyoti* to be the ultimate Supreme Absolute Truth, without knowledge that You exist behind Your spiritual effulgence in Your eternal abode. My dear Lord, You are therefore called Parabrahman. Indeed, the words *paraṁ brahman* have been used in the *Bhagavad-gītā* to identify You. Saintly persons who have completely cleansed their hearts of all material contamination can realize Your transcendental form, although You are all-pervading like the sky, unaffected by any material thing. Only the devotees can realize You, and no one else. In the impersonalists' conception of Your supreme existence, the sky is just like Your navel, fire is Your mouth, and water is Your semen. The heavenly planets are Your head, all the directions are Your ears, the earth (Urvī) is Your lotus feet, the moon is Your mind, and the sun is Your eye. As far as I am concerned, I act as Your ego. The ocean is Your abdomen, and the King of heaven, Indra, is Your arm. Trees and plants are the hairs on Your body, the clouds are the hair on Your head, and Lord Brahmā is Your intelligence. All the great progenitors, known as Prajāpatis, are Your symbolic representatives. And religion is Your heart. The impersonal feature of Your supreme body is conceived of in this way, but You are ultimately the Supreme Person. The impersonal feature of Your supreme body is only a small expansion of Your energy. You are likened to the original fire, and Your expansions are its light and heat."

Lord Śiva continued, "My dear Lord, since You are manifested universally, the different parts of the universe are the different parts of Your body, and by Your inconceivable potency You can simultaneously be both localized and universal. In the *Brahma-saṁhitā* we also find it stated that although You always remain in Your abode, Goloka Vṛndāvana, You are present everywhere. As stated in the *Bhagavad-gītā,* You appear in order to protect the devotees, and thus Your appearance indicates good fortune for all the universe. All of the demigods are directing different affairs of the universe by Your grace only. Thus the seven upper planetary systems are maintained by Your grace. At the end of this creation, all manifestations of Your energies, whether in the shape of demigods, human beings or lower animals, enter into You, and all immediate and remote causes of the cosmic manifestation rest in You without distinctive features of existence. Ultimately, there is no possibility of distinction between You and any other thing on an equal level with You or subordinate to You. You are simultaneously the cause of this cosmic manifestation and its ingredients as well. You are the Supreme Whole, one without a second. In the phenomenal manifestation there are three stages: the stage of consciousness, the stage of semiconsciousness in dreaming, and the stage of unconsciousness. But Your Lordship is transcendental to all these different material stages of existence. You exist, therefore, in a fourth dimension, and Your appearance and disappearance do not depend on anything beyond Yourself. You are the supreme cause of everything, but of You there is no cause. You Yourself cause Your own appearance and disappearance. Despite Your transcendental position, my Lord, in order to show Your six opulences and advertise Your transcendental qualities, You have appeared in Your different incarnations—fish, tortoise, boar, Nṛsiṁha, Keśava and others—by Your personal manifestation; and You have appeared as different living entities by Your separated manifestations. By Your internal potency You appear as the different incarnations of Viṣṇu, and by Your external potency You appear as the phenomenal world.

"On a cloudy day, to the common man's eyes the sun appears to be covered. But the fact is that because the sunshine creates the cloud, the sun can never actually be covered, even though the whole sky may be cloudy. Similarly, less intelligent men claim that there is no God, but when the manifestation of different living entities and their activities is visible, enlightened persons see You present in every atom and through the via media of Your external and marginal energies. Your unlimitedly potent activities are experienced by the most enlightened devotees, but those who are bewildered by the spell of Your external energy identify themselves with this material world and become attached to society, friendship and love. Thus they embrace the threefold miseries of material existence and are subjected to the dualities of pain and pleasure, sometimes drowning in the ocean of attachment and sometimes being taken out of it.

"My dear Lord, only by Your mercy and grace can the living entity get the human form of life, which is a chance to get out of the miserable condition of material existence. However, a person who possesses a human body but who cannot bring his senses under control is carried away by the waves of sensual enjoyment. As such, he cannot take shelter of Your lotus feet and thus engage in Your devotional service. The life of such a person is very unfortunate, and anyone living such a life of darkness is certainly cheating himself and thus cheating others also. Therefore, human society without Kṛṣṇa consciousness is a society of cheaters and the cheated.

"My Lord, You are actually the dearmost Supersoul of all living entities and the supreme controller of everything. The human being who is always illusioned is afraid of ultimate death. A man who is simply attached to sensual enjoyment voluntarily accepts the miserable material existence and thus wanders after the will-o'-the-wisp of sense pleasure. He is certainly the most foolish man, for he drinks poison and puts aside the nectar. My dear Lord, all the demigods, including myself and Lord Brahmā, as well as great saintly persons and sages who have cleansed their hearts of material attachment, have, by Your grace, wholeheartedly taken shelter of Your lotus feet. We have all taken shelter of You because we have accepted You as the Supreme Lord and the dearmost life and soul of all of us. You are the original cause of this cosmic manifestation, You are its supreme maintainer, and You are the cause of its dissolution also. You are equal to everyone, the most peaceful supreme friend of every living entity. You are the supreme worshipable object for every one of us. My dear Lord, let us always be engaged in Your transcendental loving service so that we may get free from this material entanglement.

"Last, my Lord, I may inform You that this Bāṇāsura is very dear to me. He has rendered valuable service unto me; therefore I want to see him always happy. Being pleased with him, I have assured him safety. I pray to You, my Lord, that as You were pleased with his forefathers King Prahlāda and Bali Mahārāja, You will also be pleased with him."

After hearing Lord Śiva's prayer, Lord Kṛṣṇa replied, "My dear Lord Śiva, I accept your statements, and I also accept your desire for Bāṇāsura. I know that this Bāṇāsura is the son of Bali Mahārāja, and as such I cannot kill him, for that is My promise. I gave a benediction to King Prahlāda that the demons who would appear in his family would never be killed by Me. Therefore, without killing this Bāṇāsura, I have simply cut off his arms to deprive him of his false prestige. The large number of soldiers he was maintaining became a burden on this earth, and I have killed them all to minimize the burden. Now he has four remaining arms, and he will remain immortal, unaffected by material pains and pleasures. I know that he is one of the chief devotees of Your Lordship, so you can now rest assured that henceforward he need have no fear of anything."

When Bāṇāsura was blessed by Lord Kṛṣṇa in this way, he

came before the Lord and bowed down before Him, touching his head to the earth. Bāṇāsura immediately arranged to have his daughter Ūṣā seated with Aniruddha on a nice chariot, and then he presented them before Lord Kṛṣṇa. After this, Lord Kṛṣṇa took charge of Aniruddha and Ūṣā, who had become very opulent materially because of the blessings of Lord Śiva. Thus, keeping forward a division of one *akṣauhiṇī* of soldiers, Kṛṣṇa proceeded toward Dvārakā. In the meantime, all the people of Dvārakā, having received the news that Lord Kṛṣṇa was returning with Aniruddha and Ūṣā in great opulence, decorated every corner of the city with flags, festoons and garlands. All the big roads and crossings were carefully cleansed and sprinkled with sandalwood pulp mixed with water. Everywhere was the fragrance of sandalwood. All the citizens joined their friends and relatives to welcome Lord Kṛṣṇa with great pomp and jubilation, and a tumultuous vibration of conchshells, drums and bugles received the Lord. In this way the Supreme Personality of Godhead, Kṛṣṇa, entered His capital, Dvārakā.

Śukadeva Gosvāmī assured King Parīkṣit that the narration of the fight between Lord Śiva and Lord Kṛṣṇa is not at all inauspicious, like ordinary fights. On the contrary, if one remembers in the morning the narration of this fight between Lord Kṛṣṇa and Lord Śiva and takes pleasure in the victory of Lord Kṛṣṇa, he will never experience defeat anywhere in his struggle of life.

This episode of Bāṇāsura's fighting with Kṛṣṇa and later being saved by the grace of Lord Śiva is confirmation of the statement in the *Bhagavad-gītā* that the worshipers of demigods cannot achieve any benediction without its being sanctioned by the Supreme Lord, Kṛṣṇa. Here in this narration we find that although Bāṇāsura was a great devotee of Lord Śiva, when he faced death by Kṛṣṇa, Lord Śiva was not able to save him. But Lord Śiva appealed to Kṛṣṇa to save his devotee, and this was sanctioned by the Lord. This is the position of Lord Kṛṣṇa. The exact words used in this connection in the *Bhagavad-gītā* are *mayaiva vihitān hi tān.* This means that without the sanction of the Supreme Lord, no demigod can award any benediction to his worshiper.

Thus ends the Bhaktivedanta purport of the Sixty-third Chapter of Kṛṣṇa, *"Lord Kṛṣṇa Fights with Bāṇāsura."*

CHAPTER SIXTY-FOUR

The Story of King Nṛga

Once the family members of Lord Kṛṣṇa, such as Sāmba, Pradyumna, Cāru, Bhānu and Gada, all princes of the Yadu dynasty, went for a long picnic in the forest near Dvārakā. In the course of their excursion, all of them became thirsty, and so they tried to find out where water was available in the forest. When they approached a well, they found no water in it, but, on the contrary, within the well was a wonderful living entity. It was a large lizard, and all of them were astonished to see such a wonderful animal. They could understand that the animal was trapped and could not escape by its own effort, so out of compassion they tried to take the large lizard out of the well. Unfortunately, they could not get the lizard out, even though they tried to do so in many ways.

When the princes returned home, their story was narrated before Lord Kṛṣṇa. Lord Kṛṣṇa is the friend of all living entities. Therefore, after hearing the appeal from His sons, He personally went to the well and easily got the great lizard out simply by extending His left hand. Immediately upon being touched by the hand of Lord Kṛṣṇa, that great lizard gave up its lizard shape and appeared as a beautiful demigod, an inhabitant of the heavenly planets. His complexion glittered like molten gold, he was decorated with fine garments, and he wore costly ornaments around his neck.

How the demigod had been obliged to accept the body of a lizard was not a secret to Lord Kṛṣṇa, but still, for others' information, the Lord inquired, "My dear fortunate demigod, now I see that your body is so beautiful and lustrous. Who are you? We can guess that you are one of the best demigods in the heavenly planets. All good fortune to you. I think that you are not meant to be in this situation. It must be due to the results of your past activities that you were put into the species of lizard life. Still, I want to hear from you how you were put in this position. If you think that you can disclose this secret, then please tell us your identity."

Actually, this large lizard was King Nṛga, and when questioned by the Supreme Personality of Godhead he immediately bowed down before the Lord, touching to the ground the helmet on his head, which was as dazzling as the sunshine. In this way, he first offered his respectful obeisances unto the Supreme Lord. He then said, "My dear Lord, I am King Nṛga, the son of King Ikṣvāku. If You have ever taken account of all charitably disposed men, I am sure You must have heard my name. My Lord, You are the supreme witness. You are aware of every bit of work done by the living entities—past, present and future. Nothing can be hidden from Your eternal cognizance. Still, You have ordered me to explain my history, and I shall therefore narrate the full story."

King Nṛga proceeded to narrate the history of his degradation, caused by his *karma-kāṇḍa* activities. He said that he had been very charitably disposed and had given away so many cows that the total was equal to the number of particles of dust on the earth, stars in the sky or drops of water in a rainfall. According to the Vedic ritualistic ceremonies, a man who is charitably disposed is recommended to give cows to the *brāhmaṇas.* From King Nṛga's statement, it appears that he followed this principle earnestly; however, as a result of a slight discrepancy he was forced to take birth as a lizard. Therefore it is recommended by the Lord in the *Bhagavad-gītā* that one who is charitably disposed and desires to derive the benefit of his charity should offer his gifts to please Kṛṣṇa. To give charity means to perform pious activities by which one may be elevated to the higher planetary systems; but promotion to the heavenly planets is no guarantee that one will never fall down. Rather, the example of King Nṛga definitely proves that fruitive activities, even if very pious, cannot give us eternal blissful life. As stated in the *Bhagavad-gītā,* the result of work, either pious or impious, is sure to bind a man unless the work is discharged as *yajña* on behalf of the Supreme Personality of Godhead.

King Nṛga said that the cows he had given in charity were not ordinary cows. Each one was very young and had given birth to only one calf. They were full of milk, very peaceful and healthy. All the cows were purchased with money earned legally. Furthermore, their horns were gold-plated, their hooves were bedecked with silver plating, and they were covered with necklaces and with silken wrappers embroidered with pearls. He stated that these valuably decorated cows had not been given to any worthless persons but had been distributed to first-class *brāhmaṇas,* whom he had also decorated with nice garments and gold ornaments. The *brāhmaṇas* were well qualified, and since none of them were rich, their family members were always in want for the necessities of life. A real *brāhmaṇa* never hoards money for a luxurious life, like the *kṣatriyas* or the *vaiśyas,* but always keeps himself poverty-stricken, knowing that money diverts the mind to materialistic ways of life. To live in this way is the vow of a qualified *brāhmaṇa,* and all of these *brāhmaṇas* were well situated in that exalted vow. They were well learned in Vedic knowledge. They executed the required austerities and penances in their lives and were liberal, meeting the standard of qualified *brāhmaṇas.* They were equally friendly to everyone; above all, they were young and quite fit to act as qualified *brāhmaṇas.* Besides the cows, they were also given land, gold, houses, horses and elephants. Those who were not married were given wives, maidservants, grain, silver, utensils, garments, jewels, household furniture, chariots, etc. This charity was nicely performed as a sacrifice according to the Vedic rituals. The King also stated that not only had he bestowed gifts upon the *brāhmaṇas,* but he had performed other pious activities, such as digging wells, planting trees on the roadside and installing ponds along the highways.

The King continued, "In spite of all this, unfortunately one of the *brāhmaṇas'* cows that I had given in charity chanced to enter amongst my other cows. Not knowing this, I again gave it in charity, to another *brāhmaṇa.* As the cow was being taken away by this *brāhmaṇa,* its former master claimed it as his own, stating, 'This cow was formerly given to me, so how is it that you are taking it away?' Thus there was arguing and fighting between the two *brāhmaṇas,* and they came before me and charged that I had taken back a cow I had previously given in charity." To give something to someone and then to take it back is considered a great sin, especially in dealing with a *brāhmaṇa.* When both *brāhmaṇas* charged the King with the same complaint, he was simply puzzled as to how it had happened. Thereafter, with great humility, the King offered each of them 100,000 cows in exchange for the one cow that was causing the fight between them. He prayed to them that he was their servant and that there had been some mistake. Thus, in order to rectify it, he prayed that they be very kind upon him and accept his offer in exchange for the cow. The King fervently appealed to the *brāhmaṇas* not to cause his downfall into hell because of this mistake. A *brāhmaṇa's* property is called *brahma-sva,* and according to Manu's law it cannot be acquired even by the government. Both *brāhmaṇas,* however, insisted that the cow was theirs and could not be taken back under any condition; neither of them agreed to exchange it for the 100,000 cows. Thus disagreeing with the King's proposal, the two *brāhmaṇas* left the place in anger, thinking that their lawful possession had been usurped.

After this incident, when the time came for the King to give up his body, he was taken before Yamarāja, the superintendent of death, who asked him whether he first wanted to enjoy the results of his pious activities or suffer the results of his impious activities. Seeing that the King had executed so many pious activities and charities, Yamarāja also hinted that he did not know the limit of the King's future enjoyment. In other words, there would be practically no end to the King's material happiness. But in spite of this hint, the King, bewildered, decided first to suffer the results of his impious activities and then to accept the results of his pious activities; therefore Yamarāja immediately turned him into a lizard.

King Nṛga had remained in the well as a big lizard for a very long time. He told Lord Kṛṣṇa, "In spite of being put into that degraded condition of life, I simply thought of You, my dear Lord, and my memory was never vanquished." It appears from these statements of King Nṛga that persons who follow the principles of fruitive activities and derive some material benefits are not very intelligent. Being given the choice by the superintendent of death, Yamarāja, King Nṛga could have first accepted the results of his pious activities. Instead, he thought it better first to receive the effects of his impious activities and then enjoy the effects of his pious activities without disturbance. On the whole, he had not developed Kṛṣṇa consciousness. The Kṛṣṇa conscious person develops love of God, Kṛṣṇa, not love for pious or impious activities; therefore he is not subjected to the results of such action. As stated in the *Brahma-saṁhitā,* a devotee, by the grace of the Lord, is not subjected to the reactions of fruitive activities.

Somehow or other, as a result of his pious activities, King Nṛga had aspired to see the Lord. He continued, "My dear Lord, I had a great desire that someday I might be able to see You personally. I think that this great desire to see You, combined with my tendency to perform ritualistic and charitable activities, has enabled me to retain the memory of who I was in my former life, even though I became a lizard. [Such a person who remembers his past life is called *jāti-smara.* In modern times also there are instances of small children recalling many details of their past lives.] My dear Lord, You are the Supersoul seated in everyone's heart. There are many great mystic *yogīs* who have the eyes to see You through the *Vedas* and *Upaniṣads.* To achieve the elevated position of realizing that they are equal in quality with You, they always meditate on You within their hearts. But although such exalted saintly persons may see You constantly within their hearts, they still cannot see You face to face. Therefore I am very much surprised that I am able to see You personally. I know that I was engaged in so many activities, especially as a king. Although I was in the midst of luxury and opulence and was subject to so much of the happiness and misery of material existence, I am so fortunate to be seeing You personally. As far as I know, when one becomes liberated from material existence, he can see You in this way."

When King Nṛga elected to receive the results of his impious activities, he was given the body of a lizard because of the mistake in his pious activities; thus he could not be directly converted to a higher status of life like a great demigod. However, along with his pious activities, he thought of Kṛṣṇa, so he was quickly released from the body of a lizard and given the body of a demigod. By worshiping the Supreme Lord, those who desire material opulences are given the bodies of powerful demigods. Sometimes these demigods can see the Supreme Personality of Godhead face to face, but they are still not yet eligible to enter into the spiritual kingdom, the

Vaikuṇṭha planets. However, if the demigods continue to be devotees of the Lord, the next chance they get they will enter into the Vaikuṇṭha planets.

Having attained the body of a demigod, King Nṛga, continuing to remember everything, said, "My dear Lord, You are the Supreme Lord and are worshiped by all the demigods. You are not one of the ordinary living entities; You are the Supreme Person, Puruṣottama. You are the source of all happiness for all living entities; therefore You are known as Govinda. You are the Lord of those living entities who have accepted material bodies and those who have not yet accepted material bodies. [Among the living entities who have not accepted material bodies are those who hover in the material world as evil spirits or live in the ghostly atmosphere. However, those who live in the spiritual kingdom, the Vaikuṇṭha-lokas, have bodics not made of material elements.] You, my Lord, are infallible. You are the Supreme, the purest of all living entities. You live in everyone's heart. You are the shelter of all living entities, Nārāyaṇa. Being seated in the heart of all living beings, You are the supreme director of everyone's sensual activities; therefore, You are called Hṛṣīkeśa.

"My dear Supreme Lord Kṛṣṇa, because You have given me this body of a demigod, I will have to go to some heavenly planet; so I am taking this opportunity to beg for Your mercy. I pray that I may have the benediction of never forgetting Your lotus feet, no matter to which form of life or planet I may be transferred. You are all-pervading, present everywhere as cause and effect. You are the cause of all causes, and Your power is unlimited. You are the Absolute Truth, the Supreme Personality of Godhead and the Supreme Brahman. I therefore offer my respectful obeisances unto You again and again. My dear Lord, Your body is full of transcendental bliss and knowledge, and You are eternal. You are the master of all mystic powers; therefore You are known as Yogeśvara. Kindly accept me as an insignificant particle of dust at Your lotus feet."

Before entering the heavenly planets, King Nṛga circumambulated the Lord, touched his helmet to the Lord's lotus feet and bowed before Him. Seeing the airplane from the heavenly planets present before him, he was given permission by the Lord to board it. After the departure of King Nṛga, Lord Kṛṣṇa expressed His appreciation for the King's devotion to the *brāhmaṇas* as well as his charitable disposition and his performance of Vedic rituals. Therefore, it is recommended that if one cannot directly become a devotee of the Lord, one should follow the Vedic principles of life. This will enable him, one day, to see the Lord by being promoted either directly to the spiritual kingdom or, indirectly, to the heavenly kingdom, where he has hope of being transferred to the spiritual planets.

At this time, Lord Kṛṣṇa was present among His relatives who were members of the *kṣatriya* class. To teach them through the exemplary character of King Nṛga, He said, "Even though a *kṣatriya* king may be as powerful as fire, it is not possible for him to usurp the property of a *brāhmaṇa* and utilize it for his own purpose. If this is so, how can ordinary kings, who falsely think themselves the most powerful beings within the material world, usurp a *brāhmaṇa's* property? I do not think that taking poison is as dangerous as taking a *brāhmaṇa's* property. For ordinary poison there is treatment—one can be relieved from its effects—but if one drinks the poison of taking a *brāhmaṇa's* property, there is no remedy for the mistake. The perfect example is King Nṛga. He was very powerful and very pious, but due to the small mistake of unknowingly usurping a *brāhmaṇa's* cow, he was condemned to the abominable life of a lizard. Ordinary poison affects only those who drink it, and ordinary fire can be extinguished simply by pouring water on it, but the *araṇi* fire ignited by the spiritual potency of a *brāhmaṇa* who is dissatisfied can burn to ashes the whole family of a person who provokes such a *brāhmaṇa.* [Formerly, the *brāhmaṇas* used to ignite the fire of sacrifice not with matches or any other external fire but with their powerful *mantras,* called *araṇi.*] If someone even touches a *brāhmaṇa's* property, his family is ruined for three generations. However, if a *brāhmaṇa's* property is forcibly taken away, the taker's family for ten generations before him and ten generations after will be subject to ruination. On the other hand, if someone becomes a pure Vaiṣṇava, or devotee of the Lord, ten generations of his family before his birth and ten generations after will be liberated."

Lord Kṛṣṇa continued, "If some foolish king who is puffed up by his wealth, prestige and power wants to usurp a *brāhmaṇa's* property, he should be understood to be clearing his path to hell; he does not know how much he has to suffer for such an unwise act. If someone takes away the property of a very liberal *brāhmaṇa* who is encumbered by a large dependent family, then such a usurper is put into the hell known as Kumbhīpāka; not only is he put into this hell, but his family members also have to accept such a miserable condition of life. A person who takes away a *brāhmaṇa's* property, whether it was originally given by him or by someone else, is condemned to live for at least sixty thousand years as a miserable insect in stool. Therefore I instruct you, all My boys and relatives present here, do not, even by mistake, take the possession of a *brāhmaṇa* and thereby pollute your whole family. If someone even wishes to possess such property, let alone attempts to take it away by force, the duration of his life will be reduced. He will be defeated by his enemies, and after being bereft of his royal position, when he gives up his body he will become a serpent, giving trouble to all other living entities. My dear boys and relatives, I therefore advise you that even if a *brāhmaṇa* becomes angry with you and calls you by ill names or curses you, still you should not retaliate. On the contrary, you should smile, tolerate him and offer your respects to the *brāhmaṇa.* You know very well that even I Myself offer My obeisances to the *brāhmaṇas* with great respect three times daily. You should therefore follow My instruction and example. I shall not forgive anyone who does not follow them, and I shall punish him. You should learn from the example of King Nṛga that even if someone unknowingly usurps the property of a *brāhmaṇa,* he is put into a miserable condition of life."

Thus Lord Kṛṣṇa, who is always engaged in purifying the conditioned living entities, gave instruction not only to His family members and the inhabitants of Dvārakā but to all the members of human society. After this, the Lord entered His palace.

Thus ends the Bhaktivedanta purport of the Sixty-fourth Chapter of Kṛṣṇa, *"The Story of King Nṛga."*

CHAPTER SIXTY-FIVE

Lord Balarāma Visits Vṛndāvana

Lord Balarāma became very anxious to see His father and mother in Vṛndāvana. Therefore, with great enthusiasm He started on a chariot for Vṛndāvana. The inhabitants of Vṛndāvana had been anxious to see Kṛṣṇa and Balarāma for a very long time. When Lord Balarāma returned to Vṛndāvana, all the cowherd boys and the *gopīs* had grown up; but still, on His arrival, they all embraced Him, and Balarāma embraced them in reciprocation. After this He came before Mahārāja Nanda and Yaśodā and offered His respectful obeisances. In response, mother Yaśodā and Nanda Mahārāja offered their blessings unto Him. They addressed Him as Jagadīśvara, or the Lord of the universe who maintains everyone. The reason for this was that Kṛṣṇa and Balarāma maintain all living entities. And yet Nanda and Yaśodā were put into such difficulties on account of Their absence. Feeling like this, they embraced Balarāma and, seating Him on their laps, began their perpetual crying, wetting Balarāma with their tears. Lord Balarāma then offered His respectful obeisances to the elderly cowherd men and accepted the obeisances of the younger cowherd men. Thus, according to their different ages and relationships, Lord Balarāma exchanged feelings of friendship with them. He shook hands with those who were His equals in age and friendship and with loud laughing embraced each one of them.

After being received by the cowherd men and boys, the *gopīs,* and King Nanda and Yaśodā, Lord Balarāma sat down, feeling satisfied, and they all surrounded Him. First Lord Balarāma inquired from them about their welfare, and then, since they had not seen Him for such a long time, they began to ask Him different questions. The inhabitants of Vṛndāvana had sacrificed everything for Kṛṣṇa, simply being captivated by the lotus eyes of the Lord. Because of their great desire to love Kṛṣṇa, they never desired anything like elevation to the heavenly planets or merging into the effulgence of Brahman to become one with the Absolute Truth. They were not even interested in enjoying a life of opulence, but were satisfied in living a simple life in the village as cowherds. They were always absorbed in thoughts of Kṛṣṇa and did not desire any personal benefits, and they were all so much in love with Him that in His absence their voices faltered when they began to inquire from Balarāmajī.

First Nanda Mahārāja and Yaśodāmāyī inquired, "My dear Balarāma, are our friends like Vasudeva and others in the family doing well? Now You and Kṛṣṇa are grown-up married men with children. In the happiness of family life, do You sometimes remember Your poor father and mother, Nanda Mahārāja and Yaśodādevī? It is very good news that the most sinful King Kaṁsa has been killed by You and that our friends like Vasudeva and the others who had been harassed have now been relieved. It is also very good news that You and Kṛṣṇa defeated Jarāsandha and Kālayavana, who is now dead, and that You are now living in a fortified residence in Dvārakā."

When the *gopīs* arrived, Lord Balarāma glanced over them with loving eyes. Being overjoyed, the *gopīs,* who had so long been mortified on account of Kṛṣṇa's and Balarāma's absence, began to ask about the welfare of the two brothers. They specifically asked Balarāma whether Kṛṣṇa was enjoying His life surrounded by the enlightened women of Dvārakā Purī. "Does He sometimes remember His father Nanda and His mother Yaśodā and the other friends with whom He so intimately behaved while in Vṛndāvana? Does Kṛṣṇa have any plans to come here to see His mother, Yaśodā, and does He remember us *gopīs,* who are now pitiably bereft of His company? Kṛṣṇa may have forgotten us in the midst of the cultured women of Dvārakā, but as far as we are concerned, we still remember Him by collecting flowers and sewing them into garlands. When He does not come, however, we simply pass our time by crying. If only He would come here and accept these garlands we have made. Dear Lord Balarāma, descendant of Dāśārha, You know that we would give up everything for Kṛṣṇa's friendship. Even in great distress one cannot give up the connection of family members, but although it might be impossible for others, we gave up our fathers, mothers, sisters and relatives. But then Kṛṣṇa, without caring a pinch for our renunciation, all of a sudden renounced us and went away. He broke off our intimate relationship without serious consideration and left for a foreign country. But He was so clever and cunning that He manufactured very nice words. He said, 'My dear *gopīs,* please do not worry. The service you have rendered Me is impossible for Me to repay.' After all, we are women, so how could we disbelieve Him? Now we can understand that His sweet words were simply for cheating us."

Protesting Kṛṣṇa's absence from Vṛndāvana, another *gopī* said, "My dear Balarāmajī, we are of course village girls, so Kṛṣṇa could cheat us in that way, but what about the women of Dvārakā? Don't think they are as foolish as we are! We village women might be misled by Kṛṣṇa, but the women in the city of Dvārakā are very clever and intelligent. Therefore I would be surprised if such city women could be misled by Kṛṣṇa and could believe His words."

Then another *gopī* began to speak. "My dear friend," she said, "Kṛṣṇa is very clever in using words. No one can compete with Him in that art. He can manufacture such colorful words and talk so sweetly that the heart of any woman would be misled. Besides that, He has perfected the art of smiling very attractively, and by seeing His smile women become mad after Him and give themselves to Him without hesitation."

Another *gopī,* after hearing this, said, "My dear friends, what is the use of talking about Kṛṣṇa? If you are at all interested in passing time by talking, let us talk on some subject other than Him. If cruel Kṛṣṇa can pass His time without us, why can't we pass our time without Kṛṣṇa? Of course, Kṛṣṇa is passing His days without us very happily, but we cannot pass our days happily without Him."

When the *gopīs* were talking in this way, their feelings for Kṛṣṇa became more and more intense, and they were experiencing Kṛṣṇa's smiling, Kṛṣṇa's words of love, Kṛṣṇa's attractive features, Kṛṣṇa's characteristics and Kṛṣṇa's embraces. By the force of their ecstatic feelings, it appeared to them that Kṛṣṇa was personally present and dancing before them. Because of their sweet remembrance of Kṛṣṇa, they could not check their tears, and they began to cry without consideration.

Lord Balarāma, of course, could understand the ecstatic feelings of the *gopīs,* and therefore He wanted to pacify them. He was expert in presenting an appeal, and thus, treating the *gopīs* very respectfully, He began to narrate the stories of Kṛṣṇa so tactfully that the *gopīs* became satisfied. To keep the *gopīs* in Vṛndāvana satisfied, Lord Balarāma stayed there continuously for two months, namely the months of Caitra (March–April) and Vaiśākha (April–May). For those two months He kept Himself among the *gopīs,* and He passed every night with them in the forest of Vṛndāvana to satisfy their desire for conjugal love. Thus Balarāma also enjoyed the *rāsa* dance with the *gopīs* during those two months. Since the season was springtime, the breeze on the bank of the Yamunā was blowing very mildly, carrying the aroma of different flowers, especially the flower known as *kaumudī.* Moonlight filled the sky and spread everywhere, and thus the banks of the Yamunā appeared very bright and pleasing, and Lord Balarāma enjoyed the company of the *gopīs* there.

The demigod known as Varuṇa sent his daughter Vāruṇī in the form of liquid honey oozing from the hollows of the trees. Because of this honey the whole forest became aromatic, and the sweet aroma of the liquid honey, *vāruṇī,* captivated Balarāmajī. Balarāmajī and all the *gopīs* became very much attracted by the taste of the *vāruṇī,* and all of them drank it together. While drinking this natural beverage, all the *gopīs* chanted the glories of Lord Balarāma, and Lord Balarāma felt very happy, as if He had become intoxicated by drinking that *vāruṇī* beverage. His eyes rolled in a pleasing attitude. He was decorated with long garlands of forest flowers, and the whole situation appeared to be a great function of happiness because of this transcendental bliss. Lord Balarāma smiled beautifully, and the drops of perspiration decorating His face appeared like soothing morning dew.

While Balarāma was in that happy mood, He desired to enjoy the company of the *gopīs* in the water of the Yamunā. Therefore He called the Yamunā to come nearby. But the Yamunā neglected the order of Balarāmajī, considering Him intoxicated. Lord Balarāma became very much displeased at the Yamunā's neglecting His order. He immediately wanted to scratch the land near the river with His plowshare. Lord Balarāma has two weapons, a plow and a club, from which He takes service when they are required. This time He wanted to bring the Yamunā by force, and He took the help of His plow. He wanted to punish the Yamunā because she did not come in obedience to His order. He addressed the Yamunā, "You wretched river! You did not care for My order. Now I shall teach you a lesson! You did not come to Me voluntarily. Now with the help of My plow I shall force you to come. I shall divide you into hundreds of scattered streams!"

When the Yamunā was threatened like this, she became greatly afraid of the power of Balarāma and immediately came in person, falling at His lotus feet and praying thus: "My dear Balarāma, You are the most powerful personality, and You are pleasing to everyone. Unfortunately, I forgot Your glorious, exalted position, but now I have come to my senses, and I remember that You hold all the planetary systems on Your head merely by Your partial expansion Śeṣa. You are the sustainer of the whole universe. My dear Supreme Personality of Godhead, You are full with six opulences. Because I forgot Your omnipotence, I have mistakenly disobeyed Your order, and thus I have become a great offender. But, my dear Lord, please know that I am a soul surrendered unto You, who are very affectionate to Your devotees. Therefore please excuse my impudence and mistakes, and, by Your causeless mercy, may You now release me."

Upon displaying this submissive attitude, the Yamunā was forgiven, and when she came nearby, Lord Balarāma enjoyed the pleasure of swimming in her waters along with the *gopīs* in the same way that an elephant enjoys himself along with his many she-elephants. After a long time, when Lord Balarāma had enjoyed to His full satisfaction, He came out of the water, and immediately a goddess of fortune offered Him a nice blue garment and a valuable necklace made of gold. After bathing in the Yamunā, Lord Balarāma, dressed in blue garments and decorated with golden ornaments, looked very attractive to everyone. Lord Balarāma's complexion is white, and when He was properly dressed He looked exactly like the white elephant of King Indra in the heavenly planets. The river Yamunā still has many small branches due to being scratched by the plowshare of Lord Balarāma. And all these branches of the river Yamunā still glorify the omnipotence of Lord Balarāma.

Lord Balarāma and the *gopīs* enjoyed transcendental pastimes together every night for two months, and time passed so quickly that all those nights appeared to be only one night. In the presence of Lord Balarāma, all the *gopīs* and other inhabitants of Vṛndāvana became as cheerful as they had been before in the presence of both brothers, Lord Kṛṣṇa and Lord Balarāma.

Thus ends the Bhaktivedanta purport of the Sixty-fifth Chapter of Kṛṣṇa, *"Lord Balarāma Visits Vṛndāvana."*

CHAPTER SIXTY-SIX

The Deliverance of Pauṇḍraka and the King of Kāśī

The story of King Pauṇḍraka is very interesting because it proves that there have always been many rascals and fools who have considered themselves God. Even in the presence of the Supreme Personality of Godhead, Kṛṣṇa, there was such a foolish person. His name was Pauṇḍraka, and he wanted to declare himself God. While Lord Balarāma was absent in Vṛndāvana, this King Pauṇḍraka, the King of Karūṣa Province, being foolish and puffed up, sent a messenger to Lord Kṛṣṇa. Lord Kṛṣṇa is accepted as the Supreme Personality of Godhead, but King Pauṇḍraka directly challenged Kṛṣṇa through the messenger, who stated that Pauṇḍraka, not Kṛṣṇa, was Vāsudeva. In the present day there are many foolish followers of such rascals. Similarly, in Pauṇḍraka's day, many foolish men accepted Pauṇḍraka as the Supreme Personality of Godhead. Because he could not estimate his own position, Pauṇḍraka falsely thought himself to be Lord Vāsudeva. Thus the messenger declared to Kṛṣṇa that King

Pauṇḍraka, the Supreme Personality of Godhead, had descended on the earth out of his causeless mercy just to deliver all distressed persons.

Surrounded by many other foolish persons, this rascal Pauṇḍraka had actually concluded that he was Vāsudeva, the Supreme Personality of Godhead. This kind of conclusion is certainly childish. When children are playing, they sometimes select a "king" amongst themselves, and the selected child may think that he is actually the king. Similarly, many foolish persons, due to ignorance, select another fool as God, and then the rascal actually considers himself God, as if God could be created by childish play or by the votes of men. Under this false impression, thinking himself the Supreme Lord, Pauṇḍraka sent his messenger to Dvārakā to challenge the position of Kṛṣṇa. The messenger reached the royal assembly of Kṛṣṇa in Dvārakā and conveyed the message given by his master, Pauṇḍraka. The message contained the following statements.

"I am the only Supreme Personality of Godhead, Vāsudeva. No man can compete with me. I have descended as King Pauṇḍraka, taking compassion on the distressed conditioned souls out of my unlimited causeless mercy. You have falsely taken the position of Vāsudeva without authority, but You should not propagate this false idea. You must give up Your position. O descendant of the Yadu dynasty, please give up all the symbols of Vāsudeva, which You have falsely assumed. And after giving up this position, come and surrender unto me. If out of Your gross impudence You do not care for my words, then I challenge You to fight. I am inviting You to a battle in which the decision will be settled."

When all the members of the royal assembly, including King Ugrasena, heard this message sent by Pauṇḍraka, they laughed very loudly for a considerable time. After enjoying the loud laughter of all the members of the assembly, Kṛṣṇa replied to the messenger as follows: "O messenger of Pauṇḍraka, you may carry My message to your master: 'You are a foolish rascal. I directly call you a rascal, and I refuse to follow your instructions. I shall never give up the symbols of Vāsudeva, especially My disc. I shall use this disc to kill not only you but all your followers also. I shall destroy you and your foolish associates, who merely constitute a society of cheaters and the cheated. O foolish King, you will then have to conceal your face in disgrace, and when your head is severed from your body by My disc, it will be surrounded by meat-eating birds like vultures, hawks and eagles. At that time, instead of becoming My shelter, as you have demanded, you will be subject to the mercy of these lowborn birds. At that time your body will be thrown to the dogs, who will eat it with great pleasure.' "

The messenger carried the words of Lord Kṛṣṇa to his master, Pauṇḍraka, who patiently heard all these insults. Without waiting any longer, Lord Śrī Kṛṣṇa immediately started out on His chariot to punish the rascal Pauṇḍraka, the King of Karūṣa. Because at that time he was living with his friend the King of Kāśī, Kṛṣṇa surrounded the whole city of Kāśī.

King Pauṇḍraka was a great warrior, and as soon as he heard of Kṛṣṇa's attack, he came out of the city with two *akṣauhiṇī* divisions of soldiers. The King of Kāśī also came out, with three *akṣauhiṇī* divisions. When the two kings came before Lord Kṛṣṇa to oppose Him, Kṛṣṇa saw Pauṇḍraka face to face for the first time. Kṛṣṇa saw that Pauṇḍraka had decorated himself with the symbols of the conchshell, disc, lotus and club. He carried an imitation Śārṅga bow, and on his chest was a mock insignia of Śrīvatsa. His neck was decorated with a false Kaustubha jewel, and he wore a flower garland in exact imitation of Lord Vāsudeva's. He was dressed in yellow silken garments, and the flag on his chariot carried the symbol of Garuḍa, exactly imitating Kṛṣṇa's. He had a very valuable helmet on his head, and his earrings, like swordfish, glittered brilliantly. On the whole, however, his dress and makeup were clearly imitation. Anyone could understand that he was just like someone onstage playing the part of Vāsudeva in false dress. When Lord Śrī Kṛṣṇa saw Pauṇḍraka imitating His posture and dress, He could not check His laughter, and thus He laughed with great satisfaction.

The soldiers on the side of King Pauṇḍraka began to shower their weapons upon Kṛṣṇa. The weapons, including various kinds of tridents, clubs, poles, lances, swords, daggers and arrows, came flying in waves, and Kṛṣṇa counteracted them. He smashed not only the weapons but also the soldiers and assistants of Pauṇḍraka, just as during the dissolution of this universe the fire of devastation burns everything to ashes. The elephants, chariots, horses and infantry belonging to the opposite party were scattered by the weapons of Kṛṣṇa. Indeed, the whole battlefield became strewn with smashed chariots and the bodies of men and animals. There were fallen horses, elephants, men, asses and camels. Although the devastated battlefield appeared like the dancing place of Lord Śiva at the time of the dissolution of the world, the warriors on the side of Kṛṣṇa were very much encouraged by seeing this, and they fought with greater strength.

At this time, Lord Kṛṣṇa told Pauṇḍraka, "Pauṇḍraka, you requested Me to give up the symbols of Lord Viṣṇu, specifically My disc. Now I will give it up to you. Be careful! You falsely declare yourself Vāsudeva, imitating Me. Therefore no one is a greater fool than you." From this statement of Kṛṣṇa's it is clear that any rascal who advertises himself as God is the greatest fool in human society. Kṛṣṇa continued, "Now, Pauṇḍraka, I shall force you to give up this false representation. You wanted Me to surrender unto you. Now this is your opportunity. We shall now fight, and if I am defeated and you are victorious, I shall certainly surrender unto you." In this way, after chastising Pauṇḍraka very severely, Kṛṣṇa smashed Pauṇḍraka's chariot to pieces by shooting an arrow. Then with the help of His disc He separated Pauṇḍraka's head from his body, just as Indra shaves off the peaks of mountains by striking them with his thunderbolt. Similarly,

Kṛṣṇa also killed the King of Kāśī with His arrows. Lord Kṛṣṇa specifically arranged to throw the head of the King of Kāśī into the city of Kāśī itself so that his relatives and family members could see it. Kṛṣṇa did this just as a hurricane carries a lotus petal here and there. Lord Kṛṣṇa killed Pauṇḍraka and his friend Kāśīrāja on the battlefield, and then He returned to His capital city, Dvārakā.

When Lord Kṛṣṇa returned to the city of Dvārakā, all the Siddhas from the heavenly planets were singing His glories. As far as Pauṇḍraka was concerned, somehow or other he always thought of Lord Vāsudeva by falsely dressing himself in imitation of the Lord. Therefore Pauṇḍraka achieved *sārūpya,* one of the five kinds of liberation, and was thus promoted to the Vaikuṇṭha planets, where the devotees have the same bodily features as Viṣṇu, with four hands holding the four symbols. Factually, his meditation was concentrated on the Viṣṇu form, but because he thought himself Lord Viṣṇu, it was offensive. By his being killed by Kṛṣṇa, however, that offense was mitigated. Thus he was given *sārūpya* liberation, and he attained the same form as the Lord.

When the head of the King of Kāśī was thrown through the city gate, people gathered and were astonished to see that wonderful thing. When they found out that there were earrings on it, they could understand that it was someone's head. They conjectured as to whose head it might be. Some thought it was Kṛṣṇa's head because Kṛṣṇa was the enemy of Kāśīrāja, and they calculated that the King of Kāśī might have thrown Kṛṣṇa's head into the city so that the people might take pleasure in the enemy's having been killed. But they finally detected that the head was not Kṛṣṇa's but that of Kāśīrāja himself. When this was ascertained, the queens of the King of Kāśī immediately approached and began to lament the death of their husband. "Our dear lord," they cried, "upon your death, we have become just like dead bodies."

The King of Kāśī had a son whose name was Sudakṣiṇa.

After observing the ritualistic funeral ceremonies, he took a vow that since Kṛṣṇa was the enemy of his father, he would kill Kṛṣṇa and in this way liquidate his debt to his father. Therefore, accompanied by a learned priest qualified to help him, he began to worship Mahādeva, Lord Śiva. (Lord Śiva, who is also known as Viśvanātha, is the lord of the kingdom of Kāśī. The temple of Lord Viśvanātha is still existing in Vārāṇasī, and many thousands of pilgrims still gather daily in that temple.) By the worship of Sudakṣiṇa, Lord Śiva was very pleased, and he wanted to give a benediction to his devotee. Sudakṣiṇa's purpose was to kill Kṛṣṇa, and therefore he prayed for a specific power by which to kill Him. Lord Śiva advised that Sudakṣiṇa, assisted by the *brāhmaṇas,* execute the ritualistic ceremony for killing one's enemy. This ceremony is also mentioned in some of the *tantras.* Lord Śiva informed Sudakṣiṇa that if such a black ritualistic ceremony were performed properly, then the evil spirit named Dakṣiṇāgni would appear and then carry out any order given to him. He would have to be employed, however, to kill someone other than a qualified *brāhmaṇa.* If all these conditions were met, then Dakṣiṇāgni, accompanied by Lord Śiva's ghostly companions, would fulfill the desire of Sudakṣiṇa to kill his enemy.

When Sudakṣiṇa was encouraged by Lord Śiva in that way, he was sure that he would be able to kill Kṛṣṇa. With a determined vow of austerity, he began to execute the black art of chanting *mantras,* assisted by the priests. After this, out of the fire came a great demoniac form, whose hair, beard and mustache were exactly the color of hot copper. This form was very big and fierce. As the demon arose from the fire, cinders of fire emanated from the sockets of his eyes. The giant fiery demon appeared still more fierce due to the movements of his eyebrows. He exhibited long, sharp teeth and, sticking out his long tongue, licked his upper and lower lips. He was naked, and he carried a big trident, blazing like fire. After appearing from the fire of sacrifice, he stood wielding the trident in his hand. Instigated by Sudakṣiṇa, the demon proceeded toward the capital city, Dvārakā, with many hundreds of ghostly companions, and it appeared that he was going to burn all outer space to ashes. The surface of the earth trembled because of his striking steps. When he entered the city of Dvārakā, all the residents panicked, just like animals in a forest fire.

At that time, Kṛṣṇa was playing chess in the royal assembly council hall. All the residents of Dvārakā approached and addressed Him, "Dear Lord of the three worlds, a great fiery demon is ready to burn the whole city of Dvārakā! Please save us!" In this way all the inhabitants of Dvārakā appealed to Lord Kṛṣṇa for protection from the fiery demon who had just appeared in Dvārakā to devastate the whole city.

Lord Kṛṣṇa, who specifically protects His devotees, saw that the whole population of Dvārakā was most perturbed by the presence of the great fiery demon. He immediately smiled and assured them, "Don't worry. I shall give you all protection." The Supreme Personality of Godhead, Kṛṣṇa, is all-pervading. He is within everyone's heart, and He is also without, in the form of the cosmic manifestation. He could understand that the fiery demon was a creation of Lord Śiva, and in order to vanquish the demon He took His Sudarśana *cakra* and ordered him to take the necessary steps. The Sudarśana *cakra* appeared with the effulgence of millions of suns, his heat being as powerful as the fire created at the end of the cosmic manifestation. By his effulgence the Sudarśana *cakra* illuminated the entire universe, on the surface of the earth as well as in outer space. Then the Sudarśana *cakra* began to freeze the fiery demon created by Lord Śiva. In this way, the fiery demon was checked by the Sudarśana *cakra* of Lord Kṛṣṇa, and, being defeated in his attempt to devastate the city of Dvārakā, he turned back.

Having failed to set fire to Dvārakā, the fiery demon went back to Vārāṇasī, the kingdom of Kāśīrāja. As a result of his return, all the priests who had helped instruct the black art of *mantras,* along with their employer, Sudakṣiṇa, were burned to ashes by the glaring effulgence of the fiery demon. According to the methods of black art *mantras* instructed in the *tantras,* if the *mantra* fails to kill the enemy, then, because it must kill someone, it kills the original creator. Sudakṣiṇa was the originator, and the priests assisted him; therefore all of them were burned to ashes. This is the way of the demons: the demons create something to kill God, but by the same weapon the demons themselves are killed.

Following just behind the fiery demon, the Sudarśana *cakra* also entered Vārāṇasī. This city had been very opulent and great for a very long time. Even now, the city of Vārāṇasī is opulent and famous, and it is one of the important cities of India. There were then many big palaces, assembly houses, marketplaces and gates, with large and very important monuments by the palaces and gates. Lecturing platforms could be found at each and every crossroad. There were buildings that housed the treasury, elephants, horses, chariots and grain, and places for distribution of food. The city of Vārāṇasī had been filled with all these material opulences for a very long time, but because the King of Kāśī and his son Sudakṣiṇa were against Lord Kṛṣṇa, the *viṣṇu-cakra* Sudarśana (the disc weapon of Lord Kṛṣṇa) devastated the whole city by burning all these important places. This excursion was more ravaging than modern bombing. The Sudarśana *cakra,* having thus finished his duty, came back to his Lord, Śrī Kṛṣṇa, at Dvārakā.

This narration of the devastation of Vārāṇasī by Kṛṣṇa's disc weapon, the Sudarśana *cakra,* is transcendental and auspicious. Anyone who narrates or hears this story with faith and attention will be released from all reaction to sinful activities. This is the assurance of Śukadeva Gosvāmī, who narrated this story to Parīkṣit Mahārāja.

Thus ends the Bhaktivedanta purport of the Sixty-sixth Chapter of Kṛṣṇa, *"The Deliverance of Pauṇḍraka and the King of Kāśī."*

CHAPTER SIXTY-SEVEN

The Deliverance of Dvivida Gorilla

While Śukadeva Gosvāmī continued to speak on the transcendental pastimes and characteristics of Lord Kṛṣṇa, King Parīkṣit, upon hearing him, became more and more enthusiastic and wanted to hear further. Śukadeva Gosvāmī next narrated the story of Dvivida, the gorilla who was killed by Lord Balarāma.

This gorilla was a great friend of Bhaumāsura, or Narakāsura, who was killed by Kṛṣṇa in connection with his kidnapping sixteen thousand princesses from all over the world. Dvivida was the minister of King Sugrīva. His brother, Mainda, was also a very powerful gorilla king. When Dvivida gorilla heard the story of his friend Bhaumāsura's being killed by Lord Kṛṣṇa, he planned to create mischief throughout the country in order to avenge the death of Bhaumāsura. His first business was to set fires in villages, towns and industrial and mining places, as well as in the residential quarters of the mercantile men who were busy dairy farming and protecting cows. Sometimes he would uproot a big mountain and tear it to pieces. In this way he created great disturbances all over the country, especially in the province of Kathwar. The city of Dvārakā was situated in this Kathwar Province, and because Lord Kṛṣṇa used to live in this city, Dvivida specifically made it his target of disturbance.

Dvivida was as powerful as ten thousand elephants. Sometimes he would go to the seashore, and with his powerful hands he would create so much disturbance in the sea that he would flood the neighboring cities and villages. Often he would go to the hermitages of great saintly persons and sages and cause a great disturbance by smashing their beautiful gardens and orchards. Not only did he create disturbances in that way, but sometimes he would pass urine and stool on their sacred sacrificial arenas. He would thus pollute the whole atmosphere. He also kidnapped both men and women, taking them away from their residential places to the caves of the mountains. After putting them within the caves, he would close the entrances with large chunks of stone, like the *bhṛṅgī* insect, which arrests and carries away many flies and other insects and puts them within the holes of the trees where it lives. Thus Dvivida regularly defied the law and order of the country. Not only that, but he would sometimes pollute the female members of many aristocratic families by forcibly raping them.

While creating such great disturbances all over the country, sometimes he heard very sweet musical sounds from Raivataka Mountain, and so he entered that mountainous region. There he saw Lord Balarāma in the midst of many beautiful young girls, enjoying their company while singing and dancing. He became captivated by the beauty of Lord Balarāma's body, whose every feature was very beautiful, decorated as He was with a garland of lotus flowers. Similarly, all the young girls present, dressed and garlanded with flowers, exhibited much beauty. Lord Balarāma seemed fully intoxicated from drinking the *vāruṇī* beverage, and His eyes appeared to be rolling in a drunken state. Lord Balarāma appeared just like the king of the elephants in the midst of many she-elephants.

This gorilla by the name Dvivida could climb up into the trees and jump from one branch to another. Sometimes he would jerk the branches, creating a particular type of sound—*kilakilā*—so that Lord Balarāma was greatly distracted from the pleasing atmosphere. Sometimes Dvivida would come before the women and exhibit different types of caricatures. By nature young women are apt to enjoy everything with laughter and joking, and when the gorilla came before them they did not take him seriously but simply laughed at him. However, the gorilla was so rude that even in the presence of Balarāma he began to show the lower part of his body to the women, and sometimes he would come forward to show his teeth while moving his eyebrows. He disrespected the women, even in the presence of Balarāma. Lord Balarāma's name suggests not only that He is very powerful but that He takes pleasure in exhibiting extraordinary strength. So He took a stone and threw it at Dvivida. The gorilla, however, artfully avoided being struck by the stone. In order to insult Balarāma, the gorilla took away the earthen pot in which the *vāruṇī* was kept. Dvivida, being thus intoxicated with his limited strength, began to tear off all the valuable clothes worn by Balarāma and the accompanying young girls. He was so puffed up that he thought Balarāma could not do anything to chastise him, and he continued to offend Balarāmajī and His companions.

When Lord Balarāma saw the disturbances created by the gorilla and heard that he had already performed many mischievous activities all over the country, He became very angry and decided to kill him. Immediately He took His club in His hands. The gorilla could understand that now Balarāma was going to attack him. To counteract Balarāma, he immediately uprooted a big oak tree, and with great force he came and struck Lord Balarāma's head. Lord Balarāma, however, immediately caught hold of the big tree and remained undisturbed, just like a great mountain. To retaliate, He took His club, named Sunanda, and hit the gorilla with it, severely injuring his head. Currents of blood flowed from the gorilla's head with great force, but the stream of blood simply enhanced his beauty, like a stream of liquid manganese coming out of a great mountain. The striking of Balarāma's club did not even slightly disturb him. On the contrary, he immediately uprooted another big oak tree and, after clipping off all its leaves, again struck Balarāma's head with it. But Balarāma, with the help of His club, tore the tree to pieces. Since the gorilla was very angry, he took another tree in his hands and struck Lord Balarāma's body. Again Lord Balarāma tore the tree to pieces, and the fighting continued. Each time the gorilla would bring out a big tree to strike Balarāma, Lord Balarāma would tear the tree to pieces by the striking of His club, and the gorilla Dvivida would clutch another tree from another direction and again attack Balarāma in the same way. As a result of this continuous fighting, the forest became treeless. When no more trees were available, Dvivida took help from the hills and threw large pieces of stone, like rainfall, upon the body of Balarāma. Lord Balarāma, in a great sporting mood, began to smash those big pieces of stone into mere pebbles. The gorilla, being bereft of all trees and stone slabs, now stood before Balarāma and waved his strong fists. Then, with great force, he began to beat Lord Balarāma's chest with his fists. This time Lord Balarāma became most angry. Since the gorilla was striking Him with his hands, Lord Balarāma would not strike him back with His own weapons, the club or the plow. Simply with His fists He struck the collarbone of the gorilla. This blow proved fatal to Dvivida, who immediately vomited blood and fell unconscious upon the ground. When the gorilla fell, all the hills and forests appeared to totter.

After this horrible incident, all the Siddhas, great sages and saintly persons from the upper planetary system showered flowers on the person of Lord Balarāma and vibrated sounds glorifying His supremacy. All of them chanted, "All glories to Lord Balarāma! Let us offer our respectful obeisances unto

Your lotus feet. By killing this great demon, Dvivida, You have initiated an auspicious era for the world." All such jubilant sounds of victory were heard from outer space. After killing the great demon Dvivida and being worshiped by showers of flowers and glorious sounds of victory, Balarāma returned to His capital city, Dvārakā.

Thus ends the Bhaktivedanta purport of the Sixty-seventh Chapter of Kṛṣṇa, *"The Deliverance of Dvivida Gorilla."*

CHAPTER SIXTY-EIGHT

The Marriage of Sāmba

Duryodhana, the son of Dhṛtarāṣṭra, had a marriageable daughter by the name of Lakṣmaṇā. She was a very highly qualified girl of the Kuru dynasty, and many princes wanted to marry her. In such cases, the *svayaṁvara* ceremony is held so that the girl may select her husband according to her own choice. In Lakṣmaṇā's *svayaṁvara* assembly, when the girl was to select her husband, Sāmba appeared. He was a son of Kṛṣṇa's by Jāmbavatī, one of Lord Kṛṣṇa's chief wives. This son Sāmba was so named because he was a pet child and always lived close to his mother. The name Sāmba indicates a son who is very much his mother's pet. *Ambā* means "mother," and *sa* means "with." So this special name was given to him because he always remained with his mother. He was also known as Jāmbavatī-suta for the same reason. As previously explained, all the sons of Kṛṣṇa were as qualified as their great father. Sāmba wanted Duryodhana's daughter, Lakṣmaṇā, although she was not inclined to have him. Therefore Sāmba kidnapped Lakṣmaṇā by force from the *svayaṁvara* assembly.

Because Sāmba took Lakṣmaṇā away from the assembly by force, all the members of the Kuru dynasty, such as Dhṛtarāṣṭra, Bhīṣma, Vidura and Arjuna, thought it an insult to their family tradition that the boy, Sāmba, could possibly have kidnapped their daughter. All of them knew that Lakṣmaṇā was not at all inclined to select him as her husband and that she was not given the chance to select her own husband; instead she was forcibly taken away by this boy. Therefore, they decided that he must be punished. They unanimously declared that he was most impudent and had degraded the Kurus' family tradition. Therefore, all of them, under the counsel of the elder members of the Kuru family, decided to arrest the boy but not kill him. They concluded that the girl could not be married to any boy other than Sāmba, since she had already been touched by him. (According to the Vedic system, once being touched by some boy, a girl cannot be married or given to any other boy. Nor would anyone agree to marry a girl who had already thus associated with another boy.) The elder members of the family, such as Bhīṣma, wanted to arrest him. Thus all the members of the Kuru dynasty, especially the great fighters, joined together just to teach him a lesson, and Karṇa was made the commander in chief for this small battle.

While making the plan to arrest Sāmba, the Kurus counseled amongst themselves that upon his arrest the members of the Yadu dynasty would be very angry with them. There was every possibility of the Yadus' accepting the challenge and fighting with them. But they also thought, "If they came here to fight with us, what could they do? The members of the Yadu dynasty cannot equal the members of the Kuru dynasty because the kings of the Kuru dynasty are the emperors whereas the kings of the Yadu dynasty are able to enjoy their land only because we have granted it to them." The Kurus thought, "If they come here to challenge us because their son was arrested, we shall accept the fight and teach them a lesson, so that automatically they will be subdued under pressure, as the senses are subdued by the mystic *yoga* process, *prāṇāyāma.*" (In the mechanical system of mystic *yoga,* the airs within the body are controlled, and the senses are subdued and checked from being engaged in anything other than meditation upon Lord Viṣṇu.)

After consultation and after receiving permission from the elder members of the Kuru dynasty, such as Bhīṣma and Dhṛtarāṣṭra, five great warriors—Karṇa, Śala, Bhūri, Yajña-ketu and Duryodhana, the father of the girl—who were all *mahā-rathīs* and who were guided by the great fighter Bhīṣma-deva, attempted to arrest the boy Sāmba. There are different grades of fighters, including *mahā-rathī, eka-rathī* and *rathī,* classified according to their fighting ability. These *mahā-rathīs* could fight alone with many thousands of men. All of them combined together to arrest Sāmba. Sāmba was also a *mahā-rathī,* but he was alone and had to fight with the six other *mahā-rathīs.* Still he was not deterred when he saw all the great fighters of the Kuru dynasty coming up behind him to arrest him.

Alone, he turned toward them and took his nice bow, posing exactly as a lion stands adamant in the face of other animals. Karṇa, leading the party, challenged Sāmba, "Why are you fleeing? Just stand, and we shall teach you a lesson!" When challenged by another *kṣatriya* to stand and fight, a *kṣatriya* cannot run away; he must fight. Therefore, Sāmba accepted the challenge and stood alone before them, but as soon as he did so he was overpowered by showers of arrows shot by all the great warriors. A lion is never afraid of being chased by many wolves and jackals. Similarly, Sāmba, the glorious son of the Yadu dynasty, endowed with inconceivable potencies as the son of Lord Kṛṣṇa, became very angry at the warriors of the Kuru dynasty for improperly using arrows against him. He fought them with great talent. First of all, he struck each of the six charioteers with six separate arrows. He used another four arrows to kill the charioteers' horses, four on each chariot. Then he used one arrow to kill the driver and one arrow for Karṇa as well as the other celebrated fighters. While Sāmba so diligently fought alone with the six great warriors, they all appreciated the boy's inconceivable potency. Even in the midst of the fighting they admitted frankly that this boy Sāmba was wonderful. But the fighting was conducted in the *kṣatriya* spirit, so all together, although it was improper, they obliged Sāmba to get down from his chariot, now broken to pieces. Of the six warriors, four took care to kill Sāmba's four horses, one struck down his chariot driver, and one managed to cut the string of Sāmba's bow so that he could no longer fight with them. In this way, with great difficulty and after a severe fight, they deprived Sāmba of his chariot and were able to arrest him. Thus, the warriors of the Kuru dynasty accepted their great victory and took their daughter, Lakṣmaṇā, away from him. Thereafter, they entered the city of Hastināpura in great triumph.

The great sage Nārada immediately carried the news to the Yadu dynasty that Sāmba had been arrested and told them the whole story. The members of the Yadu dynasty became very angry at Sāmba's being arrested, and improperly so by six warriors. Now, with the permission of the head of the Yadu dynasty, King Ugrasena, they prepared to attack the capital city of the Kuru dynasty.

Although Lord Balarāma knew very well that by slight provocation people are prepared to fight with one another in the Age of Kali, He did not like the idea that the two great dynasties, the Kuru dynasty and the Yadu dynasty, would fight amongst themselves, even though they were influenced by Kali-yuga. "Instead of fighting with them," He wisely thought, "let Me go there and see the situation, and let Me try to see if the fight can be settled by mutual understanding." Balarāma's idea was that if the Kuru dynasty could be induced to release Sāmba along with his wife, Lakṣmaṇā, then the fight could be avoided. He therefore immediately arranged for a nice chariot to go to Hastināpura, accompanied by learned priests and *brāhmaṇas,* as well as by some of the elder members of the Yadu dynasty. He was confident that the members of the Kuru dynasty would agree to this marriage and avoid fighting with the Yadus. As Lord Balarāma proceeded toward Hastināpura in His chariot, accompanied by the *brāhmaṇas* and elders, He looked like the moon shining in the clear sky amongst the glittering stars. When Lord Balarāma reached the precincts of the city of Hastināpura, He did not enter but stationed Himself in a camp outside the city, in a small garden house. Then He asked Uddhava to meet with the leaders of the Kuru dynasty and inquire from them whether they wanted to fight with the Yadu dynasty or to make a settlement. Uddhava went to see the leaders of the Kuru dynasty, and he met all the important members, including Bhīṣmadeva, Dhṛtarāṣṭra, Droṇācārya, Duryodhana and Bāhlika. After offering them due respects, he informed them that Lord Balarāma had arrived at the garden outside the city gate.

The leaders of the Kuru dynasty, especially Dhṛtarāṣṭra and Duryodhana, were joyful because they knew very well that Lord Balarāma was a great well-wisher of their family. There were no bounds to their joy on hearing the news, and so they immediately welcomed Uddhava. In order to properly receive Lord Balarāma, they all took in their hands auspicious paraphernalia for His reception and went to see Him outside the city gate. According to their respective positions, they welcomed Lord Balarāma by giving Him in charity nice cows and *arghya* (a mixture of *ārati* water and an assortment of items such as honey, butter, flowers and sandalwood pulp). Because all of them knew the exalted position of Lord Balarāma as the Supreme Personality of Godhead, they bowed their heads before the Lord with great respect. They all exchanged words of reception by asking one another about their welfare, and when such formalities were finished, Lord Balarāma, in a great voice and very patiently, submitted before them the following words for their consideration: "My dear friends, this time I have come to you as a messenger with the order of the all-powerful King Ugrasena. Please, therefore, hear the order with attention and great care. Without wasting a single moment, please try to carry out the order. King Ugrasena knows very well that you warriors of the Kuru dynasty improperly fought with the pious Sāmba, who was alone, and that with great difficulty and unrighteous tactics you have arrested him. We have all heard this news, but we are not very much agitated because we are most intimately related to one another. I do not think we should disturb our good relationship; we should continue our friendship without any unnecessary fighting. Please, therefore, immediately release Sāmba and bring him, along with his wife, Lakṣmaṇā, before Me."

When Lord Balarāma spoke in a commanding tone full of heroic assertion, supremacy and chivalry, the leaders of the Kuru dynasty did not appreciate His statements. Rather, all of them became agitated, and with great anger they said, "Hello! These words are very astonishing but quite befitting the Age of Kali; otherwise how could Balarāma speak so vituperatively? The language and tone used by Balarāma are simply abusive, and due to the influence of this age it appears that the shoes befitting the feet want to rise to the top of the head, where the helmet is worn. We are connected with the Yadu dynasty by marriage, and because of this they have been given the chance to come live with us, dine with us and sleep with us; now they are taking advantage of these privileges. They had practically no position before we gave them a portion of our kingdom to rule, and now they are trying to command us. We have allowed the Yadu dynasty to use the royal insignias like the whisk, fan, conchshell, white umbrella, crown, royal throne, sitting place and bedstead, along with everything else befitting the royal order. They should not have used such royal paraphernalia in our presence, but we did not check them due to our family relationships. Now they have the audacity to order us to do things. Well, enough of their impudence! We cannot allow them to do any more of these things, nor shall we allow them to use these royal insignias. It would be best to take all these things away; it is improper to feed a snake with milk, since such merciful activities simply increase his venom. The Yadu dynasty is now trying to go against those who have fed them so nicely. Their flourishing condition is due to our gifts and merciful behavior, and still they are so shameless that they are trying to order us. How regrettable are all these activities! No one in the world can enjoy anything if members of the Kuru dynasty like Bhīṣma, Droṇācārya and Arjuna do not allow them to. Exactly as a lamb cannot enjoy life in the presence of a lion, without our desire it is not even possible for the demigods in heaven, headed by King Indra, to find enjoyment in life, what to speak of ordinary human beings!" Actually the members of the Kuru dynasty were very much puffed up due to their opulence, kingdom, aristocracy, family tradition, great warriors, family members and vast, expansive empire. They did not even observe common formalities of civilized society, and in the presence of Lord Balarāma they uttered insulting words about the Yadu dynasty. Having spoken in this unmannerly way, they returned to their city of Hastināpura.

Although Lord Balarāma patiently heard their insulting words and simply observed their uncivil behavior, from His appearance it was clear that He was burning with anger and was thinking of retaliating with great vengeance. His bodily features became so much agitated that it was difficult for anyone to look at Him. He laughed very loudly and said, "It is true that if a man becomes too much puffed up because of his family, opulence, beauty and material advancement, he no longer wants a peaceful life but becomes belligerent toward all others. It is useless to give such a person good instruction for gentle behavior and a peaceful life; on the contrary, one should search out the ways and means to punish him." Generally, due to material opulence a man becomes exactly like an animal. To give an animal peaceful instructions is useless, and the only means is *argumentum ad baculum.* In other words, the only means to keep animals in order is a stick. "Just see how impudent are the members of the Kuru dynasty! I wanted to make a peaceful settlement despite the anger of all the other members of the Yadu dynasty, including Lord Kṛṣṇa Himself. They were preparing to attack the whole kingdom of the Kuru dynasty, but I pacified them and took the trouble to come here to settle the affair without any fighting. Yet these rascals behave like this! It is clear that they do not want a peaceful settlement, for they are factually warmongers. With great pride they have repeatedly insulted Me by calling the Yadu dynasty ill names.

"Even the King of heaven, Indra, abides by the order of the Yadu dynasty; and you consider King Ugrasena, the head of the Bhojas, Vṛṣṇis, Andhakas and Yādavas, to be the leader of a small phalanx! Your conclusion is wonderful! You do not care for King Ugrasena, whose order is obeyed even by King Indra. Consider the exalted position of the Yadu dynasty. They have forcibly used both the assembly house and the *pārijāta* tree of the heavenly planets, and still you think that they cannot order you. Don't you even think that Lord Kṛṣṇa, the Supreme Personality of Godhead, can sit on the exalted royal throne and command everyone? All right! If your thinking is like that, you deserve to be taught a very good lesson. You have thought it wise that the royal insignias like the whisk, fan, white umbrella, royal throne and other princely paraphernalia not be used by the Yadu dynasty. Does this mean that even Lord Kṛṣṇa, the Lord of the whole creation and the husband of the goddess of fortune, cannot use this royal paraphernalia? The dust of Kṛṣṇa's lotus feet is worshiped by all the great demigods. The Ganges water inundates the whole world, and since it emanates from His lotus feet, its banks have turned into great places of pilgrimage. The principal deities of all planets engage in His service and consider themselves most fortunate to take the dust of the lotus feet of Kṛṣṇa on their helmets. Great demigods like Lord Brahmā, Lord Śiva and even the goddess of fortune and I are simply plenary parts of His spiritual identity, and still you think that He is not fit to use the royal insignia or even sit on the royal throne? Alas, how regrettable it is that these fools consider us, the members of the Yadu dynasty, to be like shoes and themselves like helmets. It is clear now that these leaders of the Kuru dynasty have become mad over their worldly possessions and opulence. Every statement they made was full of crazy proposals. I should immediately take them to task and bring them to their senses. If I do not take steps against them, it will be improper on My part. Therefore, on this very day I shall rid the whole world of any trace of the Kuru dynasty. I shall finish them off immediately!" While talking like this, Lord Balarāma seemed so furious that He looked as if He could burn the whole cosmic creation to ashes. He stood up steadily and, taking His plow in His hand, began striking the earth with it, separating the whole city of Hastināpura from the earth, and then He began to drag the city toward the flowing water of the river Ganges. This caused a great tremor throughout Hastināpura, as if there had been an earthquake, and it seemed that the whole city would be dismantled.

When all the members of the Kuru dynasty saw that their city was about to fall into the water of the Ganges, and when they heard their citizens howling in great anxiety, they immediately came to their senses and understood what was happening. Thus without waiting another second they brought forward their daughter Lakṣmaṇā. They also brought Sāmba, who had forcibly tried to take her away, keeping him in the forefront with Lakṣmaṇā at his back. All the members of the Kuru dynasty appeared before Lord Balarāma with folded hands just to beg the pardon of the Supreme Personality of Godhead. Now using good sense, they said, "O Lord Balarāma, reservoir of all pleasures, You are the maintainer and support of the entire cosmic situation. Unfortunately we were all unaware of Your inconceivable potencies.

Dear Lord, please consider us most foolish. Our intelligence was bewildered and not in order. Therefore we have come before You to beg Your pardon. Please excuse us. You are the original creator, sustainer and annihilator of the whole cosmic manifestation, and still Your position is always transcendental. O all-powerful Lord, great sages speak about You. You are the original puppeteer, and everything in the world is just like Your toy. O unlimited one, You have a hold on everything, and like child's play You hold all the planetary systems on Your head. When the time for dissolution comes, You close up the whole cosmic manifestation within Yourself. At that time, nothing remains but Yourself lying in the Causal Ocean as Mahā-Viṣṇu. Our dear Lord, You have appeared on this earth in Your transcendental body just for the maintenance of the cosmic situation. You are above all anger, envy and enmity. Whatever You do, even in the form of chastisement, is auspicious for the whole material existence. We offer our respectful obeisances unto You because You are the imperishable Supreme Personality of Godhead, the reservoir of all opulences and potencies. O creator of innumerable universes, let us fall down and offer You our respectful obeisances again and again. We are now completely surrendered unto You. Please, therefore, be merciful upon us and give us Your protection." When the prominent members of the Kuru dynasty, from grandfather Bhīṣmadeva to Arjuna and Duryodhana, had offered their respectful prayers in that way, the Supreme Personality of Godhead, Lord Balarāma, immediately became softened and assured them that there was no cause for fear and that they need not worry.

For the most part it was the practice of the *kṣatriya* kings to inaugurate some kind of fighting between the parties of the bride and bridegroom before the marriage. When Sāmba forcibly took away Lakṣmaṇā, the elder members of the Kuru dynasty were pleased to see that he was actually the suitable match for her. In order to see his personal strength, however, they fought with him, and without respect for the regulations of fighting, they all arrested him. When the Yadu dynasty decided to release Sāmba from the confinement of the Kurus, Lord Balarāma came personally to settle the matter, and, as a powerful *kṣatriya,* He ordered them to free Sāmba immediately. The Kauravas were superficially insulted by this order, so they challenged Lord Balarāma's power. They simply wanted to see Him exhibit His inconceivable strength. Thus with great pleasure they handed over their daughter to Sāmba, and the whole matter was settled. Duryodhana, being affectionate toward his daughter Lakṣmaṇā, had her married to Sāmba in great pomp. For her dowry, he first gave 1,200 elephants, each at least sixty years old; then he gave 10,000 nice horses, 6,000 chariots, dazzling just like the sunshine, and 1,000 maidservants decorated with golden ornaments. Lord Balarāma, the most prominent member of the Yadu dynasty, acted as guardian of the bridegroom, Sāmba, and very pleasingly accepted the dowry. Balarāma was very satisfied after His great reception from the side of the Kurus, and accompanied by the newly married couple, He started toward His capital city of Dvārakā.

Lord Balarāma triumphantly reached Dvārakā, where He met with many citizens who were all His devotees and friends. When they all assembled, Lord Balarāma narrated the whole story of the marriage, and they were astonished to hear how Balarāma had made the city of Hastināpura tremble. It is confirmed by Śukadeva Gosvāmī that in those days the river flowing through the city of Hastināpura, present-day New Delhi, was known as the Ganges, although today it is called the Yamunā. From authorities like Jīva Gosvāmī it is confirmed that the Ganges and Yamunā are the same river flowing in different courses. The part of the Ganges which flows through Hastināpura to the area of Vṛndāvana is called the Yamunā because it is sanctified by the transcendental pastimes of Lord Kṛṣṇa. The part of Hastināpura which slopes toward the Yamunā becomes inundated during the rainy season and reminds everyone of Lord Balarāma's threatening to cast the city into the Ganges.

Thus ends the Bhaktivedanta purport of the Sixty-eighth Chapter of Kṛṣṇa, *"The Marriage of Sāmba."*

CHAPTER SIXTY-NINE

The Great Sage Nārada Visits the Different Homes of Lord Kṛṣṇa

When the great sage Nārada heard that Lord Kṛṣṇa had married sixteen thousand wives after He had killed the demon Narakāsura, sometimes called Bhaumāsura, he was astonished that Lord Kṛṣṇa had expanded Himself into sixteen thousand forms and married these wives simultaneously in different palaces. Being inquisitive as to how Kṛṣṇa was managing His household affairs with so many wives, Nārada, desiring to see these pastimes, set out to visit Kṛṣṇa's different homes. When Nārada arrived in Dvārakā, he saw gardens and parks full of various flowers of different colors, and also orchards overloaded with a variety of fruits. Beautiful birds were chirping, and peacocks crowed delightfully. There were ponds full of blue and red lotus flowers, and some of these tanks were filled with varieties of lilies. The lakes were full of nice swans and cranes, and the voices of these birds resounded everywhere.

In the city there were as many as 900,000 great palaces built of first-class marble, with gates and doors made of silver. The pillars of the houses and palaces were bedecked with jewels such as touchstone, sapphires and emeralds, and the floors gave off a beautiful luster. The highways, lanes, streets, crossings and marketplaces were all beautifully decorated. The whole city was full of residential homes, assembly houses and temples, all of different architectural beauty. All of this made Dvārakā a glowing city. The big avenues, crossings, lanes and streets, and also the thresholds of every residential house, were very clean. On both sides of every path there were bushes, and at regular intervals there were large trees that shaded the avenues so that the sunshine would not bother the passersby.

In this greatly beautiful city of Dvārakā, Lord Kṛṣṇa, the Supreme Personality of Godhead, had many residential quarters. The great kings and princes of the world used to visit these palaces just to worship Him. The architectural plans were made personally by Viśvakarmā, the engineer of the demigods, and in the construction of the palaces he exhibited all of his talents and ingenuity. These residential quarters numbered more than sixteen thousand, and a different queen of Lord Kṛṣṇa resided in each of them. The great sage Nārada entered one of these houses and saw that the pillars were made of coral and the ceilings were bedecked with jewels. The walls as well as the arches between the pillars glowed from the decorations of different kinds of sapphires. Throughout the palace were many canopies made by Viśvakarmā that were decorated with strings of pearls. The chairs and other furniture were made of ivory and bedecked with gold and diamonds, and jeweled lamps dissipated the darkness within the palace. There was so much incense and fragrant gum burning that the scented fumes were coming out of the windows. The peacocks sitting on the steps became illusioned by the fumes, mistaking them for clouds, and began dancing jubilantly. There were many maidservants, all of whom were decorated with gold necklaces, bangles and beautiful saris. There were also many menservants, nicely dressed in cloaks and turbans and jeweled earrings. Beautiful as they were, the servants were all engaged in different household duties.

Nārada saw that Lord Kṛṣṇa was sitting with Rukmiṇīdevī, the mistress of that particular palace, who was holding the handle of a *cāmara* whisk. Even though there were many thousands of maidservants equally beautiful and qualified and of the same age, Rukmiṇīdevī personally was engaged in fanning Lord Kṛṣṇa. Kṛṣṇa is the Supreme Personality of Godhead, worshiped even by Nārada, yet as soon as Kṛṣṇa saw Nārada enter the palace, He got down immediately from Rukmiṇī's bedstead and stood up to honor him. Lord Kṛṣṇa is the teacher of the whole world, and in order to instruct everyone how to respect a saintly person like Nārada Muni, He bowed down, touching His helmet to the ground. Not only did Kṛṣṇa bow down, but He also touched the feet of Nārada and with folded hands requested him to sit on His chair. Lord Kṛṣṇa is the Supreme Personality, worshiped by all devotees. He is the most worshipable spiritual master of everyone. The Ganges water, which emanates from His feet, sanctifies the three worlds. All qualified *brāhmaṇas* worship Him, and therefore He is called *brahmaṇya-deva.*

Brahmaṇya means one who fully possesses the brahminical qualifications, which are said to be as follows: truthfulness, self-control, purity, mastery of the senses, simplicity, full knowledge by practical application, and engagement in devotional service. Lord Kṛṣṇa possesses all these qualities, and He is worshiped by persons who themselves possess such qualities. There are thousands and millions of names of Lord Kṛṣṇa—*Viṣṇu-sahasra-nāma*—and all of them are given to Him because of His transcendental qualities.

Lord Kṛṣṇa in Dvārakā enjoyed the pastimes of a perfect human being. Therefore, when He washed the feet of the sage Nārada and took the water on His head, Nārada did not object, knowing well that the Lord did so to teach everyone how to respect saintly persons. The Supreme Personality of Godhead, Kṛṣṇa, who is the original Nārāyaṇa and eternal friend of all living entities, thus worshiped the sage Nārada according to Vedic regulative principles. Welcoming him with sweet, nectarean words, He addressed Nārada as *bhagavān,* or one who is self-sufficient, possessing all knowledge, renunciation, strength, fame, beauty and other, similar opulences. He particularly asked Nārada, "What can I do in your service?"

Nārada replied, "My dear Lord, this kind of behavior by Your Lordship is not at all astonishing, for You are the Supreme Personality of Godhead and master of all species of living entities. You are the supreme friend of all living entities, but at the same time You are the supreme chastiser of the miscreants and the envious. I know that Your Lordship has descended to this earth for the proper maintenance of the whole universe. Your appearance, therefore, is not forced by any other agency. By Your sweet will only, You agree to appear and disappear. It is my great fortune that I have been able to see Your lotus feet today. Anyone who becomes attached to Your lotus feet is elevated to the supreme position of neutrality and is uncontaminated by the material modes of nature. My Lord, You are unlimited—there is no limit to Your opulences. Great demigods like Lord Brahmā and Lord Śiva are always busy placing You within their hearts and meditating upon You. The conditioned souls, who have now been put into the blind well of material existence, can get out of this eternal captivity only by accepting Your lotus feet. Thus, You are the only shelter of all conditioned souls. My dear Lord, You have very kindly asked what You can do for me. In answer to this I simply request that I may not forget Your lotus feet at any time. I do not care where I may be, but I pray that I constantly be allowed to remember Your lotus feet."

By asking this benediction from the Lord, the sage Nārada

showed the ideal prayer of all pure devotees. A pure devotee never asks for any kind of material or spiritual benediction from the Lord; his only prayer is that he may not forget the lotus feet of the Lord in any condition of life. A pure devotee does not care whether he is put into heaven or hell; he is satisfied anywhere, provided he can constantly remember the lotus feet of the Lord. Lord Caitanya taught this same process of prayer in His *Śikṣāṣṭaka,* in which He clearly stated that all He wanted was devotional service, birth after birth. A pure devotee does not even want to stop the repetition of birth and death. To a pure devotee, it does not matter whether he has to take birth again in the various species of life. His only ambition is that he not forget the lotus feet of the Lord in any condition of life.

After departing from the palace of Rukmiṇī, Nāradajī wanted to see further activities of Lord Kṛṣṇa's internal potency, *yogamāyā;* thus he entered the palace of another queen. There he saw Lord Kṛṣṇa engaged in playing chess with His dear wife and Uddhava. The Lord immediately got up from His personal seat and invited Nārada Muni to sit there. The Lord again worshiped him with as much paraphernalia for reception as He had used in the palace of Rukmiṇī. After worshiping him properly, Lord Kṛṣṇa acted as if He did not know what had happened in the palace of Rukmiṇī. He therefore told Nārada, "My dear sage, when Your Holiness comes here, you are full in yourself. Although We are householders and are always in need, you don't require anyone's help, for you are self-satisfied. Under the circumstances, what reception can We offer you, and what can We possibly give you? Yet, since Your Holiness is a *brāhmaṇa,* it is Our duty to offer you something as far as possible. Therefore, I beg you to please order Me. What can I do for you?"

Nāradajī knew everything about the pastimes of the Lord, so without further discussion he simply left the palace silently, in great astonishment over the Lord's activities. He then entered another palace. This time Nāradajī saw that Lord Kṛṣṇa was engaged as an affectionate father petting His small children. From there he entered another palace and saw Lord Kṛṣṇa preparing to take His bath. In this way, Saint Nārada entered each and every one of the sixteen thousand residential palaces of the queens of Lord Kṛṣṇa, and in each of them he found Kṛṣṇa engaged in different ways.

In one palace he found Kṛṣṇa offering oblations to the sacrificial fire and performing the ritualistic ceremonies of the *Vedas* as enjoined for householders. In another palace he found Kṛṣṇa performing the *pañca-yajña* sacrifice, which is compulsory for a householder. This *yajña* is also known as *pañca-sūnā.* Knowingly or unknowingly, everyone, especially the householder, commits five kinds of sinful activities. When we receive water from a water pitcher, we kill many germs that are in it. Similarly, when we use a grinding machine or eat food, we kill many germs. When sweeping a floor or igniting a fire we kill many germs, and when we walk on the street we kill many ants and other insects. Consciously or unconsciously, in all our different activities, we are killing. Therefore, it is incumbent upon every householder to perform the *pañca-sūnā* sacrifice to rid himself of the reactions to such sinful activities.

In one palace Nārada found Lord Kṛṣṇa feeding *brāhmaṇas* after performing ritualistic *yajñas.* In another palace Nārada found Kṛṣṇa silently chanting the Gāyatrī *mantra,* and in a third he found Him practicing fighting with a sword and shield. In some palaces Lord Kṛṣṇa was found riding on horses, elephants or chariots and wandering hither and thither. Elsewhere He was found lying down on His bedstead taking rest, and somewhere else He was found sitting in His chair, being praised by the prayers of His different devotees. In some of the palaces He was found consulting with ministers like Uddhava on important matters of business. In one palace He was found surrounded by many young society girls, enjoying in a swimming pool. In another palace He was found giving well-decorated cows in charity to the *brāhmaṇas,* and in another palace He was found hearing the narrations of the *Purāṇas* and of histories such as the *Mahābhārata,* which are supplementary literatures for disseminating Vedic knowledge to common people by narrating important instances in the history of the universe. Somewhere Lord Kṛṣṇa was found enjoying the company of a particular wife by exchanging joking words with her. Somewhere else He was found engaged with His wife in religious ritualistic functions. Since it is necessary for householders to increase their financial assets for various expenditures, Kṛṣṇa was found somewhere engaged in matters of economic development. Somewhere else He was found enjoying family life according to the regulative principles of the *śāstras.*

In one palace He was found sitting in meditation as if concentrating His mind on the Supreme Personality of Godhead, who is beyond these material universes. Meditation, as recommended in authorized scripture, is meant for concentrating one's mind on the Supreme Personality of Godhead, Viṣṇu. Lord Kṛṣṇa is Himself the original Viṣṇu, but because He played the part of a human being, He taught us definitely by His personal behavior what is meant by meditation. Somewhere Lord Kṛṣṇa was found satisfying elderly superiors by supplying them things they needed. Somewhere else Nāradajī found that Lord Kṛṣṇa was engaged in discussing topics of fighting, and somewhere else in making peace with enemies. Somewhere Lord Kṛṣṇa was found discussing the ultimate auspicious activity for the entire human society with His elder brother, Lord Balarāma. Nārada saw Lord Kṛṣṇa engaged in getting His sons and daughters married with suitable brides and bridegrooms in due course of time, and the marriage ceremonies were being performed with great pomp. In one palace the Lord was found bidding farewell to His daughters, and in another He was found receiving a daughter-in-law. People throughout the whole city were astonished to see such pomp and ceremonies.

Somewhere the Lord was seen performing different types of sacrifices to satisfy the demigods, who are only His qualitative expansions. Somewhere He was seen engaged in public welfare activities, establishing deep wells for the water supply, rest houses and gardens for unknown guests, and great monasteries and temples for saintly persons. These are some of the duties enjoined in the *Vedas* for householders for fulfillment of their material desires. Somewhere Kṛṣṇa was found as a *kṣatriya* king engaged in hunting animals in the forest and riding on a very beautiful Sindhī horse. According to Vedic regulations, the *kṣatriyas* were allowed to kill prescribed animals on certain occasions, either to maintain peace in the forests or to offer the animals in the sacrificial fire. *Kṣatriyas* are allowed to practice this killing art because they have to kill their enemies mercilessly to maintain peace in society. In one situation the great sage Nārada saw Lord Kṛṣṇa, the Supreme Personality of Godhead and master of mystic powers, acting as a spy by changing His usual dress in order to understand the motives of different citizens in the city and the palaces.

Saint Nārada saw all these activities of the Lord, who is the Supersoul of all living entities but who played the role of an ordinary human being to manifest the activities of His internal potency. Smiling within himself, Nārada addressed the Lord as follows: "My dear Lord of all mystic powers, object of the meditation of great mystics, the extent of Your mystic power is certainly inconceivable, even to mystics like Lord Brahmā and Lord Śiva. But by Your mercy, because of my being always engaged in the transcendental loving service of Your lotus feet, Your Lordship has very kindly revealed to me the actions of Your internal potency. My dear Lord, You are worshipable by all, and demigods and predominating deities of all fourteen planetary systems are completely aware of Your transcendental fame. Now please give me Your blessings so that I may be able to travel all over the universes singing the glories of Your transcendental activities."

The Supreme Personality of Godhead, Lord Kṛṣṇa, replied to Nārada as follows: "My dear Nārada, O sage among the demigods, you know that I am the supreme instructor and perfect follower of all religious principles, as well as the supreme enforcer of such principles. I am therefore personally executing such religious principles in order to teach the whole world how to act. My dear son, it is My desire that you not be bewildered by such demonstrations of My internal energy."

The Supreme Personality of Godhead was engaged in His so-called household affairs in order to teach people how one can sanctify one's household life although one may be attached to the imprisonment of material existence. Actually, one is obliged to continue the term of material existence because of household life. But the Lord, being very kind upon householders, demonstrated the path of sanctifying ordinary household life. Because Kṛṣṇa is the center of all activities, the life of a Kṛṣṇa conscious householder is transcendental to Vedic injunctions and is automatically sanctified.

Thus Nārada saw one single Kṛṣṇa living in sixteen thousand palaces by His plenary expansions. Due to His inconceivable energy, He was visible in the palace of each and every individual queen. Lord Kṛṣṇa has unlimited power, and Nārada's astonishment was boundless upon observing again and again the demonstration of Lord Kṛṣṇa's internal energy. Lord Kṛṣṇa behaved by His personal example as if He were very much attached to the four principles of civilized life, namely religion, economic development, sense gratification and salvation. These four principles of material existence are necessary for the spiritual advancement of human society, and although Lord Kṛṣṇa had no need to do so, He exhibited His household activities so that people might follow in His footsteps for their own interest. Lord Kṛṣṇa satisfied the sage Nārada in every way. Nārada was very much pleased by seeing the Lord's activities in Dvārakā, and thus he departed.

In narrating the activities of Lord Kṛṣṇa in Dvārakā, Śukadeva Gosvāmī explained to King Parīkṣit how Lord Kṛṣṇa, the Supreme Personality of Godhead, descends to this material universe by the agency of His internal potency and personally exhibits the principles which, if followed, can lead one to achieve the ultimate goal of life. All the queens in Dvārakā, more than sixteen thousand in number, engaged their feminine attractive features in the transcendental service of the Lord by smiling and serving, and the Lord was pleased to behave with them exactly like a perfect husband enjoying household life. One should know definitely that such pastimes cannot be performed by anyone but Lord Śrī Kṛṣṇa, who is the original cause of the creation, maintenance and dissolution of the whole cosmic manifestation. Anyone who attentively hears the narrations of the Lord's pastimes in Dvārakā or supports a preacher of the Kṛṣṇa consciousness movement will certainly find it very easy to traverse the path of liberation and taste the nectar of the lotus feet of Lord Kṛṣṇa. And thus he will be engaged in Lord Kṛṣṇa's devotional service.

Thus ends the Bhaktivedanta purport of the Sixty-ninth Chapter of Kṛṣṇa, *"The Great Sage Nārada Visits the Different Homes of Lord Kṛṣṇa."*

CHAPTER SEVENTY

Lord Kṛṣṇa's Daily Activities

From the Vedic *mantras* we learn that the Supreme Personality of Godhead has nothing to do: *na tasya kāryaṁ karaṇaṁ ca vidyate.* But if the Supreme Lord has nothing to do, how can we speak of the activities of the Supreme Lord? From the previous chapter it is clear that no one can act the way Lord Kṛṣṇa does. We should clearly note this fact: the activities of the Lord should be followed, but they cannot be imitated. For example, Kṛṣṇa's ideal life as a householder can be followed, but if one wants to imitate Kṛṣṇa by expanding into many forms, that is not possible. We should always remember, therefore, that Lord Kṛṣṇa, although playing the part of a human being, simultaneously maintains the position of the Supreme Personality of Godhead. We can follow Lord Kṛṣṇa's dealings with His wives as an ordinary human being, but His dealings with more than sixteen thousand wives at one time cannot be imitated. The conclusion is that to become ideal householders we should follow in the footsteps of Lord Kṛṣṇa as He displayed His daily activities, but we cannot imitate Him at any stage of our life.

Lord Kṛṣṇa used to lie down with His sixteen thousand wives, but He would also rise from bed very early in the morning, three hours before sunrise. By nature's arrangement the crowing of the cocks warns of the *brāhma-muhūrta* hour. There is no need of alarm clocks: as soon as the cocks crow early in the morning, it is to be understood that it is time to rise from bed. Hearing that sound, Kṛṣṇa would get up from bed, but His rising early was not very much to the liking of His wives. The wives of Kṛṣṇa were so much attached to Him that they would lie in bed embracing Him, and as soon as the cocks crowed, Kṛṣṇa's wives would be very sorry and would immediately condemn the crowing.

In the garden within the compound of each palace there were *pārijāta* flowers. The *pārijāta* is not an artificial flower. We remember that Kṛṣṇa brought the *pārijāta* trees from heaven and implanted them in all His palaces. Early in the morning, a mild breeze would carry the aroma of the *pārijāta* flower, and Kṛṣṇa would smell it just after rising from bed. Due to this aroma, the honeybees would begin their humming vibration, and the birds also would begin their sweet chirping sounds. All together it would sound like the singing of professional chanters engaged in offering prayers to Kṛṣṇa. Although Śrīmatī Rukmiṇīdevī, the first queen of Lord Kṛṣṇa, knew that *brāhma-muhūrta* is the most auspicious time in the entire day, she would feel disgusted at the appearance of *brāhma-muhūrta* because she was not very happy to have Kṛṣṇa leave her side in bed. Despite Śrīmatī Rukmiṇīdevī's disgust, Lord Kṛṣṇa would immediately get up from bed exactly on the appearance of *brāhma-muhūrta.* An ideal householder should learn from the behavior of Lord Kṛṣṇa how to rise early in the morning, however comfortably he may be lying in bed embraced by his wife.

After rising from bed, Lord Kṛṣṇa would wash His mouth, hands and feet and would immediately sit down and meditate on Himself. This does not mean, however, that we should also sit down and meditate on ourselves. We have to meditate upon Kṛṣṇa, Rādhā-Kṛṣṇa. That is real meditation. Kṛṣṇa is Kṛṣṇa Himself; therefore He was teaching us that *brāhma-muhūrta* should be utilized for meditation on Rādhā-Kṛṣṇa. By such meditation Kṛṣṇa would feel very much satisfied, and similarly we will also feel transcendentally pleased and satisfied if we utilize the *brāhma-muhūrta* period to meditate on Rādhā and Kṛṣṇa and if we think of how Śrī Rukmiṇīdevī and Kṛṣṇa acted as ideal householders to teach the whole human society to rise early in the morning and immediately engage in Kṛṣṇa consciousness. There is no difference between meditating on the eternal forms of Rādhā-Kṛṣṇa and chanting the *mahā-mantra,* Hare Kṛṣṇa. As for Kṛṣṇa's meditation, He had no alternative but to meditate on Himself. The object of meditation is Brahman, Paramātmā or the Supreme Personality of Godhead, but Kṛṣṇa Himself is all three: He is the Supreme Personality of Godhead, Bhagavān; the localized Paramātmā is His plenary partial expansion; and the all-pervading Brahman effulgence is the personal rays of His transcendental body. Therefore Kṛṣṇa is always one, and for Him there is no differentiation. That is the difference between an ordinary living being and Kṛṣṇa. For an ordinary living being there are many distinctions. An ordinary living being is different from his body, and he is different from other species of living entities. A human being is different from other human beings and different from the animals. Even in his own body, there are different bodily limbs. We have our hands and legs, but our hands are different from our legs. The hand cannot act like the leg, nor can the leg act like the hand. The ears can hear but the eyes cannot, and the eyes can see but the ears cannot. All these differences are technically called *svajātīya-vijātīya.*

The bodily limitation whereby one part of the body cannot act as another part is totally absent from the Supreme Personality of Godhead. There is no difference between His body and Himself. He is completely spiritual, and therefore there is no difference between His body and His soul. Similarly, He is not different from His millions of incarnations and plenary expansions. Baladeva is the first expansion of Kṛṣṇa, and from Baladeva expand Saṅkarṣaṇa, Vāsudeva, Pradyumna and Aniruddha. From Saṅkarṣaṇa there is an expansion of Nārāyaṇa, and from Nārāyaṇa there is a second quadruple expansion of Saṅkarṣaṇa, Vāsudeva, Pradyumna and Aniruddha. Similarly, there are innumerable other expansions of Kṛṣṇa, but all of them are one. Kṛṣṇa has many incarnations, such as Lord Nṛsiṁha, Lord Boar, Lord Fish and Lord Tortoise, but there is no difference between Kṛṣṇa's original two-handed form, like that of a human being, and these incarnations of gigantic animal forms. Nor is there any difference between the action of one part of His body and that of another. His hands can act as His legs, His eyes can act as His ears, or His nose can act as another part of His body. Kṛṣṇa's smelling and eating and hearing are all the same. We limited living entities have to use a particular part of the body for a particular purpose, but there is no such distinction for Kṛṣṇa. In the *Brahma-saṁhitā* it is said, *aṅgāni yasya sakalendriya-vṛtti-manti:* Kṛṣṇa can perform the activities of one limb with any other limb. So by analytical study of Kṛṣṇa and His person, it is concluded that He is the complete whole. When He meditates, therefore, He meditates on Himself. Self-meditation by ordinary men, designated in Sanskrit as *so 'ham,* is simply imitation. Kṛṣṇa may meditate on Himself because He is the complete whole, but we cannot imitate Him and meditate on ourselves. Our body is a designation superimposed upon our self, the soul. Kṛṣṇa's body is not a designation: Kṛṣṇa's body is also Kṛṣṇa. There is no existence of anything foreign in Kṛṣṇa. Whatever there is in Kṛṣṇa is also Kṛṣṇa. He is therefore the supreme, indestructible, complete existence, or the Supreme Truth.

Kṛṣṇa's existence is not relative existence. Everything else but Kṛṣṇa is a relative truth, but Kṛṣṇa is the Supreme Absolute Truth. Kṛṣṇa does not depend on anything but Himself for His existence. Our existence, however, is relative. For example, only when there is the light of the sun, the moon or electricity are we able to see. Our seeing, therefore, is relative, and the light of the sun and moon and electricity is also relative; they are called illuminating only because we see them as such. But dependence and relativity do not exist in Kṛṣṇa. His activities are not dependent on anyone else's appreciation, nor does He depend on anyone else's help. He is beyond the existence of limited time and space, and because He is transcendental to time and space He cannot be covered by the illusion of *māyā,* whose activities are limited. In the Vedic literature we find that the Supreme Personality of Godhead has multipotencies. Since all such potencies are emanations from Him, there is no difference between Him and His potencies. Certain philosophers say, however, that when Kṛṣṇa comes He accepts a material body. But even if it is accepted that when He comes to the material world He accepts a material body, it should be concluded also that because the material energy is not different from Him, this body does not act materially. In the *Bhagavad-gītā* it is said, therefore, that He appears by His own internal potency, *ātma-māyā.*

Kṛṣṇa is called the Supreme Brahman because He is the cause of creation, the cause of maintenance and the cause of dissolution. Lord Brahmā, Lord Viṣṇu and Lord Śiva are different expansions of these material qualities. All these material qualities can act upon the conditioned souls, but there is no such action and reaction upon Kṛṣṇa because these qualities are all simultaneously one with and different from Him. Kṛṣṇa Himself is simply *sac-cid-ānanda-vigraha,* the eternal form of bliss and knowledge, and because of His inconceivable greatness, He is called the Supreme Brahman. His meditation on Brahman or Paramātmā or Bhagavān is on Himself only and not on anything else beyond Himself. This meditation cannot be imitated by the ordinary living entity.

After His meditation, the Lord would regularly bathe early

in the morning with clear, sanctified water. Then He would change into fresh clothing, cover Himself with a wrapper and engage Himself in His daily religious functions. Out of His many religious duties, the first was to offer oblations into the sacrificial fire and silently chant the Gāyatrī *mantra.* Lord Kṛṣṇa, as the ideal householder, executed all the religious functions of a householder without deviation. When the sunrise became visible, the Lord would offer specific prayers to the sun-god. The sun-god and other demigods mentioned in the Vedic scriptures are described as different limbs of the body of Lord Kṛṣṇa, and it is the duty of the householder to offer respects to the demigods and great sages, as well as the forefathers.

As it is said in the *Bhagavad-gītā,* the Lord has no specific duty to perform in this world, and yet He acts just like an ordinary man living an ideal life within this material world. In accordance with Vedic ritualistic principles, the Lord would offer respects to the demigods. The regulative principle by which the demigods and forefathers are worshiped is called *tarpaṇa,* which means "pleasing." One's forefathers may have to take a body on another planet, but by performance of this *tarpaṇa* system they become very happy wherever they may be. It is the duty of the householder to make his family members happy, and by following this *tarpaṇa* system he can make his forefathers happy also. As the perfect exemplary householder, Lord Śrī Kṛṣṇa followed this *tarpaṇa* system and offered respectful obeisances to the elderly, superior members of His family.

His next duty was to give cows in charity to the *brāhmaṇas.* Every day Lord Kṛṣṇa used to give many groups of 13,084 cows. Each of the cows was decorated with a silken cover and pearl necklace, their horns were covered with gold plating, and their hooves were silver-plated. All of them were full of milk, due to having their first-born calves with them, and they were very tame and peaceful. When the cows were given in charity to the *brāhmaṇas,* the *brāhmaṇas* also were given nice silken garments, and each was given a deerskin and sufficient quantity of sesame seeds. The Lord is generally known as *go-brāhmaṇa-hitāya ca,* which means that His first duty is to see to the welfare of the cows and the *brāhmaṇas.* Thus He used to give cows in charity to the *brāhmaṇas,* with opulent decorations and paraphernalia. Then, wishing for the welfare of all living entities, He would touch auspicious articles such as milk, honey, ghee (clarified butter), gold, jewels and fire. Although the Lord is by nature very beautiful due to the perfect figure of His transcendental body, He would dress Himself in yellow garments and put on His necklace of Kaustubha jewels. He would wear flower garlands, smear His body with the pulp of sandalwood and decorate Himself with similar cosmetics and ornaments. It is said that the ornaments themselves became beautiful upon being placed on the transcendental body of the Lord. After decorating Himself in this way, the Lord would then look at marble statues of the cow and calf and visit temples of God or demigods like Lord Śiva. There were many *brāhmaṇas* who would come daily to see the Supreme Lord before taking their breakfast; they were anxious to see Him, and He welcomed them.

His next duty was to please all kinds of men belonging to the different castes, both in the city and within the palace compound. He made them happy by fulfilling their different desires, and when the Lord saw them happy He also became very pleased. The flower garlands, betel nuts, sandalwood pulp and other fragrant cosmetic articles offered to the Lord would be distributed by Him, first to the *brāhmaṇas* and elderly members of the family, then to the queens, and then to the ministers, and if there were still some balance He would engage it for His own personal use. By the time the Lord finished all these daily duties and activities, His charioteer Dāruka would come with His wonderful chariot to stand before the Lord with folded hands, intimating that the chariot was ready, and the Lord would come out of the palace to travel. Then the Lord, accompanied by Uddhava and Sātyaki, would ride on the chariot just as the sun-god rides on his chariot in the morning, appearing with his blazing rays on the surface of the world. When the Lord was about to leave His palaces, all the queens would look at Him with feminine gestures. The Lord would respond to their greetings with smiles, attracting their hearts so much that they would feel intense separation from Him.

Then the Lord would go to the assembly house known as Sudharmā. It may be remembered that the Sudharmā assembly house was taken away from the heavenly planets and established in the city of Dvārakā. The specific significance of the assembly house was that anyone who entered it would be freed from the six kinds of material pangs, namely hunger, thirst, lamentation, illusion, old age and death. These are the whips of material existence, and as long as one remained in that Sudharmā assembly house he would not be affected by these six material whips. The Lord would say good-bye in all the sixteen thousand palaces, and again He would become one and enter the Sudharmā assembly house in procession with other members of the Yadu dynasty. After entering the assembly house, He used to sit on the exalted royal throne and would be seen to emanate glaring rays of transcendental effulgence. In the midst of all the great heroes of the Yadu dynasty, Kṛṣṇa resembled the full moon in the sky surrounded by multiluminaries. In the assembly house were professional jokers, dancers, musicians and ballet girls, and as soon as the Lord sat on His throne they would begin their respective functions to please the Lord and put Him in a happy mood. First of all the jokers would talk in such a way that the Lord and His associates would enjoy their humor, which would refresh the morning mood. The dramatic actors would then play their parts, and the dancing ballet girls would separately display their artistic movements. All these functions would be accompanied by the beating of *mṛdaṅga* drums and the sounds of the *vīṇā,* flutes and bells, followed by the sound of the *muraja,* another type of drum. To these musical vibrations, the auspicious sound of the conchshell would be added. The professional singers called *sūtas* and *māgadhas* would sing, and others would perform their dancing art. In this way, as devotees, they would offer respectful prayers to the Supreme Personality of Godhead. Sometimes the learned *brāhmaṇas* present in that assembly would chant Vedic hymns and explain them to the audience to the best of their knowledge, and sometimes some of them would recite old historical accounts of the activities of prominent kings. The Lord, accompanied by His associates, would be very pleased to hear them.

Once upon a time, a person arrived at the gateway of the assembly house who was unknown to all the members of the assembly, and with the permission of Lord Kṛṣṇa he was admitted into the assembly by the doorkeeper. The doorkeeper was ordered to present him before the Lord, and the man appeared and offered his respectful obeisances unto the Lord with folded hands. It had happened that when King Jarāsandha conquered all other kingdoms, many kings did not bow their heads before Jarāsandha, and consequently all of them, numbering twenty thousand, were arrested and made his prisoners. The man brought before Lord Kṛṣṇa by the doorkeeper was a messenger from all these imprisoned kings. Being duly presented before the Lord, the man began to relay a message from the kings, as follows.

"'Dear Lord, You are the eternal form of transcendental bliss and knowledge. As such, You are beyond the reach of the mental speculation or vocal description of any materialistic man within this world. A slight portion of Your glories can be known by persons fully surrendered unto Your lotus feet, and, by Your grace only, such persons become freed from all material anxieties. Dear Lord, we are not among these surrendered souls; we are still within the duality and illusion of this material existence. We therefore take shelter of Your lotus feet, for we are afraid of the cycle of birth and death. Dear Lord, we think that there are many living entities like us who are eternally entangled in fruitive activities and their reactions. They are never inclined to follow Your instructions by performing devotional service, although it is pleasing to the heart and most auspicious for one's existence. On the contrary, they are against the path of Kṛṣṇa conscious life, and they are wandering within the three worlds, impelled by the illusory energy of material existence.

"'Dear Lord, who can estimate Your mercy and Your powerful activities? You are present always as the insurmountable force of eternal time, baffling the indefatigable desires of the materialists, who are thus repeatedly confused and frustrated. We therefore offer our respectful obeisances unto You in Your form of eternal time. Dear Lord, You are the proprietor of all the worlds, and You have incarnated Yourself with Your plenary expansion Lord Balarāma. It is said that Your appearance in this incarnation is for the purpose of protecting the faithful and destroying the miscreants. Under the circumstances, how is it possible that miscreants like Jarāsandha can put us into such deplorable conditions of life against Your authority? We are puzzled at the situation and cannot understand how it is possible. It may be that Jarāsandha has been deputed to give us such trouble because of our past misdeeds, but we have heard from revealed scriptures that anyone who surrenders unto Your lotus feet is immediately immune to the reactions of sinful life. We therefore offer ourselves wholeheartedly unto Your shelter, and we hope that Your Lordship will now give us full protection. We have now come to the real conclusion of our lives. Our kingly positions were nothing but the reward of our past pious activities, just as our suffering imprisonment by Jarāsandha is the result of our past impious activities. We realize now that the reactions of both pious and impious activities are temporary and that we can never be happy in this conditioned life. The material body is awarded to us by the modes of material nature, and on account of this we are full of anxieties. The material condition of life simply involves bearing the burden of this dead body. As a result of fruitive activities, we have thus been subjected to being beasts of burden for these bodies, and, being forced by conditioned life, we have given up the pleasing life of Kṛṣṇa consciousness. Now we realize that we are the most foolish persons. We have been entangled in the network of material reactions due to our ignorance. We have therefore come to the shelter of Your lotus feet, which can immediately eradicate all the results of fruitive action and thus free us from the contamination of material pains and pleasures.

"'Dear Lord, because we are now surrendered souls at Your lotus feet, You can give us relief from the entrapment of fruitive action made possible by the form of Jarāsandha. Dear Lord, it is known to You that Jarāsandha possesses the power of ten thousand elephants, and with this power he has imprisoned us, just as a lion hypnotizes a flock of sheep. Dear Lord, You have already fought with Jarāsandha eighteen times consecutively, out of which You have defeated him seventeen times by surpassing his extraordinarily powerful position. But in Your eighteenth fight You exhibited Your human behavior, and thus it appeared that You were defeated. Dear Lord, we know very well that Jarāsandha cannot defeat You at any time, for Your power, strength, resources and authority are all unlimited. No one can equal You or surpass You. Your apparent defeat by Jarāsandha in the eighteenth engagement was nothing but an exhibition of human behavior. Unfortunately, foolish Jarāsandha could not understand Your tricks, and he has since then become puffed up over his material power and prestige. Specifically, he has arrested and imprisoned us, knowing fully that as Your devotees we are subordinate to Your sovereignty.'"

The messenger concluded, "Now I have explained the awful position of the kings, and Your Lordship can consider and do whatever You like. As the messenger and representative of all those imprisoned kings, I have submitted my words before Your Lordship and presented their prayers to You. All the kings are very anxious to see You so that they can all personally surrender at Your lotus feet. My dear Lord, be merciful upon them and act for their good fortune."

At the very moment the messenger of the imprisoned kings was presenting their appeal before the Lord, the great sage Nārada arrived. Because he was a great saint, his hair was dazzling like gold, and when he entered the assembly house it appeared that the sun-god was personally present in the midst of the assembly. Lord Kṛṣṇa is the worshipable master of even Lord Brahmā and Lord Śiva, yet as soon as He saw that the sage Nārada had arrived, He immediately stood up with His ministers and secretaries to receive the great sage and offer His respectful obeisances by bowing His head. The great sage Nārada took a comfortable seat, and Lord Kṛṣṇa worshiped him with all paraphernalia, as required for the regular reception of a saintly person. While trying to satisfy Nāradajī, Lord Kṛṣṇa spoke the following words in His sweet and natural voice.

"My dear great sage among the demigods, I think that now everything is well within the three worlds. You are perfectly eligible to travel everywhere in space—in the upper, middle and lower planetary systems of this universe. Fortunately, when we meet you we can very easily take information from Your Holiness of all the news of the three worlds, for within this cosmic manifestation of the Supreme Lord there is nothing concealed from your knowledge. You know everything, and so I wish to question you. Are the Pāṇḍavas doing well, and what is the present plan of King Yudhiṣṭhira? Will you kindly let Me know what they want to do at present?"

The great sage Nārada spoke as follows: "My dear Lord, You have spoken about the cosmic manifestation created by the Supreme Lord, but I know that You are the all-pervading creator. Your energies are so extensive and inconceivable that even powerful personalities like Brahmā, the lord of this particular universe, cannot measure Your inconceivable power. My dear Lord, You are present as the Supersoul in everyone's heart by Your inconceivable potency, exactly like the fire which is present in everyone but which no one can see directly. In conditioned life, all living entities are within the jurisdiction of the three modes of material nature. As such, they are unable to see Your presence everywhere with their material eyes. By Your grace, however, I have seen many times the action of Your inconceivable potency, and therefore when You ask me for the news of the Pāṇḍavas, which is not at all unknown to You, I am not surprised at Your inquiry.

"My dear Lord, by Your inconceivable potencies You create this cosmic manifestation, maintain it and again dissolve it. Only by dint of Your inconceivable potency does this material world, although a shadow representation of the spiritual world, appear to be factual. No one can understand what You plan to do in the future. Your transcendental position is always inconceivable to everyone. As far as I am concerned, I can simply offer my respectful obeisances unto You again and again. In the bodily concept of existence, everyone is driven by material desires, and thus everyone develops new material bodies one after another in the cycle of birth and death. Being absorbed in such a concept of existence, one does not know how to get out of this encagement of the material body. By Your causeless mercy, my Lord, You descend to exhibit Your various transcendental pastimes, which are illuminating and full of glory. Therefore I have no alternative but to offer my respectful obeisances unto You.

"My dear Lord, You are the Supreme, Parabrahman, and Your pastimes as an ordinary human are another tactical resource, exactly like a play on the stage in which the actor plays parts different from his own identity. Because the Pāṇḍavas are Your cousins, You have inquired about them in the role of their well-wisher, and therefore I shall let You know about their intentions. Now please hear me.

"First I may inform You that King Yudhiṣṭhira has all material opulences which are possible to achieve in the highest planetary system, Brahmaloka. He has no material opulence for which to aspire, and yet he wants to perform the Rājasūya sacrifice only to get Your association and please You. King Yudhiṣṭhira is so opulent that he has attained all the opulences of Brahmaloka even on this earthly planet. He is fully satisfied, and he does not need anything more. He is full in everything, but now he wants to worship You to achieve Your causeless mercy, and I beg to request You to fulfill his desires. My dear Lord, in these great sacrificial performances by King Yudhiṣṭhira there will be an assembly of all the demigods and all the famous kings of the world.

"My dear Lord, You are the Supreme Brahman, the Personality of Godhead. One who engages himself in Your devotional service by the prescribed methods of hearing, chanting and remembering certainly becomes purified from the contamination of the modes of material nature, and what to speak of those who have the opportunity to see You and touch You directly. My dear Lord, You are the symbol of everything auspicious. Your transcendental name and fame have spread all over the universe, including the higher, middle and lower planetary systems. The transcendental water which washes Your lotus feet is known in the higher planetary system as Mandākinī, in the lower planetary system as Bhogavatī, and in this earthly planetary system as the Ganges. This sacred, transcendental water flows throughout the entire universe, purifying wherever it flows."

Just before the great sage Nārada arrived in the Sudharmā assembly house of Dvārakā, Lord Kṛṣṇa and His ministers and secretaries had been considering how to attack the kingdom of Jarāsandha. Because they were seriously considering this subject, Nārada's proposal that Lord Kṛṣṇa go to Hastināpura for Mahārāja Yudhiṣṭhira's great Rājasūya sacrifice did not much appeal to them. Lord Kṛṣṇa could understand the intentions of His associates because He is the ruler of even Lord

Brahmā. Therefore, in order to pacify them, He smilingly said to Uddhava, "My dear Uddhava, you are always My well-wishing confidential friend. I therefore wish to see everything through you because I believe that your counsel is always right. I believe that you understand the whole situation perfectly. Therefore I am asking your opinion. What should I do? I have faith in you, and therefore I shall do whatever you advise." It was known to Uddhava that although Lord Kṛṣṇa was acting like an ordinary man, He knew everything—past, present and future. However, because the Lord wanted to consult with him, Uddhava, in order to render service to the Lord, began to speak.

Thus ends the Bhaktivedanta purport of the Seventieth Chapter of Kṛṣṇa, *"Lord Kṛṣṇa's Daily Activities."*

CHAPTER SEVENTY-ONE

Lord Kṛṣṇa in Indraprastha City

In the presence of the great sage Nārada and all the other associates of Lord Kṛṣṇa, Uddhava considered the situation and then spoke as follows: "My dear Lord, first of all let me say that the great sage Nārada Muni has requested You to go to Hastināpura to satisfy King Yudhiṣṭhira, Your cousin, who is making arrangements to perform the great sacrifice known as Rājasūya. I think, therefore, that Your Lordship should immediately go there to help the King in this great venture. However, although to accept the invitation offered by the sage Nārada as primary is quite appropriate, at the same time, my Lord, it is Your duty to give protection to the surrendered souls. Both purposes can be served if we understand the whole situation. Unless we are victorious over all the kings, no one can perform this Rājasūya sacrifice. In other words, it is to be understood that King Yudhiṣṭhira cannot perform this great sacrifice without gaining victory over the belligerent King Jarāsandha. The Rājasūya sacrifice can be performed only by one who has gained victory over all directions. Therefore, to execute both purposes, we first have to kill Jarāsandha. I think that if we can somehow or other gain victory over Jarāsandha, all our purposes will automatically be served. The imprisoned kings will be released, and with great pleasure we shall enjoy the spread of Your transcendental fame for having saved the innocent kings whom Jarāsandha has imprisoned.

"But King Jarāsandha is not an ordinary man. He has proved a stumbling block even to great warriors because his bodily strength is equal to the strength of ten thousand elephants. If there is anyone who can conquer this king, he is none other than Bhīmasena because he also possesses the strength of ten thousand elephants. The best thing would be for Bhīmasena to fight alone with him. Then there would be no unnecessary killing of many soldiers. In fact, Jarāsandha will be very difficult to conquer when he stands with his *akṣauhiṇī* divisions of soldiers. We may therefore adopt a policy more favorable to the situation. We know that King Jarāsandha is very much devoted to the *brāhmaṇas* and very charitably disposed toward them; he never refuses any request from a *brāhmaṇa.* I think, therefore, that Bhīmasena should approach Jarāsandha in the dress of a *brāhmaṇa,* beg charity from him and then personally engage in fighting him. And in order to assure Bhīmasena's victory, I think that Your Lordship should accompany him. If the fighting takes place in Your presence, I am sure Bhīmasena will emerge victorious, for Your presence makes everything impossible possible. Indeed, Lord Brahmā creates this universe and Lord Śiva destroys it simply through Your influence.

"Actually, You create and destroy the entire cosmic manifestation; Lord Brahmā and Lord Śiva are only the superficially visible causes. Creation and destruction are actually performed by the invisible time factor, which is Your impersonal representation. Everything is under the control of this time factor. If Your invisible time factor can perform such wonderful acts through Lord Brahmā and Lord Śiva, will not Your personal presence help Bhīmasena conquer Jarāsandha?

My dear Lord, when Jarāsandha is killed, the queens of all the imprisoned kings will be so joyful at their husbands' being released by Your mercy that they will all sing Your glories, being as pleased as the *gopīs* were when released from the hands of Śaṅkhacūḍa. All the great sages; the King of the elephants, Gajendra; the goddess of fortune, Sītā; and even Your father and mother were all delivered by Your causeless mercy. We also have been thus delivered, and we always sing the transcendental glories of Your activities.

"Therefore, I think that if the killing of Jarāsandha is undertaken first, that will automatically solve many other problems. As for the Rājasūya sacrifice arranged in Hastināpura, it will be held, either because of the pious activities of the imprisoned kings or the impious activities of Jarāsandha.

"My Lord, it appears that You are to go personally to Hastināpura to conquer demoniac kings like Jarāsandha and Śiśupāla, to release the pious imprisoned kings, and also to perform the great Rājasūya sacrifice. Considering all these points, I think that Your Lordship should immediately proceed to Hastināpura."

This advice of Uddhava's was appreciated by all who were present in the assembly; everyone considered that Lord Kṛṣṇa's going to Hastināpura would be beneficial from all points of view. The great sage Nārada, the elder personalities of the Yadu dynasty, and the Supreme Personality of Godhead, Kṛṣṇa Himself, all supported the statement of Uddhava. Lord Kṛṣṇa then took permission from His father, Vasudeva, and grandfather, Ugrasena, and He immediately ordered His servants Dāruka and Jaitra to arrange for travel to Hastināpura. When everything was prepared, Lord Kṛṣṇa especially bid farewell to Lord Balarāma and the King of the Yadus, Ugrasena, and after dispatching His queens along with their children and sending their necessary luggage ahead, He mounted His chariot, which bore the flag marked with the symbol of Garuḍa.

Before starting the procession, Lord Kṛṣṇa satisfied the great sage Nārada by offering him different kinds of articles of worship. Nāradajī wanted to fall at the lotus feet of Kṛṣṇa, but because the Lord was playing the part of a human being, he simply offered his respects within his mind, and, fixing the transcendental form of the Lord within his heart, he left the assembly house by the airways. Usually the sage Nārada does not walk on the surface of the globe but travels in outer space. After the departure of Nārada, Lord Kṛṣṇa addressed the messenger who had come from the imprisoned kings and told him that they should not be worried, for He would very soon arrange to kill the King of Magadha, Jarāsandha. Thus He wished good fortune to all the imprisoned kings and the messenger. After receiving this assurance from Lord Kṛṣṇa, the messenger returned to the imprisoned kings and informed them of the happy news of the Lord's forthcoming visit. All the kings were joyful at the news and began to wait very anxiously for the Lord's arrival.

The chariot of Lord Kṛṣṇa started for Hastināpura accompanied by many other chariots, along with elephants, cavalry, infantry and similar royal paraphernalia. Bugles, drums, trumpets, conchshells and horns all produced a loud auspicious sound, which vibrated in all directions. The sixteen thousand queens, headed by the goddess of fortune Rukmiṇīdevī, the ideal wife of Lord Kṛṣṇa, and accompanied by their respective sons, all followed behind Lord Kṛṣṇa. They were dressed in costly garments decorated with ornaments, and their bodies were smeared with sandalwood pulp and garlanded with fragrant flowers. Riding on palanquins nicely decorated with silks, flags and golden lace, they followed their exalted husband, Lord Kṛṣṇa. The infantry soldiers carried shields, swords and lances in their hands and acted as royal bodyguards to the queens. In the rear of the procession were the wives and children of all the other followers, and there were many society girls also following. Many beasts of burden like bulls, buffalo, mules and asses carried the camps, bedding and carpets, and the women who followed were seated in separate palanquins on the backs of camels. This panoramic procession was accompanied by the shouts of the people and was full with the display of different colored flags, umbrellas and whisks and different varieties of weapons, dress, ornaments, helmets and armaments. Shining in the sunlight, the procession appeared just like an ocean with high waves and sharks.

In this way the procession of Lord Kṛṣṇa's party advanced toward Hastināpura (New Delhi) and gradually passed through the kingdoms of Ānarta (Gujarat Province), Sauvīra (Surat), the great desert of Rājasthān, and then Kurukṣetra. Between those kingdoms were many mountains, rivers, towns, villages, pasturing grounds and mining fields. The procession passed through all these places in its advance. On His way to Hastināpura, the Lord crossed two big rivers, the Dṛṣadvatī and the Sarasvatī. Then He crossed the province of Pañcāla and the province of Matsya. In this way, He ultimately arrived at Hastināpura, or Indraprastha.

The audience of the Supreme Personality of Godhead, Kṛṣṇa, is not at all commonplace. Therefore, when King Yudhiṣṭhira heard that Lord Kṛṣṇa had arrived in his capital city, Hastināpura, he became so joyful that all his bodily hairs stood on end in great ecstasy, and he immediately came out of the city to properly receive the Lord. He ordered the musical vibration of different instruments and songs, and the learned *brāhmaṇas* of the city began to chant the hymns of the *Vedas* very loudly. Lord Kṛṣṇa is known as Hṛṣīkeśa, the master of the senses, and King Yudhiṣṭhira went forward to receive Him exactly as the senses meet the consciousness of life. King Yudhiṣṭhira was the elder cousin of Kṛṣṇa. Naturally he had great affection for the Lord, and as soon as he saw Him, his heart became filled with great love and affection. He had not seen the Lord for many days, and therefore he thought himself most fortunate to see the Lord present before him. The King therefore embraced Lord Kṛṣṇa again and again in great affection.

The eternal form of Lord Kṛṣṇa is the everlasting residence of the goddess of fortune. As soon as King Yudhiṣṭhira embraced Him, he became free from all the contamination of material existence. He immediately felt transcendental bliss and merged in an ocean of happiness. There were tears in his eyes, and his body shook in ecstasy. He completely forgot that he was living in this material world. After this, Bhīmasena, the second brother of the Pāṇḍavas, smiled and embraced Lord Kṛṣṇa, thinking of Him as his own maternal cousin, and thus he also merged in great ecstasy. Bhīmasena was so filled with ecstasy that for the time being he forgot his material existence. Then Lord Śrī Kṛṣṇa Himself embraced the other three Pāṇḍavas, Arjuna, Nakula and Sahadeva. The eyes of all three brothers were inundated with tears, and Arjuna embraced Kṛṣṇa again and again because they were intimate friends. The two younger Pāṇḍava brothers, after being embraced by Lord Kṛṣṇa, fell down at His lotus feet to offer their respects. Lord Kṛṣṇa thereafter offered His obeisances to the *brāhmaṇas* present, as well as to the elder members of the Kuru dynasty, like Bhīṣma, Droṇa and Dhṛtarāṣṭra. There were many kings of different provinces such as Kuru, Sṛñjaya and Kekaya, and Lord Kṛṣṇa duly reciprocated greetings and respects with them. The professional reciters like the *sūtas, māgadhas* and *vandīs,* accompanied by the *brāhmaṇas,* offered their respectful prayers to the Lord. Performing artists like the Gandharvas, as well as the royal jokers, began to play their *paṇava* drums, conchshells, kettledrums, *vīṇās, mṛdaṅgas* and bugles, and they exhibited their dancing art to please the Lord. Thus the all-famous Supreme Personality of Godhead, Lord Kṛṣṇa, entered the great city of Hastināpura, which was opulent in every respect. While Lord Kṛṣṇa was entering the city, all the people talked amongst themselves about the glories of the Lord, praising His transcendental name, qualities, form and so on.

The roads, streets and lanes of Hastināpura were all sprinkled with fragrant water through the trunks of intoxicated elephants. In different places of the city there were colorful festoons and flags decorating the houses and streets. At important crossroads there were gates with golden decorations, and at the two sides of the gates there were golden water jugs. These beautiful decorations glorified the opulence of the city. Participating in this great ceremony, all the citizens gathered here and there, dressed in colorful new clothing and decorated with ornaments, flower garlands and fragrant scents. The houses were all illuminated by hundreds and thousands of lamps placed in different corners of the cornices, walls, columns, bases and architraves, and from far away the rays of the lamps appeared to be celebrating the festival of Dīpāvalī (a particular festival observed on the New Year's Day of the Hindu calendar). Within the walls of the houses, fragrant incense was burning, and smoke rose through the windows, making the entire atmosphere very pleasing. On the top of every house, flags were flapping, and the golden waterpots kept on the roofs shone brilliantly.

Lord Kṛṣṇa thus entered the city of the Pāṇḍavas, enjoyed the beautiful atmosphere and slowly proceeded ahead. When the young girls in every house heard that Lord Kṛṣṇa, the only object worth seeing, was passing on the road, they were very eager to see this all-famous personality. Their hair loosened, and their tightened saris became slack due to their hastily rushing to see Him. They gave up their household engagements, and those who were lying in bed with their husbands immediately left them and came directly down onto the street to see Lord Kṛṣṇa. The procession of elephants, horses, chariots and infantry was very crowded; some of the girls, being unable to see properly in the crowd, got up on the roofs of the houses. Pleased to see Lord Śrī Kṛṣṇa passing with His thousands of queens, they showered flowers on the procession, embraced Lord Kṛṣṇa within their minds and gave Him a hearty reception. When they saw Him in the midst of His many queens, like the full moon situated amidst many luminaries, they began to talk amongst themselves.

One girl said to another, "My dear friend, it is very difficult to guess what kind of pious activities these queens have performed, for they are always enjoying the smiling face and loving glances of Kṛṣṇa." While Lord Kṛṣṇa was thus passing on the road, at intervals some of the citizens, who were all rich, respectable and freed from sinful activities, presented auspicious articles to the Lord, just to offer Him a reception to the city. Thus they worshiped Him as humble servitors.

When Lord Kṛṣṇa entered the palace, all the ladies there were overwhelmed with affection just upon seeing Him. They immediately received Lord Kṛṣṇa with glittering eyes expressing their love and affection for Him, and Lord Kṛṣṇa smiled and accepted their feelings and gestures of reception. When Kuntī, the mother of the Pāṇḍavas, saw her nephew Lord Kṛṣṇa, the Supreme Personality of Godhead, she was overpowered by love and affection. She at once got up from her bedstead and appeared before Him with her daughter-in-law, Draupadī, and in maternal love and affection she embraced Him. As Mahārāja Yudhiṣṭhira brought Kṛṣṇa within the palace, the King became so confused in his jubilation that he practically forgot what he was to do at that time to receive Kṛṣṇa and worship Him properly. Lord Kṛṣṇa delightfully offered His respects and obeisances to Kuntī and other elderly ladies of the palace. His younger sister, Subhadrā, was also standing there with Draupadī, and both offered their respectful obeisances unto the lotus feet of the Lord. At the indication of her mother-in-law, Draupadī brought clothing, ornaments and garlands, and with this paraphernalia they received the queens Rukmiṇī, Satyabhāmā, Bhadrā, Jāmbavatī, Kālindī, Mitravindā, Lakṣmaṇā and the devoted Satyā. These principal queens of Lord Kṛṣṇa were first received, and then the other queens were also offered a proper reception. King Yudhiṣṭhira arranged for Kṛṣṇa's rest and saw to it that all who came along with Him—namely His queens, soldiers, ministers and secretaries—were comfortably situated. He had arranged that they would experience a new feature of reception every day while staying as guests of the Pāṇḍavas.

It was during this time that Lord Śrī Kṛṣṇa, with the help of Arjuna, allowed the fire-god, Agni, to devour the Khāṇḍava forest for his satisfaction. During the forest fire, Kṛṣṇa saved the demon Mayāsura, who was hiding in the forest. Upon being saved, Mayāsura felt obliged to the Pāṇḍavas and Lord Kṛṣṇa, and he constructed a wonderful assembly house within the city of Hastināpura. To please King Yudhiṣṭhira, Lord Kṛṣṇa remained in the city of Hastināpura for several months. During His stay, He enjoyed strolling here and there. He used to drive on chariots with Arjuna, and many warriors and soldiers used to follow them.

Thus ends the Bhaktivedanta purport of the Seventy-first Chapter of Kṛṣṇa, *"Lord Kṛṣṇa in Indraprastha City."*

CHAPTER SEVENTY-TWO

The Liberation of King Jarāsandha

In the great assembly of respectable citizens, friends, relatives, *brāhmaṇas*, sages, *kṣatriyas* and *vaiśyas*—in the presence of all, including his brothers—King Yudhiṣṭhira directly addressed Lord Kṛṣṇa as follows: "My dear Lord Kṛṣṇa, the sacrifice known as the Rājasūya-yajña is to be performed by the emperor, and it is considered the king of all sacrifices. By performing this sacrifice, I wish to satisfy all the demigods, who are Your empowered representatives within this material world, and I wish that You will kindly help me in this great venture so that it may be successfully executed. As far as the Pāṇḍavas are concerned, we have nothing to ask from the demigods. We are personally fully satisfied to be Your devotees. As You say in the *Bhagavad-gītā,* 'Persons bewildered by material desires worship the demigods.' But my purpose is different. I want to perform this Rājasūya sacrifice and invite the demigods to show that they have no power independent of You—that they are all Your servants and You are the Supreme Personality of Godhead. Foolish persons with a poor fund of knowledge consider Your Lordship an ordinary human being. Sometimes they try to find fault in You, and sometimes they defame You. Therefore I wish to perform this Rājasūya-yajña. I wish to invite all the demigods, beginning from Lord Brahmā, Lord Śiva and other exalted chiefs of the heavenly planets, and in that great assembly of demigods from all parts of the universe, I want to substantiate that You are the Supreme Personality of Godhead and that everyone is Your servant.

"My dear Lord, those who are constantly in Kṛṣṇa consciousness and who think of Your lotus feet or Your shoes are certainly freed from all contamination of material life. Such persons who engage in Your service in full Kṛṣṇa consciousness, who meditate upon You only and offer prayers unto You, are purified souls. Being constantly engaged in Kṛṣṇa conscious service, they are freed from the cycle of repeated birth and death. Or, even if they do not want to be freed from this material existence but desire to enjoy material opulences, their desires are also fulfilled by their Kṛṣṇa conscious activities. In fact, those who are pure devotees of Your lotus feet have no desire for material opulences. As far as we are concerned, we are fully surrendered unto Your lotus feet, and by Your grace we are so fortunate as to see You personally. Therefore, naturally we have no desire for material opulences. The verdict of the Vedic wisdom is that You are the Supreme Personality of Godhead. I want to establish this fact, and I also want to show the world the difference between accepting You as the Supreme Personality of Godhead and accepting You as an ordinary powerful historical person. I wish to show the world that one can attain the highest perfection of life simply by taking shelter at Your lotus feet, exactly as one can satisfy the branches, twigs, leaves and flowers of an entire tree simply by watering the root. If one takes to Kṛṣṇa consciousness, his life becomes fulfilled both materially and spiritually.

"This does not mean that You are partial to the Kṛṣṇa

conscious person and indifferent to the non–Kṛṣṇa conscious person. You are equal to everyone; that is Your declaration. You cannot be partial to one and not interested in others, for You sit in everyone's heart as the Supersoul and give everyone the respective results of his fruitive activities. You give every living entity the chance to enjoy this material world as he desires. As the Supersoul, You sit in the body with the living entity, giving him the results of his own actions as well as opportunities to turn toward Your devotional service by developing Kṛṣṇa consciousness. You openly declare that one should surrender unto You, giving up all other engagements, and that You will take charge of him, giving him relief from the reactions of all sins. Still, the living entity remains attached to material activities and suffers or enjoys the reactions without Your interference. You are like the desire tree in the heavenly planets, which awards benedictions according to one's desires. Everyone is free to achieve the highest perfection, but if one does not so desire, then Your awarding of lesser benedictions is not due to partiality."

On hearing this statement by King Yudhiṣṭhira, Lord Kṛṣṇa replied as follows: "My dear King Yudhiṣṭhira, O killer of enemies, O ideal justice personified, I completely support your decision to perform the Rājasūya sacrifice. After you perform this great sacrifice, your good name will remain well established forever in the history of human civilization. My dear King, I may inform you that all the great sages, your forefathers, the demigods and your relatives and friends, including Me, desire that you perform this sacrifice, and I think that it will satisfy every living entity. But I request that you first conquer all the kings of the world and collect all the requisite paraphernalia for executing this great sacrifice. My dear King Yudhiṣṭhira, your four brothers are direct representatives of important demigods like Vāyu and Indra. [It is said that Bhīma was born of the demigod Vāyu, and that Arjuna was born of the demigod Indra, whereas King Yudhiṣṭhira himself was born of the demigod Yamarāja.] As such, your brothers are great heroes, and you are the most pious and self-controlled king and are therefore known as Dharmarāja. All of you are so qualified in devotional service to Me that I have automatically been conquered by you."

Lord Kṛṣṇa told King Yudhiṣṭhira that He is conquered by the love of one who has conquered his senses. One who has not conquered his senses cannot conquer the Supreme Personality of Godhead. This is the secret of devotional service. To conquer the senses means to engage them constantly in the service of the Lord. The specific qualification of all the Pāṇḍava brothers was that they always engaged their senses in the Lord's service. One who thus engages his senses becomes purified, and with purified senses the devotee can actually render transcendental loving service to the Lord and conquer Him.

Lord Kṛṣṇa continued, "There is no one in the three worlds of the universe, including the powerful demigods, who can surpass My devotees in any of the six opulences, namely wealth, strength, reputation, beauty, knowledge and renunciation. Therefore, if you want to conquer the worldly kings, there is no possibility of their emerging victorious."

When Lord Kṛṣṇa thus encouraged King Yudhiṣṭhira, the King's face brightened like a blossoming flower because of transcendental happiness, and thus he ordered his younger brothers to conquer all the worldly kings in all directions. Lord Kṛṣṇa empowered the Pāṇḍavas to execute His great mission of chastising the infidel miscreants of the world and giving protection to His faithful devotees. In His Viṣṇu form, the Lord carries four weapons in His four hands—a lotus flower and a conchshell in two hands, and in the other two hands a club and a disc. The club and disc are meant for the infidel miscreants and demons, and the lotus flower and conchshell are for the devotees. But because the Lord is the Supreme Absolute, the result of all His weapons is one and the same.

With the club and the disc He chastises the miscreants so that they may come to their senses and know that they are not all in all, for above them there is the Supreme Lord. And by bugling with the conchshell and offering blessings with the lotus flower, He always assures the devotees that no one can vanquish them, even in the greatest calamity. King Yudhiṣṭhira, being thus assured by the indication of Lord Kṛṣṇa, ordered his youngest brother, Sahadeva, accompanied by soldiers of the Sṛñjaya tribe, to conquer the southern countries. Similarly, he ordered Nakula, accompanied by the soldiers of Matsyadeśa, to conquer the kings of the western side. He sent Arjuna, accompanied by the soldiers of Kekayadeśa, to conquer the kings of the northern side, and he ordered Bhīmasena, accompanied by the soldiers of Madradeśa (Madras), to conquer the kings on the eastern side.

It may be noted that by dispatching his younger brothers to conquer in different directions, King Yudhiṣṭhira did not actually intend that they declare war upon the kings. Actually, the brothers started for different directions to inform the respective kings about King Yudhiṣṭhira's intention to perform the Rājasūya sacrifice. The kings were thus informed that they were required to pay taxes for the execution of the sacrifice. This payment of taxes to Emperor Yudhiṣṭhira meant that the king accepted subjugation before him. In case of a king's refusal to act accordingly, there was certainly a fight. Thus by their influence and strength the brothers conquered all the kings in different directions, and they were able to bring in sufficient taxes and presentations, which they brought before King Yudhiṣṭhira.

King Yudhiṣṭhira was very anxious, however, when he heard that King Jarāsandha of Magadha did not accept his sovereignty. Seeing King Yudhiṣṭhira's anxiety, Lord Kṛṣṇa informed him of the plan explained by Uddhava for conquering King Jarāsandha. Bhīmasena, Arjuna and Lord Kṛṣṇa then started together for Girivraja, the capital city of Jarāsandha, dressing themselves in the garb of *brāhmaṇas*. This was the plan devised by Uddhava before Lord Kṛṣṇa started for Hastināpura, and now it was given practical application.

King Jarāsandha was a very dutiful householder, and he had great respect for the *brāhmaṇas.* He was a great fighter, a *kṣatriya* king, but he was never neglectful of the Vedic injunctions. According to the Vedic injunctions, the *brāhmaṇas* are considered to be the spiritual masters of all other castes. Lord Kṛṣṇa, Arjuna and Bhīmasena were actually *kṣatriyas,* but they dressed themselves as *brāhmaṇas,* and at the time when King Jarāsandha was to give charity to the *brāhmaṇas* and receive them as guests, they approached him.

Lord Kṛṣṇa, in the dress of a *brāhmaṇa,* said to the King, "We wish all glories to Your Majesty. We three guests at your royal palace have come from a great distance to ask you for charity, and we hope that you will kindly bestow upon us whatever we ask from you. We know about your good qualities. A person who is tolerant is always prepared to tolerate everything, even though distressful. Just as a criminal can perform the most abominable acts, a greatly charitable person like you can give anything and everything for which he is asked. For a great personality like you, there is no distinction between relatives and outsiders. A famous man lives forever, even after his death; therefore, any person who is completely fit and able to execute acts which will perpetuate his good name and fame and yet does not do so becomes abominable in the eyes of great persons. Such a person cannot be condemned enough, and his refusal to give charity is lamentable throughout his whole life. Your Majesty must have heard the glorious names of charitable personalities such as Hariścandra, Rantideva and Mudgala, who used to live only on grains picked up from the paddy field, and the great Mahārāja Śibi, who saved the life of a pigeon by supplying flesh from his own body. These great personalities have attained immortal fame simply by sacrificing the temporary and perishable body." Lord Kṛṣṇa, in the garb of a *brāhmaṇa,* thus convinced Jarāsandha that fame is imperishable but the body is perishable. If one can attain imperishable name and fame by sacrificing his perishable body, he becomes a very respectable figure in the history of human civilization.

While Lord Kṛṣṇa was speaking in the garb of a *brāhmaṇa* along with Arjuna and Bhīma, Jarāsandha marked that the three of them did not appear to be actual *brāhmaṇas.* There were signs on their bodies by which Jarāsandha could understand that they were *kṣatriyas.* Their shoulders were marked with impressions due to carrying bows, they had beautiful bodily structure, and their voices were grave and commanding. Thus he definitely concluded that they were not *brāhmaṇas* but *kṣatriyas.* He also thought that he had seen them somewhere before. But although these three persons were *kṣatriyas,* they had come to his door begging alms like *brāhmaṇas.* Therefore he decided that he would fulfill their desires in spite of their being *kṣatriyas,* because they had already diminished their position by appearing before him as beggars. "Under the circumstances," he thought, "I am prepared to give them anything. Even if they ask for my body, I shall not hesitate to offer it to them." In this regard, he began to think of Bali Mahārāja. Lord Viṣṇu in the dress of a *brāhmaṇa* appeared as a beggar before Bali and snatched away all of his opulence and his kingdom. He did this for the benefit of Indra, who, having been defeated by Bali Mahārāja, was bereft of his kingdom. Although Bali Mahārāja was cheated, his reputation as a great devotee able to give anything and everything in charity is still glorified throughout the three worlds. Bali Mahārāja could guess that the *brāhmaṇa* was Lord Viṣṇu Himself and had come to him just to take away his opulent kingdom on behalf of Indra. Bali's spiritual master and family priest, Śukrācārya, repeatedly warned him about this, yet Bali did not hesitate to give in charity whatever the *brāhmaṇa* wanted, and at last he gave up everything to that *brāhmaṇa.* "It is my strong determination," thought Jarāsandha, "that if I can achieve immortal reputation by sacrificing this perishable body, I must act for that purpose; the life of a *kṣatriya* who does not live for the benefit of the *brāhmaṇas* is certainly condemned."

Actually King Jarāsandha was very liberal in giving charity to *brāhmaṇas,* and thus he informed Lord Kṛṣṇa, Bhīma and Arjuna: "My dear *brāhmaṇas,* you may ask from me whatever you like. If you so desire, you may take my head also. I am prepared to give it."

After this, Lord Kṛṣṇa addressed Jarāsandha as follows: "My dear King, please note that we are not actually *brāhmaṇas,* nor have we come to ask for food or grain. We are all *kṣatriyas,* and we have come to beg a duel with you. We hope that you will agree to this proposal. You may note that here is the second son of King Pāṇḍu, Bhīmasena, and the third son of Pāṇḍu, Arjuna. As for Myself, you may know that I am your old enemy Kṛṣṇa, the cousin of the Pāṇḍavas."

When Lord Kṛṣṇa disclosed their disguise, King Jarāsandha laughed very loudly, and then in great anger and in a grave voice he exclaimed, "You fools! If you want to fight with me, I immediately grant your request. But, Kṛṣṇa, I know that You are a coward. I refuse to fight with You because You become very confused when You face me in fighting. Out of fear of me You left Your own city, Mathurā, and now You have taken shelter within the sea; therefore I must refuse to fight with You. As far as Arjuna is concerned, I know that he is younger than me and is not an equal fighter. I refuse to fight with him because he is not in any way an equal competitor. But as far as Bhīmasena is concerned, I think he is a suitable competitor to fight with me." After speaking in this way, King Jarāsandha immediately handed a very heavy club to Bhīmasena, he himself took another, and all of them went outside the city walls to fight.

Bhīmasena and King Jarāsandha engaged themselves in fighting, and with their respective clubs, which were as strong as thunderbolts, they began to strike each other very severely, both of them being eager to fight. They were both expert fighters with clubs, and their techniques of striking each other were so beautiful that they appeared to be two dramatic artists dancing on a stage. When the clubs of Jarāsandha and Bhīmasena loudly collided, the impact sounded like that of the big tusks of two fighting elephants or like a thunderbolt in a flashing electrical storm. When two elephants fight together in a sugarcane field, each of them snatches a stick of sugarcane, holds it tightly in its trunk and strikes the other. At that time the sugarcane becomes smashed by such heavy striking. Similarly, when Bhīmasena and Jarāsandha were heavily striking each other with their clubs on different parts of their bodies—namely the shoulders, arms, collarbone, chest, thighs, waist and legs—their clubs became torn to pieces. In this way, all of the clubs used by Jarāsandha and Bhīmasena became ruined, and so the two enemies prepared to fight with their strong-fisted hands. Jarāsandha and Bhīmasena were very angry, and they began to smash each other with their fists. The striking of their fists sounded like the striking of iron bars or like the sound of thunderbolts, and the two warriors appeared to be like two elephants fighting. Neither was able to defeat the other, however, for both were expert in fighting, they were of equal strength, and their fighting techniques were also equal. Neither Jarāsandha nor Bhīmasena became fatigued or defeated in the fighting, although they struck each other continuously. At the end of each day's fighting, they lived at night as friends in Jarāsandha's palace, and the next day they fought again. In this way they passed twenty-seven days in fighting.

On the twenty-eighth day, Bhīmasena told Kṛṣṇa, "My dear Kṛṣṇa, I must frankly admit that I cannot conquer Jarāsandha." Lord Kṛṣṇa, however, knew the mystery of Jarāsandha's birth. Jarāsandha had been born in two different parts from two different mothers. When his father saw that the baby was useless, he threw the two parts into the forest. There they were later found by a witch named Jarā, who was skilled in the black arts. She managed to join the two parts of the baby from top to bottom. Knowing this, Lord Kṛṣṇa therefore also knew how to kill him. He hinted to Bhīmasena that since Jarāsandha was brought to life by the joining of the two parts of his body, he could be killed by the separation of these two parts. Thus Lord Kṛṣṇa transferred His power into the body of Bhīmasena and informed him of the device by which Jarāsandha could be killed. Lord Kṛṣṇa picked up a twig from a tree, took it in His hand, and bifurcated it. In this way He hinted to Bhīmasena how Jarāsandha could be killed. Lord Kṛṣṇa, the Supreme Personality of Godhead, is omnipotent, and if He wants to kill someone, no one can save that person. Similarly, if He wants to save someone, no one can kill him.

Informed by the hints of Lord Kṛṣṇa, Bhīmasena immediately took hold of Jarāsandha's legs and threw him to the ground. When Jarāsandha fell, Bhīmasena immediately pressed one of Jarāsandha's legs to the ground and took hold of the other leg with his two hands. Catching Jarāsandha in this way, he tore his body in two, beginning from the anus up to the head. As an elephant breaks the branches of a tree in two, Bhīmasena separated the body of Jarāsandha. The audience standing nearby saw that Jarāsandha's body was now divided into two halves, so that each half had one leg, one thigh, one testicle, half a backbone, half a chest, one collarbone, one arm, one eye, one ear and half a face.

As soon as the news of Jarāsandha's death was announced, all the citizens of Magadha began to cry, "Alas! Alas!" while Lord Kṛṣṇa and Arjuna embraced Bhīmasena to congratulate him. Although Jarāsandha was killed, neither Kṛṣṇa nor the two Pāṇḍava brothers made a claim to the throne. Their purpose in killing Jarāsandha was to stop him from creating a disturbance to the proper discharge of world peace. A demon always creates disturbances, whereas a demigod always tries to keep peace in the world. The mission of Lord Kṛṣṇa is to protect the righteous and kill the demons who disturb a peaceful situation. Therefore Lord Kṛṣṇa immediately called for the son of Jarāsandha, whose name was Sahadeva, and with due ritualistic ceremonies the Lord asked him to occupy the seat of his father and reign over the kingdom peacefully. Lord Kṛṣṇa is the master of the whole cosmic creation, and He wants everyone to live peacefully and execute Kṛṣṇa consciousness. After installing Sahadeva on the throne, He released all the kings and princes who had been imprisoned unnecessarily by Jarāsandha.

Thus ends the Bhaktivedanta purport of the Seventy-second Chapter of Kṛṣṇa, *"The Liberation of King Jarāsandha."*

CHAPTER SEVENTY-THREE

Lord Kṛṣṇa Returns to the City of Hastināpura

The kings and princes released by Lord Kṛṣṇa after the death of Jarāsandha were rulers of different parts of the world. Jarāsandha was so powerful in military strength that he had conquered all these princes and kings, numbering 20,800. They were all incarcerated within a mountain cave especially constructed as a fort, and for a long time they were kept in that situation. When they were released by the grace of Lord Kṛṣṇa, they all looked very unhappy, their garments were niggardly, and their faces were almost dried up for want of proper bodily care. They were very weak due to hunger, and their faces had lost all beauty and luster. The kings' long imprisonment had caused every part of their bodies to become slack and invalid.

However, because in that miserable condition they had had the opportunity to think about Lord Kṛṣṇa, they immediately saw Him now as the Supreme Personality of Godhead, Viṣṇu. They saw that the color of the transcendental body of Lord

Kṛṣṇa resembled the hue of a newly arrived cloud in the sky. He appeared before them nicely covered by yellow silken garments, with four hands like Viṣṇu, and carrying the different symbols of the club, the conchshell, the disc and the lotus flower. His chest was marked with a golden line, and the nipples on His chest appeared like the whorls of lotus flowers. His eyes appeared to spread like the petals of a lotus, and His smiling face exhibited the symbol of eternal peace and prosperity. He wore glittering shark-shaped earrings, and His helmet was bedecked with valuable jewels. The Lord's necklace of pearls and the bangles and bracelets nicely situated on His body all shone with a transcendental beauty. The Kaustubha jewel hanging on His chest glittered with great luster, and the Lord wore a beautiful flower garland. After so much distress, when the kings and princes saw Lord Kṛṣṇa, with His beautiful transcendental features, they looked upon Him to their hearts' content, as if drinking nectar through their eyes, licking His body with their tongues, smelling the aroma of His body with their noses and embracing Him with their arms. Just by dint of their being in front of the Supreme Personality of Godhead, all reactions to their sinful activities were washed away. Therefore, without reservation, they surrendered themselves at the lotus feet of the Lord. It is stated in the *Bhagavad-gītā* that unless one is freed from all sinful reactions, one cannot fully surrender unto the lotus feet of the Lord. All the princes who saw Lord Kṛṣṇa forgot all their past tribulations. With folded hands and with great devotion, they offered prayers to Lord Kṛṣṇa, as follows.

"Dear Lord, O Supreme Personality of Godhead, master of all demigods, You can immediately remove all Your devotees' pangs because Your devotees are fully surrendered unto You. O dear Lord Kṛṣṇa, O eternal Deity of transcendental bliss and knowledge, You are imperishable, and we offer our respectful obeisances unto Your lotus feet. It is by Your causeless mercy that we have been released from the imprisonment of Jarāsandha, but now we pray that You release us from imprisonment within material existence, Your illusory energy. Please stop our continuous cycle of birth and death. We now have sufficient experience of the miserable material life in which we are fully absorbed, and having tasted its bitterness, we have come to take shelter under Your lotus feet. Therefore please give us Your protection. Dear Lord, O killer of the demon Madhu, we can now clearly see that Jarāsandha was not at fault in the least; it is actually by Your causeless mercy that we were bereft of our kingdoms, for we were very proud of calling ourselves rulers and kings. A ruler or king who becomes too much puffed up with false prestige and power gets no opportunity to understand his real constitutional position and eternal life. Under the influence of Your illusory energy, such a foolish so-called ruler or king becomes falsely proud of his position, just like a foolish person who considers a mirage in the desert a reservoir of water. Foolish persons think that their material possessions will give them protection; engaged in sense gratification, they falsely accept this material world as a place of eternal enjoyment. O Lord, O Supreme Personality of Godhead, we must admit that before this we were puffed up with our material opulences. It was as if we were intoxicated. Because we were all envious and wanted to conquer one another, we all engaged in fighting for supremacy, even at the cost of sacrificing the lives of many citizens."

This is the disease of political power. As soon as a king becomes rich in material opulences, he wants to dominate other nations by military aggression. Similarly, mercantile men want to monopolize a certain type of business and control other mercantile groups. Impelled by false prestige and infatuated by material opulences, human society, instead of striving for Kṛṣṇa consciousness, creates havoc and disrupts peaceful living. Thus men forget the real purpose of life: to attain the favor of Lord Viṣṇu, the Supreme Personality of Godhead.

The kings continued, "O Lord, we were simply engaged in the abominable task of killing citizens and alluring them to be unnecessarily killed, just to satisfy our political whims. We did not consider that Your Lordship is always present before us in the form of cruel death. We were so fooled that we became the cause of death for others, forgetting our own impending death. But, dear Lord, the force of the time element, which is Your representative, is certainly insurmountable. The time element is so strong that no one can escape its influence; therefore we have received the reactions of our atrocious activities, and we are now bereft of all opulences and stand before You like street beggars. We consider our position Your causeless, unalloyed mercy upon us because now we can understand that we were falsely proud and that our material opulences could be withdrawn from us within a second by Your will. By Your causeless mercy only, we are now able to think of Your lotus feet. This is our greatest gain. Dear Lord, everyone knows that the body is a breeding ground of diseases. Now we are aged, and instead of being proud of our bodily strength, we are getting weaker day by day. We are no longer interested in sense gratification or the false happiness derived through the material body. By Your grace, we have now come to the conclusion that hankering after such material happiness is just like searching for water in a desert mirage. We are no longer interested in the results of our pious activities, such as performing great sacrifices to be elevated to the heavenly planets. We now understand that such elevation to a higher material standard may sound very relishable, but actually there cannot be any happiness within this material world. We pray for Your Lordship to favor us by instructing us how to engage in the transcendental loving service of Your lotus feet so that we may never forget our eternal relationship with Your Lordship. We do not want liberation from the entanglement of material existence. By Your will we may take birth in any species of life; it does not matter. We simply pray that we never forget Your lotus feet under any circumstances. Dear Lord, we now surrender unto Your lotus feet by offering our respectful obeisances unto You because You are the Supreme Lord, the Personality of Godhead, Kṛṣṇa, the son of Vasudeva. You are the Supersoul in everyone's heart, and You are Lord Hari, who can take away all miserable conditions of material existence. Dear Lord, Your name is Govinda, the reservoir of all pleasure, because one who is engaged in satisfying Your senses satisfies his own senses automatically. Dear Lord, You are ever famous, for You can put an end to all the miseries of Your devotees. Please, therefore, accept us as Your surrendered servants."

After hearing the prayers of the kings released from the prison of Jarāsandha, Lord Kṛṣṇa, who is always the protector of surrendered souls and the ocean of mercy for the devotees, replied to them as follows in His sweet, transcendental voice, which was grave and full of meaning. "My dear kings," He said, "I bestow upon you My blessings. From this day forth you will be attached to My devotional service without fail. I give you this benediction, as you have desired. You may know from Me that I am always sitting within your hearts as the Supersoul, and because you have now turned your faces toward Me, I, as master of everyone, shall always give you good counsel so that you may never forget Me and so that gradually you will come back home, back to Godhead. My dear kings, your decision to give up all conceptions of material enjoyment and turn instead toward My devotional service is factually the symptom of your good fortune. Henceforward you will always be blessed with blissful life. I confirm that all you have spoken about Me in your prayers is factual. It is a fact that the materially opulent position of one who is not fully Kṛṣṇa conscious is the cause of his downfall and his becoming a victim of the illusory energy. In the past there were many rebellious kings, such as Haihaya, Nahuṣa, Vena, Rāvaṇa and Narakāsura. Some of them were demigods and some of them demons, but because of their false perception of their positions, they fell from their exalted posts, and thus they no longer remained kings of their respective kingdoms and were lost in the violence of abominable conditioned life.

"Every one of you must understand that anything material has its starting point, growth, maintenance, expansion, deterioration and, finally, disappearance. All material bodies are subject to these six conditions, and any relative acquisitions accumulated by this body are definitely subject to final destruction. Therefore, no one should be attached to perishable things. As long as one is within this material body, he should be very cautious in worldly dealings. The most perfect way of life in this material world is simply to be devoted to My transcendental loving service and to execute honestly the prescribed duties of one's particular position. As far as you are concerned, you all belong to *kṣatriya* families. Therefore, you should live honestly, according to the prescribed duties befitting the royal order, and make your citizens happy in all respects. Keep to the standard of *kṣatriya* life. Do not beget children out of sense gratification, but simply take charge of the welfare of the people in general. Everyone takes birth in this material world in continuation of his previous life, and thus he is subject to the stringent laws of nature, such as birth and death, distress and happiness, profit and loss. One should not be disturbed by duality but should always be fixed in My devotional service and thus remain balanced in mind and satisfied in all circumstances, considering all things to be given by Me. Thus one can live a very happy and peaceful life, even within this material condition. In other words, one should actually be callous to the material body and its by-products and should be unaffected by them. One should remain fully satisfied in the interests of the spirit soul and engage in the service of the Supersoul. One should engage his mind only in thinking of Me, one should simply become My devotee, one should simply worship Me, and one should offer his respectful obeisances unto Me alone. In this way, one can cross over this ocean of nescience very easily and at the end come back to Me. In conclusion, your lives should constantly be engaged in My service."

After delivering His instructions to the kings and princes, Lord Kṛṣṇa immediately arranged for their comfort and asked many servants and maidservants to take care of them. Lord Kṛṣṇa requested Sahadeva, the son of King Jarāsandha, to supply all necessities to the kings and show them all respect and honor. In pursuance of the order of Lord Kṛṣṇa, Sahadeva offered them all honor and presented them with ornaments, garments, garlands and other paraphernalia. After taking their baths and dressing very nicely, the kings appeared happy and gentle. Then they were supplied nice food. Lord Kṛṣṇa supplied everything for their comfort, as befitting their royal positions. Since the kings were so mercifully treated by Lord Kṛṣṇa, they felt great happiness, and their bright faces appeared just like the stars in the sky after the end of the rainy season. All nicely dressed and ornamented, their earrings glittering, they were then seated on chariots bedecked with gold and jewels and drawn by decorated horses. After seeing that each was taken care of, Lord Kṛṣṇa, in a sweet voice, asked them to return to their respective kingdoms. By His liberal behavior, unparalleled in the history of the world, Lord Kṛṣṇa released all the kings who had been in the clutches of Jarāsandha, and the kings, being fully satisfied, began to chant His holy name, think of His holy form and glorify His transcendental pastimes as the Supreme Personality of Godhead. Thus engaged, they returned to their respective kingdoms. The citizens of their kingdoms were greatly pleased to see them return, and when they heard of the kind dealings of Lord Kṛṣṇa, they were all very happy. The kings began to manage the affairs of their kingdoms in accordance with the instructions of Lord Kṛṣṇa, and all those kings and their subjects passed their days very happily. This is a vivid example of a Kṛṣṇa conscious society. If the people of the world, taking into account their respective material qualities, divide the whole society into four orders for material progress and four orders for spiritual progress, centering these orders on Kṛṣṇa and following the instructions of Kṛṣṇa as stated in the *Bhagavad-gītā,* the entire human society will undoubtedly be happy. This is the lesson we have to take from this incident.

After thus causing the annihilation of Jarāsandha by Bhīmasena and after being properly honored by Sahadeva, the son of Jarāsandha, Lord Kṛṣṇa, accompanied by Bhīmasena and Arjuna, returned to the city of Hastināpura. When they reached the precincts of Hastināpura, they blew their respective conchshells, and by hearing the sound vibrations and understanding who was arriving, everyone immediately became cheerful. But the enemies of Kṛṣṇa, upon hearing the conchshells, were very sorry. The citizens of Indraprastha felt their hearts become joyful simply by hearing the vibration of Kṛṣṇa's conchshell because they could understand that Jarāsandha had been killed. Now the performance of the Rājasūya sacrifice by King Yudhiṣṭhira was almost certain. Bhīmasena, Arjuna and Kṛṣṇa, the Supreme Personality of Godhead, arrived before King Yudhiṣṭhira and offered their respects to the King. King Yudhiṣṭhira attentively heard the narration of the killing of Jarāsandha and the setting free of the kings. He also heard of the tactics adopted by Kṛṣṇa to kill Jarāsandha. The King was naturally affectionate toward Kṛṣṇa, but after hearing the story he became even more bound to Him in love; tears of ecstasy glided from his eyes, and he was so stunned that he was almost unable to speak.

Thus ends the Bhaktivedanta purport of the Seventy-third Chapter of Kṛṣṇa, *"Lord Kṛṣṇa Returns to the City of Hastināpura."*

CHAPTER SEVENTY-FOUR

The Deliverance of Śiśupāla

King Yudhiṣṭhira became very happy after hearing the details of the Jarāsandha episode, and he spoke as follows: "My dear Kṛṣṇa, O eternal form of bliss and knowledge, all the exalted directors of the affairs of this material world, including Lord Brahmā, Lord Śiva and King Indra, are always eager to receive and carry out orders from You, and whenever they are fortunate enough to receive such orders, they immediately take them and keep them on their heads. O Kṛṣṇa, You are unlimited, and although we sometimes think of ourselves as royal kings and rulers of the world and become puffed up over our paltry positions, we are very poor in heart. Actually, we are fit to be punished by You, but the wonder is that instead of punishing us You so kindly and mercifully accept our orders and carry them out properly. We are all very much surprised that Your Lordship can play the part of an ordinary human being, but we can understand that You are performing these activities just like a dramatic artist. Your real position is always exalted, exactly like that of the sun, which always remains at the same temperature during both the time of its rising and the time of its setting. Although we feel the difference in temperature between the rising and the setting sun, the temperature of the sun never changes. You are always transcendentally equipoised, neither pleased nor disturbed by any condition of material affairs. You are the Supreme Brahman, the Personality of Godhead, and for You there are no relativities. My dear Mādhava, You are never defeated by anyone. Material distinctions—'This is me,' 'This is you,' 'This is mine,' 'This is yours'—are all conspicuous by dint of their absence in You. Such distinctions are visible in the lives of everyone, even the animals, but pure devotees are freed from these false distinctions. Since these distinctions are absent in Your devotees, they cannot possibly be present in You."

After satisfying Kṛṣṇa in this way, King Yudhiṣṭhira arranged to perform the Rājasūya sacrifice. He invited all the qualified *brāhmaṇas* and sages to take part and appointed them to different positions as priests in charge of the sacrificial arena. He invited the most expert *brāhmaṇas* and sages, whose names are as follows: Kṛṣṇa-dvaipāyana Vyāsadeva, Bharadvāja, Sumantu, Gautama, Asita, Vasiṣṭha, Cyavana, Kaṇva, Maitreya, Kavaṣa, Trita, Viśvāmitra, Vāmadeva, Sumati, Jaimini, Kratu, Paila, Parāśara, Garga, Vaiśampāyana, Atharvā, Kaśyapa, Dhaumya, Paraśurāma, Śukrācārya, Āsuri, Vītihotra, Madhucchandā, Vīrasena and Akṛtavraṇa. Besides all these *brāhmaṇas* and sages, he invited such respectable old men as Droṇācārya, Bhīṣma (the grandfather of the Kurus), Kṛpācārya and Dhṛtarāṣṭra. He also invited all the sons of Dhṛtarāṣṭra, headed by Duryodhana, and also the great devotee Vidura. Kings from different parts of the world, along with their ministers and secretaries, were also invited to see the great sacrifice performed by King Yudhiṣṭhira, and the citizens, comprising learned *brāhmaṇas,* chivalrous *kṣatriyas,* well-to-do *vaiśyas* and faithful *śūdras,* all visited the ceremony.

The *brāhmaṇa* priests and sages in charge of the sacrificial ceremony constructed the sacrificial arena as usual with a plow of gold, and they initiated King Yudhiṣṭhira as the performer of the great sacrifice, in accordance with Vedic rituals. Long years ago, when Varuṇa performed a similar sacrifice, all the sacrificial utensils were made of gold. Similarly, in the Rājasūya sacrifice of King Yudhiṣṭhira, all the utensils required for the sacrifice were golden.

Present by the invitation of King Yudhiṣṭhira to participate in the great sacrifice were all the exalted demigods, including Lord Brahmā, Lord Śiva and Indra, the King of heaven, accompanied by their associates, as well as the predominating deities of the higher planetary systems, including Gandharvaloka, Siddhaloka, Janoloka, Tapoloka, Nāgaloka, Yakṣaloka, Rākṣasaloka, Pakṣiloka and Cāraṇaloka, as well as famous kings and their queens. All the respectable sages, kings and demigods who assembled there agreed unanimously that King Yudhiṣṭhira was quite competent to take the responsibility of performing the Rājasūya sacrifice; no one was in disagreement on this fact. Everyone thoroughly knew the position of King Yudhiṣṭhira; because he was a great devotee of Lord Kṛṣṇa, no accomplishment was extraordinary for him. The learned *brāhmaṇas* and priests saw to it that the sacrifice by Mahārāja Yudhiṣṭhira was performed in exactly the same way as it had been in bygone ages by the demigod Varuṇa. According to the Vedic system, whenever there is an arrangement for sacrifice, the members participating are offered the juice of the *soma* plant, which is a kind of life-giving beverage. On the day for extracting the *soma* juice, King Yudhiṣṭhira very respectfully received the special priest who had been engaged to detect any mistake in the formalities of sacrificial procedure. The idea is that the Vedic *mantras* must be enunciated perfectly and chanted with the proper accent; if the priests who are engaged in this business commit any mistake, the checker, or referee priest, immediately corrects the procedure, and thus the ritualistic performances are perfectly executed. Unless perfectly executed, a sacrifice cannot yield the desired result. In this Age of Kali there is no such learned *brāhmaṇa* or priest available; therefore, all such sacrifices are forbidden. The only sacrifice recommended in the *śāstras* is the chanting of the Hare Kṛṣṇa *mantra.*

Another important procedure is that the most exalted personality in the assembly of such a sacrificial ceremony is first offered worship. After all arrangements were made for Yudhiṣṭhira's sacrifice, the next consideration was who should be worshiped first in the ceremony. This particular ceremony is called Agra-pūjā. *Agra* means "first," and *pūjā* means "worship." This Agra-pūjā is similar to the election of a president. In the sacrificial assembly, all the members were very exalted. Some proposed to elect one person as the perfect candidate for accepting Agra-pūjā, and others proposed someone else.

When the matter remained undecided, Sahadeva began to speak in favor of Lord Kṛṣṇa. He said, "Lord Kṛṣṇa, the best amongst the members of the Yadu dynasty and the protector of His devotees, is the most exalted personality in this assembly. Therefore I think that He should without any objection be offered the honor of being worshiped first. Although demigods such as Lord Brahmā, Lord Śiva, Indra and many other exalted personalities are present in this assembly, no one can be equal to or greater than Kṛṣṇa in terms of time, space, riches, strength, reputation, wisdom, renunciation or any other consideration. Anything considered an opulence is fully present in Kṛṣṇa. As an individual soul is the basic principle of the growth of his material body, Kṛṣṇa is the Supersoul of this cosmic manifestation. All Vedic ritualistic ceremonies, such as the performance of sacrifices, the offering of oblations into the fire, the chanting of the Vedic hymns and the practice of mystic *yoga,* are meant for realizing Kṛṣṇa. Whether one follows the path of fruitive activities or the path of philosophical speculation, the ultimate destination is Kṛṣṇa; all bona fide methods of self-realization are meant for understanding Kṛṣṇa. Ladies and gentlemen, it is superfluous to speak about Kṛṣṇa, because every one of you exalted personalities knows the Supreme Brahman, Lord Kṛṣṇa, for whom there are no material differences between body and soul, between energy and the energetic, or between one part of the body and another. Since everyone is part and parcel of Kṛṣṇa, there is no qualitative difference between Kṛṣṇa and all living entities. Everything is an emanation of Kṛṣṇa's energies, material and spiritual. Kṛṣṇa's energies are like the heat and light of fire; there is no difference between the quality of heat and light and the fire itself.

"Also, Kṛṣṇa can do anything He likes with any part of His body. We can execute a particular action with the help of a particular part of our body, but He can do anything and everything with any part of His body. And because His transcendental body is full of knowledge and bliss in eternity, He doesn't undergo the six kinds of material changes—birth, existence, growth, production, dwindling and vanishing. Unforced by any external energy, He is the supreme cause of the creation, maintenance and dissolution of everything that be. By the grace of Kṛṣṇa only, everyone is engaged in the practice of religion, the development of economic conditions, the satisfaction of the senses and, ultimately, the achievement of liberation from material bondage. These four principles of progressive life can be executed by the mercy of Kṛṣṇa only. He should therefore be offered the first worship in this great sacrifice, and no one should disagree. Just as by watering the root of a tree one automatically waters the branches, twigs, leaves and flowers, or as by supplying food to the stomach one automatically nourishes all parts of the body, so by offering the first worship to Kṛṣṇa we shall satisfy everyone present in this meeting, including the great demigods. If anyone is charitably disposed, it will be very good for him to give charity only to

Kṛṣṇa, who is the Supersoul of everyone, regardless of his particular body or individual personality. Kṛṣṇa is present as the Supersoul in every living being, and if we can satisfy Him, then every living being will automatically be satisfied."

Sahadeva was fortunate to know of the glories of Kṛṣṇa, and after describing them in brief, he stopped speaking. After this speech, all the members present in that great sacrificial assembly applauded, confirming his words continuously by saying, "Everything you have said is completely perfect. Everything you have said is completely perfect." King Yudhiṣṭhira, after hearing the confirmation by all present, especially by the *brāhmaṇas* and learned sages, worshiped Lord Kṛṣṇa according to the regulative principles of the Vedic injunctions. First of all, King Yudhiṣṭhira, along with his brothers, wives, children, other relatives and ministers, washed the lotus feet of Lord Kṛṣṇa and sprinkled the water on their heads. After this, he offered Lord Kṛṣṇa various kinds of yellow silken garments and presented heaps of jewelry and ornaments before Him for His use.

King Yudhiṣṭhira felt such ecstasy by honoring Kṛṣṇa, his only lovable object, that tears glided down from his eyes, and although he wanted to see Lord Kṛṣṇa, he could not see Him very well. When Lord Kṛṣṇa was thus worshiped by King Yudhiṣṭhira, all the members present in the assembly stood up with folded hands and began to chant, *"Jaya! Jaya! Namaḥ! Namaḥ!"* All joined together to offer their respectful obeisances to Kṛṣṇa, and there were showers of flowers from the sky.

In that meeting, King Śiśupāla was also present. He was an avowed enemy of Kṛṣṇa for many reasons, especially because of Kṛṣṇa's having stolen Rukmiṇī from his intended marriage ceremony. Therefore, he could not tolerate such honoring of Kṛṣṇa and glorification of His qualities. Instead of being happy to hear the glories of the Lord, he became very angry. When everyone offered respect to Kṛṣṇa by standing up, Śiśupāla remained in his seat, but as he became angrier at

Kṛṣṇa's being honored, he stood up suddenly, raised his hand and spoke very strongly and fearlessly against Lord Kṛṣṇa in such a way that Lord Kṛṣṇa could hear him distinctly.

"Ladies and gentlemen, I can appreciate now the statement of the *Vedas* that, after all, time is the predominating factor. In spite of all endeavors to the contrary, the time element executes its own plan without opposition. For example, one may try his best to live, but when the time for death comes, no one can check it. I see here that although many stalwart personalities are present in this assembly, the influence of time is so strong that they have been misled by the statement of a boy who has foolishly spoken about Kṛṣṇa. Many learned sages and elderly persons are present, but still they have accepted the statement of a foolish boy. This means that by the influence of time even the intelligence of such honored persons as those present in this meeting can be misdirected. I fully agree with the respectable persons present here that they are competent to select the personality who can be worshiped first, but I cannot agree with the statement of a boy like Sahadeva, who has spoken so highly about Kṛṣṇa and has recommended that Kṛṣṇa is fit to accept the first worship in the sacrifice. I can see that in this meeting there are many personalities who have undergone great austerities, who are highly learned, and who have performed many penances. By their knowledge and direction, they can deliver many persons who are suffering from the pangs of material existence. There are great *ṛṣis* here whose knowledge has no bounds, as well as many self-realized persons and *brāhmaṇas* also, and therefore I think that any one of them could have been selected for the first worship because they are worshipable even by the great demigods, kings and emperors. I cannot understand how you have selected this cowherd boy, Kṛṣṇa, and have left aside all these great personalities. I think Kṛṣṇa to be no better than a crow—how can He be fit to accept the first worship in this great sacrifice?

"We cannot even ascertain which caste this Kṛṣṇa belongs

to or what His actual occupational duty is." Actually, Kṛṣṇa does not belong to any caste, nor does He have to perform any occupational duty. It is stated in the *Vedas* that the Supreme Lord has nothing to do as His prescribed duty. Whatever has to be done on His behalf is executed by His different energies.

Śiśupāla continued, "Kṛṣṇa does not belong to a high family. He is so independent that no one knows His principles of religious life. Indeed, it appears that He is outside the jurisdiction of all religious principles. He always acts independently, not caring for the Vedic injunctions and regulative principles. Therefore He is devoid of all qualities." Śiśupāla indirectly praised Kṛṣṇa by saying that He is not within the jurisdiction of Vedic injunctions. This is true because He is the Supreme Personality of Godhead. That He has no qualities means that Kṛṣṇa has no material qualities, and because He is the Supreme Personality of Godhead, He acts independently, not caring for conventions in social or religious principles.

Śiśupāla continued, "Under these circumstances, how can He be fit to accept the first worship in the sacrifice? Kṛṣṇa is so foolish that He has left Mathurā, which is inhabited by highly elevated persons following the Vedic culture, and has taken shelter in the ocean, where there is not even talk of the *Vedas*. Instead of living openly, He has constructed a fort within the water and is living in a place where there is no discussion of Vedic knowledge. And whenever He comes out of the fort, He simply harasses the citizens like a dacoit, thief or rogue."

Śiśupāla went crazy because of Kṛṣṇa's being elected the supreme, first-worshiped person in that meeting, and he spoke so irresponsibly that it appeared that he had lost all his good fortune. Being overcast with misfortune, Śiśupāla continued to insult Kṛṣṇa, and Lord Kṛṣṇa patiently heard him without protest. Just as a lion does not care when a flock of jackals howl, Lord Kṛṣṇa remained silent and unprovoked. Kṛṣṇa did not reply to even a single accusation made by Śiśupāla, but all the members present in the meeting, except for a few who agreed with Śiśupāla, were very much agitated because it is the duty of any respectable person not to tolerate blasphemy against God or His devotee. Some of them, who thought that they could not properly take action against Śiśupāla, left the assembly in protest, covering their ears with their hands in order not to hear further accusations. Thus they left the meeting, condemning the action of Śiśupāla. It is the Vedic injunction that whenever there is blasphemy of the Supreme Personality of Godhead, one must immediately leave. If he does not do so, he becomes bereft of his pious activities and is degraded to a lower condition of life.

All the kings present, belonging to the Kuru dynasty, Matsya dynasty, Kekaya dynasty and Sṛñjaya dynasty, were very angry and immediately took up their swords and shields to kill Śiśupāla, who was so foolish that he was not even slightly agitated, although all the kings present were ready to kill him. Śiśupāla did not care to think of the pros and cons of his foolish talking, and instead of stopping when he saw that all the kings were ready to kill him, he stood to fight with them and took up his sword and shield. When Lord Kṛṣṇa saw that they were going to fight in the arena of the auspicious Rājasūya-yajña, He personally pacified them. Out of His causeless mercy He Himself decided to kill Śiśupāla. When Śiśupāla was abusing the kings who were about to attack him, Lord Kṛṣṇa took up His disc, as sharp as the blade of a razor, and immediately separated Śiśupāla's head from his body.

When Śiśupāla was thus killed, a great roar and howl went up from the crowd. Taking advantage of that disturbance, the few kings who were supporters of Śiśupāla quickly left the assembly out of fear for their lives. Then the fortunate Śiśupāla's spirit soul immediately merged into the body of Lord Kṛṣṇa in the presence of all, exactly as a burning meteor falls to the surface of the globe. The merging of Śiśupāla's soul into the transcendental body of Kṛṣṇa reminds us of the story of Jaya and Vijaya, who fell to the material world from the Vaikuṇṭha planets upon being cursed by the four Kumāras. For their return to the Vaikuṇṭha world, it was arranged that both Jaya and Vijaya, for three consecutive births, would act as deadly enemies of the Lord, and that at the end of these lives they would return to the Vaikuṇṭha world and serve the Lord as His associates.

Although Śiśupāla acted as the enemy of Kṛṣṇa, he was not for a single moment out of Kṛṣṇa consciousness. He was always absorbed in thought of Kṛṣṇa, and thus he first got the salvation of *sāyujya-mukti,* merging into the existence of the Supreme, and was finally reinstated in his original position of personal service. The *Bhagavad-gītā* corroborates the fact that one who is absorbed in the thought of the Supreme Lord at the time of death immediately enters the kingdom of God after quitting his material body. After the salvation of Śiśupāla, King Yudhiṣṭhira rewarded all the members present in the sacrificial assembly. He sufficiently remunerated the priests and learned sages for their engagement in the execution of the sacrifice, and after performing all this routine work, he took his bath. This bath at the end of the sacrifice is also technical. It is called the *avabhṛtha* bath.

Lord Kṛṣṇa thus enabled the performance of the Rājasūya-yajña arranged by King Yudhiṣṭhira to be successfully completed, and, being requested by His cousins and relatives, He remained in Hastināpura for a few months more. Although King Yudhiṣṭhira and his brothers were unwilling to have Lord Kṛṣṇa leave Hastināpura, Kṛṣṇa arranged to take permission from the King to return to Dvārakā, and thus He returned home along with His queens and ministers.

The story of the fall of Jaya and Vijaya from the Vaikuṇṭha planets to the material world is described in the Seventh Canto of *Śrīmad-Bhāgavatam.* The killing of Śiśupāla has a direct link with that narration of Jaya and Vijaya, but the most important instruction we get from this incident is that the Supreme Personality of Godhead, being absolute, can give salvation to everyone, whether one acts as His enemy or as His friend. It is therefore a misconception that the Lord acts with someone in relationship of friend and with someone else in the relationship of enemy. His being an enemy or friend is always on the absolute platform. There is no material distinction.

After King Yudhiṣṭhira took his bath at the conclusion of the sacrifice and stood in the midst of all the learned sages and *brāhmaṇas,* he seemed exactly like the King of heaven and thus looked very beautiful. King Yudhiṣṭhira sufficiently rewarded all the demigods who participated in the *yajña,* and, being greatly satisfied, all of them left, praising the King's activities and glorifying Lord Kṛṣṇa.

When Śukadeva Gosvāmī narrated these incidents of Kṛṣṇa's killing Śiśupāla and described the successful execution of the Rājasūya-yajña by Mahārāja Yudhiṣṭhira, he also pointed out that after the successful termination of the *yajña* only one person was unhappy. He was Duryodhana. Duryodhana by nature was very envious because of his sinful life, and he appeared in the dynasty of the Kurus like a chronic disease personified to destroy the whole family.

Śukadeva Gosvāmī assured Mahārāja Parīkṣit that the pastimes of Lord Kṛṣṇa—the killing of Śiśupāla and Jarāsandha and the releasing of the imprisoned kings—are all transcendental vibrations, and that anyone who hears these narrations from authorized persons will immediately be freed from all the reactions of the sinful activities of his life.

Thus ends the Bhaktivedanta purport of the Seventy-fourth Chapter of Kṛṣṇa, *"The Deliverance of Śiśupāla."*

CHAPTER SEVENTY-FIVE

Why Duryodhana Felt Insulted at the End of the Rājasūya Sacrifice

King Yudhiṣṭhira was known as *ajāta-śatru,* or a person who had no enemy. Therefore, when all the men, demigods, kings, sages and saints saw the successful termination of the Rājasūya-yajña performed by King Yudhiṣṭhira, they were very happy. That Duryodhana alone was unhappy was astonishing to Mahārāja Parīkṣit, and therefore he requested Śukadeva Gosvāmī to explain this.

Śukadeva Gosvāmī said, "My dear King Parīkṣit, your grandfather King Yudhiṣṭhira was a great soul. His congenial disposition attracted everyone to be his friend, and therefore he was known as *ajāta-śatru,* one who never created an enemy. He engaged all the members of the Kuru dynasty in taking charge of different departments for the management of the Rājasūya sacrifice. For example, Bhīmasena was put in charge of the kitchen department, Duryodhana in charge of the treasury department, Sahadeva in charge of the reception department, Nakula in charge of the store department, and Arjuna in charge of looking after the comforts of the elderly persons. The most astonishing feature was that Kṛṣṇa, the Supreme Personality of Godhead, took charge of washing the feet of all the incoming guests. The Queen, the goddess of fortune Draupadī, was in charge of administering the distribution of food, and because Karṇa was famous for giving charity, he was put in charge of the charity department. In this way Sātyaki, Vikarṇa, Hārdikya, Vidura, Santardana and Bhūriśravā, the son of Bāhlīka, were all engaged in different departments for managing the affairs of the Rājasūya sacrifice. They were all so bound in loving affection for King Yudhiṣṭhira that they simply wanted to please him.

After Śiśupāla died by the mercy of Lord Kṛṣṇa and merged into the spiritual existence, and after the end of the Rājasūya-yajña, when all the friends, guests and well-wishers had been sufficiently honored and rewarded, King Yudhiṣṭhira went to bathe in the Ganges. The city of Hastināpura stands today on the bank of the Yamunā, and the statement of *Śrīmad-Bhāgavatam* that King Yudhiṣṭhira went to bathe in the Ganges indicates, therefore, that during the time of the Pāṇḍavas the river Yamunā was also known as the Ganges. While the King was taking the *avabhṛtha* bath, different musical instruments vibrated, such as *mṛdaṅgas,* conchshells, *paṇava* drums, kettledrums and bugles, and the ankle bells of the dancing girls jingled. Many groups of professional singers played *vīṇās,* flutes, gongs and cymbals, and thus a tumultuous sound vibrated in the sky. The princely guests from many kingdoms, like Sṛñjaya, Kāmboja, Kuru, Kekaya and Kośala, were present with their different flags and gorgeously decorated elephants, chariots, horses and soldiers. All of them passed in a procession, with King Yudhiṣṭhira in the forefront. The executive members who had performed the sacrifice—the priests, religious ministers and *brāhmaṇas*—all loudly chanted the Vedic hymns. The demigods and the inhabitants of Pitṛloka and Gandharvaloka, as well as many sages, showered flowers from the sky. The men and women of Hastināpura, or Indraprastha, their bodies smeared with scents and floral oils, were nicely dressed in colorful garments and decorated with garlands, jewels and ornaments. Enjoying the ceremony, they threw on one another liquid substances like water, oil, milk, butter and yogurt. Some even smeared these on each other's bodies. In this way, they enjoyed the occasion. The professional prostitutes jubilantly smeared these liquid substances on the bodies of the men, and the men reciprocated in the same way. All the liquid substances had been mixed with turmeric and saffron, and their color was a lustrous yellow.

In order to observe the great ceremony, many wives of the demigods had come in different airplanes, and they were visible in the sky. Similarly, the queens of the royal family, gorgeously decorated and surrounded by bodyguards, arrived on different palanquins. During this time, Lord Kṛṣṇa, the maternal cousin of the Pāṇḍavas, and His special friend Arjuna were both throwing the liquid substances on the bodies of the queens. The queens became bashful, but at the same time their beautiful smiling brightened their faces. Because of the liquids thrown on their bodies, the saris covering them became completely wet. The different parts of their beautiful bodies, particularly their breasts and their waists, became partially visible because of the wet cloth. The queens brought buckets of the same liquid substances and with syringes sprinkled them on the bodies of their brothers-in-law. As they engaged in such jubilant activities, their hair fell loose, and the flowers decorating their bodies began to fall. When Lord Kṛṣṇa, Arjuna and the queens were thus engaged in these jubilant activities, persons who were not clean in heart were agitated by lustful desires. In other words, such behavior between pure males and females is enjoyable, but it makes persons who are materially contaminated become lustful.

King Yudhiṣṭhira, in a gorgeous chariot yoked to excellent

horses, was present there along with his queens, including Draupadī, and their features were so beautiful that it appeared as if the great Rājasūya sacrifice were standing there in person, along with the different functions of the sacrifice.

Following the Rājasūya sacrifice, there was the Vedic ritualistic duty known as *patnī-saṁyāja.* This sacrifice, which one performs along with one's wife, was also duly conducted by the priests of King Yudhiṣṭhira. As Queen Draupadī and King Yudhiṣṭhira were taking their *avabhṛtha* bath, the citizens of Hastināpura as well as the demigods began to beat on drums and blow trumpets out of feelings of happiness, and there was a shower of flowers from the sky. When the King and the Queen finished their bath in the Ganges, all the other citizens, consisting of all the *varṇas,* or castes—the *brāhmaṇas, kṣatriyas, vaiśyas* and *śūdras*—took their baths in the Ganges. Bathing in the Ganges is recommended in the Vedic literatures because by such bathing one is freed from all sinful reactions. This is still current in India, especially at particularly auspicious moments. At such times, millions of people bathe in the Ganges.

After taking his bath, King Yudhiṣṭhira dressed in a new silken cloth and wrapper and decorated himself with valuable jewelry. The King not only dressed himself and decorated himself but also gave clothing and ornaments to all the priests and the others who had participated in the *yajñas.* In this way, he worshiped them all. He constantly worshiped his friends, his family members, his relatives, his well-wishers and everyone present, and because he was a Vaiṣṇava, a great devotee of Lord Nārāyaṇa, he knew how to treat everyone well. The Māyāvādī philosophers' endeavor to see everyone as God is an artificial attempt at oneness, but a Vaiṣṇava, or a devotee of Lord Nārāyaṇa, sees every living entity as part and parcel of the Supreme Lord. Therefore, a Vaiṣṇava's treatment of other living entities is on the absolute platform. As one cannot treat one part of his body differently from another part, because they all belong to the same body, a Vaiṣṇava does not see a human being as distinct from an animal because in both he sees the soul and the Supersoul seated together.

When everyone was refreshed after bathing and was dressed in silken clothing with jeweled earrings, flower garlands, turbans, long wrappers and pearl necklaces, they looked, all together, like the demigods from heaven. This was especially true of the women, who were very nicely dressed. Each wore a golden belt around the waist. They were all smiling, with spots of *tilaka* and curling hair scattered here and there. This combination was very attractive.

Those persons who had participated in the Rājasūya sacrifice—including the most cultured priests, the *brāhmaṇas* who had assisted, the citizens of all the *varṇas,* and the kings, demigods, sages, saints and citizens of Pitṛloka—were all very much satisfied by the dealings of King Yudhiṣṭhira, and at the end they happily departed for their residences. While returning to their homes, they talked of the dealings of King Yudhiṣṭhira, and even after continuous talk of his greatness they were not satiated, just as one may drink nectar over and over again and never be satisfied. After the departure of all the others, Mahārāja Yudhiṣṭhira restrained the inner circle of his friends, including Lord Kṛṣṇa, not allowing them to leave. Lord Kṛṣṇa could not refuse the request of the King. Kṛṣṇa therefore sent back all the heroes of the Yadu dynasty, like Sāmba and others. All of them returned to Dvārakā, and Lord Kṛṣṇa personally remained to give pleasure to the King.

In the material world, everyone has a particular type of desire to be fulfilled, but one is never able to fulfill his desires to his full satisfaction. But King Yudhiṣṭhira, because of his unflinching devotion to Kṛṣṇa, could fulfill all his desires successfully by the performance of the Rājasūya sacrifice. From the description of the Rājasūya-yajña, such a function appears to be a great ocean of opulent desires. Such an ocean is not possible for an ordinary man to cross; nevertheless, by the grace of Lord Kṛṣṇa, King Yudhiṣṭhira was able to cross it very easily, and thus he became freed from all anxieties.

When Duryodhana saw that Mahārāja Yudhiṣṭhira had become very famous after performing the Rājasūya-yajña and was fully satisfied in every respect, he began to burn with the fire of envy because his mind was always poisonous. For one thing, he envied the imperial palace constructed by the demon Maya for the Pāṇḍavas. The palace was excellent in its puzzling artistic workmanship and was befitting the position of great princes, kings or leaders of the demons. In that great palace, the Pāṇḍavas lived with their family members, and Queen Draupadī served her husbands very peacefully. And because in those days Lord Kṛṣṇa was also there, the palace was also decorated by His thousands of queens. When the queens, with their heavy breasts and thin waists, moved within the palace and their ankle bells rang very melodiously with their movement, the whole palace appeared more opulent than the heavenly kingdom. Because a portion of their breasts was sprinkled with saffron powder, the pearl necklaces on their breasts appeared reddish. With their beautiful earrings and flowing hair, the queens appeared very attractive. After seeing such beauties in the palace of King Yudhiṣṭhira, Duryodhana was envious. He was especially envious and lustful upon seeing the beauty of Draupadī because he had cherished a special attraction for her from the very beginning of her marriage with the Pāṇḍavas. In the marriage selection assembly of Draupadī, Duryodhana had also been present, and along with other princes he had been very much captivated by the beauty of Draupadī, but he had failed to achieve her.

Once upon a time, King Yudhiṣṭhira was sitting on his golden throne in the palace constructed by the demon Maya. His four brothers and other relatives, as well as his great well-wisher Kṛṣṇa, the Supreme Personality of Godhead, were present, and the material opulence of King Yudhiṣṭhira seemed no less than that of Lord Brahmā. When he was sitting on the throne surrounded by his friends and the reciters were offering prayers to him in the form of nice songs,

Duryodhana came to the palace with his younger brothers. Duryodhana was decorated with a helmet, and he carried a sword in his hand. He was always in an envious and angry mood, and therefore on a slight provocation he spoke sharply with the doorkeepers and became angry. By the craftsmanship of the demon Maya, the palace was so decorated in different places that one who did not know the tricks would consider water to be land and land to be water. Duryodhana was also illusioned by this craftsmanship, and when crossing water, thinking it to be land, he fell in. When Duryodhana, out of his foolishness, had thus fallen, the queens enjoyed the incident by laughing. King Yudhiṣṭhira could understand the feelings of Duryodhana, and he tried to restrain the queens, but Lord Kṛṣṇa indicated that King Yudhiṣṭhira should not restrain them from enjoying the incident. Kṛṣṇa desired that Duryodhana be fooled in that way and that all of them enjoy his foolish behavior. When everyone laughed, Duryodhana felt very insulted, and his bodily hairs stood up in anger. Being thus insulted, he immediately left the palace, bowing his head. He was silent and did not protest. When Duryodhana left in such an angry mood, everyone regretted the incident, and King Yudhiṣṭhira also was very sorry. But despite all these occurrences, Kṛṣṇa was silent. He did not say anything against or in favor of the incident. It appeared that Duryodhana had been put into illusion by the supreme will of Lord Kṛṣṇa, and this was the beginning of the enmity between the two sects of the Kuru dynasty. This appeared to be a part of Kṛṣṇa's plan in His mission to decrease the burden of the world.

King Parīkṣit had inquired from Śukadeva Gosvāmī why Duryodhana was not satisfied after the termination of the great Rājasūya sacrifice, and thus it was explained by Śukadeva Gosvāmī.

Thus ends the Bhaktivedanta purport of the Seventy-fifth Chapter of Kṛṣṇa, *"Why Duryodhana Felt Insulted at the End of the Rājasūya Sacrifice."*

CHAPTER SEVENTY-SIX

The Battle Between Śālva and Members of the Yadu Dynasty

While Śukadeva Gosvāmī was narrating various activities of Lord Kṛṣṇa in playing the role of an ordinary human being, he also narrated the history of the battle between the dynasty of Yadu and a demon of the name Śālva, who had managed to possess a wonderful airship named Saubha. King Śālva was a great friend of Śiśupāla's. When Śiśupāla went to marry Rukmiṇī, Śālva was one of the members of the bridegroom's party. In the fight between the soldiers of the Yadu dynasty and the kings of the opposite side, Śālva was defeated by the soldiers of the Yadu dynasty. But, despite his defeat, he made a promise before all the kings that he would in the future rid the whole world of all the members of the Yadu dynasty. Since his defeat in the fight during the marriage of Rukmiṇī, he had maintained within himself an unforgettable envy of Lord Kṛṣṇa, and he was, in fact, a fool, because he had promised to kill Kṛṣṇa.

Usually such foolish demons take shelter of a demigod like Lord Śiva to execute their ulterior plans, and so in order to get strength, Śālva took refuge at the lotus feet of Lord Śiva. He underwent a severe type of austerity during which he would eat no more than a handful of ashes daily. Lord Śiva, the husband of Pārvatī, is generally very merciful, and he is very quickly satisfied if someone undertakes severe austerities to please him. So after continued austerities by Śālva for one year, Lord Śiva became pleased with him and asked him to beg for the fulfillment of his desire.

Śālva begged from Lord Śiva the gift of an airplane which would be so strong that it could not be destroyed by any demigod, demon, human being, Gandharva or Nāga, or even any Rākṣasa. Moreover, he desired that the airplane be able to fly anywhere and everywhere he would like to pilot it, and be specifically very dangerous and fearful to the dynasty of the Yadus. Lord Śiva immediately agreed to give him the benediction, and Śālva took the help of the demon Maya to manufacture this iron airplane, which was so strong and formidable that no one could crash it. It was a very big machine, almost like a big city, and it could fly so high and at such a great speed that it was almost impossible to see; so there was no question of attacking it. It appeared to be almost covered with darkness, yet the pilot could fly it anywhere and everywhere. Having acquired such a wonderful airplane, Śālva flew it to the city of Dvārakā because his main purpose in obtaining the airplane was to attack the city of the Yadus, toward whom he maintained a constant feeling of animosity.

Śālva thus attacked the city of Dvārakā from the sky, and he also surrounded the city by a large number of infantry. The soldiers on the surface attacked the beautiful spots of the city. They began to destroy the nice parks, the city gates, the palaces and skyscraper houses, .the high walls around the city, and the beautiful spots where people would gather for recreation. While the soldiers attacked on the surface, the airplane began to drop big slabs of stone, tree trunks, thunderbolts, poisonous snakes and many other dangerous things. Śālva also managed to create such a strong whirlwind within the city that all of Dvārakā became dark because of the dust that covered the sky. The airplane occupied by Śālva put the entire city of Dvārakā into distress equal to that caused on the earth long, long ago by the disturbing activities of Tripurāsura. The inhabitants of Dvārakā Purī became so harassed that they were not peaceful for even a moment.

The great heroes of Dvārakā City, headed by commanders such as Pradyumna, counterattacked the soldiers and airplane of Śālva. When he saw the extreme distress of the citizens, Pradyumna immediately arranged his soldiers and personally got up on a chariot, encouraging the citizens by assuring safety. Following his command, many warriors like Sātyaki, Cārudeṣṇa and Sāmba, all young brothers of Pradyumna, as well as Akrūra, Kṛtavarmā, Bhānuvinda, Gada, Śuka and Sāraṇa, all came out of the city to fight with Śālva. All of them were *mahā-rathīs,* great warriors able to fight with thousands of men. All were fully equipped with necessary weapons and assisted by hundreds and thousands of charioteers, elephants, horses and infantry soldiers. Fierce fighting began between the two parties, exactly like that formerly carried on between the demigods and the demons. The fighting was severe, and whoever observed the fierce nature of the fight felt his bodily hairs stand on end.

Pradyumna immediately counteracted the mystic demonstration occasioned by the airplane of Śālva, the King of Saubha. By the mystic power of the airplane, Śālva had created a darkness as dense as night, but Pradyumna all of a sudden appeared like the rising sun. As with the rising of the sun the darkness of night is immediately dissipated, with the appearance of Pradyumna the power exhibited by Śālva became null and void. Each of Pradyumna's arrows had a golden feather at the end, and the shaft was fitted with a sharp iron head. By releasing twenty-five such arrows, Pradyumna severely injured Śālva's commander in chief. He then released another one hundred arrows toward the body of Śālva. After this, he pierced each and every soldier by releasing one arrow, he killed the chariot drivers by firing ten arrows at each one of them, and he killed the carriers like the horses and elephants by the release of three arrows directed toward each one. When everyone present on the battlefield saw this wonderful feat of Pradyumna's, the great fighters on both sides praised his acts of chivalry.

But still the airplane occupied by Śālva was very mysterious. It was so extraordinary that sometimes many airplanes would appear to be in the sky, and sometimes there were apparently none. Sometimes the plane was visible and sometimes not visible, and the warriors of the Yadu dynasty were puzzled about the whereabouts of the peculiar airplane. Sometimes they would see the airplane on the ground, sometimes flying in the sky, sometimes resting on the peak of a hill, and sometimes floating on the water. The wonderful airplane flew in the sky like a whirling firebrand—it was not steady even for a moment. But despite the mysterious maneuvering of the airplane, the commanders and soldiers of the Yadu dynasty would immediately rush toward Śālva wherever he was present with his airplane and soldiers. The arrows released by the dynasty of the Yadus were as brilliant as the sun and as dangerous as the tongues of serpents. All the soldiers fighting on behalf of Śālva soon became distressed by the incessant release of arrows upon them by the heroes of the Yadu dynasty, and Śālva himself became unconscious from the attack of these arrows.

The soldiers fighting on behalf of Śālva were also very strong, and the release of their arrows also harassed the heroes of the Yadu dynasty. But still the Yadus were so strong and determined that they did not move from their strategic positions. The heroes of the Yadu dynasty were determined either to die on the battlefield or to gain victory. They were confident that if they died in the fighting they would attain a heavenly planet and if they came out victorious they would enjoy the world. The name of Śālva's commander in chief was Dyumān.

He was very powerful, and although bitten by twenty-five of Pradyumna's arrows, he suddenly attacked Pradyumna with his fierce club and struck him so strongly that Pradyumna became unconscious. Immediately there was a roaring, "Now he is dead! Now he is dead!" The force of the club on Pradyumna's chest was very severe, and it appeared as though his chest had been torn asunder.

Pradyumna's chariot was being driven by the son of Dāruka. According to Vedic military principles, the chariot driver and the hero on the chariot must cooperate during the fighting. As such, because it was the duty of the chariot driver to take care of the hero on the chariot during the dangerous and precarious fighting, Dāruka's son removed Pradyumna from the battlefield. Two hours later, in a quiet place, Pradyumna regained consciousness, and when he saw that he was in a place other than the battlefield, he addressed the charioteer and condemned him.

"Oh, you have done the most abominable act! Why have you removed me from the battlefield? My dear charioteer, I have never heard that any of our family members was ever removed from the battlefield. None of them left the battlefield while fighting. By this removal you have overburdened me with a great defamation. It will be said that I left the battlefield while fighting was going on. My dear charioteer, I must accuse you—you are a coward and emasculator! Tell me, how can I go before my uncle Balarāma and my father, Kṛṣṇa, and what shall I say before Them? Everyone will talk about me and say that I fled from the fighting place, and if they inquire from me about this, what will be my reply? My sisters-in-law will play jokes upon me with sarcastic words: 'My dear hero, how have you become such a coward? How have you become a eunuch? How have you become so low in the eyes of the fighters who opposed you?' I think, my dear charioteer, that you have committed a great offense by removing me from the battlefield."

The charioteer of Pradyumna replied, "My dear sir, I wish a long life for you. I think that I did nothing wrong, for it is the duty of the charioteer to help the fighter in the chariot when he is in a precarious condition. My dear sir, you are completely competent in the battlefield. But it is the duty of the charioteer and the warrior to protect each other in a precarious condition. I was completely aware of the regulative principles of fighting, and I did my duty. The enemy all of a sudden struck you with his club so severely that you lost consciousness. You were in a dangerous position, surrounded by your enemies. Therefore I was obliged to act as I did."

Thus ends the Bhaktivedanta purport of the Seventy-sixth Chapter of Kṛṣṇa, *"The Battle Between Śālva and Members of the Yadu Dynasty."*

CHAPTER SEVENTY-SEVEN

The Deliverance of Śālva

After talking with his charioteer, the son of Dāruka, Pradyumna could understand the real circumstances. Therefore he refreshed himself by washing his mouth and hands, and after arming himself properly with bows and arrows, he asked his charioteer to take him near the place where Śālva's commander in chief was standing. During the short absence of Pradyumna from the battlefield, Dyumān, Śālva's commander in chief, had been taking over the positions of the soldiers of the Yadu dynasty. Appearing on the battlefield, Pradyumna immediately stopped him and, smiling, shot eight arrows at him: with four arrows he killed Dyumān's four horses and with one arrow his chariot driver, with another arrow he cut his bow in two, with another he cut his flag to pieces, and with the last he severed his head from his body.

On the other fronts, heroes like Gada, Sātyaki and Sāmba were killing the soldiers of Śālva. The soldiers staying with Śālva in the airplane were also killed in the fighting, and they fell into the ocean. Each party began to strike the opposite party very severely in a fierce, dangerous battle that continued for twenty-seven days without stopping.

While the fight was going on in the city of Dvārakā, Kṛṣṇa was staying at Indraprastha with the Pāṇḍavas and King Yudhiṣṭhira. This fighting with Śālva took place after the Rājasūya-yajña had been performed by King Yudhiṣṭhira and after the killing of Śiśupāla. When Lord Kṛṣṇa understood that there was great danger in the city of Dvārakā, He took permission from the elderly members of the Pāṇḍava family, especially from His aunt Kuntīdevī, and started immediately for Dvārakā.

Lord Kṛṣṇa began to think that while He was staying in Hastināpura with Balarāma after the killing of Śiśupāla, Śiśupāla's men must have attacked Dvārakā. On reaching Dvārakā, Lord Kṛṣṇa saw that the whole city was greatly endangered. He placed Balarāmajī in a strategic position for the protection of the city, and He Himself asked His charioteer, Dāruka, to prepare to start. He said, "Dāruka, please immediately take Me to where Śālva is staying. You may know that this Śālva is a very powerful, mysterious man. Don't fear him in the least." As soon as he got his orders from Lord Kṛṣṇa, Dāruka had Him seated on the chariot and drove very quickly toward Śālva.

The chariot of Lord Kṛṣṇa was marked with the flag bearing the insignia of Garuḍa, and as soon as the soldiers and warriors of the Yadu dynasty saw the flag, they could understand that Lord Kṛṣṇa was on the battlefield. By this time, almost all the soldiers of Śālva had been killed, but when Śālva saw that Kṛṣṇa had come to the battlefield, he released a great, powerful weapon, which flew through the sky with a roaring sound like a great meteor. It was so bright that the whole sky was lit up by its presence. But as soon as Lord Kṛṣṇa appeared, He tore the great weapon into hundreds and thousands of pieces by releasing His own arrows.

Lord Kṛṣṇa struck Śālva with sixteen arrows, and with

showers of arrows He overpowered the airplane, just as the sun in a clear sky overpowers the whole sky by an unlimited number of molecules of sunshine. Śālva struck a severe blow to Kṛṣṇa's left side, where the Lord carried His bow, Śārṅga, and as a result the Śārṅga bow fell from Lord Kṛṣṇa's hand. This dropping of the bow was indeed wonderful. Great personalities and demigods who were observing the fighting between Śālva and Kṛṣṇa were most perturbed by this, and they exclaimed, "Alas! Alas!"

Śālva thought that he had become victorious, and with a roaring sound he addressed Lord Kṛṣṇa as follows: "You rascal, Kṛṣṇa! You kidnapped Rukmiṇī forcibly, even in our presence. You baffled my friend Śiśupāla and married Rukmiṇī Yourself. And in the great assembly at King Yudhiṣṭhira's Rājasūya-yajña, while my friend Śiśupāla was a little absent-minded, You took an opportunity to kill him. Everyone thinks that You are a great fighter and that no one can conquer You. So now You'll have to prove Your strength. I think that if You stand before me any longer, with my sharp arrows I shall send You to a place wherefrom You will never return."

To this Lord Kṛṣṇa replied, "Foolish Śālva, you are talking nonsensically. You do not know that the moment of death is already upon your head. Actual heroes do not talk much. They prove their prowess by practical exhibition of chivalrous activities." After saying this, Lord Kṛṣṇa, in great anger, struck Śālva on the collarbone with His club so severely that Śālva began to vomit blood and tremble as if he were going to collapse from severe cold. Before Kṛṣṇa was able to strike him again, however, Śālva became invisible by his mystic power.

Within a few moments, a mysterious, unknown man came before Lord Kṛṣṇa. Crying loudly, he bowed down at the Lord's lotus feet and said to Him, "Since You are the most beloved son of Your father, Vasudeva, Your mother, Devakī, has sent me to inform You of the unfortunate news that Śālva has arrested Your father and taken him away by force, just as a butcher mercilessly takes away an animal." When Lord Kṛṣṇa heard this unfortunate news from the unknown man, He at first became most perturbed, just like an ordinary human being. His face showed signs of grief, and He began to cry in a piteous tone, "How could that happen? My brother, Lord Balarāma, is there, and it is impossible for anyone to conquer Balarāmajī. He is in charge of Dvārakā City, and I know He is always alert. How could Śālva possibly enter the city and arrest My father in that way? Whatever Śālva may be, his power is limited, so how could it be possible that he has conquered the strength of Balarāmajī and taken away My father, arresting him as described by this man? Alas! Destiny is, after all, very powerful."

While Śrī Kṛṣṇa was thinking like this, Śālva brought before Him in custody a man exactly resembling Vasudeva, His father. These were all creations of the mystic power of Śālva.

Śālva addressed Kṛṣṇa, "You rascal, Kṛṣṇa! Look. This is Your father, who has begotten You and by whose mercy You are still living. Now just see how I kill Your father. If You have any strength, try to save him." The mystic juggler Śālva, speaking in this way before Lord Kṛṣṇa, immediately cut off the head of the false Vasudeva. Then without hesitation he took away the dead body and got into his airplane. Lord Kṛṣṇa is the self-sufficient Supreme Personality of Godhead, yet because He was playing the role of a human being, He became very depressed for a moment, as if He had actually lost His father. But at the next moment He could understand that the arrest and killing of His father were demonstrations of the mystic powers which Śālva had learned from the demon Maya. Coming to His right consciousness, He could see that there was no messenger and no head of His father but that Śālva had left in his airplane, which was flying in the sky. He then began to think of slaying Śālva.

Kṛṣṇa's reaction is a controversial point among great authorities and saintly persons. How could Kṛṣṇa, the Supreme

Personality of Godhead, the reservoir of all power and knowledge, be bewildered in such a way? Lamentation, aggrievement and bewilderment are characteristics of conditioned souls, but how can such things affect the person of the Supreme, who is full of knowledge, power and all opulence? Actually, it is not at all possible that Lord Kṛṣṇa was misled by the mystic jugglery of Śālva. He was displaying His pastime in playing the role of a human being. Great saintly persons and sages who are engaged in the devotional service of the lotus feet of Lord Kṛṣṇa and who have thus achieved the greatest perfection of self-realization have transcended the bewilderments of the bodily concept of life. Lord Kṛṣṇa is the ultimate goal of life for such saintly persons. How then could Kṛṣṇa have been bewildered by the mystic jugglery of Śālva? The conclusion is that Lord Kṛṣṇa's bewilderment was another opulence of His supreme personality.

When Śālva thought that Kṛṣṇa had been bewildered by his mystic representations, he became encouraged and began to attack the Lord with greater strength and energy by showering volleys of arrows upon Him. But the enthusiasm of Śālva can be compared to the speedy march of moths into a fire. Lord Kṛṣṇa, by hurling His arrows with unfathomable strength, injured Śālva, whose armor, bow and jeweled helmet all scattered in pieces. With a crashing blow from Kṛṣṇa's club, Śālva's wonderful airplane burst into pieces and fell into the sea. Śālva was very careful, and instead of crashing with the airplane, he managed to jump onto the land. He again rushed toward Lord Kṛṣṇa. When Śālva ran swiftly to attack Kṛṣṇa with his club, Lord Kṛṣṇa cut off his hand, which fell to the ground with the club. Finally deciding to kill him, the Lord took up His wonderful disc, which shone like the brilliant sun at the time of the dissolution of the material creation. When Lord Śrī Kṛṣṇa stood up with His disc to kill Śālva, He appeared just like a mountain with the red sun rising over it. Lord Kṛṣṇa then cut off Śālva's head, and the head, with its earrings and helmet, fell to the ground. Śālva was thus killed in the same way that Vṛtrāsura was killed by Indra, the King of heaven.

When Śālva was killed, all his soldiers and followers cried, "Alas! Alas!" While Śālva's men were thus crying, the demigods from the heavenly planets showered flowers on Kṛṣṇa and announced the victory by beating drums and blowing bugles. At that very moment, other friends of Śiśupāla, such as Dantavakra, appeared on the scene to fight with Kṛṣṇa and avenge the death of Śiśupāla and others. When Dantavakra appeared before Lord Kṛṣṇa, he was extremely angry.

Thus ends the Bhaktivedanta purport of the Seventy-seventh Chapter of Kṛṣṇa, *"The Deliverance of Śālva."*

CHAPTER SEVENTY-EIGHT

The Killing of Dantavakra, Vidūratha and Romaharṣaṇa

After the demise of Śiśupāla, Śālva and Pauṇḍraka, a foolish demoniac king of the name Dantavakra wanted to kill Kṛṣṇa to avenge the death of his friend Śālva. He became so agitated that he appeared on the battlefield without the proper arms and ammunition and without even a chariot. His only weapon was his great anger, which was red-hot. He carried only a club in his hand, but he was so powerful that when he moved, everyone felt the earth tremble. When Lord Kṛṣṇa saw him approaching in a very heroic mood, He immediately got down from His chariot, for it was a rule of military etiquette that fighting should take place only between equals. Knowing that Dantavakra was alone and armed with only a club, Lord Kṛṣṇa responded similarly and prepared Himself by taking His club in His hand. When Kṛṣṇa appeared before him, Dantavakra's heroic march was immediately stopped, just as the great, furious waves of the ocean are stopped by the beach.

At that time, Dantavakra, who was the King of Karūṣa, stood up firmly with his club and spoke to Lord Kṛṣṇa as follows: "It is a great pleasure and fortunate opportunity, Kṛṣṇa, that we are seeing each other face to face. My dear Kṛṣṇa, after all, You are my maternal cousin, and I should not kill You in this way, but unfortunately You have committed a great mistake by killing my friend Śālva. Moreover, You are not satisfied by killing my friend; I know that You want to kill me also. Because of Your determination, I must kill You by tearing You to pieces with my club. Kṛṣṇa, although You are my relative, You are foolish. You are our greatest enemy, so I must kill You today just as a person removes a boil on his body by a surgical operation. I am always very much obliged to my friends, and I therefore consider myself indebted to my dear friend Śālva. I can liquidate my indebtedness to him only by killing You."

As the caretaker of an elephant tries to control the animal by striking it with his trident, Dantavakra tried to control Kṛṣṇa simply by speaking strong words. After finishing his vituperation, he struck Kṛṣṇa on the head with his club and made a roaring sound like a lion, but Kṛṣṇa, although struck strongly by the club of Dantavakra, did not move even an inch, nor did He feel any pain. Taking His Kaumodakī club and moving very skillfully, Kṛṣṇa struck Dantavakra's chest so fiercely that Dantavakra's heart split in twain. As a result, Dantavakra began to vomit blood, his hair scattered, and he fell to the ground, spreading his hands and legs. Within only a few minutes all that remained of Dantavakra was a dead body on the ground. After the death of Dantavakra, just as at the time of Śiśupāla's death, in the presence of all the persons standing there a small particle of spiritual effulgence came out of the demon's body and very wonderfully merged into the body of Lord Kṛṣṇa.

Dantavakra had a brother named Vidūratha, who was overwhelmed with grief at Dantavakra's death. Out of grief and anger, Vidūratha was breathing very heavily, and just to avenge the death of his brother he appeared before Lord Kṛṣṇa with a sword and a shield in his hands. He wanted to kill Kṛṣṇa immediately. When Lord Kṛṣṇa understood that Vidūratha was looking for the opportunity to strike Him with his sword, He employed His Sudarśana *cakra,* His razor-sharp disc, and without delay cut off Vidūratha's head, with its helmet and earrings.

In this way, after killing Śālva and destroying his wonderful airplane and then killing Dantavakra and Vidūratha, Lord Kṛṣṇa at last entered His city, Dvārakā. It would not have been possible for anyone but Kṛṣṇa to kill these great heroes, and therefore all the demigods from heaven and the human beings on the surface of the globe were glorifying Him. Great sages and ascetics, the denizens of the Siddha and Gandharva planets, the denizens known as Vidyādharas, Vāsuki and the Mahānāgas, the beautiful angels, the inhabitants of Pitṛloka, the Yakṣas, the Kinnaras and the Cāraṇas all showered flowers upon Him and sang songs of His victory in great jubilation. Decorating the entire city very festively, the citizens of Dvārakā held a great celebration, and when Lord Kṛṣṇa passed through the city, all the members of the Vṛṣṇi dynasty and the heroes of the Yadu dynasty followed Him with great respect. These are some of the transcendental pastimes of Lord Kṛṣṇa, the master of all mystic power and the Lord of all cosmic manifestations. Those who are fools, who are like animals, sometimes think that Kṛṣṇa is defeated, but factually He is the Supreme Personality of Godhead, and no one can defeat Him. He always remains victorious over everyone. He alone is God, and all others are His subservient order-carriers.

Once upon a time, Lord Balarāma heard that an arrangement was being made for a fight between the two rival parties in the Kuru dynasty, one headed by Duryodhana and the other by the Pāṇḍavas. He did not like the idea that He was to be only a mediator to stop the fighting. Finding it unbearable not to take an active part on behalf of either of the parties, He left Dvārakā on the plea of visiting various holy places of pilgrimage. He first of all visited the place of pilgrimage known as Prabhāsa-kṣetra. He took His bath there, and He pacified the local *brāhmaṇas* and offered oblations to the demigods, Pitās, great sages and people in general, in accordance with Vedic ritualistic ceremonies. That is the Vedic method of visiting holy places. After this, accompanied by some respectable *brāhmaṇas,* He decided to visit different places on the bank of the river Sarasvatī. He gradually visited such places as Pṛthūdaka, Bindusara, Tritakūpa, Sudarśana-tīrtha, Viśāla-tīrtha, Brahma-tīrtha and Cakra-tīrtha. Besides these, He also visited all the holy places on the bank of the Sarasvatī River running toward the east. After this He visited all the principal holy places on the bank of the Yamunā and on the bank of the Ganges. Thus He gradually came to the holy place known as Naimiṣāraṇya.

This holy place, Naimiṣāraṇya, is still existing in India, and in ancient times it was especially used for the meetings of great sages and saintly persons with the aim of understanding spiritual life and self-realization. When Lord Balarāma visited that place there was a great sacrifice being performed by a great assembly of transcendentalists. Such meetings were planned to last thousands of years. When Lord Balarāma arrived, all the participants in the meeting—great sages, ascetics, *brāhmaṇas* and learned scholars—immediately arose from their seats and welcomed Him with great honor and respect. Some offered Him respects by standing up and then paying obeisances, and those who were elderly great sages and *brāhmaṇas* offered Him blessings after standing up. After this formality, Lord Balarāma was offered a suitable seat, and everyone present worshiped Him. Everyone in the assembly stood up in the presence of Balarāma because they knew Him to be the Supreme Personality of Godhead. Education or learning means to understand the Supreme Personality of Godhead; therefore, although Lord Balarāma appeared on the earth as a *kṣatriya,* all the *brāhmaṇas* and sages stood up because they knew who Lord Balarāma was.

Unfortunately, after being worshiped and seated in His place, Lord Balarāma saw Romaharṣaṇa, the disciple of Vyāsadeva (the literary incarnation of Godhead), still sitting on the *vyāsāsana.* He had neither gotten up from his seat nor offered Him respects. Because he was seated on the *vyāsāsana,* he foolishly thought himself greater than the Lord; therefore he did not get down from his seat or bow down before the Lord. Lord Balarāma then considered the history of Romaharṣaṇa: he was born in a *sūta* family, or a mixed family, born of a *brāhmaṇa* woman and a *kṣatriya* man. Therefore although Romaharṣaṇa considered Balarāma a *kṣatriya,* he should not have remained sitting on a higher seat; according to his position by birth he should not even have accepted the higher sitting position, because many learned *brāhmaṇas* and sages were present. Lord Balarāma also observed that Romaharṣaṇa not only refused to come down from his exalted seat but did not even stand up and offer his respects when Balarāmajī entered the assembly. Lord Balarāma did not like the audacity of Romaharṣaṇa and, becoming very angry at him, declared from His seat, "This man, Romaharṣaṇa, is so impudent that he has accepted a higher seat than that of all the respectable *brāhmaṇas* present here, although he was born in a degraded *pratiloma* family."

When a person is seated on the *vyāsāsana,* he does not generally have to stand to receive a particular person entering the assembly, but in this case the situation was different because Lord Baladeva is not an ordinary human being. Therefore, although Romaharṣaṇa Sūta was voted to the *vyāsāsana* by all the *brāhmaṇas,* he should have followed the behavior of other learned sages and *brāhmaṇas* present and should have known that Lord Balarāma is the Supreme Personality of Godhead. Respects are always due Him, even though such respects can be avoided in the case of an ordinary man. The appearance of Kṛṣṇa and Balarāma is especially meant for reestablishment of the religious principles. As stated in the *Bhagavad-gītā,* the highest religious principle is to surrender to the Supreme Personality of Godhead. *Śrīmad-Bhāgavatam* also confirms that the topmost perfection of religion is to be engaged in the devotional service of the Lord.

When Lord Balarāma saw that Romaharṣaṇa Sūta did not understand the highest principle of religion in spite of his having studied all the *Vedas,* He certainly could not support his position. Romaharṣaṇa Sūta had been given the chance to become a perfect *brāhmaṇa,* but because of his ill behavior in his relationship with the Supreme Personality of Godhead, his low birth was immediately remembered. Romaharṣaṇa Sūta had been given the position of a *brāhmaṇa,* but he had not been born in the family of a *brāhmaṇa;* he had been born in a *pratiloma* family. According to the Vedic concept, there are two kinds of mixed family heritage, called *anuloma* and *pratiloma.* When a male is united with a female of a lower caste, the offspring is called *anuloma;* but when a male unites with a woman of a higher caste, the offspring is called *pratiloma.* Romaharṣaṇa Sūta belonged to a *pratiloma* family because his father was a *kṣatriya* and his mother a *brāhmaṇa.* Because Romaharṣaṇa's transcendental realization was not perfect, Lord Balarāma remembered his *pratiloma* heritage. The idea is that any man may be given the chance to become a *brāhmaṇa,* but if he improperly uses the position of a *brāhmaṇa* without actual realization, then his elevation to the brahminical position is not valid.

After seeing the deficiency of realization in Romaharṣaṇa Sūta, Lord Balarāma decided to chastise him for being puffed up. Lord Balarāma therefore said, "This man is liable to be awarded the death punishment because although he has the good qualification of being a disciple of Lord Vyāsadeva, and although he has studied all the Vedic literature from this exalted personality, he was not submissive in the presence of the Supreme Personality of Godhead." As stated in the *Bhagavad-gītā,* a person who is actually a *brāhmaṇa* and is very learned must automatically become very gentle also. But although Romaharṣaṇa Sūta was very learned and had been given the chance to become a *brāhmaṇa,* he had not become gentle. From this we can understand that one who is puffed up by material acquisitions cannot acquire the gentle behavior befitting a *brāhmaṇa.* The learning of such a person is as good as a valuable jewel decorating the hood of a serpent. Despite the valuable jewel on the hood, a serpent is still a serpent and is as fearful as an ordinary serpent. If a person does not become meek and humble, all his studies of the *Vedas* and *Purāṇas* and his vast knowledge of the *śāstras* are simply outward dress, like the costume of a theatrical artist dancing on the stage. Lord Balarāma considered, "I have appeared in order to chastise false persons who are internally impure but externally pose themselves to be very learned and religious. My killing of such persons is proper, to check them from further sinful activity."

Lord Balarāma had avoided taking part in the Battle of Kurukṣetra, and yet because of His position as an incarnation, the reestablishment of religious principles was His prime duty. Considering these points, He killed Romaharṣaṇa Sūta simply by striking him with a *kuśa* straw, which was nothing but a blade of grass. If someone questions how Lord Balarāma could kill Romaharṣaṇa Sūta simply by striking him with a blade of *kuśa* grass, the answer is given in *Śrīmad-Bhāgavatam* by the use of the word *prabhu* ("master"). The Lord's position is always transcendental, and because He is omnipotent He can act as He likes, without being obliged to follow the material laws and principles. Thus it was possible for Him to kill Romaharṣaṇa Sūta simply by striking him with a blade of *kuśa* grass.

At the death of Romaharṣaṇa Sūta, everyone present became much aggrieved and cried out, "Alas! Alas!" Although all the *brāhmaṇas* and sages present knew Lord Balarāma to be the Supreme Personality of Godhead, they did not hesitate to protest the Lord's action. They humbly submitted, "Our dear Lord, we think that Your action is not in line with the religious principles. Dear Lord Yadunandana, we may inform You that we *brāhmaṇas* posted Romaharṣaṇa Sūta on that exalted position for the duration of this great sacrifice. He was seated on the *vyāsāsana* by our election, and when one is seated on the *vyāsāsana,* it is improper for him to stand up to receive a person. Moreover, we awarded Romaharṣaṇa Sūta an undisturbed duration of life. Under the circumstances, since Your Lordship has killed him without knowing all these facts, we think that Your action is equal to killing a *brāhmaṇa.* Dear Lord, deliverer of all fallen souls, we know for certain that You are the knower of all Vedic principles. You are the master of all mystic powers; therefore the Vedic injunctions cannot ordinarily be applied to Your personality. But we respectfully advise You to show Your causeless mercy upon others by kindly atoning for this killing of Romaharṣaṇa Sūta. We do not, however, suggest what kind of act You should perform to atone for killing him; we simply suggest that You adopt some method of atonement so that others may follow Your action. What is done by a great personality is followed by the ordinary man."

The Lord replied, "Yes, I must atone for this action, which may have been proper for Me but is improper for others; therefore, I think it is My duty to execute a suitable act of atonement enjoined in the authorized scriptures. Simultaneously I can also give this Romaharṣaṇa Sūta life again, with a span of long duration, sufficient strength and full power of the senses. Not only this, but if you desire I shall be glad to award him anything else you may ask. I shall be very glad to grant all these boons to fulfill your desires."

This statement by Lord Balarāma definitely confirms that the Supreme Personality of Godhead is free to act in any way. Although His killing of Romaharṣaṇa Sūta may be considered improper, He could immediately counteract it with greater profit to all. Therefore, one should not imitate the actions of the Supreme Personality of Godhead; one should simply follow the instructions of the Lord. All the great, learned sages present realized that although they considered the action of Lord Balarāma improper, the Lord was immediately able to compensate with greater profits. Not wanting to detract from the mission of the Lord in killing Romaharṣaṇa Sūta, all of them prayed, "Our dear Lord, the uncommon use of Your *kuśa* weapon to kill Romaharṣaṇa Sūta may remain as it is; because You desired to kill him, he should not be brought to life again. At the same time, Your Lordship may remember that we sages and *brāhmaṇas* voluntarily gave him long life; therefore, such a benediction should not be nullified." Thus the request of all the learned *brāhmaṇas* in the assembly was ambiguous because they wanted to keep intact their benediction that Romaharṣaṇa Sūta would continue to live until the end of the great sacrifice, but at the same time they did not want to nullify Balarāma's killing him.

The Supreme Personality of Godhead therefore solved the problem in a manner befitting His exalted position. He said, "Because the son is produced from the body of the father, the *Vedas* enjoin that the son is the father's representative. Therefore I say that Ugraśravā Sūta, the son of Romaharṣaṇa Sūta, should henceforth take his father's position and continue the discourses on the *Purāṇas,* and because you wanted Romaharṣaṇa to have a long duration of life, this benediction will be transferred to his son. The son, Ugraśravā, will therefore have all the facilities you offered—a long duration of life in a good and healthy body, with no disturbances and full strength of all the senses."

Lord Balarāma then implored all the sages and *brāhmaṇas*

that aside from the benediction offered to the son of Romaharṣaṇa, they should ask from Him any other benediction, and He would be prepared to fulfill it immediately. The Lord thus placed Himself in the position of an ordinary *kṣatriya* and informed the sages that He did not know in what way He could atone for His killing of Romaharṣaṇa, but whatever they would suggest He would be glad to accept.

The *brāhmaṇas* could understand the purpose of the Lord, and thus they suggested that He atone in a manner beneficial to them. They said, "Our dear Lord, there is a very powerful demon of the name Balvala. He is the son of Ilvala, and he visits this sacred place of sacrifice every fortnight on the full moon and moonless days and creates a great disturbance to the discharge of our duties in the sacrifice. O descendant of the Daśārha family, we all request You to kill this demon. We think that if You kindly kill him, that will be Your atonement on our behalf. The demon occasionally comes here and profusely throws upon us contaminated, impure things like pus, blood, stool, urine and wine; he pollutes this sacred place by showering such filth upon us. After killing Balvala, You may continue touring all the sacred places of pilgrimage for twelve months, and in that way You will be completely freed from all contamination. That is our prescription."

Thus ends the Bhaktivedanta purport of the Seventy-eighth Chapter of Kṛṣṇa, *"The Killing of Dantavakra, Vidūratha and Romaharṣaṇa."*

CHAPTER SEVENTY-NINE

The Liberation of Balvala, and Lord Balarāma's Touring the Sacred Places

Lord Balarāma prepared Himself to meet the demon Balvala. At the time when the demon usually attacked the sacred place, there appeared a great hailstorm, the whole sky became covered with dust, and the atmosphere became surcharged with a filthy smell. Just after this, the mischievous demon Balvala began to shower torrents of stool and urine and other impure substances on the arena of sacrifice. After this onslaught, the demon himself appeared with a great trident in his hand. He was a gigantic person, and his black body was like a huge mass of carbon. His hair, his beard and his mustache appeared reddish like copper, and because of his great beard and mustache, his mouth appeared dangerous and fierce. As soon as He saw the demon, Lord Balarāma prepared to attack him. He first considered how He could smash the great demon to pieces. Lord Balarāma then called for His plow and club, and they immediately appeared before

Him. The demon Balvala was flying in the sky, and at the first opportunity Lord Balarāma dragged him down with His plow and angrily smashed the demon's head with His club. Balarāma's striking fractured the demon's forehead, making blood flow profusely. Screaming loudly, the demon, who had been such a great disturbance to the pious *brāhmaṇas,* fell to the ground like a great mountain with a red oxide peak being struck and smashed to the ground by a thunderbolt.

The inhabitants of Naimiṣāraṇya, learned sages and *brāhmaṇas,* became most pleased by seeing this, and they offered their respectful prayers to Lord Balarāma. They offered their heartfelt blessings to the Lord, and all agreed that none of Lord Balarāma's attempts to do something would ever be a failure. The sages and *brāhmaṇas* then performed a ceremonial bathing of Lord Balarāma, just as the demigods bathe King Indra when he is victorious over the demons. The *brāhmaṇas* and sages honored Lord Balarāma by presenting Him with first-class new clothing and ornaments and the lotus garland of victory; this garland was the reservoir of all beauty and was everlasting—it was never to be dried up.

After this incident, Lord Balarāma took permission from the *brāhmaṇas* assembled at Naimiṣāraṇya and, accompanied by other *brāhmaṇas,* went to the bank of the river Kauśikī. After taking His bath in this holy place, He proceeded toward the river Sarayū and visited the source of the river. Traveling on the bank of the Sarayū River, He gradually reached Prayāga, where there is a confluence of three rivers—the Ganges, Yamunā and Sarasvatī. Here also He took His bath, and then He worshiped in the local temples of the demigods and, as enjoined in the Vedic literature, offered oblations to the forefathers and sages. He gradually reached the *āśrama* of the sage Pulaha and from there went to the rivers Gaṇḍakī and Gomatī. After this He took His bath in the river Vipāśā. Then He gradually came to the bank of the Śoṇa River. (The Śoṇa River is still running as one of the big rivers in Bihar

Province.) He also took His bath there and performed the Vedic ritualistic ceremonies. He continued His travels and gradually came to the pilgrimage city of Gayā, where there is a celebrated Viṣṇu temple. According to the advice of His father, Vasudeva, He offered oblations to the forefathers in this Viṣṇu temple. From here He traveled to the delta of the Ganges, where the sacred river Ganges mixes with the Bay of Bengal. This sacred place is called Gaṅgāsāgara, and at the end of January every year there is still a great assembly of saintly persons and pious men, just as there is an assembly of saintly persons in Prayāga every year called the Māgha-melā fair.

After finishing His bathing and ritualistic ceremonies at Gaṅgāsāgara, Lord Balarāma proceeded toward the mountain known as Mahendra Parvata, where He met Paraśurāma, the incarnation of Lord Kṛṣṇa, and offered Him respect by bowing down before Him. After this He turned toward southern India and visited the banks of the river Godāvarī. After taking His bath in the river Godāvarī and performing the necessary ritualistic ceremonies, He gradually visited the other rivers—the Veṇā, Pampā and Bhīmarathī. On the bank of the river Bhīmarathī is the deity called Svāmī Kārttikeya. After visiting Kārttikeya, Lord Balarāma gradually proceeded to Śailapura, a pilgrimage city in the province of Mahārāṣṭra. Śailapura is one of the biggest districts in Mahārāṣṭra Province. He then gradually proceeded toward Draviḍa-deśa. Southern India is divided into five parts, called Pañca-draviḍa. Northern India is also divided into five parts, called Pañca-gauḍa. All the important *ācāryas* of the modern age—namely Śaṅkarācārya, Rāmānujācārya, Madhvācārya, Viṣṇu Svāmī and Nimbārka—advented themselves in these Draviḍa provinces. Lord Caitanya, however, appeared in Bengal, which is part of the five Gauḍa-deśas.

The most important place of pilgrimage in southern India, or Draviḍa, is Veṅkaṭācala, commonly known as Bālajī. After visiting this place Lord Balarāma proceeded toward Viṣṇu-kāñcī, and from there He proceeded on the bank of the Kāverī. While going to Viṣṇukāñcī, He visited Śivakāñcī. Lord Balarāma took His bath in the river Kāverī; then He gradually reached Raṅgakṣetra. The biggest Viṣṇu temple in the world is in Raṅgakṣetra, and the Viṣṇu Deity there is celebrated as Raṅganātha. There is a similar temple of Raṅganātha in Vṛndāvana. Although not as big as the temple in Raṅgakṣetra, it is the biggest in Vṛndāvana.

After visiting Raṅgakṣetra, Lord Balarāma gradually proceeded toward Madurai, commonly known as the Mathurā of southern India. After visiting this place, He gradually proceeded toward Setubandha, the place where Lord Rāmacandra constructed the stone bridge from India to Laṅkā (Ceylon). In this particularly holy place, Lord Balarāma distributed ten thousand cows to the local *brāhmaṇa* priests. It is the Vedic custom that when a rich visitor goes to any place of pilgrimage he gives the local priests houses, cows, ornaments and garments as gifts of charity. This system of visiting places of pilgrimage and providing the local *brāhmaṇa* priests with all necessities of life has greatly deteriorated in this Age of Kali. The richer section of the population, because of its degradation in Vedic culture, is no longer attracted by these places of pilgrimage, and the *brāhmaṇa* priests who depended on such visitors have also deteriorated in their professional duty of helping the visitors. These *brāhmaṇa* priests in the places of pilgrimage are called *paṇḍā* or *paṇḍita.* This means that they were formerly very learned *brāhmaṇas* and used to guide the visitors in all details of the purpose of coming there, and thus both the visitors and the priests benefited by mutual cooperation.

It is clear from the description of *Śrīmad-Bhāgavatam* that when Lord Balarāma was visiting the different places of pilgrimage He properly followed the Vedic system. After distributing cows at Setubandha, Lord Balarāma proceeded toward the Kṛtamālā and Tāmraparṇī rivers. These two rivers are celebrated as sacred, and Lord Balarāma bathed in them both. He then proceeded toward Malaya Hill. This Malaya Hill is very great, and it is said to be one of seven peaks called the Malaya Hills. The great sage Agastya used to live there, and Lord Balarāma visited him and offered His respects by bowing down before him. After taking the sage's blessings, Lord Balarāma, with the sage's permission, proceeded toward the Indian Ocean.

At the point of the cape (known today as Cape Comorin) is a big temple of goddess Durgā, who is known there as Kanyākumārī. This temple of Kanyākumārī was also visited by Lord Rāmacandra, and therefore it is to be understood that the temple has been existing for millions of years. From there, Lord Balarāma went on to visit the pilgrimage city known as Phālguna-tīrtha, which is on the shore of the Indian Ocean, or the Southern Ocean. Phālguna-tīrtha is celebrated because Lord Viṣṇu in His incarnation of Ananta is lying there. From Phālguna-tīrtha, Lord Balarāma went on to visit another pilgrimage spot, known as Pañcāpsarasa. There also He bathed according to the regulative principles and observed the ritualistic ceremonies. This site is also celebrated as a shrine of Lord Viṣṇu; therefore Lord Balarāma distributed ten thousand cows to the local *brāhmaṇa* priests.

From Cape Comorin Lord Balarāma turned toward Kerala. The country of Kerala is still existing in southern India under the name of South Kerala. After visiting this place, He came to Gokarṇa-tīrtha, where Lord Śiva is constantly worshiped. Balarāma then visited the temple of Āryādevī, which is completely surrounded by water. From that island He went on to a place known as Śūrpāraka. After this He bathed in the rivers known as Tāpī, Payoṣṇī and Nirvindhyā, and then He came to the forest known as Daṇḍakāraṇya. This is the same Daṇḍakāraṇya forest where Lord Rāmacandra lived while in exile. Lord Balarāma next came to the bank of the river Narmadā, the biggest river in central India. On the bank of this sacred Narmadā is a pilgrimage spot known as

Māhiṣmatī-purī. After bathing there according to regulative principles, Lord Balarāma returned to Prabhāsa-tīrtha, where He had begun His journey.

When Lord Balarāma returned to Prabhāsa-tīrtha, He heard from the *brāhmaṇas* that most of the *kṣatriyas* in the Battle of Kurukṣetra had been killed. Balarāma felt relieved to hear that the burden of the world had been reduced. Lord Kṛṣṇa and Balarāma appeared on this earth to lessen the burden of military strength created by the ambitious *kṣatriya* kings. This is the way of materialistic life: not being satisfied by the absolute necessities of life, people ambitiously create extra demands, and their illegal desires are checked by the laws of nature, or the laws of God, appearing as famine, war, pestilence and similar catastrophes. Lord Balarāma heard that although most of the *kṣatriyas* had been killed, the Kurus were still engaged in fighting. Therefore He returned to the battlefield just on the day Bhīmasena and Duryodhana were engaged in a personal duel. As the well-wisher of both of them, Lord Balarāma wanted to stop them, but they would not stop.

When Lord Balarāma appeared on the scene, King Yudhiṣṭhira and his younger brothers Nakula and Sahadeva, as well as Lord Kṛṣṇa and Arjuna, immediately offered Him their respectful obeisances, but they did not speak at all. The reason they were silent was that Lord Balarāma was somewhat affectionate toward Duryodhana, who had learned from Balarāmajī the art of fighting with a club. When the fighting was going on, King Yudhiṣṭhira and others thought that Balarāma might have come there to say something in favor of Duryodhana, and they therefore remained silent. Both Duryodhana and Bhīmasena were very enthusiastic in fighting with clubs, and, in the midst of a large audience, each very skillfully tried to strike the other. While attempting to do so they appeared to be dancing, but nonetheless it was clear that both of them were very angry.

Lord Balarāma, wanting to stop the fighting, said, "My

dear King Duryodhana and Bhīmasena, I know that both of you are great fighters and are well known in the world as great heroes, but still I think that Bhīmasena is superior to Duryodhana in bodily strength. On the other hand, Duryodhana is superior in the art of fighting with a club. Taking this into consideration, My opinion is that neither of you is inferior to the other in fighting. Under the circumstances, there is very little chance that one of you will be defeated by the other. Therefore I request you not to waste your time fighting in this way. I wish you to stop this unnecessary fight."

The good instruction given by Lord Balarāma to Bhīmasena and Duryodhana was intended for the equal benefit of both of them. But they were so enwrapped in anger against each other that they could remember only their long-standing personal enmity. Each thought only of killing the other, and they did not give much importance to the instruction of Lord Balarāma. Both of them then became like madmen in remembering the strong accusations and ill behavior they had exchanged with each other. Lord Balarāma, being able to understand the destiny awaiting them, was not eager to go further in the matter. Therefore, instead of staying, He decided to return to the city of Dvārakā.

When He returned to Dvārakā, He was received with great jubilation by relatives and friends, headed by King Ugrasena and other elderly persons, who all came forward to welcome Him. After this, He again went to the holy place of pilgrimage at Naimiṣāraṇya, and the sages, saintly persons and *brāhmaṇas* all stood up to receive Him. They understood that Lord Balarāma, although a *kṣatriya,* was now retired from the fighting business. The *brāhmaṇas* and sages, who were always for peace and tranquillity, were very pleased at this. All of them embraced Balarāma with great affection and induced Him to perform various kinds of sacrifices in that sacred spot of Naimiṣāraṇya. Actually Lord Balarāma had no business performing the sacrifices recommended for ordinary human beings; He is the Supreme Personality of Godhead, and therefore He Himself is the enjoyer of all such sacrifices. As such, His exemplary action in performing sacrifices was only to give a lesson to the common man to show how one should abide by the injunctions of the *Vedas.*

The Supreme Personality of Godhead, Balarāma, instructed the sages and saintly persons at Naimiṣāraṇya on the subject matter of the living entities' relationship with this cosmic manifestation, on how one should regard this whole universe, and on how one should relate with the cosmos in order to achieve the highest goal of perfection. This supreme goal is the understanding that the whole cosmic manifestation rests on the Supreme Personality of Godhead and that the Supreme Personality of Godhead is also all-pervading, even within the minutest atom, by the function of His Paramātmā feature.

Lord Balarāma then took the *avabhṛtha* bath, which is taken after finishing sacrificial performances. After taking His bath, He dressed Himself in new silken garments and decorated Himself with beautiful jewelry. Amidst His relatives and friends, He appeared to be a shining full moon amidst the luminaries in the sky. Lord Balarāma is the Personality of Godhead Ananta Himself; therefore He is beyond the scope of understanding by mind, intelligence or body. He descended exactly like a human being and behaved in that way for His own purposes; we can only explain His activities as the Lord's pastimes. No one can even estimate the extent of the unlimited demonstrations of His pastimes because He is all-powerful. Lord Balarāma is the original Viṣṇu; therefore anyone remembering these pastimes of Lord Balarāma in the morning and evening will certainly become a great devotee of the Supreme Personality of Godhead, and thus his life will be successful in all respects.

Thus ends the Bhaktivedanta purport of the Seventy-ninth Chapter of Kṛṣṇa, *"The Liberation of Balvala, and Lord Balarāma's Touring the Sacred Places."*

CHAPTER EIGHTY

The Meeting of Lord Kṛṣṇa with Sudāmā Brāhmaṇa

King Parīkṣit was hearing the narrations of the pastimes of Lord Kṛṣṇa and Lord Balarāma from Śukadeva Gosvāmī. These pastimes are all transcendentally pleasurable to hear, and Mahārāja Parīkṣit addressed Śukadeva Gosvāmī as follows: "My dear lord, the Supreme Personality of Godhead, Kṛṣṇa, is the bestower of both liberation and love of God simultaneously. Anyone who becomes a devotee of the Lord automatically attains liberation without having to make a separate attempt. Because the Lord is unlimited, His pastimes and activities for creating, maintaining and destroying the whole cosmic manifestation are also unlimited. I therefore wish to hear about other pastimes of His which you may not have described as yet. My dear master, the conditioned souls within this material world are frustrated by searching out the pleasure of happiness derived from sense gratification. Such desires for material enjoyment are always piercing the hearts of conditioned souls. But I am actually experiencing how the transcendental topics of Lord Kṛṣṇa's pastimes can relieve one from being affected by such material activities of sense gratification. I think that no intelligent person can reject this method of hearing the transcendental pastimes of the Lord again and again; simply by hearing, one can remain always steeped in transcendental pleasure. Thus one will not be attracted by material sense gratification."

In this statement, Mahārāja Parīkṣit has used two important words: *viṣaṇṇa* and *viśeṣa-jña. Viṣaṇṇa* means "morose." Materialistic people invent many ways and means to become fully satisfied, but actually they remain morose. The point may be raised that sometimes transcendentalists also remain morose. Parīkṣit Mahārāja, however, has used the word *viśeṣa-jña.* There are two kinds of transcendentalists, namely the impersonalists and the personalists. *Viśeṣa-jña* refers to the personalists, who are interested in transcendental variegatedness. The devotees become jubilant by hearing the descriptions of the personal activities of the Supreme Lord, whereas the impersonalists, who are actually more attracted by the impersonal feature of the Lord, are only superficially attracted by the Lord's personal activities. As such, in spite of coming in contact with the pastimes of the Lord, the impersonalists do not fully realize the benefit to be derived, and thus they become just as morose as the materialists do in pursuing their fruitive activities.

King Parīkṣit continued, "The ability to talk can be perfected only by describing the transcendental qualities of the Lord. The ability to work with one's hands can be successful only when one engages himself in the service of the Lord with those hands. Similarly, one's mind can be peaceful only when one simply thinks of Kṛṣṇa in full Kṛṣṇa consciousness. This does not mean that one has to have very great thinking power: one has to understand simply that Kṛṣṇa, the Absolute Truth, is all-pervasive by His localized aspect of Paramātmā. If one can simply think that Kṛṣṇa, as Paramātmā, is everywhere, even within the atom, then one can perfect the thinking, feeling and willing functions of his mind. The perfect devotee does not see the material world as it appears to material eyes, for he sees everywhere the presence of his worshipable Lord in His Paramātmā feature."

Mahārāja Parīkṣit continued by saying that the function of the ear can be perfected simply by engagement in hearing the transcendental activities of the Lord, and the function of the head can be fully utilized when the head is engaged in bowing down before the Lord and His representative. That the Lord is represented in everyone's heart is a fact, and therefore the highly advanced devotee offers his respects to every living entity, considering that the body is the temple of the Lord. But it is not possible for all men to come to that stage of life immediately, because that stage is for the first-class devotee. The second-class devotee can consider the Vaiṣṇavas, or the devotees of the Lord, to be representatives of Kṛṣṇa, and the devotee who is just beginning, the neophyte or third-class devotee, can bow his head before the Deity in the temple and before the spiritual master, who is the direct manifestation of the Supreme Personality of Godhead. Therefore, in the neophyte stage, in the intermediate stage or in the fully advanced, perfected stage, one can make the function of the head perfect by bowing down before the Lord or His representative. Similarly, one can perfect the function of the eyes by seeing the Lord and His representative. In this way, everyone can elevate the functions of the different parts of his body to the highest perfectional stage simply by engaging them in the service of the Lord or His representative. If one is able to do nothing more, he can simply bow down before the Lord and His representative and drink the *caraṇāmṛta,* the water which has washed the lotus feet of the Lord or His devotee.

On hearing these statements of Mahārāja Parīkṣit's, Śukadeva Gosvāmī was overwhelmed with devotional ecstasy because of King Parīkṣit's advanced understanding of the

Vaiṣṇava philosophy. Śukadeva Gosvāmī was already engaged in describing the activities of the Lord, and when asked by Mahārāja Parīkṣit to describe them further, he continued to narrate *Śrīmad-Bhāgavatam* with great pleasure.

There was a very nice *brāhmaṇa* friend of Lord Kṛṣṇa. As a perfect *brāhmaṇa,* he was very elevated in transcendental knowledge, and because of his advanced knowledge, he was not at all attached to material enjoyment. Therefore he was very peaceful and had achieved supreme control over his senses. This means that the *brāhmaṇa* was a perfect devotee, because unless one is a perfect devotee he cannot achieve the highest standard of knowledge. It is stated in the *Bhagavad-gītā* that a person who has come to the perfection of knowledge surrenders unto the Supreme Personality of Godhead. In other words, any person who has surrendered his life for the service of the Supreme Personality of Godhead has come to the point of perfect knowledge. The result of perfect knowledge is that one becomes detached from the materialistic way of life. This detachment means complete control of the senses, which are always attracted by material enjoyment. The senses of the devotee become purified, and in that stage the senses are engaged in the service of the Lord. That is the complete field of devotional service.

Although the *brāhmaṇa* friend of Lord Kṛṣṇa was a householder, he was not busy accumulating wealth for very comfortable living; therefore he was satisfied by the income which automatically came to him according to his destiny. This is the sign of perfect knowledge. A man in perfect knowledge knows that one cannot be happier than he is destined to be. In this material world, everyone is destined to suffer a certain amount of distress and enjoy a certain amount of happiness. The amount of happiness and distress is already predestined for every living entity. No one can increase or decrease the happiness of the materialistic way of life. The *brāhmaṇa,* therefore, did not exert himself for more material happiness; instead, he used his time for advancement of Kṛṣṇa

His Divine Grace A.C. Bhaktivedanta Swami Prabhupāda
The Founder-Ācārya of the International Society for Krishna Consciousness and the greatest exponent of Kṛṣṇa consciousness in the modern world

To negate the offense he had committed by refusing to give the Syamantaka jewel to King Ugrasena when Kṛṣṇa had asked him to do so, Satrājit presented the Lord with both the jewel and his daughter. (*pp. 10-11*)

Before Bhaumāsura could throw his trident, his head was cut off by the sharp Sudarśana *cakra* of Lord Kṛṣṇa. (*p. 38*)

After His victory over Bhaumāsura, Lord Kṛṣṇa delivered the 16,100 princesses who had been kept prisoners by this demon. (*p.42*)

When the Yamunā was threatened by Lord Balarāma, she became frightened. Coming before the Lord in person, she prayed for mercy. (*p. 109*)

Balarāma struck the collarbone of the gorilla with His fists.
This blow proved fatal to Dvivida. (*p. 122*)

Lord Balarāma angrily dug up Hastināpura with the tip of His plow and began to drag it, intending to cast the entire city into the Ganges. (*p. 132*)

Being inquisitive as to how Kṛṣṇa was managing His household affairs, Nārada Muni set out to visit Kṛṣṇa's different homes. (*p. 136*)

In His Dvārakā pastimes, Lord Kṛṣṇa was engaged in household affairs like an ordinary human being. (*p. 142*)

Bhīmasena immediately pressed one of Jarāsandha's legs to the ground and took hold of the other leg with his two hands. Catching Jarāsandha in this way, he tore his body in two. (*p. 179*)

At the magnificent Rājasūya sacrifice performed by King Yudhiṣṭhira, Lord Kṛṣṇa received the honor of first worship. (*p. 194*)

When Śiśupāla was abusing the kings who were about to attack him, Lord Kṛṣṇa took up His disk, as sharp as the blade of a razor, and immediately separated Śiśupāla's head from his body. (*p. 197*)

When Lord Balarāma saw the demon Balvala flying in the sky, He immediately called for His plow and club and prepared Himself to kill him. (*p. 229-230*)

Lord Kṛṣṇa had His *brāhmaṇa* friend seated on His own bedstead and personally brought him all kinds of fruits and drinks, as is proper in receiving worshipable guests. (*p. 243*)

When the demon Vṛkāsura was preparing to cut off his head, Lord Śiva became very compassionate with him and appeared from the sacrificial fire in order to save him from suicide. (*p. 427*)

consciousness. Externally he appeared very poor because he had no rich clothes and could not provide rich clothes for his wife. Because their material condition was not very opulent, they were not even eating sufficiently, and thus both he and his wife appeared very thin. The wife was not anxious for her personal comfort, but she felt concerned for her husband, who was such a pious *brāhmaṇa.* She trembled due to her weak health, and although she did not like to dictate to her husband, she spoke as follows.

"My dear lord, I know that Lord Kṛṣṇa, the husband of the goddess of fortune, is your personal friend. You are also a devotee of Lord Kṛṣṇa, and He is always ready to help His devotee. Even if you think that you are not rendering any devotional service to the Lord, still you are surrendered to Him, and the Lord is the protector of the surrendered soul. Moreover, I know that Lord Kṛṣṇa is the ideal personality of Vedic culture. He is always in favor of brahminical culture and is very kind to the qualified *brāhmaṇas.* You are the most fortunate person because you have as your friend the Supreme Personality of Godhead. Lord Kṛṣṇa is the only shelter for personalities like you because you are fully surrendered unto Him. You are saintly, learned and fully in control of your senses. Under the circumstances, Lord Kṛṣṇa is your only shelter. Please, therefore, go to Him. I am sure that He will immediately understand your impoverished position. You are a householder; therefore without money you are in distress. But as soon as He understands your position, He will certainly give you sufficient riches so that you can live very comfortably. Lord Kṛṣṇa is now the King of the Bhoja, Vṛṣṇi and Andhaka dynasties, and I have heard that He never leaves His capital city, Dvārakā. He is living there without outside engagements. He is so kind and liberal that He immediately gives everything, even His personal self, to any person who surrenders unto Him. Since He is prepared to give Himself personally to His devotee, there is nothing wonderful in giving some material riches. Of course, He does not give much material wealth to His devotee if the devotee is not very much fixed, but I think that in your case He knows perfectly well how much you are fixed in devotional service. Therefore He will not hesitate to award you some material benefit for the bare necessities of life."

In this way, the wife of the *brāhmaṇa* again and again requested, in great humility and submission, that he go to Lord Kṛṣṇa. The *brāhmaṇa* thought that there was no need to ask any material benefit from Lord Śrī Kṛṣṇa, but he was induced by the repeated requests of his wife. Moreover, he thought, "If I go there I shall be able to see the Lord personally. That will be a great opportunity, even if I don't ask any material benefit from Him." When he had decided to go to Kṛṣṇa, he asked his wife if she had anything in the home that he could offer to Kṛṣṇa, because he must take some presentation for his friend. The wife immediately collected four palmfuls of chipped rice from her neighborhood friends and tied it in a small cloth, like a handkerchief, and gave it to her husband to present to Kṛṣṇa. Without waiting any longer, the *brāhmaṇa* took the presentation and proceeded toward Dvārakā to see his Lord. He was absorbed in the thought of how he would be able to see Lord Kṛṣṇa. He had no thought within his heart other than Kṛṣṇa.

It was of course very difficult to reach the palaces of the kings of the Yadu dynasty, but *brāhmaṇas* were allowed to visit. When the *brāhmaṇa* friend of Lord Kṛṣṇa went there, he, along with other *brāhmaṇas,* had to pass through three military encampments. In each camp there were very big gates, and he also had to pass through them. After the gates and the camps, there were sixteen thousand big palaces, the residential quarters of the sixteen thousand queens of Lord Kṛṣṇa. The *brāhmaṇa* entered one palace which was very gorgeously decorated. When he entered this beautiful palace, he felt that he was swimming in the ocean of transcendental pleasure. He felt himself constantly diving and surfacing in that transcendental ocean.

At that time, Lord Kṛṣṇa was sitting on the bedstead of Queen Rukmiṇī. Even from a considerable distance He could see the *brāhmaṇa* coming to His home, and He could recognize him as His friend. Lord Kṛṣṇa immediately left His seat and came forward to receive His *brāhmaṇa* friend and, upon reaching him, embraced the *brāhmaṇa* with His two arms. Lord Kṛṣṇa is the reservoir of all transcendental pleasure, yet He Himself felt great pleasure upon embracing the poor *brāhmaṇa* because He was meeting His very dear friend. Lord Kṛṣṇa had him seated on His own bedstead and personally brought all kinds of fruits and drinks to offer him, as is proper in receiving a worshipable guest. Lord Śrī Kṛṣṇa is the supreme pure, but because He was playing the role of an ordinary human being, He immediately washed the *brāhmaṇa's* feet and, for His own purification, sprinkled the water onto His head. After this the Lord smeared the body of the *brāhmaṇa* with different kinds of scented pulp, such as sandalwood, *aguru* and saffron. He immediately burned several kinds of scented incense and, as is usual, offered him *ārati* with burning lamps. After thus offering him an adequate welcome and after the *brāhmaṇa* had taken food and drink, Lord Kṛṣṇa said, "My dear friend, it is a great fortune that you have come here."

The *brāhmaṇa,* being very poor, was not dressed nicely; his clothing was torn and dirty, and his body was very lean and thin. He appeared not very clean, and because of his weak body, his bones were distinctly visible. The goddess of fortune Rukmiṇīdevī personally began to fan him with the *cāmara* fan, but the other women in the palace were astonished at Lord Kṛṣṇa's behavior in receiving the *brāhmaṇa* in that way. They were surprised to see how eager Lord Kṛṣṇa was to welcome this particular *brāhmaṇa.* They wondered how Lord Kṛṣṇa could personally receive a *brāhmaṇa* who was poor, not very neat or clean, and poorly dressed; but at the same time they could realize that the *brāhmaṇa* was not an ordinary living being. They knew that he must have performed great pious activities; otherwise why was Lord Kṛṣṇa, the husband of the goddess of fortune, taking care of him so much? They were still more surprised to see that the *brāhmaṇa* was seated on the bedstead of Lord Kṛṣṇa. They were especially surprised to see that Lord Kṛṣṇa had embraced him exactly as He embraced His elder brother, Balarāmajī, because Lord Kṛṣṇa used to embrace only Rukmiṇī or Balarāma, and no one else.

After the *brāhmaṇa* had been received nicely and seated on Lord Kṛṣṇa's own cushioned bed, he and Kṛṣṇa took each other's hands and began to talk about their early life, when they had both lived under the protection of the *gurukula* (a boarding school). Lord Kṛṣṇa said, "My dear *brāhmaṇa* friend, you are a most intelligent personality, and you know very well the principles of religious life. I believe that after you finished your education at the house of our teacher and after you sufficiently remunerated him, you must have gone back to your home and accepted a suitable wife. I know very well that from the beginning you were not at all attached to the materialistic way of life, nor did you desire to be very opulent materially, and therefore you are in need of money. In this material world, persons who are not attached to material opulence are very rarely found. Such unattached persons haven't the least desire to accumulate wealth and prosperity for sense gratification, but sometimes they are found to collect money just to exhibit the exemplary life of a householder. They show how by proper distribution of wealth one can become an ideal householder and at the same time a great devotee. Such ideal householders are to be considered followers of My footsteps. I hope, My dear *brāhmaṇa* friend, that you remember all those days of our school life when you and I were living together at the boarding school. Actually, whatever knowledge you and I received in life was accumulated in our student life.

"If a man is sufficiently educated in student life under the guidance of a proper teacher, his life becomes successful in the future. He can very easily cross over the ocean of nescience, and he is not subject to the influence of the illusory energy.

My dear friend, everyone should consider his father to be his first teacher because by the mercy of one's father one gets this body. The father is therefore the natural spiritual master. Our next spiritual master is he who initiates us into transcendental knowledge, and he is to be worshiped as much as I am. The spiritual master may be more than one. The spiritual master who instructs the disciple about spiritual matters is called the *śikṣā-guru,* and the spiritual master who initiates the disciple is called the *dīkṣā-guru.* Both of them are My representatives. There may be many spiritual masters who instruct, but the initiator spiritual master is one. A human being who takes advantage of these spiritual masters and, receiving proper knowledge from them, crosses the ocean of material existence is to be understood as having properly utilized his human form of life. He has practical knowledge that the ultimate interest of life, which is to be gained only in this human form, is to achieve spiritual perfection and thus be transferred back home, back to Godhead.

"My dear friend, I am Paramātmā, the Supersoul present in everyone's heart, and it is My direct order that human society follow the principles of *varṇa* and *āśrama.* As I have stated in the *Bhagavad-gītā,* human society should be divided into four *varṇas,* according to quality and action. Similarly, everyone should divide his life into four parts. One should utilize the first part of life in becoming a bona fide student, receiving adequate knowledge and keeping oneself in the vow of *brahmacarya,* so that one may completely devote his life for the service of the spiritual master without indulging in sense gratification. A *brahmacārī* is meant to lead a life of austerities and penance. The householder is meant to live a regulated life of sense gratification, but no one should remain a householder for the third stage of life. In that stage, one has to return to the austerities and penances formerly practiced in *brahmacārī* life and thus relieve himself of the attachment to household life. After being relieved of his attachments to the materialistic way of life, one may accept the order of *sannyāsa.*

"As the Supersoul of the living entities, I sit in everyone's heart and observe everyone's activity in every stage and order of life. Regardless of which stage one is in, when I see that one is engaged seriously and sincerely in discharging the duties ordered by the spiritual master and is thus dedicating his life to the service of the spiritual master, that person becomes most dear to Me. As far as the life of *brahmacarya* is concerned, if one can continue the life of a *brahmacārī* under the direction of a spiritual master, that is extremely good; but if in *brahmacārī* life one feels sex impulses, he should take leave of his spiritual master, satisfying him according to the *guru's* desire. According to the Vedic system, a gift is offered to the spiritual master, which is called *guru-dakṣiṇā.* Then the disciple should take to householder life and accept a wife according to religious rites."

These instructions given by Lord Kṛṣṇa while talking with His friend the learned *brāhmaṇa* are very good for the guidance of human society. A system of human civilization that does not promote *varṇa* and *āśrama* is nothing but a polished animal society. Indulgence in sex life by a man or woman living single is never acceptable in human society. A man should strictly follow the principles of *brahmacārī* life or, with the permission of the spiritual master, should get married. Single life with illicit sex is animal life, for the animals have no such institution as marriage.

Modern society does not aim at fulfilling the mission of human life, which is to go back home, back to Godhead. To fulfill this mission, the system of *varṇa* and *āśrama* must be followed. When the system is followed rigidly and consciously, it fulfills this mission, but when followed indirectly, without the guidance of superior authority, it simply creates a disturbing condition in human society, and there is no peace and prosperity.

Kṛṣṇa continued to talk with His *brāhmaṇa* friend: "My dear friend, I think you remember our activities during the days when we were living as students. You may remember that once we went to collect fuel from the forest on the order of the *guru's* wife. While collecting the dried wood, we entered the dense forest and by chance became lost. There was an unexpected dust storm and then clouds and lightning in the sky and the explosive sound of thunder. Then sunset came, and we were lost in the dark jungle. After this, there was severe rainfall; the whole ground was overflooded with water, and we could not trace out the way to return to our *guru's āśrama.* You may remember that heavy rainfall—it was not actually rainfall but a sort of devastation. On account of the dust storm and the heavy rain, we began to feel greatly pained, and in whichever direction we turned we were bewildered. In that distressed condition, we took each other's hand and tried to find our way out. We passed the whole night in that way, and early in the morning, when our absence became known to our *gurudeva,* he sent his other disciples to search us out. He also came with them, and when they reached us in the jungle they found us very much distressed.

"With great compassion our *gurudeva* said, 'My dear boys, it is very wonderful that you have suffered so much trouble for me. Everyone likes to take care of his body as the first consideration, but you are so good and faithful to your *guru* that without caring for bodily comforts you have taken so much trouble for me. I am also glad to see that bona fide students like you will undergo any kind of trouble for the satisfaction of the spiritual master. That is the way for a bona fide disciple to become free from his debt to the spiritual master. It is the duty of the disciple to dedicate his life to the service of the spiritual master. My dear best of the twice-born, I am greatly pleased by your acts, and I bless you: May all your desires and ambitions be fulfilled. May the understanding of the *Vedas* which you have learned from me always continue to remain within your memory, so that at every moment you can remember the teachings of the *Vedas* and quote their instructions without difficulty. Thus you will never be disappointed in this life or in the next.' "

Kṛṣṇa continued, "My dear friend, you may remember that many such incidents occurred while we were in the *āśrama* of our spiritual master. Both of us can realize that without the blessings of the spiritual master no one can be happy. By the mercy of the spiritual master and by his blessings, one can achieve peace and prosperity and be able to fulfill the mission of human life."

On hearing this, the learned *brāhmaṇa* replied, "My dear Kṛṣṇa, You are the Supreme Lord and the supreme spiritual master of everyone, and since I was fortunate enough to live with You in the house of our *guru,* I think I have nothing more to do in the matter of prescribed Vedic duties. My dear Lord, the Vedic hymns, ritualistic ceremonies, religious activities and all other necessities for the perfection of human life, including economic development, sense gratification and liberation, are all derived from one source: Your supreme personality. All the different processes of life are ultimately meant for understanding Your personality. In other words, they are the different parts of Your transcendental form. And yet You played the role of a student and lived with us in the house of the *guru.* This means that You adopted all these pastimes for Your pleasure only; otherwise there was no need for Your playing the role of a human being."

Thus ends the Bhaktivedanta purport of the Eightieth Chapter of Kṛṣṇa, *"The Meeting of Lord Kṛṣṇa with Sudāmā Brāhmaṇa."*

CHAPTER EIGHTY-ONE

The Brāhmaṇa Sudāmā Blessed by Lord Kṛṣṇa

Lord Kṛṣṇa, the Supreme Personality of Godhead, the Supersoul of all living entities, knows everyone's heart very well. He is especially inclined to the *brāhmaṇa* devotees. Lord Kṛṣṇa is also called *brahmaṇya-deva,* which means that He is worshiped by the *brāhmaṇas.* Therefore it is understood that a devotee who is fully surrendered unto the Supreme Personality of Godhead has already acquired the position of a *brāhmaṇa.* Without becoming a *brāhmaṇa,* one cannot approach the Supreme Brahman, Lord Kṛṣṇa. Kṛṣṇa is especially concerned with vanquishing the distress of His devotees, and He is the only shelter of pure devotees.

Lord Kṛṣṇa engaged for a long time in talking with Sudāmā Vipra about their past association. Then, just to enjoy the company of an old friend, Lord Kṛṣṇa began to smile and asked, "My dear friend, what have you brought for Me? Has your wife given you some nice eatable for Me?" While addressing His friend, Lord Kṛṣṇa looked upon him and smiled with great love. He continued, "My dear friend, you must have brought some presentation for Me from your home."

Lord Kṛṣṇa knew that Sudāmā was hesitating to present Him with the paltry chipped rice, which was actually unfit for His eating. Understanding the mind of Sudāmā Vipra, the Lord said, "My dear friend, I am certainly not in need of anything, but if My devotee gives Me something as an offering of love, even though it may be very insignificant, I accept it with great pleasure. On the other hand, if a person is not a devotee, even though he may offer Me very valuable things, I do not like to accept them. I actually accept only things offered to Me in devotion and love; otherwise, however valuable a thing may be, I do not accept it. If My pure devotee offers Me even the most insignificant things—a little flower, a little piece of leaf, a little water—but saturates the offering in devotional love, then not only do I gladly accept such an offering, but I eat it with great pleasure."

Lord Kṛṣṇa assured Sudāmā Vipra that He would be very glad to accept the chipped rice he had brought from home, yet out of great shyness Sudāmā Vipra hesitated to present it to the Lord. He was thinking, "How can I offer such an insignificant thing to Kṛṣṇa?" and he simply bowed his head.

Lord Kṛṣṇa, the Supersoul, knows everything in everyone's heart. He knows everyone's determination and everyone's want. He knew, therefore, the reason for Sudāmā Vipra's coming to Him. He knew that, driven by extreme poverty, he had come there at the request of his wife. Thinking of Sudāmā as His very dear class friend, He knew that Sudāmā's love for Him as a friend was never tainted by any desire for material benefit. Kṛṣṇa thought, "Sudāmā has not come asking anything from Me; being obliged by the request of his wife, he has come to see Me just to please her." Lord Kṛṣṇa therefore decided that He would give more material opulence to Sudāmā Vipra than could be imagined even by the King of heaven.

He then snatched the bundle of chipped rice which was hanging on the shoulder of the poor *brāhmaṇa,* packed in one corner of his wrapper, and said, "What is this? My dear friend, you have brought Me nice, palatable chipped rice!" He encouraged Sudāmā Vipra, saying, "I consider that this quantity of chipped rice will satisfy not only Me but the whole creation." It is understood from this statement that Kṛṣṇa, being the original source of everything, is the root of the entire creation. As watering the root of a tree immediately distributes water to every part of the tree, so an offering made to Kṛṣṇa, or any action done for Kṛṣṇa, is to be considered the highest welfare work for everyone, because the benefit of such an offering is distributed throughout the creation. Love for Kṛṣṇa is distributed to all living entities.

While Lord Kṛṣṇa was speaking to Sudāmā Vipra, He ate one morsel of chipped rice from his bundle, and when He attempted to eat a second morsel, Rukmiṇīdevī, the goddess of fortune herself, checked the Lord by catching hold of His hand. After touching the hand of Kṛṣṇa, Rukmiṇī said, "My dear Lord, this one morsel of chipped rice is sufficient to cause him who offered it to become very opulent in this life and to continue his opulence in the next life. My Lord, You are so kind to Your devotee that even this one morsel of chipped rice pleases You very greatly, and Your pleasure assures the devotee opulence in both this life and the next." This indicates that when food is offered to Lord Kṛṣṇa with love and devotion and He is pleased and accepts it from the devotee, Rukmiṇīdevī, the goddess of fortune, becomes so greatly obliged to the devotee that she has to go personally to the devotee's home to turn it into the most opulent home in the world. If one feeds Nārāyaṇa sumptuously, the goddess of fortune, Lakṣmī, automatically becomes a guest in one's house, which means that one's home becomes opulent. The learned *brāhmaṇa* Sudāmā passed that night at the house of Lord Kṛṣṇa, and while there he felt as if he were living on a Vaikuṇṭha planet. Actually he was living in Vaikuṇṭha, because wherever Lord Kṛṣṇa, the original Nārāyaṇa, and Rukmiṇīdevī, the goddess of fortune, live is not different from the spiritual planets, Vaikuṇṭhaloka.

The learned *brāhmaṇa* Sudāmā did not appear to have received anything substantial from Lord Kṛṣṇa while at His palace, yet he did not ask anything from the Lord. The next morning he started for his home, thinking always about his reception by Kṛṣṇa, and thus he merged in transcendental bliss. All the way home he simply remembered the dealings of Lord Kṛṣṇa, and he felt very happy to have seen the Lord.

The *brāhmaṇa* thought, "It is most pleasurable to see Lord Kṛṣṇa, who is most devoted to the *brāhmaṇas.* How great a lover He is of the brahminical culture! He is the Supreme Brahman Himself, yet He reciprocates with the *brāhmaṇas.* He also respects the *brāhmaṇas* so much that He embraced to His chest such a poor *brāhmaṇa* as me, although He never embraces anyone to His chest except the goddess of fortune. How can there be any comparison between me, a poor, sinful *brāhmaṇa,* and the Supreme Lord Kṛṣṇa, who is the only shelter of the goddess of fortune? And yet, considering me a *brāhmaṇa,* He embraced me with heartfelt pleasure in His two transcendental arms. Lord Kṛṣṇa was so kind to me that He allowed me to sit down on the same bedstead where the goddess of fortune lies down. He considered me His real brother. How can I appreciate my obligation to Him? When I was tired, Śrīmatī Rukmiṇīdevī, the goddess of fortune, began to fan me, holding the *cāmara* whisk in her own hand. She never considered her exalted position as the first queen of Lord Kṛṣṇa. I was rendered service by the Supreme Personality of Godhead because of His high regard for the *brāhmaṇas,* and by massaging my legs and feeding me with His own hand, He practically worshiped me! Aspiring for elevation to the heavenly planets, liberation, all kinds of material opulence, or perfection in the powers of mystic *yoga,* everyone throughout the universe worships the lotus feet of Lord Kṛṣṇa. Yet the Lord was so kind to me that He did not give me even a farthing, knowing very well that I am a poverty-stricken man who, if I got some money, might become puffed up and mad after material opulence and so forget Him."

The statement of the *brāhmaṇa* Sudāmā is correct. An ordinary man who is very poor and prays to the Lord for benediction in material opulence, and who somehow or other becomes richer in material opulence, immediately forgets his obligation to the Lord. Therefore, the Lord does not offer opulences to His devotee unless the devotee is thoroughly tested. Rather, if a neophyte devotee serves the Lord very sincerely and at the same time wants material opulence, the Lord keeps him from obtaining it.

Thinking in this way, the learned *brāhmaṇa* gradually reached his own home. But there he saw that everything was wonderfully changed. He saw that in place of his cottage there were big palaces made of valuable stones and jewels, glittering like the sun, moon and rays of fire. Not only were there big palaces, but at intervals there were beautifully decorated parks, in which many beautiful men and women were strolling. In those parks there were nice lakes full of lotus flowers and beautiful lilies, and there were flocks of multicolored birds. Seeing the wonderful conversion of his native place, the *brāhmaṇa* began to think to himself, "How am I seeing all these changes? Does this place belong to me or to someone else? If it is the same place where I used to live, then how has it so wonderfully changed?"

While the learned *brāhmaṇa* was considering this, a group of beautiful men and women with features resembling those of the demigods, accompanied by musical chanters, approached to welcome him. All were singing auspicious songs. The wife of the *brāhmaṇa* was very glad on hearing the tidings of her husband's arrival, and with great haste she came out of the palace. The *brāhmaṇa's* wife appeared so beautiful that it seemed as if the goddess of fortune herself had come to receive him. As soon as she saw her husband present before her, tears of joy fell from her eyes, and her voice became so choked up that she could not even address her husband. She simply closed her eyes in ecstasy. But with great love and affection she bowed down before her husband, and within herself she thought of embracing him. She was fully decorated with a gold necklace and ornaments, and while standing among the maidservants she appeared like a demigod's wife just alighting from an airplane. The *brāhmaṇa* was surprised to see his wife so beautiful, and in great affection and without saying a word he entered the palace with her.

When the *brāhmaṇa* entered his personal apartment in the palace, he saw that it was not an apartment but the residence of the King of heaven. The palace was surrounded by many columns of jewels. The couches and the bedsteads were made of ivory and bedecked with gold and jewels, and the bedding was as white as the foam of milk and as soft as a lotus. There were many whisks hanging from golden rods, and many golden thrones with sitting cushions as soft as lotus flowers. In various places there were velvet and silken canopies with laces of pearls hanging all around. The structure of the building stood on excellent transparent marble, with engravings made of emerald stones. All the women in the palace carried lamps made of valuable jewels. The flames and the jewels combined to produce a wonderfully brilliant light. When the *brāhmaṇa* saw his position suddenly changed to one of opulence, and when he could not determine the cause for such a sudden change, he began to consider very gravely how it had happened.

He thus began to think, "From the beginning of my life I have been extremely poverty-stricken, so what could be the cause of such great and sudden opulence? I do not find any cause other than the all-merciful glance of my friend Lord Kṛṣṇa, the chief of the Yadu dynasty. Certainly these are gifts of Lord Kṛṣṇa's causeless mercy. The Lord is self-sufficient, the husband of the goddess of fortune, and thus He is always full with six opulences. He can understand the mind of His devotee, and He sumptuously fulfills the devotee's desires. All these are acts of my friend Lord Kṛṣṇa. My beautiful dark friend Kṛṣṇa is far more liberal than the cloud, which can fill the great ocean with water. Without disturbing the cultivator with rain during the day, the cloud brings liberal rain at night just to satisfy him. And yet when the cultivator wakes up in the morning, he thinks that it has not rained enough. Similarly, the Lord fulfills the desire of everyone according to his position, yet one who is not in Kṛṣṇa consciousness considers all the gifts of the Lord to be less than his desire. On the other hand, when the Lord receives a little thing in love and affection from His devotee, He considers it a great and valuable gift. I am a vivid example of this: I simply offered Him a morsel of chipped rice, and in exchange He has given me opulences greater than the opulence of the King of heaven."

What the devotee actually offers the Lord is not needed by the Lord, for He is self-sufficient. If the devotee offers something to the Lord, it acts for his own interest because whatever a devotee offers the Lord comes back in a quantity a million times greater than what was offered. One does not become a loser by giving to the Lord; one becomes a gainer by millions of times.

The *brāhmaṇa,* feeling great obligation to Kṛṣṇa, thought, "I pray to have the friendship of Lord Kṛṣṇa and to engage in His service, and to surrender fully unto Him in love and affection, life after life. I do not want any opulence. I only desire not to forget His service. I simply wish to be associated with His pure devotees. May my mind and activities be always engaged in His service. The unborn Supreme Personality of Godhead, Kṛṣṇa, knows that many great personalities have fallen from their positions because of extravagant opulence. Therefore, even when His devotee asks for some opulence from Him, the Lord sometimes does not give it. He is very cautious about His devotees. Because a devotee in an immature position of devotional service may, if offered great opulence, fall from his position due to being in the material world, the Lord does not offer opulence to him. This is another manifestation of the causeless mercy of the Lord upon His devotee. His first interest is that the devotee not fall. He is exactly like a well-wishing father who does not give much wealth into the hand of his immature son, but who, when the son is grown up and knows how to spend money, gives him the whole treasury house."

The learned *brāhmaṇa* thus concluded that whatever opulences he had received from the Lord should be used not for his extravagant sense gratification but for the service of the Lord. The *brāhmaṇa* accepted his newly acquired opulence, but he did so in a spirit of renunciation, remaining unattached to sense gratification, and thus he lived very peacefully with his wife, enjoying all the facilities of opulence as the *prasādam* of the Lord. He enjoyed varieties of food by offering it to the Lord and then taking it as *prasādam.* Similarly, if by the grace of the Lord we get such opulences as material wealth, fame, power, education and beauty, it is our duty to consider that they are all gifts of the Lord and must be used for His service, not for our sense enjoyment. The learned *brāhmaṇa* remained in that position, and thus his love and affection for Lord Kṛṣṇa increased day after day; it did not deteriorate due to great opulence. Material opulence can be the cause of degradation and also the cause of elevation, according to the purposes for which it is used. If opulence is used for sense gratification it is the cause of degradation, and if used for the service of the Lord it is the cause of elevation.

It is evident from Lord Kṛṣṇa's dealings with Sudāmā Vipra that the Supreme Personality of Godhead is very, very pleased with a person who possesses brahminical qualities. A qualified *brāhmaṇa* like Sudāmā Vipra is naturally a devotee of Lord Kṛṣṇa. Therefore it is said, *brāhmaṇo vaiṣṇavaḥ:* a *brāhmaṇa* is a Vaiṣṇava. Or sometimes it is said, *brāhmaṇaḥ paṇḍitaḥ. Paṇḍita* means a highly learned person. A *brāhmaṇa* cannot be foolish or uneducated. Therefore there are two divisions of *brāhmaṇas,* namely Vaiṣṇavas and *paṇḍitas.* Those who are simply learned are *paṇḍitas* but not yet devotees of the Lord, or Vaiṣṇavas. Lord Kṛṣṇa is not especially pleased with them. Simply the qualification of being a learned *brāhmaṇa* is not sufficient to attract the Supreme Personality of Godhead. Not only must a *brāhmaṇa* be well qualified according to the requirements stated in scriptures such as *Śrīmad Bhagavad-gītā* and *Śrīmad-Bhāgavatam,* but at the same time he must be a devotee of Lord Kṛṣṇa. The vivid example is Sudāmā Vipra. He was a qualified *brāhmaṇa,* unattached to all sorts of material sense enjoyment, and at the same time he was a great devotee of Lord Kṛṣṇa. Lord Kṛṣṇa, the enjoyer of all sacrifices and penances, is very fond of a *brāhmaṇa* like Sudāmā Vipra, and we have seen by the actual behavior of Lord Kṛṣṇa how much He adores such a *brāhmaṇa.* Therefore, the ideal stage of human perfection is to become a *brāhmaṇa-vaiṣṇava* like Sudāmā Vipra.

Sudāmā Vipra realized that although Lord Kṛṣṇa is unconquerable, He nevertheless agrees to be conquered by His devotees. He realized how kind Lord Kṛṣṇa was to him, and he was always in trance, constantly thinking of Kṛṣṇa. By such constant association with Lord Kṛṣṇa, whatever darkness of material contamination remained within his heart was completely cleared away, and very shortly he was transferred to the spiritual kingdom, which is the goal of all saintly persons in the perfectional stage of life.

Śukadeva Gosvāmī has stated that all persons who hear this history of Sudāmā Vipra and Lord Kṛṣṇa will know how affectionate Lord Kṛṣṇa is to *brāhmaṇa* devotees like Sudāmā. Therefore anyone who hears this history gradually becomes as qualified as Sudāmā Vipra, and he is thus transferred to the spiritual kingdom of Lord Kṛṣṇa.

Thus ends the Bhaktivedanta purport of the Eighty-first Chapter of Kṛṣṇa, *"The Brāhmaṇa Sudāmā Blessed by Lord Kṛṣṇa."*

CHAPTER EIGHTY-TWO

Lord Kṛṣṇa and Balarāma Meet the Inhabitants of Vṛndāvana

Once upon a time, while Lord Kṛṣṇa and Balarāma were living peacefully in Their great city of Dvārakā, there was the rare occasion of a full solar eclipse, such as takes place at the end of every *kalpa,* or day of Brahmā. At the end of every *kalpa* the sun is covered by a great cloud, and incessant rain covers the lower planetary systems up to Svargaloka. By astronomical calculation, people were informed about this great eclipse prior to its taking place, and therefore everyone, both men and women, decided to assemble at the holy place in Kurukṣetra known as Samanta-pañcaka.

The Samanta-pañcaka pilgrimage site is celebrated because Lord Paraśurāma performed great sacrifices there after killing all the *kṣatriyas* in the world twenty-one times. When Lord Paraśurāma killed all the *kṣatriyas,* their accumulated blood flowed like a stream. Lord Paraśurāma dug five big lakes at Samanta-pañcaka and filled them with this blood. Lord Paraśurāma is *viṣṇu-tattva.* As stated in the *Īśopaniṣad, viṣṇu-tattva* cannot be contaminated by any sinful activity. Yet although Lord Paraśurāma is fully powerful and uncontaminated, in order to exhibit ideal character He performed great sacrifices at Samanta-pañcaka to atone for His so-called sinful killing of the *kṣatriyas.* By His example, Lord Paraśurāma established that the killing art, although sometimes necessary, is not good. Lord Paraśurāma considered Himself culpable for the sinful killing of the *kṣatriyas;* therefore, how much more culpable are we for such abominable unsanctioned acts. Thus, the killing of living entities is prohibited from time immemorial all over the world.

Taking advantage of the occasion of the solar eclipse, all important persons from all parts of Bhārata-varṣa visited the holy place of pilgrimage. Some of the important personalities are mentioned as follows. Among the elderly persons were Akrūra, Vasudeva and Ugrasena, and among the younger generation were Gada, Pradyumna, Sāmba and many other members of the Yadu dynasty who had come there with a view to atone for sinful activities accrued in the course of discharging their respective duties. Because almost all the members of the Yadu dynasty went to Kurukṣetra, some important personalities, like Aniruddha, the son of Pradyumna, and Kṛtavarmā, the commander in chief of the Yadu dynasty, along with Sucandra, Śuka and Sāraṇa, remained in Dvārakā to protect the city.

All the members of the Yadu dynasty were naturally very beautiful, yet on this occasion, when they appeared duly decorated with gold necklaces and flower garlands, dressed in valuable clothing and properly armed with their respective weapons, their natural beauty and personalities were a hundred times enhanced. The members of the Yadu dynasty came to Kurukṣetra in their gorgeously decorated chariots, which resembled the airplanes of the demigods and which were pulled by big horses that moved like the waves of the ocean. Some Yadus rode on sturdy, stalwart elephants that moved like the clouds in the sky. Their wives were carried on beautiful palanquins by beautiful men whose features resembled those of the Vidyādharas. The entire assembly looked as beautiful as an assembly of the demigods of heaven.

After arriving in Kurukṣetra, the members of the Yadu dynasty took their baths ceremoniously, with self-control, as enjoined in the *śāstras,* and they observed fasting for the whole period of the eclipse in order to nullify the reactions of their sinful activities. Since it is a Vedic custom to give in charity as much as possible during the hours of the eclipse, the members of the Yadu dynasty distributed many hundreds of cows in charity to the *brāhmaṇas.* All those cows were fully decorated with nice dress and ornaments. The special feature of these cows was that they had golden ankle bells and flower garlands on their necks.

After the eclipse, all the members of the Yadu dynasty again took their baths in the lakes created by Lord Paraśurāma. Then they sumptuously fed the *brāhmaṇas* with first-class cooked food, all prepared in butter. According to the Vedic system, there are two classes of food. One is called raw food, and the other is called cooked food. "Raw food" does not indicate raw vegetables and raw grains but food boiled in water, whereas cooked food is made in ghee. *Capātīs,* dhal, rice and ordinary vegetables are called raw foods, as are fruits and salads. But *purīs, kachaurīs, samosās,* sweet balls and so on are called cooked foods. All the *brāhmaṇas* invited on that occasion by the members of the Yadu dynasty were fed sumptuously with cooked food.

The ceremonial functions performed by the members of the Yadu dynasty externally resembled the ritualistic ceremonies performed by the *karmīs.* When a *karmī* performs some ritualistic ceremony, his ambition is sense gratification—good position, good wife, good house, good children or good wealth—but the ambition of the members of the Yadu dynasty was different. Their ambition was to offer perpetual faith and devotion to Kṛṣṇa. All the members of the Yadu dynasty were great devotees. As such, after many births of accumulated pious activities, they were given the chance to associate with Lord Kṛṣṇa. In going to take their baths in the place of pilgrimage at Kurukṣetra, in observing the regulative principles during the solar eclipse, or in feeding the *brāhmaṇas*—in all their activities—they simply thought of devotion to Kṛṣṇa. Their ideal worshipable Lord was Kṛṣṇa, and no one else.

After the *brāhmaṇas* are fed, it is the custom for the host, with their permission, to accept *prasādam.* Thus, with the permission of the *brāhmaṇas,* all the members of the Yadu dynasty took lunch. Then they selected resting places underneath big shady trees, and when they had taken sufficient rest, they prepared to receive visitors, among whom were relatives and friends, as well as many subordinate kings and rulers. There were the rulers of Matsya Province, Uśīnara Province, Kośala Province, Vidarbha Province, Kuru Province, Sṛñjaya Province, Kāmboja Province, Kekaya Province, Madras Province, Kuntī Province, Ānarta Province, Kerala Province and many other countries and provinces. Some of the rulers belonged to opposing parties, and some were friends. But above all, the visitors from Vṛndāvana were most prominent. The residents of Vṛndāvana, headed by Nanda Mahārāja, had been living in great anxiety because of separation from Kṛṣṇa and Balarāma. Taking advantage of the solar eclipse, they all came to see their life and soul, Kṛṣṇa and Balarāma.

The inhabitants of Vṛndāvana were well-wishers and intimate friends of the Yadu dynasty. This meeting of the two parties after long separation was a very touching incident. All the Yadus and the residents of Vṛndāvana felt such great pleasure in meeting and talking together that it was a unique scene. Meeting after long separation, they were all jubilant; their hearts throbbed, and their faces appeared like freshly bloomed lotus flowers. Drops of tears fell from their eyes, the hair on their bodies stood on end, and because of their extreme ecstasy, they were temporarily speechless. In other words, they dove into the ocean of happiness.

While the men were meeting in that way, the women also met one another in the same manner. They embraced one another in great friendship, smiling very mildly, and looked at one another with much affection. When they were embracing one another in their arms, the saffron and *kuṅkuma* spread on their breasts was exchanged from one person to another, and they all felt heavenly ecstasy. Due to such heart-to-heart embracing, torrents of tears glided down their cheeks. The juniors were offering obeisances to the elders, and the elders were offering their blessings to the juniors. They thus welcomed one another and asked after one another's welfare. Ultimately, however, all their talk was only of Kṛṣṇa. All the neighbors and relatives were connected with Lord Kṛṣṇa's pastimes in this world, and as such Kṛṣṇa was the center of all their activities. Whatever activities they performed—social, political, religious or conventional—were transcendental.

The real elevation of human life rests on knowledge and renunciation. As stated in the First Canto of *Śrīmad-Bhāgavatam,* devotional service rendered to Kṛṣṇa automatically produces perfect knowledge and renunciation. The family members of the Yadu dynasty and the cowherds of Vṛndāvana had their minds fixed on Kṛṣṇa. That is the symptom of perfect knowledge. And because their minds were always engaged in Kṛṣṇa, they were automatically freed from all material activities. This stage of life is called *yukta-vairāgya,* as enunciated by Śrīla Rūpa Gosvāmī. Knowledge and renunciation, therefore, do not mean dry speculation and renunciation of activities. Rather, one must start speaking and acting only in relationship with Kṛṣṇa.

In this meeting at Kurukṣetra, Kuntīdevī and Vasudeva, who were sister and brother, met after a long separation, along with their respective sons and daughters-in-law, children and other family members. By talking among themselves, they soon forgot all their past miseries. Kuntīdevī especially addressed her brother Vasudeva as follows: "My dear brother, I am very unfortunate because not one of my desires has ever been fulfilled; otherwise how could it happen that although I have such a saintly brother as you, perfect in all respects, you did not inquire from me as to how I was passing my days in a distressed condition of life?" It appears that Kuntīdevī was remembering the miserable days when she had been banished with her sons through the mischievous plans of Dhṛtarāṣṭra and Duryodhana. She continued, "My dear brother, I can understand that when providence goes against someone, even one's nearest relatives forget him. In such a condition, even one's father, one's mother or one's own children will forget him. Therefore, my dear brother, I do not accuse you."

Vasudeva replied to his sister, "My dear sister, do not be sorry, and do not blame me in that way. We should always remember that we are all only toys in the hands of providence. Everyone is under the control of the Supreme Personality of Godhead. It is under His control only that all kinds of fruitive actions and their reactions take place. My dear sister, you know that we were very much harassed by King Kaṁsa, and by his persecutions we were scattered here and there. We were always full of anxieties. Only in the last few days have we returned to our own places, by the grace of God."

After this conversation, Vasudeva and Ugrasena received the kings who came to see them, and they sufficiently welcomed them all. Seeing Lord Kṛṣṇa present on the spot, all the visitors felt transcendental pleasure and became very peaceful. Some of the prominent visitors were as follows: Bhīṣmadeva, Droṇācārya, Dhṛtarāṣṭra, Duryodhana, Gāndhārī along with her sons, King Yudhiṣṭhira along with his wife, and the Pāṇḍavas along with Kuntī, as well as Sañjaya, Vidura, Kṛpācārya, Kuntībhoja, Virāṭa, Bhīṣmaka, King Nagnajit, Purujit, Drupada, Śalya, Dhṛṣṭaketu, the King of Kāśī, Damaghoṣa,

Viśālākṣa, the King of Mithilā, the King of Madras (formerly known as Madra), the King of Kekaya, Yudhāmanyu, Suśarmā, Bāhlika along with his sons, and many other rulers subordinate to King Yudhiṣṭhira.

When the visitors saw Lord Kṛṣṇa with His thousands of queens, they were fully satisfied at the sight of such beauty and transcendental opulence. All who were there personally visited Lord Balarāma and Kṛṣṇa, and being properly welcomed by Them, they began to glorify the members of the Yadu dynasty, especially Kṛṣṇa and Balarāma. Because Ugrasena was the King of the Bhojas, he was considered the chief Yadu, and therefore the visitors specifically addressed him: "Your Majesty Ugrasena, King of the Bhojas, factually the Yadus are the only persons within this world who are perfect in all respects. All glories unto you! All glories unto you! The specific condition of your perfection is that you always see Lord Kṛṣṇa, who is sought by many mystic *yogīs* undergoing severe austerities and penances for great numbers of years. All of you are in direct touch with Lord Kṛṣṇa at every moment.

"All the Vedic hymns glorify the Supreme Personality of Godhead, Kṛṣṇa. The Ganges water is considered sanctified because of its being the water used to wash the lotus feet of Lord Kṛṣṇa. The Vedic literatures are nothing but the injunctions of Lord Kṛṣṇa. The purpose of the study of all the *Vedas* is to know Kṛṣṇa; therefore, the words of Kṛṣṇa and the message of His pastimes are always purifying. By the influence of time and circumstances, all the opulences of this world were almost completely wiped out, but since Kṛṣṇa has appeared on this planet, all auspicious features have again appeared due to the touch of His lotus feet. Because of His presence, all our ambitions and desires are gradually being fulfilled. Your Majesty, King of the Bhojas, you are related with the Yadu dynasty by matrimonial relationship, and by blood relationship also. As a result, you are constantly associating with

Lord Kṛṣṇa, and you have no difficulty in seeing Him or touching Him at any time. Lord Kṛṣṇa moves with you, talks with you, sits with you, rests with you and dines with you. The Yadus appear to be always engaged in worldly affairs, which are considered to be the royal road to hell, but due to the presence of Lord Kṛṣṇa, the original Personality of Godhead in the Viṣṇu category, who is omniscient, omnipresent and omnipotent, all of you are factually relieved from all material contamination and are situated in the transcendental position of liberation and Brahman existence."

When Nanda Mahārāja and the other residents of Vṛndāvana had heard that Kṛṣṇa would be present in Kurukṣetra because of the solar eclipse and that all the members of the Yadu dynasty would also be there, they had immediately prepared to go there. King Nanda, accompanied by his cowherd men, had loaded all their necessary paraphernalia on bullock carts, and all of the Vṛndāvana residents had come to Kurukṣetra to see their beloved sons Lord Balarāma and Lord Kṛṣṇa. When the cowherd men of Vṛndāvana arrived in Kurukṣetra, all the members of the Yadu dynasty were most pleased. As soon as they saw the residents of Vṛndāvana, they stood up to welcome them and appeared to have regained their life. All the Yadus and Vṛndāvana residents had been very eager to meet, and when they actually came forward and met, they embraced one another to their hearts' satisfaction and remained in embrace for a considerable time.

As soon as Vasudeva saw Nanda Mahārāja, Vasudeva jumped up and ran over to him and embraced him very affectionately. Vasudeva began to narrate his own past history—how he had been imprisoned by King Kaṁsa, how his babies had been killed, how immediately after Kṛṣṇa's birth he had carried Kṛṣṇa to the place of Nanda Mahārāja, and how Kṛṣṇa and Balarāma had been raised by Nanda Mahārāja and his queen, Yaśodā, as their own children. Similarly, Lord Balarāma and Kṛṣṇa also embraced King Nanda and mother

Yaśodā, and then They offered Their respect unto their lotus feet by bowing down. Because of Their feeling affection for Nanda and Yaśodā, Lord Kṛṣṇa and Balarāma became choked up, and for a few seconds They could not speak. The most fortunate King Nanda and mother Yaśodā placed their sons on their laps and began to embrace Them to their full satisfaction. Because of separation from Kṛṣṇa and Balarāma, King Nanda and Yaśodā had been merged in great distress for a very long time. Now, after meeting Them and embracing Them, all their sufferings were mitigated.

Then Kṛṣṇa's mother, Devakī, and Balarāma's mother, Rohiṇī, both embraced mother Yaśodā. They said, "Dear Queen Yaśodādevī, you and Nanda Mahārāja have been great friends to us, and when we remember you we are immediately overwhelmed by the thought of your friendly activities. We are so indebted to you that even if we were to return your benediction by giving you the opulence of the King of heaven, it would not be enough to repay you for your friendly behavior. We shall never forget your kindly behavior toward us. When Kṛṣṇa and Balarāma were born, before They even saw Their real father and mother, They were entrusted to your care, and you raised Them as your own children, fostering Them as birds take care of their offspring in the nest. You have nicely fed, nourished and loved Them and have performed many auspicious religious ceremonies for Their benefit.

"Actually They are not our sons; They belong to you. Nanda Mahārāja and you are the real father and mother of Kṛṣṇa and Balarāma. As long as They were under your care They had not even a pinch of difficulty. Under your protection, They were completely out of the way of all kinds of fear. This most affectionate care which you have taken for Them is completely befitting your elevated position. The most noble personalities do not discriminate between their own sons and the sons of others, and there cannot be any personalities more noble than Nanda Mahārāja and you."

As far as the *gopīs* of Vṛndāvana were concerned, from the very beginning of their lives they did not know anything beyond Kṛṣṇa. Kṛṣṇa and Balarāma were their life and soul. The *gopīs* were so attached to Kṛṣṇa that they could not even tolerate not seeing Him momentarily when their eyelids blinked and impeded their vision. They condemned Brahmā, the creator of the body, because he foolishly made eyelids which blinked and checked their seeing Kṛṣṇa. Because they had been separated from Kṛṣṇa for so many years, the *gopīs,* having come along with Nanda Mahārāja and mother Yaśodā, felt intense ecstasy upon seeing Kṛṣṇa. No one can even imagine how eager the *gopīs* were to see Kṛṣṇa again. As soon as Kṛṣṇa became visible to them, they took Him inside their hearts through their eyes and embraced Him to their full satisfaction. Even though they were embracing Kṛṣṇa only mentally, they became so ecstatic and overwhelmed with joy that for the time being they completely forgot themselves. The ecstatic trance they achieved simply by mentally embracing Kṛṣṇa is impossible to achieve even for great *yogīs* constantly engaged in meditation on the Supreme Personality of Godhead. Kṛṣṇa could understand that the *gopīs* were rapt in ecstasy by embracing Him in their minds, and therefore, since He is present in everyone's heart, He reciprocated the embracing from within.

Kṛṣṇa was sitting with mother Yaśodā and His other mothers, Devakī and Rohiṇī, but when the mothers engaged in talking, He took the opportunity and went to a secluded place to meet the *gopīs.* As soon as He approached the *gopīs,* the Lord smiled, and after embracing them and inquiring about their welfare, He began to encourage them, saying, "My dear friends, you know that Lord Balarāma and I left Vṛndāvana just to please Our relatives and family members. Thus We were long engaged in fighting with Our enemies and were obliged to forget you, who were so much attached to Me in love and affection. I can understand that I have been ungrateful to you, but still I know that you are faithful to Me. May I inquire if you have been thinking of Us, although We had to leave you behind? My dear *gopīs,* do you now dislike remembering Me, considering Me to have been ungrateful to you? Do you take My misbehavior with you very seriously?

"After all, you should know that it was not My intention to leave you; our separation was ordained by Providence, who after all is the supreme controller and does as He desires. He causes the intermingling of different persons, and again disperses them as He desires. Sometimes we see that a strong wind will mingle together clouds, atomic particles of dust or broken pieces of cotton, and after the strong wind subsides, all the clouds, particles of dust and pieces of cotton are again separated, scattered in different places. Similarly, the Supreme Lord is the creator of everything. The objects we see are different manifestations of His energy. By His supreme will we are sometimes united and sometimes separated. We can therefore conclude that ultimately we are absolutely dependent on His will.

"Fortunately, you have developed loving affection for Me, which is the only way to achieve the transcendental position of association with Me. Any living entity who develops such unalloyed devotional affection for Me certainly at the end goes back home, back to Godhead. In other words, unalloyed devotional service and affection for Me are the cause of supreme liberation.

"My dear *gopī* friends, you may know from Me that it is My energies only which are acting everywhere. Take, for example, an earthen pot. It is nothing but a combination of earth, water, air, fire and sky. It is always of the same physical composition, whether in its beginning, during its existence or after its annihilation. When it is created, the earthen pot is made of earth, water, fire, air and sky, while it remains it is the same in composition, and when it is broken and annihilated its different ingredients are conserved in different parts of the material energy. Similarly, at the creation of this cosmic manifestation, during its maintenance and after its dissolution, everything is but a different manifestation of My energy. And because the energy is not separate from Me, it is to be concluded that I am existing in everything.

"In the same way, the body of a living being is nothing but a composition of the five elements, and the living entity embodied in the material condition is also part and parcel of Me. The living entity is imprisoned in the material condition on account of his false conception of himself as the supreme enjoyer. This false ego of the living entity is the cause of his imprisonment in material existence. As the Supreme Absolute Truth, I am transcendental to the living entity, as well as to his material embodiment. The two energies, material and spiritual, both act under My supreme control. My dear *gopīs,* I request that instead of being afflicted, you try to accept everything with a philosophical attitude. Then you will understand that you are always with Me and that there is no cause of lamentation in our being separated from one another."

This important instruction by Lord Kṛṣṇa to the *gopīs* can be utilized by all devotees engaged in Kṛṣṇa consciousness. The whole philosophy is considered on the basis of inconceivable, simultaneous oneness and difference. In the *Bhagavad-gītā* the Lord says that He is present everywhere in His impersonal feature. Everything exists in Him, but still He is not personally present everywhere. The cosmic manifestation is nothing but a display of Kṛṣṇa's energy, and because the energy is not different from the energetic, nothing is different from Kṛṣṇa. When this absolute consciousness, Kṛṣṇa consciousness, is absent, we are separated from Kṛṣṇa; but, fortunately, if this Kṛṣṇa consciousness is present, then we are not separated from Kṛṣṇa. The process of devotional service is the revival of Kṛṣṇa consciousness, and if the devotee is fortunate enough to understand that the material energy is not separate from Kṛṣṇa, then he can utilize the material energy and its products in the service of the Lord. But in the absence of Kṛṣṇa consciousness, the forgetful living entity, although part and parcel of Kṛṣṇa, falsely puts himself in the position of enjoyer of the material world and, being thus implicated in material entanglement, is forced by the material energy to continue his material existence. This is confirmed in the *Bhagavad-gītā.* Although a living entity is forced to act by the material energy, he falsely thinks that he is the all-in-all and the supreme enjoyer.

If the devotee knows perfectly that the *arcā-vigraha,* or Deity form of Lord Kṛṣṇa in the temple, is exactly the same *sac-cid-ānanda-vigraha* as Kṛṣṇa Himself, then his service to the temple Deity becomes direct service to the Supreme Personality of Godhead. Similarly, the temple itself, the temple paraphernalia and the food offered to the Deity are also not separate from Kṛṣṇa. One has to follow the rules and regulations prescribed by the *ācāryas,* and thus, under superior guidance, Kṛṣṇa-realization is fully possible, even in this material existence.

The *gopīs,* having been instructed by Kṛṣṇa in this philosophy of simultaneous oneness and difference, remained always in Kṛṣṇa consciousness and thus became liberated from all material contamination. The consciousness of the living entity who falsely presents himself as the enjoyer of the material world is called *jīva-kośa,* which means imprisonment by the false ego. Not only the *gopīs* but anyone who follows these instructions of Kṛṣṇa is immediately freed from the *jīva-kośa* imprisonment. A person in full Kṛṣṇa consciousness is always liberated from false egoism; he utilizes everything for Kṛṣṇa's service and is not at any time separated from Kṛṣṇa.

The *gopīs* therefore prayed to Kṛṣṇa, "Dear Kṛṣṇa, from Your navel emanated the original lotus flower, which is the birthsite of Brahmā, the creator. No one can estimate Your glories or Your opulence, which therefore remain always a mystery even to the highest thoughtful men, the masters of all yogic power. However, the conditioned soul fallen in the dark well of this material existence can very easily take shelter of Your lotus feet. Thus his deliverance is guaranteed."

The *gopīs* continued, "Dear Kṛṣṇa, we are always busy in our family affairs. We therefore request that You remain within our hearts as the rising sun. That will be Your greatest benediction." The *gopīs* are always liberated souls because they are fully in Kṛṣṇa consciousness. They only pretended to be entangled in household affairs in Vṛndāvana. Because of their separation from Kṛṣṇa, He might have asked them to return with Him to His capital city, Dvārakā. But the inhabitants of Vṛndāvana, the *gopīs,* were not interested in the idea of going with Kṛṣṇa to Dvārakā. They wanted to remain busy in Vṛndāvana and thus feel the presence of Kṛṣṇa in every step of their lives. They immediately invited Kṛṣṇa to come back to Vṛndāvana. This transcendental emotional existence of the *gopīs* is the basic principle of Lord Caitanya's teaching. The Ratha-yātrā festival observed by Lord Caitanya is the emotional process of taking Kṛṣṇa back to Vṛndāvana. Śrīmatī Rādhārāṇī refused to go with Kṛṣṇa to Dvārakā to enjoy His company in the atmosphere of royal opulence, for She wanted to enjoy His company in the original Vṛndāvana atmosphere. Lord Kṛṣṇa, being profoundly attached to the *gopīs,* never goes away from Vṛndāvana, and the *gopīs* and other residents of Vṛndāvana remain fully satisfied in Kṛṣṇa consciousness.

Thus ends the Bhaktivedanta purport of the Eighty-second Chapter of Kṛṣṇa, *"Lord Kṛṣṇa and Balarāma Meet the Inhabitants of Vṛndāvana."*

CHAPTER EIGHTY-THREE

Draupadī Meets the Queens of Kṛṣṇa

There were many visitors who came to see Kṛṣṇa, and among them were the Pāṇḍavas, headed by King Yudhiṣṭhira. After talking with the *gopīs* and bestowing upon them the greatest benediction, Lord Kṛṣṇa welcomed King Yudhiṣṭhira and other relatives who had come to see Him. He first of all inquired from them whether their situation was auspicious. Actually, there is no question of ill fortune for anyone who sees the lotus feet of Lord Kṛṣṇa, yet when Lord Kṛṣṇa, as a matter of etiquette, inquired from King Yudhiṣṭhira about his welfare, the King became very happy by such a reception and addressed the Lord thus: "My dear Lord Kṛṣṇa, great personalities and devotees in full Kṛṣṇa consciousness always think of Your lotus feet and remain fully satisfied by drinking the nectar of transcendental bliss. The nectar which they constantly drink sometimes comes out of their mouths and is sprinkled on others as the narration of Your transcendental activities. This nectar coming from the mouth of a devotee is so powerful that if one is fortunate enough to have the opportunity to drink it, he is immediately freed from the continuous journey of birth and death. Our material existence is caused by our forgetfulness of Your personality, but fortunately the darkness of forgetfulness is immediately dissipated if one is privileged to hear about Your glories. Therefore, my dear Lord, where is the possibility of ill fortune for one who is constantly engaged in hearing Your glorious activities?

"Since we are fully surrendered unto You and have no other shelter than Your lotus feet, we are always confident of our good fortune. My dear Lord, You are the ocean of unlimited knowledge and transcendental bliss. The reactions of mental concoctions in the three phases of material life—wakefulness, sleep and deep sleep—cannot exist in Kṛṣṇa consciousness. All such reactions are invalidated by the practice of Kṛṣṇa consciousness. You are the ultimate destination of all liberated persons. Out of Your independent will only, You have descended to this earth by the use of Your own internal potency, *yogamāyā,* and to reestablish the Vedic principles of life You have appeared just like an ordinary human being. Since You are the Supreme Person, there cannot be any ill luck for one who has fully surrendered unto You."

When Lord Kṛṣṇa was busy meeting various kinds of visitors and while they were engaged in offering prayers to the Lord, the female members of the Kuru dynasty and the Yadu dynasty took the opportunity to meet with one another and engage in talk of Lord Kṛṣṇa's transcendental pastimes. The first inquiry was made by Draupadī to the wives of Lord Kṛṣṇa. She addressed them, "My dear Rukmiṇī, Bhadrā, Jāmbavatī, Satyā, Satyabhāmā, Kālindī, Śaibyā (Mitravindā), Lakṣmaṇā, Rohiṇī and all other wives of Lord Kṛṣṇa, will you please let us know how Lord Kṛṣṇa, the Supreme Personality of Godhead, accepted you as His wives and married you in pursuance of the marriage ceremonies of ordinary human beings?"

To this question, the chief of the queens, Rukmiṇīdevī, replied, "My dear Draupadī, it was practically a settled fact that princes like Jarāsandha wanted me to marry King Śiśupāla, and, as is usual, all the princes present during the marriage ceremony were prepared with their armor and weapons to fight with any rival who dared to stop the marriage. But the Supreme Personality of Godhead kidnapped me the way a lion takes away a lamb from the flock. This was not, however, a very wondrous act for Lord Kṛṣṇa, because anyone who claims to be a great hero or king within this world is subordinate to the lotus feet of the Lord. All kings touch their helmets to the lotus feet of Lord Kṛṣṇa. My dear Draupadī, it is my eternal desire that life after life I be engaged in the service of Lord Kṛṣṇa, who is the reservoir of all pleasure and beauty. This is my only desire and ambition in life."

After this, Satyabhāmā began to speak. She said, "My dear Draupadī, my father was very much afflicted by the death of his brother, Prasena, and he falsely accused Lord Kṛṣṇa of killing his brother and stealing the Syamantaka jewel, which had actually been taken by Jāmbavān. Lord Kṛṣṇa, in order to establish His pure character, fought with Jāmbavān and rescued the Syamantaka jewel, which He later delivered to my father. My father was very much ashamed and sorry for accusing Lord Kṛṣṇa of his brother's death. After getting back the Syamantaka jewel, he thought it wise to rectify his mistake, so although he had promised others my hand in marriage, he submitted the jewel and me at the lotus feet of Kṛṣṇa, and thus I was accepted as His maidservant and wife."

After this, Jāmbavatī replied to Draupadī's question. She said, "My dear Draupadī, when Lord Kṛṣṇa attacked my father, Jāmbavān, the King of the *ṛkṣas,* my father did not know that Lord Kṛṣṇa was his former master, Lord Rāmacandra, the husband of Sītā. Not knowing the identity of Lord Kṛṣṇa, my father fought with Him continuously for twenty-seven days. After this period, when he became fatigued, he could understand that since no one but Lord Rāmacandra could defeat him, his opponent, Lord Kṛṣṇa, must be the same Lord Rāmacandra. He thus came to his senses and immediately returned the Syamantaka jewel. Furthermore, to satisfy the Lord, he presented me to Him to become His wife. In this way I was married to the Lord, and thus my desire to be a servitor of Kṛṣṇa life after life was fulfilled."

After this, Kālindī said, "My dear Draupadī, I was engaged in great austerities and penances to get Lord Kṛṣṇa as my husband. When He became aware of this fact, He very kindly came to me with His friend Arjuna and accepted me as His wife. Lord Kṛṣṇa then took me away from the bank of the Yamunā, and since then I have been engaged in the house of Lord Kṛṣṇa as a sweeper. And the Lord is treating me as His wife."

After this, Mitravindā said, "My dear Draupadī, there was a great assembly of princes at my *svayaṁvara* ceremony [the personal selection of a husband]. Lord Kṛṣṇa was also present in that meeting, and He accepted me as His maidservant by defeating all the princes there. He immediately took me away to Dvārakā, exactly as a lion takes its prey from a pack of dogs. When I was thus taken away by Lord Kṛṣṇa, my brothers wanted to fight Him, and later they were defeated. Thus my desire to become the maidservant of Kṛṣṇa life after life was fulfilled."

After this, Satyā addressed Draupadī in this way: "My dear Draupadī, my father arranged for an assembly for my *svayaṁvara,* and to test the strength and heroism of the prospective bridegrooms, he stipulated that they each fight with his seven ferocious bulls, which had long, sharp horns. Many heroic prospects tried to defeat the bulls, but unfortunately they were all severely struck, and they returned to their homes as defeated invalids. When Lord Śrī Kṛṣṇa came and fought with the bulls, they were just like playthings for Him. He captured the bulls and roped each one of them by the nostrils. Thus they came under His control, just as a goat's small kids come very easily under the control of children. My father was very pleased and married me to Lord Kṛṣṇa in great pomp, giving as my dowry many divisions of soldiers, horses, chariots and elephants, along with hundreds of maidservants. Thus Lord Kṛṣṇa brought me to His capital city, Dvārakā. On the way back, He was assaulted by many princes, but Lord Kṛṣṇa defeated all of them, and thus I have the privilege of serving His lotus feet as a maidservant."

After this, Bhadrā began to speak. She said, "My dear Draupadī, Lord Kṛṣṇa is the son of my maternal uncle. Fortunately, I became attracted to His lotus feet. When my father understood these feelings of mine, he personally arranged for my marriage, inviting Lord Kṛṣṇa to marry me and giving Him in dowry one *akṣauhiṇī,* or division of armed forces, along with many maidservants and other royal paraphernalia. I do not know whether I shall be able to have the shelter of Lord Kṛṣṇa life after life, but still I pray to the Lord that wherever I may take my birth I may not forget my relationship with His lotus feet."

Then Lakṣmaṇā said, "My dear Queen, many times I heard the great sage Nārada glorifying the pastimes of Lord Kṛṣṇa. I became attracted to the lotus feet of Kṛṣṇa when I heard Nārada say that the goddess of fortune, Lakṣmī, was also attracted to His lotus feet. Since then I have always been thinking of Him, and thus my attraction for Him has increased. My dear Queen, my father was very affectionate toward me. When he understood that I was attracted to Kṛṣṇa, he devised a plan like that devised by your father: during the *svayaṁvara,* the prospective bridegrooms had to pierce the eyes of a fish with their arrows. The difference between the competition in your *svayaṁvara* and mine was that in yours the fish was hanging openly on the ceiling, in clear view, but in mine the fish was covered with a cloth and could only be seen by the reflection of the cloth in a pot of water. That was the special feature of my *svayaṁvara.*

"The news of this device spread all over the world, and when the princes heard of it they arrived at my father's capital city from all directions, fully equipped with armor and guided by their military instructors. Each one of them desired to win me as his wife, and one after another they raised the bow and arrow left there for piercing the fish. Many could not even join the bowstring to the two ends of the bow, and without attempting to pierce the fish, they simply left the bow as it was and went away. Some with great difficulty drew the string from one end to the other, but being unable to tie the other end, they were suddenly knocked down by the springlike bow. My dear Queen, you will be surprised to know that at my *svayaṁvara* meeting there were many famous kings and heroes present. Heroes like Jarāsandha, Ambaṣṭha, Śiśupāla, Bhīmasena, Duryodhana and Karṇa were, of course, able to string the bow, but they could not pierce the fish, because it was covered, and they could not trace it out from the reflection. The celebrated hero of the Pāṇḍavas, Arjuna, was able to see the reflection of the fish on the water, but although with great care he traced out the location of the fish and shot an arrow, he did not pierce the fish in the right spot. But his arrow at least touched the fish, and so he proved himself better than all the other princes.

"All the princes who tried to pierce the target were disappointed, being baffled in their attempts, and some candidates even left the place without making an attempt, but when at last Lord Kṛṣṇa took up the bow, He was able to tie the bowstring very easily, just as a child plays with a toy. He placed the arrow, and looking only once at the reflection of the fish in the water, He shot the arrow, and the pierced fish immediately fell down. This victory of Lord Kṛṣṇa was accomplished at noon, during the moment called *abhijit,* which is astronomically calculated as auspicious. At that time the vibration of 'Jaya! Jaya!' was heard all over the world, and from the sky came sounds of drums beaten by the denizens of heaven. Great demigods were overwhelmed with joy and showered flowers on the earth.

"At that time, I entered the arena of competition, and

the ankle bells on my legs sounded very melodious as I walked. I was nicely dressed with new silken garments, flowers decorated my hair, and because of Lord Kṛṣṇa's victory I was in ecstatic joy and smiling very pleasingly. I carried in my hands a golden necklace bedecked with jewels, which glittered at intervals. My curling hair encircled my face, which shone with a bright luster due to the reflection of my various earrings. My eyes blinking, I first observed all the princes present, and when I reached my Lord I very slowly placed the golden necklace on His neck. As I have already informed you, from the very beginning my mind was attracted by Lord Kṛṣṇa, and thus I considered the garlanding of the Lord my great victory. As soon as I placed my garland on the neck of the Lord, there sounded immediately the combined vibration of *mṛdaṅgas, paṭaha* and *ānaka* drums, conchshells, kettle-drums and other instruments, causing a tumultuous sound, and while the music played, expert male and female dancers began to dance, and singers began to sing sweetly.

"My dear Draupadī, when I accepted Lord Kṛṣṇa as my worshipable husband and He accepted me as His maidservant, there was a tumultuous roaring among the disappointed princes. All of them were very agitated because of their lusty desires, but without caring for them, my husband, in His form as the four-handed Nārāyaṇa, immediately took me on His chariot, which was drawn by four excellent horses. Expecting opposition from the princes, He armored Himself and took up His bow, named Śārṅga, and then our celebrated driver, Dāruka, drove the beautiful chariot, without a moment's delay, toward the city of Dvārakā. Thus, in the presence of all the princes, I was carried away very quickly, exactly as a deer is carried away from the flock by a lion. Some of the princes, however, wanted to check our progress, and thus, equipped with proper weapons, they opposed us, just as dogs try to oppose the progressive march of a lion. At that time, due to the arrows released by the Śārṅga bow of Lord Kṛṣṇa, some of the princes lost their hands, some of them lost their legs, some lost their heads and their lives, and others fled from the battlefield.

"The Supreme Personality of Godhead then entered the most celebrated city of the universe, Dvārakā, and as He entered the city He appeared like the shining sun. The whole city of Dvārakā was profusely decorated on that occasion. There were so many flags and festoons and gates all over Dvārakā that the sunshine could not even enter the city. I have already told you that my father was very affectionate to me, so when he saw that my desire had been fulfilled by my getting Lord Kṛṣṇa as my husband, in great happiness he began to distribute to friends and relatives various kinds of gifts, such as valuable garments, ornaments, bedsteads and sitting carpets. Lord Kṛṣṇa is always self-sufficient, yet my father, out of his own accord, offered my husband a dowry consisting of riches, soldiers, elephants, chariots, horses and many rare and valuable weapons. He presented all these to the Lord with great enthusiasm. My dear Queen, at that time I could guess that in my previous life I must have performed some wonderfully pious activity, and as a result I can in this life be one of the maidservants in the house of the Supreme Personality of Godhead."

When all the principal queens of Lord Kṛṣṇa had finished their statements, Rohiṇī, as the representative of the other sixteen thousand queens, began to narrate the incident of their becoming wives of Kṛṣṇa.

"My dear Queen, when Bhaumāsura was conquering all the world, he collected wherever possible all the beautiful daughters of the kings and kept us arrested within his palace. When news of our imprisonment reached Lord Kṛṣṇa, He fought with Bhaumāsura and released us. Lord Kṛṣṇa killed Bhaumāsura and all his soldiers, and although He had no need to accept even one wife, He nevertheless, by our request, married all sixteen thousand of us. My dear Queen, our only qualification was that we were always thinking of the lotus feet of Lord Kṛṣṇa, which is the way to release oneself from the bondage of repeated birth and death. My dear Queen Draupadī, please take it from us that we are not after any opulence such as a kingdom, an empire or a position of heavenly enjoyment. We do not want to enjoy such material opulences, nor do we desire to achieve the yogic perfections, nor the exalted post of Lord Brahmā. Nor do we want any of the different kinds of liberation—*sārūpya, sālokya, sārṣṭi, sāmīpya* or *sāyujya.* We are not at all attracted by any of these opulences. Our only ambition is to bear on our heads life after life the dust particles attached to the lotus feet of Lord Kṛṣṇa. The goddess of fortune also desires to keep that dust on her breasts, along with fragrant saffron. We simply desire this dust, which accumulates underneath the lotus feet of Kṛṣṇa as He travels on the land of Vṛndāvana as a cowherd boy. The *gopīs* especially, and also the cowherd men and the aborigine tribeswomen, always desire to become the grass and straw on the streets of Vṛndāvana, to be trampled on by the lotus feet of Kṛṣṇa. My dear Queen, we wish to remain as such life after life, without any other desire."

Thus ends the Bhaktivedanta purport of the Eighty-third Chapter of Kṛṣṇa, *"Draupadī Meets the Queens of Kṛṣṇa."*

CHAPTER EIGHTY-FOUR

Sacrificial Ceremonies Performed by Vasudeva

Among the women present at Kurukṣetra during the solar eclipse were Kuntī, Gāndhārī, Draupadī, Subhadrā and the queens of many other kings, as well as the *gopīs* from Vṛndāvana. When the different queens of Lord Kṛṣṇa were submitting their statements as to how they had been married and accepted by Lord Kṛṣṇa as His wives, all the female members of the Kuru dynasty were struck with wonder. They were filled with admiration at how all the queens of Kṛṣṇa were attached to Him with love and affection. When they heard about the queens' intensity of love and affection for Kṛṣṇa, they could not check their eyes from filling with tears.

While the women were engaged in conversations among themselves and the men were similarly engaged in conversation, there arrived from all directions almost all the important sages and ascetics, who had come for the purpose of seeing Lord Kṛṣṇa and Balarāma. Chief among the sages were Kṛṣṇa-dvaipāyana Vyāsa, the great sage Nārada, Cyavana, Devala, Asita, Viśvāmitra, Śatānanda, Bharadvāja, Gautama,

Lord Paraśurāma (along with His disciples), Vasiṣṭha, Gālava, Bhṛgu, Pulastya, Kaśyapa, Atri, Mārkaṇḍeya, Bṛhaspati, Dvita, Trita, Ekata, the four Kumāra sons of Brahmā (Sanaka, Sanandana, Sanātana and Sanat-kumāra), Aṅgirā, Agastya, Yājñavalkya and Vāmadeva.

As soon as the sages and ascetics arrived, all the kings, including Mahārāja Yudhiṣṭhira and the other Pāṇḍavas and Lord Kṛṣṇa and Balarāma, immediately got up from their seats and offered respects by bowing down to the universally respected sages. After this, the sages were properly welcomed by being offered seats and water for washing their feet. Palatable fruits, garlands of flowers, incense and sandalwood pulp were presented, and all the kings, led by Kṛṣṇa and Balarāma, worshiped the sages according to the Vedic rules and regulations. When all the sages were comfortably seated, Lord Kṛṣṇa, who descended for the protection of religion, began to address them on behalf of all the kings. When Kṛṣṇa began to speak, all became silent, being eager to hear and understand His welcoming words to the sages.

Lord Kṛṣṇa spoke thus: "All glories to the assembled sages and ascetics! Today we all feel that our lives have become successful. Today we have achieved the desired goal of life because we now see face to face all the exalted, liberated sages and ascetics, whom even the great demigods in the heavens desire to see. Persons who are neophytes in devotional service and who simply offer their respectful obeisances to the Deity in the temple but cannot realize that the Lord is situated in everyone's heart, and those who simply worship different demigods for fulfillment of their own lusty desires, are unable to understand the importance of these sages. They cannot take advantage of receiving these sages by seeing them with their eyes, by touching their lotus feet, by inquiring about their welfare or by diligently worshiping them."

Neophyte devotees or religionists cannot understand the importance of great *mahātmās*. They go to the temple as a matter of formality and pay their respectful obeisances unto the Deity. But when one is promoted to the next platform of transcendental consciousness, one can understand the importance of *mahātmās* and devotees, and in that stage one tries to please them. Therefore, Lord Kṛṣṇa said that the neophyte cannot understand the importance of great sages, devotees or ascetics.

Lord Kṛṣṇa continued, "One cannot purify himself merely by traveling to holy places of pilgrimage and taking a bath there or by seeing the demigods' forms in the temples. But if one happens to meet a great devotee, a *mahātmā* who is a representative of the Personality of Godhead, one is immediately purified. To become purified, one is enjoined to worship the fire, the sun, the moon, the earth, the water, the air, the sky and the mind. By worshiping all the elements and their predominating deities, one can gradually become free from the influence of envy, but all the sins of an envious person can be nullified immediately simply by serving a great soul. My dear revered sages and respectable kings, you can take it from Me that a person who accepts this material body made of three elements—mucus, bile and air—as his own self, who considers his family and relatives his own, who accepts material things as worshipable, or who visits holy places of pilgrimage just to take a bath there but never associates with great personalities, sages and *mahātmās*—such a person, even though in the form of a human being, is nothing but an animal like an ass."

When the supreme authority, Lord Kṛṣṇa, was thus speaking with great gravity, all the sages and ascetics remained in dead silence. They were amazed upon hearing Him speak the absolute philosophy of life in such a concise way. Unless one is very much advanced in knowledge, one thinks his body to be his self, his family members to be his own, and the land of his birth to be worshipable. From this concept of life, the modern ideology of nationalism has sprung up. Lord Kṛṣṇa condemned such ideas, and He also condemned persons who take the trouble to go to holy places of pilgrimage just to take a bath and come back without taking the opportunity to associate with the great devotees and *mahātmās* living there. Such persons are compared to the most foolish animal, the ass. All those who heard considered the speech of Lord Kṛṣṇa for some time, and they concluded that Lord Kṛṣṇa was actually the Supreme Personality of Godhead playing the role of an ordinary human being, who is forced to take a certain type of body as a result of the reactions of his past deeds. He was assuming this pastime as an ordinary human simply to teach the people in general how they should live for perfection of the human mission.

Having concluded that Kṛṣṇa was the Supreme Personality of Godhead, the sages addressed Him thus: "Dear Lord, we, the leaders of human society, are supposed to possess the proper philosophy of life, yet we are bewildered by the spell of Your external energy. We are surprised to see Your behavior, which is just like that of an ordinary human being and which conceals Your real identity as the Supreme Personality of Godhead, and we therefore consider Your pastimes to be all-wonderful.

"Our dear Lord, by Your own energy You create, maintain and annihilate the whole cosmic manifestation of different names and forms, in the same way that the earth creates many forms of stone, trees and other varieties of names and forms and yet remains the same. Although You create varieties of manifestations through Your energy, You are unaffected by all those actions. Our dear Lord, we are simply stunned to see Your wonderful acts. Although You are transcendental to this entire material creation and are the Supreme Lord and the Supersoul of all living entities, You appear on this earth by Your internal potency to protect Your devotees and destroy the miscreants. By such an appearance You reestablish the principles of eternal religion, which human society forgets by long association with the material energy. Our dear Lord, You are the creator of the social orders and spiritual statuses of human society according to quality and work, and when these orders are misguided by unscrupulous persons, You appear and set them right.

"Dear Lord, the Vedic knowledge is the representation of Your pure heart. Austerities, study of the *Vedas,* and meditative trances lead to different realizations of Your Self in Your manifested and nonmanifested aspects. The entire phenomenal world is a manifestation of Your impersonal energy, but You Yourself, as the original Personality of Godhead, are not manifested there. You are the Supreme Soul, the Supreme Brahman. Persons who are situated in brahminical culture, therefore, can understand the truth about Your transcendental form. Thus You always hold the *brāhmaṇas* in respect, and You are considered to be the topmost of all followers of brahminical culture. You are therefore known as *brahmaṇya-deva.* Our dear Lord, You are the last word in good fortune and the last resort of all saintly persons; therefore we all consider that we have achieved the perfection of our life, education, austerity and acquisition of transcendental knowledge by meeting You. Factually, You are the ultimate goal of all transcendental achievements.

"Our dear Lord, there is no end to Your unlimited knowledge. Your form is transcendental, eternally existing in full bliss and knowledge. You are the Supreme Personality of Godhead, the Supreme Brahman, the Supreme Soul. Being covered by the spell of Your internal potency, *yogamāyā,* You are now temporarily concealing Your unlimited potencies, but still we can understand Your exalted position, and therefore all of us offer You our respectful obeisances. Dear Lord, You are enjoying Your pastimes in the role of a human being, concealing Your real character of transcendental opulence; therefore, none of the kings present here, even the members of the Yadu dynasty who constantly mingle with You, eat with You and sit with You, can understand that You are the original cause of all causes, the soul of everyone, the original cause of all creation.

"When a person dreams at night, hallucinatory figures

created by the dream are accepted as real, and the imaginary dream body is accepted as one's real body. For the time being, one forgets that besides the body created in hallucination, there is another, real body in his awakened state. Similarly, in the awakened state also, the bewildered conditioned soul considers sense enjoyment to be real happiness.

"By the process of enjoying the senses of the material body, the spirit soul is covered, and his consciousness becomes materially contaminated. It is due to material consciousness that one cannot understand the Supreme Personality of Godhead, Kṛṣṇa. All great mystic *yogīs* endeavor to revive their Kṛṣṇa consciousness by mature practice of the *yoga* system just to understand Your lotus feet. They meditate upon Your transcendental form to counteract their accumulated sinful reactions. It is said that the water of the Ganges can vanquish volumes of a person's sinful reactions, but the Ganges water is glorious only due to Your lotus feet. The Ganges water flows as perspiration from the lotus feet of Your Lordship. And we are all so fortunate that today we have been able to see Your lotus feet directly. Dear Lord, we are all surrendered souls, devotees of Your Lordship; therefore, please be kind and bestow Your causeless mercy upon us. We know well that persons who have become liberated by constant engagement in Your devotional service are no longer contaminated by the material modes of nature; thus they have become eligible to be promoted to the kingdom of God in the spiritual world."

After first offering prayers to Lord Kṛṣṇa, the assembled sages wanted to take permission from King Dhṛtarāṣṭra and King Yudhiṣṭhira and then depart for their respective *āśramas.* At that time, however, Vasudeva, the father of Lord Kṛṣṇa and the most celebrated of all pious men, approached the sages and with great humility offered his respects by falling down at their feet. Vasudeva said, "My dear great sages, you are more respected than the demigods. I therefore offer my respectful obeisances unto you. I wish for you to accept my one request, if you so desire. I shall consider it a great blessing if you kindly explain the supreme fruitive activity by which one can counteract the reactions of all other activities."

The great sage Nārada was the leader of all the sages present. Therefore he began to speak. "My dear sages," he said, "it is not very difficult to understand that because of his great goodness and simplicity, Vasudeva, who has become the father of the Personality of Godhead by accepting Kṛṣṇa as his son, is inclined to ask us about his welfare. It is said that familiarity breeds contempt. As such, Vasudeva, having Kṛṣṇa as his son, does not regard Kṛṣṇa with awe and veneration. Sometimes it is seen that persons living on the bank of the Ganges do not consider the Ganges very important, and they go far away to take their baths at a place of pilgrimage. There is no need for Vasudeva to ask us for instruction when Lord Kṛṣṇa is personally present, because His knowledge is never second in any circumstance. His knowledge is not affected by the process of creation, maintenance and annihilation, nor is it ever influenced by any agency beyond Himself, nor is it agitated by the interactions of the material qualities or changed in the course of time. His transcendental form is full of knowledge which never becomes agitated by ignorance, pride, attachment, envy or sense enjoyment. His knowledge is never subject to the laws of *karma* regarding pious or impious activities, nor is it influenced by the three modes of material energy. No one is greater than or equal to Him, because He is the supreme authority, the Personality of Godhead.

"The ordinary conditioned human being may think that the conditioned soul, who is covered by his materialistic senses, mind and intelligence, is equal to Kṛṣṇa, but Lord Kṛṣṇa is just like the sun, which, although it sometimes may appear to be so, is never covered by the cloud, snow or fog, or by other planets during an eclipse. When the eyes of less intelligent men are covered by such influences, they think the sun to be invisible. Similarly, persons who are influenced by senses addicted to material enjoyment cannot have a clear vision of the Supreme Personality of Godhead."

The sages present then began to address Vasudeva in the presence of Lord Kṛṣṇa, Balarāma and many other kings, and, as requested by him, they gave their instructions: "To counteract the reactions of fruitive activities and the desires impelling one to fruitive activities, one must with faith and devotion execute the prescribed sacrifices meant for worshiping Lord Viṣṇu. Lord Viṣṇu is the beneficiary of the results of all sacrificial performances. Great personalities and sages who are able to see everything clearly through the eyes of the revealed scriptures and possess vision of the three phases of the time element, namely past, present and future, have unanimously recommended that to purify the dust of material contamination accumulated in the heart and to clear the path of liberation and thereby achieve transcendental bliss, one must please Lord Viṣṇu. For everyone living as a householder in one of the higher social orders (*brāhmaṇa, kṣatriya* and *vaiśya*), this worship of the Supreme Personality of Godhead, Lord Viṣṇu, who is known as Puruṣottama, the original person, is recommended as the only auspicious path.

"All conditioned souls within this material world have deep-rooted desires to lord it over the resources of material nature. Everyone wants to accumulate riches, everyone wants to enjoy life to the greatest extent, everyone wants a wife, home and children, and everyone wants to become happy in this world and be elevated to the heavenly planets in the next life. But these desires are the causes of one's material bondage. Therefore, to get liberation from this bondage, one has to sacrifice his honestly earned riches for the satisfaction of Lord Viṣṇu.

"The only process to counteract all sorts of material desires is to engage oneself in the devotional service of Lord Viṣṇu. In this way a self-controlled person, even while remaining in householder life, should give up the three kinds of material desires, namely the desire for the acquisition of material opulences, for the enjoyment of wife and children, and for elevation to higher planets. Eventually he should give up householder life and accept the renounced order, engaging himself completely in the devotional service of the Lord. Everyone, even if born in a higher status as a *brāhmaṇa, kṣatriya* or *vaiśya,* is certainly indebted to the demigods, to the sages, to the forefathers and to other living entities, and in order to liquidate all these debts, one has to perform sacrifices, study the Vedic literature and generate children in religious householder life. If somehow one accepts the renounced order of life without liquidating these debts, he certainly falls down from his position. Today you have already liquidated your debts to your forefathers and the sages. Now, by performing sacrifices, you can free yourself from indebtedness to the demigods and thus take complete shelter of the Supreme Personality of Godhead. My dear Vasudeva, certainly you have already performed many pious activities in your previous lives. Otherwise, how could you be the father of Kṛṣṇa and Balarāma, the Supreme Personality of Godhead?"

Saintly Vasudeva, after hearing all the sages, offered his respectful obeisances unto their lotus feet. In this way he pleased the sages, and then he requested them to perform the *yajñas.* When the sages were selected as priests of the sacrifices, they in turn induced Vasudeva to collect the required paraphernalia for executing the *yajñas* in that place of pilgrimage. When Vasudeva was thus persuaded to start to perform the *yajñas,* all the members of the Yadu dynasty took their baths, dressed themselves very nicely, decorated themselves beautifully and garlanded themselves with lotus flowers. Vasudeva's wives, dressed with nice garments and ornaments and golden necklaces, approached the arena of sacrifice carrying in their hands the required articles to offer in the sacrifice.

When everything was complete, there was heard the vibration of *mṛdaṅgas,* conchshells, kettledrums and other musical instruments. Professional dancers, both male and female, began to dance. The *sūtas* and *māgadhas,* who were professional singers, began to offer prayers by singing. And the

Gandharvas and their wives, whose voices were very sweet, began to sing many auspicious songs. Vasudeva anointed his eyes with black cosmetic, smeared butter over his body and then, along with his eighteen wives, headed by Devakī, sat before the priests to be purified by the *abhiṣeka* ceremony. While the ceremony was being observed strictly according to the principles of the scriptures, Vasudeva resembled the moon encircled by stars. Because he was being initiated for the sacrifice, he was dressed in a deerskin, but all his wives were dressed with very nice saris, bangles, necklaces, ankle bells, earrings and many other ornaments. Vasudeva looked very beautiful surrounded by his wives, exactly like the King of heaven when he performs such sacrifices.

At that time, when Lord Kṛṣṇa and Lord Balarāma, along with Their wives, children and relatives, sat down in that great sacrificial arena, it appeared that the Supreme Personality of Godhead was present along with all the living entities and multienergies that are part of Him. We have heard from the *śāstras* that Lord Kṛṣṇa has multienergies and parts and parcels, but now, in that sacrificial arena, all could actually experience how the Supreme Personality of Godhead eternally exists with His different energies. At that time, Lord Kṛṣṇa appeared as Lord Nārāyaṇa, and Lord Balarāma appeared as Saṅkarṣaṇa, the reservoir of all living entities.

Vasudeva satisfied Lord Viṣṇu by performing different kinds of sacrifices, such as Jyotiṣṭoma and Darśa-pūrṇamāsa. Some of these *yajñas* are called *prākṛta,* and some of them are known as *śaurya-satra* or *vaikṛta.* Thereafter, the other sacrifices, known as *agnihotra,* were also performed, and the prescribed articles were offered in the proper way. Thus Lord Viṣṇu was pleased. The ultimate purpose of offering oblations in sacrifice is to please Lord Viṣṇu. But in this Age of Kali it is very difficult to collect the different articles required for offering sacrifices. People have neither the means to collect the required paraphernalia nor the necessary knowledge or tendency to offer such sacrifices. Therefore, in this Age of

Kali, when people are mostly unfortunate, full of anxieties and disturbed by various kinds of calamities, the only sacrifice recommended is the performance of *saṅkīrtana-yajña*. Worshiping Lord Caitanya by this *saṅkīrtana-yajña* is the only recommended process in this age.

After the performance of the different sacrifices, Vasudeva offered ample riches, clothing, ornaments, cows, land and maidservants to the priests. Thereafter, all the wives of Vasudeva took their *avabhṛtha* baths and performed the part of the sacrificial duties known as *patnī-saṁyāja*. After finishing the offering with all the required paraphernalia, they all took their baths together in the lakes constructed by Paraśurāma, which are known as the Rāma-hrada. After Vasudeva and his wives took their baths, all the garments and ornaments they had worn were distributed to the subordinate persons engaged in singing, dancing and similar activities. We may note that the performance of sacrifice necessitates the profuse distribution of riches. Charity is offered to the priests and the *brāhmaṇas* in the beginning, and used garments and ornaments are offered in charity to the subordinate assistants after the performance of the sacrifice.

After offering the used articles to the singers and reciters, Vasudeva and his wives, dressed with new ornaments and garments, fed everyone very sumptuously, from the *brāhmaṇas* down to the dogs. After this, all the friends, family members, wives and children of Vasudeva assembled together, along with all the kings and members of the Vidarbha, Kośala, Kuru, Kāśī, Kekaya and Sṛñjaya dynasties. The priests, the demigods, the people in general, the forefathers, the ghosts and the Cāraṇas were all sufficiently remunerated by being offered ample gifts and respectful honor. Then all the persons assembled there took permission from Lord Kṛṣṇa, the husband of the goddess of fortune, and while glorifying the perfection of the sacrifice made by Vasudeva, they departed to their respective homes.

At that time, when King Dhṛtarāṣṭra, Vidura, Yudhiṣṭhira,

Bhīma, Arjuna, Bhīṣmadeva, Droṇācārya, Kuntī, Nakula, Sahadeva, Nārada, Lord Vyāsadeva and many other relatives and kinsmen were about to depart, they felt separation and therefore embraced each and every member of the Yadu dynasty with great feeling. Many others who were assembled in that sacrificial arena also departed. After this, Lord Kṛṣṇa and Lord Balarāma, along with King Ugrasena, satisfied the inhabitants of Vṛndāvana, headed by Mahārāja Nanda and the cowherd men, by profusely offering all kinds of gifts to worship them and please them. Out of their great feelings of friendship, the inhabitants of Vṛndāvana remained there for a considerable time with the members of the Yadu dynasty.

After performing this sacrifice, Vasudeva felt so satisfied that there was no limit to his happiness. All the members of his family were with him, and in their presence he caught hold of the hands of Nanda Mahārāja and addressed him thus: "My dear brother, the Supreme Personality of Godhead has created a great tie of bondage known as the bondage of love and affection. I think that it is a very difficult job for even the great sages and saintly persons to cut such a tie of love. My dear brother, you have exhibited feelings of love for me that I was not able to return. I think, therefore, that I am ungrateful. You have behaved exactly as is characteristic of saintly persons, but I shall never be able to repay you. I have no means to repay you for your friendly dealings. Nevertheless I am confident that our tie of love will never break. Our friendship must ever continue, in spite of my inability to repay you. I hope you will excuse me for this inability.

"My dear brother, in the beginning, due to my being imprisoned, I could never serve you as a friend, and although at the present moment I am very opulent, because of my material prosperity I have become blind. I therefore cannot satisfy you properly even at this time. My dear brother, you are so nice and gentle that you offer all respect to others, but you don't care for any respect for yourself. A person seeking auspicious progress in life must avoid possessing too much material opulence so that he will not become blind and puffed up, and he should take care of his friends and relatives."

When Vasudeva was speaking to Nanda Mahārāja in this way, he was influenced by a great feeling for the friendship of Nanda Mahārāja and the beneficial activities executed by King Nanda on his behalf. As such, his eyes filled with tears, and he began to cry. Nanda Mahārāja, desiring to please his friend Vasudeva and being affectionately bound with love for Lord Kṛṣṇa and Balarāma, passed three months in their association. At the end of this time, all the members of the Yadu dynasty tried to please the inhabitants of Vṛndāvana to their hearts' content. The members of the Yadu dynasty tried to satisfy Nanda Mahārāja and his associates by offering them clothing, ornaments and many other valuable articles, and they all became fully satisfied. Vasudeva, Ugrasena, Lord Kṛṣṇa, Lord Balarāma, Uddhava and all other members of the Yadu dynasty presented their individual gifts to Nanda Mahārāja and his associates. After Nanda Mahārāja received these farewell presentations, he, along with his associates, started for Vrajabhūmi, Vṛndāvana. The minds of the inhabitants of Vṛndāvana remained, however, with Kṛṣṇa and Balarāma, and therefore all of them started for Vṛndāvana without their minds.

When the members of the Vṛṣṇi family saw all their friends and visitors departing, they observed that the rainy season was approaching, and thus they decided to return to Dvārakā. They were fully satisfied, for they regarded Kṛṣṇa as everything. When they returned to Dvārakā, they described with great satisfaction the sacrifice performed by Vasudeva, their meeting with various friends and well-wishers, and various other incidents that had occurred during their travels in the places of pilgrimage.

Thus ends the Bhaktivedanta purport of the Eighty-fourth Chapter of Kṛṣṇa, *"Sacrificial Ceremonies Performed by Vasudeva."*

CHAPTER EIGHTY-FIVE

Spiritual Instruction for Vasudeva, and the Return of the Six Dead Sons of Devakī by Lord Kṛṣṇa

It is a Vedic custom that the junior members of the family should offer respects to the elders every morning. The children or disciples especially should offer their respects to their parents or spiritual master in the morning. In pursuance of this Vedic principle, Lord Kṛṣṇa and Balarāma used to offer Their obeisances to Their parents, Vasudeva and Devakī. One day, after having returned from the sacrificial performances at Kurukṣetra, when Lord Kṛṣṇa and Balarāma went to offer Their respects to Vasudeva, Vasudeva took the opportunity to appreciate the exalted position of his two sons. Vasudeva had the opportunity to understand the position of Kṛṣṇa and Balarāma from the great sages who had assembled in the arena of the sacrifice. Not only did he hear from the sages, but on many occasions he actually experienced that Kṛṣṇa and Balarāma were not ordinary human beings but were very extraordinary. Thus he believed the words of the sages that his sons Kṛṣṇa and Balarāma were the Supreme Personality of Godhead.

With firm faith in his sons, he addressed Them thus: "My dear Kṛṣṇa, You are the *sac-cid-ānanda-vigraha* Supreme Personality of Godhead. And my dear Balarāma, You are Saṅkarṣaṇa, the master of all mystic powers; therefore I have now understood that You are eternal. Both of You are transcendental to this material manifestation and to its cause, the Supreme Person, Mahā-Viṣṇu. You are the original controller of all. You are the resting place of this cosmic manifestation. You are its creator, and You are also its creative ingredients. You are the master of this cosmic manifestation, and actually this manifestation is created for Your pastimes only.

"The different material phases that are manifest from the beginning to the end of the cosmos under different formulas of time are also Your Self because You are both the cause and effect of this manifestation. The two features of this material world, the predominator and the predominated, are also You, and You are the supreme transcendental controller who stands above them. Therefore, You are beyond the perception of our senses. You are the Supreme Soul, unborn and unchanging. You are not affected by the six kinds of transformations which occur in the material body. The wonderful varieties of this material world are also created by You, and You have entered as the Supersoul into all of them, down to the atom. You are the vital force of all these manifestations and also their supreme cognition. As such, You are the maintainer of everything.

"The vital force—the life principle in everything—and the creative force derived from it are not acting independently but are dependent upon You, the Supreme Person behind these forces. Without Your will, they cannot work. Material energy has no cognizance. It cannot act independently without being agitated by You. Because the material nature is dependent upon You, the living entities can only attempt to act. But without Your sanction and will they cannot perform anything or achieve the results they desire.

"The original energy is only an emanation from You. My dear Lord, the shining of the moon, the heat of fire, the rays of the sun, the glittering of the stars, and the electric lightning, which are all manifested as very powerful, as well as the gravity of the mountains and the energy and fragrance of the earth—all are different manifestations of You. The pure taste of water, the water itself and the vital force which maintains all life are also features of Your Lordship.

"My dear Lord, although the forces of the senses, the mental power of thinking, willing and feeling, and the strength, movement and growth of the body appear to be performed by different movements of the airs within the body, they are all ultimately manifestations of Your energy. The vast expanse of outer space rests in You. The vibration of the sky (its thunder), the supreme sound (*oṁkāra*) and the arrangement of different words to distinguish one thing from another are all symbolic representations of You. The senses, the controllers of the senses (the demigods) and the acquisition of knowledge, which is the purpose of the senses, as well as the subject matter of knowledge—all are You. The resolution of intelligence and the sharp memory of the living entity are also You. You are the egoistic principle of ignorance, which is the cause of this material world, the egoistic principle of passion, which is the cause of the senses, and the egoistic principle of goodness, which is the origin of the different controlling deities of this material world. The illusory energy, or *māyā,* which is the cause of the conditioned soul's perpetual transmigration from one form to another, is You.

"My dear Supreme Personality of Godhead, You are the original cause of all causes, exactly as the earth is the original cause of different kinds of trees, plants and similar varieties of manifestation. As the earth is present in everything, so

You are present throughout this material manifestation as the Supersoul. You are the supreme cause of all causes, the eternal principle. Everything, in fact, is a manifestation of Your one energy. The three qualities of material nature—*sattva, rajas* and *tamas*—and the result of their interaction are linked up with You by Your agency of *yogamāyā.* They are supposed to be independent, but actually the total material energy rests upon You, the Supersoul. Since You are the supreme cause of everything, the interactions of the material manifestation—birth, growth, existence, transformation, deterioration and annihilation—are all absent in You. Your supreme energy, *yogamāyā,* is acting in variegated manifestations, but because *yogamāyā* is Your energy, You are therefore present in everything."

In the *Bhagavad-gītā,* this fact is very nicely explained in the Ninth Chapter, wherein the Lord says, "In My impersonal form I am spread all over the material energy; everything is resting in Me, but I am not there." This very statement is also given by Vasudeva. To say that the Lord is not present everywhere means that He is aloof from everything although His energy is acting everywhere. This can be understood by a crude example: In a big establishment, the energy, or the organization of the supreme boss, is working in every nook and corner of the business, but that does not mean that the original proprietor is present there. Although in every department the presence of the proprietor is felt by the workers, the physical presence of the proprietor in every department is a formality only. Actually his energy is working everywhere. Similarly, the omnipresence of the Supreme Personality of Godhead is felt in the action of His energies. Therefore the philosophy of inconceivable, simultaneous oneness with and difference from the Supreme Lord is confirmed everywhere. The Lord is one, but His energies are diverse.

Vasudeva said, "This material world is like a great flowing river, and its waves are the three material modes of nature—goodness, passion and ignorance. This material body, as well as the senses, the faculties of thinking, feeling and willing and the stages of distress, happiness, attachment and lust—all are different products of these three qualities of nature. The foolish person who cannot realize Your transcendental identity above all these material reactions continues in the entanglement of fruitive activity and is subjected to the continuous process of birth and death without a chance of being freed."

This is confirmed in a different way by the Lord in the Fourth Chapter of the *Bhagavad-gītā.* There it is said that anyone who knows the appearance and activities of the Supreme Lord Kṛṣṇa is freed from the clutches of material nature and goes back home, back to Godhead. Therefore Kṛṣṇa's transcendental name, form, activities and qualities are not products of this material nature.

"My dear Lord," Vasudeva continued, "despite all these defects of the conditioned soul, if someone somehow or other comes in contact with devotional service, he achieves the civilized human form of body with developed consciousness and thereby becomes capable of executing further progress in devotional service. And yet, illusioned by the external energy, people generally do not utilize this advantage of the human form of life. Thus they miss the chance of eternal freedom and unnecessarily spoil the progress they have made after thousands of births.

"In the bodily concept of life, due to false egotism one is attached to the offspring of the body, and thus everyone in conditioned life is entrapped by false relationships and false affection. The whole world is moving under this false impression and suffering material bondage. I know that neither of You is my son; both of You are the original chief and progenitor, the Personality of Godhead, the Puruṣa with *pradhāna.* But You have appeared on the surface of this globe to minimize the burden of the world by killing the *kṣatriya* kings who are unnecessarily increasing their military strength. You have already informed me about this in the past. My dear Lord,

You are the shelter of the surrendered soul, the supreme well-wisher of the meek and humble. I am therefore taking shelter of Your lotus feet, which alone can give one liberation from the entanglement of material existence.

"For a long time I have simply considered this body to be myself, and although You are the Supreme Personality of Godhead, I have considered You my son. My dear Lord, at the very moment when You first appeared in Kaṁsa's prison house, You informed me that You were the Supreme Personality of Godhead and that You had descended for the protection of the principles of religion as well as the destruction of the unfaithful. Although unborn, You descend in every millennium to execute Your mission. My dear Lord, as in the sky there are many forms, appearing and disappearing, You also appear in many eternal forms and then disappear. Who, therefore, can understand Your pastimes or the mystery of Your appearance and disappearance? Our only business should be to glorify Your supreme greatness."

When Vasudeva was addressing his divine sons in that way, Lord Kṛṣṇa and Balarāma were smiling. Because They are very affectionate to Their devotees, They accepted all the appreciation of Vasudeva with a kindly, smiling attitude. Kṛṣṇa then confirmed all of Vasudeva's statements as follows: "My dear father, whatever you may say, We are, after all, your sons. What you have said about Us is certainly a highly philosophical understanding of spiritual knowledge. I accept it *in toto,* without exception."

Vasudeva was in the complete perfection of life in considering Lord Kṛṣṇa and Balarāma to be his sons, but because the sages assembled in the place of pilgrimage at Kurukṣetra had spoken about the Lord as the supreme cause of everything, Vasudeva simply repeated it out of his love for Kṛṣṇa and Balarāma. Lord Kṛṣṇa did not wish to detract from His relationship with Vasudeva as father and son; therefore in the very beginning of His reply He accepted the fact that He is the eternal son of Vasudeva and that Vasudeva is the eternal father of Kṛṣṇa. After this, Lord Kṛṣṇa informed His father of the spiritual identity of all living entities. He continued, "My dear father, everyone and everything, including Me and My brother Balarāma, as well as all the inhabitants of the city of Dvārakā and the whole cosmic manifestation, are exactly as you have already explained, but all of us are also qualitatively one."

Lord Kṛṣṇa intended for Vasudeva to see everything in the vision of a *mahā-bhāgavata,* a first-class devotee, who sees that all living entities are part and parcel of the Supreme Lord and that the Supreme Lord is situated in everyone's heart. In fact, every living entity has a spiritual identity, but in contact with material existence one becomes influenced by the material modes of nature. He becomes covered by the concept of bodily life, forgetting that his spirit soul is of the same quality as the Supreme Personality of Godhead. One mistakenly considers one individual to be different from another simply because of their material bodily coverings. Because of differences between bodies, the spirit soul appears before us differently.

Lord Kṛṣṇa then gave a nice example in terms of the five material elements. The total material elements, namely the sky, air, fire, water and earth, are present in everything in the material world, whether in an earthen pot or in a mountain or in the trees or in an earring. These five elements are present in everything, in different proportions and quantities. A mountain is a gigantic form of the combination of these five elements, and a small earthen pot is made of the same elements, but in a smaller quantity. Therefore all material items, although in different shapes or different quantities, are of the same ingredients. Similarly, the living entities—beginning from Lord Kṛṣṇa and including millions of Viṣṇu forms, and then the living entities in different forms, from Lord Brahmā down to the small ant—are all of the same quality in spirit. Some are great in quantity, and some are small, but qualitatively they are of the same nature. It is therefore confirmed in the *Upaniṣads* that Kṛṣṇa, or the Supreme Lord, is the chief among all living entities and that He maintains them and supplies them with all necessities of life. Anyone who knows this philosophy is in perfect knowledge. The Vedic version *tat tvam asi,* "Thou art the same," means not that everyone is God but that everyone is qualitatively of the same nature as God.

After hearing Kṛṣṇa speak the entire philosophy of spiritual life in an abbreviated summation, Vasudeva was exceedingly pleased with his son. Being thus elated, he could not speak but remained silent. In the meantime, Devakī, the mother of Lord Kṛṣṇa, sat by the side of her husband. Previously she had heard that Kṛṣṇa and Balarāma were so kind to Their teacher that They had brought back the teacher's dead son from the clutches of the superintendent of death, Yamarāja. Since she had heard of this incident, she had also been thinking of her own sons who were killed by Kaṁsa, and while remembering them she was overwhelmed with grief.

In compassion for her dead sons, Devakī appealed to Lord Kṛṣṇa and Balarāma thus: "My dear Balarāma, Your very name suggests that You give all pleasure and all strength to everyone. Your unlimited potency is beyond the reach of our minds and words. And, my dear Kṛṣṇa, You are the master of all mystic *yogīs.* I know that You are the master of the Prajāpatis like Brahmā and his assistants, and You are the original Personality of Godhead, Nārāyaṇa. I also know for certain that You have descended to annihilate all kinds of miscreants who have been misled in the course of time. They have lost control of their minds and senses, have fallen from the quality of goodness and have deliberately neglected the direction of the revealed scriptures by living a life of extravagance and impudence. You have descended on the earth to minimize the burden of the world by killing such miscreant rulers. My dear Kṛṣṇa, I know that Mahā-Viṣṇu, who is lying in the Causal Ocean of the cosmic manifestation and who is the source of this whole creation, is simply an expansion of Your plenary portion. The creation, maintenance and annihilation of this cosmic manifestation are effected only by Your plenary portion. I therefore take shelter of You without reservation. I have heard that when You wanted to reward Your teacher, Sāndīpani Muni, and he asked You to bring back his dead son, You and Balarāma immediately brought him from the custody of Yamarāja, although he had been dead for a very long time. By this act I understand You to be the supreme master of all mystic *yogīs.* I therefore ask You to fulfill my desire in the same way. In other words, I am asking You to bring back all my sons who were killed by Kaṁsa; upon Your bringing them back, my heart will be content, and it will be a great pleasure for me just to see them once."

After hearing Their mother speak in this way, Lord Balarāma and Kṛṣṇa immediately called for the assistance of *yogamāyā* and started for the lower planetary system known as Sutala. Formerly, in His incarnation of Vāmana, the Supreme Personality of Godhead had been satisfied by the King of the demons, Bali Mahārāja, who donated to Him everything he had. Bali Mahārāja was then given the whole of Sutala for his residence and kingdom. Now when this great devotee, Bali Mahārāja, saw that Lord Balarāma and Kṛṣṇa had come to his planet, he immediately merged in an ocean of happiness. As soon as he saw Lord Kṛṣṇa and Balarāma in his presence, he and all his family members stood up from their seats and bowed down at the lotus feet of the Lords. Bali Mahārāja offered Lord Kṛṣṇa and Balarāma the best seat he had in his possession, and when both Lords were seated comfortably, he began to wash Their lotus feet. He then sprinkled the water on his head and on the heads of his family members. The water used to wash the lotus feet of Kṛṣṇa and Balarāma can purify even the greatest demigods, such as Lord Brahmā.

After this, Bali Mahārāja brought valuable garments, ornaments, sandalwood pulp, betel nuts, lamps and various nectarean foods, and along with his family members he worshiped the Lords according to the regulative principles and offered his riches and body unto Their lotus feet. King Bali was feeling such transcendental pleasure that he repeatedly grasped the Lords' lotus feet and kept them on his chest, and sometimes he put them on the top of his head. In this way he felt transcendental bliss. Tears of love and affection began to flow from his eyes, and all his bodily hairs stood on end. He began to offer prayers to the Lords in a voice which choked up intermittently.

"My Lord Balarāma, You are the original Anantadeva. You are so great that Anantadeva Śeṣa and other transcendental forms have originally emanated from You. And You, Lord Kṛṣṇa, are the original Personality of Godhead, with an eternal form that is all-blissful and full of complete knowledge. You are the creator of the whole world. You are the original initiator and propounder of the systems of *jñāna-yoga* and *bhakti-yoga.* You are the Supreme Brahman, the original Personality of Godhead. I therefore with all respect offer my obeisances unto both of You. My dear Lords, it is very difficult for the living entities to get to see You, yet when You are merciful upon Your devotees You are easy for them to see. As such, only out of Your causeless mercy have You agreed to come here and be visible to us, who are generally influenced by the qualities of ignorance and passion.

"My dear Lord, we belong to the *daitya,* or demon, category. The demons or demoniac persons—the Gandharvas, the Siddhas, the Vidyādharas, the Cāraṇas, the Yakṣas, the Rākṣasas, the Piśācas, the ghosts and the hobgoblins—are by nature incapable of worshiping You or becoming Your devotees. Instead of becoming Your devotees, they are simply impediments on the path of devotion. But You are the Supreme Personality of Godhead, representing all the *Vedas,* and are situated in the mode of uncontaminated goodness. Your position is always transcendental. For this reason, some of us, although born of the modes of passion and ignorance, have taken shelter of Your lotus feet and have become devotees. Some of us are actually pure devotees, and some of us have taken shelter of Your lotus feet because we desire to gain something from devotion.

"By Your causeless mercy only are we demons in direct contact with Your personality. This contact is not possible even for the great demigods. No one knows how You act through Your *yogamāyā* potency. Even demigods cannot calculate the expanse of the activities of Your internal potency, so how is it possible for us to know it? I therefore place my humble prayers before You: Please be kind to me, who am fully surrendered unto You, and favor me with Your causeless mercy so that I may simply remember Your lotus feet, birth after birth. My only ambition is that I may live alone just like the *paramahaṁsas* who travel alone here and there in great peace of mind, depending simply upon Your lotus feet. I also desire that if I have to associate with anyone, I may associate only with Your pure devotees and no one else, for Your pure devotees are always well-wishers of all living entities.

"My dear Lord, You are the supreme master and director of the whole world. Please, therefore, engage me in Your service and let me thus become freed from all material contaminations. You can purify me in that way because if someone engages himself in the loving service of Your Lordship, he is immediately free from all kinds of regulative principles enjoined in the *Vedas.*"

The word *paramahaṁsa* mentioned here means "the supreme swan." It is said that the swan can draw milk from a reservoir of water; it can take only the milk portion and reject the watery portion. Similarly, a person who can draw out the spiritual portion from this material world and who can live alone, depending only on the Supreme Spirit, not on the material world, is called a *paramahaṁsa.* When one achieves the *paramahaṁsa* platform, he is no longer under the regulative principles of the Vedic injunctions. A *paramahaṁsa* accepts only the association of pure devotees and rejects others, who are too much materially addicted. In other words, those who are materially addicted cannot understand the value of the *paramahaṁsa,* but those who are fortunate—who are advanced in a spiritual sense—take shelter of the *paramahaṁsa* and successfully complete the mission of human life.

After Lord Kṛṣṇa heard the prayers of Bali Mahārāja, He spoke as follows: "My dear King of the demons, in the millennium of Svāyambhuva Manu, the Prajāpati known as Marīci begot six sons, all demigods, in the womb of his wife, Ūrṇā. Once upon a time, Lord Brahmā became captivated by the beauty of his daughter and was following her, impelled by sex desire. At that time, these six demigods looked at the action of Lord Brahmā with abhorrence. This criticism of Brahmā's action by the demigods constituted a great offense on their part, and for this reason they were condemned to take birth as the grandsons of the demon Hiraṇyakaśipu. These grandsons of Hiraṇyakaśipu were thereafter put into the womb of mother Devakī, and as soon as they took their birth Kaṁsa killed them one after another. My dear King of the demons, mother Devakī is very anxious to see these six dead sons again, and she is very much aggrieved on account of their early death at the hand of Kaṁsa. I know that all of them are living with you. I have decided to take them with Me to pacify My mother, Devakī. After seeing My mother, all six of these conditioned souls will be liberated, and thus in great pleasure they will be transferred to their original planet. The names of these six conditioned souls are as follows: Smara, Udgītha, Pariṣvaṅga, Pataṅga, Kṣudrabhṛt and Ghṛṇī. They will be reinstated in their former position as demigods."

After thus informing the King of the demons, Kṛṣṇa stopped speaking, and Bali Mahārāja understood the Lord's purpose. He worshiped the Lord sufficiently, and thereafter Lord Kṛṣṇa and Lord Balarāma took away the six conditioned souls and returned to the city of Dvārakā, where Lord Kṛṣṇa presented them as little babies before His mother, Devakī.

Mother Devakī was overwhelmed with joy and was so ecstatic in motherly feeling that milk immediately began to flow from her breasts, and she fed the babies with great satisfaction. She took them on her lap again and again, smelling their heads and thinking, "I have gotten my lost children back!" For the time being she was overpowered by the energy of Viṣṇu, and in great motherly affection she enjoyed the company of her lost children.

The milk from the breasts of Devakī was transcendental nectar because the same milk had been sucked by Lord Kṛṣṇa. As such, the babies who sucked the breasts of Devakījī, which had touched the body of Lord Kṛṣṇa, immediately became self-realized persons. The babies therefore began to offer their obeisances unto Lord Kṛṣṇa, Balarāma, their father Vasudeva and their mother Devakī. After this, they were immediately transferred to their respective heavenly planets.

After they departed, Devakī was stunned with wonder that her dead children had come back and had again been transferred to their respective planets. She could adjust the events only by thinking that Lord Kṛṣṇa can perform anything wonderful in His pastimes because His potencies are all inconceivable. Without accepting the inconceivable, unlimited potencies of the Lord, one cannot understand that Lord Kṛṣṇa is the Supreme Soul. By His unlimited potencies He performs unlimited pastimes, and no one can describe them in full, nor can anyone know them all. Sūta Gosvāmī, speaking *Śrīmad-Bhāgavatam* before the sages of Naimiṣāraṇya, headed by Śaunaka Ṛṣi, gave his verdict in this connection as follows.

"Great sages, please understand that the transcendental pastimes of Lord Kṛṣṇa are all eternal. They are not ordinary narrations of historical incidents. Such narrations are identical with the Supreme Personality of Godhead Himself. Anyone, therefore, who hears such narrations of the Lord's pastimes is immediately freed from the contamination of material existence. And those who are pure devotees enjoy these narrations as nectar entering into their ears." Such narrations were spoken by Śukadeva Gosvāmī, the exalted son of Vyāsadeva, and anyone who hears them, as well as anyone who repeats them for the hearing of others, becomes Kṛṣṇa conscious. And only the Kṛṣṇa conscious persons are eligible to go back home, back to Godhead.

Thus ends the Bhaktivedanta purport of the Eighty-fifth Chapter of Kṛṣṇa, *"Spiritual Instruction for Vasudeva, and the Return of the Six Dead Sons of Devakī by Lord Kṛṣṇa."*

CHAPTER EIGHTY-SIX

The Kidnapping of Subhadrā, and Lord Kṛṣṇa's Visiting Śrutadeva and Bahulāśva

After hearing of the incidents described in the last chapter, King Parīkṣit became more inquisitive to hear about Kṛṣṇa and His pastimes, and thus he inquired from Śukadeva Gosvāmī how his grandmother Subhadrā was kidnapped by his grandfather Arjuna at the instigation of Lord Kṛṣṇa. King Parīkṣit was very eager to learn about his grandfather's kidnapping and marriage of his grandmother.

Thus Śukadeva Gosvāmī began to narrate the story as follows: Once upon a time, King Parīkṣit's grandfather Arjuna, the great hero, was visiting several holy places of pilgrimage, and while thus traveling all over he happened to come to Prabhāsa-kṣetra. In Prabhāsa-kṣetra he heard the news that Lord Balarāma was negotiating the marriage of Subhadrā, the daughter of Arjuna's maternal uncle, Vasudeva. Although her father, Vasudeva, and her brother Kṛṣṇa were not in agreement with Him, Balarāma was in favor of marrying Subhadrā to Duryodhana. Arjuna, however, desired to gain Subhadrā's hand. As he thought of Subhadrā and her beauty, Arjuna became more and more captivated with the idea of marrying her, and with a plan in mind he dressed himself like a Vaiṣṇava *sannyāsī,* carrying a *tridaṇḍa* in his hand.

The Māyāvādī *sannyāsīs* take one *daṇḍa,* or one rod, whereas the Vaiṣṇava *sannyāsīs* take three *daṇḍas,* or three rods. The three rods, or *tridaṇḍa,* indicate that a Vaiṣṇava *sannyāsī* vows to render service to the Supreme Personality of Godhead by his body, mind and words. The system of *tridaṇḍa-sannyāsa* has been in existence for a long time, and the Vaiṣṇava *sannyāsīs* are called *tridaṇḍīs,* or sometimes *tridaṇḍi-svāmīs* or *tridaṇḍi-gosvāmīs.*

Sannyāsīs are generally meant to travel all over the country for preaching work, but during the four months of the rainy season in India, from July through October, they do not travel but take shelter in one place and remain there without moving. This nonmovement of the *sannyāsī* is called Cāturmāsya-vrata. When a *sannyāsī* stays in one place for these four months, the local inhabitants of that place take advantage of his presence to become spiritually advanced.

Arjuna, in the dress of a *tridaṇḍi-sannyāsī,* remained in the city of Dvārakā for the four months of the rainy season, devising a plan whereby he could get Subhadrā as his wife. None of the inhabitants of Dvārakā, including Lord Balarāma, could recognize the *sannyāsī* to be Arjuna; therefore all of them offered their respects and obeisances to the *sannyāsī* without knowing the actual situation.

One day Lord Balarāma invited this particular *sannyāsī* to lunch at His home. Balarāmajī very respectfully offered him all kinds of palatable dishes, and the so-called *sannyāsī* was eating sumptuously. While eating at the home of Balarāmajī, Arjuna was simply looking at beautiful Subhadrā, who was very enchanting to great heroes and kings. Out of love for her, Arjuna's eyes brightened, and he looked at her with glittering eyes. Arjuna decided that somehow or other he would achieve Subhadrā as his wife, and his mind became agitated on account of this strong desire.

Arjuna, the grandfather of Mahārāja Parīkṣit, was himself extraordinarily beautiful, and his bodily structure was very attractive to Subhadrā, who decided within her mind that she would accept only Arjuna as her husband. As a simple girl, she was smiling with great pleasure, looking at Arjuna. Thus Arjuna also became more and more attracted by her. In this way, Subhadrā dedicated herself to Arjuna, and he resolved to marry her by any means. He then became absorbed twenty-four hours a day in thought of how he could get Subhadrā as his wife. He was afflicted with the thought of getting Subhadrā and had not a moment's peace of mind.

Once upon a time, Subhadrā, seated on a chariot, came out of the palace fort to see the gods in the temple. Arjuna took this opportunity, and with the permission of Vasudeva and Devakī he kidnapped her. After getting on Subhadrā's chariot, he prepared himself for a fight. Taking up his bow and holding off with his arrows the soldiers ordered to check him, Arjuna took Subhadrā away. While Subhadrā was thus being kidnapped by Arjuna, her relatives and family members began to cry, but still he took her, just as a lion takes his prey and departs. When it was disclosed to Lord Balarāma that the so-called *sannyāsī* was Arjuna, who had planned such a device simply to take away Subhadrā, and that he had actually taken her, He became very angry. Just as the waves of the ocean become agitated on a full-moon day, Lord Balarāma became greatly disturbed.

Lord Kṛṣṇa was in favor of Arjuna; therefore, along with other members of the family, He tried to pacify Balarāma by falling at His feet and begging Him to pardon Arjuna. Kṛṣṇa convinced Lord Balarāma that Subhadrā was attached to Arjuna, and thus Balarāma became pleased to know that she wanted Arjuna as her husband. The matter was settled, and to please the newly married couple Lord Balarāma arranged to send a dowry consisting of an abundance of riches, including elephants, chariots, horses, menservants and maidservants.

Mahārāja Parīkṣit was very eager to hear more about Lord Kṛṣṇa, and so, after finishing the narration of Arjuna's kidnapping Subhadrā, Śukadeva Gosvāmī began to narrate another story, as follows.

There was a householder *brāhmaṇa* in the city of Mithilā, the capital of the kingdom of Videha. This *brāhmaṇa,* whose name was Śrutadeva, was a great devotee of Lord Kṛṣṇa. Because he was fully Kṛṣṇa conscious and always engaged in the service of the Lord, he was completely peaceful in mind and detached from all material attraction. He was very learned and had no desire other than to be fully situated in Kṛṣṇa consciousness. Although in the order of householder life, he never took great pains to earn anything for his livelihood; he was satisfied with whatever he could achieve without much endeavor, and somehow or other he lived in that way. Every day he would get the necessities of life in just the quantity required, and not more. That was his destiny. The *brāhmaṇa* had no desire to get more than what he needed, and thus he was peacefully executing the regulative principles of a *brāhmaṇa's* life, as enjoined in the revealed scriptures.

Fortunately, the King of Mithilā was as good a devotee as the *brāhmaṇa.* The name of this famous king was Bahulāśva. He was very well established in his reputation as a good king, and he was not at all ambitious to extend his kingdom for the sake of sense gratification. As such, both the *brāhmaṇa* and King Bahulāśva remained pure devotees of Lord Kṛṣṇa in Mithilā.

Since Lord Kṛṣṇa was very merciful toward these two devotees, King Bahulāśva and the *brāhmaṇa* Śrutadeva, He one day asked His driver, Dāruka, to take His chariot into the capital city of Mithilā. Lord Kṛṣṇa was accompanied by the great sages Nārada, Vāmadeva, Atri, Vyāsadeva, Paraśurāma, Asita, Aruṇi, Śukadeva, Bṛhaspati, Kaṇva, Maitreya, Cyavana and others. Lord Kṛṣṇa and the sages passed through many villages and towns, and everywhere the citizens would receive them with great respect and offer them articles in worship. When the citizens came to see the Lord and all of them assembled together in one place, it seemed as though the sun were present along with his various satellite planets. In that journey, Lord Kṛṣṇa and the sages passed through the kingdoms of Ānarta, Dhanva, Kuru-jāṅgala, Kaṅka, Matsya, Pāñcāla, Kunti, Madhu, Kekaya, Kośala and Arṇa, and thus all the citizens of these places, both men and women, could see Lord Kṛṣṇa face to face. In this way they enjoyed celestial happiness, with open hearts full of love and affection for the Lord, and when they saw the face of the Lord, it seemed to them that they were drinking nectar through their eyes. When they saw Kṛṣṇa, all the ignorant misconceptions of their lives dissipated. When the Lord passed through the various countries and the people came to visit Him, simply by glancing over them the Lord would bestow all good fortune upon them and liberate them from all kinds of ignorance. In some places the demigods would join with the human beings, and their glorification of the Lord would cleanse all directions of all inauspicious things. In this way, Lord Kṛṣṇa gradually reached the kingdom of Videha.

When the citizens received the news of the Lord's arrival, they all felt unlimited happiness and came to welcome Him, taking gifts in their hands to offer. As soon as they saw Lord Kṛṣṇa, their hearts immediately blossomed in transcendental bliss, just like lotus flowers upon the rising of the sun. Previously they had simply heard the names of the great sages but had never seen them. Now, by the mercy of Lord Kṛṣṇa, they had the opportunity of seeing both the great sages and the Lord Himself.

King Bahulāśva and the *brāhmaṇa* Śrutadeva, knowing well that the Lord had come there just to grace them with favor, immediately fell at the Lord's lotus feet and offered their respects. With folded hands, the King and the *brāhmaṇa* each simultaneously invited Lord Kṛṣṇa and all the sages to his home. In order to please both of them, Lord Kṛṣṇa expanded Himself into two and went to the houses of each one of them; yet neither the King nor the *brāhmaṇa* could understand that the Lord had gone to the house of the other. Both thought that the Lord had gone only to his own house. That He and His companions were present in both houses, although both the *brāhmaṇa* and the King thought He was present in one house only, is another opulence of the Supreme Personality of Godhead. This opulence is described in the revealed scriptures as *vaibhava-prakāśa.* When Lord Kṛṣṇa married sixteen thousand wives, He expanded Himself into sixteen thousand forms, each one of them as powerful as He Himself. Similarly, in Vṛndāvana, when Brahmā stole Kṛṣṇa's calves and cowherd boys, Kṛṣṇa expanded Himself into many new calves and boys.

Bahulāśva, the King of Videha, was very intelligent and was a perfect gentleman. He was astonished that so many great sages, along with the Supreme Personality of Godhead, were personally present in his home. He knew perfectly well that conditioned souls engaged in worldly affairs cannot be one hundred percent pure, whereas the Supreme Personality of Godhead and His pure devotees are always transcendental to worldly contamination. Therefore, when he found that the Supreme Personality of Godhead, Kṛṣṇa, and all the great sages were at his home, he was astonished, and he began to thank Lord Kṛṣṇa for His causeless mercy.

Feeling very much obliged and wanting to receive his guests to the best of his ability, he called for nice chairs and cushions, and Lord Kṛṣṇa, along with all the sages, sat down very comfortably. At that time, King Bahulāśva's mind was very restless, not because of any problems but because of great ecstasy of love and devotion. His heart was filled with love and affection for the Lord and His associates, and his eyes were filled with tears of ecstasy. He washed the feet of his divine guests, and afterward he and his family members sprinkled the water on their own heads. After this, he offered the guests nice flower garlands, sandalwood pulp, incense, new garments, ornaments, lamps, cows and bulls. In a manner just befitting his royal position, he worshiped each one of them in this way. When all had been fed sumptuously and were sitting very comfortably, Bahulāśva came before Lord Kṛṣṇa and caught His lotus feet. He placed them on his lap and, while massaging the feet with his hands, began to speak about the glories of the Lord in a sweet voice.

"My dear Lord, You are the Supersoul of all living entities, and as the witness within the heart You are cognizant of everyone's activities. Thus we are duty-bound to always think of Your lotus feet so that we can remain in a secure position and not deviate from Your eternal service. As a result of our continuous remembrance of Your lotus feet, You have kindly visited my place personally to favor me with Your causeless mercy. We have heard, my dear Lord, that by Your various statements You confirm Your pure devotees to be more dear to You than Lord Balarāma or Your constant servitor the goddess of fortune. Your devotees are dearer to You than Your first son, Lord Brahmā, and I am sure that You have so kindly visited my place in order to prove Your divine statement. I cannot imagine how people can be godless and demoniac even after knowing of Your causeless mercy and affection for Your devotees who are constantly engaged in Kṛṣṇa consciousness. How can they forget Your lotus feet?

"My dear Lord, it is known to us that You are so kind and liberal that when a person leaves everything just to engage in Kṛṣṇa consciousness, You sometimes give Yourself in exchange for that unalloyed service. You have appeared in the Yadu dynasty to fulfill Your mission of reclaiming all conditioned souls rotting in the sinful activities of material existence, and this appearance is already famous all over the world. My dear Lord, You are the ocean of unlimited mercy, love and affection. Your transcendental form is full of bliss, knowledge and eternity. You can attract everyone's heart by Your beautiful form as Śyāmasundara, Kṛṣṇa. Your knowledge is unlimited, and to teach all people how to execute devotional service You have sent Your incarnation Nara-Nārāyaṇa, who is engaged in severe austerities and penances at Badarīnārāyaṇa. Kindly, therefore, accept my humble obeisances at Your lotus feet. My dear Lord, I beg to request You and Your companions, the great sages and *brāhmaṇas,* to remain at my place at least for a few days so that this family of the famous King Nimi may be sanctified by the dust of Your lotus feet." Lord Kṛṣṇa could not refuse the request of His devotee, and thus He remained there for a few days with the sages to sanctify the city of Mithilā and all its citizens.

Meanwhile, the *brāhmaṇa* Śrutadeva, simultaneously receiving Lord Kṛṣṇa and His associates at his home, was transcendentally overwhelmed with joy. After offering his guests nice sitting places, the *brāhmaṇa* began to dance, waving around his wrap. Śrutadeva, being not at all rich, offered only mattresses, wooden planks, straw carpets and so on to his distinguished guests, Lord Kṛṣṇa and the sages, but he welcomed them to the best of his ability. He spoke very highly of the Lord and the sages, and he and his wife washed the feet of each one of them. After this, he took the water and sprinkled it over all the members of his family, and although the *brāhmaṇa* appeared very poor, he was at that time most fortunate. While Śrutadeva was welcoming Lord Kṛṣṇa and His associates, he simply forgot himself in transcendental joy. After welcoming the Lord and His companions, according to his ability he brought fruits, incense, scented water, scented clay, *tulasī* leaves, *kuśa* straw and lotus flowers. They were not costly items and could be secured very easily, but because they were offered with devotional love, Lord Kṛṣṇa and His associates accepted them gladly. The *brāhmaṇa's* wife cooked simple foods like rice and dhal, and Lord Kṛṣṇa and His followers were very pleased to accept them because they were offered in devotional love. When Lord Kṛṣṇa and His associates were fed in this way, the *brāhmaṇa* Śrutadeva was thinking thus: "I have fallen into the deep, dark well of householder life and am the most unfortunate person. How has it become possible that Lord Kṛṣṇa, who is the Supreme Personality of Godhead, and His associates, the great sages, whose very presence makes a place as sanctified as a pilgrimage site, have agreed to come to my place?" While the *brāhmaṇa* was thinking in this way, the guests finished their lunch and sat back very comfortably. At that time, the *brāhmaṇa* Śrutadeva and his wife, children and other relatives appeared there to render service to the distinguished guests. While touching the lotus feet of Lord Kṛṣṇa, the *brāhmaṇa* began to speak.

"My dear Lord," he said, "You are the Supreme Person, Puruṣottama, transcendentally situated beyond the manifested and unmanifested material creation. The activities of this material world and of the conditioned souls have nothing to do with Your position. We can appreciate that not only today have You given me Your audience, but You are associating with all the living entities as Paramātmā since the beginning of creation."

This statement by the *brāhmaṇa* is very instructive. It is a fact that the Supreme Lord, the Personality of Godhead, in His Paramātmā feature, enters the creation of this material world as Mahā-Viṣṇu, Garbhodakaśāyī Viṣṇu and Kṣīrodakaśāyī Viṣṇu, and in a very friendly attitude the Lord sits along with the conditioned soul in the body. Therefore, every living entity has the Lord with him from the very beginning, but due to his mistaken consciousness of life, the living entity cannot understand this. When his consciousness, however, is changed into Kṛṣṇa consciousness, he can immediately understand how Kṛṣṇa is trying to assist the conditioned souls to get out of the material entanglement.

Śrutadeva continued, "My dear Lord, You have entered this material world as if sleeping. A conditioned soul, while sleeping, creates false or temporary worlds in his mind; he becomes busy in many illusory activities—sometimes becoming a king, sometimes being murdered or sometimes going to an unknown city—and all these are simply temporary affairs. Similarly, Your Lordship, apparently also in a sleeping condition, enters this material world to create a temporary manifestation, not for Your personal necessities but for the conditioned soul who wants to imitate Your Lordship as enjoyer. The conditioned soul's enjoyment in the material world is temporary and illusory. And yet the conditioned soul is by himself unable to create such a temporary situation for his illusory enjoyment. To fulfill his desires, although they are temporary and illusory, You enter this temporary manifestation to help him. Thus from the beginning of the conditioned soul's entering into the material world, You are his constant companion. When, therefore, the conditioned soul comes in contact with a pure devotee and takes to devotional service, beginning from the process of hearing Your transcendental pastimes, glorifying Your transcendental activities, worshiping Your eternal form in the temple, offering prayers to You and engaging in discussion to understand Your transcendental position, he gradually becomes freed from the contamination of material existence. And as his heart becomes cleansed of all material dust, You gradually become visible there. Although You are constantly with the conditioned soul, only when he becomes purified by devotional service do You become revealed to him. Others, who are bewildered by fruitive activities, either by Vedic injunction or by customary dealings, and who do not take to devotional service, are captivated by the external happiness of the bodily concept of life. You are not revealed to such persons. Rather, You remain far, far away from them. But for one who engages in Your devotional service and purifies his heart by constant chanting of Your holy name, You are very easily understood as his eternal, constant companion.

"It is said that Your Lordship, sitting in the heart of a devotee, gives him direction by which he can very quickly come back home, back to You. This direct dictation by You reveals Your existence within the heart of the devotee. Only a devotee can immediately appreciate Your existence within his heart, whereas for a person who has only a bodily concept of life and is engaged in sense gratification, You always remain covered by the curtain of *yogamāyā.* Such a person cannot realize that You are very near, sitting within his heart. For a nondevotee, You are appreciated only as ultimate death. The difference is like the difference between a cat's carrying its kittens in its mouth and carrying a rat in its mouth. In the mouth of the cat, the rat feels its death, whereas the kittens in the mouth of the cat feel motherly affection. Similarly, You are present to everyone, but the nondevotee feels You as ultimate cruel death, whereas for a devotee You are the supreme instructor and philosopher. The atheist, therefore, understands the presence of God as death, but the devotee understands the presence of God always within his heart, takes dictation from You and lives transcendentally, unaffected by the contamination of the material world.

"You are the supreme controller and superintendent of the material nature's activities. The atheistic class of men simply observe the activities of material nature but cannot find You as the original background. A devotee, however, can immediately see Your hand in every movement of material nature. The curtain of *yogamāyā* cannot cover the eyes of the devotee of Your Lordship, but it can cover the eyes of the nondevotee. The nondevotee is unable to see You face to face, just as a person whose eyes are blocked by the covering of a cloud cannot see the sun, although persons flying above the cloud can see the sunshine brilliantly, as it is. My dear Lord, I offer my respectful obeisances unto You. My dear self-effulgent Lord, I am Your eternal servitor. Therefore, kindly order me—what can I do for You? The conditioned soul feels the pangs of material contamination as the threefold miseries as long as You are not visible to him. And as soon as You are visible by development of Kṛṣṇa consciousness, all miseries of material existence are simultaneously vanquished."

The Supreme Personality of Godhead, Kṛṣṇa, is naturally very much affectionately inclined to His devotees. When He heard Śrutadeva's prayers of pure devotion, He was very pleased and immediately caught his hands and addressed him thus: "My dear Śrutadeva, all these great sages, *brāhmaṇas* and saintly persons have been very kind to you by personally coming here to see you. You should consider this opportunity to be a great fortune for you. They are so kind that they are traveling with Me, and wherever they go they immediately make the whole atmosphere as pure as transcendence simply by the touch of the dust of their feet. People are accustomed to go to the temples of God. They also visit holy places of pilgrimage, and after prolonged association with such activities for many days by touch and by worship, they gradually become purified. But the influence of great sages and saintly persons is so great that by seeing them one immediately becomes completely purified.

"Moreover, the very purifying potency of pilgrimages or worship of different demigods is also achieved by the grace of saintly persons. A pilgrimage site becomes a holy place because of the presence of the saintly persons. My dear Śrutadeva, when a person is born as a *brāhmaṇa,* he immediately becomes the best of all human beings. And if such a *brāhmaṇa,* remaining self-satisfied, practices austerities, studies the *Vedas* and engages in My devotional service, as is the duty of the *brāhmaṇa*—or in other words, if a *brāhmaṇa* becomes a Vaiṣṇava—how wonderful is his greatness! My feature of four-handed Nārāyaṇa is not so pleasing or dear to Me as is a *brāhmaṇa* Vaiṣṇava. *Brāhmaṇa* means 'one well conversant with Vedic knowledge.' A *brāhmaṇa* is the insignia of perfect knowledge, and I am the full-fledged manifestation of all gods. Less intelligent men do not understand Me, nor do they understand the influence of the *brāhmaṇa* Vaiṣṇava. They are influenced by the three modes of material nature and thus dare to criticize Me and My pure devotees. A *brāhmaṇa* Vaiṣṇava, or a devotee already on the brahminical platform, can realize Me within his heart, and therefore he definitely concludes that the whole cosmic manifestation and its different features are effects of different energies of the Lord. Thus he has a clear conception of the whole material nature and the total material energy, and in every action such a devotee sees Me only, and nothing else.

"My dear Śrutadeva, you may therefore accept all these great saintly persons, *brāhmaṇas* and sages as My bona fide representatives. By worshiping them faithfully, you will be worshiping Me more diligently. I consider worship of My devotees to be better than direct worship of Me. If someone attempts to worship Me directly without worshiping My devotees, I do not accept such worship, even though it may be presented with great opulence."

In this way both the *brāhmaṇa* Śrutadeva and the King of Mithilā, under the direction of the Lord, worshiped both Kṛṣṇa and His followers, the great sages and saintly *brāhmaṇas,* on an equal level of spiritual importance. Both *brāhmaṇa* and King ultimately achieved the supreme goal of being transferred to the spiritual world. The devotee does not know anyone except Lord Kṛṣṇa, and Kṛṣṇa is most affectionate to His devotee. Lord Kṛṣṇa remained in Mithilā both at the house of the *brāhmaṇa* Śrutadeva and at the palace of King Bahulāśva. And after favoring them lavishly by His transcendental instructions, He went back to His capital city, Dvārakā.

The instruction we receive from this incident is that King Bahulāśva and Śrutadeva the *brāhmaṇa* were accepted by the Lord on the same level because both were pure devotees. This is the real qualification for being recognized by the Supreme Personality of Godhead. Because it has become the fashion of this age to be falsely proud of having taken birth in the family of a *kṣatriya* or a *brāhmaṇa,* we see persons without any qualification other than birth claiming to be a *brāhmaṇa* or *kṣatriya* or *vaiśya.* But as stated in the scriptures, *kalau śūdra-sambhavaḥ:* "In this Age of Kali, everyone is born a *śūdra.*" This is because there is no performance of the purificatory processes known as *saṁskāras,* which begin from the time of the mother's pregnancy and continue up to the point of the individual's death. No one can be classified as a member of a particular caste, especially of a higher caste—*brāhmaṇa, kṣatriya* or *vaiśya*—simply by birthright. If one is not purified by the process of the seed-giving ceremony, or *garbhādhāna-saṁskāra,* he is immediately classified amongst the *śūdras* because only the *śūdras* do not undergo this purificatory process. Sex life without the purificatory process of Kṛṣṇa consciousness is merely the seed-giving process of the *śūdras* or the animals. Kṛṣṇa consciousness is therefore the best process of purification. By this process everyone can come to the platform of a Vaiṣṇava, which includes having all the qualifications of a *brāhmaṇa.* The Vaiṣṇavas are trained to become freed from the four kinds of sinful activities—illicit sex, indulgence in intoxicants, gambling and eating animal foods. One cannot be on the brahminical platform without having these preliminary qualifications, and without becoming a qualified *brāhmaṇa,* one cannot become a pure devotee.

Thus ends the Bhaktivedanta purport of the Eighty-sixth Chapter of Kṛṣṇa, *"The Kidnapping of Subhadrā, and Lord Kṛṣṇa's Visiting Śrutadeva and Bahulāśva."*

CHAPTER EIGHTY-SEVEN

Prayers by the Personified Vedas

King Parīkṣit inquired from Śukadeva Gosvāmī about a very important topic in understanding transcendental subject matter. His question was, "Since Vedic knowledge generally deals with the subject matter of the three qualities of the material world, how then can it approach the subject matter of transcendence, which is beyond the approach of the three material modes? Since the mind is material and the vibration of words is a material sound, how can the Vedic knowledge, expressing by material sound the thoughts of the material mind, approach transcendence? Description of a subject matter necessitates describing its source of emanation, its qualities and its activities. Such description can be possible only by thinking with the material mind and by vibrating material words. Brahman, or the Absolute Truth, has no material qualities, but our power of speaking does not go beyond the material qualities. How then can Brahman, the Absolute Truth, be described by your words? I do not see how it is possible to understand transcendence from such expressions of material sound."

The purpose of King Parīkṣit's inquiry was to ascertain from Śukadeva Gosvāmī whether the *Vedas* ultimately describe the Absolute Truth as impersonal or as personal. Understanding of the Absolute Truth progresses in three features—impersonal Brahman, Paramātmā localized in everyone's heart, and, at last, the Supreme Personality of Godhead, Kṛṣṇa.

The *Vedas* deal with three departments of activities. One is called *karma-kāṇḍa,* or activities under Vedic injunction, which gradually purify one to understand his real position; the next is *jñāna-kāṇḍa,* the process of understanding the Absolute Truth by speculative methods; and the third is *upāsanā-kāṇḍa,* or worship of the Supreme Personality of Godhead and sometimes of the demigods also. The worship of the demigods recommended in the *Vedas* is ordered with the understanding of the demigods' relationship to the Personality of Godhead. The Supreme Personality of Godhead has many parts and parcels; some are called *svāṁśas,* or His personal expansions, and some are called *vibhinnāṁśas,* the living entities. All such expansions, both *svāṁśas* and *vibhinnāṁśas,* are emanations from the original Personality of Godhead. *Svāṁśa* expansions are called *viṣṇu-tattva,* whereas the *vibhinnāṁśa* expansions are called *jīva-tattva.* The different demigods are *jīva-tattva.* The conditioned souls are generally put into the activities of the material world for sense gratification; therefore, as stated in the *Bhagavad-gītā,* to regulate those who are very much addicted to different kinds of sense gratification, the worship of demigods is sometimes recommended. For example, for persons very much addicted to meat-eating, the Vedic injunction recommends that after worshiping the form of goddess Kālī and sacrificing a goat (not any other animal) under *karma-kāṇḍa* regulation, the worshipers may be allowed to eat meat. The idea is not to encourage one to eat meat but to allow one who insists on eating meat to eat it under certain restricted conditions. Therefore, worship of the demigods is not worship of the Absolute Truth, but by worshiping the demigods one gradually comes to accept the Supreme Personality of Godhead in an indirect way. This indirect acceptance is described in the *Bhagavad-gītā* as *avidhi. Avidhi* means "not bona fide." Since demigod worship is not bona fide, the impersonalists stress concentration on the impersonal feature of the Absolute Truth. King Parīkṣit's question was, Which is the ultimate target of Vedic knowledge—this concentration on the impersonal feature of the Absolute Truth or concentration on the personal feature? After all, both the impersonal and the personal feature of the Supreme Lord are beyond our material conception. The impersonal feature of the Absolute, the Brahman effulgence, is but the rays of the personal body of Kṛṣṇa. These rays of the personal body of Kṛṣṇa are cast all over the creation of the Lord, and the portion of the effulgence which is covered by the material cloud is called the created cosmos of the three material qualities—*sattva, rajas* and *tamas.* How can persons who are within this clouded portion, called the material world, conceive of the Absolute Truth by the speculative method?

In answering King Parīkṣit's question, Śukadeva Gosvāmī replied that the Supreme Personality of Godhead has created the mind, senses and living force of the living entity for the purpose of sense gratification and transmigration from one kind of body to another, as well as for the purpose of allowing liberation from the material conditions. In other words, one can utilize the senses, mind and living force for sense gratification and transmigration from one body to another or for the matter of liberation. The Vedic injunctions are there just to give the conditioned souls the chance for sense gratification under regulative principles, and thereby also to give them the chance for promotion to higher conditions of life; ultimately, if the consciousness is purified, one comes to his original position and goes back home, back to Godhead.

The living entity is intelligent. One therefore has to utilize his intelligence over the mind and the senses. When the mind and senses are purified by the proper use of intelligence, then the conditioned soul is liberated; otherwise, if the intelligence is not properly utilized in controlling the senses and mind, the conditioned soul continues to transmigrate from one kind of body to another simply for sense gratification. Another point clearly stated in the answer of Śukadeva Gosvāmī is that it is the mind, senses and intelligence of the individual living entity that the Lord created. It is not stated that the living entities themselves were ever created. Just as the shining particles of the sun's rays always exist with the sun, the living entities exist eternally as parts and parcels of the Supreme Personality of Godhead. But just as the sunrays are sometimes covered by a cloud, which is created by the sun, so the conditioned souls, although eternally existing as parts of the Supreme Lord, are sometimes put within the cloud of the material concept of life, in the darkness of ignorance. The whole Vedic process is to alleviate that darkened condition. Ultimately, when the senses and mind of the conditioned being are fully purified, he then comes to the original position, called Kṛṣṇa consciousness, and that is liberation.

In the *Vedānta-sūtra,* the first *sūtra,* or code, questions about the Absolute Truth. *Athāto brahma-jijñāsā:* What is the nature of the Absolute Truth? The next *sūtra* answers that the nature of the Absolute Truth is that He is the origin of everything. Whatever we experience, even in this material condition of life, is but an emanation from Him. The Absolute Truth created the mind, senses and intelligence. This means that the Absolute Truth is not without mind, intelligence and senses. In other words, He is not impersonal. The very word *created* means that He has transcendental intelligence. For example, when a father begets a child, the child has senses because the father also has senses. The child is born with hands and legs because the father also has hands and legs. Sometimes it is said that man is made after the image of

God. The Absolute Truth is therefore the Supreme Personality, with transcendental mind, senses and intelligence. When one's mind, intelligence and senses are purified of material contamination, one can understand the original feature of the Absolute Truth as a person.

The Vedic process is to promote the conditioned soul gradually from the mode of ignorance to the mode of passion, and from the mode of passion to the mode of goodness. In the mode of goodness there is sufficient light for understanding things as they are. For example, from earth a tree grows, and from the wood of the tree, fire is ignited. In that igniting process we first of all find smoke, and the next stage is heat, and then fire. When there is actually fire, we can utilize it for various purposes; therefore, fire is the ultimate goal. Similarly, in the gross material stage of life the quality of ignorance is very prominent. Dissipation of this ignorance takes place in the gradual progress of civilization from the barbarian stage to civilized life, and when one comes to the form of civilized life he is said to be in the mode of passion. In the barbarian stage, or in the mode of ignorance, the senses are gratified in a very crude way, whereas in the mode of passion, or in civilized life, the senses are gratified in a polished manner. But when one is promoted to the mode of goodness, one can understand that the senses and the mind are engaged in material activities only due to being covered by perverted consciousness. When this perverted consciousness is gradually transformed into Kṛṣṇa consciousness, then the path of liberation is opened. So it is not that one is unable to approach the Absolute Truth by the senses and the mind. The conclusion is, rather, that the senses, mind and intelligence in the gross stage of contamination cannot appreciate the nature of the Absolute Truth, but when purified, the senses, mind and intelligence can understand what the Absolute Truth is. The purifying process is called devotional service, or Kṛṣṇa consciousness.

In the *Bhagavad-gītā* it is clearly stated that the purpose of Vedic knowledge is to understand Kṛṣṇa, and Kṛṣṇa is understood by devotional service, beginning with the process of surrender. As stated in the *Bhagavad-gītā,* one has to think of Kṛṣṇa always, one has to render loving service to Kṛṣṇa always, and one always has to worship and bow down before Kṛṣṇa. By this process only can one enter into the kingdom of God, without any doubt.

One who is enlightened in the mode of goodness by the process of devotional service is freed from the modes of ignorance and passion. In answering King Parīkṣit's question, Śukadeva Gosvāmī used the word *ātmane,* which indicates the stage of brahminical qualification in which one is allowed to study the Vedic literatures known as the *Upaniṣads.* The *Upaniṣads* describe in different ways the transcendental qualities of the Supreme Lord. The Absolute Truth, the Supreme Lord, is called *nirguṇa.* That does not mean He has no qualities. It is only because He has qualities that the conditioned living entities can have qualities. The purpose of studying the *Upaniṣads* is to understand the transcendental qualities of the Absolute Truth, as opposed to the material qualities of ignorance, passion and goodness. That is the way of Vedic understanding. Great sages like the four Kumāras, headed by Sanaka, followed these principles of Vedic knowledge and came gradually from impersonal understanding to the platform of personal worship of the Supreme Lord. It is therefore recommended that we must follow the great personalities. Śukadeva Gosvāmī is also one of the great personalities, and his answer to the inquiry of Mahārāja Parīkṣit is authorized. One who follows in the footsteps of such great personalities surely walks very easily on the path of liberation and ultimately goes back home, back to Godhead. That is the way of perfecting this human form of life.

Śukadeva Gosvāmī continued to speak to Parīkṣit Mahārāja. "My dear King," he said, "in this regard I shall narrate a nice story. This story is important because it is in connection with Nārāyaṇa, the Supreme Personality of Godhead. This narration is a conversation between Nārāyaṇa Ṛṣi and the great sage Nārada." Nārāyaṇa Ṛṣi still resides in Badarīkāśrama and is accepted as an incarnation of Nārāyaṇa. Badarīkāśrama is situated in the northernmost part of the Himalayan Mountains and is always covered with snow. Religious Indians still go to visit this place during the summer season, when the snowfall is not very severe.

Once when Nārada, the great devotee and ascetic amongst the demigods, was traveling among different planets, he desired to meet the ascetic Nārāyaṇa personally in Badarīkāśrama and offer Him respects. This great sage incarnation of Godhead, Nārāyaṇa Ṛṣi, has been undergoing great penances and austerities from the very beginning of the creation to teach the inhabitants of Bhārata-varṣa how to attain the highest perfectional stage of going back to Godhead. His austerities and penances are exemplary practices for the human being. The incarnation of God Nārāyaṇa Ṛṣi was sitting amongst many devotees in the village known as Kalāpagrāma. Of course, these were not ordinary sages sitting with Him, and the great sage Nārada also appeared there. After offering his respects to Nārāyaṇa Ṛṣi, Nārada asked Him exactly the same question King Parīkṣit asked Śukadeva Gosvāmī. Then the Ṛṣi answered by following in the footsteps of His predecessors. He narrated a story of how the same question had been discussed on the planet known as Janoloka, which is above the Svargaloka planets, such as the moon and Venus. On this planet, great sages and saintly persons live, and they once discussed the same point regarding the understanding of Brahman and His real identity.

The great sage Nārāyaṇa began to speak. "My dear Nārada," He said, "I shall tell you a story which took place long, long ago. There was a great meeting of the denizens of the heavenly planets, and almost all the important *brahmacārīs,* such as the four Kumāras—Sanandana, Sanaka, Sanātana and Sanat-kumāra—attended. Their discussion was on the subject matter of understanding the Absolute Truth, Brahman. You were not present at that meeting because you had gone to see My expansion Aniruddha, who lives on the island of Śvetadvīpa. In this meeting, all the great sages and *brahmacārīs* very elaborately discussed the point about which you have asked Me, and it was very interesting. The discussion was so delicate that even the *Vedas* were unable to answer the intricate questions raised."

Nārāyaṇa Ṛṣi told Nāradajī that the same question Nāradajī had raised had been discussed in that meeting on Janoloka. This is the way of understanding through the *paramparā,* or disciplic succession. Mahārāja Parīkṣit questioned Śukadeva Gosvāmī, and Śukadeva Gosvāmī referred the matter to Nārada, who had in the same way questioned Nārāyaṇa Ṛṣi, who had put the matter to still higher authorities on the planet of Janoloka, where it was discussed among the great Kumāras—Sanātana, Sanaka, Sanandana and Sanatkumāra. These four *brahmacārīs,* the Kumāras, are recognized scholars in the *Vedas* and other *śāstras.* Their unlimited volumes of knowledge, backed by austerities and penances, are exhibited by their sublime, ideal character. They are very amiable and gentle in behavior, and for them there is no distinction between friends, well-wishers and enemies. Being transcendentally situated, such personalities as the Kumāras are above all material considerations and are always neutral in respect to material dualities. In the discussions held among the four brothers, one of them, namely Sanandana, was selected to speak, and the other brothers became the audience to hear him.

Sanandana said, "After the dissolution of the whole cosmic manifestation, the entire energy and the whole creation in its nucleus form enter into the body of Garbhodakaśāyī Viṣṇu. The Lord at that time remains asleep for a long, long time, and when there is again necessity of creation, the *Vedas* personified assemble around the Lord and begin to glorify Him, describing His wonderful transcendental pastimes, exactly like servants of a king: when the king is asleep in the morning, the appointed reciters come around his bedroom and begin to sing of his chivalrous activities, and while hearing of his glorious activities, the king gradually awakens.

"The Vedic reciters, or the personified *Vedas,* sing thus: 'O unconquerable Lord, You are the Supreme Personality. No one is equal to You or greater than You. No one can be more glorious in his activities. All glories unto You! All glories unto You! By Your own transcendental nature You fully possess all six opulences. As such, You are able to deliver all conditioned souls from the clutches of *māyā.* O Lord, we fervently pray that You kindly do so. All the living entities, being Your parts and parcels, are naturally joyful, eternal and full of knowledge, but due to their own faults they imitate You by trying to become the supreme enjoyer. Thus they disobey Your supremacy and become offenders. And because of their offenses, Your material energy has taken charge of them. Thus their transcendental qualities of joyfulness, bliss and wisdom have been covered by the clouds of the three material qualities. This cosmic manifestation, made of the three material qualities, is just like a prison house for the conditioned souls. The conditioned souls are struggling very hard to escape from material bondage, and according to their different conditions of life they have been given different types of engagement. But since all engagements are based on knowledge supplied by You, the conditioned souls can execute pious activities only when You mercifully inspire them to do so. Therefore, without taking shelter at Your lotus feet one cannot surpass the influence of material energy. Actually, we, as personified Vedic knowledge, are always engaged in Your service by helping the conditioned souls understand You.' "

This prayer of the *Vedas* personified illustrates that the *Vedas* are meant for helping the conditioned souls to understand Kṛṣṇa. All the *śrutis,* or personified *Vedas,* offered glories to the Lord again and again, singing, "Jaya! Jaya!" This indicates that the Lord is the most glorious. Of all His glories, the most important is His causeless mercy upon the conditioned souls in reclaiming them from the clutches of *māyā.*

There are unlimited numbers of living entities in different varieties of bodies, some moving and some standing in one place, and the conditioned life of these living entities is due only to their forgetfulness of their eternal relationship with the Supreme Personality of Godhead. When the living entity wants to lord it over the material energy by imitating the position of Kṛṣṇa, he is immediately captured by the material energy and, according to his desire, is offered one variety of the 8,400,000 different kinds of bodies. Although undergoing the threefold miseries of material existence, the illusioned living entity falsely thinks himself the master of all he surveys. Under the spell of the material energy, represented by the threefold material qualities, the living entity is so entangled that he is not at all able to become free unless he is graced by the Supreme Lord. The living entity cannot conquer the influence of the material modes of nature by his own endeavor, but because material nature is working under the control of the Supreme Lord, the Lord is beyond its jurisdiction. Except for Him, all living entities, beginning from Brahmā down to the ant, are conquered by the contact of material nature.

Because the Lord possesses in full the six opulences of wealth, strength, fame, beauty, knowledge and renunciation, He alone is beyond the spell of material nature. Unless the living entity is situated in Kṛṣṇa consciousness, he cannot approach the Supreme Personality of Godhead. Yet the Lord, by His omnipotency, can dictate from within as the Supersoul how a living entity can gradually come to Him even while performing his ordinary work. As the Lord advises in the *Bhagavad-gītā,* "Whatever you do, do it for Me; whatever you eat, first offer it to Me; whatever charity you want to give, first give it to Me; and whatever austerities and penances you want to perform, perform them for Me." In this way the *karmīs* are directed gradually to develop Kṛṣṇa consciousness. Similarly, Kṛṣṇa directs the philosophers to approach Him gradually by discriminating between Brahman and *māyā,* for at last, when one is mature in knowledge, he surrenders unto

Kṛṣṇa. As Kṛṣṇa says in the *Bhagavad-gītā,* "After many, many births, the wise philosopher surrenders unto Me." The *yogīs* are also directed to concentrate their meditation upon Kṛṣṇa within the heart, and by such a continued process of Kṛṣṇa consciousness they can also become free from the clutches of the material energy. The devotees, however, are engaged in devotional service with love and affection from the very beginning, and therefore the Lord personally directs them so that they can approach Him without difficulty or deviation. This is stated in the *Bhagavad-gītā.* Only by the grace of the Lord can the living entity understand the exact position of Brahman, Paramātmā and Bhagavān.

The statements of the personified *Vedas* give clear evidence that the Vedic literature is presented only for understanding Kṛṣṇa. The *Bhagavad-gītā* confirms that through all the *Vedas* it is Kṛṣṇa alone who has to be understood. Kṛṣṇa is always enjoying, either in the material world or in the spiritual world; because He is the supreme enjoyer, for Him there is no distinction between the material and spiritual worlds. The material world is an impediment for the ordinary living entities because they are under its control, but Kṛṣṇa, being the controller of the material world, has nothing to do with the impediments it offers. Therefore, in different parts of the *Upaniṣads,* the *Vedas* declare, "The Supreme Brahman is eternal, full of all knowledge and all bliss. That one Supreme Personality of Godhead exists in the heart of every living entity." Because of His all-pervasiveness, He is able to enter not only into the hearts of the living entities, but even into the atoms also. As the Supersoul, He is the controller of all activities of the living entities. He lives within all of them and witnesses their actions, allowing them to act according to their desires and also giving them the results of their different activities. He is the living force of all things, but He is transcendental to the material qualities. He is omnipotent; He is expert in manufacturing everything, and on account of His superior, natural knowledge, He can bring everyone under His control. As such, He is everyone's master. He is sometimes manifest on the surface of the globe, but He is simultaneously within all matter. Desiring to expand Himself in multiforms, He glanced over the material energy, and thus innumerable living entities became manifest. Everything is created by His superior energy, and everything in His creation appears to be perfectly done, without deficiency. Those who aspire for liberation from this material world must therefore worship the Supreme Personality of Godhead, the ultimate cause of all causes. He is just like the total mass of earth, from which varieties of earthly pots are manufactured: the pots are made of earthly clay, they rest on the earth, and after being destroyed, their elements ultimately merge back into earth, the original cause of all varieties of manifestation.

Employing this analogy of Brahman with earth, the impersonalists especially stress the Vedic statement *sarvaṁ khalv idaṁ brahma:* "Everything is Brahman." The impersonalists do not take into account the varieties of manifestation emanating from the supreme cause, Brahman. They simply consider that everything emanates from Brahman and after destruction merges into Brahman and that the intermediate stage of manifestation is also Brahman. But although the Māyāvādīs believe that prior to its manifestation the cosmos was in Brahman, after creation it remains in Brahman, and after destruction it merges into Brahman, they do not know what Brahman is. The *Brahma-saṁhitā,* however, clearly describes Brahman: "The living entities, space, time and the material elements like fire, earth, sky, water and mind constitute the total cosmic manifestation, known as Bhūḥ, Bhuvaḥ and Svaḥ, which is manifested by Govinda. It flourishes on the strength of Govinda and after annihilation enters into and is conserved in Govinda." Lord Brahmā therefore says, "I worship Lord Govinda, the original personality, the cause of all causes."

The word "Brahman" indicates the greatest of all and the maintainer of everything. The impersonalists are attracted by the greatness of the sky, but because of their poor fund of knowledge they are not attracted by the greatness of Kṛṣṇa. In our practical life, however, we are attracted by the greatness of a person and not by the greatness of a big mountain. Thus the term "Brahman" actually applies to Kṛṣṇa only; therefore in the *Bhagavad-gītā* Arjuna admitted that Lord Kṛṣṇa is the Parabrahman, or the supreme resting place of everything.

Kṛṣṇa is the Supreme Brahman because of His unlimited knowledge, unlimited potencies, unlimited strength, unlimited influence, unlimited beauty and unlimited renunciation. Ultimately, therefore, the word "Brahman" can be applied to Kṛṣṇa only. Arjuna affirms that because the impersonal Brahman is the effulgence emanating as rays of Kṛṣṇa's transcendental body, Kṛṣṇa is the Parabrahman. Everything rests on Brahman, but Brahman itself rests on Kṛṣṇa. Therefore Kṛṣṇa is the ultimate Brahman, or Parabrahman. The material elements are accepted as the inferior energy of Kṛṣṇa. By their interaction the cosmic manifestation takes place, rests on Kṛṣṇa, and after dissolution again enters into the body of Kṛṣṇa as His subtle energy. Kṛṣṇa is therefore the cause of both manifestation and dissolution.

Sarvaṁ khalv idaṁ brahma means that everything is Kṛṣṇa in the sense that everything is His energy. That is the vision of the *mahā-bhāgavatas.* They see everything in relation to Kṛṣṇa. The impersonalists argue that Kṛṣṇa Himself has been transformed into many and that therefore everything is Kṛṣṇa and worship of anything is worship of Him. This false argument is answered by Kṛṣṇa in the *Bhagavad-gītā:* although everything is a transformation of the energy of Kṛṣṇa, He is not present everywhere. He is simultaneously present and not present. By His energy He is present everywhere, but as the energetic He is not present everywhere. This simultaneous presence and nonpresence is inconceivable to our present senses. But a clear explanation is given in the beginning of the *Īśopaniṣad,* in which it is stated that the Supreme Lord is so complete that although unlimited energies and their transformations emanate from Kṛṣṇa, Kṛṣṇa's personality is not in the least bit transformed. Therefore, since Kṛṣṇa is the cause of all causes, intelligent persons should take shelter of His lotus feet.

Kṛṣṇa advises everyone just to surrender unto Him alone, and that is the way of Vedic instruction. Since Kṛṣṇa is the cause of all causes, He is worshiped by all kinds of sages and saints through observance of the regulative principles. As far as meditation is concerned, great personalities meditate on the transcendental form of Kṛṣṇa within the heart. In this way the minds of great personalities are always engaged in Kṛṣṇa. With minds engaged in Kṛṣṇa, naturally the captivated devotees simply talk of Kṛṣṇa.

Talking of Kṛṣṇa or singing of Kṛṣṇa is called *kīrtana.* Lord Caitanya recommends, *kīrtanīyaḥ sadā hariḥ,* which means always thinking and talking of Kṛṣṇa and nothing else. That is called Kṛṣṇa consciousness. Kṛṣṇa consciousness is so sublime that anyone who takes to this process is elevated to the highest perfection of life—far, far beyond the concept of liberation. In the *Bhagavad-gītā,* therefore, Kṛṣṇa advises everyone always to think of Him, render devotional service to Him, worship Him and offer obeisances to Him. In this way a devotee becomes fully Kṛṣṇa-ized and, being always situated in Kṛṣṇa consciousness, ultimately goes back to Kṛṣṇa.

Although the *Vedas* have recommended worship of different demigods as different parts and parcels of Kṛṣṇa, it is to be understood that such instructions are meant for less intelligent men who are still attracted by material sense enjoyment. But the person who actually wants perfect fulfillment of the mission of human life should simply worship Lord Kṛṣṇa, and that will simplify the matter and completely guarantee the success of his human life. Although the sky, the water and the land are all part of the material world, when one stands on the solid land his position is more secure than when he stands in the sky or the water. An intelligent person, therefore, does not stand under the protection of different demigods, although they are part and parcel of Kṛṣṇa. Rather, he stands on the solid ground of Kṛṣṇa consciousness. That makes his position sound and secure.

Impersonalists sometimes give the example that if one stands on a stone or a piece of wood one certainly stands on the surface of the land, because the stone and wood both rest on the surface of the earth. But it may be replied that if one stands directly on the surface of the earth he is more secure than if he stands on the wood or stone, which rest on the earth. In other words, taking shelter of Paramātmā or taking shelter of impersonal Brahman is not as secure a course as taking direct shelter of Kṛṣṇa in Kṛṣṇa consciousness. The position of the *jñānīs* and *yogīs* is therefore not as secure as the position of the devotees of Kṛṣṇa. Lord Kṛṣṇa has therefore advised in the *Bhagavad-gītā* that only a person who has lost his sense takes to the worship of demigods. And regarding persons attached to the impersonal Brahman, *Śrīmad-Bhāgavatam* says, "My dear Lord, those who think of themselves as liberated by mental speculation are not yet purified of the contamination of material nature because of their inability to find the shelter of Your lotus feet. Although they rise to the transcendental situation of existence in impersonal Brahman, they certainly fall from that exalted position because they deride Your lotus feet." Lord Kṛṣṇa therefore advises that the worshipers of the demigods are not very intelligent persons because they derive only temporary, exhaustible results. Their endeavors are those of less intelligent men. On the other hand, the Lord assures that His devotee has no fear of falling.

The personified *Vedas* continued to pray: "Dear Lord, considering all points of view, if a person has to worship someone superior to himself, then just out of good behavior he should stick to the worship of Your lotus feet because You are the ultimate controller of creation, maintenance and dissolution. You are the controller of the three worlds, Bhūḥ, Bhuvaḥ and Svaḥ; You are the controller of the fourteen upper and lower worlds; and You are the controller of the three material qualities. Demigods and persons advanced in spiritual knowledge always hear and chant about Your transcendental pastimes because this process has the specific potency of nullifying the accumulated results of sinful life. Intelligent persons factually dip into the ocean of Your nectarean activities and very patiently hear about them. Thus they immediately become freed from the contamination of the material qualities; they do not have to undergo severe penances and austerities for advancement in spiritual life. This chanting and hearing of Your transcendental pastimes is the easiest process for self-realization. Simply by submissive aural reception of the transcendental message, one's heart is cleansed of all dirty things. Thus Kṛṣṇa consciousness becomes fixed in the heart of a devotee." The great authority Bhīṣmadeva has also given the opinion that this process of chanting and hearing about the Supreme Personality of Godhead is the essence of all Vedic ritualistic performances.

"Dear Lord," the personified *Vedas* continued, "the devotee who wants to elevate himself simply by this process of devotional activities, especially by hearing and chanting, very soon comes out of the clutches of the dualities of material existence. By this simple process of penance and austerity, the Supersoul within the devotee's heart is very pleased and gives the devotee directions so that he may go back home, back to Godhead." It is stated in the *Bhagavad-gītā* that one who engages all his activities and senses in the devotional service of the Lord becomes completely peaceful because the Supersoul is satisfied with him; thus the devotee becomes transcendental to all dualities, such as heat and cold, honor and dishonor. Being freed from all dualities, he feels transcendental bliss, and he no longer suffers cares and anxieties due to material existence. The *Bhagavad-gītā* confirms that the devotee always absorbed in Kṛṣṇa consciousness has no anxieties for his maintenance or protection. Being constantly absorbed in Kṛṣṇa consciousness, he ultimately achieves the highest perfection. While in material existence, he lives very peacefully and blissfully without cares and anxieties, and after quitting this body he goes back home, back to Godhead. The Lord confirms in the *Bhagavad-gītā,* "My supreme abode is a transcendental place from which, having gone, one never returns to this material world. Anyone who attains the supreme perfection, being engaged in My personal devotional service in the eternal abode, reaches the highest perfection of human life and does not have to come back to the miserable material world."

The personified *Vedas* continued, "Dear Lord, it is imperative that the living entities be engaged in Kṛṣṇa consciousness, always rendering devotional service by such prescribed methods as hearing and chanting and executing Your orders. If a person is not engaged in Kṛṣṇa consciousness and devotional service, it is useless for him to exhibit the symptoms of life. Generally if a person is breathing he is accepted to be alive. But a person without Kṛṣṇa consciousness may be compared to a bellows in a blacksmith's shop. The big bellows is a bag of skin which exhales and inhales air, and a human being who simply lives within the bag of skin and bones without taking to Kṛṣṇa consciousness and loving devotional service is no better than the bellows. Similarly, a nondevotee's long duration of life is compared to the long existence of a tree, his voracious eating capacity is compared to the eating of dogs and hogs, and his enjoyment in sex life is compared to that of hogs and goats."

The cosmic manifestation has been made possible because of the entrance of the Supreme Personality of Godhead as Mahā-Viṣṇu within this material world. The total material energy is agitated by the glance of Mahā-Viṣṇu, and only then does the interaction of the three material qualities begin. Therefore it should be concluded that whatever material facilities we are trying to enjoy are available only due to the mercy of the Supreme Personality of Godhead.

Within the body there are five different departments of existence, known as *anna-maya, prāṇa-maya, mano-maya, vijñāna-maya* and, at last, *ānanda-maya.* In the beginning of life, every living entity is food conscious. A child or an animal is satisfied only by getting nice food. This stage of consciousness, in which the goal is to eat sumptuously, is called *anna-maya. Anna* means "food." After this one lives in the consciousness of being alive. If one can continue his life without being attacked or destroyed, one thinks himself happy. This stage is called *prāṇa-maya,* or consciousness of one's existence. After this stage, when one is situated on the mental platform, his consciousness is called *mano-maya.* The materialistic civilization is primarily situated in these three stages, *anna-maya, prāṇa-maya* and *mano-maya.* The first concern of civilized persons is economic development, the next concern is defense against being annihilated, and the next consciousness is mental speculation, the philosophical approach to the values of life.

If by the evolutionary process of philosophical life one happens to reach the platform of intellectual life and understands that he is not this material body but a spiritual soul, he is situated in the *vijñāna-maya* stage. Then, by evolution in spiritual life, he comes to the understanding of the Supreme Lord, or the Supreme Soul. When one develops his relationship with Him and executes devotional service, that stage of life is called Kṛṣṇa consciousness, the *ānanda-maya* stage. *Ānanda-maya* is the blissful life of knowledge and eternity. As it is said in the *Vedānta-sūtra, ānanda-mayo 'bhyāsāt.* The Supreme Brahman and the subordinate Brahman, or the Supreme Personality of Godhead and the living entities, are both joyful by nature. As long as the living entities are situated in the lower four stages of life—*anna-maya, prāṇa-maya, mano-maya* and *vijñāna-maya*—they are considered to be in the material condition of life, but as soon as one reaches the stage of *ānanda-maya,* he is a liberated soul. This *ānanda-maya* stage is explained in the *Bhagavad-gītā* as the *brahma-bhūta* stage. There it is said that in the *brahma-bhūta* stage of life there is no anxiety and no hankering. This stage begins when one is equally disposed toward all living entities, and it then expands to the stage of Kṛṣṇa consciousness, in which one always hankers to render service unto the Supreme Personality of Godhead. This hankering for advancement in devotional service is not the same as hankering for sense gratification in material existence. In other words, hankering remains in spiritual life, but it becomes purified. Similarly, when our senses are purified, they are freed from all material stages, namely *anna-maya, prāṇa-maya, mano-maya* and *vijñāna-maya,* and they become situated in the highest stage—*ānanda-maya,* or blissful life in Kṛṣṇa consciousness. The Māyāvādī philosophers consider *ānanda-maya* to be the state of being merged in the Supreme. To them, *ānanda-maya* means that the Supersoul and the individual soul become one. But the real fact is that oneness does not mean merging into the Supreme and losing one's own individual existence. Merging into the spiritual existence is the living entity's realization of qualitative oneness with the Supreme Lord in His aspects of eternity and knowledge. But the actual *ānanda-maya* (blissful) stage is attained when one is engaged in devotional service. That is confirmed in the *Bhagavad-gītā: mad-bhaktiṁ labhate parām.* Here Lord Kṛṣṇa states that the *brahma-bhūta ānanda-maya* stage is complete only when there is an exchange of love between the Supreme and the subordinate living entities. Unless one comes to this *ānanda-maya* stage, his breathing is like the breathing of a bellows in a blacksmith's shop, his duration of life is like that of a tree, and he is no better than the lower animals like the camels, hogs and dogs.

Undoubtedly the eternal living entity cannot be annihilated at any point. But the lower species of life exist in a miserable condition, whereas one who is engaged in the devotional service of the Supreme Lord is situated in the pleasurable, or *ānanda-maya,* status of life. The different stages described above are all in relationship with the Supreme Personality of Godhead. Although in all circumstances there exist both the Supreme Personality of Godhead and the living entities, the difference is that the Supreme Personality of Godhead always exists in the *ānanda-maya* stage, whereas the subordinate living entities, because of their minute position as fragmental portions of the Supreme Lord, are prone to fall to the other stages of life. Although in all the stages both the Supreme Lord and the living entities exist, the Supreme Personality of Godhead is always transcendental to our concept of life, whether we are in bondage or in liberation. The whole cosmic manifestation becomes possible by the grace of the Supreme Lord, it exists by the grace of the Supreme Lord, and when annihilated it merges into the existence of the Supreme Lord. As such, the Supreme Lord is the supreme existence, the cause of all causes. Therefore the conclusion is that without development of Kṛṣṇa consciousness one's life is simply a waste of time.

For those who are very materialistic and cannot understand the situation of the spiritual world, the abode of Kṛṣṇa, great sages have recommended the yogic process whereby one gradually rises from meditation on the abdomen, which is called *mūlādhāra* or *maṇipūraka* meditation. *Mūlādhāra* and *maṇipūraka* are technical terms which refer to the intestines within the abdomen. Grossly materialistic persons think that economic development is of foremost importance because they are under the impression that a living entity exists only by eating. Such grossly materialistic persons forget that although we may eat as much as we like, if the food is not digested it produces the troubles of indigestion and acidity. Therefore, eating is not in itself the cause of the vital energy of life. For digestion of eatables we have to take shelter of another, superior energy, which is mentioned in the *Bhagavad-gītā* as *vaiśvānara.* Lord Kṛṣṇa says in the *Bhagavad-gītā* that He helps the digestion in the form of *vaiśvānara.* The Supreme Personality of Godhead is all-pervasive; therefore, His presence in the stomach as *vaiśvānara* is not extraordinary.

Kṛṣṇa is actually present everywhere. The Vaiṣṇava, therefore, marks his body with temples of Viṣṇu: he first marks a *tilaka* temple on the abdomen, then on the chest, then between the collarbones, then on the forehead, and gradually he marks the top of the head, the *brahma-randhra.* The thirteen temples of *tilaka* marked on the body of a Vaiṣṇava are known as follows: On the forehead is the temple of Lord Keśava, on the belly is the temple of Lord Nārāyaṇa, on the chest is the temple of Lord Mādhava, and on the throat, between the two collarbones, is the temple of Lord Govinda. On the right side of the waist is the temple of Lord Viṣṇu, on the right arm the temple of Lord Madhusūdana, and on the right side of the collarbone the temple of Lord Trivikrama. Similarly, on the left side of the waist is the temple of Lord Vāmanadeva, on the left arm the temple of Śrīdhara, on the left side of the collarbone the temple of Hṛṣīkeśa, on the upper back the temple called Padmanābha, and on the lower back the temple called Dāmodara. On the top of the head is the temple called Vāsudeva. This is the process of meditation on the Lord's situation in the different parts of the body, but for those who are not Vaiṣṇavas, great sages recommend meditation on the bodily concept of life—meditation on the intestines, on the heart, on the throat, on the eyebrows, on the forehead and then on the top of the head. Some of the sages in the disciplic succession from the great saint Aruṇa meditate on the heart, because the Supersoul stays within the heart along with the living entity. This is confirmed in the *Bhagavad-gītā,* Fifteenth Chapter, wherein the Lord states, "I am situated in everyone's heart."

As part of devotional service, Vaiṣṇavas protect the body for the service of the Lord, but those who are gross materialists accept the body as the self. They worship the body by the yogic process of meditation on the different bodily parts, such as *maṇipūraka, dahara* and *hṛdaya,* gradually rising to the *brahma-randhra,* on the top of the head. The first-class *yogī* who has attained perfection in the practice of the *yoga* system ultimately passes through the *brahma-randhra* to any one of the planets in either the material or spiritual worlds. How a *yogī* can transfer himself to another planet is vividly described in the Second Canto of *Śrīmad-Bhāgavatam.*

In this regard, Śukadeva Gosvāmī has recommended that the beginners worship the *virāṭ-puruṣa,* the gigantic universal form of the Lord. One who cannot believe that the Lord can be worshiped with equal success in the Deity, or *arcā* form, or who cannot concentrate on this form is advised to worship the universal form of the Lord. The lower part of the universe is considered the feet and legs of the Lord's universal form, the middle part of the universe is considered the navel or abdomen of the Lord, the upper planetary systems such as Janoloka and Maharloka are the heart of the Lord, and the topmost planetary system, Brahmaloka, is considered the top of the Lord's head. There are different processes recommended by great sages according to the position of the worshiper, but the ultimate aim of all meditational yogic processes is to go back home, back to Godhead. As stated in the *Bhagavad-gītā,* anyone who reaches the highest planet, the abode of Kṛṣṇa, or even the Vaikuṇṭha planets, never has to come down again to this miserable material condition of life.

The Vedic recommendation, therefore, is that one make the lotus feet of Viṣṇu the target of all one's efforts. *Tad viṣṇoḥ paramaṁ padam:* the Viṣṇu planets, or Viṣṇuloka, are situated above all the material planets. These Vaikuṇṭha planets are known as *sanātana-dhāma,* and they are eternal. They are never annihilated, not even by the annihilation of this material world. The conclusion is that if a human being does not fulfill the mission of his life by worshiping the Supreme Lord and does not go back home, back to Godhead, it is to be understood that he is breathing just like a blacksmith's bellows, living just like a tree, eating just like a camel and having sex just like the dogs and hogs. Thus he has been frustrated in fulfilling the specific purpose of human life.

The next prayer of the personified *Vedas* to the Lord concerns His entering into different species of life. It is stated in the *Bhagavad-gītā,* Fourteenth Chapter, that in every species and form of life the spiritual part and parcel of the Supreme Lord is present. The Lord Himself claims in the *Gītā* that He is the seed-giving father of all forms and species, who therefore must all be considered sons of the Lord. The entrance of the Supreme Lord into everyone's heart as Paramātmā sometimes bewilders the impersonalists into thinking in terms of the equality of the living entities with the Supreme Lord. They think, "Both the Supreme Lord and the individual soul enter into the various bodies; so where is the distinction? Why should individual souls worship the Paramātmā, or Supersoul?" According to them, the Supersoul and the individual soul are on the same level; they are one, without any difference between them. There is a difference, however, between the Supersoul and the individual soul, and this is explained in the *Bhagavad-gītā,* Fifteenth Chapter, wherein the Lord says that although He is situated with the living entity in the same body, He is superior. He is dictating or giving intelligence to the individual soul from within. It is clearly stated in the *Gītā* that the Lord gives intelligence to the individual soul and that both memory and forgetfulness are due to the influence of the Supersoul. No one can act independently of the sanction of the Supersoul. The individual soul acts according to his past *karma,* reminded by the Lord. The nature of the individual soul is forgetfulness, but the presence of the Lord within the heart reminds him of what he wanted to do in his past life. The intelligence of the individual soul is exhibited like fire in wood. Although fire is always fire, it is exhibited in a size proportionate to the size of the wood. Similarly, although the individual soul is qualitatively one with the Supreme Lord, he exhibits himself according to the limitations of his present body. But the Supreme Lord, or the Supersoul, is unlimited. He is said to be *eka-rasa. Eka* means "one," and *rasa* means "mellow." The transcendental position of the Supreme Lord is that of eternity, bliss and full knowledge. His position of *eka-rasa* does not change in the slightest when He becomes a witness and advisor to the individual soul in each individual body.

But the individual soul, from Lord Brahmā down to the ant, exhibits his spiritual potency according to his present body. The demigods are in the same category with the individual souls in the bodies of human beings or in the bodies of lower animals. Intelligent persons, therefore, do not worship different demigods, who are simply infinitesimal representatives of Kṛṣṇa manifest in conditioned bodies. The individual soul can exhibit his power only in proportion to the shape and constitution of the body. The Supreme Personality of Godhead, however, can exhibit His full potencies in any shape or form without any change. The Māyāvādī philosophers' thesis that God and the individual soul are one and the same cannot be accepted because the individual soul has to develop his power according to the development of different types of bodies. The individual soul in the body of a baby cannot show the full power of a grown man, but the Supreme Personality of Godhead, Kṛṣṇa, even when lying on the lap of His mother as a baby, could exhibit His full power by killing Pūtanā and other demons who tried to attack Him. Thus the spiritual potency of the Supreme Personality of Godhead is said to be *eka-rasa,* or without change. The Supreme Personality of Godhead, therefore, is the only worshipable object, and this is perfectly known to persons who are uncontaminated by the modes of material nature. In other words, only the liberated souls can worship the Supreme Personality of Godhead. Less intelligent Māyāvādīs take to the worship of the demigods, thinking that the demigods and the Supreme Personality of Godhead are on the same level.

The personified *Vedas* continued to offer their obeisances. "Dear Lord," they prayed, "after many, many births, those who have actually become wise take to the worship of Your lotus feet in complete knowledge." This is confirmed in the *Bhagavad-gītā,* wherein the Lord says that after many, many births, a great soul, or *mahātmā,* surrenders unto the Lord, knowing well that Vāsudeva, Kṛṣṇa, is the cause of all causes. The *Vedas* continued, "As already explained, since the mind, intelligence and senses have been given to us by God, when these instruments are actually purified there is no alternative but to engage them all in the devotional service of the Lord. A living entity's entrapment in different species of life is due to the misapplication of his mind, intelligence and senses in material activities. Various kinds of bodies are awarded as the result of a living entity's actions, and they are created by the material nature according to the living entity's desire. Because a living entity desires and deserves a particular kind of body, it is given to him by the material nature, under the order of the Supreme Lord."

In *Śrīmad-Bhāgavatam,* Third Canto, it is explained that under the control of superior authority a living entity is put within the semen of a male and injected into the womb of a particular female in order to develop a particular type of body. A living entity utilizes his senses, intelligence, mind and so on in a specific way of his own choosing and thus develops a particular type of body, within which he becomes encaged. In this way the living entity becomes situated in different species of life, either in a demigod, human or animal body, according to different situations and circumstances.

It is explained in the Vedic literatures that the living entities entrapped in different species of life are part and parcel of the Supreme Lord. The Māyāvādī philosophers mistake the living entity for the Paramātmā, who is actually sitting with the living entity as a friend. Because the Paramātmā (the localized aspect of the Supreme Personality of Godhead) and the individual living entity are both within the body, a misunderstanding sometimes takes place that there is no difference between the two. But there is a definite difference between the individual soul and the Supersoul, and it is explained in the *Varāha Purāṇa* as follows. The Supreme Lord has two kinds of parts and parcels: the living entity is called *vibhinnāṁśa,* and the Paramātmā, or the plenary expansion of the Supreme Lord, is called *svāṁśa.* The *svāṁśa* plenary expansion of the Supreme Personality is as powerful as the Supreme Personality of Godhead Himself. There is not even the slightest difference between the potency of the Supreme Person and that of His plenary expansion as Paramātmā. But the *vibhinnāṁśa* parts and parcels possess only a minute portion of the potencies of the Lord. The *Nārada Pañcarātra* states that the living entities, who are the marginal potency of the Supreme Lord, are undoubtedly of the same quality of spiritual existence as the Lord Himself, but they are prone to be tinged with the material qualities. Because the minute living entity is prone to be subjected to the influence of material qualities, he is called *jīva,* and sometimes the Supreme Personality of Godhead is also known as Śiva, the all-auspicious one. So the difference between Śiva and *jīva* is that the all-auspicious Personality of Godhead is never affected by the material qualities, whereas the minute portions of the Supreme Personality of Godhead are prone to be affected by the qualities of material nature.

The Supersoul within the body of a particular living entity, being a plenary portion of the Lord, is worshipable by the individual living entity. Great sages have therefore concluded that the process of meditation is designed so that the individual living entity may concentrate his attention on the lotus feet of the Supersoul form (Viṣṇu). That is the real form of *samādhi.* The living entity cannot become liberated from material entanglement by his own effort. He must therefore take to the devotional service of the lotus feet of the Supreme Lord, or the Supersoul within himself. Śrīdhara Svāmī, the great commentator on *Śrīmad-Bhāgavatam,* has composed a nice verse in this regard, the meaning of which is as follows: "My dear Lord, I am eternally a part of You, but I have been entrapped by the material potencies, which are also an emanation from You. As the cause of all causes, You have entered my body as the Supersoul, and I have the prerogative of enjoying the supreme blissful life of knowledge along with You. Therefore, my dear Lord, please order me to render You loving service so that I can again be brought to my original position of transcendental bliss."

Great personalities understand that a living entity entangled in this material world cannot be freed by his own efforts. With firm faith and devotion, such great personalities engage themselves in rendering transcendental loving service to the Lord. That is the verdict of the personified *Vedas.*

The personified *Vedas* continued, "Dear Lord, it is very difficult to achieve perfect knowledge of the Absolute Truth. Your Lordship is so kind to the fallen souls that You appear in different incarnations and execute different activities. You appear even as a historical personality of this material world, and Your pastimes are very nicely described in the Vedic literatures. Such pastimes are as attractive as the ocean of transcendental bliss. People in general have a natural inclination to read narrations in which ordinary *jīvas* are glorified, but when they become attracted by the Vedic literatures which delineate Your eternal pastimes, they actually dip into the ocean of transcendental bliss. As a fatigued man feels refreshed by dipping into a reservoir of water, so the conditioned soul who is very much disgusted with material activities becomes refreshed and forgets all the fatigue of material activities simply by dipping into the transcendental ocean of

Your pastimes. And eventually he merges into the ocean of transcendental bliss. The most intelligent devotees, therefore, do not take to any means of self-realization except devotional service and constant engagement in the nine different processes of devotional life, especially hearing and chanting. When hearing and chanting about Your transcendental pastimes, Your devotees do not care even for the transcendental bliss derived from liberation or from merging into the existence of the Supreme. Such devotees are not interested even in so-called liberation, and they certainly have no interest in material activities for elevation to the heavenly planets for sense gratification. Pure devotees seek only the association of *paramahaṁsas,* or great liberated devotees, so that they can continuously hear and chant about Your glories. For this purpose the pure devotees are prepared to sacrifice all comforts of life, even giving up the material comforts of family life and so-called society, friendship and love. Those who have tasted the nectar of devotion by relishing the transcendental vibration of chanting Your glories—Hare Kṛṣṇa, Hare Kṛṣṇa, Kṛṣṇa Kṛṣṇa, Hare Hare/ Hare Rāma, Hare Rāma, Rāma Rāma, Hare Hare—do not care for any other spiritual bliss or for material comforts, which appear to the pure devotee as less important than the straw in the street."

The personified *Vedas* continued, "Dear Lord, when a person is able to purify his mind, senses and intelligence by engaging himself in devotional service in full Kṛṣṇa consciousness, his mind becomes his friend. Otherwise, his mind is always his enemy. When the mind is engaged in the devotional service of the Lord, it becomes the intimate friend of the living entity because the mind can then think of the Supreme Lord always. Your Lordship is eternally dear to the living entity, so when the mind is engaged in thought of You one immediately feels the great satisfaction for which he has been hankering life after life. When one's mind is thus fixed on the lotus feet of the Supreme Personality of Godhead, one does not take to any kind of inferior worship or inferior process of self-realization. By attempting to worship a demigod or by taking to any other process of self-realization, the living entity becomes a victim of the cycle of birth and death, and no one can estimate how much the living entity becomes degraded by entering abominable species of life such as cats and dogs."

Śrī Narottama dāsa Ṭhākura has sung that persons who do not take to the devotional service of the Lord but are attracted to the process of philosophical speculation and fruitive activities drink the poisonous results of such actions. Such persons eat all kinds of obnoxious things, such as meat, and take pleasure in alcohol and other intoxicants, and after death they are forced to take birth in lower species of life. Materialistic persons generally worship the transient material body and forget the welfare of the spirit soul within the body. Some take shelter of materialistic science to improve bodily comforts, and some take to the worship of demigods to be promoted to the heavenly planets. Their goal in life is to make the material body comfortable, but they forget the interest of the spirit soul. Such persons are described in the Vedic literature as suicidal, because attachment for the material body and its comforts forces the living entity to wander through the process of birth and death perpetually and suffer the material pangs as a matter of course. The human form of life is a chance for one to understand his position. Therefore the most intelligent person takes to devotional service just to engage his mind, senses and body in the service of the Lord without deviation.

The personified *Vedas* continued, "Dear Lord, there are many mystic *yogīs* who are very learned and deliberate in achieving the highest perfection of life. They engage themselves in the yogic process of controlling the life air within the body. Concentrating the mind upon the form of Viṣṇu and controlling the senses very rigidly, they practice the *yoga* system, but even after much laborious austerity, penance and regulation, they achieve the same destination as persons inimical toward You. In other words, both the *yogīs* and the great, wise philosophical speculators ultimately attain the impersonal Brahman effulgence, which is automatically attained by the demons who are regular enemies of the Lord. Demons like Kaṁsa, Śiśupāla and Dantavakra also attain the Brahman effulgence because they constantly meditate upon the Supreme Personality of Godhead out of enmity. The real point is to concentrate the mind on the Supreme Personality of Godhead. Women such as the *gopīs* were attached to Kṛṣṇa, being captivated by His beauty, and their mental concentration on Kṛṣṇa was provoked by lust. They wanted to be embraced by the arms of Kṛṣṇa, which resemble the beautiful round shape of a snake. Similarly, we, the Vedic hymns, simply concentrate our minds on the lotus feet of Your Lordship. Women like the *gopīs* concentrate upon You under the dictation of lust, and we concentrate upon Your lotus feet to go back home, back to Godhead. Your enemies also concentrate upon You, thinking always of how to kill You, and *yogīs* undertake great penances and austerities just to attain Your impersonal effulgence. All these different persons, although concentrating their minds in different ways, achieve spiritual perfection according to their different perspectives because You, O Lord, are equal to all Your devotees."

Śrīdhara Svāmī has composed a nice verse in this regard: "My dear Lord, to be engaged always in thinking of Your lotus feet is very difficult. It is possible for great devotees who have already achieved love for You and are engaged in transcendental loving service. My dear Lord, I wish that my mind may also be fixed somehow or other on Your lotus feet, at least for some time."

The attainment of spiritual perfection by different spiritualists is explained in the *Bhagavad-gītā,* wherein the Lord says that He grants the perfection the devotee desires in proportion to the devotee's surrender unto Him. The impersonalists, *yogīs* and enemies of the Lord enter into the Lord's transcendental effulgence, but the personalists who follow in the footsteps of the inhabitants of Vṛndāvana or strictly follow the path of devotional service are elevated to the personal abode of Kṛṣṇa, Goloka Vṛndāvana, or to the Vaikuṇṭha planets. Both the impersonalists and the personalists enter the spiritual realm, the spiritual sky, but the impersonalists are given their place in the impersonal Brahman effulgence, whereas the personalists are given a position in the Vaikuṇṭha planets or in the Vṛndāvana planet, according to their desire to serve the Lord in different mellows.

The personified *Vedas* stated that persons born after the creation of this material world cannot understand the existence of the Supreme Personality of Godhead by manipulating their material knowledge. Just as a person born in a particular family cannot understand the position of his great-grandfather, who lived before the birth of the recent generation, we are unable to understand the Supreme Personality of Godhead, Nārāyaṇa, or Kṛṣṇa, who exists eternally in the spiritual world. In the Eighth Chapter of the *Bhagavad-gītā* it is clearly said that the Supreme Person, who lives eternally in the spiritual kingdom of God (*sanātana-dhāma*), can be approached only by devotional service.

As for the material creation, Brahmā is the first created person. Before Brahmā there was no living creature within this material world; it was void and dark until Brahmā was born on the lotus flower that sprouted from the abdomen of Garbhodakaśāyī Viṣṇu. Garbhodakaśāyī Viṣṇu is an expansion of Kāraṇodakaśāyī Viṣṇu, Kāraṇodakaśāyī Viṣṇu is an expansion of Saṅkarṣaṇa, and Saṅkarṣaṇa is an expansion of Balarāma, who is an immediate expansion of Lord Kṛṣṇa. After the creation of Brahmā, the two kinds of demigods were born: demigods like the four brothers Sanaka, Sanātana, Sanandana and Sanat-kumāra, who are representatives of renunciation of the world, and demigods like Marīci and their descendants, who are meant to enjoy this material world. From these two kinds of demigods were gradually manifested all other living entities, including the human beings. Thus all living creatures within this material world, including Brahmā, all the demigods and all the Rākṣasas, are to be considered modern. This means that they were all born recently. Therefore, just as a person born recently in a family cannot understand the situation of his distant forefather, no one within this material world can understand the position of the Supreme Lord in the spiritual world, because the material world has only recently been created. Although they have a long duration of existence, all the manifestations of the material world—namely the time element, the living entities, the *Vedas* and the gross and subtle material elements—are created at some point. Thus any process manufactured within this created situation as a means for understanding the original source of creation is to be considered modern.

Therefore by the process of self-realization or God realization through fruitive activities, philosophical speculation or mystic *yoga,* one cannot actually approach the supreme source of everything. When the creation is completely terminated, when there is no existence of the *Vedas,* no existence of material time, and no existence of the gross and subtle material elements, and when all the living entities are in the nonmanifested stage, resting within Nārāyaṇa, then all these manufactured processes become null and void and cannot act. Devotional service, however, is eternally going on in the eternal spiritual world. Therefore the only factual process of self-realization or God realization is devotional service, and one who takes to this process takes to the real process of God realization.

In this regard, Śrīla Śrīdhara Svāmī has composed a verse which conveys the idea that the supreme source of everything, the Supreme Personality of Godhead, is so great and unlimited that it is not possible for the living entity to understand Him by any material acquisition. One should therefore pray to the Lord to be engaged in His devotional service eternally, so that by the grace of the Lord one can understand the supreme source of creation. The supreme source of creation, the Supreme Lord, reveals Himself only to the devotees. In the Fourth Chapter of the *Bhagavad-gītā* the Lord says to Arjuna, "My dear Arjuna, because you are My devotee and because you are My intimate friend, I shall reveal to you the process of understanding Me." In other words, the supreme source of creation, the Supreme Personality of Godhead, cannot be understood by our own endeavor. We have to please Him with devotional service, and then He will reveal Himself to us. Then we can understand Him to some extent.

There are different kinds of philosophers who have tried to understand the supreme source by their mental speculation. There are generally six kinds of mental speculators, whose speculations are called *ṣaḍ-darśana.* All these philosophers are impersonalists and are known as Māyāvādīs. Every one of them has tried to establish his own opinion, although they all have later compromised and stated that all opinions lead to the same goal and that every opinion is therefore valid. According to the prayers of the personified *Vedas,* however, none of them is valid because their process of knowledge is created within the temporary material world. They have all missed the real point: the Supreme Personality of Godhead, or the Absolute Truth, can be understood only by devotional service.

One class of philosophers, known as Mīmāṁsakas, represented by sages such as Jaimini, have concluded that everyone should engage in pious activities or prescribed duties and that such activities will lead one to the highest perfection. But this is contradicted in the Ninth Chapter of the *Bhagavad-gītā,* where Lord Kṛṣṇa says that by pious activities one may be elevated to the heavenly planets, but that as soon as one's accumulation of pious activities is used up, one has to leave the enjoyment of a higher standard of material prosperity in the heavenly planets and immediately come down again to these lower planets, where the duration of life is very short and where the standard of material happiness is of a lower grade. The exact words used in the *Bhagavad-gītā* are *kṣīṇe puṇye martya-lokaṁ viśanti.* Therefore the conclusion of the Mīmāṁsaka philosophers that pious activities will lead one to the Absolute Truth is not valid. Although a pure devotee is by nature inclined to perform pious activities, no one can attain the favor of the Supreme Personality of Godhead by pious activities alone. Pious activities may purify one of the contamination caused by ignorance and passion, but this purification is automatically attained by a devotee constantly engaged in hearing the transcendental message of Godhead in the form of the *Bhagavad-gītā, Śrīmad-Bhāgavatam* or similar scriptures. From the *Bhagavad-gītā* we understand that even a person who is not up to the standard of pious activities but who is absolutely engaged in devotional service is to be considered well situated on the path of spiritual perfection. It is also said in the *Bhagavad-gītā* that a person who is engaged in devotional service with love and faith is guided from within by the Supreme Personality of Godhead. The Lord Himself as Paramātmā, or the spiritual master sitting within one's heart, gives the devotee exact directions by which he can gradually go back to Godhead. The conclusion of the Mīmāṁsaka philosophers is not actually the truth which can lead one to real understanding.

Similarly, there are Sāṅkhya philosophers—metaphysicians or materialistic scientists who study this cosmic manifestation by their invented scientific method and do not recognize the supreme authority of God as the creator of the cosmic manifestation. They wrongly conclude that the reactions of material elements are the original cause of creation. The *Bhagavad-gītā,* however, does not accept this theory. It is clearly said therein that behind the cosmic activities is the direction of the Supreme Personality of Godhead. This fact is corroborated by the Vedic injunction *sad vā saumyedam agra āsīt,* which means that the origin of the creation existed before the cosmic manifestation. Therefore, the material elements cannot be the cause of the material creation. Although the material elements are accepted as immediate causes, the ultimate cause is the Supreme Personality of Godhead Himself. The *Bhagavad-gītā* says, therefore, that material nature works under the direction of Kṛṣṇa.

The conclusion of the atheistic Sāṅkhya philosophy is that because the effects—the phenomena of this material world—are temporary, or illusory, the cause is therefore also illusory. The Sāṅkhya philosophers are in favor of voidism, but the actual fact is that the original cause is the Supreme Personality of Godhead and that this cosmic manifestation is the temporary manifestation of His material energy. When this temporary manifestation is annihilated, its cause, the eternal existence of the spiritual world, continues as it is, and therefore the spiritual world is called *sanātana-dhāma,* the eternal abode. The conclusion of the Sāṅkhya philosophers is therefore invalid.

Then there are the philosophers headed by Gautama and Kaṇāda. They have minutely studied the cause and effect of the material elements and have ultimately come to the conclusion that atomic combination is the original cause of creation. At present the materialistic scientists follow in the footsteps of Gautama and Kaṇāda, who propounded this theory, called Paramāṇuvāda. This theory, however, cannot be supported, for the original cause of everything is not inert atoms. This is confirmed in the *Bhagavad-gītā* and *Śrīmad-Bhāgavatam,* as well as in the *Vedas,* wherein it is stated, *eko nārāyaṇa āsīt:* "Only Nārāyaṇa existed before the creation." *Śrīmad-Bhāgavatam* and the *Vedānta-sūtra* also say that the original cause is sentient and both indirectly and directly cognizant of everything within this creation. In the *Bhagavad-gītā* Kṛṣṇa says, *ahaṁ sarvasya prabhavaḥ,* "I am the original cause of everything," and *mattaḥ sarvaṁ pravartate,* "From Me everything comes into existence." Therefore, atoms may form the basic combinations of material existence, but these atoms are generated from the Supreme Personality of Godhead. Thus the philosophy of Gautama and Kaṇāda cannot be supported.

Similarly, impersonalists headed by Aṣṭāvakra and later by Śaṅkarācārya accept the impersonal Brahman effulgence as the cause of everything. According to their theory, the material manifestation is temporary and unreal, whereas the impersonal Brahman effulgence is reality. But this theory cannot be supported either, because the Lord Himself says in the *Bhagavad-gītā* that the Brahman effulgence rests on His personality. It is confirmed in the *Brahma-saṁhitā* that the Brahman effulgence is the personal bodily rays of Kṛṣṇa. As such, impersonal Brahman cannot be the original cause of the cosmic manifestation. The original cause is the all-perfect, sentient Personality of Godhead, Govinda.

The most dangerous theory of the impersonalists is that when God comes as an incarnation He accepts a material body created by the three modes of material nature. This Māyāvāda theory has been condemned by Lord Caitanya as most offensive. He has said that anyone who accepts the transcendental body of the Personality of Godhead to be made of material nature commits the greatest offense at the lotus feet of Viṣṇu. Similarly, the *Bhagavad-gītā* also states that when the Personality of Godhead descends in a human form, only fools and rascals deride Him. This actually occurred when Lord Kṛṣṇa, Lord Rāma and Lord Caitanya moved within human society as human beings.

The personified *Vedas* condemn the impersonal conception as a gross misrepresentation. In the *Brahma-saṁhitā,* the body of the Supreme Personality of Godhead is described as *ānanda-cinmaya-rasa.* The Supreme Personality of Godhead possesses a spiritual body, not a material body. He can enjoy anything through any part of His body, and therefore He is omnipotent. The limbs of a material body can perform only a particular function; for example, the hands can hold but cannot see or hear. But because the body of the Supreme Personality of Godhead is made of *ānanda-cinmaya-rasa* and is thus *sac-cid-ānanda-vigraha,* He can enjoy anything and do everything with any of His limbs. Acceptance of the spiritual body of the Lord as material is dictated by the tendency to make the Supreme Personality of Godhead equal to the conditioned soul. The conditioned soul has a material body. Therefore, if God also has a material body, then the impersonalistic theory that the Supreme Personality of Godhead and the living entities are one and the same can be very easily propagated.

Factually, when the Supreme Personality of Godhead comes He exhibits a nonmaterial body, and thus there is no difference between His childish body when He is lying on the lap of His mother Yaśodā and His so-called grown-up body when He is fighting with the demons. In His childhood body He also fought with demons, such as Pūtanā, Tṛṇāvarta and Aghāsura, with strength equal to that with which He fought in His youth against demons like Dantavakra and Śiśupāla. In material life, as soon as a conditioned soul changes his body he forgets everything of his past body, but from the *Bhagavad-gītā* we understand that because Kṛṣṇa has a *sac-cid-ānanda* body, He did not forget instructing the sun-god about the *Bhagavad-gītā* millions of years ago. The Lord is therefore known as Puruṣottama because He is transcendental to both material and spiritual existence. That He is the cause of all causes means that He is the cause of the spiritual world and of the material world as well. The Supreme Personality of Godhead is omnipotent and omniscient. Therefore, because a material body can be neither omnipotent nor omniscient, the Lord's body is surely not material. The Māyāvāda theory that the Personality of Godhead comes within this material world with a material body cannot be supported by any means.

It can be concluded that all the theories of the materialistic philosophers are generated from temporary, illusory existence, like the conclusions in a dream. Such conclusions certainly cannot lead us to the Absolute Truth. The Absolute Truth can be realized only through devotional service. As the Lord says in the *Bhagavad-gītā, bhaktyā mām abhijānāti:* "Only by devotional service can one understand Me." Śrīla Śrīdhara Svāmī has composed a nice verse in this regard, which states, "My dear Lord, let others engage in false argument and dry speculation, theorizing upon great philosophical theses. Let them loiter in the darkness of ignorance and illusion, falsely enjoying as if very learned scholars, although they are without knowledge of the Supreme Personality of Godhead. As far as I am concerned, I wish to be liberated simply by chanting the holy names of the all-beautiful Supreme Personality of Godhead—Mādhava, Vāmana, Trinayana, Saṅkarṣaṇa, Śrīpati and Govinda. Simply by chanting Your transcendental names, O Lord Madhupati, let me become free from the contamination of this material existence."

In this way the personified *Vedas* said, "Dear Lord, when a living entity, by Your grace only, comes to the right conclusion about Your exalted transcendental position, he no longer bothers with the different theories manufactured by the mental speculators or so-called philosophers." This is a reference to the speculative theories of Gautama, Kaṇāda, Patañjali and Kapila (*nirīśvara*). There are actually two Kapilas: one Kapila, the son of Kardama Muni, is an incarnation of God, and the other is an atheist of the modern age. The atheistic Kapila is often misrepresented to be the Supreme Personality of Godhead. Lord Kapila the incarnation of Godhead appeared as the son of Kardama Muni long, long ago, during the time of Svāyambhuva Manu; the modern age is the age of Vaivasvata Manu.

According to Māyāvāda philosophy, this manifested world, or material world, is *mithyā* or *māyā,* false. The Māyāvādī preaching principle is *brahma satyaṁ jagan mithyā:* "Only the Brahman effulgence is true, and the cosmic manifestation is illusory, or false." But according to Vaiṣṇava philosophy, this cosmic manifestation is true because it is created by the Supreme Personality of Godhead. In the *Bhagavad-gītā* the Lord says that He enters within this material world by one of His plenary portions and thus the creation takes place. From the *Vedas* also we can understand that this *asat,* or temporary cosmic manifestation, is an emanation from the supreme *sat,* or fact. From the *Vedānta-sūtra* also it is understood that everything has emanated from the Supreme Brahman. As such, the Vaiṣṇavas do not take this cosmic manifestation to be false. Because the Supreme Personality of Godhead has entered this cosmic manifestation in the form of His plenary expansion and caused the creation, the Vaiṣṇava philosophers see everything in this material world in relationship with the Supreme Lord.

This conception of the material world is very nicely explained by Śrīla Rūpa Gosvāmī, who says that when persons renounce the material world as illusory or false without knowing that the material world is a manifestation of the Supreme Lord, their renunciation is of no value. The Vaiṣṇavas, however, are free of attachment to this world because although the material world is generally accepted as an object of sense gratification, the Vaiṣṇavas are not in favor of sense gratification and are therefore not attached to material activities. The Vaiṣṇava accepts this material world according to the regulative principles of the Vedic injunctions and works without attachment. Since the Supreme Personality of Godhead is the original cause of everything, the Vaiṣṇava sees everything in relationship with Kṛṣṇa, even in this material world. By such advanced knowledge, everything becomes spiritualized. In other words, everything in the material world is already spiritual, but due to our lack of knowledge we see things as material.

The personified *Vedas* presented the example that those seeking gold do not reject gold earrings, gold bangles or anything else made of gold simply because they are shaped differently from the original gold. All living entities are part and parcel of the Supreme Lord and are qualitatively one, but they are now differently shaped in 8,400,000 species of life, just like many different ornaments manufactured from the same source of gold. As one who is interested in gold accepts all the differently shaped gold ornaments, so a Vaiṣṇava, knowing well that all living entities are of the same quality as the Supreme Personality of Godhead, accepts all living entities as eternal servants of God. As a Vaiṣṇava, then, one has ample opportunity to serve the Supreme Personality of Godhead simply by reclaiming these conditioned, misled living entities, training them in Kṛṣṇa consciousness and leading them back home, back to Godhead. The fact is that the minds of the living entities are now agitated by the three material qualities, and the living entities are therefore transmigrating, as if in dreams, from one body to another. When their consciousness is changed into Kṛṣṇa consciousness, however, they immediately fix Kṛṣṇa within their hearts, and thus their path toward liberation becomes clear.

In all the *Vedas* the Supreme Personality of Godhead and the living entities are stated to be of the same quality—*cetana,* or spiritual. This is confirmed in the *Padma Purāṇa,* wherein it is said that there are two kinds of spiritual entities: one is called the *jīva,* and the other is called the Supreme Lord. From Lord Brahmā down to the ant, all living entities are *jīvas,* whereas the Lord is the supreme four-handed Viṣṇu, or Janārdana. Strictly speaking, the word *ātmā* can be applied only to the Supreme Personality of Godhead, but because the living entities are His parts and parcels, sometimes the word *ātmā* is applied to them also. The living entities are therefore called *jīvātmā,* and the Supreme Lord is called Paramātmā. Both the Paramātmā and the *jīvātmā* are within this material world, and therefore this material world has a purpose other than sense gratification. The conception of a life of sense gratification is illusion, but the conception of service by the *jīvātmā* to the Paramātmā, even in this material world, is not at all illusory. A Kṛṣṇa conscious person is fully aware of this fact, and thus he does not take this material world to be false but acts in the reality of transcendental service. The devotee therefore sees everything in this material world as an opportunity to serve the Lord. He does not reject anything as material but dovetails everything in the service of the Lord. Thus a devotee is always in the transcendental position, and everything he uses becomes spiritually purified by being used in the Lord's service.

Śrīdhara Svāmī has composed a nice verse in this regard: "I worship the Supreme Personality of Godhead, who is always manifested as reality even within this material world, which is considered by some to be false." The conception of the falsity of this material world is due to a lack of knowledge, but a person advanced in Kṛṣṇa consciousness sees the Supreme Personality of Godhead in everything. This is actual realization of the Vedic aphorism *sarvaṁ khalv idaṁ brahma:* "Everything is Brahman."

The personified *Vedas* continued, "Dear Lord, less intelligent men take to other ways of self-realization, but actually there is no chance of becoming purified from material contamination or of stopping the repeated cycle of birth and death unless one is a thoroughly pure devotee. Dear Lord, everything rests on Your different potencies, and everyone is supported by You, as stated in the *Vedas: eko bahūnāṁ yo vidadhāti kāmān.* Therefore Your Lordship is the supporter and maintainer of all living entities—demigods, human beings and animals. Everyone is supported by You, and You are also situated in everyone's heart. In other words, You are the root of the whole creation. Therefore those who engage in Your devotional service without deviation, who always worship You, actually pour water on the root of the universal tree. By devotional service, therefore, one satisfies not only the Personality of Godhead but also all others, because everyone is maintained and supported by Him. Because a devotee understands the all-pervasive feature of the Supreme Personality of Godhead, he is the most practical philanthropist and altruist. Such pure devotees, thoroughly engaged in Kṛṣṇa consciousness, very easily overcome the cycle of birth and death, and they as much as jump over the head of death."

A devotee is never afraid of death or of changing his body; his consciousness is transformed into Kṛṣṇa consciousness, and even if he does not go back to Godhead, even if he transmigrates to another material body, he has nothing to fear. A vivid example is Bharata Mahārāja. Although in his next life he became a deer, in the life after that he became completely free from all material contamination and was elevated to the kingdom of God. The *Bhagavad-gītā* affirms, therefore, that a devotee is never vanquished. A devotee's path to the spiritual kingdom, back home, back to Godhead, is guaranteed. Even though a devotee slips in one birth, the continuation of his Kṛṣṇa consciousness elevates him further and further, until he goes back to Godhead. Not only does a pure devotee purify his own personal existence, but whoever becomes his disciple also becomes purified and is ultimately able to enter the kingdom of God without difficulty. In other words, not only can a pure devotee easily surpass death, but by his grace his followers can also do so without difficulty. The power of devotional service is so great that a pure devotee can electrify another person by his transcendental instruction on crossing over the ocean of nescience.

The instructions of a pure devotee to his disciple are also very simple. No one feels any difficulty in following in the footsteps of a pure devotee of the Lord. Anyone who follows in the footsteps of recognized devotees, such as Lord Brahmā, Lord Śiva, the Kumāras, Manu, Kapila, King Prahlāda, King Janaka, Śukadeva Gosvāmī, Yamarāja and their followers in disciplic succession, very easily finds the door of liberation open. On the other hand, those who are not devotees but are engaged in uncertain processes of self-realization, such as *jñāna, yoga* and *karma,* are understood to be still contaminated. Such contaminated persons, although apparently advanced in self-realization, cannot even liberate themselves, what to speak of those who follow them. Such nondevotees are compared to chained animals, for they are not able to go beyond the jurisdiction of the formalities of a certain type of faith. In the *Bhagavad-gītā* they are condemned as *veda-vāda-rata.* They cannot understand that the *Vedas* deal with activities of the material modes of nature—goodness, passion and ignorance. But as Lord Kṛṣṇa advised Arjuna, one has to go beyond the jurisdiction of the duties prescribed in the *Vedas* and take to Kṛṣṇa consciousness, devotional service. The Lord says in the *Bhagavad-gītā, nistrai-guṇyo bhavārjuna:* "My dear Arjuna, just try to become transcendental to the Vedic rituals." This transcendental position beyond the Vedic ritualistic performances is devotional service. In the *Bhagavad-gītā* the Lord clearly says that persons who are engaged in His devotional service without adulteration are situated in Brahman. Actual Brahman realization means Kṛṣṇa consciousness and engagement in devotional service. The devotees are therefore real *brahmacārīs* because their activities are always in Kṛṣṇa consciousness, devotional service.

The Kṛṣṇa consciousness movement therefore issues a supreme call to all kinds of religionists, asking them with great authority to join this movement, by which one can learn how to love God and thus surpass all formulas and formalities of scriptural injunction. A person who cannot overcome the jurisdiction of stereotyped religious principles is compared to an animal chained up by his master. The purpose of all religion is to understand God and develop one's dormant love of Godhead. If one simply sticks to the religious formulas and formalities but does not become elevated to the position of love of God, he is considered to be a chained animal. In other words, if one is not in Kṛṣṇa consciousness, he is not eligible for liberation from the contamination of material existence.

Śrīla Śrīdhara Svāmī has composed a nice verse in this regard: "Let others engage in severe austerities, let others fall to the land from the tops of hills and give up their lives, let others travel to many holy places of pilgrimage for salvation, or let them engage in deep study of philosophy and Vedic literatures. Let the mystic *yogīs* engage in their meditational service, and let the different sects engage in unnecessary arguing as to which is the best. But it is a fact that unless one is Kṛṣṇa conscious, unless one is engaged in devotional service, and unless one has the mercy of the Supreme Personality of Godhead, he cannot cross over this material ocean." An intelligent person, therefore, gives up all stereotyped ideas and joins the Kṛṣṇa consciousness movement for factual liberation.

The personified *Vedas* continued their prayers: "Dear Lord, Your impersonal feature is explained in the *Vedas.* You have no hands, but You can accept all sacrifices offered to You. You have no legs, but You can walk more swiftly than anyone else. Although You have no eyes, You can see whatever happens in the past, present and future. Although You have no ears, You can hear everything that is said. Although You have no mind, You know everyone and everyone's activities, past, present and future, and yet no one knows who You are. You know everyone, but no one knows You; therefore, You are the oldest and supreme personality."

Similarly, in another part of the *Vedas* it is said, "You have nothing to do. You are so perfect in Your knowledge and potency that everything becomes manifest simply by Your will. There is no one equal to or greater than You, and everyone acts as Your eternal servant." Thus the Vedic statements describe that the Absolute has no legs, no hands, no eyes, no ears and no mind, and yet He can act through His potencies and fulfill the needs of all living entities. As stated in the *Bhagavad-gītā,* His hands and legs are everywhere, for He is all-pervasive. The hands, legs, ears and eyes of all living entities are acting and moving by the direction of the Supersoul sitting within the living entity's heart. Unless the Supersoul is present, it is not possible for the hands and legs to be active. The Supreme Personality of Godhead is so great, independent and perfect that even without having any eyes, legs and ears, He is not dependent on others for His activities.

On the contrary, others are dependent on Him for the activities of their different sense organs. Unless the living entity is inspired and directed by the Supersoul, he cannot act.

The fact is that ultimately the Absolute Truth is the Supreme Person. But because He acts through His different potencies, which are impossible for the gross materialists to see, the materialists accept Him as impersonal. For example, one can observe the personal artistic work in a painting of a flower, and one can understand that the color adjustment, the shape and so on have demanded the minute attention of an artist. The artist's work is clearly exhibited in a painting of different blooming flowers. But the gross materialist, without seeing the hand of God in such artistic manifestations as the actual flowers blooming in nature, concludes that the Absolute Truth is impersonal. Actually, the Absolute is personal, but He is independent. He does not require to personally take a brush and colors to paint the flowers, for His potencies act so wonderfully that it appears as if flowers have come into being without the aid of an artist. The impersonal view of the Absolute Truth is accepted by less intelligent men, because unless one is engaged in the service of the Lord one cannot understand how the Supreme is acting—one cannot even know the Lord's name. Everything about the Lord's activities and personal features is revealed to the devotee only through his loving service attitude.

In the *Bhagavad-gītā* it is clearly said, *bhoktāraṁ yajña-tapasām:* "The Lord is the enjoyer of all sacrifices and the results of all austerities." Then again the Lord says, *sarva-loka-maheśvaram:* "I am the proprietor of all planets." So that is the position of the Supreme Personality of Godhead. While He is present in Goloka Vṛndāvana enjoying transcendental pleasure in the company of His eternal associates—the *gopīs* and the cowherd boys—all over the creation His potencies are acting under His direction, without disturbing His eternal pastimes.

Only through devotional service can one understand how the Supreme Personality of Godhead, by His inconceivable potencies, simultaneously acts impersonally and as a person. He acts just like the supreme emperor, and many thousands of kings and chiefs work under Him. The Supreme Personality of Godhead is the supreme independent controlling person, and all the demigods, including Lord Brahmā, Lord Śiva, Indra (the King of heaven), the king of the moon planet and the king of the sun planet, work under His direction. The *Vedas* confirm that it is out of fear of the Supreme Personality of Godhead that the sun is shining, the wind is blowing, and fire is distributing heat. The material nature produces all kinds of movable and immovable objects within the material world, but none of them can independently act or create without the direction of the Supreme Lord. All of them act as His tributaries, just like subordinate kings who offer their annual taxes to the emperor.

The Vedic injunctions state that every living entity lives by eating the remnants of food offered to the Personality of Godhead. In great sacrifices the injunction is that Nārāyaṇa should be present as the supreme predominating Deity of the sacrifice, and after the sacrifice is performed the remnants of food are distributed amongst the demigods. This is called *yajña-bhāga.* Every demigod has an allotment of *yajña-bhāga,* which he accepts as *prasādam.* The conclusion is that the demigods are not independently powerful: they are posted as different executives under the order of the Supreme Personality of Godhead, and they eat *prasādam,* or the remnants of sacrifices. They execute the order of the Supreme Lord exactly according to His plan. The Supreme Personality of Godhead is in the background, and because His orders are carried out by others, it appears that He is impersonal. In our grossly materialistic way, we cannot conceive how the Supreme Person is above the impersonal activities of material nature. Therefore the Lord explains in the *Bhagavad-gītā* that there is nothing superior to Him and that the impersonal Brahman is subordinately situated as a manifestation of His personal rays. Śrīpāda Śrīdhara Svāmī has therefore composed a nice verse in this regard: "Let me offer my respectful obeisances unto the Supreme Personality of Godhead, who has no material senses but through whose direction and will all the material senses are working. He is the supreme potency of all material senses or sense organs. He is omnipotent, and He is the supreme performer of everything. Therefore He is worshipable by everyone. Unto that Supreme Person do I offer my respectful obeisances."

Kṛṣṇa Himself declares in the *Bhagavad-gītā* that because He is transcendental to all sentient and insentient beings, He is known as Puruṣottama, which means the Supreme Personality. (*Puruṣa* means "person," and *uttama* means "supreme" or "transcendental.") In another place the Lord says that as the air is situated in the all-pervading sky, everyone is situated in Him, and everyone is acting under His direction.

The *Vedas* personified continued. "Dear Lord," they prayed, "You are equal to all, with no partiality toward a particular type of living entity. It is due to their own material desires that all living entities enjoy or suffer in different conditions of life. As Your parts and parcels, they are just like the sparks of a fire. Just as sparks dance in a blazing fire, all living entities are dancing on Your support. You are providing them with everything they desire, and yet You are not responsible for their position of enjoyment or suffering. There are different types of living entities—demigods, human beings, animals, trees, birds, beasts, germs, worms, insects and aquatics—and all enjoy or suffer in life while resting on You."

The living entities are of two kinds: one class is called *nitya-mukta,* ever liberated, and the other is called *nitya-baddha,* ever conditioned. The *nitya-mukta* living entities are in the spiritual kingdom, and the *nitya-baddhas* are in the material world. In the spiritual world both the living entities and the Lord are manifest in their original status, like live sparks in a blazing fire. But in the material world, although the Lord is all-pervasive in His impersonal feature, the living entities have forgotten their Kṛṣṇa consciousness to a greater or lesser degree, just as sparks sometimes fall from a blazing fire and lose their original brilliant condition. The sparks fall into different conditions and retain more or less of their original brilliance. Some sparks fall onto dry grass and thus ignite another big fire. This is a reference to the pure devotees who take compassion on the poor and innocent living entities. The pure devotee ignites Kṛṣṇa consciousness in the hearts of the conditioned souls, and thus the blazing fire of the spiritual world becomes manifest even within this material world. Some sparks fall onto water; they immediately lose their original brilliance and become extinct. They are comparable to the living entities who take their birth in the midst of gross materialists, in which case their original Kṛṣṇa consciousness becomes extinct. Some sparks fall to the ground and remain midway between the blazing and extinct conditions. Thus some living entities are without Kṛṣṇa consciousness, some are between having and not having Kṛṣṇa consciousness, and some are actually situated in Kṛṣṇa consciousness. The demigods in the higher planets—Lord Brahmā, Indra, Candra, the sun-god and various other demigods—are all Kṛṣṇa conscious. Human society is between the demigods and the animals, and thus some are more or less Kṛṣṇa conscious, and some are completely forgetful of Kṛṣṇa consciousness. The third-grade living entities, namely the animals, beasts, plants, trees and aquatics, have completely forgotten Kṛṣṇa consciousness. This example stated in the *Vedas* regarding the sparks of a blazing fire is very appropriate for understanding the condition of different types of living entities. But above all other living entities is the Supreme Personality of Godhead, Kṛṣṇa, or Puruṣottama, who is always liberated from all material conditions.

The question may be raised as to why the living entities

have fallen by chance into different conditions of life. To answer this question, we first have to understand that there cannot be any influence of chance for the living entities; chance is for nonliving entities. According to the Vedic literatures, living entities have knowledge, and thus they are called *cetana,* which means "in knowledge." Their situation in different conditions of life, therefore, is not accidental. It is by their choice, because they have knowledge. In the *Bhagavad-gītā* the Lord says, "Give up everything and just surrender unto Me." This process of realizing the Supreme Personality of Godhead is open for everyone, but still it is the choice of the particular living entity whether to accept or reject this proposal. In the last portion of the *Bhagavad-gītā,* Lord Kṛṣṇa very plainly says to Arjuna, "My dear Arjuna, now I have spoken everything to you. Now you may choose to accept it or not." Similarly, the living entities who have come down to this material world have made their own choice to enjoy this material world. It is not that Kṛṣṇa sent them into this world. The material world was created for the enjoyment of living entities who wanted to give up the eternal service of the Lord to become the supreme enjoyer themselves. According to Vaiṣṇava philosophy, when a living entity desires to gratify his senses and forgets the service of the Lord, he is given a place in the material world to act freely according to his desire, and therefore he creates a condition of life in which he either enjoys or suffers. We should definitely know that both the Lord and the living entities are eternally cognizant. There is no birth and death for either the Lord or the living entities. When creation takes place, this does not mean that the living entities are created. The Lord creates the material world to give the conditioned souls a chance to elevate themselves to the higher platform of Kṛṣṇa consciousness. If a conditioned soul does not take advantage of this opportunity, after the dissolution of this material world he enters into the body of Nārāyaṇa and remains there in deep sleep until the time of another creation.

In this connection the example of the rainy season is very appropriate. Seasonal rainfall may be taken as the agent for creation because after the rainfall the wet fields are favorable for growing different types of vegetation. Similarly, as soon as there is creation by the Lord's glancing over the material nature, immediately the living entities spring up in their different living conditions, just as different types of vegetation grow after a rainfall. The rainfall is one, but the creation of the different plants is varied. The rain falls equally on the whole field, but the different plants sprout up in different shapes and forms according to the seeds planted. Similarly, the seeds of our desires are varied. Every living entity has a different type of desire, and that desire is the seed which causes his growth in a certain type of body. This is explained by Rūpa Gosvāmī by the word *pāpa-bīja. Pāpa* means "sinful." All our material desires are to be taken as *pāpa-bīja,* or the seeds of sinful desires. The *Bhagavad-gītā* explains that our sinful desire is that we do not surrender unto the Supreme Lord. The Lord therefore says in the *Bhagavad-gītā,* "I shall give you protection from the reactions of sinful desires." These sinful desires are manifested in different types of bodies; therefore, no one can accuse the Supreme Lord of partiality in giving one type of body to a certain type of living entity and another type of body to another living entity. All the bodies of the 8,400,000 species are created according to the mental condition of the individual living entities. The Supreme Personality of Godhead, Puruṣottama, only gives them a chance to act according to their desires. Therefore, the living entities act by taking advantage of the facility given by the Lord.

At the same time, the living entities are born from the transcendental body of the Lord. This relationship between the Lord and the living entities is explained in the Vedic literatures, wherein it is said that the Supreme Lord maintains all His children, giving them whatever they want. Similarly, in the *Bhagavad-gītā* the Lord says, "I am the seed-giving father of all living entities." It is very simple to understand that the father gives birth to the children but the children act according to their own desires. Therefore the father is never responsible for the different futures of his children. Each child can take advantage of the father's property and instruction, but even though the inheritance and instruction may be the same for all the children, out of their different desires each child creates a different life and thereby suffers or enjoys.

Similarly, the *Bhagavad-gītā's* instructions are equal for everyone: everyone should surrender unto the Supreme Lord, and He will take charge of one and protect one from sinful reactions. The facilities of living in the creation of the Lord are equally offered to all living entities. Whatever there is, either on the land, on water or in the sky, is equally given to all living entities. Since all living beings are sons of the Supreme Lord, everyone can enjoy the material facilities given by the Lord, but unfortunate living entities create unfavorable conditions of life by fighting among themselves. The responsibility for this fighting and creating favorable and unfavorable situations lies with the living entities, not with the Supreme Personality of Godhead. Therefore, if the living entities take advantage of the Lord's instructions as given in the *Bhagavad-gītā* and develop Kṛṣṇa consciousness, then their lives become sublime, and they can go back to Godhead.

One may argue that because this material world is created by the Lord, He is therefore responsible for its condition. Certainly He is indirectly responsible for the creation and maintenance of this material world, but He is never responsible for the different conditions of the living entities. The Lord's creation of this material world is compared to a cloud's creation of vegetation. In the rainy season the cloud creates different varieties of vegetation. The cloud pours water on the surface of the earth, but it never touches the earth directly. Similarly, the Lord creates this material world simply by glancing over the material energy. This is confirmed in the *Vedas:* "He threw His glance over the material nature, and thus there was creation." In the *Bhagavad-gītā* it is also confirmed that simply by His transcendental glance over the material nature, He creates different varieties of entities, both movable and immovable, living and dead.

The creation of the material world can therefore be taken as one of the pastimes of the Lord; it is called one of the Lord's pastimes because He creates this material world whenever He desires. This desire of the Supreme Personality of Godhead is also extreme mercy on His part because it gives the conditioned souls another chance to develop their original consciousness and thus go back to Godhead. Therefore no one can blame the Supreme Lord for creating this material world.

From the subject matter under discussion, we can gain a clear understanding of the difference between the impersonalists and the personalists. The impersonal conception recommends merging into the existence of the Supreme, and the voidist philosophy recommends making all material varieties void. Both these philosophies are known as Māyāvāda. Certainly the cosmic manifestation comes to a close and becomes void when the living entities merge into the body of Nārāyaṇa to rest until another creation, and this may be called an impersonal condition, but these conditions are never eternal. The cessation of the variegatedness of the material world and the merging of the living entities into the body of the Supreme are not permanent because the creation will take place again, and the living entities who merged into the body of the Supreme without having developed their Kṛṣṇa consciousness will again appear in this material world when there is another creation. The *Bhagavad-gītā* confirms the fact that this material world is created and annihilated perpetually and that conditioned souls without Kṛṣṇa consciousness come back again and again, whenever the material creation is manifest. If such conditioned souls take advantage of this opportunity and develop Kṛṣṇa consciousness under the direct instruction of the Lord, then they are transferred to the spiritual world and do not have to come back to the material creation. It is said, therefore, that the voidists and the impersonalists are not very intelligent because they do not take shelter under the lotus feet of the Lord. Because they are less intelligent, these voidists and impersonalists take to different types of austerities, either to attain the stage of *nirvāṇa,* which means finishing the material conditions of life, or to attain oneness by merging into the body of the Lord. All of them again fall down because they neglect the lotus feet of the Lord.

In the *Caitanya-caritāmṛta,* the author, Kṛṣṇadāsa Kavirāja Gosvāmī, after studying all the Vedic literatures and hearing from all authorities, has given his opinion that Kṛṣṇa is the only supreme master and that all living entities are His eternal servants. His statement is confirmed in the prayers by the personified *Vedas.* The conclusion is, therefore, that everyone is under the control of the Supreme Personality of Godhead, everyone is serving under the supreme direction of the Lord, and everyone is afraid of the Supreme Personality of Godhead. It is out of fear of Him that activities are rightly executed. Everyone's position is to be subordinate to the Supreme Lord, yet the Lord has no partiality in His view of the living entities. He is just like the unlimited sky; as the sparks of a fire dance in the fire, similarly, all living entities are like birds flying in the unlimited sky of the Supreme Lord. Some of them are flying very high, some are flying at a lesser altitude, and some are flying at a still lesser altitude. The different birds are flying in different positions according to their respective abilities, but the sky has nothing to do with this ability. In the *Bhagavad-gītā* the Lord confirms that He awards different positions to different living entities according to their proportionate surrender. This proportionate reward by the Personality of Godhead to the living entities is not partiality. Therefore, in spite of the living entities' always being under the control of the Supreme Personality of Godhead in their different positions, spheres and species of life, He is never responsible for their different living conditions. It is foolish and artificial, therefore, to think oneself equal to the Supreme Lord, and it is still more foolish to think that one has not seen God. Everyone is seeing God according to his capacity; the only difference is that the theist sees God as the Supreme Personality, the most beloved, Kṛṣṇa, and the atheist sees the Absolute Truth as ultimate death.

The personified *Vedas* continued to pray. "Dear Lord," they said, "from all Vedic information it is understood that You are the supreme controller and all living entities are controlled. Both the Lord and the living entities are called *nitya,* eternal, and so are qualitatively one, yet the singular *nitya,* or the Supreme Lord, is the controller, whereas the plural *nityas* are controlled. The individual controlled living entity resides within the body, and the supreme controller, as Supersoul, is also present there, but the Supersoul controls the individual soul. That is the verdict of the *Vedas.* If the individual soul were not controlled by the Supersoul, then how could one explain the Vedic version that a living entity transmigrates from one body to another, enjoying and suffering the effects of his past deeds, sometimes being promoted to a higher standard of life and sometimes being degraded to a lower standard? Thus the conditioned souls are not only under the control of the Supreme Lord, but are also conditioned by the control of the material nature. This relationship of the living entities with the Supreme Lord as the controlled and the controller definitely proves that although the Supersoul is all-pervasive, the individual living entities are never all-pervasive. If the individual souls were all-pervasive, there would be no question of their being controlled. The theory that the Supersoul and the individual soul are equal is therefore a polluted conclusion, and no sensible person accepts it; rather, one should try to understand the distinctions between the supreme eternal and the subordinate eternals."

The personified *Vedas* therefore concluded, "O Lord, You

are the unlimited eternal (*dhruva*), and the living entities are the limited eternals." The form of the unlimited eternal is sometimes conceived as the universal form, and in Vedic literatures like the *Upaniṣads* the form of the limited eternal is vividly described. It is said therein that the original, spiritual form of the living entity is one ten-thousandth the size of the tip of a hair. It is also stated that spirit is greater than the greatest and smaller than the smallest. The individual living entities, who are eternally part and parcel of God, are smaller than the smallest. With our material senses we can perceive neither the Supreme, who is greater than the greatest, nor the individual soul, who is smaller than the smallest. We have to understand both Him who is greater than the greatest and him who is smaller than the smallest from the authoritative sources of Vedic literature. The Vedic literature states that the Supersoul is sitting within the heart of every living entity's body and is as big as a thumb. Therefore the argument may be put forward, How can something the size of a thumb be accommodated within the heart of an ant? The answer is that this thumb measurement of the Supersoul is imagined in proportion to the body of the living entity. In no circumstance, therefore, can the Supersoul and the individual living entity be taken as one, although both of them enter within the material body of a living entity. The Supersoul lives within the heart to direct or control the individual living entity. Although both are *dhruva,* or eternal, the living entity is always under the direction of the Supreme.

It may be argued that because the living entities are born of the material nature, they are all equal and independent. In the Vedic literature, however, it is said that the Supreme Personality of Godhead impregnates the material nature with the living entities, and then they come out. Therefore, the appearance of the individual living entities is not factually due to material nature alone, just as a child produced by a woman is not her independent production. A woman is first impregnated by a man, and then a child is produced. As such, the child produced by the woman is part and parcel of the man. Similarly, the living entities are apparently produced by the material nature, but not independently. It is due to the impregnation of the material nature by the supreme father that the living entities are present. Therefore the argument that the individual living entities are not parts and parcels of the Supreme cannot stand. For example, the different parts of the body cannot be taken as equal to the whole; rather, the whole body is the controller of the different limbs. Similarly, the parts and parcels of the supreme whole are always dependent and are always controlled by the source of the parts and parcels. It is confirmed in the *Bhagavad-gītā* that the living entities are parts and parcels of Kṛṣṇa: *mamaivāṁśaḥ.* No sane man, therefore, will accept the theory that the Supersoul and the individual soul are of the same category. They are equal in quality, but quantitatively the Supersoul is always the Supreme, and the individual soul is always subordinate to the Supersoul. That is the conclusion of the *Vedas.*

The significant word used in this connection is *yan-maya,* or *cin-maya.* In Sanskrit grammar, the word *mayaṭ* is used in the sense of "transformation," and also in the sense of "sufficiency." The Māyāvādī philosophers interpret that the word *yan-maya,* or *cin-maya,* indicates that the living entity is always equal to the Supreme. But one has to consider whether this affix, *mayaṭ,* is used for "sufficiency" or for "transformation." The living entity never possesses anything exactly in the same proportion as the Supreme Personality of Godhead. Therefore, this *mayaṭ* affix cannot be used to mean that the individual living entity is sufficient. The individual living entity never has sufficient knowledge; otherwise, how could he have come under the control of *māyā,* or the material energy? The word "sufficient" can be accepted, therefore, only in proportion to the magnitude of the living entity. The spiritual oneness of the Supreme Lord and the living entities is never to be accepted as homogeneity. Each and every living entity is individual. If homogeneous oneness is accepted, then by the liberation of one individual soul, all other individual souls would have been liberated immediately. But the fact is that every individual soul is differently enjoying and suffering in the material world.

As mentioned above, the word *mayaṭ* is also used in the sense of "transformation"; sometimes it is also used to mean "by-product." The impersonalist theory is that Brahman Himself has accepted different types of bodies and that this is His *līlā,* or pastime. There are, however, many hundreds and thousands of species of life in different standards of living conditions, such as human beings, demigods, animals, birds and beasts, and if all of them were plenary expansions of the Supreme Absolute Truth, then there would be no question of liberation, because Brahman would already be liberated. Another interpretation put forward by the Māyāvādīs is that in every millennium different types of bodies are manifest, and when the millennium is closed all the different bodies, or expansions of Brahman, automatically become one, ending all different manifestations. Then in the next millennium, according to this theory, Brahman again expands in different bodily forms. If we accept this theory, then Brahman becomes subject to change. But this cannot be accepted. From the *Vedānta-sūtra* we understand that Brahman is by nature joyful. He cannot, therefore, change Himself into a body which is subject to so many painful conditions. Actually, the living entities are infinitesimal parts and parcels of Brahman, and as such they are prone to be covered by the illusory energy. As explained before, the particles of Brahman are like sparks blissfully dancing within a fire, but there is a chance of their falling from the fire to smoke, although smoke is another condition of fire. This material world is just like smoke, and the spiritual world is like a blazing fire. The innumerable living entities are prone to fall down to the material world from the spiritual world when influenced by the illusory energy, and it is also possible for the living entity to be liberated again when by cultivation of real knowledge he becomes completely freed from the contamination of the material world.

The theory of the *asuras* is that the living entities are born of material nature, or *prakṛti,* in touch with the *puruṣa.* This theory also cannot be accepted, because both the material nature and the Supreme Personality of Godhead are eternally existing. Neither the material nature nor the Supreme Personality of Godhead can be born. The Supreme Lord is known as *aja,* or unborn. Similarly, the material nature is called *ajā.* Both these terms, *aja* and *ajā,* mean "unborn." Because both the material nature and the Supreme Lord are unborn, it is not possible that they can beget the living entities. But it is accepted in the Vedic literature that as water in contact with air sometimes presents innumerable bubbles, so a combination of the material nature and the Supreme Person causes the appearance of the living entities within this material world. As bubbles in the water appear in different shapes, the living entities also appear in the material world in different shapes and conditions, influenced by the modes of material nature. As such, it is not improper to conclude that the living entities appearing within this material world in different shapes, such as human beings, demigods, animals, birds and beasts, all get their respective bodies due to different desires. No one can say when such desires were awakened in them, and therefore it is said, *anādi-karma:* the cause of such material existence is untraceable. No one knows when material life began, but it is a fact that it does have a point of beginning because originally every living entity is a spiritual spark. As a spark's falling onto the ground from a fire has a beginning, so a living entity's coming to this material world has a beginning, but no one can say when. Even though during the time of dissolution all the conditioned living entities remain merged in the spiritual existence of the Lord, as if in deep sleep, their original desires to lord it over the material nature do not subside. Again, when there is cosmic manifestation, they come out to fulfill the same desires, and therefore they appear in different species of life.

The living entities merged into the Supreme at the time of dissolution are compared to honey. In the honeycomb, the tastes of different flowers are conserved. When one drinks honey, one cannot distinguish what sort of honey has been collected from what sort of flower, but the palatable taste of the honey presupposes that the honey is not homogeneous but is a combination of different tastes. Another example is that although different rivers ultimately mix with the water of the sea, this does not mean that the individual identities of the rivers are thereby lost. Although the water of the Ganges and the water of the Yamunā mix with the water of the sea, the river Ganges and river Yamunā still continue to exist independently. The merging of different living entities into Brahman at the time of dissolution involves the dissolution of different types of bodies, but the living entities, along with their different tastes, remain individually submerged in Brahman until another manifestation of the material world. As the salty taste of seawater and the sweet taste of Ganges water are different and this difference continuously exists, so the difference between the Supreme Lord and the living entities continuously exists, even though at the time of dissolution they appear to merge. The conclusion is, therefore, that even when the living entities become free from all contamination of material conditions and merge into the spiritual kingdom, their individual tastes in relationship with the Supreme Lord continue to exist.

The personified *Vedas* continued, "Dear Lord, it is therefore our conclusion that all living entities are attracted by Your material energy, and only due to their mistakenly identifying themselves as products of the material nature are they transmigrating from one kind of body to another in forgetfulness of their eternal relationship with You. Because of ignorance, these living entities misidentify themselves in different species of life, and especially when elevated to the human form of life, they identify with a particular class of men, or a particular nation or race or so-called religion, forgetting their real identity as eternal servants of Your Lordship. Due to this faulty conception of life, they are undergoing repeated birth and death. Out of many millions of them, if one becomes intelligent enough, by association with pure devotees, he comes to the understanding of Kṛṣṇa consciousness and comes out of the jurisdiction of the material misconception."

In the *Caitanya-caritāmṛta* it is confirmed by Lord Caitanya that the living entities are wandering within this universe in different species of life, but that if one of them becomes intelligent enough, by the mercy of the spiritual master and the Supreme Personality of Godhead, Kṛṣṇa, then he begins his devotional life in Kṛṣṇa consciousness. It is said, *hariṁ vinā na mṛtiṁ taranti:* without the help of the Supreme Personality of Godhead, one cannot get out of the clutches of repeated birth and death. In other words, only the Supreme Lord, the Personality of Godhead, can relieve the conditioned souls from the cycle of repeated birth and death.

The personified *Vedas* continued to pray: "The influence of time—past, present and future—and the material miseries, such as excessive heat, excessive cold, birth, death, old age and disease, are all simply the movements of Your eyebrows. Everything is working under Your direction." It is said in the *Bhagavad-gītā* that all material activity is going on under the direction of the Supreme Personality of Godhead, Kṛṣṇa. The Vedas continued, "All the conditions of material existence are opposing elements for persons who are not surrendered unto You. But for those who are surrendered souls and are in full Kṛṣṇa consciousness, these things cannot be a source of fear." When Lord Nṛsiṁhadeva appeared, Prahlāda Mahārāja was never afraid of Him, whereas his atheist father was immediately faced with death personified and was killed. Therefore, although Lord Nṛsiṁhadeva appears as death for an atheist like Hiraṇyakaśipu, He is always kind and is the reservoir of all pleasure for devotees like Prahlāda. A pure devotee is not, therefore, afraid of birth, death, old age and disease.

Śrīpāda Śrīdhara Svāmī has composed a nice verse, the meaning of which is as follows: "My dear Lord, I am a living entity perpetually disturbed by the conditions of material existence. I have been cracked to pieces by the smashing wheel of material existence, and because of my various sinful activities while existing in this material world, I am burning in the blazing fire of material reactions. Somehow or other, my dear Lord, I have come to take shelter under Your lotus feet. Please accept me and give me protection." Śrīla Narottama dāsa Ṭhākura, also, prays like this: "My dear Lord, O son of Nanda Mahārāja, associated with the daughter of Vṛṣabhānu, I have come to take shelter under Your lotus feet after suffering greatly in the material condition of life, and I pray that You please be merciful upon me. Please do not kick me away, for I have no other shelter than You."

The conclusion is that any process of self-realization or God realization other than *bhakti-yoga,* or devotional service, is extremely difficult. Taking shelter of devotional service to the Lord in full Kṛṣṇa consciousness is therefore the only way to become free from the contamination of material, conditioned life, especially in this age. Those who are not in Kṛṣṇa consciousness are simply wasting their time, and they have no tangible proof of spiritual life.

It is said by Lord Rāmacandra, "I always give confidence and security to anyone who surrenders unto Me and decides definitely that He is My eternal servant, for that is My natural inclination." Similarly, Lord Kṛṣṇa says in the *Bhagavad-gītā,* "The influence of the material nature is insurmountable, but anyone who surrenders unto Me can verily overcome the influence of material nature." The devotees are not at all interested in arguing with the nondevotees to nullify their theories. Rather than wasting time, they always engage themselves in the transcendental loving service of the Lord in full Kṛṣṇa consciousness.

The personified *Vedas* continued, "Dear Lord, although great mystic *yogīs* may have full control over the elephant of the mind and the hurricane of the senses, unless they take shelter of a bona fide spiritual master they fall victim to the material influence and are never successful in their attempts at self-realization. Such unguided persons are compared to merchants going to sea on a ship without a captain." By one's personal attempts, therefore, one cannot get free from the clutches of material nature. One has to accept a bona fide spiritual master and work according to his direction. Then it is possible to cross over the nescience of material conditions. Śrīpāda Śrīdhara Svāmī has composed a nice verse in this connection, in which he says, "O all-merciful spiritual master, representative of the Supreme Personality of Godhead, when my mind will be completely surrendered unto your lotus feet, at that time, only by your mercy, I shall be able to get relief from all obstacles to spiritual life, and I shall be situated in blissful life."

Actually, ecstatic *samādhi,* or absorption in the Supreme Personality of Godhead, can be achieved by constant engagement in His service, and this constant engagement in devotional service can be performed only when one works under the direction of a bona fide spiritual master. The *Vedas* therefore instruct that in order to know the science of devotional service one has to submit himself unto the bona fide spiritual master. The bona fide spiritual master is he who knows the science of devotional service in disciplic succession. This disciplic succession is called *śrotriya.* The prime symptom of one who has become a spiritual master in disciplic succession is that he is one hundred percent fixed in *bhakti-yoga.* Sometimes people neglect to accept a spiritual master, and instead they endeavor for self-realization by mystic *yoga* practice, but there are many instances of failure, even by great *yogīs* like Viśvāmitra. Arjuna said in the *Bhagavad-gītā* that controlling the mind is as impractical as stopping the blowing of a hurricane. Sometimes the mind is compared to a maddened elephant. Without following the direction of a spiritual master one cannot control the mind and the senses. In other words, if one practices *yoga* mysticism and does not accept a bona fide spiritual master, he will surely fail. He will simply waste his valuable time. The Vedic injunction is that no one can have full knowledge without being under the guidance of an *ācārya. Ācāryavān puruṣo veda:* one who has accepted an *ācārya* knows what is what. The Absolute Truth cannot be understood by arguments. One who has attained the perfect brahminical stage naturally becomes renounced; he does not strive for material gain because by spiritual knowledge he has come to the conclusion that in this world there is no insufficiency. Everything is sufficiently provided by the Supreme Personality of Godhead. A real *brāhmaṇa,* therefore, does not endeavor for material perfection; rather, he approaches a bona fide spiritual master to accept orders from him. A spiritual master's qualification is that he is *brahma-niṣṭha,* which means that he has given up all other activities and has dedicated his life to working only for the Supreme Personality of Godhead, Kṛṣṇa. When a bona fide student approaches a bona fide spiritual master, he submissively prays to the spiritual master, "My dear lord, kindly accept me as your student and train me in such a way that I will be able to give up all other processes of self-realization and simply engage in Kṛṣṇa consciousness, devotional service."

The devotee engaged by the direction of the spiritual master in the transcendental loving service of the Lord contemplates as follows: "My dear Lord, You are the reservoir of pleasure. Since You are present, what is the use of the transient pleasure derived from society, friendship and love? Persons unaware of the supreme reservoir of pleasure falsely engage in deriving pleasure from sense gratification, but this is transient and illusory." In this connection, Vidyāpati, a great Vaiṣṇava devotee and poet, says, "My dear Lord, undoubtedly there is some pleasure in the midst of society, friendship and love, although it is materially conceived, but such pleasure cannot satisfy my heart, which is like a desert." In a desert there is need of an ocean of water. But if only a drop of water is poured on the desert, what is the value of such water? Similarly, our material hearts are full of multidesires, which cannot be fulfilled by materialistic society, friendship and love. When our hearts begin to derive pleasure from the supreme reservoir of pleasure, then we can be satisfied. That transcendental satisfaction is possible only in devotional service, in full Kṛṣṇa consciousness.

The personified *Vedas* continued, "Dear Lord, You are *sac-cid-ānanda-vigraha,* the ever-blissful form of knowledge, and because the living entities are parts and parcels of Your personality, their natural state of existence is to be fully conscious of You. In this material world, anyone who has developed such Kṛṣṇa consciousness is no longer interested in the materialistic way of life. A Kṛṣṇa conscious being becomes uninterested in family life, where there is some concession for sense enjoyment. In other words, he is no longer interested in sense gratification. The perfection of human life is based on knowledge and renunciation, but it is very difficult to attempt to reach the stage of knowledge and renunciation while in family life. Kṛṣṇa conscious persons therefore take shelter of the association of devotees or sanctified places of pilgrimage. Such persons are aware of the relationship between the Supersoul and the individual living entities, and they are never in the bodily concept of life. Because they always carry You in full consciousness within their hearts, they are so purified that any place they go becomes a holy place of pilgrimage, and the water which washes their feet is able to deliver many sinful persons loitering within this material world."

When Prahlāda Mahārāja was asked by his atheistic father

to describe something very good which he had learned, he replied to his father, "For a materialistic person who is always full of anxieties due to being engaged in temporary and relative truths, the best course is to give up the blind well of family life and go to the forest to take shelter of the Supreme Lord." Those who are actually pure devotees are celebrated as *mahātmās,* or great sages, personalities perfect in knowledge. They always think of the Supreme Lord and His lotus feet, and thus they automatically become liberated. Devotees who are always situated in that position become electrified by the inconceivable potencies of the Lord, and thus they themselves become the source of liberation for their followers and devotees. A Kṛṣṇa conscious person is fully electrified spiritually, and therefore anyone who touches or takes shelter of such a pure devotee becomes similarly electrified with spiritual potencies. Such devotees are never puffed up with material opulences. Generally, the material opulences are good parentage, education, beauty and riches, but although a devotee of the Lord may possess all four of these material opulences, he is never carried away by the pride of possessing such distinctions. Great devotees of the Lord travel all over the world from one place of pilgrimage to another, and on their way they meet many conditioned souls and deliver them by their association and distribution of transcendental knowledge. They generally reside in places like Vṛndāvana, Mathurā, Dvārakā, Jagannātha Purī and Navadvīpa because only devotees assemble in such places. In this way they give saintly association to one another and thus advance. So that every living entity can take advantage of the association of Kṛṣṇa conscious persons, such great devotees open temples and *āśramas* where Kṛṣṇa's devotees assemble. By such association, people can develop more and more in Kṛṣṇa consciousness. Such advancement is not possible in ordinary household life, which is devoid of Kṛṣṇa consciousness.

The personified *Vedas* continued, "Dear Lord, there are two classes of transcendentalists, the impersonalists and the personalists. The opinion of the impersonalists is that this material manifestation is false and that only the Absolute Truth is factual. The view of the personalists, however, is that the material world, although very temporary, is nevertheless not false but factual. Such transcendentalists have different arguments to establish the validity of their philosophies. Factually, the material world is simultaneously both truth and untruth. It is truth because everything is an expansion of the Supreme Absolute Truth, and it is untruth because the existence of the material world is temporary: it is created, and it is annihilated. Because of its different conditions of existence, the cosmic manifestation has no fixed position." Those who advocate acceptance of this material world as false are generally known by the maxim *brahma satyaṁ jagan mithyā.* They put forward the argument that everything in the material world is prepared from matter. For example, there are many things made of clay, such as earthen pots, dishes and bowls. After their annihilation, these things may be transformed into many other material objects, but in all cases their existence as clay continues. An earthen water jug, after being broken, may be transformed into a bowl or dish, but either as a dish, bowl or water jug, the earth itself continues to exist. Therefore, the forms of a water jug, bowl or dish are false, but their existence as earth is real. This is the impersonalists' version. This cosmic manifestation is certainly produced from the Absolute Truth, but because its existence is temporary, it is false; the impersonalists' understanding is that the Absolute Truth, which is always present, is the only truth. In the opinion of other transcendentalists, however, this material world, being produced of the Absolute Truth, is also truth. The impersonalists argue that this is not a fact, for it is sometimes found that matter is produced from spirit soul and sometimes that spirit soul is produced from matter. Such philosophers push forward the argument that although cow dung is dead matter, sometimes it is found that scorpions come out of cow dung. Similarly, dead matter like nails and hair comes out of the living body. Therefore, things produced of a certain thing are not always of the same quality as that thing. On the strength of this argument, Māyāvādī philosophers establish that although this cosmic manifestation is certainly an emanation from the Absolute Truth, the cosmic manifestation does not necessarily have truth in it. According to this view, the Absolute Truth, Brahman, should therefore be accepted as truth, whereas the cosmic manifestation, although a product of the Absolute Truth, cannot be taken as truth.

The view of the Māyāvādī philosopher, however, is stated in the *Bhagavad-gītā* to be the view of the *asuras,* or demons. The Lord says in the *Bhagavad-gītā, asatyam apratiṣṭhaṁ te jagad āhur anīśvaram/ aparaspara-sambhūtaṁ kim anyat kāma-haitukam:* "The *asuras'* view of this cosmic manifestation is that the whole creation is false. The *asuras* think that the mere interaction of matter is the source of the creation and that there is no controller or God." But actually this is not the fact. From the Seventh Chapter of the *Bhagavad-gītā* we understand that the five gross elements—earth, water, fire, air and sky—plus the subtle elements—mind, intelligence and false ego—are the eight separated energies of the Supreme Lord. Beyond this inferior, material energy is a spiritual energy, known as the living entities. The living entities are accepted as the superior energy of the Lord. The whole cosmic manifestation is a combination of the inferior and superior energies, and the source of the energies is the Supreme Personality of Godhead. The Supreme Personality of Godhead has many different types of energies. This is confirmed in the *Vedas: parāsya śaktir vividhaiva śrūyate.* "The transcendental energies of the Lord are variegated." And because such varieties of energies have emanated from the Supreme Lord, they cannot be false. The Lord is ever-existing, and the energies are ever-existing. Some of the energy is temporary—sometimes manifested and sometimes unmanifested—but this does not mean that it is false. The example may be given that when a person is angry he does things which are different from his normal condition of life, but the fact that the mood of anger appears and disappears does not mean that the energy of anger is false. As such, the argument of the Māyāvādī philosophers that this world is false is not accepted by the Vaiṣṇava philosophers. The Lord Himself confirms that the view that there is no supreme cause of this material manifestation, that there is no God, and that everything is only the creation of the interaction of matter is a view of the *asuras.*

The Māyāvādī philosopher sometimes puts forward the argument of the snake and the rope. In the dark of evening, a curled-up rope is sometimes, due to ignorance, taken for a snake. But mistaking the rope for a snake does not mean that the rope or the snake is false, and therefore this example, used by the Māyāvādīs to illustrate the falsity of the material world, is not valid. When a thing is taken as fact but actually has no existence at all, it is called false. But if something is mistaken for something else that exists, that does not mean that it is false. The Vaiṣṇava philosophers use a very appropriate example, comparing this material world to an earthen pot. When we see an earthen pot, it does not at once disappear and turn into something else. It may be temporary, but the earthen pot is taken into use for bringing water, and we continue to see it as an earthen pot. Therefore, although the earthen pot is temporary and different from the original earth, we cannot say that it is false. We should therefore conclude that the earthen pot and the entire earth are both truths because one is the product of the other. We understand from the *Bhagavad-gītā* that after the dissolution of this cosmic manifestation, the material energy enters into the Supreme Personality of Godhead. The Supreme Personality of Godhead is ever-existing with His varied energies. Because the material creation is an emanation from Him, we cannot say that this cosmic manifestation is a product of something void. Kṛṣṇa is not void. Whenever we speak of Kṛṣṇa, He is present with His form, qualities, name, entourage and paraphernalia. Therefore, Kṛṣṇa is not impersonal. The original cause of everything is neither void nor impersonal but is the Supreme Person. Demons may say that this material creation is *anīśvara,* without a controller or God, but such arguments ultimately cannot stand.

The example given by the Māyāvādī philosophers that inanimate matter like nails and hair comes from the living body is not a very sound argument. Nails and hair are undoubtedly inanimate, but they come not from the animate living being but from the inanimate material body. Similarly, the argument that the scorpion comes from cow dung, meaning that a living entity comes from matter, is also unsound. The scorpion which comes out of the cow dung is certainly a living entity, but the living entity does not come out of the cow dung. Only the living entity's material body, or the body of the scorpion, comes out of the cow dung. The sparks of the living entities, as we understand from the *Bhagavad-gītā,* are injected into material nature, and then they come out. The body of the living entity in different forms is supplied by material nature, but the living entity himself is supplied by the Supreme Lord. The father and mother give the body necessary for the living entity under certain conditions. The living entity transmigrates from one body to another according to his different desires, which in the subtle form of intelligence, mind and false ego accompany him from body to body. By superior arrangement a living entity is put into the womb of a certain type of material body, and then he develops a similar body. Therefore, the spirit soul is not produced from matter; it takes on a particular type of body under superior arrangement. According to our present experience, this material world is a combination of matter and spirit. The spirit is moving the matter. The spirit soul (the living entity) and matter are different energies of the Supreme Lord, and since both the energies are products of the Supreme Eternal, or the Supreme Truth, they are factual, not false. Because the living entity is part and parcel of the Supreme, he exists eternally.

Therefore, for him there cannot be any question of birth or death. So-called birth and death occur because of the material body. The Vedic version *sarvaṁ khalv idaṁ brahma* means that since both the energies have emanated from the Supreme Brahman, everything we experience is nondifferent from Brahman.

There are many arguments about the existence of this material world, but the Vaiṣṇava philosophical conclusion is the best. The example of the earthen pot is very suitable: the form of the earthen pot may be temporary, but it has a specific purpose. The purpose of the earthen pot is to carry water from one place to another. Similarly, this material body, although temporary, has a special use. The living entity is given a chance from the beginning of the creation to evolve different kinds of material bodies according to the reserve desires he has accumulated from time immemorial. The human form of body is a special chance in which the developed form of consciousness can be utilized.

Sometimes the Māyāvādī philosophers push forward the argument that if this material world is truth, then why are householders advised to give up their connection with this material world and take *sannyāsa*? But the Vaiṣṇava philosopher's view of *sannyāsa* is not that because the world is false one must therefore give up material activities. The purpose of Vaiṣṇava *sannyāsa* is to utilize things as they are intended to be utilized. Śrīla Rūpa Gosvāmī has given transcendentalists two formulas for dealing with this material world. When a Vaiṣṇava renounces the materialistic way of life and takes to *sannyāsa,* it is not on the conception of the falsity of the material world but to devote himself fully to engaging everything in the service of the Lord. Śrīla Rūpa Gosvāmī therefore gives this formula: "One should be unattached to the material world because material attachment is meaningless. The entire material world, the entire cosmic manifestation, belongs to God, Kṛṣṇa. Therefore, everything should be utilized for Kṛṣṇa, and the devotee should remain unattached to material things." This is the purpose of Vaiṣṇava *sannyāsa.* A materialist sticks to the world for sense gratification, but a Vaiṣṇava *sannyāsī,* although not accepting anything for his personal sense gratification, knows the art of utilizing everything for the service of the Lord. Śrīla Rūpa Gosvāmī has therefore criticized the Māyāvādī *sannyāsīs* with his second formula: "Because the Māyāvādīs do not know that everything has a utilization for the service of the Lord, they take the world to be false and falsely think they are liberated from the contamination of the material world." Since everything is an expansion of the energy of the Supreme Lord, the expansions are as real as the Supreme Lord is.

That the cosmic world is only temporarily manifested does not mean that it is false or that the source of its manifestation is false. Since the source of its manifestation is truth, the manifestation is also truth, but one must know how to utilize it. The example of the earthen pot may be cited again: the earthen pot produced from the whole earth is temporary, but when used for a proper purpose the earthen pot is not false. The Vaiṣṇava philosophers know how to utilize the temporary construction of this material world, just as a sane man knows how to utilize the temporary construction of the earthen pot. When the earthen pot is used for a wrong purpose, that is false. Similarly, this human form of body or this material world, when used for sense gratification, is false. But if this human body and the material creation are used for the service of the Supreme Lord, their activities are never false. It is therefore confirmed in the *Bhagavad-gītā* that even slightly using this body and the material world for the service of the Lord can deliver a person from the gravest danger. When properly utilized, neither the superior nor inferior energies emanating from the Supreme Personality of Godhead are false.

As far as fruitive activities are concerned, they are mainly based on the platform of sense gratification. Therefore an advanced Kṛṣṇa conscious person does not take to them. The result of fruitive activities can elevate one to the higher planetary system, but as it is said in the *Bhagavad-gītā,* foolish persons, after exhausting the results of their pious activities in the heavenly kingdom, come back again to this lower planetary system and then again try to go to the higher planetary system. Their only profit is to take the trouble of going and coming back, just as at present many material scientists are spoiling their time by trying to go to the moon planet and again coming back. Those who are engaged in fruitive activities are described by the *Vedas* personified as *andha-paramparā,* or blind followers of the Vedic ritualistic ceremonies. Although such ceremonies are certainly mentioned in the *Vedas,* they are not meant for the intelligent class of men. Men who are too much attached to material enjoyment are captivated by the prospect of being elevated to the higher planetary system, and so they take to such ritualistic activities. But persons who are intelligent, who have taken shelter of a bona fide spiritual master to see things as they are, do not take to fruitive activities but engage themselves in the transcendental loving service of the Lord.

Persons who are not devotees take to the Vedic ritualistic ceremonies for materialistic reasons, and then they are bewildered. A vivid example may be given: an intelligent person possessing one million dollars in currency notes does not hold the money without using it, even though he knows perfectly well that the currency notes in themselves are nothing but paper. When one has one million dollars in currency notes, he is actually holding only a huge bunch of papers, but if he utilizes it for a purpose, then he benefits. Similarly, although this material world may be false, just like the paper, it has its proper beneficial utilization. Because the currency notes, although paper, are issued by the government, they have full value. Similarly, this material world may be false or temporary, but because it is an emanation from the Supreme Lord, it has its full value. The Vaiṣṇava philosopher acknowledges the full value of this material world and knows how to utilize it properly, whereas the Māyāvādī philosopher fails to do so, just as those who mistake a currency note for ordinary paper discard it and cannot utilize the money. Śrīla Rūpa Gosvāmī therefore declares that if one rejects this material world as false, not considering the importance of this material world as a means to serve the Supreme Personality of Godhead, such renunciation has very little value. A person who knows the intrinsic value of this material world for the service of the Lord, who is not attached to the material world, and who renounces the material world by not accepting it for sense gratification is situated in real renunciation. This material world is an expansion of the material energy of the Lord. Therefore it is real. It is not false, as sometimes concluded from the example of the snake and the rope.

The personified *Vedas* continued, "The cosmic manifestation, because of the flickering nature of its impermanent existence, appears to less intelligent men to be false." The Māyāvādī philosophers take advantage of the flickering nature of this cosmic manifestation to try to prove their thesis that this world is false. According to the Vedic version, before the creation this world had no existence, and after dissolution the world will no longer be manifested. Voidists also take advantage of this Vedic version and conclude that the cause of this material world is void. But the Vedic injunctions do not say that it is void. The Vedic injunctions define the source of creation and dissolution as *yato vā imāni bhūtāni jāyante,* "He from whom this cosmic manifestation has emanated and in whom, after annihilation, everything will merge." The same is explained in the *Vedānta-sūtra* and in the first verse of the First Chapter of *Śrīmad-Bhāgavatam* by the words *janmādy asya yataḥ,* "He from whom all things emanate." All these Vedic injunctions indicate that the cosmic manifestation is due to the Supreme Absolute Personality of Godhead and that when it is dissolved it merges into Him. The same principle is confirmed in the *Bhagavad-gītā:* "The cosmic manifestation comes into existence and again dissolves, and after dissolution it merges into the existence of the Supreme Lord." This statement definitely confirms that the particular energy known as *bahir-aṅga-māyā,* or the external energy, although of flickering nature, is the energy of the Supreme Lord, and as such it cannot be false. It simply appears false. The Māyāvādī philosophers conclude that because the material nature has no existence in the beginning and is nonexistent after dissolution, it is false. But by the example of the earthen pots and dishes the Vedic version is presented: although the existence of the particular by-products of the Absolute Truth is temporary, the energy of the Supreme Lord is permanent. The earthen pot or water jug may be broken or transformed into another shape, such as that of a dish or bowl, but the ingredient, or the material basis, namely the earth, continues to be the same. The basic principle of the cosmic manifestation is always the same: Brahman, or the Absolute Truth; therefore, the Māyāvādī philosophers' theory that it is false is certainly only a mental concoction. That the cosmic manifestation is flickering and temporary does not mean that it is false. The definition of falsity is "that which never had any existence but which exists only in name." For instance, the eggs of a horse or the horn of a rabbit or the flower in the sky are phenomena which exist only in name. There are no horse's eggs, there is no rabbit's horn, and there are no flowers growing in the sky. There are many things which exist in name or imagination but actually have no factual manifestation. Such things may be called false. But the Vaiṣṇava cannot take this material world to be false simply because of its temporary nature, its manifesting and again dissolving.

The personified *Vedas* continued by saying that the Supersoul and the individual soul, or Paramātmā and *jīvātmā,* cannot be equal in any circumstance, although both of them sit within the same body, like two birds sitting in the same tree. As declared in the *Vedas,* these two birds, although sitting as friends, are not equal. One is simply a witness. This bird is Paramātmā, or the Supersoul. And the other bird is eating the fruit of the tree. That is the *jīvātmā.* When there is cosmic manifestation, the *jīvātmā,* or the individual soul, appears in the creation in different forms, according to his previous fruitive activities, and due to his long forgetfulness of real existence, he identifies himself with a particular form awarded to him by the laws of material nature. After assuming a material form, he becomes subject to the three material modes of nature and acts accordingly to continue his existence in the material world. While he is enwrapped in such ignorance, his natural opulences become almost extinct. The opulences of the Supersoul, or the Supreme Personality of Godhead, however, are not diminished, although He appears within this material world. He maintains all opulences and perfections in full while keeping Himself apart from all the tribulations of this material world. The conditioned soul becomes enwrapped in the material world, whereas the Supersoul, or the Supreme Personality of Godhead, leaves it without being affected, just as a snake sheds his skin. The distinction between the Supersoul and the conditioned individual soul is that the Supersoul, or the Supreme Personality of Godhead, maintains His natural opulences, known as *ṣaḍ-aiśvarya, aṣṭa-siddhi* and *aṣṭa-guṇa.*

Because of their poor fund of knowledge, the Māyāvādī philosophers forget the fact that Kṛṣṇa is always full with six opulences, eight transcendental qualities and eight kinds of perfection. The six opulences are wealth, strength, beauty, fame, knowledge and renunciation. No one is greater than or equal to Kṛṣṇa in these six opulences. The first of Kṛṣṇa's eight transcendental qualities is that He is always untouched by the contamination of material existence. This is also mentioned in the *Īśopaniṣad: apāpa-viddham.* Just as the sun is never polluted by any contamination, the Supreme Lord is never polluted by any sinful activities. Although Kṛṣṇa's actions may sometimes seem impious, He is never polluted by such actions. The second transcendental quality is that Kṛṣṇa never dies. In the *Bhagavad-gītā,* Fourth Chapter, He informs Arjuna that both He and Arjuna had many appearances in this material world, but that He alone remembers all such activities—past, present and future. This means that He never dies. Forgetfulness is due to death. As we die, we change our bodies and forget. Kṛṣṇa, however, is never forgetful. He can remember everything that has happened in the past. Otherwise, how could He remember that He first taught the *yoga* system of the *Bhagavad-gītā* to the sun-god, Vivasvān? Therefore, He never dies. Nor does He ever become an old man. Although Kṛṣṇa was a great-grandfather when He appeared on the Battlefield of Kurukṣetra, He did not appear like an old man. Kṛṣṇa cannot be polluted by any sinful activities, Kṛṣṇa never dies, Kṛṣṇa never becomes old, Kṛṣṇa is never subject to lamentation, Kṛṣṇa is never hungry, and He is never thirsty. Whatever He desires is perfectly lawful, and whatever He decides cannot be changed by anyone. These are the eight transcendental qualities of Kṛṣṇa. Besides that, Kṛṣṇa is known as Yogeśvara. He has all the opulences or facilities of mystic powers, such as *aṇimā-siddhi,* the power to become smaller than the smallest. It is stated in the *Brahma-saṁhitā* that Kṛṣṇa has entered even within the atom (*aṇḍāntara-stha-paramāṇu-cayāntara-stham*). Similarly, Kṛṣṇa, as Garbhodakaśāyī Viṣṇu, is within the gigantic universe, and He is lying in the Causal Ocean as Mahā-Viṣṇu, in a body so gigantic that when He exhales, millions and trillions of universes emanate from His body. This is called *mahimā-siddhi.* Kṛṣṇa also has the perfection of *laghimā:* He can become the lightest. It is stated in the *Bhagavad-gītā* that it is because Kṛṣṇa enters within this universe and within the atoms that all the planets are floating in the air. That is the explanation of weightlessness. Kṛṣṇa also has the perfection of *prāpti:* He can get whatever He likes. Similarly, He has the facility of *īśitā,* controlling power. He is called the supreme controller, Parameśvara. In addition, Kṛṣṇa can bring anyone under His influence. This is called *vaśitā.*

In this way, Kṛṣṇa is endowed with all opulences, transcendental qualities and mystic powers. No ordinary living being can compare to Him. Therefore, the Māyāvādīs' theory that the Supersoul and the individual soul are equal is only a misconception. The conclusion is, therefore, that Kṛṣṇa is worshipable and that all other living entities are simply His servants. This understanding is called self-realization. Any other realization of one's self beyond this relationship of eternal servitorship to Kṛṣṇa is impelled by *māyā.* It is said that the last snare of *māyā* is to dictate to the living entity to try to become equal to the Supreme Personality of Godhead. The Māyāvādī philosopher claims to be equal to God, but he cannot reply to the question of why he has fallen into material entanglement. If he is the Supreme God, then how is it that he has been overtaken by impious activities and thereby subjected to the tribulations of the law of *karma*? When the Māyāvādīs are asked about this, they cannot properly answer. The speculation that one is equal to the Supreme Personality of Godhead is another symptom of sinful life. One cannot take to Kṛṣṇa consciousness unless one is completely freed from all sinful activities. The very fact that the Māyāvādī claims to be one with the Supreme Lord means that he is not yet freed from the reactions of sinful activities. *Śrīmad-Bhāgavatam* says that such persons are *aviśuddha-buddhayaḥ,* which means that because they falsely think themselves liberated and at the same time think themselves equal with the Absolute Truth, their intelligence is not purified. The personified *Vedas* said that if the *yogīs* and the *jñānīs* do not free themselves from sinful desires, then their particular process of self-realization will never be successful.

"Dear Lord," the personified *Vedas* continued, "if saintly persons do not take care to eradicate completely the roots of sinful desires, they cannot experience the Supersoul, although He is sitting side by side with the individual soul. *Samādhi,* or meditation, means that one has to find the Supersoul within himself. One who is not free from sinful reactions cannot see the Supersoul. If a person has a jeweled locket in his necklace but forgets the jewel, it is almost as though he does not possess it. Similarly, if an individual soul meditates but does not actually perceive the presence of the Supersoul within himself, he has not realized the Supersoul." Persons who have taken to the path of self-realization must therefore be very careful to avoid contamination by the influence of *māyā.* Śrīla Rūpa Gosvāmī says that a devotee should be completely free from all sorts of material desires. A devotee should not be affected by the results of *karma* and *jñāna.* One has to simply understand Kṛṣṇa and carry out His desires. That is the pure devotional stage. The personified *Vedas* continued, "Mystic *yogīs* who still have contaminated desires for sense gratification are never successful in their attempt, nor can they realize the Supersoul within the individual self. As such, the so-called *yogīs* and *jñānīs* who are simply wasting their time in different types of sense gratification, either by mental speculation or by exhibition of limited mystic powers, will never be liberated from conditioned life and will continue to go through repeated births and deaths. For such persons, both this life and the next life are sources of tribulation. Such sinful persons are already suffering tribulation in this life, and because they are not perfect in self-realization they will be plagued with further tribulation in the next life. Despite all endeavors to attain perfection, such *yogīs,* contaminated by desires for sense gratification, will continue to suffer in this life and the next."

Śrīla Viśvanātha Cakravartī Ṭhākura remarks in this connection that if *sannyāsīs* (persons in the renounced order of life, who have left their homes for self-realization) do not engage themselves in the devotional service of the Lord but become attracted by philanthropic work, such as opening educational institutions, hospitals or even monasteries, churches or temples of demigods, they find only trouble from such engagements, not only in this life but in the next. *Sannyāsīs* who do not take advantage of this life to realize Kṛṣṇa simply waste their time and energy in activities outside the jurisdiction of the renounced order. A devotee's attempt to engage his energies in such activities as constructing a Viṣṇu temple, however, is never wasted. Such engagements are called *kṛṣṇārthe akhila-ceṣṭā,* variegated activities performed to please Kṛṣṇa. A philanthropist's opening a school building and a devotee's constructing a temple are not on the same level. Although a philanthropist's opening an educational institution may be pious activity, it comes under the laws of *karma,* whereas constructing a temple for Viṣṇu is devotional service.

Devotional service is never within the jurisdiction of the law of *karma.* As stated in the *Bhagavad-gītā, sa guṇān samatītyaitān brahma-bhūyāya kalpate:* "Devotees of the Personality of Godhead transcend all the reactions of the three modes of material nature and are situated on the transcendental platform of Brahman realization." The devotees are liberated in both this life and the next. Any work done in this material world for Yajña (Viṣṇu, or Kṛṣṇa) is considered to be liberated work, but without connection with Acyuta, the infallible Supreme Personality of Godhead, there is no possibility of stopping the resultant actions of the law of *karma.* The life of Kṛṣṇa consciousness is the life of liberation. The conclusion is that a devotee, by the grace of the Lord, is liberated in both this life and the next, whereas *karmīs, jñānīs* and *yogīs* are never liberated, either in this life or in the next.

The personified *Vedas* continued, "Dear Lord, anyone who by Your grace has understood the glories of Your lotus feet is callous to material happiness and distress." The material pangs are inevitable as long as we exist within the material world, but a devotee does not divert his attention to such actions and reactions, which are the results of pious and impious activities. Nor is a devotee very much disturbed or pleased by praise or condemnation from people in general. A devotee is sometimes greatly praised because of his transcendental activities, and sometimes he is criticized, even though there is no reason for adverse criticism. The pure devotee, however, is always callous to praise or condemnation by ordinary people. Actually, the devotee's activities are on the transcendental plane. He is not interested in the praise or condemnation of people engaged in material activities. If the devotee can thus maintain his transcendental position, his liberation in this life and the next is guaranteed by the Supreme Personality of Godhead. A devotee's transcendental position within this material world is maintained in the association of pure devotees, simply by hearing the glorious activities enacted by the Lord in different ages and in different incarnations.

The Kṛṣṇa consciousness movement is based on this principle. Śrīla Narottama dāsa Ṭhākura has sung, "My dear Lord, let me be engaged in Your transcendental loving service, as indicated by the previous *ācāryas,* and let me live in the association of pure devotees. That is my desire, life after life." In other words, a devotee does not much care whether or not he is liberated; he is eager only for devotional service. Devotional service means that one does not do anything independently of the sanction of the *ācāryas.* The actions of the Kṛṣṇa consciousness movement are directed by the previous *ācāryas,* headed by Śrīla Rūpa Gosvāmī; in the association of devotees following these principles, a devotee is able to perfectly maintain his transcendental position.

In the *Bhagavad-gītā* the Lord says that a devotee who knows Him perfectly is very dear to Him. Four kinds of pious men take to devotional service. If a pious man is in distress, he approaches the Lord for mitigation of his distress. If a pious man is in need of material help, he prays to the Lord for such help. If a pious man is actually inquisitive about the science of God, he approaches the Supreme Personality of Godhead, Kṛṣṇa. Similarly, a pious man who is simply eager to know the science of Kṛṣṇa also approaches the Supreme Lord. Out of these four classes of men, the last is praised by Kṛṣṇa Himself in the *Bhagavad-gītā.* A person who tries to understand Kṛṣṇa with full knowledge and devotion by following in the footsteps of previous *ācāryas* conversant with scientific knowledge of the Supreme Lord is praiseworthy. Such a devotee can understand that all conditions of life, favorable and unfavorable, are created by the supreme will of the Lord. And when he has fully surrendered unto the lotus feet of the Supreme Lord, he does not care whether his condition of life is favorable or unfavorable. A devotee takes even an unfavorable condition to be the special favor of the Personality of Godhead. Actually, there are no unfavorable conditions for a devotee. He sees everything coming by the will of the Lord as favorable, and in any condition of life he is simply enthusiastic to discharge his devotional service. This devotional attitude is explained in the *Bhagavad-gītā:* a devotee is never distressed in reverse conditions of life, nor is he overjoyed in favorable conditions. In the higher stages of devotional service, a devotee is not even concerned with the list of do's and do not's. Such a position can be maintained only by following in the footsteps of the *ācāryas.* Because a pure devotee follows in the footsteps of the *ācāryas,* any action he performs to discharge devotional service should be understood to be on the transcendental platform. Lord Kṛṣṇa therefore instructs us that an *ācārya* is above criticism. A neophyte devotee should not consider himself to be on the same plane as the *ācārya.* It should be accepted that the *ācāryas* are on the same platform as the Supreme Personality of Godhead, and as such neither Kṛṣṇa nor His representative *ācārya* should be subject to any adverse criticism by the neophyte devotees.

The personified *Vedas* thus worshiped the Supreme Personality of Godhead in different ways. Offering worship to the Supreme Lord by praying means remembering His transcendental qualities, pastimes and activities. But the Lord's pastimes and qualities are unlimited. It is not possible for us to remember all the qualities of the Lord. Therefore, the personified *Vedas* worshiped to the best of their ability, and at the end they spoke as follows.

"Dear Lord, although Lord Brahmā, the predominating deity of the highest planet, Brahmaloka, and King Indra, the predominating demigod of the heavenly planets, as well as the predominating deities of such planets as the sun and the moon, are all very confidential directors of this material world, they have very little knowledge about You. Then what can ordinary human beings and mental speculators know of You? It is not possible for anyone to enumerate the unlimited transcendental qualities of Your Lordship. No one, not even the mental speculators and the demigods in higher planetary systems, is actually able to estimate the length and breadth of Your form and characteristics. We think that even Your Lordship does not have complete knowledge of Your transcendental qualities. The reason is that You are unlimited. Although it is not befitting to say that You do not know Yourself, it is practical to understand that because You have unlimited qualities and energies and because Your knowledge is also unlimited, there is unlimited competition between Your knowledge and Your expansion of energies."

The idea is that because God and His knowledge are both unlimited, as soon as God is cognizant of some of His energies, He perceives that He has still more energies. In this way, both His energies and His knowledge increase. Because both of them are unlimited, there is no end to the energies and no end to the knowledge with which to understand the energies. God is undoubtedly omniscient, but the personified *Vedas* say that even God Himself does not know the full extent of His energies. This does not mean that God is not omniscient. When an actual fact is unknown to a certain person, this is called ignorance or lack of knowledge. This is not applicable to God, however, because He knows Himself perfectly. But still, as His energies and activities increase, He also increases His knowledge to understand them. Both are increasing unlimitedly, and there is no end to it. In that sense it can be said that even God Himself does not know the limit of His energies and qualities.

How God is unlimited in His expansion of energies and activities can be roughly calculated by any sane and sober living entity. It is said in the Vedic literature that innumerable universes issue forth when Mahā-Viṣṇu exhales in His *yoga-nidrā* and that innumerable universes enter His body when He again inhales. We have to imagine that these universes, which according to our limited knowledge are expanded unlimitedly, are so great that the gross and subtle ingredients—the five elements of the cosmic manifestation, namely earth, water, fire, air and sky, along with the total material energy and false ego—are not only within the universe but cover the universe in seven layers, each layer ten times bigger than the previous one. In this way, each and every universe is very securely packed, and there are numberless universes. All these universes float within the innumerable pores of the transcendental body of Mahā-Viṣṇu. It is stated that just as the atoms and particles of dust are floating within the air along with the birds and their number cannot be calculated, so innumerable universes are floating within the pores of the transcendental body of the Lord. For this reason, the *Vedas* say that God is beyond the grasp of our knowledge. *Avāṅ-mānasa-gocara:* to understand the length and breadth of God is beyond the jurisdiction of our mental speculation. Therefore, a person who is actually learned and sane does not claim to be God but tries to understand God, making distinctions between spirit and matter. By such careful discrimination, one can clearly understand that the Supreme Soul is transcendental to both the superior and inferior energies although He has a direct connection with both. In the *Bhagavad-gītā,* Lord Kṛṣṇa explains that although everything is resting on His energy, He is different or separate from the energy.

Nature and the living entities are sometimes designated as *prakṛti* and *puruṣa* respectively. The whole cosmic manifestation is an amalgamation of *prakṛti* and *puruṣa.* Nature is the ingredient cause, and the living entities are the effective cause. These two causes combine together, and the effect is this cosmic manifestation. When one is fortunate enough to come to the right conclusion about this cosmic manifestation and everything going on within it, he knows it to be caused directly and indirectly by the Supreme Personality of Godhead Himself. It is concluded in the *Brahma-saṁhitā,* therefore, *īśvaraḥ paramaḥ kṛṣṇaḥ sac-cid-ānanda-vigrahaḥ/ anādir ādir govindaḥ sarva-kāraṇa-kāraṇam.*

After much deliberation and consideration, when one has attained the perfection of knowledge, one comes to the conclusion that Kṛṣṇa, or God, is the original cause of all causes. Instead of speculating about the measurement of God—whether He is so long or so wide—or falsely philosophizing, one should come to the conclusion of the *Brahma-saṁhitā:* "Kṛṣṇa, or God, is *sarva-kāraṇa-kāraṇam,* the cause of all causes." That is the perfection of knowledge.

Thus the *Veda-stuti,* or the prayers offered by the personified *Vedas* to Garbhodakaśāyī Viṣṇu, were first narrated in disciplic succession by Sanandana to his brothers, all of whom were born of Brahmā at the beginning of the universe. The four Kumāras were the first-born sons of Brahmā; therefore they are known as *pūrva-jāta.* It is stated in the *Bhagavad-gītā* that the *paramparā* system, or the disciplic succession, begins with Kṛṣṇa Himself. Similarly, here, in the prayers of the personified *Vedas,* it is to be understood that the *paramparā* system begins with the Personality of Godhead Nārāyaṇa Ṛṣi. We should remember that this *Veda-stuti* is narrated by Kumāra Sanandana, and the narration is repeated by Nārāyaṇa Ṛṣi in Badarīkāśrama. Nārāyaṇa Ṛṣi is the incarnation of Kṛṣṇa for showing us the path of self-realization by undergoing severe austerities. In this age Lord Caitanya demonstrated the path of pure devotional service by putting Himself in the role of a pure devotee. Similarly, in the past Lord Nārāyaṇa Ṛṣi was an incarnation of Kṛṣṇa who performed severe austerities in the Himalayan ranges. Śrī Nārada

Muni was hearing from Him. So in the statement given by Nārāyaṇa Ṛṣi to Nārada Muni, as narrated by Kumāra Sanandana in the form of the *Veda-stuti,* it is understood that God is the one supreme and that all others are His servants.

In the *Caitanya-caritāmṛta* it is stated, *ekale īśvara kṛṣṇa:* "Kṛṣṇa is the only Supreme God." *Āra saba bhṛtya:* "All others are His servants." *Yāre yaiche nācāya, se taiche kare nṛtya:* "The Supreme Lord, as He desires, is engaging all the living entities in different activities, and thus they exhibit their different talents and tendencies." This *Veda-stuti* is thus the original instruction regarding the relationship existing between the living entity and the Supreme Personality of Godhead. The highest platform of realization for the living entity is the attainment of devotional life. One cannot be engaged in devotional life, or Kṛṣṇa consciousness, unless one is fully free from material contamination. Nārāyaṇa Ṛṣi informed Nārada Muni that the essence of all the *Vedas* and Vedic literatures (namely, the four *Vedas,* the *Upaniṣads* and the *Purāṇas*) is to render transcendental loving service to the Lord. In this connection Nārāyaṇa Ṛṣi has used one particular word—*rasa.* In devotional service this *rasa* is the via medium or the basic principle for the exchange of dealings between the Lord and the living entity. *Rasa* is also described in the *Vedas: raso vai saḥ.* "The Supreme Lord is the reservoir of all pleasure." All the Vedic literatures, including the *Purāṇas,* the *Vedas,* the *Upaniṣads* and the *Vedānta-sūtra,* teach the living entities how to attain the stage of *rasa.* The *Bhāgavatam* also says that the statements in the *Mahā-purāṇa* (*Śrīmad-Bhāgavatam*) constitute the essence (*rasa*) of all Vedic literature. *Nigama-kalpa-taror galitaṁ phalam:* the *Bhāgavatam* is the essence of the ripened fruit of the tree of the Vedic literature.

We understand that with the breathing of the Supreme Personality of Godhead there issued forth the four *Vedas,* namely the *Ṛg Veda,* the *Yajur Veda,* the *Sāma Veda* and the

Atharva Veda, and also the histories like the *Mahābhārata* and all the *Purāṇas,* which are considered to be the history of the world. The Vedic histories like the *Purāṇas* and *Mahābhārata* are called the fifth *Veda.*

The twenty-eight verses of the *Veda-stuti* are to be considered the essence of all Vedic knowledge. The four Kumāras and all other authorized sages know perfectly that devotional service in Kṛṣṇa consciousness is the essence of all Vedic literatures, and they preach this on different planets, traveling in outer space. It is stated herein that such sages, including Nārada Muni, hardly ever travel on land; they perpetually travel in space.

Sages like Nārada and the Kumāras travel throughout the universe to educate the conditioned souls that their business in the world is not that of sense gratification but of reinstating themselves in their original position of devotional service to the Supreme Personality of Godhead. It is stated in several places that the living entities are like sparks of the fire and the Supreme Personality of Godhead is like the fire itself. If the sparks somehow or other fall out of the fire, they lose their natural illumination; thus it is ascertained that the living entities come into this material world exactly as sparks fall from a great fire. The living entity wants to imitate Kṛṣṇa and tries to lord it over material nature in order to enjoy sense gratification; thus he forgets his original position, and his illuminating power, his spiritual identity, is extinguished. However, if a living entity takes to Kṛṣṇa consciousness, he is reinstated in his original position. To preach this process of devotional service, sages and saints like Nārada and the Kumāras travel all over the universe educating people and increasing their disciples. Their aim is that all the conditioned souls may be educated to revive their original consciousness, or Kṛṣṇa consciousness, and thus gain relief from the miserable conditions of material life.

Śrī Nārada Muni is a *naiṣṭhika-brahmacārī.* There are four

types of *brahmacārīs.* The first is called *sāvitra,* which refers to a *brahmacārī* who after initiation and the sacred thread ceremony must observe at least three days of celibacy. The next is called *prājāpatya,* which refers to a *brahmacārī* who strictly observes celibacy for at least one year after initiation. The next is called *brāhma-brahmacārī,* which refers to a *brahmacārī* who observes celibacy from the time of initiation up to the time of the completion of his study of the Vedic literature. The next stage is called *naiṣṭhika,* which refers to a *brahmacārī* who is celibate throughout his whole life. Out of these, the first three are *upakurvāṇa,* which means that the *brahmacārī* can marry later, after the *brahmacārī* period is over. The *naiṣṭhika-brahmacārī,* however, is completely reluctant to have any sex life; therefore the Kumāras and Nārada are known as *naiṣṭhika-brahmacārīs.* Such *brahmacārīs* are called *vīra-vrata* because their vow of celibacy is as heroic as the vows of the *kṣatriyas.* The *brahmacārī* system of life is especially advantageous in that it increases the power of memory and determination. It is specifically mentioned in this connection that because Nārada was a *naiṣṭhika-brahmacārī* he could remember whatever he heard from his spiritual master and would never forget it. One who can remember everything perpetually is called *śruta-dhara.* A *śruta-dhara brahmacārī* can repeat verbatim all that he has heard, without notes and without reference to books. The great sage Nārada has this qualification, and therefore, having taken instructions from Nārāyaṇa Ṛṣi, he is engaged in propagating the philosophy of devotional service all over the world. Because such great sages can remember everything, they are thoughtful, self-realized and completely fixed in the service of the Lord.

Thus the great sage Nārada, after hearing from his spiritual master Nārāyaṇa Ṛṣi, became completely realized. He became established in the truth, and he became so happy that he offered prayers to Nārāyaṇa Ṛṣi. Nārada Muni addressed Nārāyaṇa Ṛṣi as an incarnation of Kṛṣṇa and specifically addressed Him as the supreme well-wisher of the conditioned souls. It is stated in the *Bhagavad-gītā* that Lord Kṛṣṇa descends in every millennium just to give protection to His devotees and to annihilate the nondevotees. Nārāyaṇa Ṛṣi, being an incarnation of Kṛṣṇa, is also addressed as the well-wisher of the conditioned souls. As stated in the *Bhagavad-gītā,* everyone should know that there is no well-wisher like Kṛṣṇa. Everyone should understand that Lord Kṛṣṇa is the supreme well-wisher of everyone and should take shelter of Him. In this way one can become completely confident and satisfied, knowing that he has someone who is able to give him all protection. Kṛṣṇa Himself, His incarnations and His plenary expansions are all supreme well-wishers of the conditioned souls, but Kṛṣṇa is the well-wisher even of the demons, for He gave salvation to all the demons who came to kill Him in Vṛndāvana; therefore Kṛṣṇa's welfare activities are absolute, for whether He annihilates a demon or gives protection to a devotee, the result of His activities is one and the same. It is said that the demon Pūtanā was elevated to the same position as Kṛṣṇa's mother. When Kṛṣṇa kills a demon, the demon is supremely benefited, as much as a pure devotee is benefited by always being protected by the Lord.

Nārada Muni, after offering respects to Nārāyaṇa Ṛṣi, his spiritual master, went to the *āśrama* of Vyāsadeva, his disciple. Being properly received by Vyāsadeva in his *āśrama* and seated very comfortably, Nārada Muni narrated the entire story of what he had heard from Nārāyaṇa Ṛṣi. In this way Śukadeva Gosvāmī informed Mahārāja Parīkṣit of the answers to his questions regarding the essence of Vedic knowledge and what is considered to be the ultimate goal in the *Vedas.* The supreme goal of life is to achieve the transcendental blessings of the Supreme Personality of Godhead and thus become engaged in the loving service of the Lord. One should follow in the footsteps of Śukadeva Gosvāmī and all the other Vaiṣṇavas in the disciplic succession and should pay respectful obeisances unto Lord Kṛṣṇa, the Supreme Personality of Godhead, Hari. The four sects of Vaiṣṇava disciplic succession, namely the Madhva-sampradāya, the Rāmānuja-sampradāya, the Viṣṇu-svāmi-sampradāya and the Nimbārka-sampradāya, in pursuance of all Vedic conclusions, agree that one should surrender unto the Supreme Personality of Godhead.

The Vedic literatures are divided into two parts: the *śrutis* and the *smṛtis.* The *śrutis* are the four *Vedas—Ṛg, Sāma, Atharva* and *Yajur*—and the *Upaniṣads,* and the *smṛtis* are the *Purāṇas* and the *Itihāsas* like the *Mahābhārata,* which includes the *Bhagavad-gītā.* The conclusion of all these is that one should know Śrī Kṛṣṇa as the Supreme Personality of Godhead. He is the Parama-puruṣa, or the Supreme Personality of Godhead, under whose superintendence material nature works. For creation, maintenance and annihilation, the Supreme Lord incarnates into three—Lord Brahmā, Lord Viṣṇu and Lord Śiva—after manifesting the material cosmos. All of these take charge of the three qualities of material nature, but the ultimate direction is in the hand of Lord Viṣṇu. The complete activities of material nature under the three modes are conducted under the direction of the Supreme Personality of Godhead, Kṛṣṇa. This is confirmed in the *Bhagavad-gītā* (*mayādhyakṣeṇa*) and in the *Vedas* (*sa aikṣata*).

The atheistic Sāṅkhyaite philosophers will of course offer their arguments that the material cosmic manifestation is due to *prakṛti* and *puruṣa*—material nature and the living entity, or the material cause and the effective cause. But Kṛṣṇa is the cause of all causes. He is the cause of both the material and the effective causes. *Prakṛti* and *puruṣa* are not the ultimate cause. Superficially it appears that a child is born due to the combination of the father and mother, but the ultimate cause of both the father and the mother is Kṛṣṇa. He is therefore the original cause, or the cause of all causes, as confirmed in the *Brahma-saṁhitā.*

Both the Supreme Lord and the living entities enter into

the material nature. The Supreme Lord, Kṛṣṇa, by one of His plenary expansions, manifests as Kāraṇodakaśāyī, Mahā-Viṣṇu, the gigantic Viṣṇu form lying in the Causal Ocean. Then from that gigantic form of Mahā-Viṣṇu, Garbhodakaśāyī Viṣṇu expands and enters into every universe. From Him, Brahmā, Viṣṇu and Śiva expand. Viṣṇu as Kṣīrodakaśāyī enters into the hearts of all living entities, as well as into all material elements, including the atom. The *Brahma-saṁhitā* says, *aṇḍāntara-stha-paramāṇu-cayāntara-stham:* "The Lord is within this universe and also within every atom."

The living entity has a small material body taken in various species and forms, and similarly the whole universe is but the material body of the Supreme Personality of Godhead. This body is described in the *śāstras* as *virāṭ-rūpa.* As the individual living entity maintains his particular body, the Supreme Personality of Godhead maintains the whole cosmic creation, entering within it. As soon as the individual living entity leaves the material body, the body is immediately annihilated, and similarly as soon as Lord Viṣṇu leaves the cosmic manifestation, everything is annihilated. Therefore only when the individual living entity surrenders unto the Supreme Personality of Godhead is his liberation from material existence possible. This is confirmed in the *Bhagavad-gītā: mām eva ye prapadyante māyām etāṁ taranti te.* Surrendering unto the Supreme Personality of Godhead, and nothing else, is therefore the cause of liberation. How the living entity becomes liberated from the modes of material nature after surrendering unto the Supreme Personality of Godhead is illustrated by the example of a sleeping man within a room. When a man is sleeping, everyone sees that he is present within the room, but actually the man himself is not within that body, for while sleeping a man forgets his bodily existence, although others may see that his body is present. Similarly, a liberated person engaged in devotional service to the Lord may be seen by others to be engaged in the household duties of the material world, but since his consciousness is fixed in Kṛṣṇa, he does not live within this world. His engagements are different, exactly as the sleeping man's engagements are different from his bodily engagements. It is confirmed in the *Bhagavad-gītā* that a devotee engaged full time in the transcendental loving service of the Lord has already surpassed the influence of the three modes of material nature. He is already situated on the Brahman platform and is in the transcendental realm, although he appears to be living within the body or within the material world.

In this connection, Śrīla Rūpa Gosvāmī states in his *Bhakti-rasāmṛta-sindhu* that the person whose only desire is to serve the Supreme Personality of Godhead may be situated in any condition in the material world, but he is to be understood as *jīvan-mukta;* that is to say, he is to be considered liberated while living within the body or the material world. The conclusion, therefore, is that a person fully engaged in Kṛṣṇa consciousness is a liberated person. Such a person actually has nothing to do with his material body or the material world. Those who are not in Kṛṣṇa consciousness are called *karmīs* and *jñānīs,* and they hover on the bodily and mental platforms and thus are not liberated. This situation is called *kaivalya-nirasta-yoni.* But a person situated on the transcendental platform is freed from the repetition of birth and death. This is confirmed in the *Bhagavad-gītā,* Fourth Chapter: "Simply by knowing the transcendental nature of the Supreme Personality of Godhead, Kṛṣṇa, one becomes free from the chains of the repetition of birth and death, and after quitting his present body he goes back home, back to Godhead." This is the conclusion of all the *Vedas.* Thus after understanding the prayers offered by the personified *Vedas,* one should surrender unto the lotus feet of Lord Kṛṣṇa.

Thus ends the Bhaktivedanta purport of the Eighty-seventh Chapter of Kṛṣṇa, *"Prayers by the Personified* Vedas."

CHAPTER EIGHTY-EIGHT

The Deliverance of Lord Śiva

As a great devotee of Kṛṣṇa, King Parīkṣit was already liberated, but for clarification he was asking various questions of Śukadeva Gosvāmī. In the previous chapter, King Parīkṣit's question was, "What is the ultimate goal of the *Vedas*?" And Śukadeva Gosvāmī explained the matter, giving authoritative descriptions from the disciplic succession, from Sanandana down to Nārāyaṇa Ṛṣi, Nārada, Vyāsadeva and then Śukadeva himself. The conclusion was that devotional service, or *bhakti,* is the ultimate goal of the *Vedas.* A neophyte devotee may question, "If the ultimate goal of life, or the conclusion of the *Vedas,* is to elevate oneself to the platform of devotional service, then why is it observed that a devotee of Lord Viṣṇu is generally not very prosperous materially, whereas a devotee of Lord Śiva is found to be very opulent?" In order to clarify this matter, Parīkṣit Mahārāja asked Śukadeva Gosvāmī, "My dear Śukadeva Gosvāmī, it is generally found that those who engage in the worship of Lord Śiva, whether in human, demoniac or demigod society, become materially very opulent, although Lord Śiva himself lives just like a poverty-stricken person. On the other hand, the devotees of Lord Viṣṇu, who is the controller of the goddess of fortune, do not appear very prosperous, and sometimes they are even found living without any material opulence at all. Lord Śiva lives underneath a tree or in the snow of the Himalayan Mountains. He does not even construct a house for himself, but still the worshipers of Lord Śiva are very rich. Kṛṣṇa, or Lord Viṣṇu, however, lives very opulently, whether in Vaikuṇṭha or in the material world, but His devotees appear poverty-stricken. Why is this so?"

Mahārāja Parīkṣit's question is very intelligent. The two classes of devotees, namely the devotees of Lord Śiva and the devotees of Lord Viṣṇu, are always in disagreement. Even today in India these two classes of devotees still criticize each other, and especially in South India the followers of Rāmānujācārya and the followers of Śaṅkarācārya hold occasional meetings for understanding the Vedic conclusion. Generally, the followers of Rāmānujācārya come out victorious in such meetings. So Parīkṣit Mahārāja wanted to clarify the situation by asking this question of Śukadeva Gosvāmī. That Lord Śiva lives as a poor man although his devotees appear very opulent, whereas Lord Kṛṣṇa, or Lord Viṣṇu, is always opulent and yet His devotees appear poverty-stricken, is a situation which appears contradictory and puzzling to a discriminating person.

Replying to King Parīkṣit's inquiry, Śukadeva Gosvāmī said that Lord Śiva is the master of the material energy. The material energy is represented by goddess Durgā, and because Lord Śiva happens to be her husband, goddess Durgā is completely under his subjugation. Thus Lord Śiva is understood to be the master of this material energy. The material energy is manifested in three qualities, namely goodness, passion and ignorance, and therefore Lord Śiva is the master of these three qualities. Although he is in association with these qualities for the benefit of the conditioned soul, Lord Śiva is the director and is not affected. In other words, although the conditioned soul is affected by the three qualities, Lord Śiva, being their master, is not.

From the statements of Śukadeva Gosvāmī we can understand that the effects of worshiping different demigods are not, as some less intelligent persons suppose, the same as the effects of worshiping Lord Viṣṇu. Śukadeva Gosvāmī clearly states that by worshiping Lord Śiva one achieves one reward, whereas by worshiping Lord Viṣṇu one achieves a different reward. This is confirmed in the *Bhagavad-gītā:* "Those who worship the different demigods achieve the desired results the respective demigods can reward. Similarly, those who worship the material energy receive the suitable reward for such activities, and those who worship the *pitṛs* receive similar results. But those who engage in devotional service or worship the Supreme Lord—Viṣṇu, or Kṛṣṇa—go to the Vaikuṇṭha planets or Kṛṣṇaloka." One cannot approach the transcendental region, or *paravyoma,* the spiritual sky, by worshiping Lord Śiva or Brahmā or any other demigod.

Since this material world is a product of the three qualities of material nature, all varieties of manifestations come from those three qualities. With the aid of materialistic science, modern civilization has created many machines and comforts, yet they are only varieties of the interactions of the three material qualities. Although the devotees of Lord Śiva are able to obtain many material acquisitions, we should know that such devotees are simply collecting products manufactured by the three qualities. The three qualities are again subdivided into sixteen, namely the ten senses (five working senses and five knowledge-acquiring senses), the mind, and the five elements (earth, water, fire, air and sky). These sixteen items are extensions of the three qualities. Material happiness or opulence means gratification of the senses, especially the genitals, the tongue and the mind. By exercising our minds we create many pleasurable things just for enjoyment by the genitals and the tongue. The opulence of a person within this material world is estimated in terms of his exercise of the genitals and the tongue, or, in other words, how well he is able to utilize his sexual capacities and how well he is able to satisfy his fastidious taste by eating palatable dishes. Material advancement of civilization necessitates creating objects of enjoyment by mental concoction just to become happy on the basis of these two principles: pleasures for the genitals and pleasures for the tongue. Herein lies the answer to King Parīkṣit's question to Śukadeva Gosvāmī as to why the worshipers of Lord Śiva are so opulent.

The devotees of Lord Śiva are opulent only in terms of the material qualities. Factually, such so-called advancement of civilization is the cause of entanglement in material existence. It is actually not advancement but degradation. The conclusion is that because Lord Śiva is the master of the three qualities, his devotees are given things manufactured by the interactions of these qualities for the satisfaction of the senses. In the *Bhagavad-gītā,* however, we get instruction from Lord Kṛṣṇa that one has to transcend this qualitative existence. *Nistrai-guṇyo bhavārjuna:* the mission of human life is to become transcendental to the three qualities. Unless one is *nistrai-guṇya,* he cannot get free from material entanglement. In other words, favors received from Lord Śiva are not actually beneficial to the conditioned souls, although materially such facilities seem opulent.

Śukadeva Gosvāmī continued, "The Supreme Personality of Godhead, Hari, is transcendental to the three qualities of material nature." In the *Bhagavad-gītā* the Lord states that anyone who surrenders unto Him surpasses the control of the three qualities of material nature. Therefore, since Hari's devotees are transcendental to the control of the three material qualities, certainly He Himself is transcendental. In *Śrīmad-Bhāgavatam* it is therefore stated that Hari, or Kṛṣṇa, is the original Supreme Personality. There are two kinds of *prakṛtis,* or potencies, namely the internal potency and the external potency, and Kṛṣṇa is the overlord of both. He is *sarva-dṛk,* or the overseer of all the actions of the internal and external potencies, and He is also described as *upadraṣṭā,* the supreme advisor. Because He is the supreme advisor, He is above all the demigods, who merely follow the directions of the supreme advisor. As such, if one directly follows the instructions of the Supreme Lord, as inculcated in the *Bhagavad-gītā* and *Śrīmad-Bhāgavatam,* then one gradually becomes *nirguṇa,* or above the interactions of the material qualities. To be *nirguṇa* means to be bereft of material opulences because, as we have explained, material opulence means an increase of the actions and reactions of the three material qualities. By worshiping the Supreme Personality of Godhead, instead of being puffed up with material opulences one becomes enriched with spiritual advancement of knowledge in Kṛṣṇa consciousness. To become *nirguṇa* means to achieve eternal peace, fearlessness, religiousness, knowledge and renunciation. All these are symptoms of becoming free from the contamination of the material qualities.

Śukadeva Gosvāmī, in answering Parīkṣit Mahārāja's question, went on to cite a historical instance regarding Parīkṣit Mahārāja's grandfather, King Yudhiṣṭhira. He said that after finishing the Aśvamedha sacrifice in the great sacrificial arena, King Yudhiṣṭhira, in the presence of great authorities, inquired from Lord Kṛṣṇa on that very same point: how is it that the devotees of Lord Śiva become materially opulent, whereas the devotees of Lord Viṣṇu do not? Śukadeva Gosvāmī specifically referred to King Yudhiṣṭhira as "your grandfather" so that Mahārāja Parīkṣit would be encouraged to think that he was related to Kṛṣṇa and that his grandfathers were intimately connected with the Supreme Personality of Godhead.

Although Kṛṣṇa is always very satisfied by nature, when Mahārāja Yudhiṣṭhira asked this question the Lord became even more satisfied because this question and its answer would bear a great meaning for the entire Kṛṣṇa conscious society. Whenever Lord Kṛṣṇa speaks about something to a specific devotee, it is meant not only for that devotee but for the entire human society. Instructions by the Supreme Personality of Godhead are important even to Lord Brahmā, Lord Śiva and the other demigods, and one who does not take advantage of the instructions of the Supreme Personality of Godhead, who descends within this world for the benefit of all living entities, is certainly very unfortunate.

Lord Kṛṣṇa answered the question of Mahārāja Yudhiṣṭhira as follows: "If I especially favor a devotee and especially wish to care for him, the first thing I do is take away his riches. When the devotee becomes a penniless pauper or is put into a comparatively poverty-stricken position, his relatives and family members no longer take interest in him, and in most cases they give up their connection with him. The devotee then becomes doubly unhappy." First of all the devotee becomes unhappy because his riches have been taken away by Kṛṣṇa, and he is made even more unhappy when his relatives desert him because of his poverty. We should note, however, that when a devotee falls into a miserable condition in this way, it is not due to past impious activities, known as *karma-phala;* the poverty of the devotee is a creation of the Personality of Godhead. Similarly, when a devotee becomes materially opulent, that is also not due to his pious activities. In either case, whether the devotee becomes poorer or richer, the arrangement is made by the Supreme Personality of Godhead. This arrangement is especially made by Kṛṣṇa for His devotee just to make him completely dependent upon Him and to free him from all material obligations. He can then concentrate his energies, mind and body—everything—for the service of the Lord, and that is pure devotional service. In the *Nārada-pañcarātra* it is therefore explained, *sarvopādhi-vinirmuktam,* which means "being freed from all designations." Works performed for family, society, community, nation or humanity are all designated: "I belong to this society,"

"I belong to this community," "I belong to this nation," "I belong to this species of life." Such identities are all merely designations. When by the grace of the Lord a devotee is freed from all designations, his devotional service is actually *naiṣkarmya. Jñānīs* are very much attracted by the position of *naiṣkarmya,* in which one's actions no longer have material effect. The devotee's activities are freed from material effects, and so these activities are no longer in the category of *karma-phalam,* or fruitive activities. As explained before by the personified *Vedas,* the happiness and distress of a devotee are produced by the Personality of Godhead, and the devotee therefore does not care whether he is in happiness or in distress. He goes on with his duties in executing devotional service. Although his behavior seems to be subject to the actions and reactions of fruitive activities, he is actually freed from the results of action.

It may be questioned why a devotee is put into such tribulation by the Personality of Godhead. The answer is that this kind of arrangement by the Lord is just like a father's sometimes becoming unkind to his sons. Because the devotee is a surrendered soul and is taken charge of by the Supreme Lord, whatever condition of life the Lord puts him in—whether one of distress or of happiness—it is to be understood that behind this arrangement is a large plan designed by the Personality of Godhead. For example, Lord Kṛṣṇa put the Pāṇḍavas into a distressed condition so acute that even grandfather Bhīṣma could not comprehend how such distress could occur. He lamented that although the whole Pāṇḍava family was headed by King Yudhiṣṭhira, the most pious king, and protected by the two great warriors Bhīma and Arjuna, and although, above all, the Pāṇḍavas were all intimate friends and relatives of Lord Kṛṣṇa, they still had to undergo such tribulations. Later, however, it was proved that this was planned by the Supreme Personality of Godhead, Kṛṣṇa, as part of His great mission to annihilate the miscreants and protect the devotees.

Another question may be raised: What is the difference

between a devotee and a common man, since both are put into different kinds of happy and distressful conditions—the devotee by the arrangement of the Personality of Godhead, and the common man as a result of his past deeds? How is the devotee any better than the ordinary *karmī*? The answer is that the *karmīs* and the devotees are not on the same level. In whatever condition of life the *karmī* may be, he continues in the cycle of birth and death because the seed of *karma,* or fruitive activity, is there, and it fructifies whenever there is an opportunity. By the law of *karma* a common man is perpetually entangled in repeated birth and death, whereas a devotee's distress and happiness, not being under the laws of *karma,* are part of a temporary arrangement by the Supreme Lord which does not entangle the devotee. Such an arrangement is made by the Lord only to serve a temporary purpose. If a *karmī* performs auspicious acts he is elevated to the heavenly planets, and if he acts impiously he is put into a hellish condition. But whether a devotee acts in a so-called pious or impious manner, he is neither elevated nor degraded but is transferred to the spiritual kingdom. Therefore a devotee's happiness and distress and a *karmī's* happiness and distress are not on the same level. This fact is corroborated by a speech by Yamarāja to his servants in connection with the liberation of Ajāmila. Yamarāja advised his followers that only persons who have never uttered the holy name of the Lord or remembered the form, quality and pastimes of the Lord should be approached by his watchguards. Yamarāja also advised his servants never to approach the devotees. On the contrary, he instructed his messengers that if they meet a devotee they should offer their respectful obeisances. So there is no question of a devotee's being promoted or degraded within this material world. As there is a gulf of difference between the punishment awarded by the mother and the punishment awarded by an enemy, so a devotee's distress is not the same as the distress of a common *karmī.*

Here another question may be raised: If the Supreme Lord is all-powerful, why should He try to reform His devotee by putting him in distress? The answer is that when the Supreme Personality of Godhead puts His devotee in distress, it is not without purpose. Sometimes the purpose is that in distress a devotee's feelings of attachment to Kṛṣṇa are magnified. For example, when Kṛṣṇa, before leaving the capital of the Pāṇḍavas for His home, asked Kuntīdevī for permission to leave, she said, "My dear Kṛṣṇa, in our distress You were always present with us. Now, because we have been elevated to a royal position, You are leaving us. I would therefore prefer to live in distress than to lose You." When a devotee is put into a situation of distress, his devotional activities are accelerated. Therefore, to show special favor to a devotee, the Lord sometimes puts him into distress. Besides that, it is stated that the sweetness of happiness is sweeter to those who have tasted bitterness. The Supreme Lord descends to this material world just to protect His devotees from distress. In other words, if devotees were not in a distressed condition, the Lord would not have come down. As for His killing the demons or the miscreants, this can be easily done by His various energies, just as many *asuras* are killed by His external energy, goddess Durgā. Therefore the Lord does not need to come down personally to kill such demons, but when His devotee is in distress He must come. Lord Nṛsiṁhadeva appeared not in order to kill Hiraṇyakaśipu but to save Prahlāda and to give him blessings. In other words, because Prahlāda Mahārāja was put into very great distress, the Lord appeared.

When after the dense, dark night there is finally sunrise in the morning, it is very pleasant; when there is scorching heat, cold water is very pleasant; and when there is freezing winter, hot water is very pleasant. Similarly, when a devotee, after experiencing the distress of the material world, relishes the spiritual happiness awarded by the Lord, his position is still more pleasant and enjoyable.

The Lord continued, "When My devotee is bereft of all material riches and is deserted by his relatives, friends and family members, because he has no one to look after him he completely takes shelter of the lotus feet of the Lord." Śrīla Narottama dāsa Ṭhākura has sung in this connection, "My dear Lord Kṛṣṇa, O son of Nanda Mahārāja, You are now standing before me with Śrīmatī Rādhārāṇī, the daughter of King Vṛṣabhānu. I am now surrendering unto You. Please accept me. Please do not kick me away. I have no shelter other than You."

When a devotee is thus put into so-called miserable conditions and bereft of riches and family, he tries to revive his original position of material opulence. But although he tries again and again, Kṛṣṇa again and again takes away all his resources. Thus he finally becomes disappointed in material activities, and in that stage of frustration in all endeavors, he can fully surrender unto the Supreme Personality of Godhead. Such persons are advised by the Lord from within to associate with devotees. By associating with devotees they naturally become inclined to render service to the Personality of Godhead, and they immediately get all facilities from the Lord to advance in Kṛṣṇa consciousness. The nondevotees, however, are very careful about preserving their material condition of life. Generally, therefore, such nondevotees do not come to worship the Supreme Personality of Godhead, but worship Lord Śiva or other demigods for immediate material profit. In the *Bhagavad-gītā* it is said, therefore, *kāṅkṣantaḥ karmaṇāṁ siddhiṁ yajanta iha devatāḥ:* "The *karmīs,* in order to achieve success within this material world, worship the various demigods." It is also stated by Lord Kṛṣṇa that those who worship the demigods are not mature in their intelligence. The devotees of the Supreme Personality of Godhead, therefore, because of their strong attachment for Him, do not foolishly go to the demigods.

Lord Kṛṣṇa said to King Yudhiṣṭhira, "My devotee is not

deterred by any adverse conditions of life; he always remains firm and steady. Therefore I give Myself to him, and I favor him so that he can achieve the highest success of life." The mercy bestowed upon the tried devotee by the Supreme Personality is described as *brahma,* which indicates that the greatness of that mercy can be compared only to the all-pervasive greatness of Brahman. *Brahma* means unlimitedly great and unlimitedly expanding. That mercy is also described as *paramam,* for it has no comparison within this material world, and it is also called *sūkṣmam,* very fine. Not only is the Lord's mercy upon the tried devotee great and unlimitedly expansive, but it is of the finest quality of transcendental love between the devotee and the Lord. Such mercy is further described as *cin-mātram,* completely spiritual. The use of the word *mātram* indicates absolute spirituality, with no tinge of material qualities. That mercy is also called *sat* (eternal) and *anantakam* (unlimited). Since the devotee of the Lord is awarded such unlimited spiritual benefit, why should he worship the demigods? A devotee of Kṛṣṇa does not worship Lord Śiva or Brahmā or any other, subordinate demigod. He completely devotes himself to the transcendental loving service of the Supreme Personality of Godhead.

Śukadeva Gosvāmī continued, "The demigods, headed by Lord Brahmā and Lord Śiva and including Lord Indra, Candra, Varuṇa and others, are apt to be very quickly satisfied or very quickly angered by the good or ill behavior of their devotees. But this is not so with the Supreme Personality of Godhead, Viṣṇu." This means that every living entity within this material world, including the demigods, is conducted by the three modes of material nature, and therefore the qualities of ignorance and passion are very prominent within the material world. Those devotees who take blessings from the demigods are also infected with the material qualities, especially passion and ignorance. Lord Śrī Kṛṣṇa has therefore stated in the *Bhagavad-gītā* that to take blessings from the demigods is less intelligent because when one takes benedictions from the demigods the results of such benedictions are temporary. It is easy to get material opulence by worshiping the demigods, but the result is sometimes disastrous. As such, the benedictions derived from demigods are appreciated only by the less intelligent class of men. Persons who derive benedictions from the demigods gradually become puffed up with material opulence and neglectful of their benefactors.

Śukadeva Gosvāmī addressed King Parīkṣit thus: "My dear King, Lord Brahmā, Lord Viṣṇu and Lord Śiva, the principal trio of the material creation, are able to bless or curse anyone. Of this trio, Lord Brahmā and Lord Śiva are very easily satisfied but also very easily angered. When satisfied they give benedictions without consideration, and when angry they curse the devotee without consideration. But Lord Viṣṇu is not like that. Lord Viṣṇu is very considerate. Whenever a devotee wants something from Lord Viṣṇu, Lord Viṣṇu first considers whether such a benediction will ultimately be good for the devotee. Lord Viṣṇu never bestows any benediction which will ultimately prove disastrous to the devotee. By His transcendental nature, He is always merciful; therefore, before giving any benediction, He considers whether it will prove beneficial for the devotee. Since the Supreme Personality of Godhead is always merciful, even when it appears that He has killed a demon, or even when He apparently becomes angry toward a devotee, His actions are always auspicious. The Supreme Personality of Godhead is therefore known as all-good. Whatever He does is good."

As for the benedictions given by demigods like Lord Śiva, there is the following historical incident cited by great sages. Once, Lord Śiva, after giving a benediction to a demon named Vṛkāsura, the son of Śakuni, was himself entrapped in a very dangerous position. Vṛkāsura was searching after a benediction and trying to decide which of the three presiding deities to worship in order to get it. In the meantime he happened to meet the great sage Nārada and consulted with him as to whom he should approach to achieve quick results from his austerity. He inquired, "Of the three deities, namely Lord Brahmā, Lord Viṣṇu and Lord Śiva, who is most quickly satisfied?" Nārada could understand the plan of the demon, and he advised him, "You had better worship Lord Śiva; then you will quickly get the desired result. Lord Śiva is very quickly satisfied and very quickly dissatisfied also. So you try to satisfy Lord Śiva." Nārada also cited instances wherein demons like Rāvaṇa and Bāṇāsura were enriched with great opulences simply by satisfying Lord Śiva with prayers. Because the great sage Nārada was aware of the nature of the demon Vṛkāsura, he did not advise him to approach Viṣṇu or Lord Brahmā. Persons such as Vṛkāsura, who are situated in the material mode of ignorance, cannot stick to the worship of Viṣṇu.

After receiving instruction from Nārada, the demon Vṛkāsura went to Kedāranātha. The pilgrimage site of Kedāranātha still exists near Kashmir. It is almost always covered by snow, but for part of the year, during the month of July, it is possible to see the deity, and devotees go there to offer their respects. Kedāranātha is for the devotees of Lord Śiva. According to the Vedic principle, when something is offered to the deities to eat, it is offered in a fire. Therefore a fire sacrifice is necessary in all sorts of ceremonies. It is specifically stated in the *śāstras* that gods are to be offered something to eat through the fire. The demon Vṛkāsura therefore went to Kedāranātha and ignited a sacrificial fire to please Lord Śiva.

After igniting the fire in the name of Śiva, he began to offer his own flesh by cutting it from his body to please Lord Śiva. Here is an instance of worship in the mode of ignorance. In the *Bhagavad-gītā,* different types of sacrifices are mentioned. Some sacrifices are in the mode of goodness, some are in the mode of passion, and some are in the mode of ignorance. There are different kinds of *tapasya* and worship because there are different kinds of people within this world.

But the ultimate *tapasya,* Kṛṣṇa consciousness, is the topmost *yoga* and the topmost sacrifice. As confirmed in the *Bhagavad-gītā,* the topmost *yoga* is to think always of Lord Kṛṣṇa within the heart, and the topmost sacrifice is to perform the *saṅkīrtana-yajña.*

In the *Bhagavad-gītā* it is stated that the worshipers of the demigods have lost their intelligence. As revealed later in this chapter, Vṛkāsura wanted to satisfy Lord Śiva for a third-class materialistic objective, which was temporary and without real benefit. The *asuras,* or persons within the mode of ignorance, will accept such benedictions from the demigods. In complete contrast to this sacrifice in the mode of ignorance, the *arcana-vidhi* process for worshiping Lord Viṣṇu or Kṛṣṇa is very simple. Lord Kṛṣṇa says in the *Bhagavad-gītā* that He accepts from His devotee even a little fruit, a flower or some water, which can be gathered by any person, rich or poor. Of course, those who are rich are not expected to offer only a little water, a little piece of fruit or a little leaf to the Lord; a rich man should offer according to his position. But if the devotee happens to be a very poor man, the Lord will accept even the most meager offering. The worship of Lord Viṣṇu or Kṛṣṇa is very simple, and it can be executed by anyone in this world. But worship in the mode of ignorance, as exhibited by Vṛkāsura, is not only very difficult and painful but is also a useless waste of time. Therefore the *Bhagavad-gītā* says that the worshipers of the demigods are bereft of intelligence; their process of worship is very difficult, and at the same time the result obtained is flickering and temporary.

Although Vṛkāsura continued his sacrifice for six days, he was unable to personally see Lord Śiva, which was his objective; he wanted to see him face to face and ask him for a benediction. Here is another contrast between demons and devotees. A devotee is confident that whatever he offers to the Deity in full devotional service is accepted by the Lord, but a demon wants to see his worshipable deity face to face so that he can directly take the benediction. A devotee does not worship Viṣṇu or Lord Kṛṣṇa for any benediction. Therefore a devotee is called *akāma,* free of desire, and a nondevotee is called *sarva-kāma,* or desirous of everything. On the seventh day, the demon Vṛkāsura decided that he should cut off his head and offer it to satisfy Lord Śiva. Thus he took a bath in a nearby lake, and without drying his body and hair, he prepared to cut off his head. According to the Vedic system, an animal to be offered as a sacrifice has to be bathed first, and while the animal is wet it is sacrificed. When the demon was thus preparing to cut off his head, Lord Śiva became very compassionate. This compassion is a symptom of the quality of goodness. Lord Śiva is called *tri-liṅga,* "a mixture of the three material qualities." Therefore his manifestation of the nature of compassion is a sign of the quality of goodness. This compassion, however, is present in every living entity. The compassion of Lord Śiva was aroused not because the demon was offering his flesh into the sacrificial fire but because he was about to commit suicide. This is natural compassion. Even if a common man sees someone preparing to commit suicide, he will try to save him. He does so automatically. There is no need to appeal to him. Therefore when Lord Śiva appeared from the fire to check the demon from suicide, it was not done as a very great favor to him.

Lord Śiva's touch saved the demon from committing suicide; his bodily injuries immediately healed, and his body became as it was before. Then Lord Śiva told the demon, "My dear Vṛkāsura, you do not need to cut off your head. You may ask from me any benediction you like, and I shall fulfill your desire. I do not know why you wanted to cut off your head to satisfy me. I become satisfied even by an offering of a little water." Actually, according to the Vedic process, the *śiva-liṅga* in the temple or the form of Lord Śiva in the temple is worshiped simply by offering Ganges water, because it is said that Lord Śiva is greatly satisfied when Ganges water is poured upon his head. Generally, devotees offer Ganges water and the leaves of the *bilva* tree, which are especially meant for offering to Lord Śiva and goddess Durgā. The fruit of this tree is also offered to Lord Śiva. Lord Śiva assured Vṛkāsura that he is satisfied by a very simple process of worship. Why then was he so eager to cut off his head, and why was he taking so much pain by cutting his body to pieces and offering it in the fire? There was no need of such severe penances. Anyway, out of compassion and sympathy, Lord Śiva prepared to give him any benediction he liked.

When the demon was offered this facility by Lord Śiva, he asked for a fearful and abominable benediction. The demon was very sinful, and sinful persons do not know what sort of benediction should be asked from the deity. Therefore he asked Lord Śiva to be blessed with such power that as soon as he would touch anyone's head, it would immediately crack and the man would die. The demons are described in the *Bhagavad-gītā* as *duṣkṛtīs,* or miscreants. *Kṛtī* means "very meritorious," but when *duḥ* is added it means "abominable." Instead of surrendering unto the Supreme Personality of Godhead, the *duṣkṛtīs* worship different demigods to derive abominable material benefits. Although the *duṣkṛtīs* have brain power and merit, their merit and brain power are used for abominable activities. Sometimes, for example, materialistic scientists invent a lethal weapon. The scientific research for such an invention certainly requires a very good brain, but instead of inventing something beneficial to human society they invent something to accelerate death, which is already assured to every man. They cannot show their meritorious power by inventing something which can save man from death; instead they invent weapons which accelerate the process of death. Similarly, Vṛkāsura, instead of asking Lord Śiva for something beneficial to human society, asked for something very dangerous to human society. Lord Śiva is powerful enough to give any benediction, so the demon could have asked something beneficial from him, but for his personal interest he asked that anyone whose head would be touched by his hand would at once die. Lord Śiva could understand the motive of the demon, and he was very sorry that he had assured him whatever benediction he liked. He could not withdraw his promise, but he was very sorry in his heart that he was to offer him a benediction so dangerous to human society. Devotees of the Personality of Godhead never ask any benediction from Lord Viṣṇu, or Kṛṣṇa, and even if they ask something from the Lord, it is not at all dangerous for human society. That is the difference between the demons and the devotees, or the worshipers of Lord Śiva and the worshipers of Lord Viṣṇu.

While Śukadeva Gosvāmī was narrating the history of Vṛkāsura, he addressed Mahārāja Parīkṣit as Bhārata, referring to King Parīkṣit's birth in a family of devotees. Mahārāja Parīkṣit was saved by Lord Kṛṣṇa while in his mother's womb. Later, he could have asked Lord Kṛṣṇa to save him again, from the curse of a *brāhmaṇa,* but he did not do so. The demon, however, wanted to become immortal by killing everyone with the touch of his hand. Lord Śiva could understand this, but because he had promised, he gave him the benediction.

The demon, however, being very sinful, immediately decided that he would use the benediction to kill Lord Śiva and take away Gaurī (Pārvatī) for his personal enjoyment. He immediately decided to place his hand on the head of Lord Śiva. Thus Lord Śiva was put into an awkward position because he was endangered by his own benediction to a demon. This is an instance of a materialistic devotee's misusing the power derived from the demigods.

Without further deliberation, the demon Vṛkāsura approached Lord Śiva to place his hand on Lord Śiva's head. Lord Śiva was so afraid of him that his body trembled, and he fled from the land to the sky and from the sky to other planets, until he reached the limits of the universe, above the higher planetary systems. Lord Śiva fled from one place to another, but the demon Vṛkāsura continued to chase him.

The predominating deities of other planets, such as Brahmā, Indra and Candra, could not find any way to save Lord Śiva from the impending danger. Wherever Lord Śiva went, they remained silent.

At last Lord Śiva approached Lord Viṣṇu, who is situated within this universe on the planet known as Śvetadvīpa. Śvetadvīpa is the local Vaikuṇṭha planet, beyond the jurisdiction of the influence of the external energy. Lord Viṣṇu in His all-pervasive feature remains everywhere, but wherever He remains personally is the Vaikuṇṭha atmosphere. In the *Bhagavad-gītā* it is stated that the Lord remains within the heart of all living entities. As such, the Lord remains within the heart of many lowborn living entities, but that does not mean He is lowborn. Wherever He remains is transformed into Vaikuṇṭha. So the planet within this universe known as Śvetadvīpa is also Vaikuṇṭhaloka. It is said in the *śāstras* that residential quarters within the forest are in the mode of goodness, residential quarters in big cities, towns and villages are in the mode of passion, and residential quarters in an atmosphere wherein indulgence in the four sinful activities of illicit sex, intoxication, meat-eating and gambling predominates are in the mode of ignorance. But residential quarters in a temple of Viṣṇu, the Supreme Lord, are in Vaikuṇṭha. It doesn't matter where the temple is situated; the temple itself, wherever it may be, is Vaikuṇṭha. Similarly, the Śvetadvīpa planet, although within the material jurisdiction, is Vaikuṇṭha.

Lord Śiva finally entered Śvetadvīpa Vaikuṇṭha. In Śvetadvīpa there are great saintly persons who are completely freed from the envious nature of the material world and are beyond the jurisdiction of the four principles of material activity, namely religiosity, economic development, sense gratification and liberation. Anyone who enters into that Vaikuṇṭha planet never returns to this material world. Lord Nārāyaṇa is celebrated as a lover of His devotees, and as soon as He understood that Lord Śiva was in great danger, He appeared as a *brahmacārī* and personally approached Lord Śiva to receive him from a distant place. The Lord appeared as a perfect *brahmacārī,* with a belt around His waist, a sacred thread, a deerskin, a *brahmacārī* stick and *raudra* beads. (*Raudra* beads are different from *tulasī* beads. *Raudra* beads are used by the devotees of Lord Śiva.) Dressed as a *brahmacārī,* Lord Nārāyaṇa stood before Lord Śiva. The shining effulgence emanating from His body attracted not only Lord Śiva but also the demon Vṛkāsura.

Lord Nārāyaṇa offered His respects and obeisances unto Vṛkāsura just to attract his sympathy and attention. Thus stopping the demon, the Lord addressed him as follows: "My dear son of Śakuni, you appear very tired, as if coming from a very distant place. What is your purpose? Why have you come so far? I see that you are fatigued, so I request you to take a little rest. You should not unnecessarily tire your body. Everyone greatly values his body because with this body only can one fulfill all the desires of one's mind. We should not, therefore, unnecessarily give trouble to this body."

The *brahmacārī* addressed Vṛkāsura as the son of Śakuni just to convince him that He was known to his father, Śakuni. Vṛkāsura then took the *brahmacārī* to be someone known to his family, and therefore the *brahmacārī's* sympathetic words appealed to him. Before the demon could argue that he had no time to take rest, the Lord informed him about the importance of the body, and the demon was convinced. Any man, especially a demon, takes his body to be very important. Thus Vṛkāsura became convinced about the importance of his body.

Then, just to pacify the demon, the *brahmacārī* told him, "My dear lord, if you think that you can disclose the mission for which you have taken the trouble to come here, maybe I shall be able to help you so that your purpose will be easily served." Indirectly, the Lord informed him that because the Lord is the Supreme Brahman, He would certainly be able to adjust the awkward situation created by Lord Śiva.

The demon was greatly pacified by the sweet words of Lord Nārāyaṇa in the form of a *brahmacārī,* and at last he disclosed all that had happened in regard to the benediction offered by Lord Śiva. The Lord replied to the demon as follows: "I Myself cannot believe that Lord Śiva has in truth given you such a benediction. As far as I know, Lord Śiva is not in a sane mental condition. When he had a quarrel with his father-in-law, Dakṣa, he was cursed to become a *piśāca* (ghost). Thus he has become the leader of the ghosts and hobgoblins. Therefore I cannot put any faith in his words. But if you still have faith in the words of Lord Śiva, my dear King of the demons, then why don't you make an experiment by putting your hand on your own head? If the benediction proves false, then you can at once kill this liar, Lord Śiva, so that in the future he will not dare give out false benedictions."

In this way, by Lord Nārāyaṇa's sweet words and by the expansion of His superior illusion, the demon became bewildered, and he actually forgot the power of Lord Śiva and his benediction. He was thus very easily persuaded to put his hand on his own head. As soon as the demon did that, his head cracked, as if struck by thunder, and he immediately died. The demigods from heaven showered flowers on Lord Nārāyaṇa, praising Him with shouts of "All glories!" and "All thanksgiving!" and they offered their obeisances to the Lord. On the death of Vṛkāsura, all the denizens in the higher planetary systems, namely the demigods, the *pitṛs,* the Gandharvas and the inhabitants of Janoloka, showered flowers on the Personality of Godhead.

Thus Lord Viṣṇu in the form of a *brahmacārī* released Lord Śiva from the impending danger and saved the whole situation. Lord Nārāyaṇa then informed Lord Śiva that this demon, Vṛkāsura, was killed as the result of his sinful activities. He was especially sinful and offensive because he wanted to experiment on his own master, Lord Śiva. Lord Nārāyaṇa then told Lord Śiva, "My dear lord, a person who commits an offense to great souls cannot continue to exist. He is vanquished by his own sinful activities, and this is certainly true of this demon, who has committed such an offensive act against you."

Thus by the grace of the Supreme Personality of Godhead, Nārāyaṇa, who is transcendental to all material qualities, Lord Śiva was saved from being killed by a demon. Anyone who hears this history with faith and devotion is certainly liberated from material entanglement as well as from the clutches of his enemies.

Thus ends the Bhaktivedanta purport of the Eighty-eighth Chapter of Kṛṣṇa, *"The Deliverance of Lord Śiva."*

CHAPTER EIGHTY-NINE

The Superexcellent Power of Kṛṣṇa

Long, long ago, there was an assembly of great sages on the bank of the river Sarasvatī who performed a great sacrifice of the name Satra. In such assemblies, the great sages present usually discuss Vedic subject matters and philosophical topics, and in this particular meeting the following question was raised: The three predominating deities of this material world, namely Lord Brahmā, Lord Viṣṇu and Lord Śiva, are directing all the affairs of this cosmos, but who among them is the Supreme? After much discussion on this question, the great sage named Bhṛgu, the son of Lord Brahmā, was deputed to test all three predominating deities and report to the assembly as to who is the greatest.

Being thus deputed, the great sage Bhṛgu Muni first of all went to his father's residence in Brahmaloka. The three deities are the controllers of the three material qualities, namely the qualities of goodness, passion and ignorance. The plan decided upon by the sages was for Bhṛgu to test which one of the predominating deities possesses the quality of goodness in full. Therefore, when Bhṛgu Muni reached his father, Lord Brahmā, because Bhṛgu wanted to test whether Brahmā had the quality of goodness, he purposely did not offer his respects to his father, either by offering obeisances or by offering prayers. It is the duty of a son or a disciple to offer respects and recite suitable prayers when he approaches his father or spiritual master. But Bhṛgu Muni purposely failed to offer respects, just to see Lord Brahmā's reaction to this negligence. Lord Brahmā was very angry at his son's impudence, and he showed signs which definitely proved this to be so. He was even prepared to condemn Bhṛgu by cursing him, but because Bhṛgu was his son, Lord Brahmā controlled his anger with his great intelligence. This means that although the quality of passion was prominent in Lord Brahmā, he had the power to control it. Lord Brahmā's anger and his controlling his anger are likened to fire and water. Water is produced from fire at the beginning of creation, but fire can be extinguished with water. Similarly, although Lord Brahmā was very angry due to his quality of passion, he could still control his passion because Bhṛgu Muni was his son.

After testing Lord Brahmā, Bhṛgu Muni went directly to Mount Kailāsa, where Lord Śiva resides. Bhṛgu Muni happened to be Lord Śiva's brother. Therefore, as soon as Bhṛgu Muni approached, Lord Śiva was very glad and personally rose to embrace him. But when Lord Śiva approached, Bhṛgu Muni refused to embrace him. "My dear brother," he said, "you are always very impure. Because you smear your body with ashes, you are not very clean. Please do not touch me." When Bhṛgu Muni refused to embrace his brother, saying that Lord Śiva was impure, the latter became very angry with him. It is said that an offense can be committed either with the body, with the mind or by speech. Bhṛgu Muni's first offense, committed toward Lord Brahmā, was an offense with the mind. His second offense, committed toward Lord Śiva by insulting him, criticizing him for unclean habits, was an offense by speech. Because the quality of ignorance is prominent in Lord Śiva, when he heard Bhṛgu's insult his eyes immediately became red with anger. With uncontrollable rage, he took up his trident and prepared to kill Bhṛgu Muni. At that time Lord Śiva's wife, Pārvatī, was present. Her personality, like Lord Śiva's, is a mixture of the three qualities, and therefore she is called Triguṇamayī. In this case, she saved the situation by evoking Lord Śiva's quality of goodness. She fell down at the feet of her husband, and with her sweet words she talked him out of killing Bhṛgu Muni.

After being saved from the anger of Lord Śiva, Bhṛgu Muni went directly to the planet Śvetadvīpa, where Lord Viṣṇu was lying on a bed of flowers in the company of His wife, the goddess of fortune, who was engaged in massaging His lotus feet. There Bhṛgu Muni purposely committed the greatest sin by offending Lord Viṣṇu by his bodily activities. The first offense committed by Bhṛgu Muni was mental, the second offense was vocal, and the third offense was corporal. These different offenses are progressively greater in degree. An offense committed within the mind is a positive offense, the same offense committed verbally is comparatively more grave, and when committed by bodily action it is superlative in offensiveness. So Bhṛgu Muni committed the greatest offense by kicking the chest of the Lord with his foot in the presence of the goddess of fortune. Of course, Lord Viṣṇu is all-merciful. He did not become angry at the activities of Bhṛgu Muni, for Bhṛgu Muni was a great *brāhmaṇa.* A *brāhmaṇa* is to be excused even if he sometimes commits an offense, and Lord Viṣṇu set the example. Yet it is said that from the time of this incident the goddess of fortune, Lakṣmī, has not been very favorably disposed toward the *brāhmaṇas,* and therefore, because the goddess of fortune withholds her benedictions from them, the *brāhmaṇas* are generally very poor. Bhṛgu Muni's kicking the chest of Lord Viṣṇu with his foot was certainly a great offense, but Lord Viṣṇu is so great that He did not care. The so-called *brāhmaṇas* of the Kali-yuga are sometimes very proud that a great *brāhmaṇa* like Bhṛgu Muni could touch the chest of Lord Viṣṇu with his foot. But in fact when Bhṛgu Muni kicked the chest of Lord Viṣṇu with his foot, it was the greatest offense, although Lord Viṣṇu, being greatly magnanimous, did not take it very seriously.

Instead of being angry or cursing Bhṛgu Muni, Lord Viṣṇu immediately got up from His bed along with His wife, the goddess of fortune, and offered respectful obeisances to the *brāhmaṇa.* He addressed Bhṛgu Muni as follows: "My dear *brāhmaṇa*, it is My greatest fortune that you have come here. Please, therefore, sit down on this cushion for a few minutes. My dear *brāhmaṇa,* I am very sorry that when you first entered My home I could not receive you properly. It was a great offense on My part, and I beg you to pardon Me. You are so pure and great that the water which washes your feet can purify even the places of pilgrimage. Therefore, I request you to purify the Vaikuṇṭha planet where I live with My associates. My dear father, O great sage, I know that your feet are very soft, like a lotus flower, and that My chest is as hard as a thunderbolt. I am therefore afraid that you may have felt some pain by kicking My chest with your feet. Let Me touch your feet to relieve the pain you have suffered." Lord Viṣṇu then began to massage the feet of Bhṛgu Muni.

The Lord continued to address Bhṛgu Muni. "My dear lord," He said, "My chest has now become sanctified because of the touch of your feet, and I am now assured that the goddess of fortune, Lakṣmī, will be very glad to live there perpetually." Another name for Lakṣmī is Cañcalā, indicating that she does not stay in one place for a long time. Therefore, we see that a rich man's family sometimes becomes poor after a few generations, and sometimes we see that a poor man's family becomes very rich. Lakṣmī, the goddess of fortune, is Cañcalā in this material world, whereas in the Vaikuṇṭha planets she eternally lives at the lotus feet of the

Lord. Because Lakṣmī is famous as Cañcalā, Lord Nārāyaṇa indicated that she might not have been living perpetually by His chest, but because His chest had been touched by the feet of Bhṛgu Muni, it was now sanctified, and there was no chance that the goddess of fortune would leave. Bhṛgu Muni, however, could understand his position and that of the Lord, and he was struck with wonder at the behavior of the Supreme Personality of Godhead. Because of his gratitude, his voice choked up, and he was unable to reply to the words of the Lord. Tears glided from his eyes, and he could not say anything. He simply stood silently before the Lord.

After testing Lord Brahmā, Lord Śiva and Lord Viṣṇu, Bhṛgu Muni returned to the assembly of great sages on the bank of the river Sarasvatī and described his experience. After hearing him with great attention, the sages concluded that of all the predominating deities, Lord Viṣṇu is certainly the greatest. In *Śrīmad-Bhāgavatam* these great sages are described as *brahma-vādinām. Brahma-vādinām* means those who talk about the Absolute Truth but have not yet come to a conclusion. Generally *brahma-vādī* refers to the impersonalists or to those who are students of the *Vedas.* It is to be understood, therefore, that all the gathered sages were serious students of the Vedic literature but had not come to definite conclusions as to who is the Supreme Absolute Personality of Godhead. But after hearing of Bhṛgu Muni's experience in meeting all three predominating deities—Lord Śiva, Lord Brahmā and Lord Viṣṇu—the sages concluded that Lord Viṣṇu is the Supreme Truth, the Personality of Godhead. It is said in *Śrīmad-Bhāgavatam* that after hearing the details from Bhṛgu Muni, the sages were astonished because although Lord Brahmā and Lord Śiva were immediately agitated, Lord Viṣṇu, in spite of being kicked by Bhṛgu Muni, was not agitated in the least. The example is given that small lamps may be agitated by a slight breeze, but the greatest lamp or the greatest illuminating source, the sun, is never moved, even by the greatest hurricane. One's greatness has to be estimated by one's ability to tolerate provoking situations. The sages gathered on the bank of the river Sarasvatī concluded that if one wants actual peace and freedom from all fear, he should take shelter of the lotus feet of Viṣṇu. Since Lord Brahmā and Lord Śiva lost their peaceful attitude upon a slight provocation, how can they maintain the peace and tranquillity of their devotees? As for Lord Viṣṇu, however, it is stated in the *Bhagavad-gītā* that anyone who accepts Lord Viṣṇu or Kṛṣṇa as the supreme friend attains the highest perfection of peaceful life.

The sages thus concluded that by following the principles of *vaiṣṇava-dharma* one becomes actually perfect, but that if one follows all the religious principles of a particular sect and does not become advanced in understanding the Supreme Personality of Godhead, Viṣṇu, all such labor of love is fruitless. To execute religious principles means to come to the platform of perfect knowledge. If one comes to the platform of perfect knowledge, then he will be uninterested in material affairs. Perfect knowledge means knowledge of one's own self and the Supreme Self. The Supreme Self and the individual self, although one in quality, are different in quantity. This analytical understanding of knowledge is perfect. Simply to understand "I am not matter; I am spirit" is not perfect knowledge. The real religious principle is devotional service, or *bhakti.* This is confirmed in the *Bhagavad-gītā,* where Lord Kṛṣṇa says, "Give up all other religious principles and simply surrender unto Me." Therefore, the term *dharma* applies only to *vaiṣṇava-dharma,* or *bhagavad-dharma,* following which all other good qualities and advancements in life are automatically achieved.

The highest perfectional knowledge is knowledge of the Supreme Lord. He cannot be understood by any process of religion other than devotional service; therefore, the immediate result of perfect knowledge is achieved by executing devotional service. After attainment of knowledge, one becomes uninterested in the material world. This is not because of dry philosophical speculation. The devotees become uninterested in the material world not simply because of theoretical understanding but because of practical experience. When a devotee realizes the effect of association with the Supreme Lord, he naturally hates the association of so-called society, friendship and love. This detachment is not dry but is due to achieving a higher status of life by relishing transcendental mellows. It is further stated in *Śrīmad-Bhāgavatam* that after attainment of such knowledge and such detachment from material sense gratification, one's advancement in the eight opulences attained through mystic *yoga* practice, such as the *aṇimā, laghimā* and *prāpti siddhis,* is also achieved without separate effort. The perfect example is Mahārāja Ambarīṣa. He was not a mystic *yogī* but a great devotee, yet in a disagreement with Mahārāja Ambarīṣa, the great mystic Durvāsā was defeated in the presence of the King's devotional attitude. In other words, a devotee does not need to practice the mystic *yoga* system to achieve power. The power is behind him by the grace of the Lord, just as when a small child is surrendered to a powerful father, all the powers of the father are behind him.

When a person becomes famous as a devotee of the Lord, his reputation is never to be extinguished. Lord Caitanya, when discoursing with Rāmānanda Rāya, questioned, "What is the greatest fame?" Rāmānanda Rāya replied that to be known as a pure devotee of Lord Kṛṣṇa is the perfect fame. The conclusion, therefore, is that *viṣṇu-dharma,* or the religion of devotional service unto the Supreme Personality of Godhead, is meant for persons who are thoughtful. By proper utilization of thoughtfulness, one comes to the stage of thinking of the Supreme Personality of Godhead. By thinking of the Supreme Personality of Godhead, one becomes free from the contamination of the faulty association of the material world, and thus one becomes peaceful. The world is in a disturbed condition because of a scarcity of such peaceful devotees in human society. Unless one is a devotee, one cannot be equal to all living entities. A devotee is equally disposed toward the animals, the human beings and all living entities because he sees every living entity as a part and parcel of the Supreme Lord. In the *Īśopaniṣad* it is clearly stated that one who has come to the stage of seeing all living beings equally does not hate anyone or favor anyone. The devotee does not hanker to possess more than he requires. Devotees are therefore *akiñcana;* in any condition of life a devotee is satisfied. It is said that a devotee is even-minded whether he is in hell or in heaven. A devotee is callous to all subjects other than his engagement in devotional service. This mode of life is the highest perfectional stage, from which one can be elevated to the spiritual world, back home, back to Godhead. The devotees of the Supreme Personality of Godhead are especially attracted by the highest material quality, goodness, and the qualified *brāhmaṇa* is the symbolic representation of this goodness. Therefore, a devotee is attached to the brahminical stage of life. He is not very interested in passion or ignorance, although these qualities also emanate from the Supreme Lord, Viṣṇu. In *Śrīmad-Bhāgavatam* the devotees are described as *nipuṇa-buddhayaḥ,* which means that they are the most intelligent class of men. Uninfluenced by attachment or hatred, the devotee lives very peacefully and is not agitated by the influence of passion and ignorance.

It may be questioned here why a devotee should be attached to the quality of goodness in the material world if he is transcendental to all material qualities. The answer is that there are different kinds of people existing in the modes of material nature. Those in the mode of ignorance are called Rākṣasas, those in the mode of passion are called *asuras,* and those in the mode of goodness are called *suras,* or demigods. Under the direction of the Supreme Lord, these three classes of men are created by material nature, but those in the mode of goodness have a greater chance to be elevated to the spiritual world, back home, back to Godhead.

Thus all the sages who assembled on the bank of the river Sarasvatī to try to determine who is the supreme predominating deity became freed from all doubts about Viṣṇu worship. All of them thereafter engaged in devotional service, and thus they achieved the desired result and went back to Godhead.

Those who are actually eager to be liberated from material entanglement would do well to accept at once the conclusion given by Śrī Śukadeva Gosvāmī. In the beginning of *Śrīmad-Bhāgavatam,* which is spoken by Śukadeva Gosvāmī, it is said that hearing *Śrīmad-Bhāgavatam* is extremely conducive to liberation. The same fact is now confirmed by Sūta Gosvāmī: if anyone who is traveling aimlessly within this material world cares to hear the nectarean words spoken by Śukadeva Gosvāmī, certainly he will come to the right conclusion, which is that simply by discharging devotional service to the Supreme Personality of Godhead one will be able to stop the fatigue of perpetually migrating from one material body to another. In other words, one who becomes fixed in loving devotional service to Viṣṇu will certainly be able to get relief from this journey of material life, and the process is very simple: one has to give aural reception to the sweet words spoken by Śukadeva Gosvāmī in the form of *Śrīmad-Bhāgavatam.*

Another conclusion is that we should never consider the demigods, even Lord Śiva and Lord Brahmā, to be on an equal level with Lord Viṣṇu. If we do this, then according to the *Padma Purāṇa* we are immediately categorized as atheists. Also, in the Vedic literature known as *Hari-vaṁśa* it is stated that only the Supreme Personality of Godhead, Viṣṇu, is to be worshiped and that the Hare Kṛṣṇa *mahā-mantra,* or any such *viṣṇu-mantra,* is always to be chanted. In the Second Canto of *Śrīmad-Bhāgavatam,* Lord Brahmā says, "Both Lord Śiva and I are engaged by the Supreme Personality of Godhead to act in different capacities under His direction." In the *Caitanya-caritāmṛta* it is also stated that the only master is

Kṛṣṇa and that all others in all categories of life are servants of Kṛṣṇa only.

In the *Bhagavad-gītā* it is confirmed by the Lord that there is no truth superior to Kṛṣṇa. Śukadeva Gosvāmī also, in order to draw attention to the fact that among all *viṣṇu-tattva* forms Lord Kṛṣṇa is one hundred percent the Supreme Personality of Godhead, narrated the story of an incident which took place when Lord Kṛṣṇa was present.

Once upon a time in Dvārakā, a *brāhmaṇa's* wife gave birth to a child. Unfortunately, however, just after being born and touching the ground, the child immediately died. The *brāhmaṇa* father took the child and went directly to the palace of the King. The *brāhmaṇa* was very upset because of the untimely death of the child in the presence of his young father and mother. Thus his mind became very much disturbed. Formerly, when there were responsible kings, up to the time of Dvāpara-yuga, when Lord Kṛṣṇa was present, the king was liable to be blamed for the untimely death of a child in the presence of his parents. Similarly, such responsibility was there during the time of Lord Rāmacandra. As we have explained in the First Canto of *Śrīmad-Bhāgavatam,* the king was so responsible for the comforts of the citizens that he was to see that there was not even excessive heat or cold. Now the *brāhmaṇa* whose child had died, thinking there was no fault on his own part, immediately went to the palace door with the dead child in his arms and accused the King as follows.

"The present King, Ugrasena, is envious of the *brāhmaṇas*!" The exact word used in this connection is *brahma-dviṣaḥ.* One who is envious of the *Vedas,* of a qualified *brāhmaṇa* or of the *brāhmaṇa* caste is called *brahma-dviṣ.* So the King was accused of being *brahma-dviṣ.* He was also accused of being *śaṭha-dhī,* falsely intelligent. The executive head of a state must be very intelligent to see to the comforts of the citizens, but according to the *brāhmaṇa* the King was not at all intelligent, although he was occupying the royal throne. Therefore the *brāhmaṇa* also called him *lubdha,* which means "greedy." In other words, a king or an executive head of state should not occupy the exalted post of president or king if he is greedy and self-interested. But it is natural that an executive head becomes self-interested when he is attached to material enjoyment. Therefore, another word used here is *viṣayātmanaḥ.*

The *brāhmaṇa* also accused the King of being *kṣatra-bandhu,* which refers to a person born in the family of *kṣatriyas,* or the royal order, but lacking the qualifications of a royal personality. A king should protect brahminical culture and should be very alert to the welfare of his citizens; he should not be greedy due to attachment to material enjoyment. If a person with no qualifications represents himself as a *kṣatriya* of the royal order, he is not called a *kṣatriya* but a *kṣatra-bandhu.* Similarly, if a person is born of a *brāhmaṇa* father but has no brahminical qualification, he is called a *brahma-bandhu* or *dvija-bandhu.* This means that a *brāhmaṇa* or a *kṣatriya* is not accepted simply by birth. One has to qualify himself for the particular position; only then is he accepted as a *brāhmaṇa* or a *kṣatriya.*

Thus the *brāhmaṇa* charged that his newly born baby was dead due to the disqualifications of the King. The *brāhmaṇa* took it to be most unnatural, and therefore he held the King responsible. We also find in Vedic history that if a *kṣatriya* king was irresponsible, sometimes a consulting board of *brāhmaṇas* maintained by the monarchy would dethrone him. Considering all these points, it appears that the post of monarch in the Vedic civilization is a very responsible one.

The *brāhmaṇa* therefore said, "No one should offer respects or worship to a king whose only business is envy. Such a king spends his time either hunting and killing animals in the forest or killing citizens for criminal acts. He has no self-control and possesses bad character. If such a king is worshiped or honored by the citizens, the citizens will never be happy. They will always remain poor, full of anxieties and aggrievement, and always unhappy." In modern politics the post of monarch has been abolished, and the president is not held responsible for the comforts of the citizens. In this Age of Kali, the executive head of a state somehow or other gets votes and is elected to an exalted post, but the condition of the citizens continues to be full of anxiety, distress, unhappiness and dissatisfaction.

The *brāhmaṇa's* second child also died at birth, and the third also. He had nine children, who all died at birth, and each time he came to the gate of the palace to accuse the King. When the *brāhmaṇa* came to accuse the King of Dvārakā for the ninth time, Arjuna happened to be present with Kṛṣṇa. On hearing that a *brāhmaṇa* was accusing the King of not properly protecting him, Arjuna became inquisitive and approached the *brāhmaṇa.* He said, "My dear *brāhmaṇa,* why do you say that there are no proper *kṣatriyas* to protect the citizens of your country? Is there not even someone who can pretend to be a *kṣatriya,* who can carry a bow and arrow at least to make a show of protection? Do you think that all the royal personalities in this country simply engage in performing sacrifices with the *brāhmaṇas* but have no chivalrous power?" Thus Arjuna indicated that *kṣatriyas* should not sit back comfortably on the pretext of performing Vedic rituals but must rather be very chivalrous in protecting the citizens. *Brāhmaṇas,* being engaged in spiritual activities, are not expected to do anything which requires physical endeavor. Therefore, they need to be protected by the *kṣatriyas* so that they will not be disturbed in the execution of their higher occupational duties.

"If the *brāhmaṇas* feel unwanted separation from their wives and children," Arjuna continued, "and the *kṣatriya* kings do not take care of them, then such *kṣatriyas* are to be considered no more than stage players. In dramatic performances in the theater, an actor may play the part of a king, but no one expects any benefits from such a make-believe king. Similarly, if the king or the executive head of a state cannot give protection to the head of the social structure, he is considered merely a bluffer. Such executive heads simply live for their own livelihood while occupying exalted posts as chiefs of state. My lord, I promise that I shall give protection to your children, and if I am unable to do so, then I shall enter into blazing fire so that the sinful contamination which has infected me will be counteracted."

Upon hearing Arjuna speak in this way, the *brāhmaṇa* replied, "My dear Arjuna, Lord Balarāma is present, but He could not give protection to my children. Lord Kṛṣṇa is also present, but He also could not give them protection. There are also many other heroes, such as Pradyumna and Aniruddha, carrying bows and arrows, but they could not protect my children." The *brāhmaṇa* directly hinted that Arjuna could not do that which was impossible for the Supreme Personality of Godhead. He felt that Arjuna was promising something beyond his power. The *brāhmaṇa* said, "I consider your promise to be like that of an inexperienced child. I cannot put my faith in your promise."

Arjuna then understood that the *brāhmaṇa* had lost all faith in the *kṣatriya* kings. Therefore, to encourage him, Arjuna spoke as if criticizing even his friend Lord Kṛṣṇa. While Lord Kṛṣṇa and others were listening, he specifically attacked Kṛṣṇa by saying, "My dear *brāhmaṇa,* I am neither Saṅkarṣaṇa nor Kṛṣṇa nor one of Kṛṣṇa's sons like Pradyumna or Aniruddha. My name is Arjuna, and I carry the bow known as Gāṇḍīva. You cannot insult me, for I have satisfied even Lord Śiva by my prowess when we were both hunting in the forest. I had a fight with Lord Śiva, who appeared before me as a hunter, and when I satisfied him by my prowess he gave me the weapon known as Pāśupata. Do not doubt my chivalry. I shall bring back your sons even if I have to fight with death personified." When the *brāhmaṇa* was assured by Arjuna in such exalted words, he was somehow or other convinced, and thus he returned home.

When the *brāhmaṇa's* wife was to give birth to another child, the *brāhmaṇa* began to chant, "My dear Arjuna, please come now and save my child." After hearing him, Arjuna immediately prepared himself by touching sanctified water and uttering holy *mantras* to protect his bows and arrows from danger. He specifically took the arrow presented to him by Lord Śiva, and while going out he remembered Lord Śiva and his great favor. In this way, he appeared in front of the maternity home, equipped with his bow, known as Gāṇḍīva, and with various other weapons.

Arjuna, who apparently had not left Dvārakā because he had to fulfill his promise to the *brāhmaṇa,* was called at night when the *brāhmaṇa's* wife was to give birth to the child. While going to the maternity home to attend to the delivery case of the *brāhmaṇa's* wife, Arjuna remembered Lord Śiva, and not his friend Kṛṣṇa; he thought that since Kṛṣṇa could not give protection to the *brāhmaṇa,* it was better to take shelter of Lord Śiva. This is another instance of how a person takes shelter of the demigods. This is explained in the *Bhagavad-gītā: kāmais tais tair hṛta-jñānāḥ prapadyante 'nya-devatāḥ.* "A person who loses his intelligence because of greed and lust forgets the Supreme Personality of Godhead and takes shelter of the demigods." Of course, Arjuna was not an ordinary living entity, but because of his friendly dealings with Kṛṣṇa he thought that Kṛṣṇa was unable to give protection to the *brāhmaṇa* and that he would do better to remember Lord Śiva. Later it was proved that Arjuna's taking shelter of Lord Śiva instead of Kṛṣṇa was not at all successful. Arjuna, however, did his best by chanting different *mantras,* and he shot arrows up and down to guard the maternity home from all directions. The *brāhmaṇa's* wife delivered a male child, and as usual the child began to cry. But suddenly, within a few minutes, both the child and Arjuna's arrows disappeared into the sky.

It appears that the *brāhmaṇa's* house was near Kṛṣṇa's

residence and that Lord Kṛṣṇa was enjoying everything that was taking place, apparently in defiance of His authority. It was He who played the trick of taking away the *brāhmaṇa's* baby as well as the arrows, including the one given by Lord Śiva, of which Arjuna was so proud. *Anta-vat tu phalaṁ teṣāṁ tad bhavaty alpa-medhasām:* "Less intelligent men take shelter of the demigods due to bewilderment and are satisfied with the temporary benefits they award."

In the presence of Lord Kṛṣṇa and others, the *brāhmaṇa* began to accuse Arjuna: "Everyone see my foolishness! I put my faith in the words of Arjuna, who is impotent and who is expert only in false promises. How foolish I was to believe Arjuna. He promised to protect my child when even Pradyumna, Aniruddha, Lord Balarāma and Lord Kṛṣṇa had failed. If such great personalities could not protect my child, then who can do so? I therefore condemn Arjuna for his false promise, and I also condemn his celebrated bow Gāṇḍīva and his impudence in declaring himself greater than Lord Balarāma, Lord Kṛṣṇa, Pradyumna and Aniruddha. How can anyone save my child, who has already been transferred to another planet? Due to sheer foolishness only, Arjuna thought he could bring back my child from another planet."

Thus condemned by the *brāhmaṇa,* Arjuna empowered himself with a mystic *yoga* perfection so that he could travel to any planet to find the *brāhmaṇa's* baby. It seems that Arjuna had mastered the mystic *yoga* power by which *yogīs* can travel to any planet they desire. He first of all went to the planet known as Yamaloka, where the superintendent of death, Yamarāja, lives. There he searched for the *brāhmaṇa's* baby, but was unable to find him. He then immediately went to the planet where the King of heaven, Indra, lives. When unable to find the baby there, he went to the planet of the fire demigod, then to the planet of the Nirṛti demigod, and then to the moon planet. Then he went to Vāyuloka and Varuṇaloka. When unable to find the baby on those planets, he went down to the Rasātala planet, the lowest of the planetary systems. After traveling to all these different planets, he finally went to Brahmaloka, where even mystic *yogīs* cannot go. By the grace of Lord Kṛṣṇa, Arjuna had that power, and he went above the heavenly planets to Brahmaloka. When he was unable to find the baby even after searching all possible planets, he then attempted to throw himself into a fire, since he had promised the *brāhmaṇa* he would do so if unable to bring back his baby. Lord Kṛṣṇa, however, was very kind toward Arjuna because Arjuna was the most intimate friend of the Lord. Lord Kṛṣṇa persuaded Arjuna not to enter the fire in disgrace. Kṛṣṇa indicated that since Arjuna was His friend, if he were to enter the fire in hopelessness, indirectly it would be a blemish on Him. Lord Kṛṣṇa therefore checked Arjuna, assuring him that He would find the baby. He told Arjuna, "Do not foolishly commit suicide."

After addressing Arjuna in this way, Lord Kṛṣṇa called for His transcendental chariot. He mounted it along with Arjuna and began to proceed north. Lord Kṛṣṇa, the all-powerful Personality of Godhead, could have brought the child back without effort, but we should always remember that He was playing the part of a human being. As a human being has to endeavor to achieve certain results, so Lord Kṛṣṇa, like an ordinary human being, or like His friend Arjuna, left Dvārakā to bring back the *brāhmaṇa's* baby. By appearing in human society and exhibiting His pastimes as a human being, Kṛṣṇa definitely showed that there was not a single personality greater than He. "God is great." That is the definition of the Supreme Personality of Godhead. So at least within this material world, while He was present, Kṛṣṇa proved that there was no greater personality within the universe.

Seated on His chariot with Arjuna, Kṛṣṇa proceeded north, crossing over many planetary systems. These are described in *Śrīmad-Bhāgavatam* as *sapta-dvīpa. Dvīpa* means "island." These planets are sometimes described in the Vedic literature as *dvīpas*. The planet on which we are living is called Jambūdvīpa. Outer space is taken as a great ocean of air, and within that great ocean of air there are many islands, which are the different planets. On each and every planet there are oceans also. On some of the planets the oceans are of salt water, and on some of them there are oceans of milk. On others there are oceans of liquor, and on others there are oceans of ghee or oil. There are different kinds of mountains also. Each and every planet has a different type of atmosphere.

Kṛṣṇa passed over all these planets and reached the covering of the universe. This covering is described in *Śrīmad-Bhāgavatam* as great darkness. The material world as a whole is described as dark. In the open space there is sunlight, and therefore it is illuminated, but in the covering, because of the absence of sunlight, it is naturally dark. When Kṛṣṇa approached the covering layer of this universe, the four horses which were drawing His chariot—Śaibya, Sugrīva, Meghapuṣpa and Balāhaka—all hesitated to enter the darkness. This hesitation is also a part of the pastimes of Lord Kṛṣṇa because the horses of Kṛṣṇa are not ordinary; it is not possible for ordinary horses to go all over the universe and then enter into its outer covering layers. As Kṛṣṇa is transcendental, His chariot and His horses and everything about Him is also transcendental, beyond the qualities of this material world. We should always remember that Kṛṣṇa was playing the part of an ordinary human being, and His horses also, by the will of Kṛṣṇa, played the parts of ordinary horses in hesitating to enter the darkness.

Kṛṣṇa is known as Yogeśvara, as stated in the last portion of the *Bhagavad-gītā*. *Yogeśvaro hariḥ:* all mystic powers are under His control. In our experience we can see many human beings who have yogic mystic power and who sometimes perform very wonderful acts, but Kṛṣṇa is understood to be the master of all mystic power. Therefore, when He saw that His horses were hesitant to proceed into the darkness, He immediately released His disc, known as the Sudarśana *cakra,* which illuminated the sky a thousand times brighter than sunlight. The darkness of the covering of the universe is also a creation of Kṛṣṇa's, and the Sudarśana *cakra* is Kṛṣṇa's constant companion. Thus He penetrated the darkness by keeping the Sudarśana *cakra* before Him. *Śrīmad-Bhāgavatam* states that the Sudarśana *cakra* penetrated the darkness just as an arrow released from the Śārṅga bow of Lord Rāmacandra penetrated the army of Rāvaṇa. *Su* means "very nice," and *darśana* means "observation"; by the grace of Lord Kṛṣṇa's disc, Sudarśana, everything can be seen very nicely, and nothing can remain in darkness. Thus Lord Kṛṣṇa and Arjuna crossed over the great region of darkness covering the material universes.

Arjuna then saw the effulgence of light known as the *brahmajyoti.* The *brahmajyoti* is situated outside the covering of the material universes, and because it cannot be seen with our present eyes, this *brahmajyoti* is sometimes called *avyakta.* This spiritual effulgence is the ultimate destination of the impersonalists known as Vedāntists. The *brahmajyoti* is also described as *ananta-pāram,* unlimited and unfathomed. When Lord Kṛṣṇa and Arjuna reached this region of the *brahmajyoti,* Arjuna could not tolerate the glaring effulgence, and he closed his eyes. Lord Kṛṣṇa's and Arjuna's reaching the *brahmajyoti* region is described in the *Hari-vaṁśa.* In that portion of the Vedic literature, Kṛṣṇa informs Arjuna, "My dear Arjuna, the glaring effulgence, the transcendental light you are seeing, is My bodily rays. O chief of the descendants of Bharata, this *brahmajyoti* is I Myself." As the sun disc and the sunshine cannot be separated, Kṛṣṇa and His bodily rays, the *brahmajyoti,* cannot be separated. Thus Kṛṣṇa claims that the *brahmajyoti* is He Himself. This is clearly stated in the *Hari-vaṁśa,* when Kṛṣṇa says *ahaṁ saḥ.* The *brahmajyoti* is a combination of the minute particles known as spiritual sparks, or the living entities, known as *cit-kaṇa.* The Vedic words *so 'ham,* or "I am the *brahmajyoti,*" can also be applied to the living entities, who can also claim to belong to the *brahmajyoti.* In the *Hari-vaṁśa,* Kṛṣṇa further explains, "This *brahmajyoti* is an expansion of My spiritual energy."

Kṛṣṇa told Arjuna, "The *brahmajyoti* is beyond the region of My external energy, known as *māyā-śakti.*" When one is situated within the material world, it is not possible for him to experience this Brahman effulgence. In other words, in the material world this effulgence is not manifested, whereas in the spiritual world it is manifested. That is the purport of the words *vyakta-avyakta* in the *Hari-vaṁśa.* In the *Bhagavad-gītā* it is said, *avyakto 'vyaktāt sanātanaḥ:* both these energies are eternally manifested.

After this, Lord Kṛṣṇa and Arjuna entered a vast spiritual water. This spiritual water is called the Kāraṇa Ocean, which means that this ocean is the origin of the creation of the material world; this place is also known as Virajā, because it is free from the influence of the three qualities of the material world. In the *Mṛtyuñjaya-tantra,* a Vedic literature, there is a vivid description of this Kāraṇa Ocean, or Virajā. It is stated there that the highest planetary system within the material world is Satyaloka, or Brahmaloka, beyond which are Rudraloka and Mahā-Viṣṇuloka. Regarding this Mahā-Viṣṇuloka, it is stated in the *Brahma-saṁhitā, yaḥ kāraṇārṇava-jale bhajati sma yoga-nidrām ananta-jagad-aṇḍa-sa-roma-kūpaḥ:* "Lord Mahā-Viṣṇu is lying in the Kāraṇa Ocean. When He exhales, innumerable universes come into existence, and when He inhales, innumerable universes enter within Him." In this way, the material creation is generated and again withdrawn. When Lord Kṛṣṇa and Arjuna entered the water, it appeared that there was a strong hurricane of transcendental effulgence blowing, and the water of the Kāraṇa Ocean was greatly agitated. By the grace of Lord Kṛṣṇa, Arjuna had the unique experience of being able to see the very beautiful Kāraṇa Ocean.

Accompanied by Kṛṣṇa, Arjuna saw a large palace within the water. There were many thousands of pillars and columns made of valuable jewels, and the glaring effulgence of those columns was so beautiful that Arjuna was charmed by it. Within that palace, Arjuna and Kṛṣṇa saw the gigantic form of Anantadeva, who is also known as Śeṣa. Lord Anantadeva, or Śeṣa Nāga, was in the form of a great serpent with thousands of hoods, each one decorated with valuable, effulgent jewels, beautifully dazzling. Each of Anantadeva's hoods had two eyes, which appeared very fearful. His body was as white as the mountaintop of Kailāsa, which is always covered with snow. His necks were bluish, as were His tongues. Thus Arjuna saw the Śeṣa Nāga form, and he also saw that on the very soft, white body of Śeṣa Nāga, Lord Mahā-Viṣṇu was lying very comfortably. He appeared all-pervading and very powerful, and Arjuna could understand that the Supreme Personality of Godhead in that form is known as Puruṣottama. He is known as Puruṣottama, the supreme or best Personality of Godhead, because from this form emanates within the material world another form of Viṣṇu, known as Garbhodakaśāyī Viṣṇu. The Mahā-Viṣṇu form of the Lord is also called Puruṣottama (Puruṣa-uttama) because He is beyond the material world. *Tama* means "darkness," and *ut* means "above, transcendental"; therefore, *uttama* means "above the darkest region of the material world." Arjuna saw that the bodily color of Puruṣottama, Mahā-Viṣṇu, was as dark as a new cloud in the rainy season. He was dressed in very nice yellow clothing, His face was beautifully smiling, and His eyes, which were like lotus petals, were very attractive. Lord Mahā-Viṣṇu's helmet was bedecked with valuable jewels, and His beautiful earrings enhanced the beauty of the curling hair on His head. Lord Mahā-Viṣṇu had eight arms, all very long, reaching to His knees. His neck was decorated with the Kaustubha jewel, and His chest was marked with the symbol of Śrīvatsa, which means "the resting place of the goddess of fortune." The Lord wore a garland of lotus flowers down to His knees. This long garland is known as a Vaijayantī garland.

The Lord was attended by His personal associates Nanda

and Sunanda, and the personified Sudarśana disc was also standing by Him. As stated in the *Vedas,* the Lord has innumerable energies, and they also stood there in their personified forms. The most important among them were as follows: Puṣṭi, the energy for nourishment; Śrī, the energy of beauty; Kīrti, the energy of reputation; and Ajā, the energy of material creation. All these energies are invested in the administrators of the material world, namely Lord Brahmā, Lord Śiva and Lord Viṣṇu, and also in Indra (the King of the heavenly planets), Candra, Varuṇa and the sun-god. In other words, all these demigods, being empowered by the Lord with certain energies, engage in the transcendental loving service of the Supreme Personality of Godhead. The Mahā-Viṣṇu feature is an expansion of Kṛṣṇa's body. The *Brahma-saṁhitā* confirms that Mahā-Viṣṇu is a portion of a plenary expansion of Kṛṣṇa. All such expansions are nondifferent from the Personality of Godhead, but since Kṛṣṇa appeared within this material world to manifest His pastimes as a human being, He and Arjuna immediately offered their respects to Lord Mahā-Viṣṇu by bowing down before Him. It is stated in *Śrīmad-Bhāgavatam* that Lord Kṛṣṇa offered respect to Mahā-Viṣṇu; this means that Kṛṣṇa offered obeisances unto none other than Himself, because Lord Mahā-Viṣṇu is nondifferent from Kṛṣṇa Himself. This offering of obeisances by Kṛṣṇa to Mahā-Viṣṇu is not, however, the form of worship known as *ahaṅgrahopāsanā,* which is sometimes recommended for persons trying to elevate themselves to the spiritual world by performing the sacrifice of knowledge. Such persons are also mentioned in the *Bhagavad-gītā: jñāna-yajñena cāpy anye yajanto mām upāsate.*

Although there was no necessity for Kṛṣṇa to offer obeisances, because He is the master teacher He taught Arjuna just how respect should be offered to Lord Mahā-Viṣṇu. Arjuna, however, became very much afraid upon seeing the gigantic form of everything, distinct from the material experience. Seeing Kṛṣṇa offering obeisances to Lord Mahā-

Viṣṇu, he immediately followed Him and then stood before the Lord with folded hands. After this, the gigantic form of Mahā-Viṣṇu, greatly pleased, smiled pleasingly and spoke as follows.

"My dear Kṛṣṇa and Arjuna, I was very eager to see you both, and therefore I arranged to take away the babies of the *brāhmaṇa* and keep them here. I have been expecting to see you both at this palace. You have appeared in the material world as My incarnations in order to minimize the force of the demoniac persons who burden the world. Now, after killing all these unwanted demons, you will please come back to Me. The two of you are incarnations of the great sage Nara-Nārāyaṇa. Although you are both complete in yourselves, to protect the devotees and to annihilate the demons, and especially to establish religious principles in the world so that peace and tranquillity may continue, you are teaching the basic principles of factual religion so that the people of the world may follow you and thereby be peaceful and prosperous."

Lord Kṛṣṇa and Arjuna then offered their obeisances to Lord Mahā-Viṣṇu, and, taking back the *brāhmaṇa's* children, they returned to Dvārakā via the same route by which they had entered the spiritual world. All the children of the *brāhmaṇa* had duly grown up. After returning to Dvārakā, Lord Kṛṣṇa and Arjuna delivered to the *brāhmaṇa* all of his sons.

Arjuna, however, was struck with great wonder after visiting the transcendental world by the grace of Lord Kṛṣṇa. And by the grace of Kṛṣṇa he could understand that whatever opulence there may be within this material world is an emanation from Him. Any opulent position a person may have within this material world is due to Kṛṣṇa's mercy. One should therefore always be in Kṛṣṇa consciousness, in complete gratefulness to Lord Kṛṣṇa, because whatever one may possess is all bestowed by Him.

Arjuna's wonderful experience due to the mercy of Kṛṣṇa is one of the many thousands of pastimes performed by Lord

Kṛṣṇa during His stay in this material world. They were all unique and have no parallel in the history of the world. All these pastimes prove fully that Kṛṣṇa is the Supreme Personality of Godhead. Yet while present within this material world He played just like an ordinary man with many worldly duties. He played the part of an ideal householder possessing more than 16,000 wives, 16,000 palaces and 160,000 children, and in that role He performed many sacrifices just to teach the royal order how to live in the material world for the welfare of humanity. As the ideal Supreme Personality, He fulfilled the desires of everyone, from the *brāhmaṇas,* the highest persons in human society, down to the ordinary living entities, including the lowest of men. Just as King Indra is in charge of distributing rain all over the world to satisfy everyone in due course, so Lord Kṛṣṇa satisfies everyone by pouring down His causeless mercy. His mission was to give protection to the devotees and to kill the demoniac kings. Therefore He killed many hundreds and thousands of demons. Some of them He killed personally, and some were killed by Arjuna, who was deputed by Kṛṣṇa. In this way He established many pious kings such as Yudhiṣṭhira at the helm of world affairs. Thus, by His divine arrangement, He created the good government of King Yudhiṣṭhira, and there ensued peace and tranquillity.

Thus ends the Bhaktivedanta purport of the Eighty-ninth Chapter of Kṛṣṇa, *"The Superexcellent Power of Kṛṣṇa."*

CHAPTER NINETY

Summary Description of Lord Kṛṣṇa's Pastimes

After returning from the spiritual kingdom, which he was able to visit personally with Kṛṣṇa, Arjuna was very much astonished. He thought to himself that although he was only an ordinary living entity, by the grace of Kṛṣṇa it had been possible for him to see the spiritual world. Not only had he seen the spiritual world, but he had also personally seen the original Mahā-Viṣṇu, the cause of the material creation. It is said that Kṛṣṇa never goes out of Vṛndāvana: *vṛndāvanaṁ parityajya pādam ekaṁ na gacchati.* Kṛṣṇa is supreme in Mathurā, He is more supreme in Dvārakā, and He is most supreme in Vṛndāvana. Kṛṣṇa's pastimes in Dvārakā are displayed by His Vāsudeva portion, yet there is no difference between the Vāsudeva portion manifested in Mathurā and Dvārakā and the original manifestation of Kṛṣṇa in Vṛndāvana. In the beginning of this book we have discussed that when Kṛṣṇa appears, all His incarnations, plenary portions and portions of the plenary portions come with Him. Thus some of His different pastimes are manifested not by the original Kṛṣṇa Himself but by His expansions.

Why Arjuna was puzzled by Kṛṣṇa's going to see Kāraṇārṇavaśāyī Viṣṇu in the spiritual world is fully discussed in the commentaries of Śrīla Viśvanātha Cakravartī Ṭhākura, as follows. It is understood from the speech of Mahā-Viṣṇu that He was very eager to see Kṛṣṇa. It may be said, however, that since Mahā-Viṣṇu took away the *brāhmaṇa's* sons, He must certainly have gone to Dvārakā to do so. Therefore, why did He not see Kṛṣṇa there? A possible answer is that unless Kṛṣṇa gives His permission, He cannot be seen even by Mahā-Viṣṇu lying in the Causal Ocean of the spiritual world. Thus Mahā-Viṣṇu took away the *brāhmaṇa's* sons one after another just after their births so that Kṛṣṇa would come personally to the Causal Ocean to retrieve them, and then Mahā-Viṣṇu would be able to see Him there. If that is so, the next question is this: Why would Mahā-Viṣṇu come to Dvārakā personally if He were not able to see Kṛṣṇa? Why did He not send some of His associates to take away the sons of the *brāhmaṇa*? A possible answer is that it is very difficult to put any of the citizens of Dvārakā into trouble in the presence of Kṛṣṇa. Therefore, because it was not possible for any of Mahā-Viṣṇu's associates to take away the *brāhmaṇa's* sons, He personally came to take them.

Another question may also be raised: The Lord is known as *brahmaṇya-deva,* the worshipable Deity of the *brāhmaṇas,* so why was He inclined to put a *brāhmaṇa* into such a terrible condition of lamentation over one son after another until the tenth son was taken away? The answer is that Lord Mahā-Viṣṇu was so eager to see Kṛṣṇa that He did not hesitate even to give trouble to a *brāhmaṇa.* Although giving trouble to a *brāhmaṇa* is a forbidden act, Lord Viṣṇu was prepared to do anything in order to see Kṛṣṇa—He was so eager to see Him. After losing each of his sons, the *brāhmaṇa* would come to the gate of the palace and accuse the King of not being able to give the *brāhmaṇas* protection and of thus being unfit to sit on the royal throne. It was Mahā-Viṣṇu's plan that the *brāhmaṇa* would accuse the *kṣatriyas* and Kṛṣṇa, and Kṛṣṇa would be obliged to come see Him to take back the *brāhmaṇa's* sons.

Still another question may be raised: If Mahā-Viṣṇu cannot see Kṛṣṇa, then how was Kṛṣṇa obliged to come before Him after all to take back the sons of the *brāhmaṇa*? The answer is that Lord Kṛṣṇa went to see Lord Mahā-Viṣṇu not exactly to take away the sons of the *brāhmaṇa* but only for Arjuna's sake. His friendship with Arjuna was so intimate that when Arjuna prepared himself to die by entering a fire, Kṛṣṇa wanted to give him complete protection. Arjuna, however, would not desist from entering the fire unless the sons of the *brāhmaṇa* were brought back. Therefore Kṛṣṇa promised him, "I shall bring back the *brāhmaṇa's* sons. Do not try to commit suicide."

If Lord Kṛṣṇa were going to see Lord Viṣṇu only to reclaim the sons of the *brāhmaṇa,* then He would not have waited until the tenth son was taken. But when the tenth son was taken away by Lord Mahā-Viṣṇu, and when Arjuna was therefore ready to enter the fire because his promise was going to prove false, that serious situation made Lord Kṛṣṇa decide to go with Arjuna to see Mahā-Viṣṇu. It is said that Arjuna is an empowered incarnation of Nara-Nārāyaṇa. He is even sometimes called Nara-Nārāyaṇa. The Nara-Nārāyaṇa incarnation is also one of Lord Viṣṇu's plenary expansions. Therefore, when Kṛṣṇa and Arjuna went to see Lord Viṣṇu, it is to be understood that Arjuna visited in his Nara-Nārāyaṇa capacity, just as Kṛṣṇa, when He displayed His pastimes in Dvārakā, acted in His Vāsudeva capacity.

After visiting the spiritual world, Arjuna concluded that whatever opulence anyone can show within the material or spiritual worlds is all a gift of Lord Kṛṣṇa. Lord Kṛṣṇa is manifested in various forms, as *viṣṇu-tattva* and *jīva-tattva,* or, in other words, as *svāṁśa* and *vibhinnāṁśa. Viṣṇu-tattva* is known as *svāṁśa,* and *jīva-tattva* is known as *vibhinnāṁśa.* He can, therefore, display Himself by His different transcendental pastimes, in the portion of either *svāṁśa* or *vibhinnāṁśa,* as He likes, but still He remains the original Supreme Personality of Godhead.

The concluding portion of Kṛṣṇa's pastimes is found in the Ninetieth Chapter of the Tenth Canto of *Śrīmad-Bhāgavatam,* and in this chapter Śukadeva Gosvāmī wanted to explain how Kṛṣṇa lived happily at Dvārakā with all opulences. Kṛṣṇa's opulence of strength has already been displayed in His different pastimes, and now it will be shown how His residence at Dvārakā displayed His opulences of wealth and beauty. In this material world the opulences of wealth and beauty are considered the highest of all opulences, yet they are only a perverted reflection of these opulences in the spiritual world. Therefore, while Kṛṣṇa stayed on this planet as the Supreme Personality of Godhead, His opulences of wealth and beauty had no comparison within the three worlds. Kṛṣṇa enjoyed sixteen thousand beautiful wives, and it is most significant that He lived at Dvārakā as the only husband of these thousands of beautiful women. This is specifically stated—that He was the only husband of sixteen thousand wives. It is of course not unheard of in the history of the world that a powerful king would keep many hundreds of queens, but although such a king might be the only husband of so many wives, he could not enjoy all of them at one time. Lord Kṛṣṇa, however, enjoyed all of His sixteen thousand wives simultaneously.

Although it may be said that *yogīs* also can expand their bodies into many forms, the *yogī's* expansion and Lord Kṛṣṇa's expansion are not the same. Kṛṣṇa is therefore sometimes called Yogeśvara, the master of all *yogīs.* In the Vedic literature we find that the *yogī* Saubhari Muni expanded himself into eight. But that expansion was like a television expansion. The television image is manifested in millions of expansions, but those expansions cannot act differently; they are simply reflections of the original and can only act exactly as the original does. Kṛṣṇa's expansion is not material, like the expansion of the television or the *yogī.* When Nārada visited the different palaces of Kṛṣṇa, he saw that Kṛṣṇa, in His different expansions, was variously engaged in each and every palace of the queens.

It is also said that Kṛṣṇa lived in Dvārakā as the husband of the goddess of fortune. Queen Rukmiṇī is the goddess of fortune, and all the other queens are her expansions. So Kṛṣṇa, the chief of the Vṛṣṇi dynasty, enjoyed with the goddess of fortune in full opulence. The queens of Kṛṣṇa are described as permanently youthful and beautiful. Although Kṛṣṇa had grandchildren and great-grandchildren, neither Kṛṣṇa nor His queens looked older than sixteen or twenty years of age. The young queens were so beautiful that when they moved they appeared like lightning moving in the sky. They were always dressed with excellent ornaments and garments and were always engaged in sportive activities like dancing, singing or playing ball on the roofs of the palaces. The dancing and tennis playing of girls in the material world are perverted reflections of the original pastimes of the original Personality of Godhead, Kṛṣṇa, and His wives.

The roads and streets of the city of Dvārakā were always crowded with elephants, horses, chariots and infantry soldiers. When elephants are engaged in service, they are given liquor to drink, and it is said that the elephants in Dvārakā were given so much liquor that they would sprinkle a great quantity of it on the road and walk on the streets intoxicated. The infantry soldiers passing on the streets were profusely decorated with golden ornaments, and horses and golden chariots plied along the streets. In all directions of Dvārakā City, wherever one would turn his eyes he would find green parks and gardens, each of them filled with trees and plants laden with fruits and flowers. Because there were so many nice trees of fruits and flowers, all the sweetly chirping birds and buzzing bumblebees joined together to make sweet vibrations. The city of Dvārakā thus fully displayed all opulences. The heroes in the dynasty of Yadu used to think themselves the most fortunate residents of the city, and actually they enjoyed all transcendental facilities.

All the sixteen thousand palaces of Kṛṣṇa's queens were situated in this beautiful city of Dvārakā, and Lord Kṛṣṇa, the supreme eternal enjoyer of all these facilities, expanded Himself into sixteen thousand forms and simultaneously engaged in different family affairs in those sixteen thousand palaces. In each and every one of the palaces there were nicely decorated gardens and lakes. The crystal-clear water of the lakes contained many blooming lotus flowers of different colors like blue, yellow, white and red, and the saffron powder from the lotus flowers was blown all around by the breeze. All the lakes were full of beautiful swans, ducks and cranes, crying occasionally with melodious sounds. Lord Śrī Kṛṣṇa sometimes entered those lakes or the rivers with His wives and enjoyed swimming pastimes with them in full jubilation. Sometimes the wives of Lord Kṛṣṇa, who were all goddesses of fortune, would embrace the Lord in the midst of the water while swimming or taking a bath, and the red vermilion of *kuṅkuma* decorating their beautiful breasts would adorn the chest of the Lord with a reddish color.

The impersonalists would not dare believe that in the spiritual world there are such varieties of enjoyment, but in order to demonstrate the factual, ever-blissful enjoyment in the spiritual world, Lord Kṛṣṇa descended on this planet and showed that the spiritual world is not devoid of such pleasurable facilities of life. The only difference is that in the spiritual world such facilities are eternal, never-ending occurrences, whereas in the material world they are simply impermanent perverted reflections. When Lord Kṛṣṇa was engaged in such enjoyment, the Gandharvas and professional musicians would glorify Him with melodious musical concerts, accompanied by kettledrums, *mṛdaṅgas* and other drums, along with stringed instruments and brass bugles, and the whole atmosphere would change into a greatly festive celebration. In a festive mood, the wives of the Lord would sometimes sprinkle water on His body with a syringelike instrument, and the Lord would similarly wet the bodies of the queens. When Kṛṣṇa and the queens engaged themselves in these pastimes, it seemed as if the heavenly king Yakṣarāja were engaged in pastimes with his many wives. (Yakṣarāja is also known as Kuvera and is considered the treasurer of the heavenly kingdom.) When the wives of Lord Kṛṣṇa thus became wet, their breasts and thighs would increase in beauty a thousand times, and their long hair would fall down to decorate those parts of their bodies. The beautiful flowers placed in their hair would fall, and the queens, being seemingly harassed by the Lord's throwing water at them, would approach Him on the plea of snatching the syringelike instrument. This attempt would create a situation wherein the Lord could embrace them as they willingly approached Him. Upon being embraced, the wives of the Lord would feel on their mouths a clear indication of conjugal love, and this would create an atmosphere of spiritual bliss. When the garland on the neck of the Lord then touched the breasts of the queens, their whole bodies became covered with saffron yellow. Being engaged in their celestial pastimes, the queens forgot themselves, and their loosened hair appeared like beautiful waves of a river. When the queens sprinkled water on the body of Kṛṣṇa or He sprinkled water on the bodies of the queens, the whole situation appeared just like that of an elephant enjoying in a lake with many she-elephants.

After enjoying fully amongst themselves, the queens and Lord Kṛṣṇa would come out of the water, and they would give up their wet garments, which were very valuable, to be taken away by the professional singers and dancers. These singers and dancers had no means of subsistence other than the rewards of valuable garments and ornaments left by the queens and kings on such occasions. The whole system of society was so well planned that all the members of society in their different positions as *brāhmaṇas, kṣatriyas, vaiśyas* and *śūdras* had no difficulty in earning their livelihood. There was no competition among the divisions of society. The original conception of the caste system was so planned that a group of men engaged in a particular type of occupation would not compete with another group of men engaged in a different occupation.

In this way, Lord Kṛṣṇa used to enjoy the company of His sixteen thousand wives. Some devotees of the Lord who want to love the Supreme Personality of Godhead in the mellow of conjugal love are elevated to the position of becoming wives of Kṛṣṇa, and Kṛṣṇa keeps them always attached to Him by His kind behavior. Kṛṣṇa's behavior with His wives—His movements, His talking with them, His smiling, His embracing and similar other activities, which are just like those of a loving husband—kept them always very much attached to Him. That is the highest perfection of life. If someone remains always attached to Kṛṣṇa, it is to be understood that he is liberated, and his life is successful. With any devotee who loves Kṛṣṇa with his heart and soul, Kṛṣṇa reciprocates in such a way that the devotee cannot but remain attached to Him. The reciprocal dealings of Kṛṣṇa and His devotees are so attractive that a devotee cannot think of any subject matter other than Kṛṣṇa.

For all the queens, Kṛṣṇa was their only worshipable objective. They were always absorbed in thought of Kṛṣṇa, the lotus-eyed and beautifully blackish Personality of Godhead. Sometimes, in thought of Kṛṣṇa, they remained silent, and in great ecstasy of *bhāva* and *anubhāva* they sometimes spoke as if in delirium. Sometimes, even in the presence of Lord Kṛṣṇa, they vividly described the pastimes they had enjoyed in the lake or river with Him. Some of such talk is described here.

The queens said, "Dear *kurarī* bird, now it is very late at night. Everyone is sleeping. The whole world is now calm and peaceful. At this time, the Supreme Personality of Godhead is sleeping, although His knowledge is undisturbed by any circumstance. Then why are you not sleeping? Why are you lamenting like this throughout the whole night? Dear friend, is it that you are also attracted by the lotus eyes of the Supreme Personality of Godhead and by His sweet smiling and attractive words, exactly as we are? Do those dealings of the Supreme Personality of Godhead pinch your heart as they do ours?

"Hello, *cakravākī.* Why have you closed your eyes? Are you searching after your husband, who may have gone to foreign countries? Why are you lamenting so pitiably? Alas, it appears that you are very much aggrieved. Or is it a fact that you also are willing to become an eternal servitor of the Supreme Personality of Godhead? We think that you are anxious to put a garland on the lotus feet of the Lord and then place it on your hair.

"O dear ocean, why are you roaring all day and night? Don't you like to sleep? We think you have been attacked by insomnia, or, if we are not wrong, our dear Śyāmasundara has tactfully taken away your gravity and power of forbearance, which are your natural qualifications. Is it a fact that for this reason you are suffering from insomnia like us? Yes, we admit that there is no remedy for this disease.

"Dear moon-god, we think you have been attacked by a severe type of tuberculosis. For this reason, you are becoming thinner and thinner day by day. O lord, you are now so weak that your thin rays cannot dissipate the darkness of night. Or is it a fact that, just like us, you have been stunned by the mysteriously sweet words of our Lord Śyāmasundara? Is it a fact that it is because of this severe anxiety that you are so grave?

"O breeze from the Himalayas, what have we done to you that you are so intent on teasing us by awakening our lust to meet Kṛṣṇa? Do you not know that we have already been injured by the crooked policy of the Personality of Godhead? Dear Himalayan breeze, please know that we have already been stricken. There is no need to injure us more and more.

"Dear beautiful cloud, the color of your beautiful body exactly resembles the bodily hue of our dearmost Śyāmasundara. We think, therefore, that you are very dear to our Lord, the chief of the dynasty of the Yadus, and because you are so dear to Him, you are absorbed in meditation, exactly as we are. We can appreciate that your heart is full of anxiety for Śyāmasundara. You appear excessively eager to see Him, and we see that for this reason only, drops of tears are gliding down from your eyes, just as they are from ours. Dear black cloud, we must admit frankly that to establish an intimate relationship with Śyāmasundara means to purchase unnecessary anxieties while we are otherwise comfortable at home."

Generally the cuckoo sounds its cooing vibration at the end of night or early in the morning. When the queens heard the cooing of the cuckoo at the end of night, they said, "Dear cuckoo, your voice is very sweet. As soon as you vibrate your sweet voice, we immediately remember Śyāmasundara because your voice exactly resembles His. We must frankly admit that your voice is imbued with nectar, and it is so invigorating that it is competent to bring back life to those who are almost dead in separation from their dearmost friend. So we are very much obliged to you. Please let us know how we can welcome you or how we can do something for you."

The queens continued talking like that, and they addressed the mountain as follows: "Dear mountain, you are very generous. By your gravity only, the whole crust of this earth is properly maintained, although because you are discharging your duties very faithfully, you do not know how to move. Because you are so grave, you do not move hither and thither, nor do you say anything. Rather, you always appear in a thoughtful mood. It may be that you are always thinking of a very grave and important subject matter, but we can guess very clearly what you are thinking of. We are sure that you are thinking of placing the lotus feet of Śyāmasundara on your raised peaks, as we want to place His lotus feet on our raised breasts.

"Dear dry rivers, we know that because this is the summer season, all your beds are dry, and you have no water. Because all your water has now been dried up, you are no longer beautified by blooming lotus flowers. At the present moment, you appear very lean and thin, so we can understand that your position is exactly like ours. We have lost everything due to being separated from Śyāmasundara, and we no longer hear His pleasing words. Our hearts no longer work properly, and therefore we also have become very lean and thin. We think, therefore, that you are just like us. You have turned lean and thin because you are not getting any water from your husband, the ocean, through the clouds." The example given herewith by the queens is very appropriate. The riverbeds become dry when the ocean no longer supplies water through the clouds. The ocean is supposed to be the husband of the river and therefore is supposed to support her. Unless a woman is supported by her husband with the necessities of life, she also becomes as dry as a dry river.

One queen addressed a swan as follows: "My dear swan, please come here, come here. You are welcome. Please sit down and take some milk. My dear swan, can you tell me if you have any message from Śyāmasundara? I take you to be a messenger from Him. If you have any such news, please tell me. Our Śyāmasundara is always very independent. He never comes under the control of anyone. We have all failed to control Him, and therefore we ask you, Is He keeping Himself well? I may inform you that Śyāmasundara is very fickle. His friendship is always temporary; it breaks even by slight agitation. But would you kindly explain why He is so unkind to me? Formerly He said that I alone am His dearmost wife. Does He remember this assurance? Anyway, you are welcome. Please sit down. But I cannot accept your entreaty to go to Śyāmasundara. When He does not care for me, why should I be mad after Him? I am very sorry to let you know that you have become the messenger of a poor-hearted soul. You are asking me to go to Him, but I am not going. What is that? You talk of His coming to me? Does He desire to come here to fulfill my long expectation for Him? All right. You may bring Him here. But don't bring with Him His most beloved goddess of fortune. Do you think that He cannot be separated from the goddess of fortune even for a moment? Could He not come here alone, without Lakṣmī? His behavior is very displeasing. Does it mean that without Lakṣmī, Śyāmasundara cannot be happy? Can't He be happy with any other wife? Does it mean that the goddess of fortune has the ocean of love for Him and none of us can compare to her?"

All the wives of Lord Kṛṣṇa were completely absorbed in thought of Him. Kṛṣṇa is known as Yogeśvara, the master of all *yogīs,* and all the wives of Kṛṣṇa at Dvārakā used to keep this Yogeśvara within their hearts. Instead of trying to be master of all yogic mystic powers, it is better if one simply keeps the supreme Yogeśvara, Kṛṣṇa, within his heart. Thus one's life can become perfect, and one can very easily be transferred to the kingdom of God. It is to be understood that all the queens of Kṛṣṇa who lived with Him at Dvārakā were in their previous lives very greatly exalted devotees who wanted to establish a relationship with Kṛṣṇa in conjugal love. Thus they were given the chance to become His wives and enjoy a constant loving relationship with Him. Ultimately, they were all transferred to the Vaikuṇṭha planets.

The Supreme Absolute Truth Personality of Godhead is never impersonal. All the Vedic literatures glorify the transcendental performance of His various personal activities and pastimes. It is said that in the *Vedas* and in the *Rāmāyaṇa,* only the activities of the Lord are described. Everywhere in the Vedic literature, His glories are sung. As soon as soft-hearted people such as women hear those transcendental pastimes of Lord Kṛṣṇa, they immediately become attracted to Him. Soft-hearted women and girls are therefore very easily drawn to the Kṛṣṇa consciousness movement. One who is thus drawn to the Kṛṣṇa consciousness movement and tries to keep himself in constant touch with such consciousness certainly gets the supreme salvation, going back to Kṛṣṇa in Goloka Vṛndāvana. If simply by developing Kṛṣṇa consciousness one can be transferred to the spiritual world, one can simply imagine how blissful and blessed were the queens of Lord Kṛṣṇa, who talked with Him personally and saw Lord Kṛṣṇa face to face. No one can properly describe the fortune of the wives of Lord Kṛṣṇa. They took care of Him personally by rendering various transcendental services like bathing Him, feeding Him, pleasing Him and serving Him. Thus no one's austerities can compare to the service of the queens at Dvārakā.

Śukadeva Gosvāmī informed Mahārāja Parīkṣit that for self-realization the austerities and penances performed by the queens at Dvārakā have no comparison. The objective of self-realization is one: Kṛṣṇa. Therefore, although the dealings of the queens with Kṛṣṇa appear just like ordinary dealings between husband and wife, the principal point to be observed is the queens' attachment for Kṛṣṇa. The entire process of austerity and penance is meant to detach one from the material world and enhance one's attachment to Kṛṣṇa, the Supreme Personality of Godhead. Kṛṣṇa is the shelter of all persons advancing in self-realization. As an ideal householder, He lived with His wives and performed the Vedic rituals just to show less intelligent persons that the Supreme Lord is never impersonal. Kṛṣṇa lived with wives and children in all opulence, exactly like an ordinary conditioned soul, just to teach those souls who are actually conditioned that they must enter into the family circle of Kṛṣṇa, where He is the center. For example, the members of the Yadu dynasty lived in the family of Kṛṣṇa, and Kṛṣṇa was the center of all their activities.

Renunciation is not as important as enhancing one's attachment to Kṛṣṇa. The Kṛṣṇa consciousness movement is especially meant for this purpose. We are preaching the principle that it does not matter whether a man is a *sannyāsī* or a *gṛhastha* (householder). One simply has to increase his attachment for Kṛṣṇa, and then his life is successful. Following in the footsteps of Lord Śrī Kṛṣṇa, one can live with his family members or within the society or nation, not for the purpose of indulging in sense gratification but to realize Kṛṣṇa by advancing in attachment for Him. There are four principles of elevation from conditioned life to the life of liberation, which are technically known as *dharma, artha, kāma* and *mokṣa* (religion, economic development, sense gratification and liberation). If one lives a family life following in the footsteps of Lord Kṛṣṇa's family members, one can achieve all four of these principles of success simultaneously by making Kṛṣṇa the center of all activities.

It is already known to us that Kṛṣṇa had 16,108 wives. All these wives were exalted liberated souls, and among them Queen Rukmiṇī was the chief. After Rukmiṇī there were seven other principal wives, and the names of the sons of these eight principal queens have already been mentioned. Besides the sons born of these eight queens, Lord Kṛṣṇa had ten sons by each of the other queens. Thus altogether Kṛṣṇa's sons numbered 16,108 times ten. One should not be astonished to hear that Kṛṣṇa had so many sons. One should always remember that Kṛṣṇa is the Supreme Personality of Godhead and that He has unlimited potencies. He claims all living entities as His sons, so the fact that He had 161,080 sons attached to Him personally should be no cause for astonishment.

Among Kṛṣṇa's greatly powerful sons, eighteen sons were *mahā-rathas*. The *mahā-rathas* could fight alone against many thousands of foot soldiers, charioteers, cavalry and elephants. The reputations of these eighteen sons are very widespread and are described in almost all the Vedic literatures. The eighteen *mahā-ratha* sons are listed as Pradyumna, Aniruddha, Dīptimān, Bhānu, Sāmba, Madhu, Bṛhadbhānu, Citrabhānu, Vṛka, Aruṇa, Puṣkara, Vedabāhu, Śrutadeva, Sunandana, Citrabāhu, Virūpa, Kavi and Nyagrodha. Of these eighteen *mahā-ratha* sons of Kṛṣṇa, Pradyumna is considered the foremost. Pradyumna happened to be the eldest son of Queen Rukmiṇī, and he inherited all the qualities of his great father, Lord Kṛṣṇa. He married the daughter of his maternal uncle,

Rukmī, and from that marriage Aniruddha was born. Aniruddha was so powerful that he could fight against ten thousand elephants. He married the granddaughter of Rukmī, the brother of his grandmother Rukmiṇī. Because the relationship between these cousins was distant, such a marriage was not uncommon. Aniruddha's son was Vajra. When the whole Yadu dynasty was destroyed by the curse of some *brāhmaṇas,* only Vajra survived. Vajra had one son, whose name was Pratibāhu. The son of Pratibāhu was named Subāhu, the son of Subāhu was named Śāntasena, and the son of Śāntasena was Śatasena.

It is stated by Śukadeva Gosvāmī that all the members of the Yadu dynasty had many children. Just as Kṛṣṇa had many sons, grandsons and great-grandsons, each one of the kings named herewith also had similar family extensions. Not only did all of them have many children, but all were extraordinarily rich and opulent. None of them were weak or short-lived, and above all, all the members of the Yadu dynasty were staunch devotees of the brahminical culture. It is the duty of the *kṣatriya* kings to maintain the brahminical culture and protect the qualified *brāhmaṇas,* and all these kings discharged their duties rightly. The members of the Yadu dynasty were so numerous that it would be very difficult to describe them all, even if one had a duration of life of many thousands of years. Śrīla Śukadeva Gosvāmī informed Mahārāja Parīkṣit that he had heard from reliable sources that simply to teach the children of the Yadu dynasty there were as many as 38,800,000 tutors, or *ācāryas.* If so many teachers were needed to educate their children, one can simply imagine how vast was the number of family members. As for their military strength, it is said that King Ugrasena alone had ten quadrillion soldiers as personal bodyguards.

Before the advent of Lord Kṛṣṇa within this universe, there were many battles between the demons and the demigods. Many demons died in the fighting, and they all were given the chance to take birth in high royal families on this earth. Because of their royal exalted posts, all these demons became very much puffed up, and their only business was to harass their subjects. Lord Kṛṣṇa appeared on this planet just at the end of Dvāpara-yuga to annihilate all these demoniac kings. As it is said in the *Bhagavad-gītā, paritrāṇāya sādhūnāṁ vināśāya ca duṣkṛtām:* "The Lord comes to protect the devotees and annihilate the miscreants." Some of the demigods were asked to appear on this earth to assist in the transcendental pastimes of Lord Kṛṣṇa. When Kṛṣṇa appeared, He came in the association of His eternal servitors, but some of the demigods also were requested to come down to assist Him, and thus they took their births in the Yadu dynasty. The Yadu dynasty had 101 clans in different parts of the country. All the members of these different clans respected Lord Kṛṣṇa in a manner befitting His divine position, and all of them were His devotees heart and soul. Thus all the members of the Yadu dynasty were very opulent, happy and prosperous, and they had no anxieties. Because of their implicit faith in and devotion to Lord Kṛṣṇa, they were never defeated by any other kings. Their love for Kṛṣṇa was so intense that in their regular activities—in sitting, sleeping, traveling, talking, sporting, cleansing, bathing—they were simply absorbed in thoughts of Kṛṣṇa and paid no attention to bodily necessities. That is the symptom of a pure devotee of Lord Kṛṣṇa. Just as when a man is fully absorbed in some particular thought he sometimes forgets his other bodily activities, the members of the Yadu dynasty acted automatically for their bodily necessities, but their actual attention was always fixed on Kṛṣṇa. Their bodily activities were performed mechanically, but their minds were always absorbed in Kṛṣṇa consciousness.

Śrīla Śukadeva Gosvāmī has concluded the Ninetieth Chapter of the Tenth Canto of *Śrīmad-Bhāgavatam* by pointing out five particular excellences of Lord Kṛṣṇa. The first excellence is that before Lord Kṛṣṇa's appearance in the Yadu family, the river Ganges was known as the purest of all things; even impure things could be purified simply by touching the water of the Ganges. This superexcellent power of the Ganges water was due to its having emanated from the toe of Lord Viṣṇu. But when Lord Kṛṣṇa, the Supreme Viṣṇu, appeared in the family of the Yadu dynasty, He traveled personally throughout the kingdom of the Yadus, and by His intimate association with the Yadu dynasty, the whole family not only became very famous but also became more effective in purifying others than the water of the Ganges.

The next excellence of Lord Kṛṣṇa's appearance was that although He apparently gave protection to the devotees and annihilated the demons, both the devotees and the demons achieved the same result. Lord Kṛṣṇa is the bestower of five kinds of liberation, of which *sāyujya-mukti,* or the liberation of becoming one with the Supreme, was given to demons like Kaṁsa, whereas the *gopīs* were given the chance to associate with Him personally. The *gopīs* kept their individuality to enjoy the company of Lord Kṛṣṇa, but Kaṁsa was accepted into His impersonal *brahmajyoti.* In other words, both the demons and the *gopīs* were spiritually liberated, but because the demons were enemies and the *gopīs* were friends, the demons were killed and the *gopīs* protected.

The third excellence of Lord Kṛṣṇa's appearance was that the goddess of fortune, who is worshiped by demigods like Lord Brahmā, Indra and Candra, remained always engaged in the service of the Lord, even though the Lord gave more preference to the *gopīs.* Lakṣmījī, the goddess of fortune, tried her best to be on an equal level with the *gopīs,* but she was not successful. Nevertheless, she remained faithful to Kṛṣṇa, although she generally does not remain in one place even if worshiped by demigods like Lord Brahmā.

The fourth excellence of Lord Kṛṣṇa's appearance concerns the glories of His name. It is stated in the Vedic literature that by chanting the different names of Lord Viṣṇu a thousand times, one may be bestowed with the same benefits as by thrice chanting the holy name of Lord Rāma. And by chanting the holy name of Lord Kṛṣṇa only once, one receives the same benefit. In other words, of all the holy names of the Supreme Personality of Godhead, including Viṣṇu and Rāma, the holy name of Kṛṣṇa is the most powerful. The Vedic literature therefore specifically stresses the chanting of the holy name of Kṛṣṇa: Hare Kṛṣṇa, Hare Kṛṣṇa, Kṛṣṇa Kṛṣṇa, Hare Hare/ Hare Rāma, Hare Rāma, Rāma Rāma, Hare Hare. Lord Caitanya introduced this chanting of the holy name of Kṛṣṇa in this age, thus making liberation much more easily obtainable than in other ages. In other words, Lord Kṛṣṇa is more excellent than His incarnations, although all of them are equally the Supreme Personality of Godhead.

The fifth excellence of Lord Kṛṣṇa's appearance is that He established the most excellent of all religious principles by His one statement in the *Bhagavad-gītā* that simply by surrendering unto Him one can discharge all the principles of religious rites. In the Vedic literature there are twenty kinds of religious principles mentioned, and each of them is described in different *śāstras.* But Lord Kṛṣṇa is so kind to the fallen conditioned souls of this age that He personally appeared and asked everyone to give up all kinds of religious rites and simply surrender unto Him. It is said that this Age of Kali is three-fourths devoid of religious principles. Hardly one fourth of the principles of religion are still observed in this age. But by the mercy of Lord Kṛṣṇa, not only has this void of Kali-yuga been completely filled, but the religious process has been made so easy that simply by rendering transcendental loving service unto Lord Kṛṣṇa by chanting His holy names, Hare Kṛṣṇa, Hare Kṛṣṇa, Kṛṣṇa Kṛṣṇa, Hare Hare/ Hare Rāma, Hare Rāma, Rāma Rāma, Hare Hare, one can achieve the highest result of religion, namely, being transferred to the highest planet within the spiritual world, Goloka Vṛndāvana. Considering all this, one can immediately appreciate the benefit of Lord Kṛṣṇa's appearance on the earth and understand that His giving relief to the people of the world by His appearance was not at all extraordinary.

Śrīla Śukadeva Gosvāmī thus concludes his description of

the superexalted position of Lord Kṛṣṇa by glorifying Him in the following way: "O Lord Kṛṣṇa, all glories unto You. You are present in everyone's heart as Paramātmā. Therefore You are known as Jananivāsa, one who lives in everyone's heart." As confirmed in the *Bhagavad-gītā, īśvaraḥ sarva-bhūtānāṁ hṛd-deśe 'rjuna tiṣṭhati:* "The Supreme Lord in His Paramātmā feature lives within everyone's heart." This does not mean, however, that Kṛṣṇa has no separate existence as the Supreme Personality of Godhead. The Māyāvādī philosophers accept the all-pervading feature of Parabrahman, but when Parabrahman, or the Supreme Lord, appears, they think that He appears under the control of material nature. Because Lord Kṛṣṇa appeared as the son of Devakī, the Māyāvādī philosophers accept Kṛṣṇa to be an ordinary living entity who takes birth within this material world. Therefore Śukadeva Gosvāmī warns them: *devakī-janma-vāda,* which means that although Kṛṣṇa is famous as the son of Devakī, actually He is the Supersoul, or the all-pervading Supreme Personality of Godhead. The devotees, however, take this word *devakī-janma-vāda* in a different way. The devotees understand that actually Kṛṣṇa was the son of mother Yaśodā. Although Kṛṣṇa first appeared as the son of Devakī, He immediately transferred Himself to the lap of mother Yaśodā, and His childhood pastimes were blissfully enjoyed by mother Yaśodā and Nanda Mahārāja. This fact was admitted by Vasudeva himself when he met Nanda Mahārāja and Yaśodā at Kurukṣetra. He admitted that Kṛṣṇa and Balarāma were actually the sons of mother Yaśodā and Nanda Mahārāja. Vasudeva and Devakī were only Their official father and mother. Their actual father and mother were Nanda and Yaśodā. Therefore Śukadeva Gosvāmī describes Lord Kṛṣṇa as *devakī-janma-vāda.*

Śukadeva Gosvāmī then glorifies the Lord as one who is honored by the *yadu-vara-pariṣat,* the assembly house of the Yadu dynasty, and as the killer of different kinds of demons. Kṛṣṇa, the Supreme Personality of Godhead, could have killed all the demons by employing His different material energies, but He wanted to kill them personally, to give them salvation. There was no need of Kṛṣṇa's coming to this material world to kill the demons; simply by His willing, many hundreds and thousands of demons could have been killed without His personal endeavor. But actually He descended for His pure devotees, to play as a child with mother Yaśodā and Nanda Mahārāja and to give pleasure to the inhabitants of Dvārakā. By killing the demons and giving protection to the devotees, Lord Kṛṣṇa established the real religious principle, which is simply love of God. By following the factual religious principle of love of God, even the living entities known as *sthira-cara* were also delivered of all material contamination and transferred to the spiritual kingdom. *Sthira* means the trees and plants, which cannot move, and *cara* means the moving animals, especially the cows. When Kṛṣṇa was present, He delivered all the trees, monkeys and other plants and animals who happened to see Him and serve Him both in Vṛndāvana and in Dvārakā.

Lord Kṛṣṇa is especially glorified for giving pleasure to the *gopīs* and the queens of Dvārakā. Śukadeva Gosvāmī glorifies Lord Kṛṣṇa for His enchanting smile, by which He enchanted not only the *gopīs* of Vṛndāvana but also the queens of Dvārakā. The exact words used in this connection are *vardhayan kāma-devam.* In Vṛndāvana, as the boyfriend of many *gopīs,* and in Dvārakā, as the husband of many queens, Kṛṣṇa increased their lusty desires to enjoy with Him. For God realization or self-realization, one generally has to undergo severe austerities and penances for many, many thousands of years, and then it may be possible to realize God. But the *gopīs* and the queens of Dvārakā, simply by enhancing their lusty desires to enjoy Kṛṣṇa as their boyfriend or husband, received the highest type of salvation.

This behavior of Lord Kṛṣṇa with the *gopīs* and queens is unique in the history of self-realization. Usually people understand that for self-realization one has to go to the forest or mountains and undergo severe austerities and penances.

But the *gopīs* and the queens, simply by being attached to Kṛṣṇa in conjugal love and enjoying His company in a so-called sensuous life full of luxury and opulence, achieved the highest salvation, which is impossible to achieve even for great sages and saintly persons. Similarly, demons such as Kaṁsa, Dantavakra and Śiśupāla, who all treated Kṛṣṇa as an enemy, also got the highest benefit of being transferred to the spiritual world.

In the beginning of *Śrīmad-Bhāgavatam,* Śrīla Vyāsadeva offered his respectful obeisances to the Supreme Truth, Vāsudeva, Kṛṣṇa. After that he taught his son, Śukadeva Gosvāmī, to preach *Śrīmad-Bhāgavatam.* It is in this connection that Śukadeva Gosvāmī glorifies the Lord with the word *jayati.* Following in the footsteps of Śrīla Vyāsadeva, Śukadeva Gosvāmī and all the *ācāryas* in disciplic succession, the whole population of the world should glorify Lord Kṛṣṇa, and for their best interest they should take to this Kṛṣṇa consciousness movement. The process is easy and helpful. It is simply to chant the *mahā-mantra,* Hare Kṛṣṇa, Hare Kṛṣṇa, Kṛṣṇa Kṛṣṇa, Hare Hare/ Hare Rāma, Hare Rāma, Rāma Rāma, Hare Hare. Lord Caitanya has therefore recommended that one be callous to the material ups and downs. Material life is temporary, and so the ups and downs of life may come and go. When they come, one should be as tolerant as a tree and as humble and meek as the straw in the street, but certainly he must engage himself in Kṛṣṇa consciousness by chanting Hare Kṛṣṇa, Hare Kṛṣṇa, Kṛṣṇa Kṛṣṇa, Hare Hare/ Hare Rāma, Hare Rāma, Rāma Rāma, Hare Hare.

The Supreme Personality of Godhead, Kṛṣṇa, the Supersoul of all living entities, out of His causeless mercy comes down and manifests His different transcendental pastimes in different incarnations. Hearing the attractive pastimes of Lord Kṛṣṇa's different incarnations is a chance for liberation for the conditioned soul, and the most fascinating and pleasing activities of Lord Kṛṣṇa Himself are still more attractive because Lord Kṛṣṇa personally is all-attractive.

Following in the holy footsteps of Śrīla Śukadeva Gosvāmī, we have tried to present this book, *Kṛṣṇa,* for being read and heard by the conditioned souls of this age. By hearing the pastimes of Lord Kṛṣṇa, one is sure and certain to get salvation and be transferred back home, back to Godhead. It is stated by Śukadeva Gosvāmī that as we hear the transcendental pastimes of the Lord, we gradually cut the knots of material contamination. Therefore, regardless of what one is, if one wants the association of Lord Kṛṣṇa in the transcendental kingdom of God for eternity in blissful existence, one must hear about the pastimes of Lord Kṛṣṇa and chant the *mahā-mantra,* Hare Kṛṣṇa, Hare Kṛṣṇa, Kṛṣṇa Kṛṣṇa, Hare Hare/ Hare Rāma, Hare Rāma, Rāma Rāma, Hare Hare.

The transcendental pastimes of the Supreme Personality of Godhead, Kṛṣṇa, are so powerful that simply by hearing, reading and memorizing this book, *Kṛṣṇa,* one is sure to be transferred to the spiritual world, which is ordinarily very difficult to achieve. The description of the pastimes of Lord Kṛṣṇa is so attractive that it automatically gives us an impetus to study repeatedly, and the more we study the pastimes of the Lord, the more we become attached to Him. This very attachment to Kṛṣṇa makes one eligible to be transferred to His abode, Goloka Vṛndāvana. As we have learned from the previous chapter, to cross over the material world is to cross over the stringent laws of material nature. The stringent laws of material nature cannot check the progress of one who is attracted by the spiritual nature. This is confirmed in the *Bhagavad-gītā* by the Lord Himself: "Although the stringent laws of material nature are very difficult to overcome, one who surrenders unto the Lord can very easily cross over nescience." There is no influence of material nature in the spiritual world. As we have learned from the Second Canto of *Śrīmad-Bhāgavatam,* the ruling power of the demigods and the influence of material nature are conspicuous by their absence in the spiritual world.

Śrīla Śukadeva Gosvāmī has therefore advised Mahārāja Parīkṣit in the beginning of the Second Canto that every conditioned soul should engage himself in hearing and chanting the transcendental pastimes of the Lord. Śrīla Śukadeva Gosvāmī also informed King Parīkṣit that previously many other kings and emperors went to the jungle to prosecute severe austerities and penances in order to go back home, back to Godhead. In India it is still a practice that many advanced transcendentalists give up their family lives and go to Vṛndāvana to live there alone and completely engage in hearing and chanting the holy pastimes of the Lord. This system is recommended in *Śrīmad-Bhāgavatam,* and the six Gosvāmīs of Vṛndāvana followed it, but at the present moment many *karmīs* and pseudo devotees have overcrowded the holy place of Vṛndāvana just to imitate this process recommended by Śukadeva Gosvāmī. It is said that many kings and emperors formerly went to the forest for this purpose, but Śrīla Bhaktisiddhānta Sarasvatī Ṭhākura does not recommend that one take up this solitary life in Vṛndāvana prematurely.

One who prematurely goes to Vṛndāvana to live in pursuance of the instructions of Śukadeva Gosvāmī again falls victim to *māyā,* even while residing in Vṛndāvana. To check such unauthorized residence in Vṛndāvana, Śrīla Bhaktisiddhānta Sarasvatī Ṭhākura has sung a nice song in this connection, the purport of which is as follows: "My dear mind, why are you so proud of being a Vaiṣṇava? Your solitary chanting of the holy name of the Lord is based on a desire for cheap popularity, and therefore your chanting is only a pretension. Such an ambition for a cheap reputation may be compared to the stool of a hog because such popularity is another extension of the influence of *māyā.*" One may go to Vṛndāvana for cheap popularity, and instead of being absorbed in Kṛṣṇa consciousness, one may always think of money and women, which are simply temporary sources of happiness. It is better that one engage whatever money and women he may have in his possession in the service of the Lord, because sense enjoyment is not for the conditioned soul.

The master of the senses is Hṛṣīkeśa, Lord Kṛṣṇa. Therefore, the senses should always be engaged in His service. As for material reputation, there were many demons like Rāvaṇa who wanted to go against the laws of material nature, but they all failed. One should therefore not take to the demoniac activity of claiming to be a Vaiṣṇava just for false prestige, without performing service to the Lord. But when one engages oneself in the devotional service of the Lord, automatically the Vaiṣṇava reputation comes to him. There is no need to be envious of the devotees who are engaged in preaching the glories of the Lord. We have practical experience of being advised by the so-called *bābājīs* in Vṛndāvana that there is no need to preach and that it is better to live in Vṛndāvana in a solitary place and chant the holy name. Such *bābājīs* do not know that if one is engaged in preaching, or in glorifying the Supreme Personality of Godhead, the good reputation of a preacher automatically follows one. One should not, therefore, prematurely give up the honest life of a householder to lead a life of debauchery in Vṛndāvana. Śrīla Śukadeva Gosvāmī's recommendation to leave home and go to the forest in search of Kṛṣṇa is not for immature persons. Mahārāja Parīkṣit was mature. Even in his householder life, or from the very beginning of his life, he worshiped Lord Kṛṣṇa's *mūrti*. In his childhood he worshiped the Deity of Lord Kṛṣṇa, and later, although he was a householder, he was always detached, and therefore when he got the notice of his death, he immediately gave up all connection with household life and sat down on the bank of the Ganges to hear *Śrīmad-Bhāgavatam* in the association of devotees.

Thus ends the Bhaktivedanta purport of the Ninetieth Chapter of Kṛṣṇa, *"Summary Description of Lord Kṛṣṇa's Pastimes."*

Appendixes

A Note About This Edition

Śrīla Prabhupāda completed *Kṛṣṇa, the Supreme Personality of Godhead* (popularly known as *Kṛṣṇa* book) in 1970, and his Bhaktivedanta Book Trust published it that year in two volumes and soon again in three. In 1986, the BBT published a one-volume edition with minor revisions.

For the present edition, the editors have gone back to the original tapes of Śrīla Prabhupāda's dictation of the text and compared them word-for-word with the previous edition. In the course of their work they found that the original transcribers and editors had for the most part done an excellent job. Occasionally, however, they erred, perhaps owing to Śrīla Prabhupāda's heavily accented English, the uneven quality of the recordings, or the difficult philosophical concepts in some passages of the Tenth Canto. These errors, constituting less than one percent of the total text, have now been corrected, so that an already perfect book has become even more perfect for its increased fidelity to Śrīla Prabhupāda's original words.

The Author

His Divine Grace A. C. Bhaktivedanta Swami Prabhupāda appeared in this world in 1896 in Calcutta, India. He first met his spiritual master, Śrīla Bhaktisiddhānta Sarasvatī Gosvāmī, in Calcutta in 1922. Bhaktisiddhānta Sarasvatī was a prominent religious scholar and the founder of the Gauḍīya Maṭha (a Vaiṣṇava movement with sixty-four centres) in India. He liked this educated young man and convinced him to dedicate his life to teaching Vedic knowledge. Śrīla Prabhupāda became his student and, in 1933, received initiation as his disciple.

At their first meeting Śrīla Bhaktisiddhānta Sarasvatī requested Śrīla Prabhupāda to broadcast Vedic knowledge in English. In the years that followed, Śrīla Prabhupāda wrote a commentary on the *Bhagavad-gītā* and assisted the Gauḍīya Maṭha in its work. In 1944, he started *Back to Godhead,* a fortnightly magazine in English. Singlehandedly, Śrīla Prabhupāda edited it, typed the manuscripts, checked the galley proofs and even distributed the individual copies. The magazine now continues to be published by his disciples throughout the world in different languages.

In 1950, Śrīla Prabhupāda retired from domestic life to devote more time to his studies and writing. He travelled to the holy town of Vṛndāvana, where he lived in humble circumstances in the historic temple of Rādhā-Dāmodara. There, for several years, he engaged in deep study and writing. He accepted the renounced order of life (*sannyāsa*) in 1959. It was at the Rādhā-Dāmodara temple that Śrīla Prabhupāda began to work on his life's masterpiece: a multivolume translation of the eighteen-thousand verse *Śrīmad-Bhāgavatam* (*Bhāgavata Purāṇa*) with full commentary. After publishing three volumes of the *Bhāgavatam,* Śrīla Prabhupāda travelled by freighter to

New York City. He was practically penniless, but he had faith that the mission of his spiritual master could be successful. On the day he landed in America and saw the grey mists hanging over the towering skyscrapers, he penned these words in his diary: "My dear Lord Kṛṣṇa, I am sure that when this transcendental message penetrates their hearts, they will certainly feel gladdened and thus become liberated from all unhappy conditions of life." He was sixty-nine years old, alone and with few resources, but the wealth of spiritual knowledge and devotion he possessed was an unwavering source of strength and inspiration.

"At a very advanced age, when most people would be resting on their laurels," writes Harvey Cox, Harvard University theologian and author, "Śrīla Prabhupāda harkened to the mandate of his own spiritual teacher and set out on the difficult and demanding voyage to America. Śrīla Prabhupāda is, of course, only one of thousands of teachers. But in another sense, he is one in a thousand, maybe one in a million."

In 1966, Śrīla Prabhupāda founded the International Society for Krishna Consciousness, which became the formal name for the Hare Kṛṣṇa movement.

In the years that followed, Śrīla Prabhupāda gradually attracted tens of thousands of followers, started more than a hundred temples and *āśramas,* and published scores of books. His achievement is remarkable in that he transplanted India's ancient spiritual culture to the twentieth-century Western world.

In 1968, Śrīla Prabhupāda sent three devotee couples to bring Kṛṣṇa consciousness to the U.K. At first, these devotees were cared for by Hindu families who appreciated their mission, but soon they became well-known in London for the street chanting in Oxford Street. A headline in the *Times* announced, "Kṛṣṇa Chant Startles London." But the *mahā-mantra* soon became popular. Former-Beatle, George Harrison, who had known Śrīla Prabhupāda and the chanting before the devotees came to England, wanted to help. He arranged to produce a recording of the *mantra* on the Beatles' Apple label. It reached the Top Ten in Britain and number one in some other countries.

When Śrīla Prabhupāda arrived in England, he was the guest of John Lennon at his estate in Tittenhurst, while work was progressing on the temple in Bloomsbury, near the British Museum. In November 1969, Śrīla Prabhupāda opened the temple—the first Rādhā-Kṛṣṇa temple in Europe. The movement grew from strength to strength. Once again, George Harrison offered to help by donating a beautiful mock-Tudor manor house and estate in Hertfordshire. Now named Bhaktivedanta Manor, it is the Society's main training centre in Britain.

New devotees of Kṛṣṇa soon became highly visible in all the major cities around the world by their public chanting and their distribution of Śrīla Prabhupāda's books of Vedic knowledge. They began staging joyous cultural festivals throughout the year and serving millions of plates of delicious food offered to Kṛṣṇa (known as *prasādam*) throughout the world. As a result, ISKCON has significantly influenced the lives of hundreds of thousands of people. The late A.L. Basham, one of the world's leading authorities on Indian history and culture, wrote, "The Hare Kṛṣṇa movement arose out of next to nothing in less than twenty years and has become known all over the West. This is an important fact in the history of the Western world."

In just twelve years, despite his advanced age, Śrīla Prabhupāda circled the globe fourteen times on lecture tours that took him to six continents. Yet this vigorous schedule did not slow his prolific literary output. His writings constitute a veritable library of Vedic philosophy, religion, literature and culture.

Indeed, Śrīla Prabhupāda's most significant contribution is his books. Highly respected by academics for their authority, depth and clarity, they are used as textbooks in numerous university courses.

Garry Gelade, a professor at Oxford University's Department of Philosophy, wrote of them: "These texts are to be treasured. No one of whatever faith or philosophical persuasion who reads these books with an open mind can fail to be moved and impressed." And Dr. Larry Shinn, Dean of the College of Arts and Sciences at Bucknell University, wrote, "Prabhupāda's personal piety gave him real authority. He exhibited complete command of the scriptures, an unusual depth of realisation and an outstanding personal example, because he actually lived what he taught."

His writings have been translated into over 70 languages. The Bhaktivedanta Book Trust, established in 1972 to publish the works of His Divine Grace, has thus become the world's largest publisher of books in the field of Indian religion and philosophy. By the end of 1991, 450 million copies had been sold.

Before he passed away on the 14th of November 1977, he had guided ISKCON and seen it grow to a worldwide confederation of more than one hundred *āśramas,* schools, temples, institutes and farm communities.

Glossary

Ācārya—a spiritual master who teaches by his own personal behavior.

Asura—a demon or nondevotee.

Ātmārāma—a self-satisfied sage.

Avatāra—an incarnation of Godhead who descends from the spiritual world.

Bhagavad-gītā—the book that records the spiritual instructions given by Kṛṣṇa to His friend Arjuna on the Battlefield of Kurukṣetra.

Bhakta—a devotee.

Bhakti-yoga—the *yoga* of devotional service to the Lord.

Brahmā—the first created living being in the universe.

Brahmacārī—a celibate student under the guidance of a spiritual master.

Brahmajyoti—the impersonal effulgence that emanates from the body of Kṛṣṇa.

Brahman—the impersonal feature of the Absolute Truth.

Brāhmaṇas—the spiritual order of society whose occupation is the cultivation of Vedic knowledge.

Brahma-saṁhitā—a scripture written by Lord Brahmā in which his authoritative prayers to the Lord are recorded.

Caitanya Mahāprabhu—the incarnation of Kṛṣṇa as His own devotee who comes in this age to teach the process of devotional service by chanting the holy names of God.

Cāmara—a yak-tail whisk.

Deva—a demigod or devotee.

Ekādaśī—a day of fasting which occurs twice a month and which is meant for increasing Kṛṣṇa consciousness.

Gandharvas—celestial denizens of the heavenly planets who sing very beautifully.
Garuḍa—the giant bird-carrier of Viṣṇu.
Gopīs—cowherd girls, specifically the transcendental girlfriends of Lord Kṛṣṇa.
Gṛhastha—one who is in the householder order of life.
Guru—a spiritual master.

Jaya—victory.
Jñānī—someone who engages in mental speculation in pursuit of knowledge.

Kadamba—a tree which bears a round yellow flower and which is generally seen only in the Vṛndāvana area.
Karma—fruitive activities or their reactions.
Karmī—a fruitive worker.
Kaumudī—an especially fragrant flower found on the bank of the Yamunā River.
Kaustubha—a transcendental jewel worn around the neck of the Supreme Personality of Godhead.
Kṛṣṇa-kathā—narrations spoken by or about Kṛṣṇa.
Kṣatriyas—the spiritual order of society whose occupation is governmental administration and military protection of the citizens.
Kuṅkuma—a sweetly flavored reddish powder which is thrown upon the bodies of worshipable persons.

Līlā—pastimes.

Māgadhas—professional singers present at sacrifices.
Mahā-bhāgavata—a highly advanced devotee.
Mahā-mantra—the Hare Kṛṣṇa *mantra:* Hare Kṛṣṇa, Hare Kṛṣṇa, Kṛṣṇa Kṛṣṇa, Hare Hare/ Hare Rāma, Hare Rāma, Rāma Rāma, Hare Hare.
Mantra—a transcendental sound vibration.
Māyā (Mahāmāyā)—the external, material energy of the Su-

preme Lord, which covers the conditioned soul and does not allow him to understand the Supreme Personality of Godhead.

Māyāvādī—one who adheres to impersonalist or voidist philosophy and does not accept the eternal existence of the transcendental form of the Lord.

Mukti—liberation.

Mukunda—Lord Kṛṣṇa, who awards liberation and whose smiling face is like a *kunda* flower.

Nirguṇa—literally, without qualities (used to describe the Supreme Lord, who has no material qualities).

Pāṇḍavas—the five sons of King Pāṇḍu (Yudhiṣṭhira, Arjuna, Bhīma, Nakula and Sahadeva).

Paramahaṁsa—(literally, the supreme swan) a devotee who can appreciate the spiritual essence of life, just as a swan extracts milk from a mixture of milk and water.

Paramātmā—the expansion of the Supreme Lord who lives in the heart of all living entities.

Pārijāta—a type of flower found on the heavenly planets.

Prakṛta-sahajiyā—pseudodevotees of Kṛṣṇa who fail to understand His absolute, transcendental position.

Prāṇāyāma—the yogic breathing exercises.

Prasādam—food first offered to the Supreme Lord and then distributed.

Rasa—a transcendental relationship between the individual soul and the Supreme Lord.

Rāsa-līlā—Lord Kṛṣṇa's transcendental pastime of dancing with the *gopīs.*

Samādhi—trance; deep absorption in meditation upon the Supreme.

Saṅkīrtana-yajña—the chanting of the holy names of God, which is the recommended sacrifice for this age.

Sannyāsī—one who is in the renounced order of spiritual life.
Śāstras—revealed scriptures.
Sāyujya-mukti—the liberation of merging into the existence of the Supreme Lord.
Siddhi—a mystic yogic perfection.
Śiva—the demigod in charge of annihilation and the mode of ignorance.
Śrīmad-Bhāgavatam—the authoritative Vedic scripture that deals exclusively with the pastimes of the Personality of Godhead and His devotees.
Sudarśana—the wheel that is the personal weapon of Viṣṇu or Kṛṣṇa.
Śūdras—the spiritual order of society who are not very intelligent and are unqualified for any work other than menial service.
Śyāmasundara—a name of Kṛṣṇa. *Śyāma* means "blackish," and *sundara* means "very beautiful."

Tapasya—austerity.
Tilaka—a clay mark that decorates the faces of Kṛṣṇa and His devotees.
Tulasī—a great devotee in the form of a plant, who is very dear to Lord Kṛṣṇa.

Vaiṣṇava—a devotee of the Supreme Lord Viṣṇu or Kṛṣṇa.
Vaiśyas—the agricultural community in Vedic culture, who protect cows and cultivate crops.
Viṣṇu—the Supreme Lord; an expansion of Lord Kṛṣṇa for the creation and maintenance of the material world.

Yajña—sacrifice.
Yoga—the process of linking with the Supreme.
Yogamāyā—the principal internal (spiritual) potency of the Supreme Lord.
Yogī—one who practices *yoga*.

Sanskrit Pronunciation Guide

The system of transliteration used in this book conforms to a system which scholars have accepted to indicate the pronunciation of each sound in the Sanskrit language.

The short vowel **a** is pronounced like the **u** in b**u**t, long **ā** like the **a** in f**a**r. Short **i** is pronounced as **i** in p**i**n, long **ī** as in p**i**que, short **u** as in p**u**ll and long **ū** as in r**u**le. The vowel **ṛ** is pronounced like **ri** in **ri**m, **e** like the **ey** in th**ey**, **o** like the **o** in g**o**, **ai** like the **ai** in **ai**sle and **au** like the **ow** in h**ow**. The *anusvāra* (**ṁ**) is pronounced like the **n** in the French word *bo***n**, and *visarga* (**ḥ**) is pronounced as a final **h** sound. At the end of a couplet, **aḥ** is pronounced **aha** and **iḥ** is pronounced **ihi**.

The guttural consonants—**k, kh, g, gh** and **ṅ**—are pronounced from the throat in much the same manner as in English. **K** is pronounced as in **k**ite, **kh** as in E**ckh**art, **g** as in **g**ive, **gh** as in di**g-h**ard and **ṅ** as in si**ng**.

The palatal consonants—**c, ch, j, jh** and **ñ**—are pronounced with the tongue touching the firm ridge behind the teeth. **C** is pronounced as in **ch**air, **ch** as in staun**ch-h**eart, **j** as in **j**oy, **jh** as in he**dgeh**og and **ñ** as in ca**n**yon.

The cerebral consonants—**ṭ, ṭh, ḍ, ḍh** and **ṇ**—are pronounced with the tip of the tongue turned up and drawn back against the dome of the palate. **Ṭ** is pronounced as in **t**ub, **ṭh** as in ligh**t-h**eart, **ḍ** as in **d**ove, **ḍh** as in re**d-h**ot and **ṇ** as in **n**ut.

The dental consonants—**t, th, d, dh** and **n**—are pronounced in the same manner as the cerebrals, but with the forepart of the tongue against the teeth.

The labial consonants—**p, ph, b, bh** and **m**—are pronounced with the lips. **P** is pronounced as in **p**ine, **ph** as in u**ph**ill, **b** as in **b**ird, **bh** as in ru**b-h**ard and **m** as in **m**other.

The semivowels—**y, r, l** and **v**—are pronounced as in **y**es,

run, **l**ight and **v**ine respectively. The sibilants—**ś**, **ṣ** and **s**—are pronounced, respectively, as in the German word **s***prechen* and the English words **sh**ine and **s**un. The letter **h** is pronounced as in **h**ome.

Centres of the International Society for Krishna Consciousness

Founder-*Ācārya:* His Divine Grace
A.C. Bhaktivedanta Swami Prabhupāda

November 1995

UNITED KINGDOM AND IRELAND

Belfast, Northern Ireland – Brookland, 140 Upper Dunmurray Lane, BT17 OHE/ Tel. +44 (1232) 620530

Birmingham, England – 84 Stanmore Rd., Edgbaston, B16 9TB/ Tel. +44 (121) 420-4999

Bristol, England – 2 Perry Rd., Bristol BS1 5BQ/ Tel. +44 (1275) 853788

Coventry, England – Sri Sri Radha Krishna Cultural Centre, Kingfield Rd., Radford (mail: 19 Gloucester St., CV1 3BZ)/ Tel. +44 (1203) 555420

Dublin, Ireland – Hare Krishna Centre, 56 Dame St., Dublin 2/ Tel. +353 (1) 6791306

Glasgow, Scotland – Karuna Bhavan, Bankhouse Road, Lesmahagow, Lanarkshire ML11 OES/ Tel. +44 (1555) 894790

Leicester, England – 21/21A Thoresby St., North Evington, Leicester LE5 4GU/ Tel. +44 (116) 2762587

Liverpool, England – 114 Bold Street, Liverpool L1 4HY/ Tel. +44 (151) 708-9400

London, England (City) – Sri Sri Radha Krishna Temple, 10 Soho St., London W1V 5DA/ Tel. +44 (171) 4373662

London, England (Country) – Bhaktivedanta Manor, Letchmore Heath, Watford, Hertfordshire WD2 8EP/ Tel. +44 (1923) 857244

London (south) – 42 Enmore Road, South Norwood, London SE25 Tel. +44 (181) 6564296

Manchester, England – 20 Mayfield Rd., Whalley Range, Manchester M16 8FT/ Tel. +44 (161) 2264416

Newcastle upon Tyne, England – Hare Krishna Centre, 21 Leazes Park Rd., NE1 4PF/ Tel. +44 (191) 2220150

FARM COMMUNITIES

Lisnaskea, Northern Ireland – Hare Krishna Island BT92 9GN Lisnaskea, Co. Fremanagh/ Tel. +44 (13657) 21512

London, England – (contact Bhaktivedanta Manor)

Rathgorragh, Ireland – Kiltegan, County Wicklow/ Tel. +353 (508) 73305

RESTAURANTS

London, England – Govinda's (at ISKCON London, City)

Manchester, England – Krishna's, 20 Cyril St., Manchester 14

Kṛṣṇa conscious programmes are held regularly in more than twenty other cities in the U.K. For information, contact Bhaktivedanta Books Ltd., Reader Services Dept., P.O. Box 324, Borehamwood, Herts. WD6 1NB/ Tel. (0181) 9051244.

NORTH AMERICA

CANADA

Calgary, Alberta–313 Fourth St. N.E., T2E 3S3/ Tel. +1 (403) 238-0602
Montreal, Quebec–1626 Pie IX Boulevard, H1V 2C5/ Tel. +1 (514) 521-1301
Ottawa, Ontario–212 Somerset St. E., K1N 6V4/ Tel. +1 (613) 565-6544
Regina, Saskatchewan–1279 Retallack St., S4T 2H8/ Tel. +1 (306) 525-1640
Toronto, Ontario–243 Avenue Rd., M5R 2J6/ Tel. +1 (416) 922-5415
Vancouver, B.C.–5462 S.E. Marine Dr., Burnaby V5J 3G8/ Tel. +1 (604) 433-9728

FARM COMMUNITY

Ashcroft, B.C.–Saranagati Dhama, Box 99, Ashcroft, B.C. V0K 1A0

RESTAURANTS

Ottawa–(at ISKCON Ottawa)
Toronto–Hare Krishna Dining Room (at ISKCON Toronto)
Vancouver–Hare Krishna Buffet (at ISKCON Vancouver)
Vancouver–The Hare Krishna Place, 46 Begbie St., New Westminster

USA

Atlanta, Georgia–1287 South Ponce de Leon Ave. N.E., 30306/ Tel. +1 (404) 378-9234
Baltimore, Maryland–200 Bloomsbury Ave., Catonsville, 21228/ Tel. +1 (410) 744-1624 or 4069
Boise, Idaho–1615 Martha St., 83706/ Tel. +1 (208) 344-4274
Boston, Massachusetts–72 Commonwealth Ave., 02116/ Tel. +1 (617) 247-8611
Champaign, Illinois–608 W. Elm St., 61801/ Tel. +1 (217) 344-2562
Chicago, Illinois–1716 W. Lunt Ave., 60626/ Tel. +1 (312) 973-0900
Columbus, Ohio–379 W. Eighth Ave., 43201/ Tel. +1 (614)421-1661
Dallas, Texas–5430 Gurley Ave. 75223/ Tel. +1 (214) 827-6330
Denver, Colorado–1400 Cherry St., 80220/ Tel. +1 (303) 333-5461
Detroit, Michigan–383 Lenox Ave., 48215/ Tel. +1 (313) 824-6000
Encinitas, California–468 First St., 92024/ Tel. +1 (619) 634-1698
Gainesville, Florida–214 N.W. 14th St., 32603/ Tel. +1 (904) 336-4183
Gurabo, Puerto Rico–Route 181, P.O. Box 8440 HC-01, 00778-9763/ Tel. +1 (809) 737-1658
Hartford, Connecticut–1683 Main St., E. Hartford, 06108/ Tel. +1 (203) 289-7252
Honolulu, Hawaii–51 Coelho Way, 96817/ Tel. +1 (808) 595-3947
Houston, Texas–1320 W. 34th St., 77018/ Tel. +1 (713) 686-4482
Laguna Beach, California–285 Legion St. 92651/ Tel. +1 (714) 494-7029
Long Island, New York–197 S. Ocean Ave., Freeport, 11520/ Tel. +1 (516) 223-4909
Los Angeles, California–3764 Watseka Ave., 90034/ Tel. +1 (310) 836-2676
Miami, Florida–3220 Virginia St., 33133 (mail: P.O. Box 337, Coconut Grove, FL 33233)/ Tel. +1 (305) 442-7218
New Orleans, Louisiana–2936 Esplanade Ave., 70119/ Tel. +1 (504) 586-9379
New York, New York–305 Schermerhorn St., Brooklyn, 11217/ Tel. +1 (718) 855-6714
New York, New York–26 Second Avenue, 10003/ Tel. +1 (212) 420-8803
Philadelphia, Pennsylvania–529 South St., 19147/ Tel. +1 (215) 829-0077
St. Louis, Missouri–3926 Lindell Blvd., 63108/ Tel. +1 (314) 535-8085
San Diego, California–1030 Grand Ave., Pacific Beach, 92109/ Tel. +1 (619) 483-2500
San Francisco, California–84 Carl St., 94117/ Tel. +1 (415) 661-7320
San Francisco, California–2334 Stuart St., Berkeley, 94705/ Tel. +1 (510) 540-9215
Seattle, Washington–1420 228th Ave. S.E., Issaquah, 98027/ Tel. +1 (206) 391-3293
Tallahassee, Florida–1323 Nylic St. (mail: P.O. Box 20224, 32304)/ Tel. +1 (904) 681-9258
Topanga, California–20395 Callon Dr. 90290/ Tel. +1 (213) 455-1658
Towaco, New Jersey–(mail: P.O. Box 109, 07082)/ Tel. +1 (201) 299-0970
Tucson, Arizona–711 E. Blacklidge Dr., 85719/ Tel. +1 (602) 792-0630
Walla Walla, Washington–314 E. Poplar, 99362/ Tel. +1 (509) 525-7133
Washington, D.C.–600 Ninth St., NE, 20002/ Tel. +1 (202) 547-1444
Washington, D.C.–10310 Oaklyn Dr., Potomac, Maryland 20854/ Tel. +1 (301) 299-2100

FARM COMMUNITIES

Alachua, Florida (New Ramana-reti)–Box 819, Alachua, 32615/ Tel. +1 (904) 462-2017
Carriere, Mississippi (New Talavan)–31492 Anner Road, 39426/ Tel. +1 (601) 799-1354
Gurabo, Puerto Rico (New Govardhana Hill)–(contact ISKCON Gurabo)
Hillsborough, North Carolina (New Goloka)–1032 Dimmocks Mill Rd., 27278/ Tel. +1 (919) 732-6492
Mulberry, Tennessee (Murari-sevaka)–Rt. No. 1, Box 146-A, 37359/ Tel. +1 (615) 759-6888
Port Royal, Pennsylvania (Gita Nagari)–R.D. No. 1, Box 839, 17082/ Tel. (717) 527-4101

RESTAURANTS

Atlanta, Georgia–The Hare Krishna Dinner Club (at ISKCON Atlanta)

Boise, Idaho – Govinda's, 500 W. Main St./ Tel. +1 (208) 338-9710
Chicago, Illinois – Govinda's Buffet (at ISKCON Chicago)
Columbus, Ohio – (at ISKCON Columbus)
Dallas, Texas – Kalachandji's (at ISKCON Dallas)
Denver, Colorado – Govinda's (at ISKCON Denver)
Eugene, Oregon – Govinda's Vegetarian Buffet, 270 W. 8th St., 97401/ Tel. +1 (503) 686-3531
Gainesville, Florida – Radha's, 125 NW 23rd Ave., 32609/ Tel. +1 (904) 376-9012
Gainesville, Florida – Govinda's, 1222 West University Avenue, 32602/ Tel. +1 (904) 376-9393
Honolulu, Hawaii, – Gauranga's Vegetarian Dining (at ISKCON Honolulu)
Laguna Beach, California – Gauranga's (at ISKCON Laguna Beach)
Los Angeles, California – Govinda's (at ISKCON Los Angeles)
Miami, Florida – (at ISKCON Miami)
New Orleans, Louisiana – (at ISKCON New Orleans)
St. Louis, Missouri – Govinda's (at ISKCON St. Louis)
San Diego, California – Govinda's at the Beach (at ISKCON San Diego)/ Tel. +1 (619) 483-5266
Tucson, Arizona – (at ISKCON Tucson)
Ukiah, California – 111 S. State St., 95482/ Tel. +1 (707) 462-0244

AUSTRALASIA

AUSTRALIA

Adelaide – 227 Henley Beach Road, Torrensville, S.A. 5031 Adelaide/ Tel. +61 (8) 2341378
Brisbane – 95 Bank Rd., Graceville, QLD (mail: P.O. Box 83, Indooroopilly 4068)/ Tel. +61 (7) 379-5455
Canberra – (mail: P.O. Box 1411, Canberra ACT 2060)/ Tel. +61 (6) 290-1869
Melbourne – 197 Danks St., Albert Park, Victoria 3206 (mail: P.O. Box 125)/ Tel. +61 (3) 699-5122
Perth – 356 Murray St., Perth (mail: P.O. Box 102, Bayswater, W.A. 6053)/ Tel. +61 (9) 481-1114 or 370-1552
Sydney – 180 Falcon St., North Sydney, N.S.W. 2060 (mail: P. O. Box 459, Cammeray, N.S.W. 2062)/ Tel. +61 (2) 959-4558

FARM COMMUNITIES

Bambra (New Nandagram) – Oak Hill, Dean's Marsh Road, Bambra, VIC 3241/ Tel. +61 (52) 88-7383
Millfield, N.S.W. – New Gokula Farm, Lewis Lane (off Mt. View Rd. Millfield, near Cessnock), N.S.W. (mail: P.O. Box 399, Cessnock, N.S.W. 2325)/ Tel. +61 (49) 98-1800
Murwillumbah (New Govardhana) – Tyalgum Rd., Eungella, via Murwillumbah, N.S.W. 2484 (mail: P.O. Box 687)/ Tel. +61 (66) 72-6579

RESTAURANTS

Brisbane – Govinda's, 99 Elizabeth St., 1st floor/ Tel. +61 (7) 210-0255
Melbourne – Crossways, 123 Swanston St., Melbourne, VIC 3000/ Tel. +61 (3) 965 02939
Melbourne – Gopal's, 139 Swanston St., Melbourne, VIC 3000/ Tel. +61 (3) 965 01578
Perth – Hare Krishna Food for Life, 200 William St., Northbridge, W.A. 6003/ Tel. +61 (9) 227-1684
Sydney – Govinda's Upstairs and Govinda's Take-Away, 112 Darlinghurst Rd., Darlinghurst, N.S.W. 2010/ Tel. +61 (2) 380-5162
Sydney – 3296 King St., Newtown, N.S.W. 2042/ Tel. +61 (2) 550-6524
Sydney – Gopal's (at ISKCON Sydney, 180 Falcon St.)

NEW ZEALAND AND FIJI

Christchurch, New Zealand – 83 Bealey Ave. (mail: P.O. Box 25-190 Christchurch/ Tel. +64 (3) 3665-174
Labasa, Fiji – Delailabasa, Labasa (mail: P.O. Box 133, Labasa)/ Tel. +679-812912
Lautoka, Fiji – 5 Tavewa Ave., Lautoka (mail: P.O. Box 125, Lautoka)/ Tel. +679-664112
Port Moresby, Papua New Guinea – Section 23, Lot 46, Gordonia St., Hohola (mail: P.0. Box 571, POM NCD)/ Tel. +675 259213
Rakiraki, Fiji – Rewasa, Rakiraki (mail: P.O. Box 204)/ Tel. +679-694243
Suva, Fiji – Nasinu 7½ miles (P.O. Box 7315, Suva)/ Tel. +679-393599
Wellington, New Zealand – 60 Wade St., Wadestown, Wellington (mail: P.O. Box 2753, Wellington)/ Tel. +64 (4) 4720510

FARM COMMUNITY

Auckland, New Zealand (New Varshan) – Hwy. 18, Riverhead, next to Huapai Golf Course (mail: R.D. 2, Kumeu, Auckland)/ Tel. +64 (9) 4128075

RESTAURANTS

Auckland, New Zealand – Gopal's, 1st floor, Civic House, 291 Queen St./ Tel. +64 (9) 3034885
Christchurch, New Zealand – Gopal's, 143 Worcester St./ Tel. +64 (3) 3667-035
Labasa, Fiji – Govinda's, Naseakula Road/ Tel. +679-811364
Lautoka, Fiji – Gopal's, Corner of Yasawa St. and Naviti St./ Tel. +679-662990

Suva, Fiji – Gopal's, 18 Pratt St./ Tel. +679-314154

EUROPE

GERMANY

Berlin – Johannisthaler Chausee 78, 12259 Berlin (Britz)/ Tel. +49 (30) 6312400
Flensburg – Neuhörup 1, 24980 Hörup/ Tel. +49 (4639) 7336
Hamburg – Mühlenstr. 93, 25421 Pinneberg/ Tel. +49 (4101) 23931
Heidelberg – Center for Vedic Studies, Kurfürsten Anlage 5, 69115 Heidelberg/ Tel. +49 (6221) 165101
Cologne – ISKCON (info centre), Taunusstr. 40, 51105 Köln-Gremberg/ Tel. +49 (221) 8303778, Fax +49 (221) 8370485

There are also centres in Wiesbaden, Hannover, Leipzig, Dresden, Munich, Nuremberg and Stuttgart. Please contact the info centre in Cologne for further information.

FARM COMMUNITY

Jandelsbrunn – Nava-Jiyada-Nrsimha-Ksetra, Zielberg 20, 94118 Jandelsbrunn/ Tel. +49 (8583) 316

RESTAURANTS

Berlin – Higher Taste, Kurfürstendamm 157/158, 10709 Berlin/ Tel. +49 (30) 8929917
Heidelberg – Higher Taste (at ISKCON Heidelberg)
Cologne – Govinda (at ISKCON Cologne)

ITALY

Asti – Roatto, Frazione Valle Reale 20/ Tel. +39 (141) 938406
Bergamo – Villaggio Hare Krishna, Via Galileo Galilei 41, 24040 Chignolo D'isola (BG)/ Tel. +39 (35) 490706
Bologna – Via Ramo Barchetta 2, 40010 Bentivoglio (BO)/ Tel. +39 (51) 863924
Catania – Via San Nicolo al Borgo 28, 95128 Catania, Sicilia/ Tel. +39 (95) 522-252
Naples – Via Vesuvio, N33, Ercolano LNA7/ Tel. +39 (81) 739-0398
Rome – Nepi, Sri Gaura Mandala, Via Mazzanese Km. 0,700 (dalla Cassia uscita Calcata), Pian del Pavone (Viterbo)/ Tel. +39 (761) 527038
Vicenza – Via Roma 9, 36020 Albettone (Vicenza)/ Tel. +39 (444) 790573 or 790566

FARM COMMUNITY

Florence (Villa Vrindavan) – Via Communale degli Scopeti 108, S. Andrea in Percussina, San Casciano, Val di Pesa (FI) 5002/ Tel. +39 (55) 820-054

RESTAURANTS

Catania – Govinda's (at ISKCON Catania)
Milan – Govinda's, Via Valpetrosa 3/5, 20123 Milano/ Tel. +39 (2) 862-417

SWEDEN

Gothenburg – Höjdgatan 22, 43136 Mölndal/ Tel. +46 (31) 879648, Fax: 879657
Grödinge – Korsnäs Gård, 14792 Grödinge/ Tel. +46 (8) 53029151
Karlstad – Govindas, Västra Torggatan 16, Box 5155, 65005 Karlstad/ Tel. +46 (54) 152000, Fax: 152001
Malmö – Hare Krishna Temple, Gustav Adolfs Torg 10A, 21139 Malmö/ Tel. +46 (40) 127181
Stockholm – Fridhemsgatan 22, 11240 Stockholm/ Tel. +46 (8) 6549002
Uppsala – Nannaskolan sal F 3, Kungsgatan 22, 75332 Uppsala (mail: P.O. Box 833, 75108 Uppsala)/ Tel. +46 (18) 102924
Lund – Bredgatan 28 ipg, 22221 Lund/ Tel. +46 (46) 120413, Fax 188804

FARM COMMUNITY

Järna – Almviks Gård, 15395 Järna/ Tel. +46 (8) 55152050 or 55152073

RESTAURANTS

Gothenburg – Govindas Restaurang, Viktoriagatan 2A, 41125 Göteborg/ Tel. +46 (31) 139698
Malmö – Higher Taste, Amiralsgatan 6, 21155 Malmö/ Tel. +46 (40) 970600
Stockholm – Govindas (at ISKCON Stockholm)
Uppsala – Govindas (at ISKCON Uppsala)
Lund – Govindas i Lund (at ISKCON Lund)

SWITZERLAND

Basel – Hammerstrasse 11, 4058 Basel/ Tel. +41 (61) 6932638
Bern – Govinda, Marktgasse 7, 3011 Bern/ Tel. +41 (31) 3123825

Lugano – Via ai Grotti, 6862 Rancate (TI)/ Tel. +41 (91) 466616
Zürich – Bergstrasse 54, 8030 Zürich/ Tel. +41 (1) 2623388

RESTAURANT

Zürich – Preyergasse 16, 8001 Zürich/ Tel. +41 (1) 2518851

OTHER COUNTRIES

Amsterdam, The Netherlands – Van Hilligaertstr. 17, 1072 JX/ Tel. +31 (20) 6751404
Antwerp, Belgium – Amerikalei 184, 2000 Antwerpen/ Tel. +32 (3) 2370037
Athens, Greece – Bhakti-yoga Centre, Methimnis 18, Kipseli, 11257 Athens/ Tel. +30 (1) 8658384
Barcelona, Spain – c/de L'Oblit 67, 08026 Barcelona/ Tel. +34 (93) 347-9933
Belgrade, Serbia – VVZ-Veda, Custendilska 17, 11000 Beograd/ Tel. +381 (11) 781-695
Budapest, Hungary – Hare Krishna Temple, Mariaremetei ut. 77, Budapest 1028 II/ Tel. +36 (1) 1768774
Cakovec, Croatia – Radnicka 2, Savska Ves 42300 Cakovec/ Tel. +385 (42) 311195
Debrecen, Hungary – L. Hegyi Mihalyne U62, Debrecen 4030/ Tel. +36 (52) 342-496
Dôle, France – Château Bellevue, 39700 Châtenois / Tel. + 33 (84) 728235
Dunajská Lužná, Slovakia – ISKCON, Dunajská Lužná 707, 90042/ Tel. +42 (7) 986516
Gdansk, Poland – ISKCON Temple Gdansk, ul. Cedrowa 5, Gdansk 80-125 (mail: MTSK, 80-958 Gdansk 50, skr. poczt. 364)/ Tel./Fax +48 (58) 329665
Helsinki, Finland – Ruoholahdenkatu 24d, 00180, Helsinki/ Tel. +358 (0) 6949879
Hillerød, Denmark – Bauneholm, Baunevej 23, Bendstrup, 3400 Hillerød/ Tel. +45 (42) 286446, Fax (42) 287331
Iasi, Romania – Stradela Moara De Vint 72, 6600 Iasi
Kaunas, Lithuania – Savanoriu 37, 3000 Kaunas/ Tel. +370 (7) 222574
Krakow, Poland – ul. Podedworze 23a, 30-686 Krakow-Piaski Wielkie/ Tel. +48 (12) 588283
Lisbon, Portugal – Rua Fernao Lopes 6, Cascais 2750 (mail: Apartado 2489, Lisboa 1112)/ Tel. +351 (11) 286713
Ljubljana, Slovenia – Hare Krišna center, Žibertova 27, 61000 Ljubljana/ Tel. +386 (61) 1312319 or 1312124, Fax 1311225
Madrid, Spain – Espíritu Santo 19, 28004 Madrid/ Tel. +34 (91) 521-3096
Málaga, Spain – Ctra. Alora, 3 int., 29140 Churriana/ Tel. +34 (952) 621038
Osijek, Croatia – Bartola Kasica 32, 5400 Osijek/ Tel. +385 (54) 127829
Oslo, Norway – Jonsrudveien 1G, 0274 Oslo/ Tel. +47 (22) 552243
Paris, France – 31 Rue Jean Vacquier, 93160 Noisy-le-Grand/ Tel. +33 (1) 43043263
Plovdiv, Bulgaria – ul. Prosveta 56, kv. Proslav, Plovdiv 4015/ Tel. +359 (32) 446962
Porto, Portugal – Rua S. Miguel, 19 C.P. 4000 (mail: Apartado 4108, 4002 Porto Codex)/ Tel. +351 (2) 2005469
Prague, Czech Republic – Jilova 290, Praha 5-Zlicin 155 21/ Tel. +42 (2) 3021282 or 3021608
Pula, Croatia – Vinkuran centar 58, 52000 Pula/ Tel. +385 (52) 541425
Riga, Latvia – Krishyana Barona 56, LV 1001 Riga/ Tel. +371 (2) 272490
Rijeka, Croatia – Bhaktivedanta Cultural Centre, Boze Starca Juričeva 5, 51000 Rijeka (mail: Rijeka PP 61)/ Tel. +385 (51) 335893
Rotterdam, The Netherlands – Braamberg 45, 2905 BK Capelle a/d Ijssel/ Tel. +31 (10) 4580873
Santa Cruz de Tenerife, Spain – C/ Castillo 44, Santa Cruz 38003, Tenerife/ Tel. +34 (922) 241035
Sarajevo, Bosnia-Herzegovina – Saburina 11, 71000 Sarajevo/ Tel. +381 (71) 531 154
Septon-Durbuy, Belgium – Château de Petite Somme, 6940 Septon (Durbuy)/ Tel. +32 (86) 322926
Skopje, Macedonia – Roze Luksemburg 13, 91000 Skopje / Tel. +389 (91) 201451
Sofia, Bulgaria – ul. Zelen bor 3, kv. Simeonovo–Iztok, Sofia 1434/ Tel. +359 (2) 6352608
Split, Croatia – Hinduvaisnavska zajednica, Cesta Mutogras 20, 58312 Podstrana (mail: P.P. 290, 58001 Split)/ Tel. +385 (21) 651265
Timisoara, Romania – Porumbescu 92, 1900 Timisoara, Romania/ Tel. +40 (961) 54776
Turku, Finland – Kaurakatu 39, 20740 Turku 74/ Tel. +358 (21) 364 055
Vilnius, Lithuania – Raugyklos 23, 2024 Vilnius/ Tel. +370 (2) 661218
Warsaw, Poland – Mysiadlo k. Warszawy, ul. Zakret 11, 05-500 Piaseczno/ Tel. +48 (22) 562-711
Wroclaw, Poland – ul. Nowowiejska 87/8, 50-340 Wroclaw/ Tel./Fax +48 (71) 225704
Zagreb, Croatia – Centar za Vedske Studije, I Bizek 5, 41090 Zagreb (mail: P.P. 68, 41001 Zagreb)/ Tel. +385 (41) 190548

FARM COMMUNITIES

Czech Republic – Krsnův Dvůr c. 1, 257 28 Chotysany
France (La Nouvelle Mayapura) – Domaine d'Oublaisse, 36360, Lucay le Mâle/ Tel. +33 (54) 402481
Poland (New Santipura) – Czarnow 21, k. Kamiennej gory, woj. Jelenia Gora/ Tel. +48 (8745) 1892
Spain (New Vraja Mandala) – (Santa Clara) Brihuega, Guadalajara/ Tel. +34 (911) 280018

RESTAURANTS

Barcelona, Spain – Restaurante Govinda, Plaza de la Villa de Madrid 4-5, 08002 Barcelona
Copenhagen, Denmark – Govinda's Vegetarisk Restaurant, Nørre Farimagsgade 82, København/ Tel. +45 (33) 337444

Oslo, Norway – Krishna's Cuisine, Kirkevejen 59b, 0364 Oslo/ Tel. +47 (22) 606250
Prague, Czech Republic – Govinda's, Nahrázi 5, 180 00 Praha 8/ Tel. +42 (2) 6837226
Prague, Czech Republic – Soukenická 27, 110 00 Praha 1/Tel. +42 (2) 4816016
Septon-Durbuy, Belgium – Gopinatha's Garden (at ISKCON Septon-Durbuy)
Tallinn, Estonia – Damodara, Lauteri 1, EE 0001 Tallinn/ Tel. +372 (2) 442650
Vienna, Austria – Govinda, Lindengasse 2A, 1070 Wien/ Tel. +43 (1) 5222817

COMMONWEALTH OF INDEPENDENT STATES

RUSSIA

Moscow – Khoroshevskoye shosse d. 8, korp. 3, 125 284, Moscow/ Tel. +7 (095) 255-67-11
Nijni Novgorod – ul. Ivana Mochalova, 7-69, 603904 Nijni Novgorod/ Tel. +7 (8312) 252592
Novosibirsk – ul. Leningradskaya 111-20, Novosibirsk
Perm (Ural Region) – Pr. Mira, 113-142, 614065 Perm/ Tel. +7 (3442) 335740
St. Petersburg – ul. Burtseva 20-147, St. Petersburg 190000/ Tel. +7 (812) 1502880
Ulyanovsk – ul. Glinki, 10/ Tel. +7 (0842) 221-42-89
Vladivostok – ul. Ridneva 5-1, 690087 Vladivostok/ Tel. +7 (4232) 268943

UKRAINE

Dnepropetrovsk – ul. Ispolkomovskaya, 56A, 320029 Dnepropetrovsk/ Tel. +7 (0562) 445029
Donetsk – ul. Treneva, 3 Flat N44, Donetsk
Kharkov – ul. Verchnegijevskaya, 43, 310015 Kharkov
Kiev – Menjinskogo, 21-B., 252 054 Kiev/ Tel. +7 (044) 2444944
Lvov – 292066 Lvivska obl. Buski rajon. S. Zbolotni Chuchmani
Odessa – Klubnichny Per., Vinogradny Tupik, Sanatory "Rodina," 8 Kor.
Vinnitza – Chkalov St., 5, Vinnitza 26800/ Tel. +7 (4322) 23152

OTHER COUNTRIES

Alma Ata, Kazakstan – Per Kommunarov, 5, 480022 Alma Ata/ Tel. +7 (3272) 353830
Baku, Azerbaijan – pos. 8-oy km, per. Zardabi 2, 370060 Baku/ Tel. +7 (8922) 212376
Bishkek, Kyrgizstan – Per. Omski, 5, 720000 Bishkek/ Tel. +7 (3312) 472683
Kishinev, Moldavia – ul. George Asaki, 68/1 Flat 105, 277028 Kishinev/ Tel. +7 (127) 737024
Minsk, Byelorussia – ul. Pavlova 11, 220 053 Minsk
Sukhumi, Georgia – Pr. Mira 274, Sukhumi
Tashkent, Uzbekistan – ul. Babadjanova, 36 Flat 34, 700097 Tashkent
Tbilisi, Georgia – ul. Kacharava, 16, 380044 Tbilisi/ Tel. +7 (8832) 623326

ASIA

INDIA

Agartala, Tripura – Assam-Agartala Rd., Banamalipur, 799001
Ahmedabad, Gujarat – Satellite Rd., Gandhinagar Highway Crossing, Ahmedabad 380 054/ Tel. +91 (79) 649945 or 649982
Allahabad, U.P. – 403 Baghambari Housing Scheme, Bharadwaj Puram, Allahapur, Allahabad 211006/ Tel. +91 (532) 609213 or 607885
Bamanbore, Gujarat – N.H. 8A, Surendranagar District
Bangalore, Karnataka – Hare Krishna Hill, 1 'R' Block, Chord Road, Rajaji Nagar 560 010/ Tel. +91 (80) 321 956 or 342 818 or 322 346
Bhayandar, Maharashtra – Shivaji Chowk, Station Road, Bhayandar (West), Thane 401101/ Tel. +91 (22) 8191920
Bhubaneswar, Orissa – National Highway No. 5, Nayapali, 751001/ Tel. +91 (674) 413517 or 413475
Bombay, Maharashtra – Hare Krishna Land, Juhu 400 049/ Tel. +91 (22) 6206860
Calcutta, W. Bengal – 3C Albert Rd., 700 017/ Tel. +91 (33) 2473757 or 2476075
Chandigarh, Punjab – Hare Krishna Land, Dakshin Marg, Sector 36-B, 160 036/ Tel. +91 (172) 601590 or 603232
Coimbatore, Tamil Nadu – Padmam 387, VGR Puram, Alagesan Road 1, 641011/ Tel. +91 (422) 445978 or 442749
Gauhati, Assam – Ulubari Charali, Gauhati 781 001/ Tel. +91 (361) 31208
Guntur, A.P. – Opp. Sivalayam, Peda Kakani 522 509
Hyderabad, A.P. – Hare Krishna Land, Nampally Station Rd., 500 001/ Tel. +91 (40) 592018 or 552924
Imphal, Manipur – Hare Krishna Land, Airport Road, 795 001/ Tel. +91 (385) 21587
Kurukshetra, Haryana – 369 Gudri Muhalla, Main Bazaar, 132118/ Tel. +91 (1744) 32806 or 33529
Madras, Tamil Nadu – 59, Burkit Rd., T. Nagar, 600 017/ Tel. +91 443266

Mayapur, W. Bengal – Shree Mayapur Chandrodaya Mandir, Shree Mayapur Dham, Dist. Nadia (mail: P.O. Box 10279, Ballyganj, Calcutta 700 019)/ Tel. +91 (3472) 45239 or 45240 or 45233
Moirang, Manipur – Nongban Ingkhon, Tidim Rd./ Tel. +91 795133
Nagpur, Maharashtra – 70 Hill Road, Ramnagar, 440 010/ Tel. +91 (712) 529932
New Delhi – Sant Nagar Main Road (Garhi), behind Nehru Place Complex (mail: P.O. Box 7061), New Delhi 110 065/ Tel. +91 (11) 6419701 or 6412058
New Delhi – 14/63, Punjabi Bagh, 110 026/ Tel. +91 (11) 5410782
Pandharpur, Maharashtra – Hare Krishna Ashram (across Chandrabhaga River), Dist. Sholapur, 413 304/ Tel. +91 (218) 623473
Patna, Bihar – Rajendra Nagar Road No. 12, 800 016/ Tel. +91 (612) 50765
Pune, Maharashtra – 4 Tarapoor Rd., Camp, 411 001/ Tel. +91 (212) 667259
Puri, Orissa – Sipasurubuli Puri, Dist. Puri
Puri, Orissa – Bhakti Kuthi, Swargadwar, Puri/ Tel. +91 (6752) 23740
Secunderabad, A.P. – 27 St. John's Road, 500 026/ Tel. +91 (40) 805232
Silchar, Assam – Ambikapatti, Silchar, Cachar Dist., 788004
Siliguri, W. Bengal – Gitalpara 734 401/ Tel. +91 (353) 26619
Surat, Gujarat – Rander Rd., Jahangirpura, 395 005/ Tel. +91 (261) 685516 or 685891
Tirupati, A.P. – K.T. Road, Vinayaka Nagar 517 507/ Tel. +91 (8574) 20114
Trivandrum, Kerala – T.C. 224/1485, WC Hospital Rd., Thycaud, 695 014/ Tel. +91 (471) 68197
Udhampur, Jammu and Kashmir – Srila Prabhupada Ashram, Prabhupada Marg, Prabhupada Nagar, Udhampur 182 101/ Tel. +91 (199) 298
Vallabh Vidyanagar, Gujarat – ISKCON Hare Krishna Land, Vallabh Vidyanagar 338 120/ Tel. +91 (2692) 30796
Vrindavana, U.P. – Krishna-Balaram Mandir, Bhaktivedanta Swami Marg, Raman Reti, Mathura Dist. 281124/ Tel. +91 (565) 442-478 or 442-355

FARM COMMUNITIES

Ahmedabad District, Gujarat – Hare Krishna Farm, Katwada (contact ISKCON Ahmedabad)
Assam – Karnamadhu, Dist. Karimganj
Chamorshi, Maharashtra – 78 Krishnanagar Dham, District Gadhachiroli, 442 603
Hyderabad, A.P. – P.O. Dabilpur Village, Medchal Tq., R.R. District, 501 401/ Tel. +91 552924
Mayapur, W. Bengal – (contact ISKCON Mayapur)
Shimoga Dist., Karnataka – Vallor Valley, P.O. Nagodi, Hosanagar Taluq 577425, Shimoga Dist., Karnataka

RESTAURANTS

Bombay – Govinda's (at Hare Krishna Land)
Calcutta – Hare Krishna Karma-Free Confectionary, 6 Russel Street, Calcutta 700 071
Mayapur – Govinda's (at ISKCON Mayapur)
Vrindavana – Krishna-Balaram Mandir Guesthouse

OTHER COUNTRIES

Bali, Indonesia – (contact ISKCON Jakarta)
Bangkok, Thailand – 139 Soi Puttha Osotha, New Road (near GPO), Bangkok 10500
Cagayan de Oro, Philippines – 30 Dahlia St., Ilaya Carmen, 900 Cagayan de Oro (c/o Sepulveda's Compound)
Chittagong, Bangladesh – Caitanya Cultural Society, Sri Pundarik Dham, Mekhala, Hathazari (mail: GPO Box 877, Chittagong)/ Tel. +880 (31) 225822
Colombo, Sri Lanka – 188 New Chetty St., Colombo 13/ Tel. +94 (1) 433325
Dhaka, Bangladesh – 5 Chandra Mohon Basak St., Banagram, Dhaka 1203/ Tel. +880 (2) 252428
Hong Kong – 27 Chatam Road South, 6/F, Kowloon/ Tel. +852 7396818
Iloilo City, Philippines – 13-1-1 Tereos St., La Paz, Iloilo City, Iloilo/ Tel. +63 (33) 73391
Jakarta, Indonesia – P.O. Box 2694, Jakarta Pusat 10001/ Tel. +62 (21) 4899646
Jessore, Bangladesh – Nitai Gaur Mandir, Kathakhali Bazaar, P.O. Panjia, Dist. Jessore
Jessore, Bangladesh – Rupa-Sanatana Smriti Tirtha, Ramsara, P.O. Magura Hat, Dist. Jessore
Kathmandu, Nepal – Budhanilkantha, Kathmandu (mail: P.O. Box 3520)/ Tel. +977 (1) 225087
Kuala Lumpur, Malaysia – Lot 9901, Jalan Awan Jawa, Taman Yarl, off 5½ Mile, Jalan Kelang Lama, Petaling/ Tel. +60 (3) 780-7355, -7360, -7369
Manila, Philippines – 170 R. Fernandez, San Juan, Metro Manila/ Tel. +63 (2) 707410
Taipei, Taiwan – (mail: c/o ISKCON Hong Kong)
Tel Aviv, Israel – P.O. Box 48163, Tel Aviv 61480/ Tel. +972 (3) 5223718
Tokyo, Japan – 1-29-2-202 Izumi, Suginami-ku, Tokyo 168/ Tel. +81 (3) 3327-1541
Yogyakarta, Indonesia – P.O. Box 25, Babarsari YK, DIY

FARM COMMUNITIES

Indonesia – Govinda Kunja (contact ISKCON Jakarta)
Malaysia – Jalan Sungai Manik, 36000 Teluk Intan, Perak

Philippines (Hare Krishna Paradise) – 231 Pagsa-bungan Rd., Basak, Mandaue City/ Tel. +63 (32) 83254

RESTAURANTS

Cebu, Philippines – Govinda's, 26 Sanchiangko St.

Kuala Lumpur, Malaysia – Govinda's, 16-1 Jalan Bunus Enam, Masjid India/ Tel. +60 (3) 7807355 or 7807360 or 7807369

Singapore – Govinda's Restaurant, B1-19 Cuppage Plaza 5, Koek Rd., 0922/ Tel. +65 735-6755

AFRICA

Abeokuta, Nigeria – Ibadan Rd., Obanatoka (mail: P.O. Box 5177)

Benin City, Nigeria – 108 Lagos Rd., Uselu/ Tel. +234 (52) 247900

Durban, S. Africa – Chatsworth Centre, Chatsworth 4030 (mail: P.O. Box 56003)/ Tel. +27 (31) 433-328

Enugu, Nigeria – 8 Church Close, off College Rd., Housing Estate, Abakpa-Nike

Ibadan, Nigeria – 1 Ayo Akintoba St., Agbowo, University of Ibadan

Johannesburg, S. Africa – 14 Goldreich St., Hillbrow 2001 (mail: P.O. Box 10667, Johannesburg 2000)/ Tel. +27 (11) 484-3273

Jos, Nigeria – 5A Liberty Dam Close (mail: P.O. Box 6557, Jos)

Kaduna, Nigeria – 8B Dabo Rd., Kaduna South (mail: P.O. Box 1121, Kaduna)

Kampala, Uganda – Bombo Rd., near Makerere University (mail: P.O. Box 1647, Kampala)

Cape Town, S. Africa – 17 St. Andrews Rd., Rondebosch 7700/ Tel. +27 (21) 689 1529

Kisumu, Kenya – P.O. Box 547/ Tel. +254 (35) 42546

Lagos, Nigeria – 25 Jaiyeola Ajata St., Ajao Estate, off International Airport Express Rd., Lagos (mail: P.O. Box 8793)/ Tel./Fax +234 (1) 876169

Marondera, Zimbabwe – 6 Pine Street (mail: P.O. Box 339)/ Tel. +263 (28) 8877801

Mombasa, Kenya – Hare Krishna House, Sauti Ya Kenya and Kisumu Rds. (mail: P.O. Box 82224, Mombasa)/ Tel. +254 (11) 312248

Nairobi, Kenya – Muhuroni Close, off West Nagara Rd. (mail: P.O. Box 28946, Nairobi)/ Tel. +254 (2) 744365

Phoenix, Mauritius – Hare Krishna Land, Pont Fer, Phoenix (mail: P.O. Box 108, Quartre Bornes, Mauritius)/ Tel. +230 696-5804

Port Elizabeth, S. Africa – 15 Whitehall Court, Western Rd., Central Port Elizabeth 6001/ Tel./Fax +27 (41) 521-102

Port Harcourt, Nigeria – Second Tarred Road, Ogwaja Waterside (mail: P.O. Box 4429, Trans Amadi)

Warri, Nigeria – Okwodiete Village, Kilo 8, Effurun/Orerokpe Rd. (mail: P.O. Box 1922, Warri)

FARM COMMUNITY

Mauritius (ISKCON Vedic Farm) – Hare Krishna Rd., Vrindaban, Bon Acceuil/ Tel. +230 418-3955

RESTAURANTS

Durban, S. Africa – Govinda's (contact ISKCON Durban)

Johannesburg, S. Africa – (contact ISKCON Johannesburg)

LATIN AMERICA

BRAZIL

Belém, PA – Rua Lindolpho Collor, 42, Marco, CEP 66095-310

Belo Horizonte, MG – Rua St. Antonio, 45, Venda Nova, CEP 31515-100

Brasilia, DF – HIGS 706, Bloco C, Casa 29, CEP 70350-752/ Tel. +55 (61) 242-7579

Caxias Do Sul, RS – Rua Italia Travi, 601, Rio Branco, CEP 95097-710

Curitiba, PR – Comunidade Nova Goloka, Pinhais (mail: R. Cel Anibal dos Santos 67, Vila Fanny, Curitiba, CEP 81030-210)

Florianopolis, SC – Rua Joao de Souza, 200, Praia do Santinho, CEP 88056-678

Fortaleza, CE – Rua Jose Loureço, 2114, Aldeota, CEP 60115-288/ Tel. +55 (85) 266-1273

Guarulhos, SP – Rua Dom Pedro II, 195, Centro, 3rd floor, CEP 07131-418/ Tel. +55 (11) 209-6669

Manaus, AM – Av. 7 de Setembro, 1559, Centro, CEP 69005-141/ Tel. +55 (92) 232-0202

Natal, RN – Av. Praia do Timbau, 2133, Ponta Negra, CEP 59894-588

Pirajui, SP – Estr. Pirajui-Estiva, Km 2, CEP 16600-000/ Tel. +55 (142) 72-2309

Porto Alegre, RS – Rua Tomas Flores, 331, Bonfim, CEP 90035-201

Recife, PE – Rua Zenobio Lins, 70, Cordeiro, CEP 50711-300

Ribeirao, Preto – Rua dos Aliados, 155, Campos Eliseos, CEP 14080-570

Rio de Janeiro, RJ – Rua Armando C. de Freitas, 108, B. Tijuca, CEP 22628-098/ Tel. +55 (21) 399-4493

Salvador, BA – Rua Alvaro Adrono, 17, Brotas, CEP 40255-460/ Tel. +55 (71) 244-0418

Santos, SP – Rua Nabuco de Araujo, 151, Embare, CEP 11025-011/ Tel. +55 (132) 38-4655

Sao Paulo, SP – Av. Angelica, 2583, Centro, CEP 01227-200/ Tel. +55 (11) 259-7352
Teresopolis, RJ – Comunidade Vrajabhumi (contact ISKCON Rio)

FARM COMMUNITIES

Caruaru, PE – Nova Vrajadhama, Distrito de Murici (mail: C.P. 283, CEP 55000-000)
Parati, RJ – Goura Vrindavana, Sertao Indaituba (mail: 62 Parati, CEP 23970-000)
Pindamonhangaba, SP – Nova Gokula, Bairro de Ribeirao Grande (mail: C.P. 108, CEP 12400-000)/ Tel. +55 (122) 42-5002

RESTAURANTS

Brasilia – (at ISKCON Brasilia)
Caxias do Sul, RS – Av. Julio de Castilhos, 1095, Centro

MEXICO

Guadalajara – Pedro Moreno No. 1791, Sector Juarez/ Tel. +52 (36) 160775
Mexico City – Gob. Tiburcio Montiel No. 45, 11850 Mexico, D.F./ Tel. +52 (5) 271-22-23
Saltillo – Blvd. Saltillo No. 520, Col. Buenos Aires

FARM COMMUNITY

Guadalajara – contact ISKCON Guadalajara

RESTAURANTS

Guadalajara – (at ISKCON Guadalajara)
Orizaba – Restaurante Radhe, Sur 5 No. 50, Orizaba, Ver./ Tel. +52 (272) 5-75-25
Tulancingo – Restaurante Govinda, Calle Juarez 213, Tulancingo, Hgo./ Tel. +52 (775) 3-51-53

PERU

Lima – Pasaje Solea 101, Santa Maria-Chosica/ Tel. +51 (14) 910891
Lima – Schell 634 Miraflores
Lima – Av. Garcilazo de la Vega 1670-1680/ Tel. +51 (14) 259523

FARM COMMUNITY

Correo De Bella Vista – DPTO De San Martin

RESTAURANTS

Cuzco – Espaderos 128
Lima – Schell 634 Miraflores

OTHER COUNTRIES

Asunción, Paraguay – Centro Bhaktivedanta, Mariano R. Alonso 925/ Tel. +595 (21) 480-266
Bogotá, Colombia – Carrera 16, No.60-52, Bogota (mail: Apartado Aereo 58680, Zona 2, Chapinero)/ Tel. +57 (1) 2486892, 210665
Buenos Aires, Argentina – Centro Bhaktivedanta, Andonaegui 2054, 1431 Buenos Aires/ Tel. +54 (1) 521-5567 or 523-4232
Cali, Colombia – Avenida 2 EN, #24N-39/ Tel. +57 (23) 68-88-53
Caracas, Venezuela – Avenida Berlin, Quinta Tia Lola, La California Norte/ Tel. +58 (2) 225463
Chinandega, Nicaragua – Edificio Hare Krsna No 108, Del Banco Nacional 10 mts. abajo/ Tel. +505 (341) 2359
Cochabamba, Bolivia – Av. Heroinas E-0435 Apt. 3 (mail: P.O. Box 2070, Cochabamba)/ Tel./Fax +591 (42) 54346
Cuenca, Ecuador – Entrada de Las Pencas 1, Avenida de Las Americas/ Tel. +593 (7) 825211
Essequibo Coast, Guyana – New Navadvipa Dham, Mainstay, Essequibo Coast
Georgetown, Guyana – 24 Uitvlugt Front, West Coast Demerara
Guatemala, Guatemala – Apartado Postal 1534
Guayaquil, Ecuador – 6 de Marzo 226 or V.M. Rendon/ Tel. +593 (4) 308412, 309420
Managua, Nicaragua – Residencial Bolonia, De Galeria los Pipitos 75 mts. norte (mail: P.O. Box 772)/ Tel. +505 242759
Mar del Plata, Argentina – Dorrego 4019 (7600) Mar del Plata/ Tel. +54 (23) 745688
Montevideo, Uruguay – Centro de Bhakti-Yoga, Mariana Moreno 2660/ Tel. +598 (2) 477-919
Panama, Republic of Panama – Via las Cumbres, entrada Villa Zaita, frente a INPSA No. 1 (mail: P.O. Box 6-29-54, Panama)
Pereira, Colombia – Carrera 5a, #19-36
Quito, Ecuador – Inglaterra y Amazonas
Rosario, Argentina – Centro de Bhakti-Yoga, Paraguay 556, (2000) Rosario/ Tel. +54 (41) 252-630 or 264-243

San José, Costa Rica – Centro Cultural Govinda, Av. 7, Calles 1 y 3, 235 mtrs. norte del Banco Anglo, San Pedro (mail: Apdo. 166, 1002)/ Tel. +506 23-52-38

San Salvador, El Salvador – Avenida Universitaria 1132, Media Quadra al sur de la Embajada Americana (mail: P.O. box 1506)/ Tel. +503 25-96-17

Santiago, Chile – Carrera 330/ Tel. +56 (2) 698-8044

Santo Domingo, Dominican Republic – Calle Cayetano Rodriquez No. 254/ Tel. (809) 686-5665

Trinidad and Tobago, West Indies – Orion Drive, Debe/ Tel. +1 (809) 647-3165

Trinidad and Tobago, West Indies – Prabhupada Ave. Longdenville, Chaguanas

FARM COMMUNITIES

Argentina (Bhaktilata Puri) – Casilla de Correo No. 77, 1727 Marcos Paz, Pcia. Bs. As., Republica Argentina

Bolivia – contact ISKCON Cochabamba

Colombia (Nueva Mathura) – Cruzero del Guali, Municipio de Caloto, Valle del Cauca/ Tel. +57 (23) 61-26-88 en cali

Costa Rica – Nueva Goloka Vrindavana, Carretera a Paraiso, de la entrada del Jardin Lancaster (por Calle Concava), 200 metros as sur (mano derecha) Cartago (mail: Apdo. 166, 1002)/ Tel. +506 51-6752

Ecuador (Nueva Mayapur) – Ayampe (near Guayaquil)

Ecuador (Giridharidesha) – Chordeleg (near Cuenca), Cassiga Postal 01.05.1811, Cuenca/ Tel. +593 (7) 255735

El Salvador – Carretera a Santa Ana, Km. 34, Canton Los Indios, Zapotitan, Dpto. de La Libertad

Guyana – Seawell Village, Corentyne, East Berbice

RESTAURANTS

Buenos Aires, Argentina – Gusto Superior, Blanco Encalada 2722, 1428 Buenos Aires Cap. Fed./ Tel. +54 (1) 788 3023

Cochabamba, Bolivia – Gopal Restaurant, calle Espana N-0250 (Galeria Olimpia), (mail: P.O. Box 2070, Cochabamba)/ Tel. +591 (42) 26626

Guatemala, Guatemala – Callejor Santandes a una cuadra abajo de Guatel, Panajachel Solola

Quito, Ecuador – (contact ISKCON Quito)

San Salvador, El Salvador – 25 Avenida Norte 1132

Santa Cruz, Bolivia – Snack Govinda, Av. Argomosa (1 ero anillo), esq. Bolivar/ Tel.+591 (3) 345189

An Introduction to ISKCON and Devotee Lifestyle

What Is the International Society for Krishna Consciousness?

The International Society for Krishna Consciousness (ISKCON), popularly known as the Hare Kṛṣṇa movement, is a worldwide association of devotees of Kṛṣṇa, the Supreme Personality of Godhead. The same God is known by many names in the various scriptures of the world. In the Bible He is known as Jehovah ("the almighty one") in the Koran as Allah ("the great one"), and in the *Bhagavad-gītā* as Kṛṣṇa, a Sanskrit name meaning "the all-attractive one".

The movement's main purpose is to promote the well-being of human society by teaching the science of God consciousness (Kṛṣṇa consciousness) according to the timeless Vedic scriptures of India.

The best known of the Vedic texts is the *Bhagavad-gītā* ("Song of God"). It is said to date back 5,000 years to the time when Kṛṣṇa incarnated on earth to teach this sacred message. It is the philosophical basis for the Hare Kṛṣṇa movement and is revered by more than 700 million people today.

This exalted work has been praised by scholars and leaders the world over. M.K. Gandhi said, "When doubts haunt me, when disappointments stare me in the face and I see not one ray of hope, I turn to the *Bhagavad-gītā* and find a verse to comfort me." Ralph Waldo Emerson wrote, "It was the first of books; it was as if an empire spoke to us, nothing small or unworthy, but large, serene, consistent, the voice of an old intelligence which in another age and climate had pondered and thus disposed of the same questions which exercise us." And Henry David Thoreau said, "In the morning I bathe my intellect in the stupendous and cosmogonal philosophy of the *Bhagavad-gītā.*"

Lord Kṛṣṇa teaches in the *Bhagavad-gītā* that we are not these temporary material bodies but are spirit souls, or conscious entities, and that we can find genuine peace and happiness only in spiritual devotion to God. The *Gītā* and other world scriptures recommend that people joyfully chant the holy name of God. Whether one chants His name as Kṛṣṇa, Allah or Jehovah, one may become blessed with pure love of God.

A Sixteenth-Century Incarnation of Kṛṣṇa

Kṛṣṇa incarnated again in the sixteenth century as Śrī Caitanya Mahāprabhu and popularised the chanting of God's names all over India. He constantly sang these names of God, as prescribed in the Vedic literature: Hare Kṛṣṇa, Hare Kṛṣṇa, Kṛṣṇa Kṛṣṇa, Hare Hare/Hare Rāma, Hare Rāma, Rāma Rāma, Hare Hare. The Hare Kṛṣṇa *mantra* is a transcendental sound vibration. It purifies the mind and awakens the dormant love of God in the hearts of all living beings. Lord Caitanya requested His followers to spread this chanting to every town and village of the world.

Anyone can take part in the chanting of Hare Kṛṣṇa and learn the science of devotion by studying the *Bhagavad-gītā.* This easy and practical process of self-realisation will awaken our natural state of peace and happiness.

Many academics and religious leaders who understand the roots of the modern day Hare Kṛṣṇa movement have affirmed the movement's authenticity. Diana L. Eck, professor of comparative religion and Indian studies at Harvard University, describes the movement as a "tradition that commands a respected place in the religious life of humankind".

Hare Kṛṣṇa Lifestyles

The devotees seen dancing and chanting in the streets, dressed in traditional Indian robes, are, for the most part, full-time students of the Hare Kṛṣṇa movement. The vast majority of followers, however, live and work in the general community, practising Kṛṣṇa consciousness in their homes and attending temples on a regular basis.

There are about 5,000 full-time devotees throughout the world and 200,000 congregational members outside of India. The movement is presently comprised of over 300 temples, 40 rural communities, 26 schools and 45 restaurants in 71 countries. The basic principle of the Hare Kṛṣṇa lifestyle is "simple living and high thinking". A devotee of Kṛṣṇa is encouraged to use his time, energy, talents and resources in devotional service to God, and not to hanker for selfish ambitions or pleasures which result in frustration and anxiety.

Devotees try to cultivate humanity's inherent spiritual qualities of compassion, truthfulness, cleanliness and austerity. There are four regulative principles which devotees adopt to assist them to develop those qualities and also to help control the insatiable urges of the mind and senses. These are:

1. No eating of meat, fish or eggs.
2. No gambling.
3. No sex other than for procreation within marriage.
4. No intoxication, including all recreational drugs, alcohol, tobacco, tea and coffee.

According to the *Bhagavad-gītā,* indulgence in the above activities disrupts our physical, mental and spiritual well-being and increases anxiety and conflict in society.

A Philosophy for Everyone

The philosophy of the Hare Kṛṣṇa movement is a non-sectarian monotheistic tradition. It may be summarised in the following eight points:

1. By sincerely cultivating an authentic spiritual science, we can become free from anxiety and achieve a state of pure, unending, blissful consciousness.

2. Each one of us is not the material body but an eternal spirit soul, part and parcel of God (Kṛṣṇa). As such, we are all interrelated through Kṛṣṇa, our common father.

3. Kṛṣṇa is eternal, all-knowing, omnipresent, all-powerful and all-attractive. He is the seed-giving father of all living beings and the sustaining energy of the universe. He is the source of all incarnations of God.

4. The *Vedas* are the oldest scriptures in the world. The essence of the *Vedas* is found in the *Bhagavad-gītā,* a literal record of Kṛṣṇa's words spoken 5,000 years ago in India. The goal of Vedic knowledge—and of all theistic religions—is to achieve love of God.

5. We can perfectly understand the knowledge of self-realisation through the instructions of a genuine spiritual master—one who is free from selfish motives and whose mind is firmly fixed in meditation on Kṛṣṇa.

6. All that we eat should first be offered to Kṛṣṇa with a prayer. In this way Kṛṣṇa accepts the offering and blesses it for our purification.

7. Rather than living in a self-centred way, we should act for the pleasure of Kṛṣṇa. This is known as *bhakti-yoga,* the science of devotional service.

8. The most effective means for achieving God consciousness in this age is to chant the holy names of the Lord: Hare Kṛṣṇa, Hare Kṛṣṇa, Kṛṣṇa Kṛṣṇa, Hare Hare/ Hare Rāma, Hare Rāma, Rāma Rāma, Hare Hare.

Kṛṣṇa Consciousness at Home

From what we've read in *Kṛṣṇa, The Supreme Personality of Godhead,* it is clear how important it is for everyone to practise Kṛṣṇa consciousness, devotional service to Lord Kṛṣṇa. Of course, living in the association of Kṛṣṇa's devotees in a temple or *aśrama* makes it easier to perform devotional service. But if you're determined, you can follow the teachings of Kṛṣṇa consciousness at home and thus convert your home into a temple.

Spiritual life, like material life, means practical activity. The difference is that, whereas we perform material activities for the benefit of ourselves or those we consider ours, we perform spiritual activities for the benefit of Lord Kṛṣṇa, under the guidance of the scriptures and the spiritual master. Kṛṣṇa declares in the *Bhagavad-gītā* that a person can achieve neither happiness nor the supreme destination of life—going back to Godhead, back to Lord Kṛṣṇa—if he or she does not follow the injunctions of the scriptures. How to follow the scriptural rules by engaging in practical service to the Lord is explained by a bona fide spiritual master who is in an authorised chain of disciplic succession coming from Kṛṣṇa Himself.

These timeless practices which are outlined in this book have been taught to us by His Divine Grace A.C. Bhaktivedanta Swami Prabhupāda, the foremost exponent of Kṛṣṇa consciousness in our time.

The purpose of spiritual knowledge is to bring us closer to God, or Kṛṣṇa. Kṛṣṇa says in the *Bhagavad-gītā* (18.55), *bhaktyā mām abhijānāti:* "I can be known only by devotional service." Spiritual knowledge guides us in proper action to satisfy the desires of Kṛṣṇa through practical engagements in His loving service. Without practical application, theoretical knowledge is of little value.

Spiritual knowledge offers direction in all aspects of life. We should endeavour, therefore, to organise our lives in such a way as to follow Kṛṣṇa's teachings as far as possible. We should try to do our best, to do more than is simply convenient. Then it will be possible to for us rise to the spiritual plane of Kṛṣṇa consciousness, even while living far from a temple.

Chanting Hare Kṛṣṇa

The first principle in devotional service is to chant the Hare Kṛṣṇa *mahā-mantra* (*mahā* means "great"; *mantra* means "sound that liberates the mind from ignorance"):

Hare Kṛṣṇa, Hare Kṛṣṇa, Kṛṣṇa Kṛṣṇa, Hare Hare
Hare Rāma, Hare Rāma, Rāma Rāma, Hare Hare

You can chant these holy names of the Lord anywhere and at any time, but it is best to do it at a specific time of the day. Early morning hours are ideal.

The chanting can be done in two ways: singing the *mantra*, called *kīrtana* (usually done in a group), and saying the *mantra* to oneself, called *japa* (which literally means "to speak softly"). Concentrate on hearing the sound of the holy names. As you chant, pronounce the names clearly and distinctly, addressing Kṛṣṇa in a prayerful mood. When your mind wanders, bring it back to the sound of the Lord's name. Chanting is a prayer to Kṛṣṇa that means "O energy of the Lord (Hare), O all-attractive Lord (Kṛṣṇa), O supreme enjoyer (Rāma), please engage me in Your service." The more attentively and sincerely you chant these names of God, the more spiritual progress you will make.

Since God is all-powerful and all-merciful, He has kindly made it very easy for us to chant His names, and He has also invested all His powers in them. Therefore the names of God and God Himself are identical. This means that when we chant the holy names of Kṛṣṇa and Rāma we are directly associating with God and being purified by such communion. Therefore we should always try to chant with devotion and reverence. The Vedic literature states that Lord Kṛṣṇa is personally dancing on your tongue when you chant His holy name.

When you chant alone, it is best to chant on *japa* beads (available at any of the centres listed in the advertisement at the end of this book). This not only helps you fix your attention on the holy name, but also helps you count the number of times you chant the *mantra* daily. Each strand of *japa* beads contains 108 small beads and one large bead, the head bead. Begin on a bead next to the head bead and gently roll it between the thumb and middle finger of your right hand as you chant the full Hare Kṛṣṇa *mantra.* Then move to the next bead and repeat the process. In this way, chant on each of the 108 beads until you reach the head bead again. This is called one "round" of *japa.* Then, without chanting on the head bead, reverse the beads and start your second round on the last bead you chanted on.

Initiated devotees vow before the spiritual master to chant at least sixteen rounds of the Hare Kṛṣṇa *mantra* daily. But even if you can chant only one round a day, the principle is that once you commit yourself to chanting that round, you should try to complete it every day without fail. When you feel you can chant more, then increase the minimum number of rounds you chant each day—but try not to fall below that number. You can chant more than your fixed number, but you should maintain a set minimum each day. Please note that the beads are sacred and therefore should never touch the ground or be put in an unclean place. To keep your beads clean, it is best to carry them in a special bead bag, also available from any of the temples.

Aside from chanting *japa,* you can also sing the Lord's holy names in *kīrtana.* Although you can sing *kīrtana* on your own, it is generally performed with others. A melodious *kīrtana* with family or friends is sure to enliven everyone. ISKCON devotees use traditional melodies and instruments, especially in the temple, but you can chant to any melody and use any musical instruments to accompany your chanting. As Lord Caitanya said, "There are no hard and fast rules for chanting

Hare Kṛṣṇa." One thing you might want to do, however, is to obtain some *kīrtana* and *japa* audiotapes and hear the various styles of chanting.

Setting Up Your Altar

You will probably find that *japa* and *kīrtana* are more effective when done before an altar. Lord Kṛṣṇa and His pure devotees are so kind that they allow us to worship them even through their pictures. It's something like mailing a letter: You can't mail a letter by placing it in just any box; you must use the postbox authorised by the government. Similarly, we cannot concoct an image of God and worship that, but we may worship the authorised picture of God, and Kṛṣṇa accepts our worship through that picture.

Setting up an altar at home means receiving the Lord and His pure devotees as your most honoured guests. Where should you set up the altar? Well, how would you seat a guest? An ideal place would be clean, well lit and free from draughts and household disturbances. Your guest, of course, would need a comfortable chair, but for the picture of Kṛṣṇa's form a wall shelf, a mantelpiece, a corner table or the top shelf of a bookcase will do. You wouldn't seat a guest in your home and then ignore him; you'd provide a place for yourself to sit, too, where you could comfortably face him and enjoy his company, so don't make your altar inaccessible.

What do you need to set up your altar? Here are the essentials:

1. A picture of Śrīla Prabhupāda.
2. A picture of Lord Caitanya and His associates.
3. A picture of Rādhā and Kṛṣṇa.

In addition, you may want an altar cloth, water cups (one for each picture), candles with holders, a special plate for offering food, a small bell, incense, an incense holder and fresh flowers, which you may offer in vases or simply place before each picture. If you're interested in more elaborate Deity worship, ask any of the ISKCON devotees or write to the Bhaktivedanta Book Trust.

The first person we worship on the altar is the spiritual master. The spiritual master is not God. Only God is God. But because the spiritual master is His dearmost servant, God has empowered him to be His representative and therefore he deserves the same respect as that given to God. The spiritual master links the disciple with God and teaches him the process of *bhakti-yoga.* He is God's ambassador to the material world. When the Queen sends an ambassador to a foreign country, the ambassador receives the same respect as that accorded the Queen, and the ambassador's words are as authoritative as the Queen's. Similarly, we should respect the spiritual master as we would God, and revere his words as we would God's.

There are two main kinds of *guru*: the instructing *guru* and the initiating *guru.* Everyone who takes up the process of *bhakti-yoga* as a result of coming in contact with ISKCON owes an immense debt of gratitude to Śrīla Prabhupāda. Before Śrīla Prabhupāda left India in 1965 to spread Kṛṣṇa consciousness abroad, almost no one outside India knew anything about the practice of pure devotional service to Lord Kṛṣṇa. Therefore, everyone who has learned of the process through his books, his *Back to Godhead* magazine, his tapes or contact with his followers should offer respect to Śrīla Prabhupāda. As the founder and spiritual guide of the International Society for Krishna Consciousness, he is the prime instructing *guru* of all of us.

Devotees should first of all develop this spiritual understanding and their relationship with Śrīla Prabhupāda. However, the Vedic literature encourages us to become connected to the current link of the chain of spiritual masters. Following Śrīla Prabhupāda's departure, this means accepting initiation from one of Śrīla Prabhupāda's senior followers who are acknowledged as spiritual masters within the movement.

The second picture on your altar should be of the *pañca-tattva,* Lord Caitanya and His four leading associates. Lord Caitanya is the incarnation of God for this age. He is Kṛṣṇa Himself, descended in the form of His own devotee to teach us how to surrender to Him, specifically by chanting His holy names and performing other activities of *bhakti-yoga.* Lord Caitanya is the most merciful incarnation, for He makes it easy for anyone to attain love of God through the chanting of the Hare Kṛṣṇa *mantra.*

And of course, your altar should have a picture of the Supreme Personality of Godhead, Lord Śrī Kṛṣṇa, with His eternal consort, Śrīmatī Rādhārāṇī. Śrīmatī Rādhārāṇī is Kṛṣṇa's spiritual potency. She is devotional service personified, and devotees always take shelter of Her to learn how to serve Kṛṣṇa.

You can arrange the pictures in a triangle, with the picture of Śrīla Prabhupāda on the left, the picture of Lord Caitanya and His associates on the right and the picture of Rādhā and Kṛṣṇa, which, if possible, should be slightly larger than the others, on a small raised platform behind and in the centre. Or you can hang the picture of Rādhā and Kṛṣṇa on the wall above.

When you establish an altar, you are inviting Kṛṣṇa and His pure devotees to reside as the most important guests in your home. Carefully clean the altar each morning. Cleanliness is essential in the worship of Kṛṣṇa. You would not neglect to clean the room of an important guest. If you have water cups, rinse them out and fill them with fresh water daily. Then place them conveniently close to the pictures. You should remove flowers in vases as soon as they're slightly wilted, or daily if you've offered them at the base of the pictures. You should offer fresh incense at least once a day, and, if possible, light candles and place them near the pictures while you're chanting before the altar.

Please try the things we've suggested so far. It's very simple really: If you try to love God, you'll gradually realise how much He loves you. That's the essence of *bhakti-yoga.*

Prasādam: How to Eat Spiritually

By His omnipotent transcendental energies, Kṛṣṇa can actually convert matter into spirit. If we place an iron rod in a fire, soon the rod becomes red-hot and acts just like fire. In the same way, food prepared for and offered to Kṛṣṇa with love and devotion becomes completely spiritualised. Such food is called *kṛṣṇa-prasādam,* which means "the mercy of Lord Kṛṣṇa".

Eating *prasādam* is a fundamental practice of *bhakti-yoga.* In other forms of *yoga* one must artificially repress the senses, but the *bhakti-yogī* can engage his or her senses in a variety of pleasing spiritual activities, such as tasting delicious food offered to Lord Kṛṣṇa. In this way the senses gradually become spiritualised and bring the devotee more and more transcendental pleasure by being engaged in devotional service. Such spiritual pleasure far surpasses any kind of material experience.

Lord Caitanya said of *prasādam,* "Everyone has tasted these foods before. However, now that they have been prepared for Kṛṣṇa and offered to Him with devotion, these foods have acquired extraordinary tastes and uncommon fragrances. Just taste them and see the difference in experience! Apart from the taste, even the fragrance pleases the mind and makes one forget any other aroma. Therefore, it should be understood that the spiritual nectar of Kṛṣṇa's lips must have touched these ordinary foods and imparted to them all their transcendental qualities."

Eating only food offered to Kṛṣṇa is the perfection of vegetarianism. Refraining from animal flesh out of compassion for innocent creatures is certainly a praiseworthy sentiment, but when we go beyond vegetarianism to a diet of *prasādam,* our eating becomes helpful in achieving the goal of human life—reawakening the soul's original relationship with God. In the *Bhagavad-gītā* Lord Kṛṣṇa says that unless one eats only food that has been offered to Him in sacrifice, one will suffer the reactions of *karma.*

How to Prepare and Offer Prasādam

As you walk down the supermarket aisles selecting the foods you will offer to Kṛṣṇa, you need to know what is offerable and what is not. In the *Bhagavad-gītā*, Lord Kṛṣṇa states, "If one offers Me with love and devotion a leaf, a flower, a fruit or water, I will accept it." Elsewhere, it is explained that we can offer Kṛṣṇa foods prepared from milk products, vegetables, fruits, nuts and grains. (Write to the Bhaktivedanta Book Trust for one of the many Hare Kṛṣṇa cookbooks.) Meat, fish and eggs are not offerable. A few vegetarian items are also forbidden—garlic and onions, for example, because they tend to agitate the mind, making meditation more difficult. (Hing, asafoetida, is a tasty substitute for them in cooking and is available at most Indian grocers.) Nor can you offer Kṛṣṇa coffee or tea that contain caffeine. If you like these beverages, purchase caffeine-free coffee and herbal teas.

While shopping, be aware that you may find meat, fish and egg products mixed with other foods; so be sure to read labels carefully. For instance, some brands of yoghurt and sour cream contain gelatin, a substance made from the horns, hooves and bones of slaughtered animals. Most hard cheese contains rennet, an enzyme extracted from the stomach tissue of slaughtered calves. Look for such cheese labelled as being suitable for vegetarians.

Try to avoid foods cooked by nondevotees. According to the subtle laws of nature the consciousness of the cook affects the food. The principle is the same as that at work in a painting: a painting is not simply a collection of brush strokes on a canvas but an expression of the artist's state of mind, which affects the viewer. So if you eat food cooked by nondevotees such as processed foods etc. then you are likely to absorb a dose of materialism and *karma.* As far as possible in your own cooking use only fresh, natural ingredients.

In preparing food, cleanliness is the most important principle. Nothing impure should be offered to God; so keep your kitchen very clean. Always wash your hands thoroughly before entering the kitchen. While preparing food, do not taste it, for you are cooking the meal not for yourself but for the pleasure of Kṛṣṇa. Arrange portions of the food on dinnerware kept especially for this purpose; no one but the Lord should eat from those dishes. The easiest way to offer food is simply to pray, "My dear Lord Kṛṣṇa, please accept this food," and to chant each of the following prayers three times while ringing a bell (see the Sanskrit Pronunciation Guide on page 541).

1. Prayer to Śrīla Prabhupāda:

nama oṁ viṣṇu-pādāya kṛṣṇa-preṣṭhāya bhū-tale
śrīmate bhaktivedānta-svāmin iti nāmine

namas te sārasvate deve gaura-vāṇī-pracāriṇe
nirviśeṣa-śūnyavādi-pāścātya-deśa-tāriṇe

"I offer my respectful obeisances unto His Divine Grace A.C. Bhaktivedanta Swami Prabhupāda, who is very dear to Lord Kṛṣṇa, having taken shelter at His lotus feet. Our respectful obeisances are unto you, O spiritual master, servant of Bhaktisiddhānta Sarasvatī Gosvāmī. You are kindly preaching the message of Lord Caitanyadeva and delivering the Western countries, which are filled with impersonalism and voidism."

2. Prayer to Lord Caitanya:

namo mahā-vadānyāya kṛṣṇa-prema-pradāya te
kṛṣṇāya kṛṣṇa-caitanya-nāmne gaura-tviṣe namaḥ

"O most munificent incarnation! You are Kṛṣṇa Himself appearing as Śrī Kṛṣṇa Caitanya Mahāprabhu. You have assumed the golden colour of Śrīmatī Rādhārāṇī, and You are widely distributing pure love of Kṛṣṇa. We offer our respectful obeisances unto You."

3. Prayer to Lord Kṛṣṇa:

namo brahmaṇya-devāya go-brāhmaṇa-hitāya ca
jagad-dhitāya kṛṣṇāya govindāya namo namaḥ

"I offer my respectful obeisances unto Lord Kṛṣṇa, who is the worshipable Deity for all *brāhmaṇas,* the well-wisher of the cows and the *brāhmaṇas,* and the benefactor of the whole world. I offer my repeated obeisances to the Personality of Godhead, known as Kṛṣṇa and Govinda."

Remember that the real purpose of preparing and offering food to the Lord is to show your devotion and gratitude to Him. Kṛṣṇa accepts your devotion, not the physical offering itself. God is complete in Himself—He doesn't need anything—but out of His immense kindness He allows us to offer food to Him so that we can develop our love for Him.

After offering the food to the Lord, wait at least five minutes for Him to partake of the preparations. Then you should transfer the food from the special dinnerware and wash the dishes and utensils you used for the offering. Now you, your family and any guests may eat the *prasādam.* While you eat, try to appreciate the spiritual value of the food. Remember that because Kṛṣṇa has accepted it, it is nondifferent from Him, and therefore by eating it you will become purified.

Everything you offer on your altar becomes *prasādam,* the mercy of the Lord. The flowers, the incense, the water, the food—everything you offer for the Lord's pleasure becomes spiritualised. The Lord enters into the offerings, and thus the remnants are nondifferent from Him. So you should not only deeply respect the things you've offered, but you should distribute them to others as well. Distribution of *prasādam* is an essential expression of your devotion to Kṛṣṇa.

Everyday Life: The Four Regulative Principles

Anyone serious about progressing in Kṛṣṇa consciousness must try to avoid the following four sinful activities:

1. Eating meat, fish or eggs. These foods are saturated with the modes of passion and ignorance, and therefore cannot be offered to the Lord. A person who eats these foods participates in a conspiracy of violence against helpless animals and thus curtails his spiritual progress.

2. Gambling. Gambling invariably puts one into anxiety and fuels greed, envy and anger.

3. The use of intoxicants. Drugs, alcohol and tobacco, as well as any drinks or foods containing caffeine, cloud the mind, overstimulate the senses and make it impossible to understand or follow the principles of *bhakti-yoga.*

4. Illicit sex. This is sex outside of marriage or sex in marriage for any purpose other than procreation. Sex for pleasure compels one to identify with the body and prevents one from understanding Kṛṣṇa consciousness. The scriptures teach that sex attraction is the most powerful force binding us to the illusions of the material world. Anyone serious about advancing in Kṛṣṇa consciousness should therefore abstain from or regulate sexual activity according to the scriptures. In the *Bhagavad-gītā* Kṛṣṇa says that sexual union for conceiving a child to be raised in God consciousness is an act of devotion to Him.

Engagement in Practical Devotional Service

We all must work to earn our livelihood and to maintain home, family and so on. However, if we try to take the fruits of our labour for ourselves and dependents, we must also accept the karmic reactions incurred because of our work. Kṛṣṇa says in the *Bhagavad-gītā* (3.9), "Work done as a sacrifice for Viṣṇu (Kṛṣṇa) has to be performed. Otherwise work binds one to the material world."

However, it is not necessary to change our occupation, we need to change our attitude. If we are striving for Kṛṣṇa consciousness, if our home has become a temple, and if we share spiritual life with our family members, then what we earn may legitimately be spent for the maintenance of our domestic affairs and the balance engaged in promoting our and others' spiritual lives. Thus, whatever we do we can see it as being part of our devotional service to Kṛṣṇa.

Further, we may also have the opportunity to use our skills and talents directly for Kṛṣṇa. If you're a writer, write for Kṛṣṇa; if you're an artist, create for Kṛṣṇa; if you're a secretary, type for Kṛṣṇa. You may also help a local temple in your spare time, and you could sacrifice some of the fruits of your work by contributing a portion of your earnings to help maintain the temple and propagate Kṛṣṇa consciousness. Some devotees buy Hare Kṛṣṇa literature and distribute it to their friends and associates, or they engage in a variety of services at the temple. There is also a wide network of devotees who gather in each other's homes for chanting, worship and study. Write to your local temple or the Society's secretary to learn of any such programmes near you.

Additional Devotional Principles

There are many more devotional practices that can help you become Kṛṣṇa conscious. Here are two vital ones:

Studying Hare Kṛṣṇa literature. Śrīla Prabhupāda, the founder-*ācārya* of ISKCON, dedicated much of his time to writing and translating books such as *Śrīmad-Bhāgavatam.* Hearing the words—or reading the writings—of a realised spiritual master is an essential spiritual practice. So try to set aside some time every day to read Śrīla Prabhupāda's books. You can get a free catalogue of available books and tapes from the Bhaktivedanta Book Trust.

Associating with devotees. Śrīla Prabhupāda established the Hare Kṛṣṇa movement to give people in general the chance to associate with devotees of the Lord. This is the best way to gain faith in the process of Kṛṣṇa consciousness and become enthusiastic in devotional service. Conversely, maintaining intimate connections with nondevotees slows one's spiritual progress. So try to visit the Hare Kṛṣṇa centre nearest you as often as possible.

In Closing

The beauty of Kṛṣṇa consciousness is that you can take as much as you're ready for. Kṛṣṇa Himself promises in the *Bhagavad-gītā* (2.40), "In this endeavour there is no loss or diminution, and a little advancement on this path can protect one from the most dangerous type of fear." So bring Kṛṣṇa into your daily life, and we guarantee you'll feel the benefit.

Hare Kṛṣṇa!

STAY IN TOUCH

Now that you've read this book, you may like to further your interest by joining thousands of others as a member of ISKCON.

The International Society for Krishna Consciousness was founded in 1966 by the author of this book, Srila Prabhupada. The Society is dedicated to providing knowledge of Krishna and the science of Krishna consciousness as a means of achieving the highest personal happiness and spiritual fellowship among all living beings. We invite you to join us.

What Does Membership of ISKCON Mean for Me?

For an annual donation of £25 (£30 for non-UK addresses) you'll receive a membership package that will keep you fully informed and involved. Here's what you receive:

- **BACK TO GODHEAD**

The Magazine of the Hare Krishna Movement

Each issue of Back to Godhead has colourful photos and informative articles on topics such as:

- techniques of *mantra* meditation
- how the spiritual knowlegde of the *Vedas* can bring peace, satisfaction and success in your life
- recipes for a *karma*-free diet
- news of Hare Krishna devotees and devotional projects worldwide
- clear explanations of Vedic science and cosmology
- Krishna conscious perspectives on current affairs, and much more...

• THE NAMA HATTA

ISKCON UK's newsletter covering happenings in both UK and Ireland. Articles, letters and lots of news and items of interest.

• VALUABLE DISCOUNTS

All registered members will be sent a valuable 10% Membership Discount Card to use on purchases of books, audio and video tapes, posters, incense and all other items from UK Hare Krishna shops and the mail order department.

• VAISHNAVA CALENDAR

A beautifully illustrated 12-page wall calendar featuring some of the best of The Bhaktivedanta Book Trust's paintings. It will remind you of all the important festivals and celebrations of the Krishna devotee year.

Become a member today and experience the higher taste of *bhakti-yoga.*

Application for Membership

(you can write these details out on a separate piece of paper if you wish)

I wish to be included as a member of ISKCON UK, and I have enclosed payment of £25 (£30 outside UK) accordingly for the next years' membership. Please send my magazines to:

Surname Mr/Mrs/Ms ______________________________

Forenames ______________________________

Address ______________________________

____

KB2s

Postcode __________ County ______________

Please make all payments out to ISKCON:

Signed ______________ Date ______________

Please send this application to:
Membership Service Dept., ISKCON,
2 St. James Rd., Watford, WDI 8EA

BHAGAVAD-GITA AS IT IS

The World's Most Popular Edition of a Timeless Classic

Throughout the ages, the world's greatest minds have turned to the *Bhagavad-gita* for answers to life's perennial questions. Renowned as the jewel of India's spiritual wisdom, the *Gita* summarises the profound Vedic knowledge concerning man's essential nature, his environment and ultimately his relationship with God. With more than fifty million copies sold in twenty languages, *Bhagavad-gita As It Is,* by His Divine Grace A.C. Bhaktivedanta Swami Prabhupada, is the most widely read edition of the *Gita* in the world. It includes the original Sanskrit text, phonetic transliterations, word-for-word meanings, translation, elaborate commentary and many full-colour illustrations.

	Soft	Vinyl	Hard	Deluxe
UK	**£4.00**	**£6.50**	**£7.95**	**£13.95**
US	$3.90	$8.50	$10.30	$18.00
AUS		$11.00	$14.00	$28.00

EASY JOURNEY TO OTHER PLANETS

One of Srila Prabhupada's earliest books. *Easy Journey* describes how *bhakti-yoga* enables us to transfer ourselves from the material to the spiritual world.

Softbound, 96 pages

UK: £1.50; US: $1.00; AUS: $2.00

BEYOND BIRTH AND DEATH

What is the self? Can it exist apart from the physical body? If so, what happens to the self at the time of death? What about reincarnation? Liberation? *Beyond Birth and Death* answers these intriguing questions and more.

Softbound, 96 pages

UK: £1.50, US: $1.00; AUS: $2.00

THE HIGHER TASTE

A Guide to Gourmet Vegetarian Cooking and a Karma-Free Diet

Illustrated profusely with black-and-white drawings and eight full-colour plates, this popular volume contains over 60 tried and tested international recipes, together with the why's and how's of the Krishna conscious vegetarion life-style.

Softbound, 176 pages

UK: £1.50; US: $1.99; AUS: $2.00

RAJA-VIDYA: THE KING OF KNOWLEDGE

In this book we learn why knowledge of Krishna is absolute and frees the soul from material bondage.

Softbound, 128 pages

UK: £1.50; US: $1.00; AUS: $2.00

THE PERFECTION OF YOGA

A lucid explanation of the psychology, techniques, and purposes of *yoga,* a summary and comparison of the different *yoga* systems, and an introduction to meditation.

Softbound, 96 pages

UK: £1.50; US: $1.00; AUS: $2.00

COMING BACK

Coming Back answers the most profound and mysterious of all questions by presenting clear and complete explanations from the world's most authentic, timeless sources of knowledge about the afterlife. With this book you will learn the science of controlling your present, determining your future, and dramatically changing your life!

Softbound, 160 pages, 16 colour pages

UK: £1.50; US: $1.00; AUS: $2.00

GREAT

VEGETARIAN DISHES

Featuring over 100 stunning full-colour photos, this new book is for spiritually aware people who want the exquisite taste of Hare Krishna cooking without a lot of time in the kitchen. The 240 international recipes were tested and refined by world-famous Hare Krishna chef Kurma dasa.

240 recipes, 192 pages, coffee table size hardback

UK: £12.95; US: $19.95; AUS: $24.95

THE HARE KRISHNA BOOK OF

VEGETARIAN COOKING

A colourfully illustrated, practical cookbook that not only helps you prepare authentic Indian dishes at home, but also teaches you about the ancient tradition behind India's world-famous vegetarian cuisine.

130 kitchen-tested recipes, 300 pages, hardback

UK: £12.95; US: $11.60; AUS: $15.00

STAY IN TOUCH...

❒ Please send me a free information pack, including the small booklet *Krishna the Reservoir of Pleasure* and a catalogue of available books.

- ❒ Bhagavad-gita As It Is ❒ Soft ❒ Vinyl ❒ Hard ❒ Deluxe
- ❒ Great Vegetarian Dishes
- ❒ The Hare Krishna Book of Vegetarian Cooking
- ❒ The Higher Taste
- ❒ Raja-vidya: The King of Knowledge
- ❒ Easy Journey to Other Planets
- ❒ Beyond Birth and Death
- ❒ The Perfection of Yoga
- ❒ Message of Godhead

Please send me the above books. I enclose $/£ ____ to cover the cost and understand that the prices given include postage and packaging. (All prices offered here are greatly reduced from our normal retail charges!)

Name ________________________________

Address ______________________________

____________________ Postcode ______________

KB2s

Post this form with payment to:

In Europe: The Bhaktivedanta Book Trust, P.O. Box 324, Borehamwood, Herts. WD6 1NB, UK

In North America: The Bhaktivedanta Book Trust, 3764 Watseka Ave., Los Angeles, CA 90034, USA

In Australia: The Bhaktivedanta Book Trust, P.O. Box 262, Botany, NSW 2019, Australia